Diversity  & Equity
in the Classroom

Valerie Ooka Pang

CENGAGE
Learning·

Australia • Brazil • Mexico • Singapore • United Kingdom • United States

Diversity and Equity in the Classroom
Valerie Ooka Pang

Senior Product Director: Marta Lee-Perriard

Senior Product Manager: Cheri-Ann Nakamaru

Senior Content Developer: Lin Gaylord

Product Assistant: Megan Nauer

Marketing Manager: Andrew Miller

Senior Content Project Manager: Christy Frame

Senior Art Director: Helen Bruno

Senior Manufacturing Planner: Doug Bertke

Production Service and Compositor: Jill Traut, MPS Limited

Photo Researcher: Nisha Bhanu Beegum, Lumina Datamatics

Text Researcher: Venkatasubramanian Ramakrishnan, Lumina Datamatics

Copy Editor: Heather Mann

Text Designer: Dare Porter

Cover Design: Irene Morris Design

Cover Image: Young students walking in hallway: Thomas Barwick/Getty Images; World globe: rtguest/fotolia; Navigation: JJAVA, fotolia.

For product information and technology assistance, contact us at
Cengage Learning Customer & Sales Support, 1-800-354-9706

For permission to use material from this text or product, submit all requests online at **www.cengage.com/permissions**
Further permissions questions can be e-mailed to
permissionrequest@cengage.com

Unless otherwise noted, all content is © Cengage Learning

Library of Congress Control Number: 2016947228

Student Edition:

ISBN: 978-1-305-38647-1

Loose-leaf Edition:

ISBN: 978-1-337-09610-2

Cengage Learning
20 Channel Center Street
Boston, MA 02210
USA

Cengage Learning is a leading provider of customized learning solutions with employees residing in nearly 40 different countries and sales in more than 125 countries around the world. Find your local representative at **www.cengage.com**

Cengage Learning products are represented in Canada by Nelson Education, Ltd.

To learn more about Cengage Learning Solutions, visit **www.cengage.com**

Purchase any of our products at your local college store or at our preferred online store **www.cengagebrain.com**

Printed at CLDPC, USA, 04-19

Special Dedications
Carl Masami Ooka and Marie Horiuchi Ooka
Gerald C. H. Pang, Jennifer M. Pang, Matthew
A. Pang, Kari Boyum, Kathy Ooka, Cheryl Ooka,
Karen and Terry Hofman, Trish Howard, Naomi
and Greg Bang, Ariana Erwood, Cameron
Erwood, Connor Howard, Mirei Yasuda, Nicole
Howard, Sophia Hofman

Ramón Valle

Brief Contents

Contents

Chapter 3 **Culturally Relevant Teaching**   73

Chapter 6 Social Oppression: Classism and Sexism   174

Chapter 7   Human Diversity: Sexual Orientation and Gender Identity   214

**Chapter 8: Social Biases: Discrimination Based on Religion,
Immigrant Status, and Exceptionalities**   241

Chapter 10 Language Development and Acquisition 307

Chapter 11 Diversity and the Achievement Gap   336

Preface

Dear Educator,

Thank you for taking the time to read the introduction. One of my purposes in writing this book is to get all educators to think about how equity, social justice, and culture are important values in education. They influence what we think and how we teach. Most of us are proponents of social justice and equity; however, many of us do not realize that we ourselves—like our students—are members of many cultural subgroups. We all have cultures that have shaped and nurtured us, whether French culture or Vietnamese culture or Egyptian culture or Haida culture or a combination of many. We also are affected by other social elements such as social class, gender identity, religious membership, sexual orientation, exceptionalities, language, nationality, and family. Our culture influences our teaching and how we learn.

One of the goals of the book is to prompt teachers to first think about their own educational values. What are their foundational beliefs about schooling? I believe all students come to school hoping to be respected and supported as part of the learning process. Students also want to be cared for and treated fairly. Students hope that their teachers will be fair because teachers care about them. Caring for others is the foundation of our values of fairness. Students want to be members of a compassionate and collaborative community. This is why the theoretical framework that is at the center of this book brings together the constructs of caring, culture, and community with a social justice core. Students want to be affirmed. They want the opportunity to be successful. In addition, students also want to find meaning in what they are learning.

By reading this book, teachers will more fully understand how they and their students bring many cultural backgrounds to the classroom and that it is up to teachers to provide equitable educational opportunities for all. To be effective, teachers must be strong cultural mediators and advocates for all students. Teachers who appreciate diversity know that students cannot be characterized by one element such as ethnicity or language or social class. Even if a student is a Mexican American female, she may also be an exceptional chef, can speak three languages, and is a member of the local Buddhist temple. This is the **intersectionality** that each student brings into the classroom and it is this underlying perspective that informs **culturally relevant teaching** and the strategies found in this book. It is important that as educators we get away from describing a student as "that Black" student or "that Muslim" learner; students are complex cultural beings.

Like other people, teachers have heard or learned ideas about other cultural and ethnic groups that may be positive or negative. This book will assist students in unpacking their learned biases about other groups so they can eliminate those prejudices in their teaching. Ridding ourselves of bias will help us to build affirming classrooms where students are respected so we can facilitate their educational and social growth.

The text also presents examples of social oppression in society and shows teachers how to use those different views—from civil rights to "Black Lives Matter" to gender roles—to create a classroom of respect to reach all children. We live in a complicated world where answers are neither black nor white but often grey, especially when addressing sensitive issues of racism, homophobia, sexism, classism, language differences, ethnicity, and religious bias. The separation of diverse groups is artificial and is not how humans identify and what they believe about life. The text assists teachers in analyzing many cultural issues and learning how to integrate diversity into their curriculum and in the creation of supportive classroom environments.

Major Philosophies and Themes of This Book

Teachers often understand that student cultures are important in teaching, but they do not know how to incorporate culturally relevant education into their classrooms. I am on a research team with Dr. Yuji Shimogori and Dr. Gudiel Crosthwaite. We surveyed over 200 teachers in a public school district in southern California and found that most teachers believed in the importance of culturally relevant teaching, but could not explain what it is or how to implement the construct. Therefore, one of the major themes in this book is how to apply culturally relevant principles and strategies. This refers to the integration of culture in choosing curriculum content, identifying instructional-delivery methods, creating affirming classrooms, involving parents, and providing effective educational feedback. Teachers must have basic knowledge of education along with deep understandings of culturally relevant education. Therefore, the following major topics are presented so teachers can build strong, positive, motivating, and effective classrooms:

1. Analyze foundational beliefs about multicultural education including core values of caring and social justice
2. Review personal values as they relate to education, diversity, and equity
3. Assess and use culture in the classroom—what is it and why is it important to you as a teacher?
4. Employ culturally relevant teaching: theory and practice
5. Evaluate social oppression due to race (a sociopolitical construct), ethnicity, class, gender, sexual orientation, religion, language, sex, and exceptionality
6. Identify, address, and eliminate bullying and discrimination in schools
7. Integrate multilingual education
8. Create an educational environment focused on teaching the whole student
9. Address the achievement gap
10. Implement and assess effectiveness of instructional strategies
11. Build connections between students' worldviews and the content that we as teachers teach

Teachers want to know how to teach. This book is about practice and the integration of culturally relevant teaching into the curriculum. Teachers seek practical strategies that they can use in the classroom, and this text provides many stories and ideas in each chapter for them to study and implement. Many books for teachers either include too much theory with few teaching tips or too much practice without strong theoretical foundation. This book was designed to provide both theory and practice in a balanced way.

Culturally Relevant Teaching

Teachers are often aware of the need to integrate culturally relevant curriculum and instruction in the classroom but are not sure what that means. This text includes numerous examples for classroom use, from life stories appearing in Case Studies to keeping a curated teacher log of the stories students share in class discussions. Student examples from their own lives about the issues they face and the conflicts they have had to overcome can be built upon to teach social studies, language arts, literature, journalism, drama, music, sociology, psychology, civics, and art lessons.

Throughout the text your teachers will find many different examples of how to use culturally relevant teaching. For example, what if a student comes from a country that is densely populated and so he or she pushes his way in line or to get on the bus? Are teachers aware of this different behavioral expectation and the cultural conflict that it can create in school? How could they incorporate this knowledge into a lesson?

Culturally relevant teaching includes not only content but also context and delivery. Many suggestions are included in the text and special features such as Teaching Tips and Application: Know and Go Tools in the Classroom. For example, one of the most powerful ways for teachers to integrate student-lived experiences is to write notes in a teacher log so that the teacher can go back and remember what the students said. Also, when teachers record stories from as many students as they can, educators are able to present diverse accounts and experiences within the formal curriculum. This can enrich the lives of all students in the class. Another way to integrate culturally relevant teaching is to invite parents into the classroom to share their expertise. Maybe a parent is a firefighter or a skyscraper window washer. These two parents can give different ideas about careers and what they find fulfilling about their work. Teachers can also consider integrating knowledge of a discipline by integrating culturally relevant literature. Literature can present multiple perspectives about various issues and enrich the understanding of all students. Teachers also can use delivery methods such as the integration of hip hop to teach specific discipline content from history to literature. The Broadway play, *Hamilton*, is a great example of culturally relevant teaching because Lin-Manuel Miranda presents excellent content about the life of Alexander Hamilton, the first U.S. secretary of the treasury, using rap and hip-hop dance.

Cultural Models

One of the approaches within culturally relevant teaching that is discussed in the text is the use of cultural models. Your teachers may be inspired by the study of cultural models such as Rosa Parks, Martin Luther King, Jr., Cesar Chavez, Chief Joseph, Jane Addams, John Brown, Morris Dees, or Philip Vera Cruz. Their lives are stories of inspiration and describe their passion for freedom and equality. Teachers may also come to your classroom aware of many cultural models and processes; students may know how to crack an egg or dribble a soccer ball. These models used in life can be integrated into your curriculum. The cultural model of cracking an egg can represent a new beginning or transformation. Dribbling the soccer ball can be a cultural model that teaches patience and developing balance in life.

Intended Audience

Every course is unique because each instructor and class is different. This book can be used for a variety of introductory and upper division classes such as multicultural education, diversity and equity, culture in schools, culturally relevant teaching, race relations in schools, education, sociology of education, education in urban schools, introduction to teaching, human differences in schools, and anthropology in education.

Chapter Highlights

The book presents chapters as a series of building blocks so that teacher knowledge can be constructed like a house. First, there are foundational principles presented in Chapters 1–3, which act like the cement groundwork; the initial chapter discusses our democratic beliefs and constructs that include why social justice, caring, and culture must be the underpinnings of our teaching. The next two chapters describe what culture is and explains how to implement culturally relevant teaching. Many teachers think they know what culture is; however, most lack a clear understanding of culture and how to naturally incorporate it throughout their curriculum and in instruction.

The subsequent five chapters (Chapters 4–8) discuss social oppression due to race (a sociopolitical construct), sex, class, sexual orientation, exceptionalities (which includes people with developmental and intellectual disabilities, and advanced learners), and religion. There are perennial themes across social categories in which teachers must have a strong knowledge to understand the importance of their roles in a democracy. Next there is a chapter on prejudice and bullying (Chapter 9). Teachers need to know what types of prejudice and bullying are most prevalent and what strategies they can implement in their classrooms to eliminate these destructive actions. Chapter 10 discusses language acquisition as many of our students come from homes where a language other than English is spoken. The last chapter (Chapter 11) is dedicated to the achievement gap. Teachers must become aware of what it is and how all of the strategies discussed in the text can be implemented to assist them in addressing the achievement gap. This chapter also discusses using technology to address the achievement gap.

Below is a brief description of each chapter.

- In **Chapter 1** the foundations for multicultural education are presented. The United States is an extremely diverse nation. Diversity refers not only to characteristics of ethnicity, race (a sociopolitical construct), and gender, but also to areas such as sexual orientation, religion, and language. There are many misconceptions about multicultural education. Some teachers believe it is only for schools with large numbers of students of color; however, the field was created to address issues of equality and equity for all students. This chapter also discusses how multicultural education as a field developed. Principles and goals are presented. One of the most important goals of multicultural education is to eliminate the achievement gap. Few teachers understand this. Many think multicultural education is about sharing cultural elements like food and art; though these are important, they are not the major goals of the field. Educators need to identify an educational system of beliefs or a framework that guides their work. This may be equity pedagogy and/or culturally relevant teaching along with the values of social justice and the ethic of care.

- **Chapter 2** is an entire chapter on culture. What is culture? Why isn't it primarily about holidays and foods? What do teachers need to know about their students to be effective educators? Culture is a powerful element in the classroom if teachers know how to build on student cultures. This doesn't mean eating lots of yummy food. A model of culture that assists teachers in identifying three levels of culture in their learners is shared. Culture is like the air: it nurtures students, it feeds students, and it teaches them about life. That is one of the reasons why teachers need to understand student cultures and respect them. However, mainstream culture is also powerful and can convey the belief that student cultures are not important or worthy. Teachers as cultural mediators must be able to identify the many different ways that the cultures of students of color can be put down. Students also are beings where many cultures intersect. They are not members of one social group such as a "Dineh kid" or a "Latino kid." This limits their complex cultural identities that include the intersection of many social characteristics. Several excellent educational programs that affirm the cultural backgrounds of diverse students are described.

- **Chapter 3** builds on the first two chapters and describes how teachers can implement culturally relevant teaching in their own classrooms. This section of the book describes characteristics of successful culturally relevant programs such as the Algebra project and Funds of Knowledge. Culturally relevant teaching is not just about race, a sociopolitical construct, but also many other social characteristics. Culturally relevant teaching includes content and instructional delivery strategies. Using the educational theory of Vygotsky, the chapter also explains how teachers can use a variety of cultural models in their instruction. These models can also include examples from student lives, cultural stories, cultural role models, familiar family songs, civil rights issues, community history, and community issues. Students come to school already having a great deal of knowledge, and teachers can tap into their knowledge and skills in creating the classroom curriculum. Examples from the learners' lives can be some of the most powerful ways teachers scaffold student learning. This chapter will begin to get teachers to think differently about how to integrate culturally relevant teaching.

▶ **Chapter 4** discusses racism in the United States. Teachers need to understand why some of their students—whether White or students of color or from low income communities or women—feel that inequities are common in life. It is critical for all teachers to study the historical experiences of people from many different communities. Specific patterns of exclusion across racial groups, as sociopolitical communities, will emerge. While it is not possible to present the history of all ethnic communities, this book integrates coverage of particular issues in the histories of Native Americans, Latino/Hispanic Americans, African Americans, Asian American and Pacific Islander Americans, and Jewish Americans. Teachers need to know the histories of underrepresented groups not only to understand various viewpoints their own students may bring to the class but also to use historical contexts to inform lesson plans for all students.

▶ **Chapter 5** was created to expand on the discussions and strategies presented in Chapter 4. It is not enough for teachers to review major themes in regard to societal racism such as imperialism, colonialism, slavery, cultural assimilation, and nativism, but they also need to know how to teach the concept of racism in class. It is important for teachers to move away from seeing oppressed people as victims. Chapter 5 presents many civil rights activists and organizations that have worked for social justice for all. Many of the activists discussed in Chapter 5 also are representative of intersectionality. For example, James Baldwin was not only African American, but also gay and lived in Harlem, a poor community in New York City. He was persecuted for all of these social characteristics, but he still fought back in his writings and public presentations. This chapter includes historical timelines for major racial communities to identify ways that they fought for their civil rights.

▶ **Chapter 6** is about class and sex. Classism is a powerful force in our schools. Students are often judged by the economic level of their families. However, in the United States over 21 percent of the children live in poverty, including 38 percent of Black students. There are many students of color who live in families that suffer from hunger or lack of adequate shelter and healthcare. Stereotypes about children in poverty are powerful and can lead to lower teacher expectations. Teachers need to review their stereotypes about poor students. This chapter also includes discussion of inequalities dealing with sex and those women who have fought for equal rights. Many families are led by single mothers. They also must not only fight the lack of equal pay but also pervasive and continual stereotypes about women in society. Title IX is presented with a discussion about how it has led to more women in sports and has provided other opportunities such as college scholarships. A timeline highlighting those who fought for women's rights is included in this chapter.

▶ **Chapter 7** is an extensive discussion of sexual orientation and gender identity. Though recently more discussion about sexual orientation has occurred in society, many teachers need further information about the topic. In this book, we believe that LGBTQ is a cultural group, which like other cultural groups has developed a frame of reference, language, symbols, customs, and values. They also have a distinct history fighting for civil rights. Researchers believe like ethnic identity development in racial populations, LGBTQ individuals pass through stages of identity formation. Our teachers also need to know that many civil rights activists arose from this community, such as James Baldwin and Langston Hughes. This again shows intersectionality in how oppression involves various social characteristics and compounds the discrimination people are subjected to. This chapter also includes a timeline of selected events that identifies where members of the LGBTQ community fought for their civil rights.

➤ **Chapter 8** centers on religion, people with disabilities, and advanced learners as cultural groups. Freedom of religion is a First Amendment right. However, teachers often do not teach about religion. As a nation where church and state are separated, we are also mindful that one of the most devastating human tragedies of modern times was the genocide of Jews during World War II. Unfortunately, anti-Semitism, along with Islamophobia, is still strong in our nation today. Religious groups are extremely diverse as well. There are over 15 different Protestant organizations in the United States. Just as discrimination due to religious affiliation is present in today's world, prejudice toward people with disabilities is also pervasive. In this chapter, underlying beliefs of disability studies are compared with those in the area of special education. In disability studies, people with disabilities and advanced learners are seen as members of cultural groups. Have you considered this perspective? This compares with special education, which is based on the medical model. Disability studies and special education are extremely different orientations, and teachers should have backgrounds in the two positions so they can make the most informed educational decisions for their students.

➤ **Chapter 9** about prejudice and bullying is next because bullying is one of the most hurtful and inescapable behaviors that students must deal with. Prejudice is destructive to both the perpetrator and victim because it creates obstacles to building a strong, compassionate democracy. There are different levels of prejudice. How can teachers identify those levels? Prejudice when put into action becomes discrimination. How can teachers work with students to eliminate verbal, physical, emotional, and cyberbullying in the classroom? Bullying stems from prejudicial feelings and beliefs. There are many reasons why students bully each other, from wanting to be accepted by peers to needing to feel in control of a situation. Teachers can guide students to develop social consciousness and help them develop intervention strategies. However, spectators of bullying also participate in the process because they reinforce the bullying behaviors of the perpetrator.

➤ **Chapter 10** is about language acquisition and how teachers can implement instructional strategies that are most effective with English learners or duel immersion students. How do children learn language? How can teachers build on a student's first language as they learn English or a second language? These are topics covered in this chapter. Language is one of the most powerful cultural tools we learn. Language also shapes how we take in information and identify who we are. There are numerous strategies that teachers can use such as the natural approach or the cognitive academic language learning approach. One thing teachers may not understand is that though students can carry on an excellent conversation in English, it may take an English language learner up to seven years to learn the academic and high level English language required to read materials and write in disciplines like social studies or ecology. Researchers have found that bilingual programs in which students keep their home language along with learning English are the most beneficial for students; learners acquire two or more languages, cognitive strengths that can be used in a variety of linguistic and cultural environments, and enhance reading skills.

➤ **Chapter 11** is about the achievement gap and how to use technology to address it. Many students of color do not do as well as White students on reading and math assessments. This points to the lack of equal educational outcomes for students. What can teachers do? Teachers must make learning more relevant to all students and build on what students know. They must integrate student experiences and knowledge into the classroom curriculum through the use of culturally relevant teaching. Along with this, teachers must affirm the cultural backgrounds of students and engage parents in the learning process. The partnerships that teachers create with parents can be invaluable. Technology also provides teachers with new ways to interact with their students, from providing extra tutoring lectures to providing opportunities to get online and ask their teachers questions about the lesson outside of the classroom.

The entire book is dedicated to making suggestions to teachers. First, they need to develop their educational framework. Second, they must examine their own biases about different human differences. Third, teachers must educate themselves about the social oppression that still exists in our nation and world. Next, they must more fully understand the perennial issues that different populations must continually deal with, whether it is racism, homophobia, sexism, or Islamophobia. Most importantly, teachers must learn what culturally relevant teaching is and how to implement the approach into their own work. Each student must see relevance in what they are learning and connect that learning to their lives. In this way they will be affirmed and see their own future potential!

Distinctive Features

A variety of features is included to provide students with many teaching resources and hands-on suggestions, as well as opportunities to critically evaluate strategies for teaching in today's diverse classrooms.

- **Case Studies.** Multiple case studies of real-world classroom situations and challenges are presented throughout the chapters. These give students the opportunity to reflect upon solutions they might want to incorporate into their teaching. Case studies are also ways for students to learn the stories of others and how their struggles have been addressed by teachers in the classroom.

- **Teaching Tips.** These provide hands-on tips for teaching in the classroom and include general recommendations on how to examine one's own teaching, and use strategies like chunking, scaffolding, modeling, and questioning.

- **My Journal.** This feature helps students think about extremely complex issues involving culture, equity, and civil rights. It provides them with a guided portfolio of their ideas for teaching in the classroom. These can be uploaded into the e-portfolio Pathbrite app in the MindTap product and taken with the student upon completion of the course.

- **Take a Stand.** Many of these lessons present controversial issues in which students use critical thinking and decision making skills to decide on the viewpoints they will support or actions they would take. These activities give students the opportunity to examine issues from multiple perspectives and question strategies, which are critical teaching skills.

- **Checklists** are provided periodically as teaching tools for your students.

Pedagogy

In addition to bolded key terms and a running glossary, *Diversity and Equity in the Classroom* includes a number of learning aids that clarify the material in visually compelling ways, and prompt students to be self-reflective and to think critically about teaching challenges and strategies.

- **Consider this**.... These short vignettes highlight insights that teachers should consider. Students are then asked to answer questions about the situation or topic presented. For example, globalization is not westernization.

- **Data Tables.** Numerous tables are included in the book to help students access information in a succinct way. For example, there are tables illustrating the percentage of people who belong to various religions in the United States, poverty rates of children, and academic test performance of various ethnic groups.

- **Photographs.** Photographs enhance the knowledge presented. Some photos were taken by the author and her husband. These photographs show real teachers and students engaged in teaching and learning at schools in which the author took on a leadership role.

- **Timelines.** Chronological time lines are provided for African Americans, Asian Americans and Pacific Islanders, Hispanic/Latinos, Jews, the LGBT community, Native Americans, and women. The information can be analyzed to show patterns of social oppression and the consistent struggle for civil rights, and used as to create lesson plans with positive role models.

- **Videos.** Video Cases with critical thinking questions for every chapter are included in the MindTap for *Diversity and Equity in the Classroom*. The videos provide additional information about concepts like classroom motivation, cooperative learning, culturally relevant teaching, and the social and emotional development of adolescents.

- **Thinking about Intersectionality** is a section at the end of each chapter that gets teachers to think about how oppression is based on various human differences. It highlights that no child is the result of any one human characteristic. For example, students may be seen as Muslim, but they also are members of various groups like scientists, stamp collectors, and guitar players. This section is designed to get teachers to think of students in their totality.

- **Check Your Cultural Awareness** follows the Summary of each chapter and provides students with an essay question that prompts them to reflect on what they have learned in the chapter. It is important for educators to have the opportunity to test themselves and confirm their knowledge.

- **Know and Go Tools in the Classroom** is found at the very end of every chapter and provides extensive curriculum and educational ideas and tools, as well as recommendations on how teachers can integrate cultural issues into the classroom such as civil rights or culturally relevant teaching. This feature also includes technology strategies for the classroom.

Integrated Approach

The book uses an approach in which content and instructional strategies are integrated, and where issues affecting various groups are integrated within overarching chapter topics. For example, there are word webs that show how a student identifies with numerous social characteristics such as religion, ethnicity, class, martial arts, and language. History is also woven in and role models are identified throughout the text so that teachers will be able to teach their students that individuals from many different communities have fought for civil rights for all of us. Throughout the book there are also many examples of what teachers can do in their own teaching to integrate culturally relevant teaching. For instance, even though a video presented in MindTap talks about how technology can be used in the classroom, the issue being researched is civil rights role models. The themes of community, culture, and social justice are woven together as a tapestry in the book.

Focus on Intersectionality

Intersectionality must be understood and covered by teachers. It is important that they teach their students that people cannot be labeled according to stereotypes. Labels only serve to narrow perceptions of people. In order to understand others, we need to listen to them and understand them as a complicated whole. They are members of many subcultures and have many interests. In addition, unfortunately students are bullied because of numerous human differences such as sexual orientation, class, and gender.

Because the teacher is the most important element of a successful classroom, I hope to get future teachers to think about issues of diversity and equity. It takes time to develop not only one's belief system about teaching but also to create a repertoire of successful curriculum and instructional strategies for today's diverse classrooms. Each educator teaches in his or her unique way. We all have different personalities and cultural backgrounds and create our own innovative and meaningful ways to provide equity in education. We want all students to become successful learners, and we are passionate about making a difference in students' lives.

Remember, great teaching is like running a marathon; you must keep at it. There's no profession as rewarding as teaching. Seeing students think, work, and succeed warms one's heart like nothing else.

Your teachers will inspire their students and they will inspire you too!

Sending my best wishes!

Val Pang

Acknowledgments

There are numerous people to whom I am so grateful for their support throughout my career and in the creation of this text: Sumie Akizuki, Carole Norman, Jackie Maruhashi, Joe Melendez, Mario Garrett, Jack L. Nelson, Gwen Nelson, Stanley Sue, Jose Luis and Patricia Alvarado, Rick Oser, Candee Chaplin, Ellen Beck, Scot Danforth, Thanh and Curt Hopkins, Andrea Saltzman-Martin, Luke Duesbery, Lucille Hee, Donna and Alvin Wong, Cynthia and James Park, Jose Preciado, Kin and Connie Wong, E. Wayne Ross, Lynelle Hee and Venkat Shastri, Merry Merryfield, Alan Singer, A. Lin Goodwin, Bill Fernekes, Binaya Subedi, David Hursh, Yoon Pak, Clift Tanabe, Ron Rochon, Marc Pruyn, Jean Brosius, Eveline Takahashi, Karen and Doug Beahm, Ariana Erwood, Cameron Erwood, Mirei Yasuda, Connor Howard, Nicole Howard, Sophie Hofman, Alan Lau, Kevin Vinson, Leanne Quirk, Nancy and Patrick Michalowski, Martha Pedroza, Scott Mullin, Angelica Tavison Soto, Easter Finley, Debbie Marsing, Cathy Close, Kathy Mikitka Gomez, Kathy Holowach, Ceci Necoechea, Geneva Gay, Pat Larke, Jackie Jordan Irvine, John Palmer, Peter Kiang, Yuji Shimogori, Carl Grant, Franciso Rios, Maxime Dumesnil, Allen Trent, Penny Lisi, Cherry and James Banks, Jessica Gordon Nehmbhard, Ed Dial, Gregg Korematsu, Sage Ainsworth, Joe Mulson, Cheyenne Raines, Sara Barlow, Ronnie Daniels, Arturo Salazar, Hindeliza Flores, Julia Cruz, Pia Parrish, Buzz and Janice Boyum, Nikki Boyum and Seth Sligar, Peggy Han, Jason Poliak, Eric Sands, Linda Harrington, Carrie Brown, Don Masse, Logan Masse-Brown, Aurora Masse-Brown, Jace and Andre Cruz, Ally Ainsworth, Sammy Oser, Edith Oser, Gerry C. H. Pang, Jennifer M. Pang, Matthew A. Pang, Kari Boyum, Kathy Ooka, Cheryl Ooka, Karen and Terry Hofman, Trish Howard, Naomi and Greg Bang, Ryan, Cheree, Kai, Selah Rose, and Brooklyn Porter, and the thousands of teachers who I have had the opportunity to work with for over 40 years as an educator. You have taught me so much.

In addition, I would like to thank the many reviewers whose comments and suggestions helped develop this text. These include:

Ilene Allgood, Florida Atlantic University
Archie L. Blanson, Ph.D., University of St. Thomas
Dr. Bonita Cade, Roger Williams University
Dr. Irene Chen, University of Houston Downtown
Kam Chi Chan, Purdue University North Central
Lara Christoun, Carthage College
Sandra R. Ciocci, Bridgewater State University
Nedra L. Cossa, Armstrong State University
Deanna L. Cozart, University of Georgia
Ella-Mae Daniel, Florida State University, College of Education
April Dominguez, Ph.D., California State University, Bakersfield
Amy Shriver Dreussi, Ph.D., University of Akron
Maryann Dudzinski, Valparaiso University
Karla Esser, Regis University
Dr. Melinda Eudy Ratchford, Belmont Abbey College
Susan Finley, Washington State University
Susan Foley, Coastal Carolina University

Shannon L. Gooden, Florida State University

Sherry A Green, Ed. S., Georgia Highlands College

Diane Smith Grych, Ph.D., Concord University

Dr. Jeannette Jones, Texas Lutheran University

Kathleen Lazarus, Daytona State College

Tawnya L. Lubbes, Eastern Oregon University

Mary F. Mattson, Georgia Perimeter College

Heather Merrill, Glendale Community College

Laura Mitchell, Urban Education UHD

Diane B. Mitschke, University of Texas at Arlington

Inna Molitoris, Eastern Michigan University

Michael Perrotti, Ph.D, California University of Pennsylvania

Regina Rahimi, Armstrong State University

Dr. Eileen Richardson, Cameron University

Jacqueline Rippy, Florida State College at Jacksonville

Dr. Dick Robertson, St. Ambrose University

Rodrigo Joseph Rodriguez, University of Texas at El Paso

Darlene Russell, William Paterson University

Elizabeth Sandell, Minnesota State University, Mankato

Joseph Sencibaugh, Webster University

Mary Amanda Stewart, Texas Woman's University

Dr. Naomi R. Taylor, Hamline University

Dr. Shereah Taylor, Tarrant County College South Campus

Jamia Thomas-Richmond, Coastal Carolina University

Dr. Melinda Trice Cowart, Texas Woman's University

Phitsamay S. Uy, University of Massachusetts Lowell

Lillian Vega Castaneda, California State University Channel Islands

Debra T. Wiley, Albany State University

Rhonda D. Wilkins, Ph.D., Georgia Perimeter College

Dr. Lynda Wolverton, Polk State College

I would also like to thank the many professionals at Cengage who made this book possible: Cheri-Ann Nakamura, Lin Gaylord, Mark Kerr, Nick Barrows, Andrew Miller, and Christy Frame. These professionals provided exceptional recommendations and their expertise has contributed greatly to the creation of this text. Additional thanks for the production of the book go to Jill Traut of MPS Limited, the copyeditor Heather Mann, and Nick Stern for his creative illustrations. Independent consultants with Cengage, Beth Kaufman and Kate Russillo also provided outstanding guidance in the text's development.

Online Resources

The following materials are available to enhance learning for *Diversity and Equity in the Classroom.*

Instructor's Manual and Test Bank

An online Instructor's Manual accompanies this book. It contains information to assist the instructor in designing the course, including sample syllabi, discussion questions, teaching and learning activities, field experiences, learning objectives, and additional online resources. For assessment support, the test bank includes true/false, multiple-choice, matching, short-answer, and essay questions for each chapter.

Cengage Learning Testing Powered by Cognero

Cognero is a flexible online system that allows you to author, edit, and manage test bank content from multiple Cengage Learning solutions. Create multiple test versions in an instant and deliver them from your LMS, classroom, or wherever you want! No special installs or downloads needed. Create tests from school, home, the coffee shop—anywhere with Internet access.

MindTap™: The Personal Learning Experience

MindTap for *Diversity and Equity in the Classroom* represents a new approach to teaching and learning. A highly personalized, fully customizable learning platform with an integrated eportfolio, MindTap helps students to elevate thinking by guiding them to:

- Know, remember, and understand concepts critical to becoming a great teacher;
- Apply concepts, create curriculum and tools, and demonstrate performance and competency in key areas in the course, including national and state education standards;
- Prepare artifacts for the portfolio and eventual state licensure, to launch a successful teaching career; and
- Develop the habits to become a reflective practitioner.

As students move through each chapter's Learning Path, they engage in a scaffolded learning experience designed to move them up Bloom's Taxonomy from lower- to higher-order thinking skills. The Learning Path enables preservice students to develop these skills and gain confidence by:

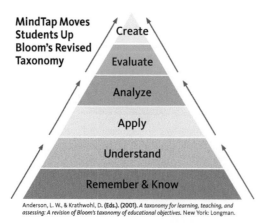

MindTap Moves Students Up Bloom's Revised Taxonomy

Create
Evaluate
Analyze
Apply
Understand
Remember & Know

Anderson, L. W., & Krathwohl, D. (Eds.). (2001). *A taxonomy for learning, teaching, and assessing: A revision of Bloom's taxonomy of educational objectives.* New York: Longman.

> Engaging them with chapter topics and activating their prior knowledge by watching and answering questions about authentic videos of teachers teaching and children learning in real classrooms;

> Checking their comprehension and understanding through Did You Get It? assessments, with varied question types that are autograded for instant feedback;

> Applying concepts through mini-case scenarios—students analyze typical teaching and learning situations, and then create a reasoned response to the issue(s) presented in the scenario; and

> Reflecting about and justifying the choices they made within the teaching scenario problem.

MindTap helps instructors facilitate better outcomes by evaluating how future teachers plan and teaching lessons in ways that make content clear and help diverse students learn, assessing the effectiveness of their teaching practice, and adjusting teaching as needed. MindTap enables instructors to facilitate better outcomes by:

> Making grades visible in real time through the Student Progress App so students and instructors always have access to current standings in the class.

> Using the Outcome Library to embed national education standards and align them to student learning activities, and also allowing instructors to add their state's standards or any other desired outcome.

> Allowing instructors to generate reports on students' performance with the click of a mouse against any standards or outcomes that are in their MindTap course.

> Giving instructors the ability to assess students on state standards or other local outcomes by editing existing or creating their own MindTap activities, and then by aligning those activities to any state or other outcomes that the instructor has added to the MindTap Outcome Library.

MindTap for *Diversity and Equity in the Classroom* helps instructors easily set their course because it integrates into the existing Learning Management System and saves instructors time by allowing them to fully customize any aspect of the learning path. Instructors can change the order of the student learning activities, hide activities they don't want for the course, and—most importantly—create custom assessments and add any standards, outcomes, or content they do want (e.g., YouTube videos, Google docs). Learn more at www.cengage.com/mindtap.

About the Author

Gerald C. H. Pang

Valerie Ooka Pang has extensive experience as a teacher and educational researcher. She began teaching in an all-Black neighborhood school in the Pacific Northwest. The students walked to school and were served breakfast at a local community center that was supported by the Black Panthers. Pang has also taught in an all-White farming community where families raised acres of corn, potatoes, and wheat. Though many of her students lived on farms, she lived in town.

Pang taught elementary school and has been involved in K–12 diversity and equity efforts since the 1970s. One of her most fun consultancies was at *Sesame Street*; she gave a workshop for the staff of Children's Television Workshop on racism and culture. During that trip, she took her family to New York City, and they met Sonia Manzano who played Maria for 44 years. Pang also had the opportunity to consult with Fred Rogers and his staff of *Mr. Roger's Neighborhood*. She provided feedback on issues of diversity and equity as they developed new programs for his show. Pang values the little red, wooden trolley that Fred Rogers gave her.

One of the most important contributions she has made in education is her work with various social studies textbook companies. A contribution to the field of social studies was to add content about the Angel Island Immigration Station on the West Coast from 1910–1940 where Chinese, Japanese, Italian, Korean, Australian, Russian, and other immigrants were processed. Now, when Ellis Island is discussed in many social studies texts, it is also standard to include descriptions of Angel Island and how many Chinese immigrants were held there for months before being allowed into the United States.

Her interest in diversity and equity arose out of her family's experiences. Her mother, a native-born American citizen, was taken away in 1942 with her brothers and parents from their home in Seattle, Washington, when Japanese Americans were forced into internment camps during World War II. Her mother and family were taken to Minidoka Incarceration Camp Idaho and were imprisoned there for about three and a half years.

Pang works toward the creation of compassionate and effective schools where students develop their potentials and contribute to a stronger democracy and peaceful world.

Pamela Moore/Getty Images

Multicultural Education: A Foundation for Schools

Learning Objectives

LO1 Describe the difference between the terms "race" and "ethnicity" and what is meant by "cultural diversity."

LO2 Discuss demographic changes in the United States.

LO3 Identify the roots and misconceptions of multicultural education.

LO4 Define and analyze the goals and concepts of multicultural education.

LO5 Discuss and evaluate the goals, major concepts, and models of multicultural education.

STANDARDS COVERED

NAEYC 6 **naeyc**

CAEP 1 *CAEP*

INTASC 1, 2, 3, 4, 5, 7, 8, 9, 10 **InTASC**

LO1 Describe the difference between the terms "race" and "ethnicity" and what is meant by "cultural diversity."

Overview of Race, Ethnicity, and Cultural Diversity

naeyc CAEP InTASC

This text is about the history, principles, and instructional practices of multicultural education, an increasingly important field of study in education. As you read the first chapter, you will gain an understanding of why multicultural education is so important to your professional development and success as a teacher. One major reason is because the demographics of the United States reveal that it is a racially and ethnically diverse nation. Race refers to the sociopolitical concepts of being Asian American and Pacific Islander, Black, Latino, Native American, and White. **Race** is a political and social construct, categorizing people based on *perceived* physical differences such as skin color; there is no basis for race in biology. During the 1700s and 1800s, race was used as a political construct that unified the British Empire and the United States in an orientation where the domination of "Anglo Saxons" as the desirable "race." This idea was supported as the basis for peace because they were seen as the most competent group to support a democratic world (Bell, 2014). There was a vague definition of race, which comprised the integration of biological and cultural roots including human evolutionary history and advancements, cognitive superiority, and physiology (Bell, 2014). This orientation perpetuated the belief that the dominance and self-importance of Anglo-Saxons was warranted because of their goal of democracy and superior intellectual abilities.

The original typology of race presented by the Swedish naturalist Carl Linneaus in his 1735 book *Systema naturea* has been shown to be fraught with biological inaccuracies, though its so-called biological ideas about race continue to be used in present times by some people (Muller-Wille, 2014). Linneaus described four categories of human races and their skin colors along with dispositions: Europeans (whitish and confident), Africans (blackish and hot tempered), Asians (tawny and melancholy), and Americans (reddish and apathetic) (Muller-Wille, 2014; Gould, 1996). Though Linneaus's views have been challenged and the biological underpinnings have been disputed (Gould, 1996; Bell, 2014), the construct has been used as a political tool in domination in society, including schools. One example is the continual segregation of students in our schools—now known as resegregation—so that students of color do not have the same opportunities as their White peers (Tatum, 2010). **Resegregation** refers to the practice of continual segregation of students of color even after many legal and social practices aimed at desegregation, from busing to court-ordered remedies, have been implemented. Beverly Daniel Tatum, an educator who is also the president of Spelman College, has identified many ways in which racial inequalities continue to plague our schools when students of color do not have the same opportunities to attend schools with high-quality teachers, well-equipped facilities, and access to high-level discipline content (2010).

Also consider how race is interwoven into many other social categories such as social class and neighborhood. **Ethnicity**, on the other hand, refers to the ancestry or national origin of a person identifying, for example, as a Mexican American, Puerto Rican, Japanese American, or Black American (Figure 1.1). Additionally, **cultural diversity** can include many different subcultures identified by ethnicity, language, social class, gender, sexual orientation, age, family, neighborhood, exceptionalities (intellectual and developmental disabilities and advanced learners), and religion. You will also learn that a student could be a member of several subcultures. For example, Maria may speak Spanish, was born in Iowa, is a member of the Buddhist Temple, comes from a high-income family, and identifies as being gay. Each subculture is complex, and when teachers place a student in a single subcultural box, such as ethnicity, then it ignores the multifaceted elements in his or her life. This action can also lead to stereotyping.

Race is a political and social construct that refers to categorizing people based on perceived physical differences such as skin color; there is no basis for race in biology.
Resegregation refers to the practice of continual segregation of students of color even after many legal and social practices aimed at desegregation, from busing to court-ordered remedies.

Ethnicity refers to a place of family-national origin such as Ireland, Japan, Croatia, Nigeria, or Mexico.
Cultural diversity is a broad term and includes subcultures such as race, ethnicity, social class, gender, religion, neighborhoods, families, language, exceptionalities, and sexual orientation.

Figure 1.1: Young people create masks to represent their cultural and ethnic identities. They wear them proudly.

Valerie Ooka Pang

A student is usually a member of many subcultures and defines him- or herself depending on the social context of the situation. If a teacher is talking about ethnic membership, the student may say she is Mexican American; however, if the instructor is discussing religion, the learner may share that she is Buddhist. Though the term "culture" is often used—the singular form of the term—your students are most likely members of many subcultures that include the concepts of race and ethnicity.

Think about how you might culturally identify yourself. If you are European American, do you want to be known only as the White teacher? Are there other aspects of your life that you identify with, such as being a surfer of Irish ancestry or speaking Spanish? Doesn't the term "White teacher" tend to stereotype you? What does that term really mean? That's why it is not best to identify students as being in one category of race. Saying something like, "He's the Black student" can be limiting and stereotypical.

This chapter is designed to help you reflect on various aspects of diversity including misconceptions about the field and foundations of multicultural education. For example, some teachers believe that multicultural education should only be included in schools with large numbers of students of color. This misunderstanding can limit an educator's knowledge of how culture influences student learning in many different subcultures. In addition, this chapter includes discussion of three major theories that are foundational to multicultural education today. These theories are made up of values, goals, concepts, and beliefs that are key elements of equitable education. The theories direct teachers to create strong trusting relationships with their students and students' parents and to facilitate the development of curriculum and instructional practices that are culturally relevant in schools as they work to provide equitable education.

Historical and Social Context

To understand the complex issues that surround the discussion of race, ethnicity, and other aspects of cultural diversity in the United States, it is important to consider the demographics of our nation. Race and ethnicity are powerful elements in schools because students bring with them a huge suitcase of beliefs about themselves and others that is founded on beliefs about race and ethnicity. You will be considering these aspects of society and how they impact your students and your perceptions of individuals in your classes. Both of these constructs will be discussed in more depth in later chapters.

Demographics: Diversity in the United States

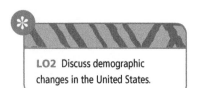

The United States of America is one of the most culturally diverse countries in the world. You will become a teacher in schools that serve many different communities; students come from different racial and ethnic families, are members of various religious communities, and may be straight, gay, able/disabled, lesbian, bisexual, or transgendered. The diversity in our schools represents the evolution over time of various cultures and subcultures that have made America home. For example, it is estimated that about 4 percent of the American adult population is a member of the gay, bisexual community as identified by the National Health Survey of 2013 of the Centers for Diseases Control and Prevention (Somashekhar, 2014). The research included over 33,000 adults from 18 to 64 years old and was one of the largest studies to collect information from gay, lesbian, and bisexual adults.

In addition, cultural diversity has always been a characteristic of the people who were indigenous to the lands now known as the United States. Before Columbus reached the Bahamas in 1492, there were hundreds of Native American tribes in existence. The people did not see themselves as "Native Americans" or "American Indians;" rather they were from the Iroquois nation or they were Wampanoag. They saw themselves as members of their specific tribe or nation. They were members of many diverse communities. Even in 2003, the National Congress of American Indians noted that there were 562 tribes; these 562 communities are federally recognized (National Congress of American Indians, 2003). Today, our population is still growing and is increasingly diverse, as you can see in Table 1.1. The table shows that there are almost 50 million K–12 students in the United States from many different racial backgrounds.

In reviewing the table, do you notice that almost half of all students in the United States are members of underrepresented groups? **Underrepresented** refers to non-White people, including African Americans, American Indians, Alaska Natives, Asian Americans, Hispanic/Latinos, Pacific Islanders, and interracial students. Sometimes **Asian American and Pacific Islander** students are placed into a large pan-Asian group and denoted by **AAPI**. It is important that teachers understand that diversity is an important element of American society.

Racial Diversity in U.S. Schools

As our country becomes more culturally diverse, so do our students. If you have visited schools in a major school district, you may have noticed the racial diversity of students in

---

LO2 Discuss demographic changes in the United States.

Underrepresented refers to non-White people, including African Americans, American Indians, Alaska Natives, Asian Americans, Hispanic/Latinos, and Pacific Islanders.
Asian American and Pacific Islander students are placed into a large general group and denoted by **AAPI**. The AAPI community includes over 50 groups such as Chinese Americans, Japanese Americans, Korean Americans, Samoan Americans, Guamanian Americans, Hawaiian Americans, Hmong Americans, Taiwanese Americans, Cambodian Americans, Laotian Americans, Vietnamese Americans, South Indian Americans, Thai Americans, and others.

Table 1.1 U.S. Kindergarten through Twelfth Grade Student Population, Racial Membership, 2011*		
Race	Total Student Numbers	Percentage
Whites	25,464,162	52.7
Hispanics	11,693,788	24
African Americans	7,782,146	16
Asian American and Pacific Islanders	2.499,233	5
American Indian and Alaska Natives	541,986	.01
Two or more races	1,265,222	2.5
Total	48,246,539	100

National Center for Educational Statistics. Table 216.55 at http://nces.ed.gov/programs/digest/d13/tables/dt13_216.55.asp.
*Due to rounding, percentages add up to more than 100%.

Consider this . . .

Almost half of the students in U.S. schools are from families of color. And in many districts, Hispanics make up almost half or more of the student population. These statistics help us to understand that as teachers, we must learn about the culture, history, behaviors, and values of students from underrepresented groups in order to teach them most effectively.

Q What can teachers do to address these demographic changes?

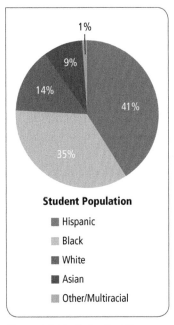

Student Population

■ Hispanic
■ Black
■ White
■ Asian
■ Other/Multiracial

Figure 1.2: **K–12 Student Population of Boston Public Schools, 2015–2016**

Source: Boston Public Schools, 2015–2016.

the classroom. In school districts in cities such as Chicago, Los Angeles, St. Louis, New Orleans, Houston, Baltimore, and Seattle, the majority of students come from communities of color. Figures 1.2 and 1.3 show the student populations of one district on the East Coast—Boston Public Schools—and one district on the West Coast—Los Angeles Unified School District. What differences and similarities do you see in the ethnic student makeup of each district?

It is not enough to know that students of color make up the majority of students in large urban districts like Boston and Los Angeles. It is also important to know that districts have different percentages of students. For example, Hispanics make up almost 65 percent of all students in Los Angeles Unified, while 8 percent are Black. In Boston, almost 35 percent of students are from African American families and about 41 percent are Hispanic. From these numbers, you can see that it is imperative teachers know about the culture, history, and lives of African American and Hispanic students if they teach in areas such as Boston or Los Angeles.

Class and Income Inequality

Social class is an element of diversity in society. A major factor of social class is income. The term *income* refers to the money one makes at his or her job. Income has also been found to be integrated with race, a sociopolitical construct as discussed at the beginning of the chapter. For example, people of color are more likely to be in the lower and middle-income groups because they have difficulty securing high-paying jobs. Historically, people of color have not had the same opportunities as others to secure high-levels of education in order to secure high-paying positions. Research shows that achievement levels in schools are highly correlated to income levels of parents and the opportunities they have for jobs and housing (Anyon, 1997).

Related to class is the issue of income inequality. The term *income inequality* refers to how the gap between the rich and others continues to grow exponentially. The recession of 2007–2008, during which the wealth of the rich greatly increased while middle- and lower-income people saw their wealth become stagnant, is an example (Frey & Kochhar, 2014). In 2013, upper-class families had wealth of about $639,400 in comparison to middle-income families who had wealth of about $96,500. Wealth is a much broader term than your salary. *Wealth* refers to the financial resources a family has such as a car, stocks, and savings, minus debts. Income refers to the salary of those in the family and profits from other sources.

The problem of income is not that children come from poor families; rather families do not have the social and political status to make changes in their lives (Anyon, 1997, 2005b). Anyon, an educational researcher, believed that positive change for low-income students could only occur if the social needs of their families were met. This included not only parent employment and family healthcare, but also improvements in housing and neighborhoods. There is a large movement in the United States protesting businesses like Walmart and McDonald's and advocating for an increase in wages to $15 an hour. Protests

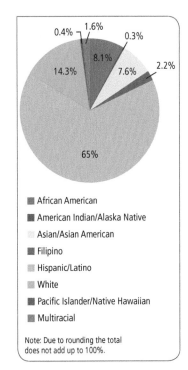

■ African American
■ American Indian/Alaska Native
☐ Asian/Asian American
■ Filipino
▨ Hispanic/Latino
▨ White
■ Pacific Islander/Native Hawaiian
■ Multiracial

Note: Due to rounding the total does not add up to 100%.

Figure 1.3: **K–12 Student Population of Los Angeles Unified School District, 2015**

Source: Kidsdata.org.

Table 1.2 Sample Minimum Wages by State for 2015

State	Minimum Wage
California	$9.00 an hour
Florida	$8.05 an hour
Illinois	$8.25 an hour
New Mexico	$7.50 an hour
New York	$8.75 an hour
Texas	$7.25 an hour
Virginia	$7.25 an hour
Washington	$9.47 an hour
Wisconsin	$7.25 an hour

Source: Raise the Minimum Wage, 2015.

have occurred in cities like New York, Chicago, Seattle, and Los Angeles. In 2015 many workers made much less than $15 an hour (Table 1.2).

Many people do not believe that these amounts are enough to support someone to live. Therefore, there is a movement toward a living wage, being led, in part, by the Service Employees International Union, which began organizing the effort in 2012 (Choi, 2015). A **living wage** is a level of income that is enough to pay for one's housing, food, utilities, and other necessities.

Income and wealth greatly dropped during the recent recession. What does it mean to be in a middle-income or high-income family? Table 1.3 provides one definition of middle-income and upper-income households. Chapter 6 discusses class and poverty and will have extensive discussions on the impact of class on achievement and how poverty can have lasting effects on children.

> **Living wage** refers to a level of income that is enough to pay for one's housing, food, utilities, and other necessities.

Sexual Orientation

Sexual orientation is another aspect of diversity in society that is being recognized by many people and organizations. In the past, many teachers believed that heterosexuality, the attraction of a woman and a man, was considered "the norm" in regards to sexual orientation. However, today many believe that there are numerous sexual orientations within society (Garbacik, 2013). One of the most common instruments used to measure sexual orientation in individuals was developed by Alfred Kinsey in 1948, but many researchers have raised questions about his work because they feel that the scale is too rigid. There are several hundred scales used to measure sexual orientation (Garbacik, 2013). Table 1.4 includes some of the various ways sexual orientation has been described.

One of the most comprehensive organizations dedicated to the inclusion of lesbian, gay, bisexual, transgender, and transgender students is GLSEN (Gay, Lesbian, Straight Education Network). You can review their website at GLSEN.org for information on how to

Table 1.3 Middle-Income and Upper-Income Households, 2013

Number in Family	1	2	3	4	5
Upper-income	$66,000	$93,300	$114.300	$132,000	$147,600
Middle Income	$22,000	$31,100	$38,100	44,000	$59,200

Source: Pew Research Center, Frey & Kochhar, 2014.

Table 1.4 Sexual Orientations: Definitions	
Lesbian	Attraction of women to each other.
Gay	Attraction of men to each other.
Bisexual	Attracted to women and men.
Transgender	Gender identity is not associated with the sex a person is born with.
Asexual	May not be attracted to others.
Queer	Negative term for some because it was, and still is, used to denigrate LGBT individuals, while others see it as a term of empowerment about being proud of who they are.
Heterosexuality	Attraction of men and women; infers that there are only two sexes.

Source: Garbacik, 2013.

include all students in classrooms through the curriculum and collaborative events. Eliminating bias because of sexual orientation is critical to the creation of a safe and effective school and classroom for everyone.

There are many destructive comments that students make about sexual orientation, such as "that homework is so gay." It is important in a diverse community to treat everyone with respect and compassion. This aspect of diversity is often one of the most difficult for teachers to address because there is less information in schools about the issue and how to deal with prejudice due to sexual orientation.

Sexual Abuse and Violence

Because diversity includes issues that affect women, one of the severe problems that females may be subjected to is sexual abuse and sexual violence. In recent years, many Americans have stood up against sexual abuse and violence by marching through the streets of their cities and towns. In 2016, protesters picketed against a judge's minimal sentence of a swimming star at Stanford University who was found to have raped a young woman on campus (Stack, 2016). Sexual abuse and violence can be directed toward women or men; however, it is usually aimed at women and girls (Blake et al., 2014). Female youth and teenagers can suffer severe physical and psychological trauma due to sexual abuse. It is a human rights issue that impacts millions of women around the world and can include issues of sex trafficking and war (Garbacik, 2013). To find out more about the support network for sexual abuse victims and their families, visit the website for RAINN, Rape, Abuse & Incest National Network, at www.rainn.org. Educators may find that they would like to gather more information about these issues.

Multicultural Education

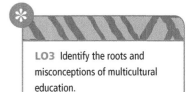

LO3 Identify the roots and misconceptions of multicultural education.

To understand the issues in multicultural education, it is valuable for you to learn about the roots of the field. How did the field evolve? What were major issues and concepts that arose? How did equity in education arise? Why do some educators believe that equity in education is so important? In addition, later in the chapter you will examine misconceptions that some educators hold about multicultural education. Maybe you think it is about knowing a culture of a student community so you are respectful to the students in class. However, the field is much more complicated than that because multicultural education includes learning theory, culturally relevant education, and prejudice reduction in schools.

Roots of Multicultural Education: Intercultural Education, Intergroup Education, the Civil Rights Movement, and Cultural Pluralism

Multicultural education is an integral part of the preparation of teachers today. However, original scholars of the field struggled to establish the discipline. Many Americans such as parents, politicians, teachers, and members of the general public (Kozol, 2005, 2010) did not believe racism was a powerful impediment to success in society and in schools, even though there were numerous schools where African American, Latino, American Indian, and Asian American students were not provided equal educational opportunity (Banks, 1984; C. A. Banks, 2005; Johnson, 2002; Pak, 2004; Pak & Johnson, forthcoming; Rivera & Poplin, 1995).

You will read in the next two sections that prior to establishment of the legitimacy of the field, the Intercultural Education (Pak, 2004, 2006; Pak & Johnson, forthcoming) and the Intergroup Education Movements (C. A. Banks, 2005) pushed for the inclusion of ethnic and racial information and content into the curriculum. This was important to the creation of culturally relevant and affirming schools. Pak explained that as the United States was coming out of the Great Depression of the 1930s, our nation had to deal with an increase in immigration and the rise of Nazism in Europe. At the same time African Americans challenged the national values of democracy and equality when segregation was a legalized and systematic process in the United States. They wanted to be considered full citizens able to access all aspects of society such as public schools and public transportation. One of the great voices at this time was philosopher Horace Kallen who taught about **cultural pluralism** and respecting people from diverse cultures and their ways of life. Kallen argued that cultural pluralism was important to our democracy because it called for multiple perspectives and that diverse cultures enriched mainstream America (Kallen, 1998).

> **Cultural pluralism** refers to respecting people from diverse cultures and their ways of life.

The field of multicultural education did not develop in a vacuum. It took many years and the hard work of numerous educators to create what we now know as multicultural education. The field of multicultural education has its roots in three major movements in the United States. The first two movements were the Intercultural Education Movement and the Intergroup Education Movement. Both developed around the same time period of the mid-1920s and 1930s. Some scholars (Caraballo, 2009) see the two as one consistent movement in education, while others believe the efforts were distinctive struggles because they had different goals and used diverse methods to address issues of equality in a democracy. The third movement, for civil rights, occurred in the 1950s. Each brought to the field a slightly different orientation to the inclusion of immigrants and people and communities of color. Research has indicated that exact dates of their origins differ from scholar to scholar, but their approximate time periods are:

- Intercultural Education Movement, 1930s through 1960s
- Intergroup Education Movement, 1930s through 1960s
- Civil Rights Movement, 1950s through present day

The next sections will discuss the goals and practices that the different movements added to the evolution of multicultural education. The three sections will be followed by a chart that describes the actions, goals, and significant places in the history of each of the movements.

Intercultural Education: Assimilation or Acculturation?

As the nation recognized the racial diversity in the United States in cities such as New York and Detroit, educators began calling for the integration of curriculum content about communities of color. They were concerned that segregation in schools, housing, and general living in the nation were unfair and did not support the values of a democracy. Many educators and other citizens believed that as a democracy, the United States needed more integration of information about groups such as Black Americans in schools.

Consider this . . .

Cultural assimilation is a process whereby new immigrants and others adopt practices, values, behaviors, and expectations of the dominant culture. Some educators believe that schools do too much of this. For example, Spanish-speaking students are told not to speak Spanish in school at any time.

Q Do you think that school practices encourage students to culturally assimilate?

Q What consequences, positive and negative, does cultural assimilation have on culturally and linguistically diverse students?

Because schools were essential in teaching democratic values to young Americans, the inclusion of racially and ethnically diverse populations had to be included in the curriculum (Johnson, 2002; Pak, 2004, 2006; Pak & Johnson, forthcoming). More specifically the inclusion of knowledge about role models and the history of groups that had been left out, such as African Americans, American Indians, and Asian Americans, was essential to provide a more equitable education (Johnson, 2002).

One of the intercultural-educator activists in the late 1930s was Rachel Davis DuBois, a Quaker (Pak, 2004). DuBois believed in the national values of equality and social justice; she did not believe in **cultural assimilation**, a process whereby new immigrants and people of color are pushed to take on the language, behaviors, values, and way of life from the dominant culture while letting go of home or heritage cultures in order to become "American" (Lal, 2006). For example, many immigrants had their names Anglicized. Instead of being known as Schmidt, the person's last name was changed to Smith, or a Seattle-born Japanese American's name was changed by a teacher from Mayako to Marie. However, DuBois was an educator who believed in acculturation. **Acculturation** refers to the exchange of cultural knowledge and skills among diverse people and organizations. This means that people can take on the dress, foods, sports, arts, music, and other aspects of a dominant culture, but at the same time keep their home cultures.

DuBois valued the concept of acculturation, and from that orientation she created and consulted on a CBS radio show series which began in 1938, "Americans All—Immigrants All"; she supported diverse cultural communities (Bohan, 2007). The show was supported by the U.S. Office of Education. She wanted to counter the general belief in the inferiority of many ethnic groups and teach people to appreciate various cultures that made up the United States such as Irish Americans, Welsh Americans, Japanese Americans, Jews, African Americans, German Americans, and other diverse communities (Figure 1.4). DuBois also founded the Service Bureau of Intercultural Education in 1934 (Johnson, 2002; Lal, 2006). She was one of the leaders in the Intercultural Education Movement and believed that educators should also fight racism and other forms of prejudice. Unlike other educators, DuBois did not believe in comprehensive cultural assimilation; rather, she believed that the exchange of knowledge between various immigrant and cultural groups would enhance interpersonal understandings.

> **Cultural assimilation** is the process by which an individual adopts language, behaviors, values, and a way of life from the dominant culture while letting go of home or heritage cultures. **Acculturation** refers to the process in which people learn about and feel comfortable with the practices and cultural ways of life of the dominant culture, but still retain their home/native cultures. It can also refer to the exchange of cultural elements such as food, art, and other aspects of culture among people from diverse groups.

Valerie Ooka Pang

Figure 1.4: Schools need to present and affirm Asian Americans in society. How can teachers highlight the contributions of Asian Americans?

There were other interculturalists who also believed in the integration of cultural information about communities other than European Americans. For example, in New York City from about 1935 to 1950, the teachers from the New York Teachers Union organized to institute intercultural studies in schools. One of these teachers was Gertrude Ayer, who became the first African American principal in New York City in 1934. She taught some of the first race-relations workshops at Teachers College, Columbia University (Johnson, 2002). William C. Crawford, a superintendent from San Diego City Schools, also believed in the integration of intercultural curriculum; he moved the district toward the development of student materials, teacher training, and the inclusion of various ethnic communities including Blacks, Whites, and Japanese Americans (Pak, 2004). Crawford saw tremendous growth in the San Diego district. When he began as superintendent in 1934, there were 30,000 students and when he left in 1953, the district was made up of 70,000 students. Crawford expanded how educators looked at intercultural education to include curricular materials. He addressed race relations by focusing on local communities, which included African Americans, American Indians, Asian Americans, and Mexican Americans (Pak, 2004). This was quite different from other programs around the nation that had a primarily Black and White orientation.

Intergroup Education

The next important movement at the foundation of multicultural education was the Intergroup Education Movement. Some scholars like Cherry Banks (2005) and Limarys Caraballo (2009) believe that Intergroup Education was part of a continuous connection with Intercultural Education. They saw them as intimately linked.

During World War II and in the years after, the number of immigrants from Europe continued to escalate. Also there was a migration of African American workers from the South to the North, which sometimes led to interracial conflicts. Intergroup educators were concerned not only about the civil strife that they witnessed but also about social prejudice and discrimination that was prevalent in the United States (Van Til, 1959). Hilda Taba, a curriculum theorist and social studies educator, wanted to address the lack of tolerance among students in schools. Intergroup educators saw cultural assimilation as a powerful force that pushed many immigrants and people of color to give up aspects of their cultures such as neighborhoods, beliefs, behaviors, recreational practices, sports, and foods. This was often done by exclusion or use of prejudicial practices. However, not all people left behind their ethnic cultures and replaced them with the dominant one. Some immigrants and other native born people like Native Americans and African Americans acculturated rather than assimilated. It became clear to some educators that acceptance of immigrants and people of color would not be easily accomplished. Though advocates like DuBois thought that the inclusion of knowledge of culturally different communities would lead to their approval by the general society, the road to appreciation of differences was one with many obstacles.

The Intergroup Education Movement shifted away from cultural pluralism toward intercultural communications and prejudice reduction. Because many Jewish organizations, such as the National Conference of Jews and Christians and the American Jewish Committee, had provided funding for intercultural programs after World War II when many immigrants were assimilating into society, they were concerned that too much discussion of differences would result in religious prejudice (C. A. Banks, 2005; Caraballo, 2009). Many educators believed that the emphasis on more effective communication skills led to the focus of many school districts on human relations. A human relations approach to diversity integrates much discussion on how to eliminate prejudice and intolerance among individuals.

Hilda Taba was a leader in the Intergroup Education Movement (Bernard-Powers, 1999). She had been a student of John Dewey, the philosopher, who wrote much about the importance of schools being a laboratory for democracy. Taba worked with teachers to develop a curriculum with the goals of teaching about diverse cultural values, conflict resolution skills, and identification of stereotypes of others (Krull, 2003). Another intergroup educator, Jean Dresden Grambs (1968), was a huge force in social studies education, bringing forth research that also looked at the impact of prejudice and stereotypes on students of color. In her work, she found that children held extensive prejudice against African Americans. For example, Grambs described a scenario in which a researcher showed a photo of a Black woman who had a flat tire to Black first-graders. When asked who would help the stranded motorist, the children told the researcher that a White man would not help her because she might have a knife and be dangerous. Grambs was concerned that the biased social messages that Black children learned about race would be a severe obstacle to intergroup relationships.

One of the strategies that Grambs suggested that teachers use in their classrooms to counteract prejudice was role playing (Grambs, 1968). A situation could include a group of all White girls who did not accept a Black child into their play group. After the role play, the teacher might say, "How would you feel if that happened to you? What would be a more fair solution?" This example shows how the Intergroup Education Movement addressed intercultural conflicts and tried to teach students how to understand that social justice in a democracy must be implemented by the actions of citizens.

The Civil Rights Movement

Following the Intercultural Education Movement and Intergroup Education Movement, the political force of the Civil Rights Movement influenced the direction of education. Civil rights activists pushed for more systematic and institutional changes in society. Though both of the former movements did push the idea of equality, most of what was accomplished had to do with curriculum and instructional practices that were integrated into schools. Equality was viewed as an essential aspect of democracy. **Equality** in education is defined as providing students with the same instruction, curriculum, counseling approaches, and other activities in school; it is about fair and equal treatment. This was followed toward the end of the twentieth century by a value of equity. Edmund Gordon (2006), former dean of Teachers College, along with Brenda X. Mejia, researcher, explained that equity is defined differently from equality. **Equity** is seen as providing students with what they need in order to be successful. One student's needs may not be the same as another student's. For example, one student may need more instruction on fractions while her classmate needs more instruction on verbs. According to the value of equity, the teacher would then deliver different lessons to ensure that each child is successful and excels. Today, many educators believe that students need equity in order to provide equal education opportunities because each student has different needs.

> **Equality** in education is defined as providing students with the same instruction, curriculum, counseling approaches, and other activities in school; it is about fair and equal treatment.
> **Equity** refers to providing students with what they need in order to excel and demonstrate equality of outcome.

The Civil Rights Movement, which grew stronger in the 1950s, was a political call for legislation that pushed our nation toward inclusion of all people, especially communities of color. It is also known to some as the African American Civil Rights Movement because of the leadership that many African Americans took in advocating for equal rights many years ago. Individuals such as Rosa Parks, Martin Luther King, Jr., and Thurgood Marshall pushed for societal changes.

In education, the Civil Rights Movement came after the two other movements. Like most social movements, there are no hard and fast dates identifying the beginning; however, for the purpose of this book, the Supreme Court decision of *Brown* v. *Board of Education of Topeka* in 1954 is recognized as one of the key events of the Civil Rights Movement as it relates to education. This case will be discussed in depth in the chapter on African American history. However, you should know that Linda Brown, an African American student, was denied entrance into a public school and the Supreme Court ruled in 1954 that "separate educational facilities are inherently unequal." In other words having separate White and Black schools was discriminatory; their financial and educational resources were not the same therefore they were not equal. Later, Title IV of the Civil Rights Act of 1964 called for the desegregation of schools. It also prohibited discrimination based on race, color, or national origin in schools, universities, or other programs that receive federal assistance.

Legislation as described above gave more impetus for equality of treatment and inclusion of students who were in the past denied participation in schools and other social institutions. As time has progressed, social movements have challenged inequalities based on race, ethnicity, gender, sexual orientation, exceptionalities, religion, and class. The field of multicultural education has benefited from the three movements, and initially progressed due to the work of curriculum specialists in the early 1970s including James A. Banks, Geneva Gay, Carl A. Grant, and the historian, Carlos Cortez. Their intellectual efforts led to the foundation of the field of multicultural education that is taught today. Their work built on the work of many others who were actively engaged in Intercultural Education and Intergroup Education, and the legislative push for educational equity through the Civil Rights Movement. As you can see from the timeline, it has taken approximately 100 years to develop a strong field of multicultural education.

Cultural Pluralism

Cultural pluralism was one of the values that many intercultural education advocates supported and believed in. Do you believe all Americans should give up their languages, customs, cultural values, and other aspects of culture? If you believe that Americans should be able to keep their home languages and cultural ways of living, then you might be a cultural pluralist. Cultural pluralism is a concept developed by Horace Kallen, a philosopher. He believed that because the United States is a democracy, people should be able to have the freedom to keep their cultural practices, languages, values, and ethnic identities. Our country has been built on a diversity of ideas rather than immigrants giving up all of their values and beliefs. Many diverse students bring to our schools strong values of community and education (Pang et al., 2010). For example, many immigrant students serve as excellent cultural bridges between their families and school personnel. They often serve as translators for their parents and act as mentors to their younger siblings because of their bilingual skills. Older students also help their parents care for their brothers and sisters. Some middle school and high school students may work alongside their parents in their businesses, contributing to the household income. The strong family values that some immigrant students bring to schools enhance the sense of community that many educators are working to build.

Multiculturalism

When the interculturalists were actively working in schools, one of their values was cultural pluralism. As you learned, this was about the acceptance and support of various culturally diverse groups. In contrast to cultural assimilation, new immigrants were encouraged to hold onto and continue to practice their cultural practices, behaviors, customs, languages, and ways of life. Not only were people of color forced to assimilate, but also new immigrant groups from Scotland, Ireland, and Italy found that many Americans pushed them to get rid of their cultures. Today, multiculturalism is used to represent the valuing of diverse social categories. These groupings have expanded beyond racial or ethnic classifications; multiculturalism is a much broader concept and can include differences based on gender, sexual orientation, exceptionalities, class, religion, and age. It can be understood using the metaphor of a symphony. In a symphony, individual and different instruments that have distinct sounds come together in unison and create a collaborative piece of music. The plurality of sounds contributes to an enriched composition.

INTERCULTURAL EDUCATION MOVEMENT, INTERGROUP EDUCATION MOVEMENT, AND CIVIL RIGHTS MOVEMENT: SELECTED EVENTS

Intercultural Education Movement

1934

Rachel David DuBois founded the Service Bureau for Intercultural Education (initially known as the Service Bureau for Human Relations) and was against drastic assimilation of immigrants. Pushed for acculturation.

- Believed in cultural democracy;
- Respect for diverse cultural and immigrant groups;
- Integration of cultural heritage such as history, holidays, customs in schools;
- Created books, skits, plays, and curriculum materials for schools

1935–1950

New York City African and Jewish teachers, grassroots movement (Johnson, 2002)

- Integration of curriculum materials about African Americans and other cultural groups;
- Better quality schools

1946–1949

San Diego City Schools, led by Superintendent Will Crawford (Pak, 2002)

- Respect of diverse cultural groups;
- Inclusion of intercultural curriculum materials;
- Focus on differences in a democracy

Intergroup Education Movement—Focus on Individual Prejudice

1944, 1945

Hilda Taba leads summer workshop at Harvard on Intergroup Education (1944) and becomes Director of the Center for Intergroup Education (1945) (Powers, 2002).

- Prepare students to participate in a democracy;
- Taught prejudice reduction skills;
- Developed tools to evaluate people's biases and views about race, ethnicity, and class;
- Developed spiral curriculum for social studies education

1945–1949

College Study in Intergroup Relations, included 20 colleges and universities

- Study of teacher behaviors, teacher beliefs, and teacher practices;
- Focus on national ideals of our democracy;
- Believed in the equality of each person;
- Researched human relations skills/attitudes

Civil Rights Movement

1954

Brown v. *Board of Education of Topeka*

- Desegregation of schools, U.S. Supreme Court Decision;
- Separate (schools) is not equal

1964

Civil Rights Act, Title IV

- Legislation addressing systematic and institutional discrimination based on race, class, and ethnicity

1968

Chicago Schools, Black high-school students, parents, and community protest (Danns, 2002)

- Integration of Black history into the curriculum;
- Hiring of Black teachers;
- Increase of Black administrators;
- Fire racist teachers

1970s–present

Scholars in education create a field of multicultural education

- Initially the integration of ethnic studies—type materials in schools
- somewhat like Intercultural Education Movement;
- Today call for total school reform—movement away from additive approach;
- Emphasis on culturally relevant education;
- Call for institutional changes that support social justice (Pang et al., 2010)

TAKE A STAND — RACHEL DAVIS DuBois

Passionate Advocate for Intercultural Education

Rachel Davis DuBois

Read through this short segment about what Rachel Davis DuBois did as a major figure in the Intercultural Education Movement.

A key member of the Intercultural Education Movement in the 1930s and 40s was Rachel Davis DuBois (Pak, 2006). She believed that the literature, music, history, and experiences of people of color, often referred to at that time as "racial minorities," should be included in the general school curriculum. Intercultural education was based on the principles of intercultural relationships and an inclusive democracy. DuBois spoke about the importance of eliminating personal prejudices and exclusionary practices. Within intercultural education, she created a curriculum that addressed racism in society and incorporated historical information about Black Americans, Chinese Americans, Japanese Americans, and Jews into school content. These materials were implemented in various school districts from Seattle, Washington, to New Orleans, Louisiana, to Cambridge Massachusetts. This curriculum challenged the strong cultural assimilation underpinning of educational content (Pak, 2006). In this context, cultural assimilation is the adoption of language, behaviors, values, norms, identity, and a way of life from the dominant culture while letting go of home or native cultures. She did not believe that one of the major goals of schools should be cultural assimilation. DuBois thought that if people knew more about each other and understood their cultural differences, they would get along and work together as part of a democracy.

TAKE A STAND ...

▶ **Write two sentences about ways in which you agree with DuBois. Now take a stand. How effective do you think her work would be today? Why?**

Misconceptions about Multicultural Education

Many teachers hold misconceptions about the field of multicultural education. For example, many think that multicultural education will cause divisiveness, create reverse discrimination, or foster a curriculum that opposes the dominant culture. These concerns may result because teachers have not had opportunities to take a class or read materials about the discipline. In addition, a few teachers feel that misconceptions about the field have developed because the field itself lacks agreement or a collaborative definition (Sheets & Fong, 2003). Part of the problem is the resistance that many teachers have because they do not have a clear understanding of the goals and principles of multicultural education (see Table 1.5).

Table 1.5 Misconceptions about Multicultural Education

Misconceptions about Multicultural Education	Goals and Principles of Multicultural Education
Multicultural education emphasizes separatism and causes divisiveness.	Multicultural education builds upon national values of equity and diversity: Unity amidst diversity; *E Pluribus Unum*.
Multicultural education creates reverse discrimination.	One of the major goals of Multicultural Education is to eliminate racism and other forms of social oppression found in schools.
Multicultural education seeks to replace U.S. culture with the cultures of ethnic groups.	People from many communities, including African Americans, Asian Pacific Americans, Latinos, and Native Americans, are a part of, have contributed to, and continue to contribute to the development and success of this nation.
Multicultural education is only for schools with high numbers of ethnic minority students or schools with racial tension.	Multicultural education is a field in education that is dedicated to equal opportunity and outcomes for all students. Even groups who appear to be monocultural are diverse with regard to characteristic such as class, gender, and language.
Multicultural education seeks to replace current school curriculum with Afrocentric curriculum that opposes the dominant society.	Multicultural education seeks total school reform so that all aspects of schools reflect our national diversity. Schools must be effective for all students. Curriculum includes lived experiences of students from underrepresented groups.
Multicultural education encourages lower standards for students from underrepresented groups.	Multicultural education seeks to eliminate the achievement gap between mainstream students and those from underrepresented communities by creating more effective schools. Standards will be raised in the process. Equity and excellence are interwoven.
Multicultural education is about food fairs, ethnic costumes, and cultural traditions.	Multicultural education is a field in education that calls for total school reform and is built on the integration of caring, culture, and a socially just community.

Obstacles can lead to misconceptions. For example, teachers may develop an internal obstacle and become reluctant to examine personal and professional values and actions for bias (with regard to areas such as culture, language, ethnicity, class, gender, exceptionalities, sexual orientation, religion, and age). When this occurs, teachers may hold onto stereotypical ideas about their students, parents, and colleagues. This could lead to misunderstandings and misconceptions about what students are capable of in their school work. In addition some individuals are unwilling to change because change takes effort and often requires people to give up long-held beliefs and views. Read through Table 1.5 and reflect upon the many misconceptions some educators have about the field. Do you hold any of these views? If so, where did you learn them?

Let's talk about one of these misconceptions. Some teachers think that multicultural education seeks to replace the current school curriculum with an Afrocentric curriculum. An Afrocentric curriculum would mean that the classroom activities would focus around African American students only. However, this is not true. As a field in education, multicultural education is founded on the belief that schools should engage in total school reform where the values of equity in education are at its core.

Multicultural education is an academic discipline that encompasses a range of views from total school reform, to curriculum infusion, to societal change. Educators need to think about how equity can be integrated into school policies, curriculum, instructional strategies, underlying principles, counseling practices, parent–teacher relationships, testing instruments, and many more areas in schools, based on the diversity teachers now find in the classroom.

Multicultural Education Defined

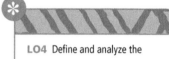

LO4 Define and analyze the goals and concepts of multicultural education.

Teaching is an inspiring and holistic profession. Like other "helping" professions, teachers focus on their learners and celebrate the importance of education. Multicultural education, as identified in the prior section on goals of the field, is about the development of responsible citizens in a democracy along with providing equity in education. Teachers want to effectively reach and teach skills and knowledge to all students. Over the years, various definitions of multicultural education have arisen. For example, it is sometimes referred to as a philosophy that emphasizes cultural pluralism, or a curriculum approach based on the inclusion of ethnic studies, or the integration of democratic processes into schools (Gay, 1994). However, as the area has been established, more scholars see multicultural education as its own field, which arose out of our national values of democracy, social justice, equality, and freedom. One of the first scholars in the field was James A. Banks. He developed a conceptual model that identified a plan of action to guide teachers in what they do in the classroom. He addressed curricular changes that he felt were needed to address instructional delivery and materials. The model includes content integration, knowledge construction, equity pedagogy, prejudice reduction, and an empowered school culture (J. A. Banks & C. A. Banks, 1997).

As the field moved forward, scholars also felt the need to identify theories that would serve as the foundation for the field. Sonia Nieto (2004), an educator, brought to the field the importance of a political orientation called *critical theory* as developed by Paulo Freire. Critical theory has numerous definitions; however, Nieto and Freire saw it as a philosophical orientation that encouraged teachers and students to develop critical thinking skills and social action skills. They would then be able to challenge extensive inequities in schools and throughout society. They saw extensive capitalism as a major reason inequalities are so prevalent in life. In regard to schooling, Nieto and Freire believed that the infusion of culture, language, and literacy development into the curriculum would not result in comprehensive school transformation that could address the massive unbalance of wealth and status found in the United States. Nieto concluded that in order for schools to address perennial educational inequities, educators needed to become more politically active.

Educators rely on theories and models to help them create effective learning environments. Though many of the early models in the field were mostly about curriculum development, it is important for teachers to understand the value of philosophical and cognitive learning theories. Pang (2005) put forth the philosophies of Nel Noddings' ethic of care and John Dewey's education for democracy as foundational to the field. She also believed in the need to include learning theory, which was Vygotsky's sociocultural theory of learning. The integration of these three theories imparts a strong base for the field. These three theories will be discussed in depth later in the chapter. However, the following definition can help you appreciate the complexities of teaching in a culturally diverse nation.

Multicultural education is defined as a field in education that calls for total school reform and is based on the belief that education is an intellectual and ethical endeavor where students are provided equity in schools (Pang, 2005). The field seeks to develop happy, creative, ethical, and fulfilled persons who work toward a more compassionate and socially just society. Students are encouraged to develop vital decision-making and intercultural communication skills, which are used to develop collaborative relationships and challenge inequities. The field includes school policies, culturally relevant curriculum and instructional practices, parent relationships, and school structures. Multicultural education, as part of a life-giving process of growth and joy, focuses on teaching the whole student with the goal of academic excellence and developing the potential of each student by integrating care theory, education for democracy, and sociocultural cognitive theory of learning.

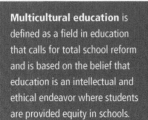

Multicultural education is defined as a field in education that calls for total school reform and is based on the belief that education is an intellectual and ethical endeavor where students are provided equity in schools.

Relationship-Centered and Culture-Centered Framework

Multicultural education is based on a relationship-centered and culture-centered framework in education (Pang, 2005). Teachers develop strong trusting and reciprocal relationships with their students and affirm their cultural backgrounds. Teachers also build on the life experiences of students in the teaching and learning processes. One of the key instructional principles of the field is its holistic perspective. Teaching is seen not only within the development of content knowledge, but also in the growth of the whole person. Teaching is an art; it is not made up of a number of isolated skills. Rather, teaching is a complex combination of skills, knowledge, and beliefs that work in sync to create an environment that encourages maximum growth in the student and the teacher.

Goals of Multicultural Education

Multicultural education as a field of study has a variety of goals. Most of them have to do with the creation of schools that deliver equality and equity in schools. Teachers work hard to ensure that every student is successful and learns not only discipline knowledge, but also critical thinking skills such as analysis, synthesis, evaluation, and problem solving.

LO5 Discuss and evaluate the goals, major concepts, and models of multicultural education.

Goals and Challenging the Lack of Diverse Viewpoints

There are numerous goals in education, such as the development of the physical and mental well-being of students (Goodlad, 1979, 2006). However in Multicultural education, three major goals are directed at the inclusion of issues of diversity and equity into all areas of schooling:

- Attain equality and equity in education
- Eliminate the achievement gap
- Develop responsible and empowered citizens

Goal: Attain Equality and Equity in Education

First, schools must be structured so that every child is provided equal opportunity and access to education. For this goal to be achieved, student outcomes are as important as student access because for learners to receive equal educational opportunity, they must also show equal outcomes. The students must learn. You must be effective in reaching students to ensure they are successful achievers. School policies are critical components to make certain that all factors work together to create a successful educational environment. Policies can require that the curriculum is taught in meaningful ways and include information that affirms contributions of communities of color. One of the strategies that teachers have developed to create equity in schools is to *detrack* students (Nasir, Cabana, Shreve, Woodbury, & Louie, 2014). **Detracking** refers to not placing students in stereotypical ability groups. Unfortunately, a higher percentage of students of color and low-income learners are found in the lower levels of ability groups or classes (Oakes, 2005). Nasir and her colleagues worked in a school where they eliminated tracking and utilized **complex instruction**, a collaborative approach to instruction that uses group work activities developed by Elizabeth Cohen. The teachers and students found that they were most successful when working together and presenting information in multiple ways.

> **Detracking** refers to not placing students in stereotypical ability groups.

> **Complex instruction** is a collaborative approach to instruction that uses group work activities.

Goal: Eliminate the Achievement Gap

The success of Nasir and her colleagues demonstrated that it was possible to address equity in learning. This leads to the second goal in multicultural education, which is to eliminate the achievement gap between students of color and their White peers. If teachers are successful in teaching all learners, then the achievement gap will decrease. Unfortunately in many national assessment studies, African American, Latino, Native American, Pacific Islander, and low-income students do not do as well on achievement measures as middle-class White learners. One of the reasons may be due to high teacher turnover in schools where students of color comprise the majority of the population (Ronfeldt, Loeb, & Wychoff, 2013). Research indicates that schools with more social challenges need a stable teaching corps to ensure policy continuity and to keep grade-level teams together. Therefore, many educators believe that numerous students of color and learners from low-income families are not being provided equal educational opportunities, access, or outcomes in education.

Goal: Develop Responsible and Empowered Citizens

As a democracy, the United States needs citizens who have a strong grasp of discipline knowledge and can also analyze the issues that challenge this nation. Citizens participate in and vote on many social issues, therefore the last major goal of multicultural education is the development of responsible and empowered citizens ready to participate in a democracy. Another way to put it is to teach students to think critically so they are prepared to make decisions on serious social issues like homelessness with compassion and understanding of other points of view. Multiple perspectives are critical to the creation of a strong democracy because the common good is at the core of the nation. Students also need to develop teamwork skills along with fostering empathy toward others (McClung, 2013). McClung, an attorney, believes we, as a nation, need informed citizens who participate in our democracy. A democracy does not grow without the work of its citizens.

In order for students to be informed citizens, King (2011), who writes on African American education, challenges teachers to include authentic information about African Americans in classes such as social studies, sociology, history, political science, and literature. She believes that cultural assimilation forces are so strong that the policies and politics that enslaved African Americans and the structure of slavery, which was once legal and systematic, have not been fully dealt with in schools today. King believes that the cultural values and contributions of African Americans are not taught in schools because the dominant voice of society determines what is taught. For example, during the Katrina crisis, King identified numerous examples of how poor, young Black men and women exemplified African American community values of generosity, collective care, and respect for elders as they helped many stranded people in New Orleans after the hurricane (King, 2011).

African Americans are often dehumanized in the media and curriculum, however. Students must be taught to critically challenge the exclusion of viewpoints of poor and racially diverse communities in schools. Teachers should consider these questions:

- Who chooses what is taught?
- What messages are conveyed by what is taught?
- Who benefits from the knowledge being taught?
- Who is marginalized by the omission of diverse perspectives?

These questions are important ones for teachers and students in a democracy to address. King (2011) and McClung (2013) believe that teachers should not only teach specific information such as the study of the United States Constitution and Bill of Rights, but also the development of cognitive and people skills. It is important for teachers to also know the ethnic communities of their students. Each neighborhood may have differences in cultural elements such as history in the United States, languages, and values about life. Otherwise, only information that has been taken from European American communities will be taught in schools. If this happens, students of color may believe that schools and teachers do not respect or accept their diverse cultural backgrounds. If only mainstream information is taught, then students who are from the dominant culture have "an edge" in that they are more familiar with the information in schools. Suppose, for example, there is a question on a standardized test about the novel, *The Phantom of the Opera*, and students had never read the French story. However, several of the learners had gone to the musical and so knew about the tale and were exposed to the information as part of their life experiences. Other students did not have the financial resources to go to the musical because the ticket was expensive. This situation shows how class can influence items on a test. Including exam questions on *The Phantom of the Opera* could represent cultural bias. This example points to how asking "whose knowledge" can help students understand test bias.

It is vital that teachers learn about the lives of their students in order to become effective cultural mediators in schools. If you know about the learners in your classes, then you will know how to connect learning to their lives. How can you do this? The checklist below will help you to more fully learn about the cultural backgrounds of your students.

Perspectives: Cultural Deficit, Cultural Asset-Based, Cultural Different, and Cultural Congruent

Have you ever heard teachers say that they believe students will not do well in school because of the color of their skin or because they are female? It is important that you

CHECKLIST: LEARNING ABOUT MY STUDENTS

This checklist was developed to help you observe and listen to your students. In this way you will have a better idea of what they value, what they know, and how they identify themselves.

Name of Student:

_____

☐ Ask student to finish this prompt: I want my teacher to know that I...
☐ Who does the student play with and talk to?
☐ How does the student identify? Does she talk about ethnic background, racial background, gender, exceptionalities, sexual orientation, neighborhood, religion, class, or something else?
☐ What does your student value the most? Her family? Her dog? Her hobbies? Her friends?

☐ Does the student need excessive attention from you the teacher? If so, how does the student get your attention? Positive ways? Negative ways?
☐ Does the student feel successful in class? How do you know?
☐ What does the student know that you do not? Think of how you can integrate the information into a reading, math, or science lesson.

❯❯ **Professional Resource Download**

see all of your students as enriching your classroom. In contrast, a damaging belief that many teachers, parents, and guardians hold is a **cultural deficit** perspective about students of color or young people from lower economic families who are seen as intellectually inferior. People with this perspective view students from underrepresented groups as coming from substandard communities. When students of color do not do well on standardized tests or in mainstream classrooms, some teachers label the culture of the students' families as being disadvantaged. These educators place the blame for student failure on children and/or their families and cultures. Some teachers blame students for doing poorly based on the fact that they come to school speaking another language like Spanish or Mandarin. Other teachers blame the cultural backgrounds of children, saying they do not value education. In many of these cases it is as if educators perceive themselves to hold little responsibility for low grades and low standardized test scores of students of color, and students from lower-income communities. Placing blame on a student's cultural background, skin color, socioeconomic background, or gender is a huge detriment to the idea of equal learning for all students, in all schools (Gay, 1994, 2013; King, 1991, 2011).

In contrast, other educators accept and embrace the cultural difference and cultural asset-based viewpoints. They believe that students come from ethnic communities that provide knowledge and values which may differ from mainstream society; however, what they bring to schools are beneficial skills and knowledge. A **cultural asset-based** orientation recognizes the strengths and benefits of what a child and his family add to the school community. Some students with diverse worldviews can experience a conflict with their school's culture. For instance, when Hmong refugees came to the United States from Laos during the Vietnam War (1955–1975), many had a preliterate tradition, meaning that they came from a culture that had not developed the use of writing. Many refugees also did not have any formal schooling. Consequently, when young Hmong students went to school, they did not know what to expect nor did they know what was expected of them, and many cultural clashes ensued. In their home culture, Hmong young people brought to the United States many assets. For example, they held strong loyalties to the family and knew how to sew, grow crops, and take care of members in the community. They may not have known about school bells or homework. Parents were reserved and unsure about their children's participation in school programs because they did not understand their purposes. In addition, parents believed they did not have the professional training needed to help their children with school related issues.

Cultural deficit viewpoint is the belief that students from underrepresented groups come with cultures and languages that place them at risk of failing in school; intellectual inferiority is often an underlying belief that links cultural differences with cultural deficiency.

Cultural asset-based orientation recognizes the cultural strengths and benefits of what a child and his family add to the school community.

Figure 1.5: For many White teachers and other educators, it is important that they learn about the history, culture, and languages of all students in their classes. This will assist in building trusting relationships between students of color and teachers.

Cultural difference viewpoint is the belief that students from underrepresented communities come with cultures that are not deficient from the dominant culture, rather they are different.

Intersectionality refers to how various aspects of oppression come together and are interrelated.

So the parents exemplified a **cultural difference** orientation that is not deficient but rather a different way of looking at life.

Within their cultural knowledge, Hmong parents believed and respected the teachers and education administrators and relied on them to do the best for their children. This did not mean that Hmong parents were unaware of how important education is; rather, that they had faith in teachers and believed that they would make sure their children learned. For example, Hmong families brought with them a strong sense of community. In fact, Hmong children are taught collective responsibility, which means that the needs of the family are more important than the needs of individual members.

King (1994, 2011) believes that the cultural difference theory still calls for the re-socialization of students of color, especially African American youth, to mainstream culture because school personnel have not changed their beliefs about the abilities of students of color. The knowledge and processes currently used still emulate mainstream society. King carefully explains that because mainstream society (including social institutions like schools) has continually oppressed African Americans and other students of color, schools must be transformed from organizations of oppression into institutions of liberation. King believes that the entire system of education should be reorganized so that it challenges the status quo and calls for emancipation of the minds of all students. For example, the inclusion of African American cultural knowledge would give all students a sense of presence of the African American community. Students can also be taught African American history, American Indian history, and the history of women. All students need to know the contributions of the diverse cultural communities that make up this democracy. (See Figure 1.5.)

Intersectionality and Cultural Diversity

The concepts of diversity and equity must also include the construct of intersectionality. **Intersectionality** refers to how various aspects of oppression come together and are interrelated. In multicultural education, the whole student is important. A student should not be placed in one social box like race or class and narrowly labeled. For example, a fifth-grade teacher may say to a colleague, "Jesus is Mexican and does not speak English well. He brings my class test scores down. He won't sit still when I am teaching. I do not want him in my class." This characterization shows the interrelated nature of ethnic membership, language capabilities, and gender. The teacher is mixing together various social biases though it may seem at first glance that she is talking about ethnic or racial bias. It is important that teachers are able to dig deep and identify the various layers of their own prejudice that may be an obstacle to reaching students. For example, all educators should ask themselves about the stereotypes they hold about various students. Everyone has some types of biases or prejudices, and to be the best teacher, we must reflect on and then extract them from our minds. Is it easy? No. But if you are committed to all of your students, this is a life-long process of change.

CASE STUDY

A New Teacher's First Year

My interest in multicultural education began when I was 20 years old. It was March and I had just received my bachelor's degree in education from a small private university. I felt like I was ready to tackle the problems of the world. My first teaching assignment was at an elementary school of 300 children located in a predominantly Black neighborhood in a large urban district. Ninety-three percent of the students were Black, three percent were Asian and Native American, and four percent were European American. All my students came from low-income households and were either on reduced-cost or free lunch. Of the 14 teachers at the school, only three had more than six years of teaching experience, 75 percent were women, and many had been teaching for fewer than three years. The upper-grade teachers fought an underlying atmosphere of frustration and hopelessness because there was violence in the neighborhood and most parents did not have time to create teacher–parent partnerships. Initially I did not understand that the majority of parents were single-parent mothers and they were trying to survive working two or three jobs. This was a tough situation.

A week after I took the job, the principal said, "We had a knifing in the parking lot last year, so be sure to lock your car." I was definitely a greenhorn. Right away, I realized that I knew little about the lives of the students in my first grade class. Although my apartment was only five miles from the school, it was as if I lived in another city. The good news was that I finished the year and taught for another full year at this school because I began to understand that though the children came from difficult circumstances, they wanted to do well in school and have a teacher who believed in them. The bad news was that I wasn't prepared to teach in a culturally diverse school. As much as I wanted to assist my students in becoming the best they could be, I was unprepared to teach in a school where the life experiences of children were so different from my own. I taught the way I had been taught and socialized.

Fortunately, the students were patient and forgiving, even though I made many mistakes. In those 16 months, I learned more from the children than they learned from me.

For example, I learned that the curriculum content the district had chosen was not appropriate for them and actually hampered their success in three ways. First, the stories in the textbook were primarily about living on a farm. Reading about raising dairy cows was new to them and not meaningful. So while they were learning how to read, they also had to simultaneously learn new and unfamiliar content. Second, the students spoke African American vernacular English, but the district mandated the use of a highly phonetic commercial reading series for the primary grades. The basal reader was built upon the phonemes and semantic structure of standard English.

Upon reflection, I realized several mistakes that I was making. First, I was attempting to teach students how to decode what they were reading without teaching them the necessary comprehension skills they needed. Second, I was also asking the children to learn a new language, standard English. Finally, I was also teaching students how to read not in their home language, but a new language. Within this context, many of the students struggled with learning the highly phonetic reading skills because the sounds and ways the sounds were put together differed from what the children knew.

The problems included my approach to reading, and the textbooks—not the kids. I had never perceived myself as being culturally disadvantaged. At that time, it was a common practice in education to label low-income, culturally diverse children as being culturally disadvantaged, which meant that Black children who were from poor families were considered to be "at-risk" or less intellectually capable than other students. Although this was not true, these powerful stereotypes shaped the views of many teachers, White and ethnically diverse, about Black students and other students of color. I now think that schools operating on these beliefs were culturally disadvantaged institutions because many teachers at the schools did not understand the life experiences or background of students. The deficiency was not in the students and their families; rather the educational system was based on a dominant perspective and teachers often saw students of color as being deficient. No one seemed to question the way schools were organized or the curriculum that was being

taught. As I thought more about these misguided and even negative beliefs, these views were entrenched in the minds of many teachers. When students of color, like all students, go to school, teachers need to believe that they bring with them a rich knowledge of their cultures and neighborhoods.

Because I lacked knowledge about my students or the community, I began to search out various African American community groups and read about African American and Native American history. I also knew it was important for me to earn the respect of parents and students. I hadn't grown up in the school's neighborhood and the parents didn't know if they could trust me, so I visited many students at home and regularly spoke with parents in order to get to know them. We created parent–teacher partnerships. All of the children, regardless of their ethnic backgrounds, spoke African American vernacular English and were bright and eager to learn. Parents slowly began to trust me because they could see that I cared and was honest. I continued to make mistakes, but the parents were open-hearted; they knew that I was a new teacher. In fact, they were extremely accessible. Jimmy's mom told me to call her in the morning because she worked in the late afternoon. I called Lisa's mother at work at the telephone company in the evening to give her an update on Lisa's reading progress. Cecilia's grandma came in regularly to read to small groups of children in the classroom.

My early teaching experiences taught me that I needed to understand the role culture plays in how students learn. I also realized that race had influenced the economic context of my students. So from my experiences, it was clear that I needed to learn about multicultural education because knowledge gained from this field would help me become a more effective teacher. I knew that a good teacher would be able to reach all students; this is how my interest in multicultural education began, and I have been teaching for over 40 years now.

Reflection Questions

Q What were the most important aspects about teaching that this new teacher learned her first year?

Q How did that knowledge help her to be a more effective teacher?

Culturally Relevant Education

In sync with the research of King (2011), Gay (2013), and Ladson-Billings (1995), educational researchers Au and Kawakami (1994) agree that schools should strive to be **culturally relevant**, similar to the orientations of **culturally responsive** and **culturally appropriate** pedagogy. Culturally relevant refers to education that builds on the cultural knowledge, values, and experiences that students bring to school (Ladson-Billings, 1995; Gay, 2013). Although Au and Kawakami do not believe that schools must imitate a student's home life, they do feel that schools must integrate knowledge and practices from students' home cultures into the curriculum and instruction of classrooms. For example, Au and Kawakami, educators from Hawaii, found that many native Hawaiian students were quiet and did not participate in class discussions. However, when the teachers saw the children in other contexts, they were playful, laughing, and spontaneous. When teachers realized that the students were more comfortable participating in the classroom when they worked together as a group, Au and Kawakami instituted a reading process called *talk story* in which all the students worked collaboratively to decode and comprehend materials. This instructional strategy has been effective in teaching reading to many native Hawaiian and Asian American students. Moll (1990) also has shown how teachers can build on the knowledge students bring to school by inviting parents to be guest speakers. This teaches all students about the abilities of a class parent while affirming cultural backgrounds of learners. How to integrate culturally relevant instruction and curriculum in your own classroom will be discussed in the last chapter of this text.

> **Culturally relevant, culturally responsive** or **culturally appropriate** teaching refers to education that builds on the cultural knowledge, values, and experiences that students bring to school.

Models and Theories

In order to understand the theories and models that multicultural education includes, it is important for you to understand that culture, community, and learning are core aspects. For the purpose of this text, a *model* is defined as an organized idea that a scholar develops to explain a specific phenomenon. In contrast, a *theory* or theoretical **framework** is a broad system of beliefs that include principles that can be used to explain a comprehensive number of situations. Theories often have been highly researched. For example, a model of a Lego wagon shows how the small block toys can be used to make a product. However, the theory of Legos would include principles of construction, facilitation, flow, facts, and fun. A framework is more complex and abstract in nature. Therefore, it is important for teachers to understand the complicated nature of learning, relationship building, cultural foundations, curriculum development, equitable policies, and many more aspects of teaching as related to multicultural education. The models and theories in this field emphasize an education that affirms students, presents effective ways to teach, and brings them all aspects of schooling in a democracy. Schools can be places were students learn to become responsible and compassionate citizens.

> **Framework** is a set of educational principles, beliefs, policies, and practices.

Your Educational Philosophy

Have you ever wondered why you are asked to study theory? You aren't the only one who may question why theory and educational principles are taught in education classes. Here are some typical comments that may come up in discussions:

"I don't have time to read about theory. It doesn't tell me what to do in the classroom."
"Get real. I teach 185 middle school students. Don't waste my time with that stuff."
"I need ideas and activities for the classroom! Forget the theory. It doesn't help!"

You might want to reconsider your approach to studying theory and research. Have you chosen a belief system to guide your personal life? Many people have chosen a

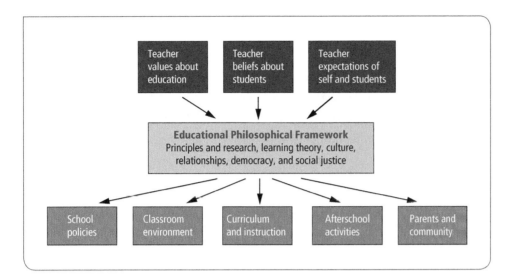

Figure 1.6: **How Teacher Values, Beliefs, and Expectations Are the Foundation of an Educational Framework**

philosophy, religious dogma, or set of ethical principles to help direct their actions. These belief systems provide guidance and rationale for people's actions. When individuals hold philosophies, they use established systems and values to advise them in making difficult decisions. Consider adopting an educational set of principles based on your beliefs and research. In today's schools, many forces continually push and pull at teachers. There are district, state, and national standards. There are subject area standards for social studies, mathematics, reading, language arts, science, physical education, character education, history, and literacy. There are district, state, and national standardized tests. There are accreditation requirements. Voucher issues are being studied. Small school forces are trying to be heard. Forces from the right and left of the political spectrum are petitioning school boards for change. Teacher unions are pushing for changes in the curriculum, and administrators are pushing for more accountability. How will you know which position to take on the issues? It is sometimes overwhelming to make decisions about the many issues teachers face. How are teachers going to be able to sort through these important concerns?

Teachers have lots of responsibilities. They work hard to connect with each student and to develop their academic skills. In order to do the best job, teachers need to choose a system of beliefs that direct them so they know which path they will take. That is where theory and an educational framework come in. If teachers have not chosen a strong framework which is their philosophy of education, they may never reach their selected destinations because they did not keep on track. A strong philosophy and instructional practices act like a map to guide your work. The set of principles will ground you and keep you driving in the best directions so you don't find yourself stuck in a ditch or dead end.

Teachers must think carefully about what is most important to them. Their values, beliefs, and expectations can lead to the development and adoption of their educational framework.

See how the process can work in Figure 1.6. This is why it is vital for teachers to identify their ideals, ethics, and principles. These aspects of their belief system can drive their behaviors and the pedagogy that they use in the classroom. Their values also guide them in what they do for students after school and how they approach parents and community members.

Five Dimensions of Multicultural Education: A Model

James Banks developed a model or construct that he used to guide teachers. Banks primarily addressed changes in the curriculum. Initially, his work focused on the integration

Consider this . . .

In 2008, 25 percent of U.S. students who started high school dropped out. The percentage was higher than countries such as Norway, Switzerland, South Korea, Ireland, Japan, and Germany. These students are more likely not to be employed. This has implications not only for the students who drop out, but also for us as a nation.

Q How does the high dropout rate in the United States hurt us as a nation?

Q How does dropping out of school hurt our young students?

U.S. Census Bureau. 2011. Education and synthetic work-life earnings estimates. *American Community Survey Reports.*

of ethnic studies into the materials that students used in the classroom. Later he built a conceptual model that identifies five avenues teachers needed to address in schools. The model includes content integration, knowledge construction, equity pedagogy, prejudice reduction, and an empowered school culture (J. A. Banks & C. A. Banks, 1997).

Content integration refers to bringing in knowledge about culturally diverse groups. As a social studies educator, Banks initially focused on the incorporation of ethnic history into all grade levels. This included teaching about important role models who fought for civil rights such as Dr. Martin Luther King, Jr.

Knowledge construction is similar to content integration. Banks was concerned that teachers had not considered that the information included in the curriculum may have been chosen by someone with a specific perspective. However, the perspective of that information was often not from someone of color. For example, many historians see history through a European American lens so they may not present perspectives of literature, history, or math from various ethnic groups.

Equity pedagogy refers to the ability of teachers to deliver knowledge in ways that are meaningful to all students. Often students of color respond to a pedagogical approach that is not necessarily used in schools. Recall the discussion of *talk story*, the approach to teaching reading in Hawaii. The students preferred to work together rather than to have one individual star in the classroom. This is an example of equity pedagogy.

Prejudice reduction refers to teaching students to eliminate racism and other types of social oppression in schools. Bias hurts everyone. Most students are aware of the hurt of prejudice and discrimination, and it is the responsibility of teachers to provide respectful classroom and school environments.

The last dimension is the creation of an *empowered school*. This is an approach to multicultural education that seems to call for total school reform. Unlike the other dimensions, which focus primarily on curriculum and instruction, this last dimension is about building a school that respects and values all students. As you assess this model, what makes it more of a model is that it does not include educational theories. Most of the ideas are about curriculum.

Ethic of Care, Sociocultural Theory of Learning, and Education for Democracy: Connecting Three Theories

The three theories of the ethic of care developed by Nel Noddings, sociocultural theory of learning as built by Lev Vygotsky, and education for democracy as created by John Dewey were brought together into one educational framework. This framework created a strong foundation for multicultural education because it includes a strong relationship orientation, a cognitive learning theory, and an educational theory about education as the core of our democratic nation. It is a comprehensive framework that focuses upon the education of the whole student. This framework is referred to as caring-centered multicultural education (Pang, 2005). (See Figure 1.7.)

Ethic of Care Theory: Noddings

Caring is a concept in schools based on the work of Carl Rogers, a psychologist, and Jerome Freiberg, an educational researcher (1994). They believed that the development of strong, caring relationships was key to a foundation for humanistic schools. Elements that they identified were:

- Teacher empathy
- Positive school climate
- Trusting relationships

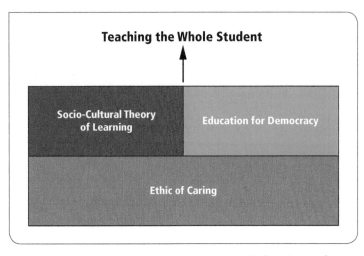

Figure 1.7: **Caring-Centered Multicultural Education**

Rogers and Freiberg thought that these characteristics fostered effective learning environments where students learned to have:

- High self-esteem
- Confidence
- Commitment to personal growth

In addition, other scholars have presented caring as a fundamental human ability to relate to others and not a sentimental or condescending notion (Chaskin & Rauner, 1995; Gilligan, 1993; Ianni, 1996; Noddings, 1984, 1992, 2013; Palmer, 2008).

Theorist Nel Noddings (1992) developed the **ethic of care** as a theory in education and believes that education is based on teachers having a moral purpose to mentor individuals who are ethical. She writes, "We should educate all our children not only for competence but also for caring. Our aim should be to encourage the growth of competent, caring, loving, and lovable people" (Noddings, 1992, p. xiv). One of the critiques of Noddings' caring theory is that the theory is colorblind while society is not. Thompson, a philosopher, cautions educators that the care theory, as described by Noddings, was created within the context of a mainstream, patriarchal orientation. Although care theorists like Noddings have referred to natural caring, this has not always been true in society (Thompson, 1998). The treatment of many people from communities of color throughout U.S. history has demonstrated that caring for others who are seen as different is not automatic or a natural human response. The institution of slavery is an example of how some people did not believe in natural caring for all humans. Therefore, it is important to reflect upon care theory along with issues of cultural discrimination and oppression such as racism. Many educators may believe in caring for students, but do not realize they must reflect on their own biases to put caring into practice.

> **Ethic of Care** is a theory developed primarily by Nel Noddings which focuses on the importance of developing trusting, reciprocal relationships in schools.

When teachers operate from the ethic of care, they consciously make a moral commitment to care for and teach students and to develop reciprocal relationships with them. These teachers create schools that are centers of care. In these schools, students, teachers, and parents form a community where relationships are at the heart of school, and where the curriculum and policies focus on compassion, respect, and community building (Figure 1.8). Students are also encouraged to care for ideas, plants, animals, distant others, and the self. In this way the care theory is a holistic orientation toward education with themes of care woven throughout the curriculum. Care theory is not only about teaching knowledge; the perspective also focuses on the whole student within an empowering and compassionate environment.

Figure 1.8: New teachers will want to develop trusting relationships with mentor educators who share valuable insights about how to create caring classroom environments that emphasize compassion, respect, and community building.

Noddings sees the care theory as an alternative approach in education. She raises critical questions such as what kinds of schools do educators value, and what would schools founded on care look like? Noddings explains that most likely schools would be very different if we could start from scratch and found a school based on care. The way that we might structure our schools would, in part, depend on our definition of caring. See Table 1.6 for a list of important characteristics of the ethic of care theory.

Noblit, Rogers, and McCadden, educators, defined *caring* as a belief that may not be easy to see in schools but is extremely important in the development of relationships. They wrote:

> Morally and culturally, caring is a belief about how we should view and interact with others. In this way, caring is essential to education and may guide the ways we instruct and discipline students, set policy, and organize the school day . . . Caring in our schools lies hidden beneath the technical and instrumental ways of viewing culture and schooling . . . [Although] more technical aspects of teaching dominate our thinking . . . Caring gives priority to relationships. (Noblit, Rogers, & McCadden, 1995, pp. 680–81)

Teachers who care for and about students want to know about their students' experiences and backgrounds, as the case study of the new teacher described. The author felt that she would have been a much more effective teacher if she had known the local community and history of African Americans.

Table 1.6 The Ethic of Care Theory: Characteristics
• Teachers make a moral commitment to students.
• Teachers develop trusting, reciprocal relationships with students and focus on ethical and intellectual development.
• Teachers get to know and affirm students, their identities, and their cultures.
• Teachers carefully reflect on their own biases.
• Teachers engage in dialogue with students.
• Teachers teach critical thinking skills used to address inequalities.
• Teachers create schools that are centers of care.

Caring teachers encourage students to develop their innate potentials. Schools become places of caring and places where students can learn how to care for themselves and others through the modeling of teachers. The next section moves to a discussion of Vygotsky's sociocultural theory of learning and how culture plays a powerful role in learning.

Sociocultural Theory of Learning: Vygotsky

Culture is one of the most important components of who we are, how we define ourselves, and how we see the world (Erickson, 2012). We are socialized into a group of people, usually our nuclear and extended families. Our cultural background arises from what the people who are closest to us teach us through their use of language and nonverbal communications. New ideas are interpreted in relation to our prior knowledge, how we identify ourselves, and our personal perspectives. The Russian psychologist Lev Vygotsky developed the **sociocultural theory of learning** to explain how learning is socially mediated. Vygotsky believed that people learn through social interactions and these interactions occur within multiple cultural contexts.

> **Sociocultural theory of learning** is a theory developed primarily by Lev Vygotsky where social interactions and language are seen as the vehicles of learning.

Psychologists and scholars, like Vygotsky, believe language and social interactions are major cultural tools needed to develop cognitive skills. Nussbaum, a humanist, writes, "We each have a language (in some cases more than one) in which we are at home, which we have usually known from infancy. We naturally feel a special affection for this language. It defines our possibilities of communication and expression. The works of literature that move us most deeply are those that exploit well the resources of that language" (1997, pp. 61–62).

Language is used to communicate important aspects of a culture such as values, beliefs, thoughts, and norms; it is a cultural tool. Thoughts and language are reciprocal, and both are needed in developing intelligence (Wink & Putney, 2002). Research has indicated that there are cultural differences in the way people think. For example Nisbett (2003), a cognitive psychologist, found that Westerners have a culture in which they have been trained to use categorization in their thinking processes so they can apply the proper rules and logic in solving problems. In contrast, East Asians often view problems in a broad context, knowing that the situation is often complex, needing the consideration of a range of elements. They think in a more circular manner and the use of linear ways of thinking to problem solve is not valued as it is in Western countries. In other words people around the world do not think in the same ways. Cultural belief systems differ because people understand and interpret the world differently.

How do language and social interactions shape what you think? As children you learned what was acceptable and valued in your culture from members of your family or those closest to you. For example, if your parents read to you every night before bedtime, their behavior taught you that they believed reading was important. An excellent example of how language and social interactions in the classroom can shape how we think comes from a study of a Mexican American, bilingual elementary-grade teacher as she taught mathematics (Gutstein, Lipman, Hernandez, & de los Reyes, 1997). Although the researchers found few references to Mexican history, Mexican cultural artifacts, or other aspects of Mexican culture, they did find that the teacher saw her classroom relationships as extending a sense of family. In other words, the teacher saw culture in a holistic way. She felt that the exercise of learning in schools could be an extension of the type of learning that happens in a family unit (Figure 1.9). Here is what the teacher, Ms. Herrera, said about teaching in a bilingual-Spanish classroom:

> I try a whole lot to connect to them, to try to understand . . . I come in here thinking from the first day, they are already a part of me, already a part of my family. That makes me want so hard to help all of them. They're part of me, my family, my culture, little bits and pieces of me . . . I know they're going to go through the same things I went through, I want to see them go beyond what's

Figure 1.9: Students who feel as if they are part of a community are more likely to enjoy learning and respect each other in the process.

Steve Debenport/E+/Getty Images

expected of them . . . it's so hard to see how a lot of Hispanics are being treated . . . I want them to stand out, be special in their own way. . . . (Gutstein et al., 1997, p. 729)

Ms. Herrera's teaching style is an effective example of how the care theory and sociocultural theory can be intimately connected.

Let's look at an example from an African American family. What if values weren't taught by reading books, but through oral tradition? What values might you have learned through this process? First, you might have been indirectly taught to respect and honor older members of the community who bestowed this information to you. Second, you would have been taught how to listen and remember. In addition, the content of your grandparents' stories would also have taught you specific family and cultural values. By using oral tradition, this family is teaching that the valuable members of the community are the elders and that it is extremely important to know how to listen. (See Figure 1.10.)

Socially Mediated Learning Michael Cole, an educator who has studied Vygotsky's work extensively, has theorized about why language is one of the most important tools we use in learning. He believes that we use cultural "tools" like language and cultural expectations to mold, shape, and filter what we think. Cole believes tools such as language, ideas, customs, behaviors, and practices all act as cultural negotiators and shape our learning. Learning is also historical. Many people have come before us and our cultural knowledge is built upon what they did in their lives and taught to us (Cole, 1996). Culture is accumulated over time and handed down from generation to generation over many years. Because people change, culture also changes and is continually being reconstructed.

We learn through the many sociocultural interactions we have in our lives. Sometimes our learning comes from inner reflection; other times it comes from working with people or ideas or objects. The teachers who follow a sociocultural learning framework create powerful communities of learners, where individuals work together, giving those who participate more opportunities to learn from each other. The discussions and nonverbal communications that pass between students convey ideas and concepts. In addition, there is a social process that may be formal, casual, or spontaneous; this social context also impacts

Figure 1.10: A grandfather shares a story with his grandson and imparts wisdom about life to him.

learning. When we bring different cultural experiences and viewpoints into the discussion, we can enhance our own learning and the growth of others (Figure 1.11). Cole suggests that cross-cultural teaching is like a bridge. In this way the bridge allows for two-way exchange of knowledge and insights. Knowledge moves in both directions. Having a diversity of students in our classrooms can enrich our schools. When there is reciprocal sharing of perspectives, information, ideas, and practices within a trusting environment, learning will be expanded.

Figure 1.11: Teacher uses a traditional, Native American guessing game to teach prediction skills to students who are members of the Chumash tribe.

Following is an example of how socially-mediated learning can enrich many lives. When a fourth-generation Japanese American tenth grader shared her family tree project with her class, the other students in the class learned about how the young girl's grandmother had been placed in a concentration camp in Idaho during World War II. Her peers were surprised to learn that the U.S. government took their own citizens, who were of Japanese ancestry, away from their homes to desolate camps in desert areas in such states as Idaho, Wyoming, and California. The student's grandmother was born in the state of Washington and had never been to Japan. Classmates of the young girl had the opportunity to learn in a personal way how history involves people they know. The granddaughter provided a bridge for other students to better understand the experience of the Japanese American community. This discussion added to the social-cultural knowledge of the classroom. In addition, sharing was beneficial to the Japanese American student, because the class asked her grandmother to come and talk to them. As a result of her grandmother's presentation to her classmates, she learned more about her grandmother and what she went through in her life.

Let's get back to Vygotsky. His sociocultural theory of development recommends that teachers use cultural knowledge to carefully develop social interactions and activities to increase learning. Research scientists like Michael Cole demonstrate that students can learn more effectively using a comprehensive orientation toward curriculum and instruction that simultaneously uses student cultural knowledge, cues, social interaction patterns, and cultural practices. In Chapters 2 and 3, you will read about several programs using culturally relevant teaching. They are called the Algebra Project, Funds of Knowledge, the Puente Project, and the Organic Reading and Writing. All of them use a holistic approach.

Zone of Proximal Development Many teachers wonder about how theory can help them in the classroom. What does it have to do with their everyday teaching? As part of his sociocultural framework for cognitive development, Vygotsky constructed the concept of the **zone of proximal development** that extends the range of a child's learning from the actual developmental level to the potential level achieved through the guidance of an adult or collaboration with a more knowledgeable peer (Tharp & Gallimore, 1988).

As the child learns skills from interactions with the teacher or others in the first phase, he or she moves into the second phase of the zone of proximal development by guiding the use of the skills on her or his own. In the third phase, the child internalizes the skill or capability; in the fourth phase, the student may have forgotten a skill and may ask the teacher for help, and the process repeats itself as follows:

1. Performance is assisted by more capable others.
2. Performance is assisted by self.
3. Performance becomes internalized or "fossilized."
4. Assistance is requested and the process begins again.

Researchers believe that mental processes arise out of sociocultural ways of knowing through social interactions in the zone of proximal development. (See Figure 1.12.) In this process, the teacher is a guide, facilitator, and evaluator. Vygotsky believed that because learning is socially mediated, interpersonal relationships are fundamental to the zone of proximal development.

Using Vygotsky's sociocultural theory of learning, reading researchers Goodman and Goodman (1990) believed that teachers should act as initiators. They share an example about how a teacher, together with her eighth-grade students, designed a unit on evolution. The teacher's objective was to assist students so that they fully understood the issues around both theories of creationism and evolution. She also

> **Zone of proximal development** is an extended range of a child's learning, from the actual developmental level to the potential level achieved through the guidance of an adult or collaboration with a more knowledgeable peer.

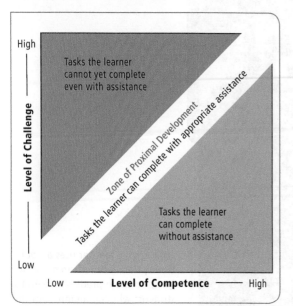

Figure 1.12: Zone of Proximal Development

Table 1.7 Sociocultural Theory of Learning: Characteristics
• Culture Shapes and Molds Our Thinking, Values, Knowledge, and Identity
• Learning Occurs through Social Interactions and Language
• Teachers Build on Student Prior Knowledge and Experiences
• Students Construct Their Own Meaning; Schools Are Laboratories of Culture
• Teacher Assists Student Performance/Achievement
• Student Become Self-Regulating

wanted to sharpen their reading comprehension and social studies skills in the process. As an initiator, the teacher assisted students by selecting materials for the unit, providing time for student discussions, and encouraging students to choose pieces of literature that would deepen their understanding of the issues. However, the teacher did not control the learning process. Her students independently defined terms such as *evolution* and *creationism* and also picked a biography about Charles Darwin to read. They were able to examine the role of science while reading the biographical novel. This instructional unit demonstrated that both process and content were important aspects of learning. Not only did students become more competent readers, but they also built on what they already knew and investigated various aspects of the issues. Their understanding of the conflict and difference in value orientations between creationism and evolution deepened while they learned reading and social studies skills, such as reading for meaning, reading for evidence, and grasping the difference between fact and opinion. Because the students learned specific skills within a larger context, their zone of proximal development increased. Their teacher helped them develop their thinking processes and challenged them to reflect beyond the acquisition of knowledge by encouraging them to examine complex issues. Learning expanded because the concepts and knowledge that students gained arose from a meaningful context.

In this process, learning occurred on two levels. First, learning is a socially-constructed phenomenon in which students learned by interacting with ideas and with other people. Second, students grew because they reflected on those experiences. They developed a metacognitive understanding; students understand their own thinking processes. Through this process, skills became automatic and internalized. When people share with each other their perspectives, information, ideas, and practices, the understanding and comprehension of students can be expanded. Students can learn on their own, but greater growth can be achieved when they are assisted by teachers or peers. The role of the teacher as an active participant in the learning process is to assist students by providing modeling, feedback, coaching, instructing, questioning, and cognitive structuring (Tharp & Gallimore, 1988).

Vygotsky theorized that the zone of learning can be increased when teachers use effective strategies and materials to help guide a student's learning beyond what they could learn on their own. According to Vygotsky, students also learn to **self-regulate**, which means they identify goals and work toward them. For example, when they're in school, students might identify goals such as higher grades or the completion of assignments. You will read more about the sociocultural theory of learning in Chapter 2. For now, review the characteristics of the sociocultural theory of learning found in Table 1.7.

Self-regulation refers to a process in which an individual or student identifies a goal and then works toward achieving or accomplishing the goal.

Culturally Relevant Education Vygotsky's research is an excellent foundation for culturally relevant education, though other researchers have not identified it as such (Pang, 2005). Culturally relevant education is especially oriented toward equity and building the curriculum and instructional strategies on the knowledge, values, and practices of culturally and linguistically diverse students. Geneva Gay, educator, explains that culturally relevant and responsive education build upon the cultural frames of reference of students of color and low-income students (2010, 2013). Through the use of culturally relevant teaching, education becomes more meaningful and is based on the rich knowledge and points of view that students of color bring to the classroom. This orientation is in opposition to a cultural deficit viewpoint (King, 2011; Gay, 2013). Much more discussion of culturally relevant education will be presented in Chapter 3 of this book.

Teachers as Cultural Mediators For teachers to understand diverse cultural values and integrate the cultural knowledge of students into the curriculum and instruction, educators must become cultural mediators. A cultural mediator can be extremely effective if he or she takes on the role of mentor or facilitator; the mediator guides students in understanding

CASE STUDY A Story to Live By: Teaching through Oral Tradition

Interview of Pia Parrish

Pia Parrish, a member of the Blackfoot community, shared how important the stories of her grandparents and other elders in the community were to her. She works with many teachers in science education. As a child, she would sit and listen to stories from the elders in the evenings. This was their way of sharing cultural values. She learned as a little tyke that their stories were the foundation for her life. These stories help to guide her beliefs today. Stories are important to many Native peoples. Since many cultural traditions developed without written languages, stories are an integral way of communicating cultural values. These social interactional patterns often differed from Pia's school culture. Here is a short sample of one of the stories she heard about change and how two people who love you may not always get along. The story may be about divorce, siblings, or community relationships. The story emphasizes the importance of mutual respect. Through the social interactions Pia had with her grandparents and the carefully chosen words they used, Pia understood the lessons they were teaching.

The Moon and the Sun
Long ago, the Moon and the Sun lived in a small house. They had a little girl named Earth. They were happy. But then they started to fight.

The Moon said, "You are too hot!"
The Sun said, "You are too cold!"
"Okay," said the Moon, "Let's live apart. But the Earth will live with me."
"No, she will get too cold without me," said the Sun.
They went to wise old Thunder. Thunder listened to the fight. Then he said, "Let the sun watch the Earth in the day. Let the Moon watch the Earth in the night."
That is why the sun shines in the day, and the moon shines at night.
When the Moon is busy, the stars shine on the Earth.

Using the oral tradition of the Blackfoot culture, Pia's elders taught her ways to look at conflicts in relationships. The story can be used to explain how children in a divorced family need both their parents to take care of them, even though they may not live in the same house. There is much symbolism in the story.

The segment of the story that says "When the Moon is busy, the stars shine on the Earth" is interpreted by some Native people to symbolize the roles of aunts and uncles. Aunts and uncles can also play important roles in childrearing. As an adult, Pia reflects back to the cultural values she was given as a child. These stories guide her life today.

Like all of us, Pia learned about life within cultural contexts. The sociocultural setting of sitting in the evening and listening to her elders and the use of the oral tradition taught her much about what her family values in life. This was a familiar cultural practice. Her grandfather and other elders used language and social interaction as a means of communicating ideas with Pia. Vygotsky, the Russian psychologist, believed that language stimulates thought and is a tool for learning (Wink & Putney, 2002). His work led to the development of the sociocultural theory of learning. This theory emphasizes the importance of language and social interactions.

Let's take a look at Pia's experiences. She learned specific cultural practices, and language was the tool that stimulated and conveyed her grandfather's ideas and beliefs. The social situation was meaningful and relevant to Pia because her grandfather was a valued person in her family, and she had been taught by her parents and culture that he had important lessons to teach. Her grandfather became a facilitator or teacher in her learning. Pia's grandfather did not explicitly say, "This story is about divorce"; rather, he allowed her to become active in the learning process and she made sense of his stories. In this way her grandfather stimulated her thoughts by teaching her how to interpret the many stories she heard from him and other members of the Blackfoot community.

Reflection Questions

Q Pia believes that elders are important in her family. How important are elders in other communities?

Q What evidence can you provide?

school expectations and practices. The facilitator is also sensitive to student cultural values and practices. They value and affirm student cultural backgrounds and know how to connect with culturally and linguistically diverse students. A mediator will see the culture as a whole system rather than isolated elements of food, dress, and customs.

The teacher as cultural mediator also helps other educators understand the values of students who may be members of cultural communities of which they have little knowledge. For example, the new teacher in the case study by Pang would have benefited from talking with a parent or educator who could explain to her about African American vernacular English, the viewpoints of African Americans in the neighborhood, and the knowledge that the role model for many African American youth in the school was Malcolm X. The mediator could explain to the new teacher reasons why he was seen as important to Black history and that the students respected his fight for civil rights and saw many parallels in his life and their own. Though the new teacher held a conflicting view of Malcom X and she may not have allowed her students to read books discussing the life of the historical figure, the mediator could have discussed students' thoughts about Malcolm X with the teacher so she could incorporate material on Malcolm X into the curriculum.

Education for Democracy: Dewey

One of the foundational values of our nation and multicultural education is social justice. John Dewey, an educational philosopher of the twentieth century, focused his work on the creation of an educated and democratic citizenry, which is his theory of **education for democracy**. As a firm advocate of democracy, Dewey believed that schools should be major institutions that mentored children to become active citizens who make just decisions based on the common good (Westbrook, 1991). Dewey saw schools as laboratories of democracy and community building where students developed communication and collaboration skills that enabled them to work with others as responsible citizens in a just society. As a result of his work, schools have become places where students are actively involved in the process of democracy. (See Figure 1.13.) Dewey believed that democracy was not a system of rules, but rather a state of collaborative living where people made decisions about the common good together. Dewey saw democracy as a process of shared inquiry where decisions must be continually reflected upon to ensure the continual growth

> **Education for democracy** is a theory developed primarily by John Dewey that identifies the values of democracy, equality, community, and justice as core values of schools.

Figure 1.13: A multicultural class engaged in classroom democracy.

Table 1.8 Education for Democracy: Characteristics
• Teachers' Use of Higher Order Thinking Skills
• Students Are Active Participants, Living in a Democracy
• Students Engage in Shared Inquiry and Decision Making
• Students Engage in Community Building, Working Toward the Common Good
• Students Value Social Justice, Civil Rights, Self-Empowerment
• Students Analyze Power Relationships for Equity
• Students Engage In Self-Direction
• Schools: Laboratories for Democracy

of society. Schools should reflect that caring, fair, and collaborative process so that children will grow up into responsible and participatory citizens.

Many practices that you may use in schools came from Dewey's work. For example, he believed in and promoted student-centered education where students work collaboratively to make schools a more just, compassionate place. Dewey did not believe that at the core of good instruction was standardized testing that emphasized rote memorization of isolated and fragmented information outside of a relevant context.

One of the key aspects of multicultural education that Dewey brought to schools was that his belief in participatory democracy (Westbrook, 1991). He posed that collaborative living, understanding, and working with people from various cultural backgrounds was possible. Because students would be in classrooms with students of many different cultural backgrounds, they would be enriched by the many viewpoints and belief systems that they shared with each other. His wife, Alice, believed in cultural and racial equality and influenced his thinking (Fallace, 2011). Dewey viewed schools not only as places where children could develop their minds and their abilities to read, write, and do mathematics, but also as places where students could learn about society and different ways of looking at the world through discussions and subject areas related to the arts, nature, and ethics.

Dewey's belief in education for democracy emphasized a curriculum that facilitates higher-order-thinking analysis skills in students so that they are able to examine such social issues as racial inequities, class struggles, and gender discrimination (Dewey, 1916; Freire, 1970; Darder, 1991; King, 1991, 2011; Pang, 2005). He proposed that schools should be places of activity where people work on common problems and establish rules collaboratively (Noddings, 2013). Education for democracy focuses on teaching students how to analyze power relationships and build collaborative communities; it also encourages social communication skills (see Table 1.8). These skills are similar to the ones that Noddings highlights in her ethic of care theory and the work of other researchers such as Joyce E. King (1991, 1994, 2011) and Geneva Gay (1994, 2010, 2013).

In order to understand how the integration of the three theories form a comprehensive framework for multicultural education, see Table 1.9. You will be able to identify relationships among the theories and see their connections. A framework links together various theories, pinpoints similarities, and unifies principles.

Global Citizens

Extending the work of John Dewey, Martha Nussbaum and Merry Merryfield, as educators, also believed that it is important for all of us to think and act beyond national or ethnic boundaries. They considered it crucial for all people to view themselves as global citizens who make ethical decisions based on understanding the perspectives of people from other countries, ethnic communities, and organizations.

How easy is it to consider multiple perspectives? Merryfield (2001) recommended that we move away from the basic assumptions of some traditional global education programs

Table 1.9 The Integration of Ethic of Care Theory, Sociocultural Theory of Learning, and Education for Democracy
The three theories complement and build on each other.

	Ethic of Care (Noddings)	Sociocultural Theory of Learning (Vygotsky)	Education for Democracy (Dewey)
Critical Thinking	Teachers guide students to develop critical thinking skills	Higher levels of thinking will develop when collaborating with others	Teachers guide students to develop critical thinking skills in order to solve social problems
The Individual	Development of a compassionate, responsible, and ethical person	Build on student knowledge and experiences; affirm student	Development of an ethical, reflective, participatory citizen for a democracy
Community	Reciprocal relationships form the foundation of a strong compassionate and ethical community.	Social interactions form the foundation for cognitive development	Development of collaborative, trusting relationships enhances democracy
Social Justice	Positive school climate is built on fairness and compassion	All students can achieve, and teachers must provide instruction that is effective	Social justice is a key value in a democratic society and all students must achieve
Culture	Learning about each other will enhance trusting relationships	Through culture students learn language and tools that are used in learning	Affirm and accept diverse cultural communities
Prejudice	Teachers must reflect on their biases in order to demonstrate true caring	Working together in dialogue creates more enriched knowledge; a class hierarchy is not accepted	Inequalities and discrimination must be eliminated in a democracy

whose aim is to educate students to continue to exert the cultural ways and political role of the United States in the world. Globalization does not mean Westernization. For example, teachers should not teach the attitude that the *American* way is the best or the only way to address global problems. An important challenge for our students and ourselves is to reconsider U.S. imperialism, political issues, and global control in the marketplace. Questions that we, as educators, can ask ourselves are:

- Will our students seek out diverse global perspectives?
- Will our students be able to understand the perspectives of people from developing countries who may have different values than those found in the United States?
- Will our students be able to work within cross-cultural situations in other countries?

In addition, as Nussbaum has argued, teachers should see themselves as citizens of humanity, instead of considering only the views of a local group like an ethnic community or only our country's needs. How easy is it to really understand another's view, especially if it conflicts with your own? It can be extremely difficult to do so because placing yourself in someone else's shoes may mean giving up, for a moment, your own beliefs. In addition, you may also have difficulty understanding other people's perspectives because of a lack of knowledge of another group different from yourself or because of unconscious prejudices (Pang, 1994). However, as Socrates explained, education must be cross-cultural; we learn from others, and our understanding of the world and of ourselves can be greatly expanded through exposure to diverse people, cultures, and ideas (Nussbaum, 1997). (See Figure 1.14.) This

Image Source/Superstock

Figure 1.14: Elementary student studies the globe and is learning how important communication skills are in building a peaceful world.

CHECKLIST: MY EDUCATIONAL PHILOSOPHY

Every teacher needs to develop a system of beliefs and values about what it means to be a great educator. Ask yourself the following questions:

☐ What do you value as a teacher?

☐ What are the most important goals of schooling?

☐ Have you identified theories that explain student learning? If not, why not? If so, what are they?

☐ How do the theories that make up your educational philosophy guide your teaching? Goals? Teacher expectations? Student expectations? Pedagogy?

≫ Professional Resource Download

is even more important today, given our close relationships to other countries in the areas of economics, politics, education, and environment. Estela Matriano, an international education specialist, also encourages educators to create a culture of peace that is more than the lack of war. She believes that all of us must work toward mutual understanding, democracy, and freedom. We all have a responsibility to serve our fellow global citizens.

Consider this . . .

Globalization does not mean Westernization.

Q What does globalization include?

Q Should Westernization be a large component of globalization? Why or why not?

TAKE A STAND BULLYING AT SCHOOL

John Dewey believed in the importance of building a strong community by teaching students the roles and responsibilities within a democratic classroom. Each student must share in the power of directing the classroom and school. We see teachers who foster democratic education through the use of classroom meetings in which students develop common goals and then take on various roles to address community goals (Nussbaum, 1997). In these schools students are encouraged to face difficult issues.

For instance, many young people face homophobic harassment, as well as harassment based on their social class. Teachers can guide students to address prejudice. In a caring, democratic community, every person has the responsibility to treat others with respect and to act justly. For example, in many schools across the nation, high school students say, "Our homework is gay." These students mean that they consider the

homework to be "bad" or not desirable, and they don't want to do it. Similarly, grade school students can often be heard taunting a male child with a label like, "John is gay; John is gay." Another common example is one child calling another child "retard" or "retarded" to hurt their feelings.

In a classroom, caring and social justice are important values. Some teachers do not feel as if it is important for them to address passing comments as these. They see their job as teaching algebra or physical education and not about stopping student remarks.

TAKE A STAND . . .

≫ **Is it the responsibility of a teacher to stop these prejudicial comments? What should teachers do?**

Thinking about Intersectionality

As a teacher do you think students are often labeled based on economic status or race? Oftentimes teachers hold bias against students based on both race and social class. The two characteristics of learners are often intimately woven together. For instance, Rank (2005) analyzed the U.S. Bureau of the Census, Current Population Reports for 2003 and found that 24.1 percent of Blacks were considered living at the poverty rate or lower. Rank also discovered that 69.5 percent of Black children who are 17-years-old in the United States have lived at least one year in poverty. Often Black American poor students attend the most segregated and inadequately funded schools (Anyon, 1997; Rank, 2005). The economic and ra-

cial stratification of students often reproduces itself from one generation to the next (Rank, 2005). Teacher bias is a factor in the achievement process.

Lower teacher expectations of students of color is an aspect of teacher prejudice. Many educators do not believe their students of color and poor students can do well in school (Kuykendall, 2012). Often teachers ignore, separate, and reject students of color by their comments, body language, and lack of effective teaching strategies. Teachers may convey the belief that poor students of color are not teachable and not smart. Students become disengaged in school and the achievement gap grows. Intersectionality plays a powerful role in education.

Summary

1. **Describe the difference between the terms "race" and "ethnicity" and what is meant by "cultural diversity."**

   Race is a political and social construct based upon perceived physical differences. There is no biological basis for racial categories such as African American, Asian American and Pacific Islanders, Latinos, Native Americans, and White Americans, though many people believe race to be an accurate biological truth. There is only one race, the human race. The book discusses race because so many people use it as a given. It is a sociopolitical construct that has often been used to divide people. Ethnicity refers to place of origin, so a student may be Puerto Rican or Cuban in ethnicity. So not only are race and ethnicity considered aspects of cultural diversity, but also people may vary due to languages, religions, exceptionalities, gender, sexual orientation, social class, or age.

2. **Discuss demographic changes in the United States.**

   Immigration has had a profound influence on the development of our nation. This is evident in the diverse racial and ethnic communities found in the United States. However, diversity is far broader and includes groupings such as gender, sexual orientation, class, religion, age, religion, and language. Students come to school speaking many different home languages. They also may have strong ties to family in other countries. They can have strong global connections to others.

3. **Identify the roots and misconceptions of multicultural education.**

   There have been several movements that have pushed schools and society to become more inclusive. They are the Intercultural Education Movement, the Intergroup Education Movement, and the Civil Rights Movement. These movements not only called for equality in schools and society, but also advocated for the inclusion of cultural diversity into school curriculum, policies, and all aspects of schooling.

4. **Define and analyze the goals and concepts of multicultural education.**

   Multicultural education is a complex field in education. One of the major goals is to ensure equal educational opportunity, access, and outcomes

   for every student. Like you, teachers in the field want to develop the potential of each child so they become happy, compassionate, and ethical citizens. Multicultural education first arose out of our national values of democracy, social justice, equality, and freedom. This led to the curriculum model that recommended that schools include content integration, knowledge construction, equity pedagogy, prejudice reduction, and an empowered school culture. As time progressed the next orientation presents a theory of multicultural education which is more politically based; this approach in highly founded upon critical theory, which mentors students to analyze power inequalities in society and work toward challenging those disparities. The third model is a theoretical framework that includes the principles of three theories: ethic of care, sociocultural theory of learning, and education for democracy. This framework includes not only principles of social justice and culturally relevant teaching, but also cognitive learning theory.

5. **Discuss and evaluate the goals, major concepts, and models of multicultural education.**

   One of the major models of multicultural education has five dimensions that primarily focus on curriculum development. Another foundation for multicultural education is based on critical theory, which advocates the examination of power inequities.

   Another theoretical framework includes theories about relationship building, cultural backgrounds, democratic values, and cognitive learning research; these elements create a strong system of educational principles. This framework guides:

   - The development and implementation of school policies that are based on equal educational opportunities and outcomes
   - A pedagogy that builds on student cultural backgrounds and cognitive research on learning
   - The integration of curriculum materials that affirm students
   - The creation of collaborative, respectful school communities that include parents

Check Your Cultural Knowledge

Reflective Essay Question

Three of the major goals of multicultural education are:

- ❯ Attain equality and equity in education
- ❯ Eliminate the achievement gap
- ❯ Develop responsible and empowered citizens

Describe your educational philosophy with principles and values to ensure that the three goals are accomplished. Explain also why you chose the philosophical principles and values you did. Be sure to include a cognitive theory so that you are aware of ways to address how students learn. You will have to make important judgments about your foundational beliefs and goals about education as a teacher.

Application

Know and Go Tools in the Classroom

It is important for teachers to address issues of prejudice and discrimination in multicultural education. Students need to know that name-calling and prejudice have no place in schools.

Students can be heard calling each other names such as the "N" word, beaner, fag, tranny, retard, rag head, and chink on the playground. The name calling is so pervasive that teachers supervising students during recess are not sure what to do.

What would you do?

Suggestions

If this is a prevalent issue in your school, it is important to bring up the name calling at your school during a faculty meeting. Have all teachers along with the administrators decide on how to tackle the issue together. There should not only be a school policy about creating a safe and respectful school environment, but strategies should be identified by the faculty as a whole so that everyone is consistent in their dealing with the issue.

If teachers let the issue continue, students will think that it is okay to name call. They also may think that social oppression is not that big of an issue.

Possible Suggestions for Classrooms

Each classroom may begin to discuss the issue of name calling with the following questions. However, if there is little trust in the classroom, teachers will need first to create trusting communities before effective discussions on social oppression can take place.

Have students discuss these questions:

What are your values regarding building community?

Have you heard students call each other negative names?

How did the victim feel?

Why do people call others names?

What is your responsibility to eradicate these prejudicial practices?

You should already have created classroom rules of behavior so students know what behaviors are expected and the consequences for poor conduct.

Following are several other possibilities to extend the discussion on name calling.

1. One way to get students to talk about prejudices and name calling is to have learners get into groups and come up with a poster to be hung around the school. Students can come up with a great "hook" or catchy phrase.

2. Great examples of sports role models against prejudice were created by the Anti-Defamation League of B'nai B'rith. One poster showed a famous basketball player jumping toward the basket with the saying, "If you really believe in America, prejudice is foul play."

3. Students may create posters with pictures of other students in solidarity at their school with a phrase such as, "If you really believe in fairness, we stand together." This could be a message shared with the entire school.

4. In addition, teachers should periodically remind students about how hurtful name-calling is. In high school, students might decide to say to those who use inappropriate labels, "That's not cool. We don't talk that way to each other." These are strategies students and teachers can build together. They arise out of values of social justice and democracy.

❮❮ Professional Resource Download

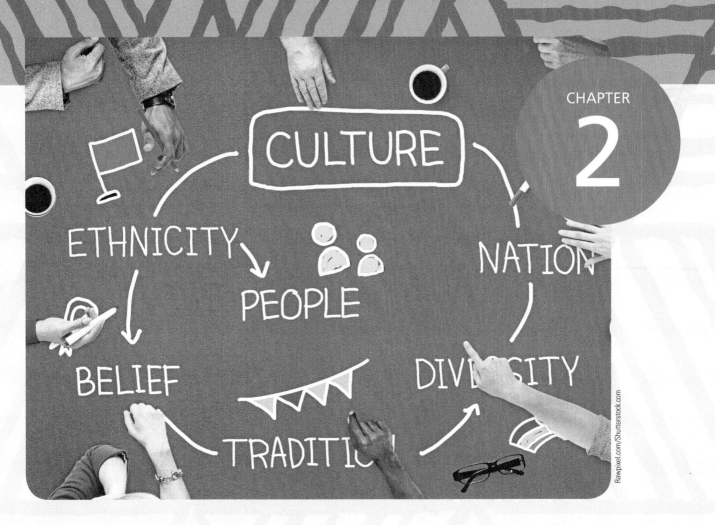

The Power of Culture

Learning Objectives

LO1 Describe the various elements of culture and explain why culture is a powerful aspect of life.

LO2 Define and explain a model of culture.

LO3 Discuss mainstream culture and subcultures in the United States.

LO4 Describe how culture is transmitted and cultural identity is developed.

LO5 Investigate culturally relevant education and evaluate examples of several programs.

STANDARDS COVERED

NAEYC 1, 4, 6
naeyc

CAEP 1 CAEP

INTASC 1, 2, 3, 4, 5, 6, 7, 8, 9, 10
InTASC

LO1 Describe the various elements of culture and explain why culture is a powerful aspect of life.

Overview

Culture is a powerful force in life. This chapter will define what culture is and how culture is important in the learning and teaching processes. In addition, this chapter will include questions so that you can reflect upon how culture influences your life. To be a successful teacher, you will need to be an effective cultural mediator. This means you will know and appreciate the cultural backgrounds of your students and can act as a link between the school and home. Teachers who know about the cultures of their students also are experts at folding student experiences and knowledge into the curriculum. They build on what students know as they teach new information and skills. Get ready to learn about how culture can be a vital aspect of your teaching "toolbox."

Culture Is All Around

Culture is like air; it is always there, but people who live in and are part of a culture may have difficulty seeing it. One way to think about culture is that it is everything that is created by humans. Don't you think that's a lot of things? That's why teachers must begin to think about what culture is and how it influences learning and teaching. (See Figure 2.1.)

Many teachers may think of culture in regard to the foods they eat, clothes they wear, holidays they celebrate, and activities they enjoy. Culture is vast in that it includes not only aspects of a community like common history, identified literature, and languages spoken, but also nonverbal behaviors such as how one stands, how one greets another, and even the motions one makes when talking. However, the most important aspect of culture revolves around our values, beliefs, attitudes, and philosophies. That is the reason that the sociopolitical construct of race is included in this book because it is a major concept in our culture, though not biologically true.

Frederick Erickson, an educational anthropologist, reminds teachers of three important aspects about culture and humans: (1) everyone is cultural; (2) everyone is multicultural; (3) culture is learned (2015). We all are members of various groups, and culture is a tool that we use in deciding how to act. Though many White teachers or European Americans

Figure 2.1: A student's culture can include spending time with family.

Monkey Business Images/Shutterstock.com

may not think of themselves as cultural beings, they, like everyone else, are shaped by various cultural elements such as the languages they speak, their geographical roots, and religious beliefs. One aspect of culture that may be different for White Americans and people of color is that though everyone is cultural, White Americans as a group often have more cultural and political power and prestige than they do.

How is everyone multicultural? Anthropologist Ward Goodenough believes, like Erickson, that each human group is culturally diverse (1976). For example, do all German Americans think and act the same? Probably not because within their cultural group, there is diversity. Goodenough sees that there are individual people within large groupings who may act and behave in many different ways. In this way he carefully explains that people should be careful not to overgeneralize. Not everyone within a specific cultural group will act and think in the same way. There is a difference between the **macroculture**, or the culture of the larger community, and the micro or subcultures of which individuals may find themselves members (Goodenough, 1976).

Valerie Ooka Pang

Figure 2.2: Two teachers use the thumbs up symbol to demonstrate a cultural practice that can be interpreted differently in various cultures.

Culture can be extremely difficult to grasp. Different behaviors and values may come about because of situational differences. Let's take a high school student who is a member of a classroom where the teacher only wants learners to speak in English. The classroom is an example of a subculture. The student then always answers her peers in English. However, in another classroom where the teacher welcomes Spanish, the young person uses Spanish to explain abstract math concepts to her classmates. This student knows the macroculture of public schools but also is a member of a subculture where Spanish is spoken and valued. She knows the expectations that her two teachers and follows specific cultural views depending on the situation.

Some teachers may see their culture as natural or neutral because they have grown up with it every day of their lives. Teachers may understand that their students are members of various cultural groups, but they may not see themselves as cultural beings. However, you as a teacher, also bring your cultural viewpoints to the classroom. Teachers and students will not always have the same worldviews or cultural expectations, and this can result in conflicts (see Figure 2.2). In order to teach the whole student, you may need to learn and understand more about the cultural communities of your students and reflect upon your own cultural background. Culture is like an onion—it has many layers, and you need to peel back each succeeding level to get at its core.

> **Macroculture** refers to the larger cultural group, which includes expectations, symbols, and behaviors.

Explicit Elements of Culture

Culture is an extremely complex concept. Defining culture is like defining who you are and all that you do, identify with, and believe in simultaneously. There are hundreds of definitions

Consider this . . .

Culture is like air; it is always there, but people who live in and are part of a culture may have difficulty seeing it.

One way to think about culture is that it is everything that is created by humans.

Q What does that mean for you as a teacher?

of culture that have been developed by anthropologists to explain the behaviors and beliefs of people (Erickson, 2015). Differences in groups were also often defined as racial and therefore genetic in nature; almost as if the civilized nature of people arose from their biology. Remember in Chapter 1 the discussion of the work of Carl Linneaus—his human taxonomy placed Europeans at the top as the most intelligent, capable, and worthy of power. It also reinforced racial superiority of Europeans. Anthropologists developed another way to describe the diversity of people around the globe that was different from race, which led to the construct of culture. Racial beliefs are and were often used to justify Western imperialism; anthropologists wanted a way to explain that people are different; however, one civilization is not superior to another (Erickson, 2015).

Culture is often defined as a social system of rules, language, customs, rituals, arts, government, expectations, norms, values, and ideals that people share (Cushner, McClelland, & Safford, 2012). Cultural values are the ideals that a group of people hold; they form the shared ethics that members of a community live by. In this book, culture will be thought of in a more organized way than a list of human elements. You will read about this in the section on models of culture because teachers need to more fully understand how culture influences the way students mature and learn.

Sometimes, people talk about **explicit culture** (Cushner et al., 2012). This term refers to cultural elements that can be seen, heard, worn, and eaten; it can also refer to factors of living that are conscious (Erickson, 2015). It may include geographical areas. These are tangible and visible factors. Explicit culture would include what you wear, the music you listen to, traditional clothes that you might wear, a country that you see as identifying your national origin, and the foods you eat. These are aspects of life that are observable.

Implicit Elements of Culture

In contrast to explicit culture is implicit culture. **Implicit culture** is made up of elements that are often hidden or embedded within a community (Erickson, 2015). It includes the values, assumptions, beliefs, and philosophies of a group. These are harder to identify because they include expectations and worldviews. For example, students usually do not come to school with a sign saying, "I am an Orthodox Jew" or "I am a Muslim." Students may reveal these inner aspects of themselves over time.

It is also important for you, as a teacher, to understand that a cultural group may not always be defined as arising out of ethnicity. A cultural group can be religious in nature or have to do with a lifestyle. For example, there are people who identify as being a member of a dairy farm or a logging community.

Sometimes people disagree on an issue because they have different implicit cultural values that they learned from their families. For example, maybe you believe it is important to intervene on the playground whenever there is a conflict. However, maybe another teacher believes it is important for students to figure out solutions to recess problems themselves. Each teacher has different views about guiding students. However, if they, as educators in the school, do not identify common values and the behaviors needed to implement them, then they may conflict as they supervise students on the playground. The actions of the two teachers may differ because of their own cultural backgrounds and how they were raised.

In addition, cultural views and explicit practices change over time. Since culture is created by people and people change, cultural knowledge and values also may shift. For example, in the past cars were primarily fueled by gasoline and driven by a person in the driver's seat. Now, there is much concern about how the burning of fossil fuels has led to pollution and the release of carbon emissions into the air. Some scientists believe the increase in carbon in the atmosphere is the primary cause of global warming. Some people are concerned about global warming, and so they choose to drive electric cars in which electricity is generated by solar, wind, hydro, and other sustainable sources.

Culture is a dynamic, shared social system of human components such as language, dress, customs, history, philosophies, behaviors, institutions, norms, and values; it also can include geographical influences.

Explicit culture refers to tangible and visible cultural elements, including food, dress, holidays, governmental systems, country of origin, history, and language.

Implicit culture is made up of elements that are often hidden: the values, assumptions, beliefs, and philosophies of a group. Implicit cultural aspects are harder to identify because they include expectations and worldviews.

Can you see from this example how our cultural values are changing and therefore leading to different practices and cultural products? Electric cars are more energy efficient than those that use gasoline. All-electric cars also do not emit pollutants into the air. Cultural views about transportation are changing. Consider the example of a cultural change in Figure 2.3. Our cultural values, knowledge, and behaviors about phones have changed in the past several decades. What can we do with a phone today? We can type a grocery list on it; we can surf the Web; we can play video games; and we can call someone. Our culture has changed with the evolution of the cell phone; however, some teachers may have used a rotary phone for much of their lives, and they grew up thinking of a telephone as one with a dial. Probably, many younger students have never dialed on a dial-type telephone. So not only have our expectations about communications changed, but also the cultural beliefs that we held about telephones, now called cell phones, have been transformed.

MOM, HOW DO YOU TEXT ON THAT?

Figure 2.3: Though cultural elements may persist over time, cultural artifacts may change. Few students have used a rotary telephone. They may not realize the cell phone is a new aspect of our culture and how we use it is different too. We cannot text on a rotary phone.

Comparing Culture and Ethnicity

Ethnicity and culture are generally understood as different but connected concepts. Depending on the discipline from anthropology to geography, definitions of the terms can vary (Hiebert, 2009). This text is based on an educational orientation, which defines culture as a dynamic, shared social system of human components such as language, dress, customs, history, philosophy, norms, institutions, and values; it also includes geographical influences. As you read in Chapter 1, ethnicity includes a sense of peoplehood and has roots in a common ancestry. Ethnicity is often connected to a socially and politically defined "racial" group (Black, Asian, White, Native American, or Hispanic/Latino) or to a country such as Ethiopia, Iran, Cuba, Mexico, Ireland, or Cambodia.

CHECKLIST: HOW DOES CULTURE INFLUENCE MY VIEWS?

Culture shapes much of who we are and what we think; it is also dynamic and changing, though it has stable elements that are taught to the next generation. It is often difficult to identify aspects of one's culture because these characteristics are part of our daily life. Consider the old black telephone, which in one generation has been replaced by cell phones. Many students may not even know how to operate a traditional rotary phone. Your answers to the following questions may help you to more fully understand how your cultural knowledge and identity have been shaped by your experiences:

☐ What is expected of me? What is my purpose in life?
Your life purpose may be influenced by what your parents or other members of your family taught you as a child. If you decide to become

a teacher, was one of your parents or other relatives teachers? Family is a critical aspect of one's cultural background.

☐ What are my ideals? What are the goals and values that guide my life?
Ideals come from a variety of cultural sources. For example, they may come from your family values, but they also may include religious beliefs. Religion is another element of culture.

☐ What choices do I make and what do those choices say about my values?
The important choices you make about your career and relationships may reflect the values you learned as a child from friends, family, and teachers.

☐ Who is my role model in life?
You may choose a role model like a teacher or a parent as you grow up. However, as you

become an adult and your knowledge of life expands, you may also choose other role models from your profession.

☐ Which groups/communities do I identify with?
You belong to many cultural subgroups. This can include an ethnic community, your family, a professional group, and many more. The groups you identify probably will represent values that you hold.

☐ What methods do I think are best to teach children?
Your teaching methods may somewhat be based on your upbringing. For example, if your parents were strict, you might have strong structure in the classroom or you may be looser with rules. It will depend on how you viewed what worked and did not work in your own experiences.

❯❯ Professional Resource Download

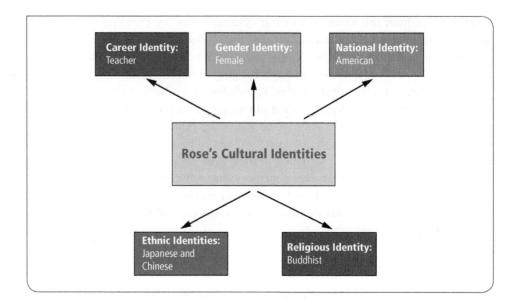

Figure 2.4: Rose's Cultural Identities

Phenotype refers to the use of outward physical characteristics to identify someone. This could be the labeling of a person as Native American or Black.

The concepts of ethnicity and culture can be hard to understand, so let's look at an example. There is a student, Rose, who was born in San Francisco and attends a public high school in the city. Rose sees herself as a member of American society, a cultural community, but her ethnic identities are Chinese American and Japanese American. China and Japan are her two ancestral heritages. Her great grandparents on her mother's side were originally from Japan. Rose's great grandparents on her father's side migrated from Canton, China. Rose has developed a complex understanding of who she is. She also identifies as a female and member of the Buddhist temple. Religious affiliations and gender identification are cultural groups, and so like many Americans, Rose has a complex cultural identity; she sees herself as a member of several cultural and ethnic groups. (See Figure 2.4.)

Some researchers believe that ethnicity and racial membership are the same (Heibert, 2009). However, there are many scholars who believe that the concept of race was erroneous and used to separate groups by dominant groups in power. *Racialization* was a process by which some groups were seen as superior and others inferior based upon physical appearance. As a socio-political construct, the use of phenotypes to identify a person is limiting, and as the United Nations has discussed, there is only one race, the human race (Heibert, 2009; Valle, 1997). **Phenotype** refers to the use of outward physical characteristics to identify someone. As part of this process, many Black Americans may choose their ethnic identity based upon the experiences of a large so-called racial group of people who were historically stigmatized and excluded based on perceived phenotypes. Many Black Americans share a communal history, language, values, and sense of peoplehood that is cultural and racial, and includes ethnic identity. This is an example of how complex the concepts of ethnicity and culture are even today.

Consider this . . .

Cultural and ethnic identities are complex concepts.

Q Which cultural groups are you a member of?

Q With which ethnic identity or identities do you feel an affiliation? Why?

Culture Defined

LO2 Define and explain a model of culture.

As you have read throughout this chapter, culture includes so many aspects of what we think, do, and are as human beings. It is not always easy to define the essentials of culture because it is complex. It is often defined as a social system that includes history, symbols such as language, behaviors, governmental structures, norms, customs, artwork, religions, foods, and so on. People share these elements, and they are taught from one generation to another. If you were to list all the things that people achieve, believe, and value, wouldn't that be a lot? The inventory that includes all that is human would be extremely long too; therefore, in the next section a model of culture is presented to help you identify and organize cultural elements that students bring to school. This model has helped many teachers understand the cultures of their students and how to build on them. Culture is a system rather than a list of aspects of life.

Three Levels of Culture

Culture is an important aspect of life, and it is vital for teachers to be able to "unpack" or peel away the many layers of student cultures. In this process, teachers will more fully understand the values and beliefs of the learners in their classrooms and will be able to develop trusting relationships with them. Sometimes teachers may say something that offends the cultural background of a student. For example, what if a teacher said she did not understand why people ate pork and had a student in class whose favorite dish was carnitas, a pork recipe often made in Mexican American families? This teacher's statement could be seen by students as judgmental.

How can you, the teacher, avoid cultural conflicts? It is important for you to think about the importance of culture to your students. The following **model of culture** can help you more fully understand the cultural systems that your students identify with and follow. Ramón Valle, an expert in Latino health, developed a model that defined culture as having three levels (1997):

Level 1: Artifacts such as dress, food, art, music, symbols, holidays, geography, language, currency, folklore, proverbs, dances, geography, and children's games (means of communication)

Level 2: Customs, practices, greetings, and interactional patterns (means of interaction and behavioral links)

Level 3: Shared values, beliefs, norms, and expectations (values driving people, groups)

This model can help you understand how various elements of culture work together in making an integrated whole. Separating culture into distinct elements like dress, art, history, language, holidays, and food tends to fragment it. However, Valle's typology can help you to understand how many different elements contribute to culture and make sense of the complex wholeness. Do you see that culture represents a complex system of thinking, behaving, and valuing?

The first level is comprised of explicit elements which can be seen on the surface. These are aspects of culture that you can easily see or hear or what some say are elements of explicit culture. The second level is made up of behaviors and interactional patterns of people. The third level represents the implicit components of culture. Breaking down the three levels further, think of them in the following way (Valle, 1997):

- *Level 1: Artifacts*—Such as language, dialects preferred, proverbs, signs, sayings, jokes, stories, myths, analogies, folklore, art forms, heroes, dances, rituals, music, children's games, currency, symbols, holidays, geography, history (family, national, and global), governmental structures. (See Figures 2.5.)
- *Layer 2: Interactional patterns, which include customs and practices (means of interaction)*— Such as verbal (tone of voice, phrases used) and nonverbal (eye contact, proximity of

Model of culture consists of three levels: Level 1, artifacts, explicit elements; Level 2, interactional patterns; and Level 3, values, beliefs, and norms.

Figure 2.5:

(a) Level 1 of Culture This symbol for the men's restroom also shows that a person who has a wheelchair can be accompanied by a woman or man. Language and symbols are elements of layer 1 of culture and are an important part of culture.

(b) Level 2 of Culture This teacher uses a whiteboard to interact with students, which is a common practice in schools in the United States.

(c) Level 3 of Culture The U.S. Constitution arises out of our national values and beliefs of social justice, equality, and democracy.

(d) Level 3 of Culture This includes our religious beliefs and attitudes.

stance, gestures) communication patterns, greetings, family behaviors, conversational styles (formal, business, casual, ritualized), friendship patterns, community roles, gender roles.

- *Layer 3: Shared values, beliefs, norms, and expectations (values driving people, groups)*— Such as attitudes, cultural values, religious and spiritual beliefs, fears, laws, standards, norms, and expectations.

Our values, beliefs, norms, and expectations guide how we live our lives, and therefore they are part of implicit culture; it is not possible to picture them. However, people may share a document or legislation that is built on the foundational values and organizational structure, such as the Constitution of the United States (Figure 2.5c). The Bill of Rights, which is contained in the Constitution, also presents many of the underlying values of our government and nation.

Consider this . . .

Teachers will be more effective if they build on the cultural knowledge that students bring to the classroom. Teachers can use student-lived experiences in scaffolding instruction.

Q How can you use student-lived experiences and cultures in building the curriculum for your classroom?

Mainstream Culture

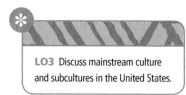

LO3 Discuss mainstream culture and subcultures in the United States.

Culture is a powerful force in society. In the previous section, you read about various examples of each level in the model of culture. You also need to know that there is a U.S. culture on the macro level; some people call it American culture. It is important to remember that the term *American* as referring exclusively to things in the United States is not true in all parts of the globe. For example, people in South America and Latin America also use the term American to refer to their cultures. Another term for U.S. American culture might be referred to in other books as **mainstream** or **dominant culture**, which arises out of the experiences and values of middle-class, Protestant Caucasians who live in this U.S. democracy (Brislin, 2000), although it also includes elements from other ethnic groups. The reason the term U.S. American culture is used in the book is to make sure you understand that people in the United States are not the only folks who use the term American.

In the U.S. American culture, holidays like the Fourth of July, Thanksgiving, Easter, and Christmas are observed; however, not everyone celebrates these days, and some U.S. Americans may celebrate other holidays such as Rosh Hashanah, Ramadan, and Kwanzaa. Our nation has a strong Judeo-Christian orientation, so many of the holidays come from that tradition; however, Buddhists, Muslims, agnostics, and atheists are members of our nation, too. Many of these holidays are part of U.S. religious subcultures. A **subculture** is a smaller community that has shared features that distinguish it from a larger social group (Cushner et al., 2012).

There are also less obvious elements of U.S. culture that affect us every day and that we may take for granted. For example, money is part of level 1 of culture. It is something that we can hold and see. Take paper money from your wallet, purse, or pocket and lay the money flat on a table with the portraits facing up. You may not have every bill, but you can look up those you do not own. This activity can be informative because you can more fully understand how elements of culture can be powerful forces in our lives. Paper money is an element in life that is extremely important. Let's move now to the paper money you have:

> Whom do you see on the $1 bill?
> Five dollar bill?
> Ten dollar bill?
> Twenty dollar bill?
> Fifty dollar bill?
> Hundred dollar bill?
> The pictures on our money are powerful role models.

Culture is composed of many everyday elements (Valle, 1997). One of those elements is our currency, or money. It is important in many people's lives because we use it to buy groceries, clothes, gas, services, and housing. As a country built on capitalism, money is valuable.

Whom did you discover pictured on our paper money? Table 2.1 lists the person who is portrayed on each note.

Each bill has the face of a U.S. statesperson. Historically, paper money reinforces the contributions of European American males and gives more political and cultural powers to European American culture. Currency is powerful, considering how often you and others use money. Therefore, mainstream culture identifies notable leaders, which reinforces a belief system that is based on cultural background and gender. Gould, the paleontologist, wrote that he believed the United States has "a truly sexist past that regarded males as standards for humanity" and ignored women (2008). Where are the women and people of color on our money?

The messages conveyed in much of our culture are hidden and yet powerful, like our paper currency. This is like the **hidden curriculum** in our schools: hidden messages about

Mainstream or **dominant culture** arises out of the experiences and values of middle-class, Protestant Caucasians who live in the U.S. democracy.

Subculture refers to a smaller community that has shared features that distinguish it from a larger social group.

Hidden curriculum refers to an implicit set of values that exist but may be found mostly by looking at behaviors and unstated practices and content.

Table 2.1 Images Found on U.S. Currency: Paper Money		
Amount of Note	Portrait	Picture on Opposite Side of Note
$1	George Washington	Great Seal of the United States
$2	Thomas Jefferson	Signing of the Declaration of Independence
$5	Abraham Lincoln	Lincoln Memorial
$10	Alexander Hamilton	U.S. Treasury Building
$20	Andrew Jackson	The White House
$50	Ulysses S. Grant	U.S. Capitol
$100	Benjamin Franklin	Independence Hall

who and what is most important in society are not always obvious. The hidden curriculum is the implicit set of values that exist but may be found mostly by looking at behaviors and unstated practices and content. In society, a good example of cryptic messages can be seen in our paper currency. Many European American men did contribute to the building of our nation from its beginning; however, Native American women and men, indigenous to what we know as the continental United States, also played roles in the development of this country. For example, the Iroquois Confederacy had a democratic governmental structure, and Benjamin Franklin studied it. He brought principles and practices from the Iroquois Confederacy to the framers of the U.S. Constitution (Weatherford, 2010). Do you think it might be a good idea to have a role model from the Iroquois League on our money to go along with Benjamin Franklin on the $100 bill and Thomas Jefferson on the $2 currency?

Figure 2.6 depicts how our paper money will be changed in order to show the diversity of our nation (Ohlheiser, 2015). This will occur by 2020 in collaboration with the 100-year anniversary of the passage of the Nineteenth Amendment (Chandler, 2015).

Figure 2.6: Our currency is an important artifact of U.S. culture. Because money is an essential aspect of life, having a variety of role models like Harriet Tubman, Martin Luther King, Jr., Eleanor Roosevelt, Sojourner Truth, Susan B. Anthony, and Elizabeth Cady Stanton on them reinforces the value of diversity in our society.

Valerie Ooka Pang

Valerie Ooka Pang

U.S. Landmarks: Level 1 of Culture

Mainstream culture reinforces basic ideas, places, artifacts, and values. For example, another important aspect of U.S. American culture is our democratic government. Our money is controlled and produced by the United States Department of the Treasury. As you probably noticed, U.S. currency also depicts many important governmental locations such as the U.S. Capitol building, the U.S. Treasury Building, and the Lincoln Memorial. These landmarks are often seen as symbols of our government. So the buildings and monuments are examples and symbols of our democracy and are aspects of the surface level of culture in Valle's model. However, the structures also represent underlying values of justice, equality, and freedom (Figure 2.7). The building designs arose out of Roman architecture, which also evolved out of the Greek designs of arcs, domes, and Corinthian columns. This shows how important European roots are to the United States' key governmental buildings.

Figure 2.7: The photo on the left is the front entrance of the United States Supreme Court, which represents values such as social justice, equality, and freedom. On the right is our Capitol building, which is a symbol of our democracy.

United States Interactional Patterns: Level 2 of Culture

Interactional patterns are also important in culture. These behaviors are learned and often passed on from one generation to another by parents and by teachers. Let's start by thinking about what happens at home. Did you learn that it was important to say "please" when requesting something and "thank you" when someone either gave you something or helped you? Manners are aspects of culture. They are often expected interactional patterns among people in the United States.

Norms of interaction at many elementary schools where the weather is often warm involve beginning the day with children lining up on the playground in specific spots depending on their room number or teacher. In this way students enter school all together in an orderly fashion. When it is snowing or rainy, however, the norm of interaction may change and teachers could have students enter the classroom as they arrive at school. Students know where to place their coats and backpacks. Students also begin their seatwork given out from the day before. When the teacher enters the room, students are busy working at their desks or at a computer. These are expected behaviors and school practices.

Let's think of middle schools. Middle school students are expected to bring notebooks with lined paper to every class period. The teacher often lectures, and students take notes of what the teacher says so they do not forget and can study the information later. Some students go home in the evening and summarize and study their notes so they more fully remember what

CASE STUDY

Cultural Solutions to Health: Bread and Tortillas

How could cultural knowledge lead to critical health solutions? These examples have aspects of the three levels of culture described by Valle.

Here are two examples of how cultural knowledge resulted in addressing the issue malnutrition in people. Scientists and health professions thought about the lifestyles of people and integrated solutions based upon the foods people ate.

1. In the 1930s, children and adults in the United States were developing pellagra, a disease caused by malnutrition. Many people were not getting the nourishment they needed because they were poor. The lack of niacin caused pellagra, which includes skin problems, dementia, and diarrhea. In 1928 and 1929, pellagra was the ninth largest cause of mortality in the United States. People who lived in the South with diets primarily made up of corn products developed pellagra more often than people in other parts of the United States (Park, Sempos, Barton, Vanderveen, & Yetley, 2000). Corn is low in niacin. Health officials tried to figure out what to do. They decided to implement food fortification practices in the creation of bread. Many people ate bread, so it was decided to put the B vitamin niacin in the flour. This led to the reduction of the mortality rate of about 1000 people per year during the early 1920s to none in the 1930s.

   This strategy of food fortification continues to be used. Many babies are born with neural birth defects due to the lack of folic acid in the diet of mothers. One approach has been to add vitamin B9, folic acid, to masa flour that is used not only to make tortillas but also corn chips and cereals. This is proving to be a viable tactic in strengthening the health of babies in the United States (Zhang, 2015).

2. In Mexico, malnutrition was a grave problem because some people lived in deep poverty (Smith, 1999). There were families who could not afford to provide much protein or fresh vegetables to their diets.

Many children did not have normal energy and were underweight because they did not have a healthy diet. Children also got sick more often, which impacted their ability to learn.

Health researchers from Mexico's Health Ministry and National Nutrition Institute and the United Nations Children's Fund searched for a cultural food element that would give more nutrition and fit in with the diet of the people.

The key was the tortilla! The tortilla is a corn-based food that has been a traditional staple for thousands of years in what we know today as Mexico. When researchers found that most families received more than two-thirds of their nutrition from tortillas, they realized that tortillas could be used as a vehicle to enrich the diet of many families. The health officials asked major cornmeal manufacturers to add six vitamins and numerous minerals to the cornmeal they sold. The addition was not that costly. This change has had a major positive impact on the health of many Mexican children and adults. People have more energy and students are doing much better in school because they are more nourished. Researchers are also studying ways in which protein can be added to the tortillas. They would like to fortify tortillas with protein-rich soy. Health officials say that the addition of soy will help increase the height, birth weight, and physical and mental ability of children (Smith, 1999).

The tortilla, like bread in the United States, was a logical solution because it is a key element of the Mexican lifestyle. The tortilla became an important nutritional tool because of the combination of scientific research and culture.

Conclusion

Health professionals thought about the cultural practices of groups of people, and this included all three levels of culture. In level 1, corn tortillas or bread are often eaten as a staple. In level 2, many individuals and corporations

Children enjoying tortilla chips.

commonly used cornmeal or flour in their cooking and products. And in level 3, corn and good health are considered valuable aspects of the Mexican culture. Similarly, nutrition is seen as important in the United States, so solving this issue was imperative in the overall health of adults and children.

Combination of Culture and Science

Food fortification, which is the addition of vitamins, minerals, and proteins, is an approach has been used around the globe for many years. In the United States, vitamins and minerals have been added to food since the 1930s to ward off disease and malnutrition. When children do not have enough vitamins, minerals, and protein, they are more apt to get sick and have a lower immune system. Today, there are many cereals, breads, and other staples that have been fortified with iron, calcium carbonate, zinc, and vitamins (C, B6, B2, B1, A, and D). Have you checked the ingredients of your breakfast cereal boxes lately?

Don't forget these examples; they might be a way to teach about the impact of culture in your own classroom.

Reflection Questions

Q How will you learn about the cultural backgrounds of your students?

Q What did these two examples teach you about how educators can build on student cultures in the classroom?

the teacher taught. These are all different practices and interactional patterns. The teacher often stands at the front of the classroom, and students sit in their desks writing what the teacher says. The underlying belief is that the teachers are there to impart knowledge that students do not have, so young people should be sitting quietly and recording what is being taught.

Capitalism and Individualism: Level 3 of Culture

Mainstream culture is complex and includes many subcultures such as economic status. Have you ever felt poor? Have you ever felt that you needed money? How much money a person has is often seen as a measure of her or his status. Economic status can be rich or poor and many places in between. Bill Gates has been on the cover of many magazines such as *Time* because he is one of the richest people in the world and founded Microsoft. Gates is currently worth about $80 billion. Another person who is often in the news is Mark Zuckerberg, the CEO of Facebook. He is young and currently worth close to $37 billion. The high social economic status of Gates and Zuckerberg also include prestige and more societal influence; in addition they are both White and male. Another CEO who is prominent in the world is Carlos Slim, a businessman and entrepreneur from Mexico. Slim has recently been identified as the richest man in the world and even surpassed Gates in some years depending on the performance of his companies (Lakhani, 2015); Slim is not often discussed in the U.S. media. Christy Walton is also one of the wealthiest people in the world and is part of the Sam Walton family that created Walmart.

These individuals' ability to gain financial success was due to their participation in **capitalism**, which refers to an economic system of production resulting in profit for private owners (Nembhard, 2014; Selwyn, 2012). One of the most important values of capitalism is individualism. In the United States, **individualism** refers to the ability and perseverance of the individual to generate his or her own success. Many Americans believe that only through individual effort and smarts can anyone become a successful entrepreneur. This value is one of the beliefs that underlie the conviction in the **American dream**, which is a belief in individualism and meritocracy: if you work hard enough and get an education, you can become economically successful because this nation is founded upon the belief in equal opportunities for all (Naranjo, Pang, & Alvarado, 2015/2016). Do you think that each person, no matter what their ethnic, racial, gender, and economic status is, has the same opportunity to become successful?

Collectivism: Level 3 of Culture

In the United States, there are many people who also believe in the values of community and collectivism. **Collectivism** refers to the identification of a person with a group or collective and its goals, behaviors, values, and general way of life. Individualism is not as important to people who hold collectivism as a core conviction. For example, some Mexican Americans believe in the needs of the group over any one individual (Cushner et al., 2012). A mother

> **Capitalism** refers to an economic system of production resulting in profit for private owners. **Individualism** is an important value in the United States and refers to the ability and perseverance of the individual to generate his or her own success. **American dream** is a belief in individualism and meritocracy: if you work hard enough and get an education, you can become economically successful because this nation is founded upon the belief in equal opportunities for all. **Collectivism** refers the identification of a person with a group or collective and its goals, behaviors, values, and general way of life.

Consider this . . .

Individualism is an important value in the United States and is the belief that a person has the ability and perseverance to generate her or his own success.

Q Have you heard the following statements made by teachers?

"It is important that you work on your own."

"Do not ask anyone else for the answers. No discussion of the assignment. That would be cheating."

"Do your own work."

"Only students who work hard do well in school."

Q Can you think of other statements that you have heard in schools that reinforce individualism?

(Maria) in a PTA meeting may feel that she does not want to oppose the new Common Core standards, though another mother (Jocelyn) is adamantly against them because they have little to do with teaching bilingual education. However, Maria, though she may not agree with everything Jocelyn said, goes along with her. Because Maria believes in collectivism, she will put aside her views and go with what the group decides. A teacher may think Mexican American mothers are not smart enough to speak up, but that is not the case. The force of the value of collectivism has entered into the dynamics of the environment because Maria believes that harmony among parents is more important than her concerns. However, if a teacher talks with her privately and in person, Maria may be willing to explain her perspective. Maria has strong beliefs, but she also sees herself as part of the larger group of Mexican American mothers and believes that it is really important for her to support the community over her personal views.

E Pluribus Unum: Level 3 of Culture

Another core ideal in U.S. culture is *e pluribus unum*. It is Latin for "Out of many, one." The phrase can be found on the U.S. Seal (Figure 2.8). One of the messages that the phrase conveys is that we are an inclusive diversity. What do you think that phrase means? How can we make sure that individualism, diversity, and community are values supported in our nation? Do they seem to be in opposition with each other?

For many scholars the phrase *e pluribus unum* refers to the development of a strong democratic community that also supports cultural pluralism (Barber, 1993; Pang, Gay, & Stanley, 1995). As this book presents, the definition of diversity continues to expand. In the past, it was primarily about race, class, and gender; however, Americans now consider diversity to also include sexual orientation, religion, languages, ethnicity, age, exceptionalities, and political viewpoints. Our cultural orientation toward diversity is increasing, and new interpretations of democratic and educational standards are developing.

In order for our nation to be united, we must have a clear understanding of how unity and diversity are integrated into who we are as one nation. This is why one of the major goals of multicultural education is to support a cohesive nation (Banks, 1993, 2014). However, it is important that our nation restructures the knowledge being taught to include information from diverse groups. For example, teaching only about the 13 colonies without the history of American Indians who are indigenous to the United States would emphasize only a certain aspect of U.S. history. Our history is comprised of the efforts and contributions of many different ethnic communities.

Common Set of National Values: Level 3 of Culture

To be a united country, we must have a common set of values that serves as the foundation of our national identity. The U.S. Constitution and its Bill of Rights are foundational statements of our values. Though many researchers have argued for the core principles of freedom, justice, equality, and human dignity (Pang et al., 1995), people may have different beliefs about how those values should be implemented in our everyday lives. If we believe in unity, do we all need to agree on the interpretation of these ideals? As you can see in Congress, senators and representatives often do not agree though they are to work for the common good. They hold diverse political views though many know their work is interdependent. Putting national goals of community above the value of individuality is part of working as a democracy. Our struggle is a collective one. As part of this expanding community, we must unite and work as one. The following beliefs are important in bringing diversity and community together and should be stressed in the classroom:

- Cultural diversity is an aspect of the human condition.
- Aspects of diversity such as race, ethnicity, gender, class, language, exceptionalities, religion, sexual orientation, culture, and age continue to be used as obstacles to full participation in our nation.
- Community must take precedence over individualism in areas of voting, housing, and education.
- Structure, processes, and programs in schools must be responsive to our diverse nation.

Library of Congress Prints and Photographs Division (LC-USZC4-2108)

Figure 2.8: The U.S. Seal represents all of us, *e pluribus unum.*

Unity can continually be strengthened. Table 2.2 shows that many diverse ethnic communities comprise the United States, and a strong democracy has developed. Our nation was considered the great experiment in 1776 when the United States broke away from England.

Today, ethnic diversity is considered a major area of unity as well as conflict. Reviewing Table 2.2, you can see that the United States is made up of many people from various ancestries. You may not have realized how ethnically diverse we are because for the most part,

Table 2.2 2011 U.S. Populations by Ethnic Background: Largest 31 Populations, Self-Identified	
Ethnic Ancestry	**Population**
German	49,206,934
African American	41,284,752
Irish	35,523,082
Mexican American	31,789,483
English	26,923,091
American (includes several ethnic backgrounds*)	19,911,467
Italian	17,558,598
Polish	9,739,653
French	9,136,092
Scottish	5,706,263
Scotch-Irish	5,102,858
American Indian/Alaska Native	4,920,336
Dutch	4,810,511
Puerto Rican	4,607,774
Norwegian	4,557,539
Swedish	4,211,644
Chinese	3,245,080
Russian	3,060,143
Asian Indian	2,781,904
West Indian	2,625,306
Filipino	2,549,545
French Canadian	2,087,970
Welsh	2,087,970
Cuban	1,764,374
Salvadorian	1,733,778
Arab	1,620,637
Vietnamese	1,576,032
Czech	1,573,608
Hungarian	1,511,926
Portuguese	1,423,139
Korean	1,422,567

*Includes people from a variety of groups that are not listed or those who do not want to identify a specific ethnic community.

Source: Infoplease, http://www.infoplease.com/ipa/A0762137.html. Original source is the American Community Survey, five-year estimates, 2007–2011.

we work well as a country. As you analyze Table 2.2, you will see that German Americans make up the largest ancestry group. The second largest community is African Americans, though they are a racial group rather than being made up of one ethnic community. The third largest group is Irish Americans, and Mexican Americans make up the fourth largest population in the United States. Are you surprised about some of the groups? Why? What did you expect? Did you hold some assumptions that might not have been true? Where did you learn these ideas? One way the table can be interpreted is that we are one nation of many people.

Review examples of culture in Table 2.3. Americans have many similar cultural elements such as knowing the game of football, what to do in an accident, and the symbolism of the flag. These examples show how Americans hold many common values though there may be aspects of culture on which we may differ.

As you can see from the table, learning culture is a complex process. A teacher will become more effective if she or he has the ability to understand the three levels of culture. The chart is designed to help you see how so many aspects in your life can be explained using Valle's model of culture. Each level is connected to and is interactive with the other two levels. Take time to think through them. Can you come up with another example and provide the three levels of culture for the situation you choose?

Table 2.3 The Three Interactive and Interlocking Levels of Culture

Examples of How to View Culture	Level 1: The Artifacts of the Culture	Level 2: The Relational and Interactional Patterns of the Culture	Level 3: The Values, Norms, and Expectations of the Culture
Football, general U.S. culture	Equipment needed: Football, uniforms, rulebook, field, goal line and goal post, 11 players, referees	Coach trains the players. Plays are called by quarterback. Players line up together facing the other team. Defenders tackle other team members. Receivers catch football. Kick ball over goal post for 3 points or 1 point. Take ball into end zone for a touchdown.	Teams want to win. Defense is an important aspect of football. A good offense is also needed to win. Teamwork is important.
Accident in a neighborhood, subculture	A child is hit at a crosswalk when walking home from school. There is a stop sign for cars and a yellow-painted crosswalk. The driver of the car did not see the child stepping off the curb into the crosswalk.	An older student calls 911. The brother of the hit student holds him. Other parents get the student onto the sidewalk. The ambulance comes to help the student. The ambulance takes the student to the hospital. The parents in the community bring food to the student's family. People leave teddy bears and flowers at the corner where the accident occurred.	Members of a school are part of a caring community. They believe in helping each other. Some people say prayers for the child because they believe in God. They also leave candles in tall glass cylinders with drawings of Jesus Christ representing their prayers and religious beliefs. Some people do not believe in God, but believe in leaving positive thoughts for him to get better, so they leave teddy bears at the corner.
The U.S. Flag, general U.S. culture	The flag has 50 stars and 13 stripes. The colors of the flags are red, white, and blue.	Citizens fly the flag on poles in front of governmental buildings. People hold poles with the flag during parades. The flag is presented during sporting events. People stand up when the flag is presented at functions and recite the Pledge of Allegiance. At various events, people will sing the "Star Spangled Banner," our national anthem.	The 50 stars represent each of the 50 states in the United States. The flag also represents U.S. values of democracy, justice, courage, loyalty, and integrity. The flag represents a united nation.

Transmission of Culture

LO4 Describe how culture is transmitted and cultural identity is developed.

Culture is transmitted to students in many ways. First they learn about family and general culture from members of their families. Children also learn elements of culture from their friends and other important people in their lives such as teachers and ministers. They also gather information about culture from the materials they read and the media they watch. Children are often bombarded by cultural messages throughout their day.

Children Learn Culture from Society

Did you learn about how to act and think from your parents, sisters, or brothers? How about from your grandparents? Did you learn how to act from friends and church members? Often we learn culture from the people with whom we socialize. This is important to understand because the people close to you have a powerful influence on what you learn, know, value, and identify with.

There is an interesting book that describes a cultural viewpoint and various assumptions about life. The text is *Ishmael*, written by ecologist Daniel Quinn (1995). His story is about a teacher and a student. One individual is a gorilla and the other is a human. Who do you think was the teacher, the human or gorilla? The teacher is Ishmael, a gorilla, and the student is a human! Surprised?

In the story, the gorilla and human have contrasting views about why the world was created. The student, a young man, thinks the world was created for humans. Ishmael asks the man how he learned that assumption. The man was not sure. The following is what Ishmael told his pupil about culture:

> Mother Culture, whose voice has been in your ear since the day of your birth, has given you an explanation of how things came *to be this way*. You know it well; everyone in your culture knows it well. But this explanation wasn't given to you all at once. No one ever sat you down and said, "Here is how things came to be this way, beginning ten or fifteen billion years ago right up to the present." Rather, you assembled this explanation like a mosaic: from a million bits of information presented to you in various ways by others who share that explanation. You assembled it from the table talk of your parents, from cartoons you watched on television, from Sunday School lessons, from your textbooks and teachers, from news broadcasts, [and] from movies. (Quinn, 1995, p. 40)

Consider this . . .

Religion is one of the areas of cultural diversity in the United States. There is great diversity in religious affiliations. Through religion many students learn values, beliefs, and norms of behaviors found in level 3 of Valle's model of culture. Take a look at the following list, which shows the self-identified breakdown of religious affiliations in 2014.

    Protestants 46.6%

    Roman Catholics 20.8%

    Mormons 1.6%

    Other Christians 0.3%

    Jews 1.6%

    Muslims 0.9%

    Buddhists 0.7%

    Hindus 0.7%

    Other faiths 1.5%

    Unaffiliated 22.8% (includes atheists, agnostics, and nothing in particular)

    Don't know/Will not answer 0.6%

Q **What surprises you about religion in the United States? Why?**

Source: The Changing Religious Composition of the United States, Pew Research Center, Retrieved from http:// www.pewforum.org/2015/05/12/chapter-1-the-changing-religious-composition-of-the-u-s/. May 12, 2015.

My Journal

Which Cultural Groups Do You Identify With?

You are a member and identify with multiple cultural groups. Maybe you use a wheelchair to get around; you may identify with others who also use one. Maybe you are a father or a mother. Maybe you have Somali roots. Think about your multiple cultural identities. This may help you to more fully understand how culture influences the behaviors and values of your students.

Q *List at least six groups and explain why that particular cultural community is important to you.*

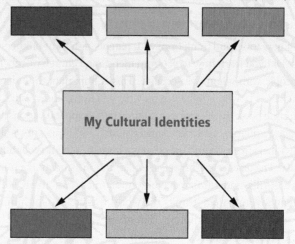

Think of your cultural identities. Place your name in the center circle and then add cultural characteristics in the other three circles. They may include your gender, education, and ethnic background.

⌄ Professional Resource Download

In this novel, Quinn wants us to think beyond the limits of our own cultural novels, sermons, plays, newspapers, and other aspects of culture. He explains that culture is all around us, and we learn from many, many elements and individuals.

What do you think Ishmael means when he says that we learned "from a million bits of information" that was presented and taught to us?

We all have developed a cultural view from the people, food, music, and all that surrounds us as we grow and live. This is what Ishmael would call a world view: upbringing so we can view life from the perspectives of others. Culture is a complex set of elements we breathe in that includes artifacts, interactional patterns, and values. Mainstream society and our participation and identification with various subcultures have taught us what to do, what to pay attention to, what to value.

Consider this . . .

We learn culture from the million bits of information that we receive from others and all that we are immersed in.

Q Where do you think your students learn about culture? Where do they learn the values they adopt? Who serves as role models? Why can culture be described as millions of bits of information? What does that mean?

Children Learn Culture at Home

Have you ever heard of the phrase "stretching your legs"? That phrase is considered cultural because it applies to the idea that people need to stretch their legs, perhaps after sitting too long. However, what if a child is in a wheelchair and cannot stretch his legs? Can you see how this cultural saying may not be applicable to all students? Though some students grow up with that phrase, it does not apply to everyone. Culture is often extremely personal and develops initially from children's interactions with their parents and other close individuals.

Initially, children learn culture from members of their families during the thousands of interactions they have with their brothers, sisters, parents, grandparents, cousins, aunts, and uncles. Family members are the holders and *teachers* of culture (Bruner, 1990). Your parents were some of your most important teachers. If you went to day care as a child, your caregivers also taught you a great deal.

Your parents and these important core caregivers taught you how to act and how to talk to and work with others in a family and daycare context. Children also learn in social and cultural contexts; sometimes others tell children how to act or think, but they also learn from talking, playing, and watching others (Bruner, 1990; Moll, 1990; Tharp & Gallimore, 1988). Have you seen a toddler watch another youngster take a cup and bang on the table? Then that child begins banging the table too. One child watched another and saw how fun it was to make a big noise.

Children also learn from interacting with others as Vygotsky has explained. Social interactions are the way youngsters learn. Children watch their peers and adults in their world, learning to pay attention to selected cultural stimuli. They perceive other stimuli as background noise and filter it out. Parents and significant others train children how to succeed in the community by teaching the **cultural worldview**, which refers to a holistic perspective based upon the history, values, and beliefs of a cultural group. Culture identifies what is important to the community—the values, beliefs, interpretations, skills, and selected ways of solving problems. This worldview may also include which groups should be dominant. As Erickson (2015) explained, many people have grown up with the cultural idea that Europeans and European Americans should be in control in the world because they are smarter and more competent. This is supported by Linneaus's human taxonomy, which is an important source of the construct of race.

Through culture, socialization occurs. **Socialization** is a process whereby individuals learn the values, expectations, and behaviors of a group. What is really interesting about the socialization process is that most people do not realize that it is happening; they are learning so much about what is appropriate behavior and norms of the community without even realizing it. They may not understand that they are learning to accept the dominance of some groups over others. Children take in all of this by observing and following the lead of others. These messages can be conveyed via cartoons, books, films, video games, magazines, and what people say. Though primary socialization takes place at home, socialization also includes learning from the many other people children come in contact with or interact with.

Do you wonder how some children grow up to be so witty and able to talk with people in authority, while other young people are quieter? The following Case Study describes

> **Cultural worldview** or perspective refers to a holistic orientation based upon the history, values, and beliefs of a cultural group.

> **Socialization** is a process whereby individuals learn the values, expectations, and behaviors of a group.

Consider this . . .

Through their interactions with others, children become socialized as to what the appropriate values, norms, behaviors, and expectations are in the community.

Q What might interactions with parents teach children?

A Predominantly Black American Low-Income Community: Child Rearing

The educational anthropologist, Shirley Brice Heath, conducted many studies on how different communities taught language and cultural knowledge. In the 1960s and 1970s, Heath studied two communities, comparing linguistic traditions of a Black American and White community in the Piedmont area of the Carolinas. Trackton is a primarily Black working-class community with roots in farming. In Trackton, when a newborn is brought home from the hospital, the baby is carried continuously for the first year of life by many different family members. The child is constantly surrounded by verbal and nonverbal communication, although it is usually not directed at the baby. During that first year, the child observes how people talk to each other. He or she sees how people posture, listens to how the pace of speaking changes, and observes how the context of a situation shapes the way a person responds in a social setting.

This community guides boys as young as 12 to 14 months old to begin to participate in public oral communication in the form of teasing, bossing, scolding, and defying. In fact, Heath (1983) explained that a young boy's esteem is measure by his ability to speak with wit. Young male toddlers learn the importance of clever language and the ability to perform for others. They learn how important it is to be verbally competent and to use the appropriate tone and nonverbal facial expressions. Girls also learn in the same way; they are constantly being carried and observe the conversations of adults, but are not encouraged to participate in conversations when they are babies. Gender makes a difference in this community.

Heath found that children learned how to deal with various situations. They were often asked, "Now what are you gonna do?" (p. 84). For example, adults often tease children, pretending to take away their candy or bottle. Because children do not have physical power, they must learn skills in dealing with

This African American baby learns language and other communication skills from his parents and family members.

others by outwitting, outtalking, or out acting their aggressors. This is all part of the cultural behaviors children learn from their interactions with adults. Children learn about the type of situations they will need to be able to cope with; they learn acceptable behavior and what to say in response.

A Predominantly White-Working Class Community in Roadville: Child Rearing

Heath was also interested in how children in Roadville were socialized. She wondered if she would find differences with what she saw in Trackton.

Roadville is a primarily White, working-class, low-income textile mill community in the Piedmont area of the Carolinas. Many of the families were originally from the Appalachian Mountains and moved to the Piedmont area in the early 1900s. In this community, people are excited about new babies and look forward to caring for them.

For the first three months of their lives, babies are placed on feeding and sleeping schedules to encourage them to learn a routine. Relatives and close friends visit the mother and her new baby regularly; they help the mother with baby duty and give her advice (Heath, 1983). These women talk with the baby, calling her or him by name and asking questions using a sing-song intonation.

how the seminal work of Shirley Brice Heath, an educational anthropologist, helped teachers to understand how different cultural family environments socialize children to interact with others and value different skills. Heath studied how parents interacted with their children from two communities: Trackton and Roadville. Although both communities believed in schooling, Heath found basic cultural differences.

Institutional Racism

Teachers also convey mainstream culture to students. Consider, for example, the literature that is taught in school; F. Scott Fitzgerald, Ernest Hemingway, and Shakespeare can shape what students think are considered great literary works. Our country has a European orientation toward literature that can support institutional racism (Brislin, 2000; Erickson, 2015; Cushner et al., 2012). **Institutional racism** is a system of legalized practices designed to keep the dominant group in power (McIntosh, 1992).

There are numerous ways for the school curriculum to reinforce institutional racism. Often the curriculum presents European American or European or Western views. These

Institutional racism is a system of legalized practices designed to keep the dominant group in power

CASE STUDY *continued*

This White child is learning nonverbal skills through interactions with her mother.

This way both baby and new mother learn how to behave and respond to each other. Mothers are encouraged to respond to their babies, but not to "spoil" them by carrying them all the time. Relatives encourage mothers to let their babies explore, talk baby talk, and make noises. When children begin talking, parents, siblings, and others teach children the names of pets, people, objects, and events. They are taught to listen, learn from others, and behave; babies learn how to talk appropriately through their interactions with adults. Socialization of the babies is shaped by these social interactions.

Trackton and Roadville: Comparing Their Socialization Processes

Did you notice the differences between how the two communities interact with babies? Heath found that the two communities of Trackton and Roadville socialized their children in contrasting ways though they are both low-income, working-class societies. It appears that in Trackton, intuitive performance is taught so youngsters learn how to joke, jest, and say funny things. However in Roadville, children are more encouraged to communicate as adults and to remember aspects of stories that present accurate representations of what happens in life. Take a look at the following table to examine different communication styles of the two groups. Which community has values and ways of behaving that may be more like what is expected in schools?

Reflection Questions

Q How do parents raise children to have different behavioral expectations?

Q How can teachers learn that childrearing practices in cultural communities may differ?

Q Why do some behavioral expectations of students differ from their teachers?

Comparing Socialization in Trackton and Roadville		
	Trackton Community	**Roadville Community**
Who interacted with the babies?	Parents, older siblings, relatives, others from the neighborhood	Primarily parents
What types of communication styles are emphasized?	Children learn to show their verbal and nonverbal abilities by being spontaneous, witty, and knowledgeable.	Children speak like adults.
Oral tradition	Children tell stories of real life events.	Children retell stories from traditional nursery rhymes and the Bible.

works are presented as the best and so should be taught in schools. For example, you probably know the work of a famous writer, William Shakespeare, who was born in England, not the United States. Despite this, his work is considered to be an important element of American culture. Shakespeare wrote many plays, such as *Romeo and Juliet*, *Hamlet*, *King Lear*, *Macbeth*, and *Julius Caesar*. The stories from these plays have also been made into modern day movies like *10 Things I Hate About You*, which is an adaptation of *Taming of the Shrew*, and *West Side Story*, which was adapted from *Romeo and Juliet*. They represent European or European American viewpoints, values, and history; the underlying message is that Shakespeare's work is better than any person of color's writings. Do you remember famous statements from Shakespeare such as "To be or not to be, that is the question," or "A rose by any other name would smell as sweet"? These famous sayings are also often taught in high school English classes. Figure 2.9 depicts famous sayings that many people have learned.

Let's compare the work of a well-known writer from the United States, Langston Hughes, with what you know about Shakespeare. Hughes wrote many poems, plays, and novels. Did you read many or even one of his works in school? Did you study his stories and

Figure 2.9: Many common sayings we now use come from the writings of William Shakespeare.

Harlem Renaissance refers to the period during the 1920s and 1930s where there was a great burst of outstanding work from artists, musicians, and writers from the Black American community. Langston Hughes was one of the great writers of the time.

poems as much as those by Shakespeare? Why or why not? Hughes was born in 1902 in Missouri, and racial oppression is one of the most powerful themes in his work. As a writer who was African American, he had to deal with extreme social and institutional racism; however, Hughes was one of the giants of the **Harlem Renaissance**. During the 1920s and 1930s, there was a great burst of outstanding work from artists, musicians, and writers from the Black American community. In one of his most well-known poems, "Dream Deferred," he talks about racism and how it has eliminated the dreams of many people. Do you know his poem?

Langston Hughes is a celebrated poet, novelist, and African American civil rights activist who wrote about the desperate feelings of thousands of people who felt the oppression of racism. Many Black Americans hoped that the United States would become that nation where everyone had freedom and was treated equally. However, African Americans were seen by many as second class citizens in their own nation. Though the Civil War was over and slavery had been abolished by the passage of the Thirteenth Amendment to the Constitution in 1865, people who were Black and from other communities of color did not have the same rights as Whites. People's dreams "dried up like a raisin in the sun" because of racial inequalities. People gave up on their dreams and their hope "sagged." Blacks still did not have opportunities and were treated with disdain in the general society. As you will read later in the book, Black students were segregated in schools for much of this country's history. Hughes expressed in his work that life continued to be a struggle and that it was important to fight for justice and equality. Read "Dream Deferred." What do you think Hughes meant when he wrote, "Or does it explode?"

Most of you are probably familiar with the sayings from the works of Shakespeare, but how many of you are familiar with the writings of Langston Hughes? Do you get a sense of how our U.S. American culture is shaped by a European orientation? What knowledge is taught in schools? Who controls what is taught in schools? Whose history is taught in schools? I hope that you consider these questions as you read through the text.

Individual Cultural Identity

People have a **cultural identity**. It means if you identify with a group or community. One's cultural identity is always in process; for most people it is never finished. Sociologist Stuart Hall believed that though some people feel they have a fixed identity based on group affiliations, true cultural identity is always in flux. Historically, Hall explained, many sociologists believed that an individual had a core identity and that core identity is enriched by social interactions with others such as parents. Hall did not believe that a person's cultural identity is fixed, rather it modifies over time (Hall et al., 1996). Therefore, the way children see themselves can also vary over time. Teachers should not believe that a student only sees him- or herself in one way or as a member of one cultural community (Voicu, 2013).

Do people from the same cultural group agree about an issue? Let's say that a predominantly Mexican American community is going to be cut in two by a new freeway. On one side of the debate, people are concerned about fragmenting the community, but because a priest of the local Catholic church assures them that the city is hearing their concerns, they decide not to openly fight the city. This part of the community choses several male members to work with city transportation officials. Those who decide to work with the governmental officials hold more traditional values about authority in working with religious leaders and trusting elected officials. However, another group of people from the same community is extremely unhappy. They write letters to the newspaper and to city officials demanding a meeting. They operate from a more bicultural perspective. Those who use more mainstream techniques such as picketing, holding news conferences, and testifying at city council meetings may be part of a bicultural group. They are able to function in both the ethnic community and mainstream society. When the two factions come together in a community meeting, the traditionalists and biculturalists cannot agree on a collaborative strategy.

The two groups fall on different places on the cultural identity continuum (Figure 2.10). Members of one group are **cultural traditionalists** and follow the ways, beliefs, and patterns of the cultural group much of the time. They may continue to speak the native language. **Bicultural identity** members retain cultural values, customs, and ways of seeing life from their ethnic culture, yet they have adopted practices and beliefs of the mainstream culture. A third group is made up of **assimilationists**. This segment of the community is made up of individuals who have culturally assimilated into society and do not identify with an ethnic group. They highly identify with mainstream society and take on a mainstream view that the new freeway benefits many other people, so it isn't as important if one neighborhood is cut in half. Although cultural identity and cultural patterns are more complicated than a linear model, Figure 2.10 does provide an understanding of how individuals within the same community may adopt different levels of cultural assimilation (Valle, 1997).

Where do you fall in the cultural identity continuum? Why do you think so? Is cultural identity important to you? Why or why not?

In summary, you probably know people who are bicultural and function in both mainstream and ethnic cultural communities. There are traditionalists who only interact with individuals from the same ethnic background. And there are assimilationists who do everything in the general society and do not engage in ethnic cultural customs or do not feel that they belong to an ethnic community. Sometimes a person may operate at various places on the continuum depending on the context.

> **Cultural identity** refers to the identity a person can develop based on affiliations with various subgroup communities. Cultural identities can be personal or public. Sometimes outsiders may adopt a cultural identity of others that can be in conflict with the person's chosen cultural identity.

> **Cultural traditionalists** follow the ways, beliefs, and patterns of the cultural group much of the time and may continue to speak the native or home language.
> **Bicultural identity** refers to members of a group who retain cultural values, customs, and ways of seeing life, yet they have adopted practices and beliefs of the mainstream culture.
> **Assimilationists** identify with mainstream society and take on mainstream views, behaviors, values, and ways of thinking. They do not relate to their ethnic or racial communities.

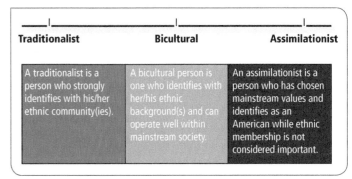

Traditionalist	Bicultural	Assimilationist
A traditionalist is a person who strongly identifies with his/her ethnic community(ies).	A bicultural person is one who identifies with her/his ethnic background(s) and can operate well within mainstream society.	An assimilationist is a person who has chosen mainstream values and identifies as an American while ethnic membership is not considered important.

Figure 2.10: **Cultural Identity Continuum**

Stereotyped Cultural Identities

Cultural identity may also be an identity that someone else places on another person. It is often one dimensional and therefore borders on a stereotypical image. For example, a Latino citizen sees a White police officer and assumes the person is biased toward people of color. He keeps his head down hoping the officer does not stop him. In contrast, maybe a White woman walks down the street and sees three teenagers of color coming toward her. One is Black, another is Latino, and the other is Asian. She thinks they might take her purse, so she ducks into the nearest coffee shop. But then the teenagers also go into the coffee shop. She is scared, but then she hears the barista yells out, "Want your regular?" They nod. She was wrong: the young men were going to get coffee, not get her.

Hall believed that one's cultural identity is always open ended. For members of modern society, life is always shifting and moving in a variety of directions especially in a global world (Hall et al., 1996). However, Hall also believes that an individual may not understand the complexity of cultural identities. He gave the example of when President George H. W. Bush in 1991 nominated Clarence Thomas to be on the Supreme Court. Bush thought conservatives would support Thomas's nomination and Blacks would support him because he was a member of the African American community. However Thomas's identity was complicated. During the hearing process, Anita Hill, a former student of Thomas, accused him of sexual misconduct. Both Hill and Thomas are Black. Many conservative females who Bush thought would have supported Thomas did not. They saw him as a sexual abuser. In addition, Bush thought Blacks would back Thomas's nomination, but while some did defend him, others saw him as an exploiter of women. Some White, liberal women who may have supported him because of his race opposed him due to the sexual allegations, while many White conservative women opposed feminists who were against Thomas and so supported his nomination. Can you see how complicated cultural identity can be?

Cultural identity is not only how a person feels about her- or himself, but it also refers to the identity that others attribute to the person. The complex nature of cultural identities also can be in conflict with each other. Cultural identities are often situational and can be attached to personal beliefs about oneself.

Subcultures and Intersectionality

Has anyone ever asked, "What are you?"

When they ask that question, usually they want to know your ethnic background. For example, the person is asking if you are Irish, Chinese, German, or Mexican. Teachers may not know that some children do not like being asked this question; many educators do not understand that ethnic identity is considered a personal aspect of people's lives. Children or adults also may not answer because they really don't know.

Some people get irritated when strangers ask, "What are you?" To counter that rude behavior of others, an individual might answer with a great deal of information about the subcultures of which he is a member. He might say, "I'm a Panamanian American dad of twins who paints and enjoys photographing the cathedrals of Italy." Like this father of two children, you are a multidimensional person, and a one-word racial or ethnic category like Black, Asian, or Caucasian is a limiting descriptor.

This question can also be compared to how you might teach multicultural education. When multicultural education is considered primarily as consisting of isolated, racial categories, stereotypes can be reinforced rather than rooted out. For example, by presenting separate categories like Black American history or the needs of students with disabilities as detached chapters in a text, teachers may not understand that their students are unique combinations of many diverse cultures. The young people you work with are distinct blends of many groupings. This is one of the reasons that it can be difficult for teachers to accurately identify student identities and affiliations without getting to know them.

Though this book only provides a limited discussion about culture, children are members of, or identify with, many subcultures. Subcultures are smaller units that have defining elements from a larger culture. Children may have connections to a larger culture, but they also may develop an identity to subcultures. For example, in the United States, people can develop strong identities with a variety of subcultures such as ethnic membership, labor status, social class, political affiliation, gender, religious beliefs, sexual orientation, and exceptionalities. A case in point can be how ethnic groups, such as African American and Cambodian American, have retained subcultures by preserving home languages, group history, geographical neighborhoods, and sense of community, though the communities are part of the larger society of the United States. Many students in schools may have strong ethnic identities. However, teachers must also realize that though a young person may appear to be strongly affiliated with a particular cultural community, the young person, more accurately, may also identify with being a member of many other subcultures such as a participant of a community volunteer group, a string quartet, and the school tennis team.

Today, young people may have a variety of interests and may identify more strongly with a particular interest rather than an ethnic group they are a member of. Because students are exposed to and identify with many different aspects of life around the world, and represent a complex union of interests and affiliations, multicultural education is moving beyond static categories of race and ethnicity.

It is important that teachers understand that stereotypical identifiers can become obstacles in teachers' ability to identify the educational needs of their students. Overgeneralizations can also act as barriers to figuring out what the behaviors of students mean. It is important that you as a teacher see the richness each student brings to the classroom; stereotypes can act as hurdles to appreciating the resources they can share. The model in Figure 2.11 illustrates the complex nature of student identities and affiliations. The person represented in the chart was born and raised in the United States, is a female, identifies with being Mexican American, feels connected to heavy metal music, sees herself as a gamer, and has worked hard to learn strategies that help her deal with her epilepsy. The intersectionality of the various subcultures she is a member of shows the interconnectedness of her various identities.

Figure 2.12 represents a European American who also may see himself as a member of several different subcultures. He is gay, identifies as a German-Swedish-English American, speaks Mandarin, earned a black belt in judo, and has strong ties to Boston, Massachusetts. Like people of color, White teachers and students also are members of diverse subcultures. We are all complex beings.

Teachers who are cultural mediators understand the complexities of the different cultures that children bring to school. As cultural liaisons, teachers can move from one cultural context to another and also bring students together if there are cultural conflicts. See the Teaching Tip for five ways that a teacher can act as a competent cultural mediator.

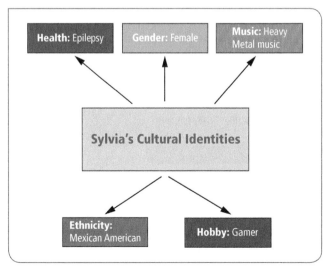

Figure 2.11: **Sylvia's Cultural Identities**

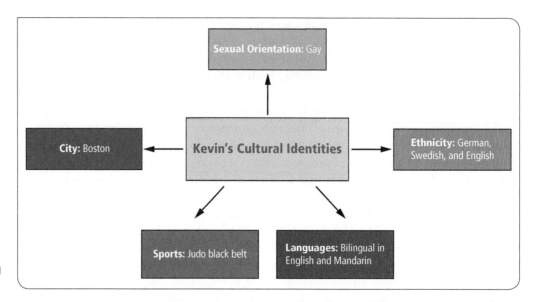

Figure 2.12: **Kevin's Cultural Identities**

Five Ways to Be a Cultural Mediator

Cultural Mediator: someone who works to establish collaborative and respectful relations across cultures

1. **Listen and Observe.** In order to understand the cultural backgrounds of a student, it is important to listen and observe her or him in the classroom and on the playground.
   a. What sports or activities does the student like to play?
   b. Does he or she do it as a group or independently?
   c. Does the student talk about playing the sport or activity with a family member?
   d. Do not stereotype a student. Ask students for information. For example, if a student is Mexican American, this does not automatically mean the student likes soccer rather than football.

2. **Learn.** Find out additional information about cultural groups from written materials, local community leaders, educators, and parents.
   a. Go to a local community function like an international festival. Get to know parents outside of the school environment.
   b. Pick up local community newspapers to learn about the issues of the community.
   c. Ask parents to serve as guest speakers in the classroom. Most parents have professional expertise, whether it is about cooking, ranching, finance, or computers.

3. **Be Open.** Have unbiased conversations with cross-cultural individuals and learn their views and values. People may see and respond to the same event or issue differently.
   a. Have a parent night activity like Family Math Night. Ask parents how you can make the event more culturally relevant.
   b. If parents need transportation, contact your principal or district office to see if a bus can pick up parents and children from the neighborhood so people can attend school events.

4. **Clarify.** In a clear and objective way, identify areas of conflict to discuss.
   a. Ask parents and students about how to make schools more effective and welcoming.
   b. Bring in parents who want to organize a volunteer program in your classroom.
   c. Maybe parents are interested in helping in the classroom, but they work. Can parents participate in the classroom even though they work during the day? What are some of limitations that parents must deal with?

5. **Collaborate.** Bring people together and establish common goals. What are the goals of parents and students? Are they the same as teachers' goals?
   a. Are parents interested in learning about college access issues?
   b. How can teachers and parents work closely for the benefit of students?

Professional Resource Download

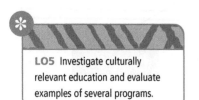

LO5 Investigate culturally relevant education and evaluate examples of several programs.

Culturally Relevant Education

naeyc **CAEP** **InTASC**

Culturally relevant education is an approach that incorporates student-lived experiences and their cultural modes of delivery into the curriculum and instructional methods of teaching. Culturally relevant teaching can also be referred to as meaningful teaching where instruction is relevant, interesting, and purposeful to all students. When teachers respect and are committed to students, educators want to listen to and know about them. This shows how we care. Looking at life from other perspectives enriches our knowledge of the world, especially in a classroom where children may speak ten different languages and come from various communities. Creating a community of learners who come from diverse backgrounds is a difficult but exciting aspect of being a teacher. This portion of the chapter will discuss several programs that take a culturally relevant education approach. In addition, culturally relevant curriculum and materials will be presented Chapter 3.

An excellent way to design culturally relevant programs for students is to ask them what their opinions are about the needs of the community and to use that information to create relevant curriculum. In Philadelphia, the University of Pennsylvania organized the West Philadelphia Improvement Corps (WPIC) after interviewing several teachers and approximately 100 students about what could be done to improve their schools and neighborhoods. From their responses, WPIC designed and implemented a plan that included landscaping, removal of graffiti, and other neighborhood beautification projects (Nothdurft, 1989).

WPIC was a coalition of the University of Pennsylvania, local corporations, community agencies, and schools, and the project rose out of the beliefs of the students; therefore, the young people could see how school and the real world were linked. They also saw that their efforts did make a difference. Through this program, students learned geometry and carpentry by being involved in rehabilitating row houses; they learned biological principles by running a greenhouse and learned economic principles by being responsible for a school store. Dropout rates decreased, and the academic achievement of students increased. Several of the WPIC schools have become community centers with outside funding. This program demonstrated that connecting learning in schools to real life is key.

Another aspect of relevancy in the classroom deals with culture. Evangelina Bustamante Jones, a literacy professor, believes that teachers must act as cultural mediators. Teachers should explain to children and help them understand the differences in values and social contexts. Thus, teachers can honor both the world of the child and the majority society. As cultural mediators, teachers can affirm both the home and school cultures. Teachers must have the ability to take school information and skills and make connections to the lives of their children. Three examples of culturally relevant educational programs follow.

The Puente Project: An Example of Culturally Relevant Education

The Puente Project is a pipeline program in California established to mentor high school and community college students to enter and graduate from four-year colleges and universities. It was started in 1982 by Felix Galaviz and Pat McGrath, who saw high dropout rates, especially among Latino students. They wanted to address the needs of culturally and linguistically diverse students who were having difficulty writing for and understanding the college admissions process. They believed that many students could do well given counseling, writing skill development, and mentoring. The Puente Project pushed to give high school students the same English/Language Arts teachers for both ninth and tenth grades. This provided continuity of learning because the teacher would know their students as they moved from ninth to the tenth grade. Students also engage in leadership training through which they became actively involved in their schools and communities. Puente high school students also work with a college counselor who assists in preparing them for college.

Puente community college students are engaged in a sequence of two courses, which cover English skills, along with preparing to transfer to a four-year university. The classes not only focus on English but also have students work on their personal and career

> **Culturally relevant education** is an approach that incorporates student-lived experiences and cultural modes of delivery into the curriculum and instructional methods of teaching. Culturally relevant teaching can also be referred to as meaningful teaching where instruction is relevant, interesting, and purposeful to all students.

TAKE A STAND: ARE SCHOOLS CULTURALLY NEUTRAL?

The United States is a culturally diverse society, and students may come to school from many different cultural and national communities. The students may be refugees from Vietnam, North Korea, Sudan, or other nations.

Many teachers believe that schools are culturally neutral institutions because they teach basic knowledge that everyone needs to know. Discuss the following questions.

TAKE A STAND . . .

▶ Are schools culturally neutral? If so, how? If not, what evidence can you present to demonstrate that schools are not culturally neutral? What is basic knowledge? Whose knowledge does it represent?

▶ I suggest that you make a table that has two columns. The first is "schools are culturally neutral" and list the evidence. In the second column, provide evidence as to why schools are not culturally neutral. What does the table teach you about schools?

▶ Do you benefit from thinking that schools are culturally neutral? Why or why not?

development. The Puente Project builds on the cultural and linguistic capital of students and holds high expectations for learners.

Puente in Spanish means bridge, and the Puente Project continues to act as a bridge between students and their families and college careers. Classes for parents are given through this project and a middle school component is being added. In order to address the science, math, and technology needs of students, a STEM (Science, Technology, Engineering, Math) component has been added. Take the time to read through the timeline of the project and learn about how the Puente Project continued to grow at http://puente.berkeley.edu/.

Harlem Children's Zone: Changing the Odds

The Harlem Children's Zone (HCZ) is a comprehensive plan to increase the educational and social opportunities of families and their children in Central Harlem in New York City (Figure 2.13). HCZ not only targets the needs of youngsters, but also those of their parents.

Figure 2.13: The Harlem Children's Zone believes it is vital to start children learning at an early age and to involve their parents in this process.

Richard Levine/Alamy Stock photo

Taking a larger view of families has made a huge difference in the impact of the program. HCZ creates strong communities dedicated to the development of healthy, highly educated children (Harlem Children's Zone, 2014).

The project (originally called Rheedlen) began in 1970 when it started a truancy prevention program. Since that time, the HCZ has grown tremendously to include a charter school, community centers, after school programs, health programs, and community development. Originally the HCZ focused on one block and now includes over 100 blocks. Geoffrey Canada, CEO of HCZ, developed a comprehensive program that addresses social, political, medical, and educational needs of the families who live within its boundaries. The program serves over 10,000 children and 7400 adults. In 2010 their budget was over $75 million.

Why is the HCZ successful? William Julius Wilson, a sociologist at Harvard, believes that the comprehensive nature of the program is the reason for its success (Wilson, 2010). Canada has created a program that follows students from birth through college. He has developed the "pipeline" for children so that they understand the importance of higher education. Here is a sample of the programs within HCZ:

- **Baby College** for expectant parents or those with preschool children. This program provides parent instruction in discipline, planning for college, and cognitive development of youngsters.
- **Path to Promise Academies** is a program for three-year-olds and their parents that targets language and cognitive development in children.
- **Harlem Gems** is a full-day preschool program that prepares children for kindergarten and teaches English, Spanish, and French.
- **The Promise Academies** are two charter schools that run from grade school through high school. The schools not only offer exceptional education but also medical and dental services. There are numerous after school activities and remedial programs.
- **Non-academy opportunities** offer students who do not attend one of the Promise Academies the chance to get involved in after school activities and summer programs.
- **College preparation program**s include instruction in college preparation, college admissions, college applications, and career counseling.
- **Community programs** for parents include how to organize block associations and how to access medical care. There are also programs about alcohol and drug abuse.

Consider this . . .

The Harlem Children's Zone Project starts as early as possible in children's lives, and the program results in a critical mass of adults in the neighborhood who can help children reach their potential and succeed.

Q Why do you think it is important for the Harlem Children's Zone to include many neighborhood mentors? What might neighborhood mentors bring to students that others might not?

The Lemon Grove Academy: Comprehensive Wellness

Local schools and programs addressing the achievement gap at the community level can also be successful. Rick Oser is principal of the K–8 school, the Lemon Grove Academy of Science and Humanities. When he first went to the school, it was the lowest achieving in

Figure 2.14: This poster is painted on the wall of the cafeteria of Lemon Grove Academy in Lemon Grove, California. The culture of the school reinforces the students' self-esteem and the importance of college.

the district. However, he brought the faculty, staff, and parents together; they developed the common goals of physical, emotional, intellectual, and social growth of their students (Oser, Beck, Alvarado, & Pang, 2014). In fact, a motto of the school faculty reinforces the importance of community networking in development of an exceptional educational environment: "If the school's not good enough for our own children, it's not good enough for the kids at school." Figure 2.14 is an example of a poster at the school where the students worked to create the idea using their own handprints and career choices. This was a way to affirm student aspirations.

Lemon Grove Academy is one of six elementary schools in a small district. Teachers, the principal, staff, and parents have transformed the achievement of the school; though a low achieving school, it is now one of the highest in the district. At the Lemon Grove Academy, teachers at each grade level work together to address the needs of individual students. They share ideas and instructional strategies and develop ways to make sure that the skills and knowledge learned from one grade to the next build upon each other. In addition, at each grade level teachers address the individual needs of students and identify particular educational needs of learners. For example, maybe certain learners need more work on fractions while others need additional instruction on reading comprehension.

In 2012, the ethnic breakdown of the students in the school was: 60 percent Latino, 19 percent Black, 11 percent White, and 5 percent Asian American and Pacific Islander. In addition, about 45 percent of the students in the school were English learners. Over 80 percent of the students were also served by the free lunch/reduced lunch program, suggesting that many families are living at poverty levels.

The work in the school is built on three theoretical frameworks. First, using Maslow's hierarchy of needs (Maslow, 1999), staff and faculty believe that students and their families must have their physical and safety needs addressed so a strong academic community can be created. Therefore, the purpose of the school's Comprehensive Wellness Program (CWP) is to improve the overall health and wellness of students and their families by increasing their access to a holistic school program that covers things such as healthcare and college readiness. In addition, the health and security of teachers and staff is included in the program, which also addresses faculty morale.

Second, the school's vision statement is "Keeping it RE²AL." The acronym represents four of the most important aspects of teaching:

1. Developing positive **relationships** with students and families
2. Having high **expectations** for **excellence**
3. Ensuring students are **actively engaged** in their learning
4. Focusing each day on **learning** (Oser, 2008)

The third theory is the caring-centered education framework that emphasizes the creation of reciprocal, trusting relationships throughout the school, the integration of culturally relevant education into the learning process, and teaching students how to develop crucial citizenship skills for a democracy (Pang, 2005; Pang, Lafferty, Pang, Griswold, & Oser, 2014).

As part of the free clinic project, the school has both a medical clinic and a dental office for all members of the school families. The free clinic project is founded on a philosophical framework that includes four core tenets, which are taught, modeled, and expected in all relationships (Beck, 2004, 2005):

1. Empowerment—creating environments where people take charge of their health and achieve health and well-being
2. Humanistic approach—respect, empathy, and self-awareness on the part of the clinician addressing needs of the body, mind, and spirit
3. Transdisciplinary work across all fields—with the child and family at the center, practice mutual respect across all multiple fields including addressing social determinants of health
4. The community as teacher—the community, the children, will teach us how to be effective teachers and healers

These belief systems form the basis for the clinic work at the school and place the development of the whole child at the center of their efforts.

The Challenge of Being an Effective Teacher and Cultural Mediator

It is a great challenge to become a cultural mediator when students represent varied ethnic communities like Somali or Hmong, where some value orientations are extremely different from majority culture. If you are a European American, you probably will be more like the child who is an immigrant from an English-speaking province of Canada, not only because of the language, but also because of the religious and political similarities of Canada and the United States. To become a strong cultural mediator, you must gain cultural knowledge about your students. Figure 2.15 is a form that you might use to collect information that will help you to learn about how your students identify themselves. You can also talk with social workers, school liaisons, or community counselors who are willing to speak with you or members of your faculty to help initiate the process of understanding some of the cultural conflicts children face in schools. It takes time to become a strong mediator, but as a life-long learner, you can continue to more fully understand the implicit cultural elements of your students.

Culture is a powerful influence in your classroom. As a teacher you need to learn how culture can provide important keys that can be used to unlock ways to connect to your students and facilitate their academic and social growth.

Thinking about Intersectionality

As you read in Chapter 1, intersectionality deals with the interconnections between various cultures and groupings. The Case Study on the subcultures of Whites and Blacks in Trackton and Roadville discusses two different ways that intersectionality influences the development of children. Both communities are low income. Both communities are also highly influenced by their ethnic cultures. The integration of ethnicity and social class has led to the creation of a subculture. The subculture includes aspects of both social class and ethnic values and behaviors. In addition, children brought up in these two communities learn attitudes about their gender and integrate those views into their identities. The children may also learn religious beliefs and doctrine, which become who they are too. Do you see how intersectionality can lead to a complex identity that students develop and bring to school?

Instructions: This form can be used to collect information about your students. As you gather this information, remember to not ask students questions like, "What are you?" Rather listen to them and let them volunteer information about themselves. Some preliminary questions might be: What is the neighborhood you live in? What is your favorite place in the neighborhood and why? What are your hobbies? You may also have students write an essay about who they are or who their role models are.

Student Names	Ethnic Communities Identified With	Ethnic Experiences Shared	Additional Information

Student Names	Neighborhoods Students Identify With	Neighborhood Activities Students Participate In	Additional Information

Student Names	Hobbies	After School Activities	Additional Information

Student Names	Historic Role Model	Living Role Model	Additional Information

Figure 2.15: Teacher Research Form: Student Culture

Source: "Colorblind Intersectionality," by Devon W. Carbado, 2013, *Signs, 38*(4), 811–845.

Professional Resource Download

Summary

1. Describe the various elements of culture and explain why culture is a powerful aspect of life.

This chapter is about the power of culture. Culture is a complex construct that is all around us. There is explicit culture, or elements of life that you observe and see, such as the food people eat or the games they play. Implicit culture is harder to identify because it includes aspects within a community or person that are hidden. It includes the expectations or beliefs of a person or group. It is not easy to explain how the many elements and aspects of culture impact learning. Children and students learn about culture from a multitude of places, such as watching what parents do and watching television programs.

2. Define and explain a model of culture.

In your classroom you may have students who speak 20 different home languages. Children come not only with various languages, but also different value systems, so Valle's model of three levels of culture helps teachers to understand its complicated nature: (1) artifacts and elements on the surface; (2) interactional patterns such as customs and expected behaviors; and (3) implicit values and beliefs that form the core of a person's way of life. It is important for teachers to understand and to learn about the cultural backgrounds of student cultures so they can build trusting relationships and create educational programs that address student cultural values and goals.

3. Discuss mainstream culture and subcultures in the United States.

Mainstream American culture is a powerful force in our nation. It includes the governmental values that are reinforced in our landmarks and flag. However, it also can be Eurocentric in that most literature presented in the classroom, such as the writings of F. Scott Fitzgerald and Ernest Hemmingway, represents European American perspectives. Though Americans have common goals such as equality, freedom, and democracy, they may not have the same viewpoint about how these values should be implemented in society. One of the most powerful aspects of American culture is our paper currency. At this time, all paper currency only has pictures of European American males on it. This may change in the future.

4. Describe how culture is transmitted and cultural identity is developed.

Most children first learn about culture from their families. The work by Heath demonstrated how socialization practices that communities used taught children the values of the community and family. For example, in Trackton most children were taught to be witty and humorous; verbal performance was valued. Infants were carried by different family members, and babies learned a great deal about verbal and nonverbal language skills. Children who were born in Roadville learned to tell stories they were read, especially stories from the Bible. They also learned to listen and talk like adults.

5. Investigate culturally relevant education and evaluate examples of several programs.

Culturally relevant education is an approach that can be used to bridge what students know and bring to school and what they are expected to learn in class. Three important comprehensive programs are the Puente Project, the Harlem Children's Zone, and the Lemon Grove Academy. These programs integrate student cultures into the educational process and demonstrate the importance of teaching students educational skills such as math and language literacy along with college preparation skills. The programs also include parents in the educational process. Student-lived experiences are used in the curriculum so that learners are affirmed and their cultural backgrounds are respected.

Check Your Cultural Knowledge

Reflective Essay Question

You are part of a grade-level team that shares their lessons and goes over curriculum standards. You have brought up the importance of including issues of diversity and culture into the curriculum. For example, you believe students may do better if teachers were effective cultural mediators. Mediators are people who make connections with students from other cultures and find bridges between home/heritage cultures and mainstream society. As you explain why this is an important responsibility of teachers, you hear an educator in the back of the room who laughs and says so everyone can hear, "It is not up to me to learn about the students. If kids want to do well in this country, they must learn what I expect and do what I say."

How would you respond to this comment? What would your educational framework include?

Application

Know & Go Tools in the Classroom

E Pluribus Unum

Culture is an important element of who students are and what they value. In your teaching toolbox, you need a variety of lessons in which the cultures of students are affirmed. Following is a possible lesson.

Encourage students to create posters that can be hung around the room or even the school. The instructional objectives are to affirm student cultures, encourage students to analyze and synthesize their knowledge of personal culture, teach how to use a word web, and teach how to organize/rank order information in various themes.

Bring many different magazines, poster paints, and butcher paper.

Have students answer the question: Who am I?

Suggestions

High school students can create a large poster that includes short essays about various aspects of their lives. These posters can also include magazine pictures, articles from the newspaper, and photos that show them participating in sports or in the ASB (associated student body) activities. Students can also draw a large pyramid and then rank their cultural identities. For example, Diana has at the top of her pyramid a photo of her and her sister because her sister is her best friend. Next might be the Diana's participation in school as the treasurer of the school student body. The third level of the pyramid might be a photo of Diana's Latino family celebrating Mexican Independence Day (September 16). The last level might show a watercolor portrait that she painted of her grandmother.

Upper-elementary students can create a word web. In each section of the web, students can paste magazine pictures that signify important elements in their lives. The word web might include religion, sports, music, ethnic background, family, and many other categories. Students can also bring photos from home.

Younger students can lie on poster paper and have the teacher draw an outline of their body. Students can then cut out their outlines and paste magazine photos or bring photos from home showing important elements of their lives. In this way children can share their families, important role models, ethnic traditions, and many other aspects of life that they identify with.

To answer the question of "Who am I?" students may want to say, "I am a brave person," or "I am African American," or "I am a Japanese-American girl who loves dogs." The possibilities of how a student might identify her- or himself are limitless. This could be a large sentence at the bottom of the poster.

Before implementing this activity into the classroom, make sure that your students will be respectful of each other and their work. You as the teacher must make it clear that you expect them to treat each other with dignity. It is important that teachers have already implemented classroom rules and positive ways to work with each other before doing this activity. Each student's responses will be different, and that is beneficial to the class because the United States is a nation of many peoples.

❯❯ Professional Resource Download

Culturally Relevant Teaching

Learning Objectives

LO1 Analyze culturally relevant teaching and theoretical frameworks.

LO2 Describe how culture influences the way people learn.

LO3 Assess culturally relevant programs, such as Funds of Knowledge and the Algebra Project, and their elements.

LO4 Investigate and plan how culturally relevant teaching can be integrated throughout the curriculum and instruction.

STANDARDS COVERED

NAEYC 1, 4, 5, 6
naeyc

CAEP 1 **CAEP**

INTASC 1, 2, 3, 4, 5, 6, 7, 8, 9, 10 **InTASC**

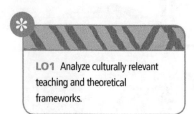

Introduction: Culturally Relevant Teaching

One evening in a teacher education class, I introduced the term *culturally relevant teaching*. During the break, James Allen, a teacher of color, came up to me and said with much emotion, "Those kids won't work. They are never ready for class. They don't even have a pencil, and I teach an English class. All they want to be are boxers and they aren't interested in what I have to say. Nothing I use seems to get through. Why do you think anything about culture is going to make any difference? I don't believe you."

James looked at me with frustration in his eyes and raised his hands in the air in desperation. You could see he cared or he wouldn't have brought up the issue. But he was concerned about the Chicano students in his class not being interested in school. As a teacher, he felt that he was failing his students. I suggested that he consider integrating culturally relevant teaching. Of course, his first question was, "What is culturally relevant teaching?"

Previous chapters have discussed how culture is an integral aspect of life. This chapter presents how culture can provide important links between the everyday experiences and knowledge of students to school knowledge, concepts, and skills. Integrating culture into the curriculum and identifying instructional practices that are culturally relevant can provide important ways for educators to more effectively teach. Not all students come to school with the same knowledge, expectations, or skills. High-quality teachers are able to build on the strengths and knowledge of their students. This means they may be aware of students' family, ethnic, religious, and racial subcultures that may contribute to how students learn and identify what is important. James was trying to identify how to tap into the interests of his students in order to motivate and interest learners in his class. He had never thought of building on the knowledge that was already important to his students.

Teachers and Student Cultures

Ethnic culture is often seen as a marginal aspect in schools. Many educators do not believe that it impacts learning. For example an effective principal told a parent that his school won an award from the district for improved test scores. He said that his large elementary school was divided into three small schools that shared the same campus. Class size had been reduced, and the curriculum was clearly articulated between the primary school and the intermediate school. However, when the parent asked the principal if student cultures were integrated in the curriculum, there was a long pause, and then he said, "No, we don't do much with culture." As a person from a nonmainstream ethnic group, the parent thought he would have a cultural thread woven throughout the school, especially since he learned English as the language of school and at home he spoke Spanish.

The principal explained that he believed that students who spoke Spanish, Vietnamese, Russian, Somali, and Lao would quickly adapt. To him, academic achievement, as measured by standardized tests, was most important. He believed that it was critical to improve student scores. It never occurred to him what students might be giving up in the process of replacing home culture with school culture. However, teachers in the school felt that students would need to give up aspects of their cultures if they wanted to do well in school. The educators did not understand how the assimilation process could negatively impact student self-identity or cause students to give up home languages, behaviors, and community affiliations with their parents and other family friends.

When the parent asked the principal about multicultural education, he said that his staff didn't think it was relevant to the education of his students, and they didn't believe in holding international potlucks. Most of the faculty did not think that families were interested in participating in the school and would not attend a school dinner. A common misconception about multicultural education is that it is mainly the presentation of cultural fairs. The principal and his staff didn't realize that multicultural education is about school reform; this includes psychological principles of learning, curriculum chosen, teaching practices, and materials that are relevant and meaningful to all students. Multicultural education is a paradigm shift from a teacher-centered to a student-centered orientation.

Many of the teachers at this school believed that the curriculum and methods of instruction were culturally neutral. They did not examine the fact that many aspects of their school taught a strong mainstream culture and that some students had to accept new cultural assumptions, beliefs, and values in order to do well in school. In the process of assimilation, students gave up vital aspects of culture such as their home language and aspects of their ethnic identify. For example, some students did not keep up their home language skills because they felt it was more important to develop their writing skills in English and become more "American." However, an approach to teaching that affirms the cultural, linguistic, and racial backgrounds of students with the major goal of getting each student to achieve in school is called culturally relevant teaching (Figure 3.1). This approach is defined in the next section.

Figure 3.1: Teachers work together to develop a culturally relevant curriculum.

Culturally Relevant Teaching: Sociocultural Theoretical Foundation

In Chapter 1, the sociocultural theory of learning was discussed. This theory is important because it is the theoretical grounding for culturally relevant teaching (Cole, 2005). Many teachers are unaware that culturally relevant teaching is built on the sociocultural theoretical framework as developed by Lev Vygotsky, the Russian psychologist, and others such as Carol D. Lee, Vera John-Steiner, Barbara Rogoff, and Michael Cole, who are cross-cultural psychologists. Most often culturally relevant teaching is presented as arising out of curriculum or an anthropological view of education (Ladson-Billings, 1995; Gay, 2013; Gonzalez, 1995). However, teachers need to consider cognitive learning theory because it explains principles of how students learn and develop (Lee, 2008). In this way educators can understand which instructional strategies are most beneficial in cross-cultural and urban classrooms. It is not the curriculum that should drive the cognition; rather, it is psychological principles and research that should direct how teachers choose the most effective instructional strategies and meaningful curriculum connections for students. Cognition is defined by educational psychologist Carol D. Lee as problem solving and thinking (2008). Let's take an example of how children learn and how teachers might build on their cultural ways of learning. If research has demonstrated that some African American students learn most successfully through oral history because they were exposed to extensive oral language and social communication activities during child-rearing (Heath, 1983), should teachers omit that method of learning?

Recall that in Chapter 2 on culture, the work of Shirley Brice Heath was presented. She studied a Black community called Trackton and found that many African American families sang, talked, and actively interacted with babies. Youngsters were expected to respond with quick wit as the children learned how to talk. The expectations, methods of communication, and behaviors taught to babies are all part of the cultural worldview that children in the community learned. Her research indicates that some African American students may be most successful in performance-type presentations. Their final projects might involve a monologue explaining the worldview of a famous scientist or politician. A learner may also enjoy being part of a play or act as if she is an author of a book explaining why she wrote the novel. She could be Walter Dean Myer who wrote the book, *Malcolm X: By Any Means Necessary*. What motivated Myer to write the book? What were his major messages?

Some scholars believe that people learn from external forces. The theory of behaviorism states that people can be trained to respond to external conditioning such as rewards or punishment (Tuckman & Monetti, 2013). One of the giants of behaviorism was B. F. Skinner, who believed that individuals learn from forces outside of themselves. Let's say the teacher asks you to write a short paper on your educational philosophy. If you earn a grade of A, this reinforcement might encourage you to write another exceptional essay.

In contrast, Vygotsky believed that individuals participate in shared social experiences with others, which become internalized (John-Steiner & Mahn, 1996). The approach builds on a sociocultural theory integrating the importance of social interactions within the process of learning. This theory also is based on the belief that learning can be improved through an apprenticeship or mentorship model when a more knowledgeable person assists another. This increases the zone of proximal development of the learner as described in Chapter 1. For example, the more knowledgeable person might be the teacher or it could also be a student peer who understands something that another child does not (Lake, 2012). Maybe the student peer verbally explains and concretely shows the other learner how to group small red blocks together to exhibit the concept of multiplication. As the learner more fully understands this mathematical procedure, the student will take on more responsibility in their mutual activity and is able to explain how the red objects are clustered together to the more knowledgeable mentor. The social interaction moves from being part of the external environment of the learner to becoming an element of the inner thinking of the individual. The reflections can also develop into more abstract thinking such as rational thought and reasoning. Therefore language, symbols, mathematical numbers, graphs, and art are other tools that are used to learn about the world and shape the inner thought of a person (John-Steiner & Mahn, 1996). Now the student understands that multiplication is the grouping of objects, which can be represented using the mathematical symbols of numbers.

Vygotsky also believed in the cultural context of the learner (John Steiner & Mahn, 1996; Lake, 2012; Marshall, 1996). People in different communities may respond to different cultural contexts (Nisbett, Pen, Choi, & Norenzayan, 2001; Oyserman, Sorenson, Reber, & Chen, 2009). For example, John-Steiner and Mahn discussed the Kamehameha Early Education Program in Hawaii. They used the "talk story" context to teach students in Hawaii (Au & Kawakami, 1994; Tharp & Gallimore, 1991). The program implemented a collaborative style that allowed for overlapping speech in small groups of five to six; Hawaiian American students took turns discussing reading material. The student leader encouraged her peers to participate in the discussions as a family. This was an effective strategy that arose out of students' cultural context (Tharp & Gallimore, 1991). The students knew what to do because the behaviors were ones used in their everyday lives. However, when Tharp and Gallimore used the same contextual strategy with a class of Navajo students, it was less successful because the children did better in pairs of same-sex partners and were not as verbal as students in Hawaii; this shows that cultural context can make a difference in the learning process. These research studies indicate that there are many ways that people learn, and in education, teachers should explore new methods of reaching students of color who may not be achieving (Lee, 2008).

One of the instructional strategies that has arisen out of recognition of the importance of social interaction in learning is the use of collaborative groups in reciprocal teaching

Consider this . . .

There are many ways to learn. Teachers should be exploring various approaches to learning that include cultural viewpoints and communication styles.

Let's say a teacher has her first-grade students sit with their knees touching in teams of two girls and two boys. The teacher believes that more discussion will occur when students work collaboratively.

Q Can you identify a possible cultural disconnect?

Q What if students have been taught that it is inappropriate to touch another person of a different gender?

(Brown, 1992). Brown, an educational psychologist, created many experiments to assess the process by which children learn and remember what they read. She believed that questioning, clarifying, summarizing, and predicting were needed to develop reading comprehension. This is what teachers taught students to do in small groups:

- Question: leader gets discussion started with a question about the reading
- Clarify: students clarify what was read, focusing on comprehension
- Summarize: leader summarizes the passage
- Predict: leader asks students what may happen in the future

Later another student in the group becomes the leader; all students take turns running the group discussion. This collaborative strategy created communities of learners that were more self-directed, in which students actively participated in their own learning. They constructed meaning, and learning became student-centered. The teacher was not seen as the authority who lectured and provided all the answers. The next section discusses a general social interaction model that teaches students how to analyze reading content and share their viewpoints.

Cultural Models

Another effective strategy based on Vygotsky's work is the use of *cultural models*. These models consider aspects of people's shared worldviews and help to organize large amounts of information (Ghassemzadeh, 2005). For example, what if you had never been to a library and looked at all of the books; you might not be able to mentally picture a huge building with rows and rows of books and many floors of books, videos, and other documents. However, if you have been to a library, no one needs to explain what it holds and what its purpose is. Let's take another cultural model. When Chinese Americans go to their friends' homes, they may bring a small present. This present may be five large, juicy oranges. Some Chinese Americans never go to visit others without a gift of some kind because bringing a gift means that a person respects and values the other individual; it is an important tradition and expectation. The number of oranges makes a difference. It is often five, but never four because the word for four sounds similar to the term for death in the Chinese language. All this is part of the cultural model that some people know. There is somewhat of an expectation to bring a gift. It is important for teachers to understand the cultural contexts of the parents. It does not mean that a teacher has to give something to students' parents; however, if the educator goes to a student's home for dinner, he or she might want to bring a small gift. Sometimes teachers don't understand that they can offend parents through their interactions. However, teachers who become knowledgeable about cultural traditions can create stories that can be used in teaching language arts, English, or social studies. (See Figure 3.2.) The narratives can describe how students and teachers may hold different viewpoints about life. Teachers use extensive new vocabulary like cultural

Figure 3.2: A teacher is able to integrate student cultures into the curriculum by having students write about their families and placing posters with definitions for language arts terms translated into Spanish on the walls.

acculturation, cultural misconceptions, cultural traditions, and cultural conflicts. In the next section of the text, the cultural modeling work of educational psychologist Carol D. Lee will be discussed to show how she built upon a cultural model from the lives of many African Americans and created a method that could be used in the curriculum.

Before discussing the Lee research, take time to read through Table 3.1. It was created to help you to more fully understand Vygotsky's research. Consider how his work can be used to help you be a more effective teacher. It will not be possible to use culturally relevant teaching if you do not know your students. You must learn about their cultures, their

Table 3.1 Culturally Relevant Teaching: Foundations from Vygotsky's Cognitive Development Theory	
Concept	**Descriptions**
Social Construction of Meaning	Children interact with people around them, and social interactions are at the core of their cognitive development.
Internalization	Child has learned the information or skill and can explain it using her or his own understandings through language; directs one's own learning through inner speech.
Language and Cultural Tools	Language, cultural tools like metaphors, cultural models, and examples are used in problem solving, understanding, and thinking.
Zone of Proximal Development	Refers to a more knowledgeable person assisting another person, increasing the zone of learning for the less-informed learner.
Scaffolding	Like the framework of a house, provides support in learning new content or skills; possible strategies include breaking task into smaller chunks, providing connections to knowledge student already has, and using graphic organizers.
Cultural Models	Integration of cultural models that can be used as bridges from student lived experiences to new concepts being taught. They might be metaphors, similes, stories, proverbs, or a larger system of interrelated concepts.

Adaptation of Tuckman and Monetti's work in *Educational Psychology*, 2013.

goals, and their lives to effectively teach in a culturally and linguistically diverse classroom (Figure 3.2). Integrating cultural relevance is not possible if you teach only from your own cultural lens. Get to know your students; really get to know them. Observe them, ask them questions, and LISTEN to what they say about their lives. What careers are your students interested in and why? What can teachers do to more fully connect with them? How can you tie in what your students tell you with the curriculum you are teaching?

The Cultural Modeling Project

Carol D. Lee developed research that provided another important example of how cultural tools can be used to teach new skills and principles. She got to know her students and transferred what they knew to teaching skills and concepts taught in mainstream classrooms. Her research is based on the work of Vygotsky. Lee developed a culturally based *cognitive apprenticeship model* with African American high school seniors that integrated both cultural content and strategies. This framework is called cultural modeling (Lee, 2000).

Using the cultural modeling philosophy, Lee worked with students so that they were able to use elements of *signifying*, a form of social discourse (communication) in the community that is often used to insult others or challenge them. "To signify within the African American community means to speak with innuendo and double meanings, to play rhetorically on the meaning and sounds of words, and to be quick and often witty in one's response" (Lee, 2000, p. 197). Lee studied the impact of students' prior knowledge of signifying in their reading and interpretation of fiction. Could elements of signifying be used as a scaffold to teach students literary interpretations? Recall from Chapter 2 the child-rearing practices in the community of Trackton. Black children in this community develop communication skills by having conversations with much older community members. They learn to tease, scold, defy, and outwit others. Carol Lee builds on students' knowledge of these communication skills in developing student literacy abilities.

Lee wanted to measure the difference in achievement of African American students. First, she observed African Americans in a classroom where traditional literacy strategies were used; no culturally relevant practices were incorporated in the teaching. The students in this group were called the control group. This classroom had the usual lectures and recitations as their primary means of instruction of European literature.

In contrast, teachers in the experimental group structured lessons so that students were responsible for analysis and discussion of African American fiction. The teacher also accessed the students' prior knowledge of signifying and the social context of the community. Students found more than one meaning to a statement or idea and used the rhythm of language as an additional means of conveying implications. Lee observed African American students in the experimental group who were taught to use their cultural knowledge in learning about literary devices such as irony, symbolism, and satire. The students were able to identify specific examples of various literary skills by reading African American literature. Later, Lee had students examine European literature for the same literary devices. It was easier for students to figure out what those literary devices were. The high school students were able to make connections between what they already knew about African American literature to elements in European literature. These literary devices were more easily discovered in reading mainstream authors because students had already developed a deep understanding of the concepts. The students in the experimental group scored significantly higher on the post-test than the African American students in the control group.

Students from both the control and experimental groups wrote essays answering questions that ranged from literal to complicated inferences. They were assessed before the instruction (pre-test) and after the instruction (post-test). Lee found that the experimental group significantly gained in achievement from pre-test to post-test measures (1995). Lee believed that the achievement differences could be explained by the use of signifying a culturally relevant strategy.

Figure 3.3: This is the entrance to the James Madison building of the Library of Congress in Washington, DC. Teachers and students can access culturally rich knowledge through the use of this library via the Internet.

Culturally relevant teaching (CRT) is an approach to instruction founded on the belief in equity education that responds to the sociocultural context of students and seeks to integrate their cultural and social capital.

Lee found that the modeling, scaffolding, coaching, and self-monitoring strategies that were taught using culturally meaningful, prior knowledge were crucial in teaching students problem-solving techniques and methods that could be applied to examine various literary genres such as poetry, short stories, rap, and European literature. Lee found that students could apply their new skills of analysis to other settings. She relied on the students' own knowledge of their culture and used it to create cross-cultural cognitive bridges. There are many cultural tools that can be used as systems of concepts for learning. For example, a teacher may use the example of going to the grocery store as a cultural tool of ideas that are linked. She may talk about finding the best bargains using math skills and may compare that model with learning about financial literacy. Buying stocks is like going to the grocery store; you want the best value for the least amount of cost.

The Library of Congress is a great source of cultural knowledge (Figure 3.3).

Culturally Relevant Teaching Defined

Let's make sure that you know what culturally relevant teaching is. Culture is a broad concept and encompasses everything that is created by people. Teachers who have chosen sociocultural theory of learning as their theoretical framework see culture as having assets that can be built on in the learning process. **Culturally relevant teaching (CRT)** can be defined as an approach to instruction founded on the belief in equity education and value of social justice. CRT responds to the sociocultural context of students and seeks to integrate their cultural and social capital, which includes student cultural backgrounds, experiences, expectations, knowledge, family knowledge, family networks, and values. CRT also takes into consideration student behaviors, interactional patterns, historical background, and learning styles. When choosing content for instruction, aspects of student lives are also integrated into the curriculum; their experiences, knowledge, events, values, role models, perspectives, history, expectations, and community issues often serve as bridges from what is known to new content. Often new content can be explained and extended by using many examples from the lives of students. In this way, what is being taught becomes more meaningful to students. CRT also includes cultural context and delivery of the material. One of the best examples of how culture can be used to teach is the Tony-award winning Broadway musical, "Hamilton." Lin-Manuel Miranda, the creator of the play, uses rap and hip-hop as the means of delivering material about Alexander Hamilton, the first U.S. Secretary of the Treasury. He also uses dance, street culture, and actors of color to create a powerful cultural context. CRT is an approach that integrates culture, context, and delivery elements.

Culturally literate teachers appreciate and work to understand the worldview of students' cultural communities. They understand that cultural elements operate simultaneously and can be used to motivate and interest students. Culturally knowledgeable teachers are keen observers of culture, understand the importance of context, identify nonverbal communication cues, and use learning style preferences of students. Write notes about your students like the sample shown in Figure 3.4. Save the information and use the information as you plan your lessons.

Student Name	Learning Style (Visual, Musical, Spatial, Mathematical, Interpersonal, Intrapersonal, Verbal, Kinesthetic, Artistic, Hands-on—Experiential)	Nonverbal Communication styles	Student Home or Heritage Language	Family Stories Shared	Family and Student Educational Expectations	Role Models	Student and Family Values (may include religion)	Community Issues Considered Important
Maria	Likes to collaborate and learns through song	May not say much, but is knowledgeable. Not flashy. Helps others.	Speaks Spanish at home. Translates for her parents.	Talks about her abuela	Parents expect her to go to college. She wants to go to Berkeley.	Martin Luther King, Jr., and Cesar Chavez and her grandmother	Baptist Education Doing homework Help take care of siblings	Being safe Good schools Loves her family Likes a public library. Believes immigration contributes to the strength of the nation.
Robert	Kinesthetic	Uses facial expressions a lot.	Speaks Black Vernacular at home.	Talks about playing football with his brothers	Parents expect him to go to college and be an engineer.	Malcolm X and his grandmother	Catholic Watches over his grandmother who is sick	Is a member of the Boy's and Girl's Club. Believes in the Black Lives Matter and Police Matter movements.

Figure 3.4: **Sample Chart of Student Cultural and Social Knowledge**

Professional Resource Download

Creating Culturally Relevant Lessons

Effective teachers integrate culturally relevant teaching because they know the approach makes their teaching more effective (King, 2001; Gay, 2013; Pang, 2010). For example, researchers like Jackie Jordan Irvine (1990, 2002) and Janice Hale-Benson (1982) have studied African American students. They found that many came to school with behaviors that contrasted with those expected in schools. Therefore, they advised teachers to observe their young people to determine whether they came with a strong cultural orientation. If so, then teachers might provide students who are expressive and higher in energy with opportunities to make presentations as a vehicle for displaying their competence rather than always being required to perform on written examinations. Researchers like Park (1997) and Litton (1999) found that Filipino American, Korean American, Vietnamese American, and Chinese American students had a learning style preference for visual learning in comparison to their European American peers. Being aware of these research findings, teachers were advised to use more three-dimensional models, graphic organizers, photographs, concept mapping, tables, and writing on the board while teaching new concepts and knowledge. It was also recommended that teachers use the strategy of chunking. **Chunking** refers to breaking up the material into smaller pieces of knowledge so that the information being taught is not overwhelming to students. This is an extremely important strategy for teaching English learners and those who are having trouble grasping complex, abstract concepts.

Because many Latinos and Asian American students are immigrants who came to the United States with different cultural understandings (Pang & Cheng, 1998), Cheng (1998), a cross-cultural researcher, recommends that teachers provide students with opportunities to practice colloquial patterns and interactional behaviors using scripted role plays. Students can create a script that describes a situation they found conflicted with others' values and behaviors. For example, in fifth grade a young man from China regularly pushed his way into the classroom after recess. His peers thought he was being extremely rude. The teacher had

Chunking refers to creating smaller pieces of knowledge so that the information being taught is not overwhelming to students.

Figure 3.5: Students can work with each other and explain differences of opinions. Teachers may need to facilitate conversations, however.

the student work in a small group to present this situation and give his viewpoint. When the young man lived in China, there were so many people that he had learned to push others to get into a cable car or bus. He thought this was normal behavior. By presenting the cultural difference in behaviors and ways of thinking in a role play, the young man learned that this behavior was not appropriate in the United States and that he did not know he was making his peers mad. This lesson provided young people the opportunity to learn how to socialize with other students and identify appropriate behaviors. (See Figure 3.5.)

Another way to integrate the lives of students is to choose issues they know about. Because many students may be immigrants, Fung (1998) suggests that teachers present interdisciplinary units on immigration. These units would infuse cultural content from all major subject areas such as mathematics, science, history, and music. For example, educators may have students compare and contrast different types of musical instruments that were brought to the United States as part of the immigration process. Many of these instruments—from violins to mandolins—are displayed at the Ellis Island Museum. Students could also be directed to study the multiple reasons for migration (Pang, Han, & Pang, 2011). All of these recommendations demonstrate the importance of adjusting teacher practices in the classroom to meet the needs of their culturally diverse students.

Before you begin to create culturally relevant lessons, consider the following four questions:

1. What are the values of your students? What motivates them? Do they work best in groups? Individually? On projects? What is their preferred learning style?
2. Have you already presented the "big picture" of the content? Will students know where this new knowledge or skill fits in with what they have already learned?
3. Do your students already know the vocabulary and concepts being taught in the lesson? If not, how can you teach the terms by using what the students have already learned?
4. What examples from the students' lives can you integrate into the lesson to create bridges from what they know to the new content and skills you are teaching? Providing clear and effective examples from students' lives is one of the most important elements of good teaching.

Provide a variety of ethnic, family, cultural examples when you are teaching to demonstrate the principle or concept. This will assist students in understanding the content more fully. One of the best ways to teach is through experiential learning. In Figure 3.6 you see a chart that students created explaining their experiences at the zoo feeding a giraffe. Student learning is enhanced when they are engaged in the learning process. That's why learners remember more when they are engaged in hands-on activities rather than a lecture. Along with experiences is the importance of examples, examples, examples. These are the key to effective instruction. All of these elements, from hands-on learning to "big picture" understanding to learning styles, make a difference in student engagement.

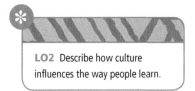

Valerie Ooka Pang

Figure 3.6: As part of experiential learning, students in this class went on a field trip to the zoo, which is a cultural and educational experience, and then wrote about the giraffe that they fed.

Culturally Relevant Principles and Practices

As explained above, teachers need to comprehensively think about how elements of culture can be integrated into the curriculum and instruction. It is not only about building upon children's knowledge but also their cultural context. What motivates students? What are your students interested in? How can teachers affirm who they are and their cultural backgrounds? Are there methods of delivery that students are experts at using?

Review Table 3.1 and Figure 3.4 that present principles and instructional practices of culturally relevant teaching. CRT is an integral characteristic of multicultural education. Read through the material carefully so you can understand the underlying principles of CRT. Then review the practices and identify how they have arisen from the core assumptions.

> **LO2** Describe how culture influences the way people learn.

Culture Shapes How People Learn

Culture shapes how people learn. The culture individuals have grown up with may have taught people different goals, and many teachers do not fully understand the diverse social contexts of their students. Research has shown that these cultural elements make a difference in how children learn. Teachers need to realize that their students may not have the same goals or cultural frames of reference as they have. Students may come to school with different cultural learning experiences. Following is a discussion of research conducted

Consider this . . .

Culturally relevant teaching is a term that has many sisters, such as culturally responsive teaching, culturally congruent teaching, culturally authentic teaching, and culturally sensitive teaching.

They have similar goals and beliefs. Different scholars have identified slightly diverse explanations.

Q What term do you think is best? Why?

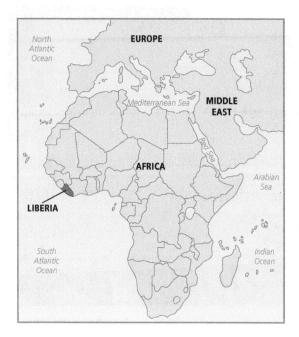

Vai People of Liberia

in Liberia, Brazil, and Alaska. The first case involves people getting others to pay them back; the second case is about being able to make a living; and the third reinforces the connections of people to their natural environment. The differences in cultural contexts result in children learning information and skills in different ways and for different purposes.

Case #1: Paying a Debt in Liberia: Personal Goals

Children learn a great deal of context-specific knowledge before coming to school. Their everyday thinking has been shaped by the specific goals of the community in which they live. Children are aware of how the needs within a community depend on what must be accomplished as part of everyday life. These functions may include having young people do the dishes, take out the garbage, or sweep the floor. Within those contexts are specific symbols, practices, skills, and tools that are used to teach children how to function and address family and community goals. For example, psychologists Sylvia Scribner and Mike Cole studied the literacy of the Vai people in Liberia, a country in West Africa (Scribner & Cole, 1981). The researchers wanted to understand the role of literacy and the use of knowledge and written language within their specific cultural contexts. They found that different cognitive skills were developed from being literate that were used in the schools and in everyday life. Many Vai who were literate also had letter-writing skills because in their lives, letters were written to secure payment for a debt (Scribner, 1984). Thus, people used the written language to reach a specific goal of being paid for a debt.

Many Vai could write letters, but they did not show a strong skill in repeating a story or remembering a list of words. However, Scribner observed that students who learned the Vai indigenous script did so more effectively by using a system of learning in which the student would learn a chain of three words at a time; this was the way young students learned. Later several chains of words would be put together. The researchers believed that their cultural practice for learning script was effective for the Vai and provided an example of literacy in their culture. Though learning was different from other communities, this practice was successful in teaching letter-writing skills to their young people. For the people in this community, work, literacy, and the written word were primarily seen in relationship to writing business letters. The purpose of their learning was clear, and context was an important aspect of shaping the way they learned.

Scribner and Cole believe that literacy skills are shaped by the everyday needs and activities of a community or cultural group. Before this study, they had believed that literacy was part of the same set of universals found in all people. After this study, they theorized that literacy represented a variety of skills and differed within various cultural contexts.

Case #2: Economic Survival and Math Skills in Brazil: Cultural Context

Another example of how culture impacts cognition comes from the work of Geoffery Saxe. As an educational psychologist, Saxe studied how children who never went to school or only attended two years of grade school developed mathematical skills (1988a, 1988b, 1994). The children were 10- to 12-year-old candy vendors on the streets of Brazil, a country in South America. Because of the high inflation rate in the country, the value of money was continually changing. The children had to mentally convert money all the time in order to sell their candy on the streets. Saxe found that these children, who would be considered by U.S. standards illiterate and unschooled, were able to compute complex math problems more accurately than students who were formally educated.

The children first had to decide how many boxes of candy they should purchase from a wholesaler. Second, the children had to purchase the candy with the proper amount of currency from the wholesaler. Next, they had to figure out the cost to sell the candy in order to make a profit as the inflation rate continued to rise. (At one point during the study, Brazil's inflation rate was 250 percent.) The children did not use pencil and paper to compute these problems correctly, even though the buying and selling of the candy necessitated that they be able to compute large numbers.

Saxe found that children developed complex mathematical problem-solving strategies based on the local currency system. The children had a specific goal, to sell candy and make money. The children could add and subtract large numbers. They could deal with the value of currency and provide accurate change. Their personal goals necessitated that they learned how to efficiently work with numbers in order to survive.

Due to the nature of changing currency rates, children had to use math quickly. For example, three Lifesaver candies might cost CR$500 (500 *cruziero*), and over time a box of candy might have cost CR$3600 to CR$20,000 because of the inflation rate. One of the tasks that Saxe created to assess the children's skills was to hand a child a stack of 17 bills that added up to CR$17,300, explaining that this money represented the amount they started the day with. Then he asked how much change would they give back if he handed them a CR$10,000 and the candy cost CR$7600. In order not to have to make change, the children developed strategies that lowered the cost to customers but increased the number of candy bars sold. For example, a child might sell two candy bars for CR$500 and five bars for CR$1000.

What were some of the strategies the children used? First, if someone gave them a series of bills (currency), the young people would group them together. For example, if they held CR$500, 200, 200, 500, and 100, the young people would place them together as such [500 + 500] and [200 + 200 + 100]. This made it easier for the children to generate a total. Regarding the use of ratios in their calculations, the children knew that when they sold three candy bars for CR$500, selling one candy bar for $200 was more because three candy bars at CR$200 would amount to CR$600. Though the students had not learned multiplication skills at school, they were able to make calculations using grouping as they sold their candy.

As Scribner has pointed out in the discussion about paying back a debt in Liberia, some skills are school oriented and other skills address the functions needed in a specific community. Although all learning is not culturally familiar, teachers need to understand that some children have learned much within a cultural context that may differ from majority culture. Teachers may be able to better reach children when using the culturally familiar content and contexts that act as bridges to school knowledge and skills.

Brazil: Street Vendors Use Mathematics

Case #3: Teaching in a Yup'ik Community: Cultural Affirmation and Identity

One of the Native communities in Alaska is the Yup'ik who live in southwestern Alaska. Jerry Lipska (1996) researched how experienced Yup'ik teachers used culturally relevant pedagogy that affirmed student ethnic identity. Overall, Lipska reported a rhythm and flow of learning in the classroom. He watched a lesson focusing on the beaver round-up festival, which signals the end of the winter. In the discussion about how to trap and skin beavers, the male students in this fifth-grade classroom spoke in animated tones and quickly explained how to stretch the beaver pelt. The teacher reinforced their responses with a short, "Right." He used the term *aqsatuyaaq* (young beaver) in his lesson.

At first, the teacher gave directions, using art materials, about how to make the beaver blanket. Then he allowed the students to make their blankets on

Yup'ik Communities

the floor or at their own desks. The teacher made his own beaver blanket at his desk. Some students went to the teacher's desk to watch the teacher. Students talked to each other as they worked. When several students came into the room from another activity, the teacher did not stop to tell them what to do. Rather, other students explained the activity to them. In this way, the teacher was a collaborator in the classroom.

The teacher asked those students surrounding his desk what they might write on the blanket when they were finished making them. To outside observers, the lesson seemed to lack substance; however, to the Yup'ik teacher the activities were carefully organized around the themes of survival, sustenance, respect, care, and patience. The teacher not only taught how a beaver is trapped, dried, and its pelt stretched, but he also taught students how they were expected to behave during the learning process (Lipska, 1996).

As you can see from the three case examples, responding to the cultural context in a classroom is challenging, especially when there are 20 different cultures represented. It is not possible to create culturally relevant lessons for all students all of the time; however, it is possible for teachers to create an affirming environment that values the cultures that students bring to school and integrate information about specific cultures naturally throughout the curriculum. Teachers can use a variety of cultural contexts to make sure students understand why what they are learning is valuable. By connecting the content and skills being taught in school with the cultural and family goals of students, culturally relevant teaching connects with abilities that students have been taught from their families that they need in life.

If you are interested in reading about other scholars who have specific programs or knowledge of what works for students from underrepresented groups, get to know the work of educators such as Okhee Lee, Lisa Delpit, Teresa L. McCarty, Donna Deyle, Bob Moses, Susan Philips, Michael Cole, and Karen Swisher. There is a list of further readings in the online Professional Resource section on MindTap. These educators began their work focusing on a question or issue that interested them and then became educational detectives. Their work can assist you in better understanding what to be sensitive to and what to look for and expect in your classrooms.

Culturally Relevant Programs

Scholars have developed strategies to incorporate the cultures of students into the curriculum and schools. Two different programs are presented in this section. First, we examine **Funds of Knowledge**, where teachers believe it is important to teach the whole student and incorporate parents in the learning process. The second program is the Algebra Project, in which student understanding of math concepts is built on cultural and everyday experiences. As you read, think of ways you could implement one or two of the strategies found in the two programs into your teaching.

Funds of Knowledge: Teaching the Whole Student

Teaching the whole student means to know the whole person, including her or his cultural background and identity. Luis Moll, an educational researcher, sees culture not as a static concept but as a dynamic one. Moll believes that culture is really about people living together in an organized system (Moll, 1990, 2000). He and his colleagues wanted to better understand the cultural resources students brought to the classroom. To study this, he developed the Funds of Knowledge project, which was founded on the belief that students come to school with a rich bank of information. (See Figure 3.7.)

Caring, culturally relevant teachers want to know about their students and view teaching as an opportunity to be part of caring encounters (Goldstein, 1999). Teachers who use a

LO3 Assess culturally relevant programs, such as Funds of Knowledge and the Algebra Project, and their elements.

Funds of Knowledge is a culturally relevant program that teaches the whole child and builds upon the knowledge that students bring to school, brings parents into the classroom, and affirms student identity and family knowledge.

Figure 3.7: Some of the students that Moll and his teachers interviewed were from families that owned horse ranches. As part of the Funds of Knowledge program, students brought information to school explaining how to care for horses, what to feed the horses, and the type of exercise they made sure the horses got daily.

pirita/Shutterstock.com

caring, culturally relevant approach to teaching are cued into the sociocultural background of students and use scaffolding as an important cognitive strategy. In order to successfully build on what students know, teachers must learn cultural analogies, metaphors, similes, and stories from the formal and informal social and economic networks of the family.

Luis Moll and his colleagues demonstrated that using a holistic orientation to learning is more effective than teaching skills in isolation (Moll, Amanti, Neff, & Gonzalez, 1992). When the curriculum and context of learning arise from the lives of students, the knowledge and culture of students become valuable school resources, and students can build on what they know. With his colleagues, James Greenberg and C. Vélez-Ibáñez, Moll studied the cultural knowledge of family relationships and the social networks of 35 Mexican families in a working-class community of Tucson, Arizona (Moll & Greenberg, 1990). Their average yearly family income was $14,500. The cultural riches of the family were called "funds of knowledge."

What did the researchers mean by funds of knowledge? Every family and community holds information about relationships and activities in everyday life. For example, funds of knowledge include information about how families use their money, prepare nourishing meals, practice ethnic traditions, and solve household problems. Every family has a large "bank" of knowledge that contains skills on how to survive. For example, Moll, Vélez-Ibáñez, and Greenberg (1988) discovered that families knew about different kinds of soils for growing vegetables, veterinary medicine, ranch economy, carpentry, masonry, herbal medicines, and midwifery. These systems of knowledge were cultural tools that teachers could use in the classroom. Students had developed and learned rich vocabulary and concepts from their parents about taking care of animals or building a home. They also had knowledge about society and could find out about school programs, enroll in local community college classes, and other community services. Researchers interviewed family members, forged trusting relationships, and built partnerships with families.

In the process of getting to know parents and children, Moll (1990) carefully explained that, although teachers need to know about the knowledge resources in the family, educators also must examine the way children construct their own meaning. Children have social worlds in which they have brought together what they have learned.

Bringing Parents into the Classroom

The Funds of Knowledge project researchers worked with a sixth-grade bilingual teacher who was in her fourth year of teaching. All her children were Mexican American and spoke Spanish. Her goal was to integrate more writing activities into her curriculum. The teacher decided to introduce a unit on construction because many of the parents had experience in building, and this unit could become a bridge between home and school knowledge. The teacher was particularly sensitive to the parents because she was concerned they did not feel welcome at school. She wanted to do something to encourage the parents to become partners in the classroom so that they would become more involved in their children's learning.

This is the process through which she took her students:

1. The class brainstormed and suggested possible topics they could research at the library.

2. Students researched the history of dwellings and how to build different kinds of structures, even using their mathematics skills to figure out how many bricks would be needed in one of the structures.

3. Students built a model of a building and then wrote a short essay explaining their research and how they built their model. One of the students compared building a house to the human body. He wrote, "Without steel rods, you couldn't maintain a house upright. It would fall to the ground like a puppet without strings to sustain it. A house without a frame would fall the same way. Nevertheless, the frame (*es-queleto*, skeleton) of a house is not constituted by bones like ours, but by reinforced steel" (Moll & Greenberg, 1990, p. 338).

4. The teacher then invited parents to school. Because their parents lacked formal schooling, the students were surprised that she would invite them as experts to share their knowledge.

5. About 20 parents (carpenters, masons, draftspersons, and others) brought their funds of knowledge about construction to the children's learning process in the classroom. For example, parents who were masons explained how they used bricks and mortar in the building of a home. The teacher had students write detailed essays about the parent visits and what they learned, such as about how to care for horses and the daily routine that some parents and their children adhered to tending to their animals.

6. Students wanted to extend the unit on construction by creating a community of many buildings. They researched extensively what made up a town. For example, they learned about how to obtain water and electricity. In addition, students had to look into the development of streets, services, parks, schools, and other public service agencies. Writing became a meaningful way to present their research.

7. At the end of the year, the teacher developed a career unit based on the work and the questions students raised during the construction unit. She guided their work with the question, "What do you see in your future?" (Moll & Greenberg, 1990, p. 344). Upper-grade students created posters showing different professions. Figure 3.8 shows a variety of careers that they were familiar with and thought about. They invited a variety of people to talk about their work and what steps they would need to take in order to get a job in that career. The unit centered upon a fund of knowledge found within the children's families. The knowledge that the people in the community shared with the students helped them to identify topics, increase their understanding of construction, and motivate them to write about what they learned. They interviewed many members of their families, engaged in much library research, and were taught important writing skills in the process. Their skills in spelling, grammar, and conceptualization improved.

The sixth graders read and wrote in both English and Spanish. Their skills of expression and analysis increased because they engaged in a series of writing assignments around a culturally meaningful topic. The activities were not isolated or unrelated. The teacher also instituted peer-editing groups and taught students how to critique each other's work so that their recommendations would help peers write more clearly. Students engaged in the third phase of the zone of proximal development, internalization/fossilization. This approach encourages a more holistic orientation to teaching, connecting the everyday life of students with the classroom.

Skills were not taught in isolation; they were taught within a comprehensive, community-based curriculum. For example, a teacher interviewed a parent who was an expert in medicinal plants (Gonzalez, 1995). The teacher then developed a language arts unit around these plants. Students wrote about various regional plants and their health benefits. In another example, Cathy Amanti found during her home visits that several of the families of her students knew about horses and how to care for them. On many ranches in Mexico, horses have contributed to cattle ranching. She developed a unit on the evolution of horses, explored animal behavior, shared information on saddles, created horse math, and used literature and movies that focused on horses (Amanti, 1995). The teacher even borrowed a video that an uncle of one of the students had filmed of his own horses. The students made true-to-size graphs of different breeds of horses and investigated their various characteristics. Students were experts on the topic and had more control in the study of the unit because the curriculum reflected their local cultural knowledge. Some of the students also visited relatives in Mexico who owned ranches. Many of the children had natural and cultural ties to this topic. In addition, family members came to the classroom to discuss their work with horses.

The Funds of Knowledge program affirms and values the knowledge of students, and relationships between students, teachers, and the community become strengthened and reciprocal. Ties of trust are built and maintained. Students are engaged in motivating instructional units that focus on higher-level thinking skills rather than recitation or drill because they become sources of information and have more control over their own learning.

The work of these researchers is extremely exciting because it guides teachers in developing anthropological and cross-cultural skills that assist them in creating motivating and effective learning contexts for students. In addition, this program centers on building trusting and reciprocal relationships with parents. Although it is not possible to go to every student's home, it is possible to learn about a community through interacting with students and parents from the neighborhood.

One of the strengths of the Funds of Knowledge approach is that it addresses the issue of school power. Many of the leading multicultural educators focus a great deal of attention on what educator Lisa Delpit (2006) calls the culture of power. The **culture of power** refers to the beliefs, behaviors, standards, and expectations for success in U.S. society as defined by the mainstream culture. Delpit believes that children in schools are asked, in both small and large ways, to give up their culture. Sometimes children give up small things, such as what they eat at lunch; sometimes the cultural elements are much larger, such as speaking Cambodian or Spanish at school. Because the Funds of Knowledge teachers build instructional units that arise out of the lived experience of their students and because they ask parents to become active instructional partners within the

Figure 3.8: Guest speakers talked about a variety of occupations such as roofer, mason, baker, candy maker, rancher, carpenter, and teacher.

Culture of power refers to the beliefs, behaviors, standards, and expectations for success in U.S. society as defined by mainstream culture.

My Journal

How Will I Integrate Culturally Relevant Teaching?

Read through the culturally relevant teaching principles. Identify the five principles that are most important to you. Explain why. Then describe how you would use the principles in your own teaching. Give an example for each principle you choose.

Culturally Relevant Teaching Principles and Practices

Principles	Practices
Educational Cultural	
Ensure that all students learn in an environment that considers multiple cultural contexts.	All children/students learn in a cultural context that can include a combination of ethnic, racial, linguistic, family, and community cultures.
Recognize that students learn skills and knowledge within cultural contexts.	Students learn within a context, and that context communicates to them what skills and knowledge they need to learn in order to be successful in life.
Recognize that language is an important cultural tool.	Language is one of the major cultural tools that shapes the way people think, learn, and identify themselves.
Use culture to construct meaningful curriculum.	Culture can be used in constructing meaningful curriculum when student cultural capital and social capital are integrated into instructional content.
Culturally Relevant Instructional	
Affirm student identities, cultural backgrounds, and linguistic heritages.	Effective teachers affirm student identities, cultural backgrounds, and linguistic heritages in their teaching.
Teach students how to self-regulate.	Exceptional educators know to teach all students how to set goals and work toward achieving them.
Build on the knowledge of students using cultural tools.	Building on the knowledge of students is critical in creating linkages with what students know and are learning; that is why the use of cultural tools like examples are key.
Teach students how to apply knowledge and skills by using culturally relevant examples.	Successful teachers use many, many culturally relevant examples in their instruction to make learning more meaningful and comprehensible to learners.
Explain concepts and skills to students and relate them into their lives.	A valuable teacher knows how to connect the curriculum to culturally relevant student stories, role models, ethnic history, family sayings, and community issues.
Engage students in active learning using student-centered methods.	Effective teachers engage students in active learning and use student-centered methods of instruction that include problem-based and issues-centered education.
Empower students to teach critical thinking and decision-making skills.	Effective teachers believe in empowering students to teach critical thinking and decision-making skills needed to succeed in a democracy and interdependent world.
Teach students how to assess their own progress.	Thriving educators know how to assess student progress using a variety of measures such as student essays, student portfolios, student projects, limited number of standardized tests, and teacher-made tests; assessments like student portfolios instruct students on how to assess themselves.
Link curriculum standards with student cultural knowledge.	Outstanding teachers know how to address curriculum standards by integrating cultural content into the curriculum.
Culturally Relevant Relationships	
Develop strong, trusting, reciprocal relationships to teach the whole student.	Effective teachers develop strong, trusting, reciprocal relationships with their students and their families, which reinforces the importance of teaching the whole student.
Hold high expectations for all students to ensure educational equity.	Effective teachers believe in educational equity and hold high expectations for all students.

classroom, the program naturally addresses this hierarchical power issue. At the same time, stronger support networks of care develop between teachers and families.

Many multiculturalists believe that the ultimate goal of schooling is to develop social action skills in students and teachers so that they become active in a changing society. While social action is a major goal of schooling, it is also important for teachers to consider whether their classroom teaching contributes to restructuring schools so that all students are academically successful. Another excellent program that teachers can learn from is the Algebra Project.

The Algebra Project: Keeping Math Real

The Algebra Project is another example of how a culturally relevant curriculum can have profound results. The Algebra Project is a culturally relevant curriculum program in math that integrates community action and math instruction. It uses an inquiry approach and was created by Robert Moses. Civil rights activist, Bob Moses, believes that all students should have equal access to education (Moses & Cobb, 2002). When Moses found that African American students were either failing algebra or not taking it, he worked with parents to develop a curriculum that used concrete student experiences or cultural models to teach mathematical skills. Like Funds of Knowledge, the Algebra Project is a holistic approach to learning. The math skills that students learned were part of a larger community project based on the values of equal access to schooling and the importance of preparing young people for college. Math was taught not only within the social context of students and their cultural knowledge, but it was part of a larger community movement.

> **The Algebra Project** is a culturally relevant curriculum program in math that integrates community action and math instruction. It use an inquiry approach and was created by Robert Moses.

This project included not only culturally familiar knowledge but also cultural information such as experiences with the subway. Moses also used social networks, which are motivations in the African American community. These are powerful social motivators for students whose elders expect them to learn math skills, because they convey the message that math skills are not just isolated skills but are needed for everyday life.

Bob Moses was concerned that African American students did not have the same access as other youth to higher-level math classes. Instead, most African American students were funneled into lower-level math courses. Algebra was a gatekeeper course for many students from underrepresented groups who wanted to go to college because students had to pass algebra to be admitted to college. Although some districts have mandated that all students have access to algebra, this has not been accomplished. Students who do not have proper preparation will not be successful in college (Silver, 1997). In addition, Moses wanted African American students to have the option to take advanced math classes in middle school and high school. Bob Moses was already committed to equality. He and his colleagues developed the transition curriculum to teach concepts in seventh and eighth grades that prepared students for higher-level courses, such as algebra, in high school.

In order to reach African American students, Moses and his colleagues felt that it was critical for young people to see the relevancy of algebra in their lives (Moses, Kamii, Swap, & Howard, 1989). Two questions that he asked parents and students to think about were: "What is algebra for?" and "Why do we want children to study it?" With Moses's direction, parents and students realized that young people needed math skills not only to get into college but also to become full members of society and develop their career dreams. Members of the community became more actively involved in schools and more aware of the importance of math skills. Moses built a strong community of people who were interested in school reform. These parents continuously participated and monitored the progress of local sites of the Algebra Project and worked with local school district teachers and administrators.

In order for the project to work, algebra had to become more than separate and unrelated theories and formulas. Moses developed a transition curriculum using the experiences of students. For example, students knew how to use the subway. The five-step instructional process is summarized in Table 3.2. Their cultural knowledge of the functions and cultural

Table 3.2 The Algebra Project: Five-Step Instructional Process
The Algebra Project uses an experiential learning process. Here are the five steps. You could also use this format to move your students from concrete to abstract understandings.
1. Students participate in a physical experience.
2. Students draw a picture or model of the experience.
3. Students discuss and write about what happened in their own words.
4. Students discuss and write about the experience in formal language.
5. Students build and use symbols to express the experience.

Moses, Robert P. & Cobb, Charles E., Jr. (2002). *Radical equations: Civil rights from Mississippi to the Algebra Project.* Boston, MA: Beacon Press.

tools like the map of the subway were used to guide learners to raise questions about math concepts such as the number line, positive and negative integers, and measuring distance. In another activity, sixth graders made lemonade from concentrate. This unit on making lemonade centered on the importance of ratio and how the concentration of the lemonade was related to proportions. Another innovative unit in the project taught ratios using African drums. Students explored the concept of proportions and ratios needed to make the drums. This particular unit used a variety of learning activities from visual, aural, and kinesthetic learning.

Using the Algebra Project, teachers guide students from concrete and meaningful knowledge to abstract concepts and theories in mathematics. Moses found that many students with whom he worked did not understand how mathematical symbols and operational signs were put together to create an idea or thought. The abstract symbols had no real meaning to some students. This project used cultural knowledge from various subgroups. The African drum unit applied ethnic knowledge to math instruction, while the units on lemonade and the subway used local and personal cultural knowledge. In all cases, the shared lives of the children were taken into consideration and affirmed the student role in constructing knowledge and learning academic skills. The results of the program were impressive. The original group of students advanced either to the college preparatory mathematics series of courses or into honors algebra or geometry (Moses et al., 1989). The students were proud of their accomplishments, and the parents and community became more involved in schools.

Common Themes in Culturally Relevant Programs

These three programs—Funds of Knowledge, The Algebra Project, and Organic Reading and Writing—provide teachers with principles and strategies that can enrich their teaching. An analysis of the programs identified shared characteristics:

- Teachers learned about their students. In each project, the educators became familiar with the culture and lives of their students within a comprehensive context. Their understanding of culture was not superficial or piece by piece.
- The lived experiences of students were integrated into the curriculum and acted as bridges to learning writing, mathematics, reading, and other academic skills and knowledge.
- Communities of learners were developed in which students became active and engaged partners and participants in the learning process.
- Parents and other community members were invited to become partners with teachers and school personnel. Some parents acted as experts and taught along with the teachers.

- Trusting and reciprocal, caring relationships were developed among students, teachers, parents, and the community, and they all became active members in the community of learners.
- Teachers created learning activities that engaged students because the activities were meaningful, relevant, and hands-on. Students understood the purpose of the units and made choices in their own learning.
- Focus was on learning and student academic success. Students were not asked to give up their culture in school and thus did not become more culturally assimilated.

These programs provide important foundational principles and practices that can be used to incorporate cross-cultural knowledge and skills within much of the district, state, and federal standards that teachers must follow in their teaching.

Consider this . . .

The Algebra Project is an ongoing program for equity in math education. Visit their website at www.algebra.org. Read about their current activities and learn about schools that have implemented the Algebra Project at their schools.

Q What do teachers in the project do to relate to the world of young people and make math relevant to their lives?

CASE STUDY — Organic Reading and Writing: Making Reading Meaningful

Culturally relevant teaching, student choice, and student life experiences are at the core of another educational program, Organic Reading and Writing. It is another holistic-oriented approach in which learning is seen within a community context. Skills are not taught in isolation; children learn to read within the context of their desire to communicate to others. This program is described by Sylvia Ashton-Warner (1986) in her book *Teacher*. Although this is an old book, the method she uses has been implemented in various formats by many teachers through the years.

Ashton-Warner described a method that she used to teach reading and writing in New Zealand, which used the vocabulary that the students suggested. Many of her students were from the Maori community. She began by having her young students identify one-word sentences. These words had great emotional value to students: for example, "Mummy," "Daddy," "ghost," "kiss," "love," "touch," "truck," and "haka" (Maori war dance). Ashton-Warner

described the best first words or key vocabulary as being the following:

- First words students learn to read must have an intense meaning.
- First words must already be part of the dynamic of life.
- First books must be made of the stuff of the child himself, whatever and wherever the child (Ashton-Warner, 1986).

Ashton-Warner found that her students could understand the importance of words quickly because the words they picked had strong meanings to them. The strong emotions of key vocabulary urged students to write complex sentences and express themselves. The stories that students wrote described life in their society. Sometimes this had to do with violence or conflict in the family or community. One of the examples a student wrote was:

> When I went to sleep.
> I dreamt about the war.
> The Chinese never won.
> The Maoris won. (Ashton-Warner, 1986)

The books they wrote were full of the drama of living and not like Dick and Jane books in which the everyday life of the characters was superficial and unreal to the students. Jane was never scared, and Dick never fell and hurt himself. Reading and writing rose out of the lives of each student and what they were afraid of and happy about.

With this method, a Maori child not only learned how to read and write but also saw that reading and writing could mean something personal and often spontaneous to them. Writing was a way to communicate with others. Reading was also a source of great individual joy. This affirmed to the students who they were and also what they could do.

Reflection Questions

Q How can you integrate student knowledge into your curriculum?

Q What have you identified that is organic to your students? The knowledge would be issues and concepts that are important and part of the everyday lives of your students.

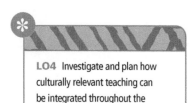

LO4 Investigate and plan how culturally relevant teaching can be integrated throughout the curriculum and instruction.

Integrating Culturally Relevant Teaching into Curriculum and Instruction

Culturally relevant teaching taps into the multiple cultures that students bring to school. As the case examples from the Yup'ik studying beavers in Alaska, Vai writing letters in West Africa, and children dealing with inflation as they sell items in Brazil demonstrate, teachers who understand the importance of culture affirm the cultural identity of students and integrate student experiences into the curriculum and instruction. In Figure 3.9, the optometrist uses culturally relevant knowledge with his patient. The young man does not want to wear classes, but the optometrist becomes a cultural mediator and reminds him that the glasses he is getting will make him look "cool" like rap artists. The optometrist tapped into the young man's subculture of rap. He was then willing to wear the glasses.

Why does using cultural elements work? Cultural elements can assist us in our teaching because they provide us with ways to enhance the learning process and make it relevant. The next section discusses how teachers can use Vygotsky's theory of the zone of proximal development and the instructional practice of scaffolding to increase the zone of learning for a student.

Using Scaffolding and Cultural Models

Cultural models and scaffolding of lessons are excellent ways that teachers can integrate the lives of their students into instruction. **Scaffolding** is the building of supports to assist students in their learning and can include visuals, explanations of how to think about a concept, modeling a skill, asking pertinent questions, and giving students feedback. Gee (1996), a sociolinguist, believes cultural tools include **cultural models**, which are systems of interconnected ideas. For example, cultural models are like videotapes or movies that are stored in a

Scaffolding refers to instructional strategies that a teacher uses to facilitate the learning of a student such as providing visuals, explaining how to think about a concept, modeling a skill, asking pertinent questions, and giving students feedback.
Cultural models are systems of interconnected ideas.

Figure 3.9: A culturally relevant optometrist knew that the student did not want to wear glasses because he did not believe wearing them was "cool." However, the optometrist became a cultural mediator by linking the new glasses to being a rapper on stage who wears sunglasses.

person's mind and represent what a person experiences in life or believes life should be. These cultural models contain a sequence or broad understanding of an aspect of life. Often, cultural models include both context and content. These tools include aspects of life such as stories, sayings, patterns of behavior, procedures or policies, and conceptual understandings. Teachers can tie into these cultural models. Here is an example from a first-grade classroom: The teacher is standing at the front of the class by the chalkboard. The children are sitting on a large rug. They have their reading textbooks open to a story they were introduced to the day before.

Teacher: What are some of the ways we read?

Rayleen: Echo reading.

Teacher: That's when we repeat after someone else.

Teacher: What's another type of reading?

Scott: Silent reading.

Teacher: How do we read silently?

Maria: We read quietly.

Teacher: Our lips are sealed and our eyes are reading. Your lips are closed. Your eyes are moving. This is silent reading.

Teacher: What's another type of reading?

Paul: Choral reading.

Teacher: Clarise, do you remember what choral reading is? That's when we do what?

Clarise: (She looks up at the teacher and doesn't answer.)

Teacher: Let's give her some wait time.

Clarise: I don't know.

Teacher: You do know. Just like when we sing together in the choir at church, we read together. That's why it is called choral reading.

In this way, Miss Valerie Grayson, a first-grade teacher, used a series of understandings. First, students knew that the people sing together as one voice. Second, they knew that people in a choir sing the same song. Third, students knew that they were to follow her lead in order for everyone to read in coordination with each other. This is an example of a cultural model. It includes a specific context—a group setting. In addition, there are particular behaviors and expectations associated with the example.

The next story is a short excerpt from a discussion in a high school English class. What cultural models does the reading evoke?

Teacher: Why did Lorraine Hansberry name her play *A Raisin in the Sun*?

Linda: I think it comes from a poem by Langston Hughes called "Harlem," in which he wrote about dreams being deferred and drying up like raisins in the sun. She is referring to how African Americans have been poorly treated.

Teacher: Why do you think Hansberry picked the image of a raisin?

Akio: Because it is the only part of Hughes's poem that could be both a negative and a positive. It could be negative in that it is rotting and drying up in the sun or it could be sweeter because as a raisin it might be more powerful.

Teacher: What is the main message of the play?

Linda: When society kills your dream, it breaks you. Walter found what was important to him. It was his family and so no matter what happened in life, his family would always be there for him and he would be there for them. His dream was to be someone, to be successful. His epiphany was that he didn't need to own a liquor store. His dream turned from owning a business to being a real part of the family.

Matt: Walter didn't want to be subservient any more. He was festering. He knew that people didn't treat him equally. Walter felt he had a dead end job. But even through all of that, he was proud of himself and didn't need the dream. He had grown past it.

Students understood the analogy of the raisin dried by the sun and presented underlying values and dreams that the raisin symbolized.

CASE STUDY   Cultural Models

A School Example

Students are expected to follow the rules in school. For example, at one particular middle school when the bell rings in the morning, the students must line up single file behind a specific number on the playground. Students wait quietly until the second bell rings, and teachers come out onto the blacktop to get their students. This way each class goes into the school in an orderly fashion.

Not only do students line up, but they know to keep their backpacks and lunch boxes with them. The students also know not to punch or touch their classmates who are also in line. They wait for the teacher to come out of the building. The teacher will then wave to the students to walk single file into the school. This is a cultural model of getting ready for school and walking into the building with good behavior.

A Family Example

When Matt was 10 years old, he went to his grandmother's eightieth birthday party in Hawaii. The family had the party at a Chinese restaurant. Everyone was smiling and talking. Matt sat next to his Auntie Sara at a round table with nine other people. This was a big birthday celebration, and the family honored their grandmother with a nine-course dinner.

Many years ago, Matt's grandmother traveled to Hawaii from Canton, China, by ship when she was only 15 years old. She was betrothed to his grandfather, who at that time was about 25 years old. The couple eventually had eight children. His grandfather died when Matt was 4 years old and left his grandmother as matriarch of the family.

In honor of the grandmother, the family had golden peach pins for everyone. Peaches symbolize long life, and so every family member was given not only pins but also vases with peaches painted on the front panel. Paper-folded cranes were also on the table to signify longevity. Cranes live a long time.

As each course of food was brought out to the table and served, Matt became fuller. He wanted to rest his stomach, so he stuck his chopsticks into his bowl of rice. The chopsticks stuck straight up. His Auntie Sara placed her hand on his shoulder and whispered, "Matt, don't do that because it means death."

Matt quickly took the chopsticks from his bowl of rice and placed them on his white dinner plate; his face was slightly red because he was embarrassed. He knew children were not supposed to do anything to bring disgrace to their family. Just like in school, children were supposed to act properly.

One of the nine courses was a noodle dish. Noodles are served at birthday parties in many Chinese and Chinese American families because noodles are long and therefore represent a long life. When the large blue platter of noodles was pushed before Matt on the table's lazy Susan, he took the large spoon and began to put noodles on his plate. However, some noodles were falling off the serving plate so he cut them with the spoon. His Auntie Sara frowned and leaned down toward Matt gently whispering in his ear. This time she said, "Matt, don't cut your noodles or you will be cutting the life of your grandmother short."

The young man quickly scooped the noodles onto his plate and pushed the lazy Susan toward the next diner.

In the course of the meal, each person was also given a small packet of dried coconut and fruit that had a sugar coating. The sweetness of the dessert represented more sweetness in life for his grandmother.

Matt learned much about the importance of long life and symbols of longevity within a cultural family context. He understood more clearly not only the explicit aspects of culture, but he also knew that he had to obey elder members of his family like his auntie. The education of children is often given not only by parents, but also grandparents, aunts, uncles, and other important family friends. It wasn't only that it took a village to educate a child, but also that he, as a child, had to treat all elders in the village with respect.

Like most children, Matt learned values and beliefs besides other cultural elements like traditions and customs through social interactions with family members. The example demonstrated that Matt grew up in a supportive extended family context. His learning came not only from direct statements from his auntie but also from other elements like tone of voice and nonverbal behaviors of other family members. The birthday party was a powerful cultural context for learning. Matt learned in more detail which behaviors were expected and accepted, while learning cultural values that emphasized longevity, respect for grandparents, and the importance of obedience and harmony in the family. This birthday party was a powerful cultural model that included many values and expected behaviors. The cultural model includes not only a specific context or situation but also cultural values.

Reflection Question

Q Can you identify another cultural model that teachers may use to teach students how to behave in school and at home?

Cultural Model of Student Preparing for School

The cultural model or "short movie" in Matt's mind in the case study included not only appropriate behavior and underlying values about family roles but also the meaning of cultural symbols such as peaches and cranes. My friend's cultural model about his grandmother's birthday included the importance of family role models such as his aunt and her authority to teach him appropriate behavior in this social context.

Here is another example of a cultural model and how cultural models may differ depending on the cultural backgrounds of students. In a mostly African American first-grade classroom, the teacher was going over test-taking skills and the importance of reading each word carefully. As you know, a cultural model of test-taking includes certain instructions about how to mark the correct answers. Tests also include vocabulary; some words are more familiar to some students than to others. One of the vocabulary words on this particular test was the term *brush*. That seemed simple to the teacher. The students were supposed to look at the picture of a hair brush on the left and then circle the correctly spelled word on the right side of the box. Many students in this class missed this item. The teacher wasn't sure why.

One of the best readers in the class was Eugene. He was able to read at a second-grade level, so the teacher couldn't understand why he missed what she thought was an easy vocabulary word.

She asked Eugene to help her stack up the tests. He smiled.

The teacher showed him the top page of the practice test and pointed to the picture of the hair brush. He looked at it and his eyes went blank.

"Eugene, do you know what this is a picture of?" He shook his head no.

She was flabbergasted. Thinking that he was teasing, the teacher looked at him again and asked in a puzzled voice, "You really don't know what this is?"

Eugene was beginning to look worried. His forehead wrinkled.

"I'm not sure."

The teacher could see from his nonverbal reaction that he was not pulling her leg, so she said, "It's a hair brush."

Immediately Eugene said, "Oh, that's right. But I don't use one. I use a pick in my hair."

This is an example of how cultural models can have different meanings depending on a person's cultural background and contexts. Eugene used a pick to style his hair, while the teacher used a brush. They had developed two different cultural models of taking care of their hair. This example showed how cultural knowledge learned at home can conflict with the cultural knowledge of schools. However, cultural knowledge can be used by teachers as examples of subject area principles being taught. The next section provides examples from the playground and shows how they can be used in a physics classroom.

Cultural Models on the Playground

People who teach math and science often have difficulty understanding the importance of culture in learning. They see math and science as value-free and culture-free. As discussed in Chapter 2, knowledge is culture bound. Scientists discover new information within a cultural context. The interpretations of one scientist may differ from those of another because of cultural background (Gould, 1996). For example, the issue of race is seen differently in biology versus the social sciences. Biologists may not see race as a social construct; however, sociologists understand race from a sociopolitical orientation. In addition, teachers may see culture only as ethnic culture. As this book has indicated, culture is much broader. Many teachers believe that when asked about the cultural backgrounds of their students, they are being asked about ethnic cultures. However, no matter where teachers live, there are likely many diverse subcultures in the area. Even if a community is all White, the individuals in the area may represent different social classes and have different hobbies and religions.

One way to connect math and science to the lives of students is to look at the cultural movies and at the tools on the playground. The cultures that students bring to school can be used to make teaching more meaningful. Figure 3.10 shows how math can be tied to the daily experiences of students.

Many children enjoy a playground, and their science and math learning can be tied to a play area. The drawings in Figure 3.10 are an excellent way to show students that math can be used to describe aspects of everyday life. These are examples of cultural models on the playground. For example, most young people know about climbing up the ladder of a slide

Figure 3.10: Tie science and math learning into play.

and then going down the incline. This is a familiar cultural model. A physics teacher can make connections between various math formulas and experiences on the playground on the swing, merry-go-round, and slide. For example, in the upper left-hand corner of the drawing, the student thinks about the time it takes to make a complete swing, forwards and backwards. The upper right corner of the drawing shows a student going down the slide and the formula given is for acceleration of the student. The lower left corner shows the young person on a merry-go-round type of ride, and she is thinking about the formula for centripetal force.

Math is the language of science, and the symbols in the drawings are good examples of how the teacher needs to understand the objects, share knowledge of the toys, and understand each situation to understand the physical concepts and formulas of the playground. Unless you studied the culture of math and physics, you probably would not understand the concepts that were explained by the formulas in the drawings. As in any classroom, when students do not understand the language, symbols, and accepted practices of schools, they, like those who had trouble translating these drawings, may find themselves unable to comprehend what teachers are trying to teach. This shows the importance of culture in learning and teaching.

Consider this . . .

Teachers can use examples from students' lives as a way to build on what students know in the learning process. Remember, using lots of culturally relevant examples is an excellent way to build a bridge from what students know to what they are learning!

Q How can you remember the examples that students share in class and use them in your own teaching?

Key Culturally Relevant Content Elements

Sometimes it is difficult to think of culturally relevant elements that connect with students' lives. Consider integrating **culturally relevant elements** into your curriculum: they include student personal experiences, role models, culturally relevant stories/legends/folktales/songs, photos/pictures, linguistic expressions, multiple perspectives, formal subject content, and community issues. Table 3.3 lists the seven elements and examples of what could be included in a lesson or unit.

> **Culturally relevant elements** that can be integrated into lessons: student personal experiences, role models, culturally relevant stories/legends/folktales/songs, photos/pictures, linguistic expressions, multiple perspectives, formal subject content, and community issues.

Teachers who value their students learn about and integrate cultural elements naturally into their teaching. This creates a more caring and comfortable environment and also builds a more effective learning atmosphere. Though textbooks provide some information, teachers can integrate numerous examples of concepts, ideas, structures, and perspectives from the lives of their students. The insertion of culturally relevant content and contexts to learning affirms student cultures and creates links in the learning process. Teachers can choose to do so in working to make learning meaningful to students. As Gee wrote, "Just as many women have sought to replace our cultural models of gender roles with new ways of thinking, interacting, and speaking, so humans at their best are always open to rethinking, to imagining newer and better, more just and more beautiful words and worlds. That is why good teaching is ultimately a moral act" (Gee, 1996, p. 89).

Integrating community issues into the curriculum can be used to teach higher-order thinking skills such as evaluation, analysis, creation, and transformation. The Take a Stand feature provides some ideas that teachers might bring into their classrooms.

Table 3.3 Key Culturally Relevant Content Elements and Examples

Element	Example 1	Example 2
Personal Experiences	Student uses words from her spelling list and writes a story about a time when she felt special.	Using grammatical rules, the student writes a story about her quinceañera and why it is important to her. What does the event represent?
Role Models	A student may choose a parent to research and write an essay. A student may also want to draw a picture of the role model.	A student may choose someone like Helen Keller, Rosa Parks, Fred Korematsu, or Cesar Chavez to research and write an essay.
Songs	A student may choose to share with her class the song, *Des Colores*, which is often sung during civil rights marches.	A student may choose to share a song his father would sing to him at bedtime.
Photos/Pictures/Drawings	A student may share a photo of when he was a baby and a picture of his family.	A student might share a photo from her family history. A student may create a photo timeline of her life.
Linguistic phrases or terms	*Des Colores* refers to unity of a community to many in the Latino community.	*Gambare* means "grin and bear it" in Japanese.
Multiple Perspectives	A student may share his view of why his home language is important to him.	A student may share various subcultural identities that she holds, from being a daughter to being a pianist.
Formal Discipline Content	A student may share her great grandmother's journal of her experiences during the internment of Japanese Americans during WWII, which can be woven into the language arts curriculum about autobiographies.	A student may share information about his religious practices and beliefs as part of the K–12 social studies curriculum. Discussion should be about religions and not endorse or belittle any particular faith.
Community Issues	A student may share her concern regarding the treatment of her sister who has Down Syndrome by the sister's peers in a middle school.	A student may share his concern about the lack of funds for an LBGTQ club at a local high school.

Adapted from *Multicultural Education: A Caring-Centered, Reflective Approach*, by Valerie Ooka Pang, 2010, San Diego, CA: Montezuma Publishing.

TAKE A STAND USING COMMUNITY ISSUES

One of the most important curriculum components of caring-centered multicultural education is the inclusion of public issues. Not only do students learn various points of views, but they also develop vital higher-order thinking skills. In a democracy, people make decisions that impact others. Take time to consider what the critical issues are in your local area.

Here are several points to consider:

▶ List three important issues that students' face today or should have the opportunity to think about.

▶ What evidence can you share to support your stand?

▶ What should students, staff, and faculty do to address this issue?

If you are unable to think of important issues that students could consider in schools, please read through the following:

Middle through High School
Subject Areas: Social Studies Political Science, Government
Issue: Immigration
Focal Unit Questions:

▶ What criteria should the United States use in deciding who should be allowed to immigrate to this country?

▶ What responsibilities do we as a country have to new immigrants? To refugees?

Grade Level: 9–12
Subject Areas: Social Studies, Civics, U.S. History, U.S. Literature
Issue: High-Stakes Testing: Scholastic Aptitude Test (SAT)
Focal Unit Questions:

▶ Are SAT scores a true predictor of how successful a student will be in college? Why or why not?

▶ What methods should be used to measure the academic competence of students?

Grade Level: 9–12
Subject Areas: Statistics, Social Studies, Sociology
Issue: Gender Equity in Sports
Focal Unit Questions:

▶ What proportion of the sports budget should women's and men's sports receive?

▶ Should the funding be the same for women and men? Why or why not?

▶ Should the funding depend on the cost of the sport? Should it depend on revenue the sport brings to the school? Why or why not?

Grade Level: 5–12
Subject Areas: Social Studies, U.S. History, Sociology, Government, Civics, Women's Studies
Issue: Women and Equity
Focal Unit Questions:

▶ What are the major contributions of women in the area of science?

▶ How have the contributions of women been taught in the schools? Why?

▶ How should teachers address this issue?

Grade Level: 5–12
Subject Areas: Social Studies, American Literature, U.S. History, Sociology, Sciences, Government, Civics, Women's Studies
Issue: Violence in Schools
Focal Unit Questions:

▶ What types of school violence are most prevalent in your school?

▶ Why does school violence exist?

▶ What can we do to prevent it?

Grade Level: 4–12
Subject Areas: Social Studies, Sociology, Government, Civics
Issue: Ethnic Segregation in the Cafeteria
Focal Unit Questions:

▶ Where do students choose to sit in the cafeteria?

▶ What are the seating patterns?

▶ Do the seating arrangements students choose show an integrated community? Why or why not?

Grade Level: 4–12
Subject Areas: Social Studies, U.S. History, Sociology, Government, Civics
Issue: Popular Music
Focal Unit Questions:

▶ What impact does rap music have on young people and their ideas about women, issues of culture/ethnicity, and aggressive behavior?

▶ Should rap be used in the curriculum? Why or why not?

Grade Level: 6–12
Subject Areas: Music, Sociology, Social Studies
Issue: Affirmative Action
Focal Unit Questions:

▶ What is the purpose of affirmative action?

▶ Should our country continue to support affirmative programs? Why or why not?

Primary and Elementary Level
Subject Areas: Social Studies, Government, Civics
Issue: Social Activism
Focal Unit Questions:

▶ Can children take leadership roles in social change? Why or why not?

▶ What leadership roles have children played in civil rights?

▶ What contributions did Ruby Bridges make to our lives?

Grade Level: 1–5
Subject Areas: Citizenship, Social Studies, Health
Issue: Name-Calling
Focal Unit Questions:

▶ Is name-calling a problem in the school?

▶ What evidence demonstrates your viewpoint?

▶ What is our responsibility when we hear people call others names?

▶ What should we do? Why?

▶ What should the school's policy be toward name-calling? Why?

Grade Level: K–12
Subject Areas: Language Arts/ English, Social Studies, Government, Civics
Issue: Heroes
Focal Unit Questions:

▶ Who is your hero?

▶ What qualities do you think a hero should have?

▶ What definition would you give for a hero?

Consider this . . .

Culture can be used in constructing meaningful curriculum when student cultural and social capital are integrated into instructional content. If you do not live in the school area, learn about your students by visiting organizations or places in their neighborhoods.

Q What things can you do as a teacher to get to know the cultural backgrounds and beliefs of your students?

Q Have you ever gone to a grocery store where you know your students and their families shop?

Q Have you ever gone to a church that you know your students and their families attend?

My Journal

Integrating Culturally Relevant Teaching into My Curriculum and Instruction

Q *Reflecting on the four holistic educational projects discussed in this chapter—Funds of Knowledge, the Algebra Project, Organic Reading and Writing, and Cultural Modeling—what are eight common elements that you found among all of the programs?*

Q *Which strategies are most important with number one being the most important to use in your teaching?*

Culturally Relevant Curriculum: Examples

The following sections give examples of culturally relevant curriculum that are hands-on and engage students. It is important for teachers to provide lessons where students get the opportunity to learn by doing.

Lesson in Science: Magnets and Coins

Science is an extremely interesting discipline, yet it can include difficult concepts to teach. However, science experiments can also be among the most effective lessons because students are engaged in hands-on activities in which they discover various properties and principles. Teachers should consider including more science in the curriculum because for many students of color and women, science is an area in which they have had little exposure or they have not had the opportunity to learn in depth. Most schools focus on reading and some math, especially in elementary school. However, because science education is an equity issue, teachers need to teach many more science lessons in their classes.

It is really important for teachers to make opportunities to integrate culturally relevant teaching into their classroom. One way to get parents and students involved in science, for example, is to put on a science learning fair each year (Pang, Lafferty, Pang, Griswold, & Oser, 2014). The learning fair can be held every year at the same time and on a Saturday so families can attend (Figure 3.11).

One example is a recent fall festival that was centered on the scientific concepts of magnetism and electromagnetism (Pang et al., 2014). Table 3.4 lists the National Science Education Standards for grades K–4 on magnetism and electricity.

Because the science learning fair is held outside, multiple teams of teachers may create a booth where they teach their lessons. The booths must include:

- Clear lesson plans with identified content standards and clear vocabulary.
- A large canopy with tables to create a learning space.

Figure 3.11: Two brothers investigate the influence of wind on a small floating boat made from a soda can.

- The title of the booth on a large banner attached to the front of the canopy in Spanish and English.
- Well-developed posters to help teach the science concepts and principles. Posters must be translated into English and Spanish, and should have photos or drawings to teach the concepts and principles.
- Science standards included on posters.
- All materials needed for the experiment.
- Prizes (optional) for students (not candy) and written flyers for parents with directions for conducting the experiments at home.

Figure 3.12 shows a banner for one of the lessons that teachers developed to involve students in discovering the properties of a magnet.

Instructional objectives:

- Students explain that a magnet has two poles, a north pole and a south pole.
- Students explain and show that magnets are attracted (pull toward) objects that have iron, nickel, or cobalt in them.
- Students explain that there are many objects that are not attracted to magnets.
- Students demonstrate that not all coins are attracted to a magnet.
- Students identify which countries have coins that are attracted to a magnet.

To extend the learning, older students can be asked to observe, predict, ask questions, and analyze their observations. Teachers give students opportunities to explore and investigate on their own as they learn about various science concepts and principles.

Figure 3.12: This is an example of one of the posters created for use at the learning fair.

Table 3.4 National Science K–4 Education Standards on Magnetism and Electricity			
Science Area	Content Standard	Fundamental Principles and Content	Discussion of Student Understanding
Physical Science	Light, Heat, Electricity, and Magnetism	Magnets attract and repel each other and certain kinds of other materials.	By experimenting with light, heat, electricity, magnetism, and sound, students begin to understand that phenomena can be observed, measured, and controlled in various ways.

National Science Education Standards, National Academy of Sciences, 1996. Retrieved from http://www.nap.edu/catalog/4962.html.

Lesson activities:

- Ask students if they have ever held a magnet and then ask them what a magnet can do.
- Explain to students that magnets are attracted to objects that have iron, nickel, and cobalt in them.
- Show students objects that have iron, nickel, and cobalt in them and how the magnet is attracted to these items.
- Ask students to place the magnet next to objects on the table that they think the magnet will be attracted to.
- Ask students to describe what happens when the object is attracted to the magnet.
- Ask students what happens when the object is not attracted to the magnet.

Inserting Cultural Relevant Elements into the Science Lesson The lesson above, however, looks pretty similar to any other lesson. How can a teacher make the lesson culturally relevant? The teachers work with lots of Spanish-speaking students in the area. Many of the children go to Mexico to visit relatives, so they know how to use U.S. coins and Mexican coins.

A group of teachers had two sets of coins on a piece of a paper labeled U.S. coins and Mexican coins. They asked all children, many of whom were Mexican American, which coins would be magnetic. All of the children in grades K–6 thought the U.S. coins would be magnetic. They did not think that the coins from Mexico would be attracted to the magnet that they held in their hand.

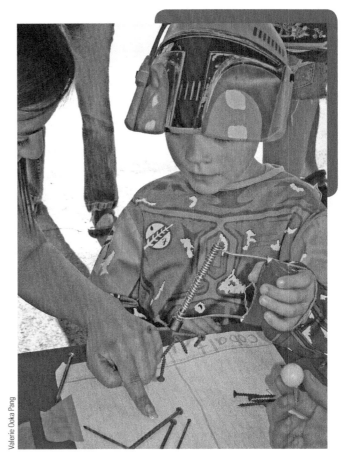

Valerie Ooka Pang

Figure 3.13: This student is experimenting with the construct of magnetism.

What do you think would happen? Take a second and think about magnets and coins.

There's something about the power of a magnet. It is fun to play with, but as the science standards explain, it is important for children to observe and think.

The children found out, like the young boy in Figure 3.13, that the coins from the United States are not magnetic. They may be made of metal, but they do not have enough iron, nickel, or cobalt in them to attract a magnet. In fact, the U.S. nickel is largely made of copper and some nickel, but not enough to be attracted to a magnet. Most U.S. coins are made primarily of copper, and that is why some pennies will turn green because the copper and oxygen oxidize. The children were surprised that Mexican money was magnetic. Many Mexican coins are made of iron. For example, the 5 and 10 cents centavos are made primarily of iron.

Young students think that anything that looks like metal must be magnetic. They do not realize that only specific metals are attracted to magnets. Using coins that children are familiar with provides them with opportunities to observe and make connections with their lives. The use of culturally relevant objects the students were already familiar with, like the centavos from Mexico, gave more relevance to students who often visited their grandparents and uncles in Tijuana. Finally, the teachers used an assessment process to measure whether students were learning the concepts about magnetism.

Assessment:

- Ask students which metals are attracted to magnets.
- Ask students how many poles magnets have and to identify their names.
- Ask students to identify which objects on the table were attracted to magnets and why.
- Ask students what it means when an objected is attracted to a magnet.
- Ask students why the Mexican centavos are attracted to magnets and why the U.S. coins were not.

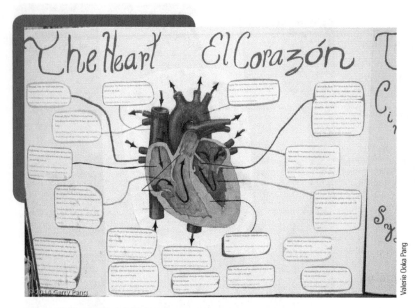

Figure 3.14: This is a bilingual poster of the heart so Spanish-speaking parents understand what was being taught in this lesson.

Pre-service teachers also created posters with both English and Spanish words to ensure that parents who did not know English well would also know which concepts were being taught at each booth. Figure 3.14 is a sample poster that has both English and Spanish and talks about how the heart works.

Lesson in Social Studies: Malcolm X: Literacy, Humanity, and Civil Rights

Integrating content that interests students can be a powerful learning tool to help teach critical thinking. A familiar figure for many students from underrepresented groups is **Malcolm X.** One teacher told the author why he chooses to incorporate the life of Malcolm X into his curriculum and classroom.

The teacher said, "I have a picture of Malcolm X and Martin Luther King, Jr., on my wall. Malcolm X and Martin are in a picture together and they are pointing at the temple of their minds; they're pointing to their minds as thinkers. No matter what went on in their life personally, they stood for their values of equality . . . and were willing to die for them. And I gear more towards Malcolm because of his experience with losing his parents and being street-wise and then converting into religion, then rising to become international and not just national . . . I use Malcolm's life as a parable."

The teacher continued to explain what students can learn from the life of Malcolm X.

"He is a hero to many African American males, especially those who are struggling in life. Malcolm is also a role model with Mexican American males . . . because of what they've been through, what their ancestors have been through . . ."

When asked to talk about what life-related issues learning about Malcolm brings to students, this teacher said, "We have to realize we're all human. We make mistakes. We have to reach down [to our inner strength]. And this is what Malcolm X did. He reached down to people [African Americans and others who have been marginalized by society. He fought racism all of his adult life]. Martin did this, too. But Martin had the degree that Caucasians respected. Malcolm got his 'degree' while in jail, studying when it was nighttime, staying up late reading the dictionary, learning the words of the slave master, and using them to protect himself when others tried to attack him . . . He studied so much that it caused him to have to wear glasses because he had strained his eyes reading for long periods at night. Malcolm knew that truth is knowledge and those without knowledge are the ones who are left behind or they're left with the left-overs . . . I tell my students that they're a slave to the system if they don't have the knowledge in order to combat ignorance."

The teacher shared his insider viewpoint and beliefs about Malcolm X. He gave a rich perspective about Malcolm X's life and how, as an African American male, he was moved by Malcolm X's work and dedication to the community.

Malcolm X is the teacher's role model, and Malcolm's life represents to him the struggle that the educator and his family go through every day. He gathers strength and a clearer understanding of his own role as a teacher from reflecting on Malcolm X's life, because Malcolm cared passionately about people, especially those whom society had abandoned.

Another colleague recommended to the teacher Theresa Perry's book, *Teaching Malcolm X*. This edited volume presents effective ways to examine and use the life and values of Malcolm X in a classroom that is based on democratic reflective thinking and dedicated to a compassionate and just society. Consider reading the text because Perry clearly explains the following important beliefs of Malcolm X:

"Reading and writing affirms one's humanity."
"Reading and writing is an act of resistance."
"Literacy is freedom."
(Perry, 1996, pp. 9, 18)

Malcolm X had a passionate love of reading and learning and became a voracious reader. As a child, he had been an excellent student and was well liked by his peers. He was someone who also believed in the equal rights and the freedoms of every citizen and was willing to speak out and ultimately to die for his beliefs. In studying Malcolm X, students understand not only the work of an individual, but also how he exemplified courage in the face of deep-seated racism and challenged members of the community to become active in their own learning and in the restructuring of a better society. Because students must be able to interpret, analyze, synthesize, and evaluate information, they must be taught how to examine complicated issues and problems.

Many teachers are unsure how an issues-centered curriculum differs from a thematic approach. Table 3.5 demonstrates the difference between a theme and an **issues-centered approach** to curriculum. The case study on Malcolm X was an example of an issue-centered approach, where students gained a broader understanding of Malcolm X's contributions and the role he played in the civil rights we enjoy today. In addition, students learned about the social context of the time.

> **Issues-centered approach**
> is a method that is taught to students so they develop skills to make important decisions in their personal lives and as citizens of a democracy and the world.

Teachers raised the following questions to guide them while developing a unit on Malcolm X:

1. How might your personal values bias your teaching of Malcolm X? How can you best present the material in a fair and responsible way?
2. What are ways to teach both the strengths and weaknesses of Malcolm X's life?

Table 3.5 Comparing a Theme Approach to an Issues-Centered Approach

Theme Topics in the Life of Malcolm X	Focal Questions of an Issues-Centered Unit on Malcolm X
The Life of Malcolm X	1. What impact did Malcolm X's parents have on his values? 2. How did Malcolm X's early life influence his later work? 3. Was civil rights important to Malcolm X? If so, how? 4. What role, if any, did Malcolm X play in the Civil Rights Movement and U.S. history? 5. Why did Malcolm X believe racism had to be addressed before Black Americans could achieve civil rights in the United States? 6. Which social issues did Malcolm X believe were the most pressing during his life time? Why? How did he suggest that the nation and African Americans address them? 7. What if Malcolm X had never lived?
Civil Rights	1. How did Malcolm X view the civil rights movement? 2. Which civil rights issues were most important to Malcolm X? Why? 3. Did literacy contribute to his participation in the civil rights movement? Why or why not? 4. Did Malcolm X believe literacy development was important to the civil rights movement? Why or why not?
Freedom	1. Did Malcolm X believe that education and freedom were linked? Why or why not? 2. How can reading and writing impact community and political roles? 3. What role does education play in a democratic nation?
Malcolm X: His Life and Work	1. Are people aware of Malcolm X's life? Why or why not? 2. Should students study his life? Why or why not? 3. If you believe that Malcolm X's life should be studied, which aspects of his life are most important?
Literacy and Self Affirmation	1. How did Malcolm X link literacy to what it means to be human? 2. How can literacy be used to affirm a person's humanity?

Table 3.6 Aligning History: Social Science Standards on Malcolm X, State of California, into Grade 11 Teaching

History Social Science Standard for California Public Schools	Content
11.10 Students analyze the development of federal civil rights and voting rights.	Examine the roles of civil rights advocates (e.g., A. Philip Randolph, Martin Luther King, Jr., Malcolm X, Thurgood Marshall, James Farmer, and Rosa Parks), including the significance of Martin Luther King, Jr.'s "Letter from Birmingham Jail" and "I Have a Dream" speech.

California Content Standards for Social Studies, 2009. Retrieved from http://www.cde.ca.gov/be/st/ss/documents/histsocscistnd.pdf.

3. How can you teach about racism and systems of privilege in a way that will not alienate students who come from privileged status groups?
4. What values of the African American community does Malcolm X represent?

Malcolm X is named in the History Social Science Standards for the State of California in Grade 11, shown in Table 3.6; this example reminds us that teachers need to examine their state standards for the inclusion of role models such as Malcolm X in the curriculum.

Table 3.7 shows how concepts such as culture, power, identity, and civic practices are part of the **National Council for the Social Studies, National Curriculum Standards for Social Studies.** The National Council for the Social Studies is the largest professional association for social studies education. All teachers should consider these if they are discussing issues of civic ideas, civic values, and civic practices.

> **National Council for the Social Studies, National Curriculum Standards for the Social Studies** is a document that identifies standards for social studies from K–12.

Teaching an Issues-Centered Unit on Malcolm X

Inquiry and decision making in issues-centered education comes from the work of educators Shirley Engle and Anna Ochoa (1988). They believed in teaching abstract-thinking skills to students. See Table 3.8 for an adaptation of their instructional models, which guide students through the identification, research, decision making, and action of an issue. It shows one way that the life and work of Malcolm X can be taught in an issues-centered classroom. There is a problem or decision that is posed at the start of the unit. Focal and subunit questions guide students while they study an issue. The questions included in this curriculum on Malcolm X are suggestions only, and your students may create other insightful ones. The more involved students become in shaping the study of an issue, the

Table 3.7 National Council for the Social Studies, National Curriculum Standards for Social Studies

Culture	Time, Continuity, and Change	Individual Development and Identity	Power, Authority, and Governance	Civic Ideals and Practices
Cultures are dynamic and change over time.	Knowledge and understanding of the past enable us to analyze the causes and consequences of events and developments, and to place these in the context of the institutions, values, and beliefs of the periods in which they took place.	Personal identity is shaped by an individual's culture, by groups, by institutional influences, and by lived experiences shared with people inside and outside the individual's own culture throughout her or his development.	The development of civic competence requires an understanding of the foundations of political thought, and the historical development of various structures of power, authority, and governance. It also requires knowledge of the evolving functions of these structures in contemporary U.S. society, as well as in other parts of the world.	An understanding of civic ideals and practices is critical to full participation in society and is an essential component of education for citizenship, which is the central purpose of social studies.

National Curriculum Standards for Social Studies: A Framework for Teaching, Learning, and Assessment, National Council for the Social Studies, 2010, Silver Springs, Maryland: National Council for the Social Studies.

Table 3.8 The Steps of An Issues-centered Approach: Teaching Malcolm X	
Orientation: Students begin to think about the life of Malcolm X.	Teacher brings in a poster of Malcolm X. **Focal Question:** • What role did Malcolm X play in the Civil Rights Movement? **Subunit questions:** • What were the social issues that Malcolm X passionately addressed in his life? Are those issues still prevalent today? • Which events in Malcolm X's life affected him the most? Why? • Did Malcolm X believe that education was freedom? Why or why not? • What impact does his race have on how people perceive Malcolm X? Teacher has students read the *Autobiography of Malcolm X* (high school/adult level) by Alex Haley or *By Any Means Necessary: Malcolm X* (middle school level) by Walter Dean Myers. Students begin to explore and clarify aspects of Malcolm X's life. They pose and answer the following questions: • Who was Malcolm X? • Before this unit, what did you know about his life? • What were his goals? Were any of them like yours? • Why are there many misconceptions about him? • Who killed him and why? • What does the *X* stand for and why doesn't he have a last name? • Was he racist?
Identification: Students identify key issues that are important to study and research. They also define terms and concepts.	Students collaboratively make a time line of Malcolm X's life. They also find other materials to read about Malcolm X. In addition, the class lists key issues that would provide important new understandings and knowledge. Students may also write statements about what they learned while discussing Malcolm X. • Through literacy people could more effectively fight social oppression. • Freedom of the mind was more important than freedom of the body. • People must work for and be committed to community and the struggle for equality. • Malcolm X fought for the rights of all people, especially people such as African Americans, who had not been treated equally. Students identify different perspectives about Malcolm X. Some people think he was an important leader in the Civil Rights Movement. Others believe he was a hoodlum and was destructive because he defied the law. They can organize the information they have found. Students can identify various communities and individuals and how they differ in their views of Malcolm X.
Evidence and Multiple Perspectives: Students seek evidence and describe multiple views and perspectives of the issue.	Students identify different perspectives about Malcolm X. They can organize the information they have found. Students can identify various communities and individuals and how they differ in their views of Malcolm X. Students review original unit focal and subunit questions to decide if they have gathered sufficient information to answer those questions.
Values and Beliefs: Students identify their own values and beliefs in relation to the person, event, or issue being studied.	Students identify and discuss their own values. Students identify and discuss the values of others. For example: • "I thought Malcolm X believed in violence. I can see that he didn't want violence. He believed in community, but also wanted to challenge the system. I agree, but I don't have the courage he had." • "Malcolm X was too angry and couldn't see part of his anger. Although I felt bad about what happened to him, I think he shouldn't have been as aggressive. That ties in so much with the stereotypes about African American men." • "I never thought that education gave me freedom in my mind. I thought it was just something I had to do." • "Malcolm X was about reading and doing. He was awesome. He is my role model now. I think I will try to do better in school because I can be somebody." • "I believe teachers are afraid to talk about him because they don't know what might happen. Maybe kids will get too aggressive." • "Malcolm knew it took courage to speak out. People should stand up to change things, not sit back and just complain about how things are."
Solutions/Perspectives and Their Consequences: Students deal with value and ethical conflicts and differences. Students begin to identify various ways to resolve a problem or make a decision and explain consequences of each.	Teacher again asks the focal question: What role did Malcolm X play in the Civil Rights Movement? What if Malcolm X had never lived, how would that have influenced the outcome of the movement? Students share their views about the impact of Malcolm X on today's youth and society. Teacher asks about consequences of each student position/decision. Possible student discussions: • "I believe Malcolm X was a critical person in our civil rights history. He challenged people to do something about unfairness in society."

(*continued*)

Table 3.8 The Steps of An Issues-centered Approach: Teaching Malcolm X (Continued)

	• "If we talk about him, people might get mad at each other. He brings up stuff from the past. What happened to Blacks in the past is over. It is only adding salt to the wound so I do not think he played an important role." • "If we don't talk about him, then we are discounting the contribution of a person from the Black community. There is already so much rage about being left out of society or not being treated fairly." • "Malcolm X's life was one of transformation and change. He was a Black man challenging a White power structure so that's why he is important to the civil rights movement. "
Take a Stand and Justify a Decision: Students provide their argument about why they chose their position.	Students reply to unit focal question in Orientation stage: • "I still believe Malcolm X is an important role model in the fight for civil rights." • "I thought Malcolm X was about violence, but he was really about education because he thought education gave people freedom, freedom of the mind, and that is what was most important." • "Malcolm X was too violent. He broke laws. Is that right? We must all follow the law or else there would be chaos. He might have gone about getting equality in other ways, more like Martin Luther King, Jr., using nonviolence." • "Malcolm X stood for all people no matter what their race. He stood for equality and justice. That goes above any one color. He played a critical role in our nation."
Action: Students develop an action plan.	• Students may write a letter to the history department in the school asking that more time be spent on the life of Malcolm X. • Students may give the autobiography to their friends to read and discuss it with them. • Students may decide to volunteer in an after school program helping younger students with their homework because they see how important education, and literacy in particular, is to kids.

❯❯ Professional Resource Download

more effective the unit/lesson will be. Decision making and inquiry learning are important strategies identified by the National Council for the Social Studies in teaching higher-order thinking skills.

Often teachers use a topic orientation of teaching content. This refers to using a theme or topic as the core of the lesson. An issues-centered approach focuses on the presentation of an issue that students grapple with and arrive at a solution. It is similar to a project-based orientation; however, the learning is shaped by the use of focal open-ended questions and identification of the learner's values in a democracy.

Back to School Night: Teaching Parents about Culturally Relevant Education

Sometimes it is not easy for teachers to explain certain educational approaches to parents. A student's parent may not have had the opportunity to learn this way when they were a child so they may need a good example, or explanation from their child's teacher. One of the best ways to teach parents about culturally relevant education is to give them a cultural model from their own lives. For example, most parents probably like to go to the movies. Sometimes they need to decide whether to take their children to the movies with them or to get a baby sitter. You have probably seen the letter ratings on movies such as "G," which means the film is for general audiences or all ages. From "G" the next rating is "PG," which means parental guidance is suggested. A "PG-13" rating suggests that children under the age of thirteen should be accompanied by a parent or guardian. Some parents might find these ratings a little difficult to decipher, so the Motion Picture Association of America wanted to make it clear to parents how to decide which movies might be most appropriate for their children. To do this they came up with the guidelines outlined in Figure 3.15.

The culturally relevant notice in Figure 3.15 gives parents more information than do the ratings of G, PG, PG-13, R, and NC-17 alone. For example, R is explained as the rating in which parents should "Think before taking your kids." These specific ideas help parents understand what each symbol represents to the Motion Picture Association of America. It also provides a concrete, culturally relevant guide that teachers can use to help parents understand what is best for their child.

Lesson Using Culturally Relevant Stories, Songs, and Literature

Culturally Relevant Stories

Culturally relevant stories, songs, and literature may come in the form of myths, legends, and folktales. These stories, often handed down from generation to generation, are not necessarily what the general society calls formal literature. An example is a story of the origin of a community such as the Haida, a Native American indigenous community in the Pacific Northwest. The community believes that they arose out of a clam shell that a raven found on the shore of the ocean (Council of the Haida Nation, 2013). The people see the raven as a trickster who was mischievous, but who also brought the Haida salmon and water. Many indigenous people believe they arose from specific animals like the bear or raven. Teachers need to think before using terms such as legend, myth, or folktale in the classroom because the stories represent important cultural accounts that communities use to guide their lives. If teachers do not understand the underlying values that the story is trying to convey, the deep cultural meanings might be lost. Students may remember the story line, but not much about the belief system of a community. Teachers can relate the stories of Native peoples somewhat to stories found in the Bible. Many people believe in what is written in the Bible and follow the teachings.

A member of the Yakima nation from the state of Washington told a group of educators that people from the majority group may refer to American Indian stories as legends or myths, which is a misconception. The consultant told educators that what others may refer to as legends or myths are actually stories of today because they suggest how people should conduct their lives from generation to generation. In expressing her cultural viewpoint, she helped educators understand that culturally grounded stories are important in people's lives today and that presenting multiple perspectives to students is vital in education. If teachers plan on using stories like these in their classrooms, they should be fully aware of the educational significance and make that clear to the student so the morals or meaning are not lost on them.

Consider the following true story that has become part of a community's cultural legacy. One holiday season a brick was thrown through the window of a Jewish home that had a menorah in the window. Several other Jewish homes in the area were also vandalized. Members of this small rural town were very upset. They wanted the vandals to stop; however, they didn't know who was at fault. After much sharing in the community, they thought of a unique solution. Members of the town decided that they would all put menorahs in their windows; then the vandals wouldn't single out any particular family. This strategy worked. The destruction stopped because everyone worked together. The town's story is used across the United States today to help students understand that it takes the moral courage of everyone in the community to stop discrimination.

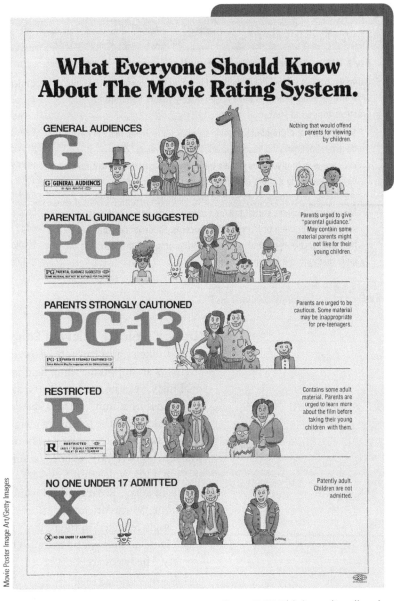

Movie Poster Image Art/Getty Images

Figure 3.15: This is a culturally relevant poster where parents are asked to decide if their children should see a movie. The poster uses information about what parents know about their children to help them make the decision.

TEACHING TIPS

Five Ways to Integrate Culturally Relevant Teaching

Using Vygotsky's sociocultural theory of learning, it is important to know what instructional practices have arisen from his work. Here are five practices for you to study.

1. **Scaffolding and Chunking.** Provide supports for learning. This can be done by simplifying the lesson, providing pacing in small "chunks" of knowledge so that students still are making meaning of the content, conveying clear student goals, and creating an environment where students are successful. Encourage students to become independent thinkers.

2. **Modeling.** Provides verbal talk or example of how the teacher is solving the problem or learning the concepts. Students can then see how the teacher is organizing her or his learning and the steps she or he is taking in the learning process.

3. **Coaching.** Provide hints, ask questions, or facilitate so students move toward successful directions in their learning. The teacher is encouraging students to analyze, synthesize, and evaluate their thinking.

4. **Feedback.** When teachers facilitate learning, they are continually providing students with feedback and encouragement. The feedback needs to ensure that students are developing strong critical thinking skills and not just being asked to give recitations to the teacher.

5. **Self-Monitoring.** Students should be self-empowered learners. Students should be encouraged to develop skills and gather knowledge so that their zone of proximal development increases. The students become independent learners, and teacher scaffolding is not needed.

 Professional Resource Download

Using Culturally Relevant Songs in the Curriculum

Songs, like stories can reflect the deep values of a cultural community. A belief in civil rights is an important value held by many African Americans. Their commitment to social justice can be seen in poetry, stories, folktales, musical styles, and songs. If a teacher is presenting a unit on the 1960s and the contributions of the Civil Rights Movement, she could teach the following song to her students. Some students may already know it; others will have the opportunity to learn a new song. It may even pique the interest of those who have little chance to sing. This song, which has strong civil rights messages, is "Lift Ev'ry Voice and Sing" by two teachers who were also brothers, James Weldon Johnson and J. Rosamond Johnson. The song is about fighting for freedom without losing hope. Many African Americans are extremely spiritual and believe in God; this belief is strongly reflected in the lyrics. This song is often called the Black National Anthem. It represents an anthem or hymn that African Americans sing about participating fully in society. The lyrics are:

Lift ev'ry voice and sing,
Till earth and heaven ring,
Ring with the harmonies of Liberty;
Let our rejoicing rise
High as the listening skies,
Let it resound loud as the rolling sea.
Sing a song full of the faith that the dark past has taught us,
Sing a song full of the hope that the present has brought us,
Facing the rising sun of our new day begun
Let us march on till victory is won.

Stony the road we trod,
Bitter the chastening rod,
Felt in the days when hope unborn had died;
Yet with a steady beat,
Have not our weary feet
Come to the place for which our fathers sighed?
We have come over a way that with tears has been watered,
We have come, treading our path through the blood of the slaughtered,
Out from the gloomy past,
Till now we stand at last
Where the white gleam of our bright star is cast.

God of our weary years,
God of our silent tears,
Thou who has brought us thus far on the way;
Thou who has by Thy might
Led us into the light,
Keep us forever in the path, we pray.
Lest our feet stray from the places, Our God, where we met Thee,
Lest, our hearts drunk with the wine of the world, we forget Thee;
Shadowed beneath Thy hand,
May we forever stand.
True to our God,
True to our native land. (NAACP, 2016)

Here are some questions that can be used in a student discussion of the lyrics of the song:

- What does the title of the song mean to you?
- What are the three main points of the song?
- Why do you think the Johnson brothers wanted to create a Black National Anthem?
- Historically, Black churches have been strong advocates of civil rights; why do you think members of churches would work for equality and freedom?
- Are there other songs that you know that give similar messages about civil rights?

After exploring the meaning of the song, have students begin to research the role of Black churches in the Civil Rights Movement. Students can create a timeline that identifies important events in U.S. history in which Black churches were powerful forces in the struggle for civil rights. Teachers may want to include the work of role models like Martin Luther King, Jr., who was also a Black minister of the Dexter Avenue Baptist Church in Montgomery, Alabama. His father, his grandfather, and his great-grandfather were also ministers.

This song not only provides a cultural story of the values of many African Americans, it also gives another perspective on the oppression African Americans have encountered and still face today. The song is direct in talking about the slaughtering of people, but also about how people rose above the terrible oppression with great faith in God.

Discussion of issues from U.S. history should include multiple perspectives because when teachers present a more comprehensive view of our nation, students gain a deeper understanding of our ongoing struggles. Because a comparative viewpoint provides students with a more comprehensive view of an event, issue, or concept, when teaching the Black National Anthem, you might consider using the lesson given in Carl Grant and Christine Sleeter's book, *Turning on Learning*, called "Our National Anthems." They have included an excellent lesson on how students can be guided to look at the issue of national anthems and review different ones (Grant & Sleeter, 1998, pp. 217–221). They suggest the following national anthems: "The Star-Spangled Banner," "Himno Nacional" (Mexican national anthem), "Lift Ev'ry Voice and Sing" (Black National Anthem), and "Bread and Roses" (women's anthem).

Using Culturally Relevant Literature in the Curriculum

It is important for teachers who have little background in the culture presented to be careful when they choose books depicting a favorite folktale to young children. For example, if teachers use the original version of the *Five Chinese Brothers* by Claire Bishop, students may learn stereotypical images of the Chinese. This book was published in 1938 and the drawings of the Chinese brothers are extremely stereotypical. For example, they depict the brothers with large teeth, small or no eyes, and everyone looking almost exactly alike. The book does not represent Chinese Americans or Chinese from China. It represents an outsider's viewpoint of another group's beliefs, their physical appearance, and story. The important message of the story, that the brothers cared for each other and that they each had a unique talent, is lost in the negative and stereotypical depiction of the brothers and the other characters in the book.

CASE STUDY

Civil Rights Song in Spanish: "De Colores"

Integrating Music into the Curriculum

Many examples of cultural phrases and expressions appear in the Spanish song, "De Colores." This song about spring includes a linguistic interpretation of the sound of the rooster, hen, and baby chicks. For example, the hen says, "Cara, cara, cara." The rooster says, "Quiri quiri quiri quiri quiri." The chick says, "Pío, pío, pío, pi." Students can compare the sounds of the animals in various languages found in the classroom.

"De Colores" is a fun song that reminds many people of their childhood. Some parents have sung this song to their children when they were toddlers. The song can reflect the warmth of parents to their children and the fun they had singing the song together, which ties in with the theme of caring and family. "De Colores" is often sung at Latino community affairs because it signifies the importance of unity. There are older Latinos who remember marching with the civil rights activist Cesar Chavez and singing this song. Like the many colors of the flowers, we as diverse people make up a beautiful rainbow. We make up a wonderful family, the human family.

Reflection Questions

Q What is this song about?

Q Why do you think it was chosen to be sung during civil rights marches?

Q How could you integrate the singing of the son in your curriculum?

De Colores

(Spanish Translation by Cynthia D. Park)

De colores
De colores se visten los campos en la primavera
De colores
De colores son los pajarillos que vienen de afuera
De colores
De colores es el arco iris que vemos lucir
Y por eso los grandes amores
De muchos colores
Me gustan a mi,
Y por eso los grandes amores
De muchos colores
Me gustan a mi
Canta el gallo
Canta el gallo con el quiri quiri quiri quiri quiri
La gallina
La gallina con el cara cara cara cara cara
Los pollitos
Los pollitos con el pío pío pío pío pi

Y por eso los grandes amores
De muchos colores
Me gustan a mi
Y por eso los grandes amores
De muchos colores
Me gustan a mi.

All the Colors

(English Translation by Cynthia D. Park)

All the colors
In springtime the countryside dresses itself in all the colors of the rainbow
All the colors
The birds which return each spring from faraway are marked by all the colors
All the colors
All the colors make up the rainbow which we see shining (across the blue sky)

For these reasons it pleases me that the greatest loves (of the world) are made up of all the colors of the rainbow.
Sings the rooster
Sings the rooster with his kiri kiri kiri kiri kiri
(Also) the hen
The hen with her cara cara cara cara cara
And the baby chicks
And the baby chicks with their pío pío pío pío pi

For these reasons it pleases me (greatly) that the greatest loves (of the world) are made up of all the colors (of the rainbow).

It's important for teachers to carefully review the materials they choose to use in the classroom. It is not possible to learn about multicultural education in one day and then the next day present "cultural" information. Like many aspects of teaching, choosing materials that are sensitive to and reflect a general perspective of the group is a skill that requires much knowledge. Cultural information and views have specific contexts, historical backgrounds, and a long tradition of values. In the Know and Go section found at the end of this chapter, there are guidelines for reviewing children's literature for racism, sexism, and classism.

Lesson in Gender Bias in Children's Literature Gender bias is an issue that all students should have the opportunity to examine and think about. Teachers read many children's books to students during their language arts and literacy periods in class. Let's look at the book, *And to Think That I Saw It on Mulberry Street* by Dr. Seuss, which was published in 1937. Do you remember this book?

Dr. Seuss wrote many fun stories and some with themes about prejudice like *The Sneetches and Other Stories*. Remember that some Sneetches had stars and they felt they were superior to those without stars.

A fifth-grade school teacher was given the book *And to Think That I Saw It on Mulberry Street* as a gift. She read through the book and laughed a couple of times to herself. The book starts out with a funny rhyme:

When I leave home to walk to school,
Dad always says to me,
"Marco, keep your eyelids up
And see what you can see."

She was laughing because the yellow horse turned into a zebra pulling a cart! Then the teacher saw a blue chariot rumbling down Mulberry Street. Next the zebra changed into a reindeer, and it was no longer pulling a cart but a sled. This led to an elephant on Mulberry Street. All of sudden there was a band playing a marching song.

That's when she stopped. The educator looked at the picture and was surprised. The pictures had all men. Between the two pages she was reading she counted eight men and no women or girls.

Turning to the next page she saw a man riding an elephant, pulling the marching band, and attached to them was a trailer with a man with a beard sitting in it.

Yikes.

The teacher then looked further, and there were three policemen riding on motor cycles, six men wearing top hats and tuxedos, two more men dumping confetti on the crowd. She counted 19 men, and then finally, she thought there was a woman flying a small airplane in the upper corner of the second page. This was quite a revelation. In the entire book there was only a picture of one woman. The teacher decided to go back and read through the text more carefully. The name of the protagonist was Marco, a young man. Marco's father was named Dad in the story. The text included "A Chinese man who eats with sticks..." (which was stereotypically drawn) and the following list of names:

Say—anyone could think of that,
Jack or Fred or Joe or Nat—
Say, Even Jane could think of that.

There is one female name in the book. It is Jane.

So if you read this story to your students, you may want to ask questions such as:

- Who are the characters in the story?
- What are they doing?
- Where are the girls?
- Would girls like to walk down Mulberry Street?
- How could you add girls or women to the story?
- What could girls do on Mulberry Street?
- If we changed the main character from a son to a daughter, what would she see?
- What would a mother ask her daughter or son about Mulberry Street?
- How is the Chinese man pictured?
- When was the book published?

In culturally relevant teaching, teachers make bridges from what students know to what they could learn. Students are careful observers if they are taught to think about gender roles and gender balance. So even with established authors like Dr. Seuss, who is enjoyed by millions of readers, teachers need to mentor students into being thinkers and critical readers. This particular book could be used to have even the youngest readers think about gender balance and presentation of racially diverse characters. It was published many years ago when few people thought about social oppression in books for children.

In addition, many of Dr. Seuss's books are also used with English learners because of the rhyming and fun patterns of the language. As the standards developed by the **International Reading Association** and the **National Council of Teachers of English** identified in Table 3.9 demonstrate, it is important that students not only are able to learn the language arts skills, but also students must become critical thinkers who can participate in a democracy and make prudent decisions about diversity and equity.

International Reading Association along with the National Council of Teachers of English have identified K–12 standards in language arts that compliment local, state, and district standards.

National Council of Teachers of English along with the International Reading Association have identified K–12 standards in language arts that complement local, state, and district standards.

Table 3.9 International Reading Association and National Council of Teachers of English Standards		
Standard 9	**Standard 10**	**Standard 12**
Students develop an understanding of and respect for diversity in language use, patterns, and dialects across cultures, ethnic groups, geographic regions, and social roles.	Students whose first language is not English make use of their first language to develop competency in the English language arts and to develop understanding of content across the curriculum.	Students use spoken, written, and visual language to accomplish their own purposes (e.g., for learning, enjoyment, persuasion, and the exchange of information).

International Reading Association and the National Council of Teachers of English. Retrieved from http://www.ncte.org/library/NCTE-Files/Resources/Books/Sample/StandardsDoc.pdf.

Concluding Thoughts

Remember James, the teacher mentioned at the beginning of this chapter who was very skeptical of culturally relevant teaching? On the last day of our college methods course, he said to me, "I didn't think it would work. I really didn't think it would." James threw up his hands and said, "But I was surprised. These big, huge kids who were boxers began coming to class prepared. They brought pencils and notebooks. They were sitting in their seats. They were ready to listen." Of course, I was anxious to find out what James was doing that was reaching his students, so I asked, "So what did you do?" James said, "I designed an issues-centered unit based on the question, 'Was Pancho Villa a hero or was he a villain as portrayed by others?'" Pancho Villa was a revolutionary leader in Mexico during the beginning of the twentieth century. He was also known as a bandit in his early years. Villa was a complex individual who lived during extreme civil unrest in Mexico (Cummings, 2008) (Figure 3.16).

"I brought in passages about Pancho Villa. They researched his life and then wrote about different aspects. In addition," James said, "because I was teaching English skills, I was able

Figure 3.16: Pancho Villa is an important role model for many students, and they are interested in learning more about him.

Photo Researchers -/Getty Images

to include various morphology skills. For example, I explained that 'er' can be added to a verb to indicate a person who does the action: box to boxer, play to player, and lead to leader. In Spanish, 'er' has a corresponding morphology, 'dor.' Therefore, when using the following examples, the students were better able to make that code switch: *correr* becomes *corredor*, *ensenar* becomes *ensenador*, and *jugar* becomes *jugador.*"

James paused and said to me, "I can't believe the students actually come to school now ready to learn. The students are Chicano and, though I didn't believe you, I was desperate so I decided to try the culture thing. I guess culture can make a difference. I didn't believe you and I'm Mexican myself, but it worked for me!"

James smiled widely.

James is primarily bringing in content based on topics that interest the students and that have roots in Mexican culture. James plans to consider other cultural aspects such as social interaction patterns, too. He now sees how culturally relevant teaching can be used to reach his students.

Thinking about Intersectionality

Intersectionality of various human elements such as race, gender, class, and sexual orientation continues to be important in evaluating how these areas are layered with social oppression. For example, a woman may find herself subjected to bias because of her gender, being Black, growing up in a poor family, and identifying as lesbian. Culturally relevant teaching is an approach that not only is used to addresses academic achievement for all students but also higher-order thinking and decision-making skills. These skills are necessary for students to foster their potentials and move forward in selected careers. It is absolutely essential that teachers are effective instructors who guide, mentor, and educate their students because education is about the growth of the whole student. Then students become self-empowered citizens who develop positive self-esteem and career skills. They are not held back by bias from others or institutional inequities.

Summary

1. **Analyze culturally relevant teaching and theoretical frameworks.**

   Culturally relevant teaching is an approach to education that is based on the sociocultural theory developed by Vygotsky. Teachers consider both cultural content and context when developing lessons and delivering instruction. One of the major cultural tools that educators use is language. Ideas are shared through social interaction, and people use metaphors, similes, examples, symbols, formulas, and other aspects of language to convey thought. Teachers can also use cultural models that represent systems of ideas that are linked such as the communication style of some African Americans who use satire, irony, and wit in their verbal interactions. This is what researcher Carol D. Lee did when she created her Cultural Modeling program.

2. **Describe how culture influences the way people learn.**

   Culture influences the way people receive, interpret, think, and create because they have grown up within specific cultural contexts. Research by Scribner and Cole demonstrated that individuals learn within cultures specific goals in life and then develop skills to accomplish those goals. Saxe found that children in Brazil figured out how to calculate exchange rates of currency daily as they fluctuated, though the young people may not know how to compute a sheet of multiplication problems. Their skill development occurred within a specific cultural context.

3. **Assess culturally relevant programs, such as Funds of Knowledge and the Algebra Project, and their elements.**

   Educators have created and implemented different culturally relevant programs that build on and integrate culturally relevant information and context into the learning process. Programs such as Funds of Knowledge, the Algebra Project, and Organic Reading are examples of how teachers can build curriculum and instruction programs that affirm the cultural knowledge of students in instruction and curriculum. The cultural context is a powerful element that instructional strategies can be built upon.

4. **Investigate and plan how culturally relevant teaching can be integrated throughout the curriculum and instruction.**

   There are numerous ways to integrate culturally relevant teaching. There are seven major ways such as the inclusion of: community issues, student-personal experiences, role models and heroes, literary tools, discipline content, photos and other visual organizers, and multiple perspectives. Culturally relevant teaching emphasizes the development of higher-order thinking skills like decision-making and evaluation skills. One of the most important models that students can learn in school is the use of an issues-centered, decision-making model so that they know how to think about complex social issues and how to solve them.

Check Your Cultural Knowledge

Reflective Essay Question

Culturally relevant teaching is a complex approach to instruction. Teachers must have knowledge about students' cultural groups and knowledge about instruction. Teachers also must understand how to use cognitive principles of learning. This is one of the reasons that many educators resort to having international food fairs or celebrating Martin Luther King, Jr.'s birthday. They stick with lower level activities that focus on outward manifestations of culture such as food, role models, and customs. However, teachers have to develop evaluative skills so they can critique why the surface items of culture do not always lead to children's understanding of the values, beliefs, and worldviews of a cultural group.

Let's take Martin Luther King, Jr.'s birthday. Of course it is important to celebrate someone who fought for civil rights. But why else is he important to our national values? What makes him different than other Americans who are also Black? As you work to transform your curriculum, think of how to address controversial issues that impact everyone every day. One of the most important issues about Dr. King is that he challenged a White power structure though he was a Black man. He was a member of a marginalized community whose history in the United States is laced with lynching, segregation, lack of voting, and denial of numerous civil rights.

So when your school or class celebrates Dr. King's birthday, what does his birthday really represent? Do you lead students in discussions that challenge unequal power within society? What are some of the inequities you see in your school or city? Do you talk about these issues throughout the year and not only Dr. King's birthday?

This entire chapter was about using culturally relevant teaching in your instruction and curriculum. Let's say you were asked by a colleague why you use culturally relevant teaching and how culture is important to learning. How would you respond? You want to teach the person, and you want to persuade her to try to incorporate the approach.

Application

Know and Go Tools in the Classroom

Ten Quick Ways to Analyze Books for Racism, Sexism, and Other Biases

You read about the Dr. Seuss book and some of the misconceptions it may have promoted. Below is a comprehensive checklist that you can use when reviewing children's literature for your classroom. The checklist works for books in which characters arise from underrepresented groups or when the core story line has to do with issues of equality or prejudice. The items on this check list have been adapted from the Council on Interracial Books for Children's *Ten Quick Ways to Analyze Books for Racism and Sexism* and their work on ageism. Pick a children's picture book and use these guidelines in assessing the volume for social oppression. How well did it do?

1. **Illustrations**
   a. **Stereotypes**—Examine the book, story, or illustrations for stereotypical images such as the savage Indian, eye-rolling "mammy," sombrero-wearing Latino, "slant eyes" Asian American, apron-wearing mother, wicked-step mother, hard of hearing older person, passive older wife, effeminate gay, or terrorist Middle Easterner. Do the illustrations reinforce stereotypes such as the savage Indian, eye-rolling "mammy," sombrero-wearing Latino, "slant-eyed" Asian American, apron-wearing mother, wicked step mother, handicapped child, useless older person, passive older wife, effeminate gay person, or terrorist Middle Easterner?
   b. **Tokenism**—Also review the illustrations for tokenism. Are people of color depicted as Whites just with "colored" skin? Are people of color portrayed stereotypically, or are they drawn as individuals with distinctive features?
   c. **Leaders and Doers**—Do the illustrations show people of color as subservient or in passive roles while showing Whites as leaders and those who act?
2. **The Story Line**
   a. **Standard for Success**—Does it take "White" or mainstream behavior and values for a person of color to be successful and get ahead?

Is making it in the dominant society portrayed as the only ideal? To gain acceptance, do people of color have to excel at sports and get As? Does the child or person of color have to be the one that who is most forgiving or understanding in a conflict?
   b. **Resolution of the Problem**—Are people of color or the communities they come from seen as "the problem"? Is the oppression that people of color and women are subjected to presented as being in conflict with social justice? Are the reasons for poverty and oppression accepted as inevitable? In the story, do the characters show passive acceptance or active resistance? Is a benevolent White person portrayed as the one who solves the problems of women or people of color?
   c. **Role of the Elderly**—Are people who are older seen as inept and feeble?
   d. **Role of Women**—Are the achievements of girls and women presented as the result of their own intelligence and initiative, or are their successes based on good looks or relationships with boys/men? Could the story be told if the gender roles were reversed? Are women who are older depicted as passive and incapable of solving problems?
3. **Look at Life Styles**—Are middle-class White ways of life depicted as the standard? If the way people of color live are different, is it shown as being negative and deficient? Are people of color shown primarily in ghettos, barrios, migrant camps, or Chinatowns? Is there an oversimplification of the lives of people of color and their life styles? Look for inaccuracies and flawed depictions of other cultures. Watch for examples of the "quaint-native- in costume" or presenting Chinatown as an exotic place rather than an area with deep poverty. Also examine clothing, customs, behaviors, and personality traits that are one dimensional and stereotypical.
4. **Weigh the Relationships among People**—Do White people have all or most of the power and are leaders in making the decisions? Do people of color or women act in supporting roles? In Black families, are mothers portrayed as always dominant? Are Latino families always shown with lots of children? If families are depicted as being separated, are reasons of unemployment and poverty given as primary reasons? Are women and men shown in nurturing family roles? Are people who are older shown as less capable and dependent?

Application (Continued)

5. **Heroes**—Are only "safe" heroes presented? These are heroes who were accepted by the White establishment. Heroes should be chosen by all; people of color and women can choose their heroes based on their values and their struggle for equality and justice. When heroes who are people of color are identified, has what they have done only benefitted White people? Whose interest is a particular hero serving?

6. **Child's Self-Image**—Do the expectations and norms presented limit a child's self-concept and aspirations? What is the effect on the self-image of African American, Asian American and Pacific Islander, Latino, and Native American children when they are continually bombarded with images of White as the ultimate beauty, cleanliness, and virtue, whereas the colors black and brown may be seen as evil, dirty, not belonging, or defiant? Does the book counteract or reinforce these stereotypes? Is the story one where a child of color and girls can readily and positively identify with?

7. **Author's Perspective**— An author cannot be entirely objective; authors write from a cultural as well as a personal point of view. Often children's books are written by members of the middle class. Read through the book to determine whether the author's perspective substantially weakens or strengthens the value of his or her written work. Is the perspective patriarchal or feminist? Is it solely Eurocentric, or are underrepresented viewpoints respected? Does the work assume heterosexuality?

8. **Loaded Words**— Words should not be "loaded" or have insulting overtones or outright oppressive terms. Examples include *savage*, *primitive*, *beaner*, *Chink*, *Jap*, *conniving*, *lazy*, *superstitious*, *treacherous*, *sneaky*, *inscrutable*, *docile*, *ancient*, *aged*, *geezer*, *old goat*, *old maid*, *helpless*, *mentally retarded*, *fags*, *dykes*, *N-word*, *tranny (very negative term)*, and *backward*. Look for sexist language in which women are ridiculed or excluded. Look for the use of the male pronoun to refer to both females and males. Does the book substitute the following words: *ancestors* for *forefathers*, *chairperson* for *chairman*, or *community* for *brotherhood*, *firefighters* for *firemen*, *manufactured* for *manmade*, and the *human family* for the *family of man*? Instead of using the term *old* consider substituting words such as *older*, *senior*, or *seasoned*.

9. **Copyright Date**—Though this is not always the case, books published before the 1970's may not present a diverse society and world. As the presence of authors of color and women who wrote about the lives of people of color and women increased, there were changes made. However, there was also resistance to the presentation of nonmainstream people in children's books. Therefore it is most important for people to read through children's books carefully and to be sensitive to the inclusion and portrayal of diverse communities. Be careful of books that show older people acting cranky or crabby and cute or adorable, to implying they are like a children.

10. **Literacy, Historical, and Cultural Perspectives**—As our lives and cultures continue to change, it is important to read folktales, stories, and literary works within the context of their time. Attitudes about women and people of color continue to change, and it is important for readers to understand that particular viewpoints are shifting toward equality and social justice.

These ideas can also be utilized in examining books for other characteristics such as exceptionalities and sexual orientation. For example, books that use a term like "mentally retarded" to refer to students with special needs is not acceptable. The term is demeaning and has been replaced with the phrase, intellectual disability. It is also important for teachers to review books for assumptions of heterosexism in stories. In addition, since about ten percent of students do not identify as being heterosexual, it is important that materials presented show a variety of beliefs about sexual orientation.

Source: Council for Interracial Children's Books.

AP Images

Race: Historical Oppression

Learning Objectives

LO1 Describe how racial oppression continues to be a powerful force in the United States.

LO2 Examine how immigrants influenced the lives of Native Americans.

LO3 Examine how Latinos/Hispanics were caught in the U.S. policy of Manifest Destiny.

LO4 Investigate the slavery of African Americans as a legal and accepted practice in the United States.

LO5 Assess the exclusion and internment of Asian Americans and Pacific Islanders in the United States.

LO6 Explain the segregation of Jewish Americans and summarize their fight for economic and political equality.

<table>
<tr><td>STANDARDS COVERED</td></tr>
<tr><td>NAEYC 5, 6
naeyc</td></tr>
<tr><td>CAEP 1 CAEP</td></tr>
<tr><td>InTASC 3, 4, 5, 6, 7, 8, 9, 10
InTASC</td></tr>
</table>

Social Context

Race is a powerful sociopolitical construct used to exclude people in the United States. This book offers discussion about the intersectionality of diverse social categories. For the purposes of this chapter and the next, it important for teachers to understand that though race is often seen in isolation, it has deep ties to categories such as class, religion, ethnicity, and geography.

Some teachers believe we do not need to discuss racial issues or have chapters on racism. Other educators believe that without understanding the patterns of racial oppression, it is difficult for teachers to understand the perspectives of many people of color who may be their students or students' parents. Since it is not possible to present and analyze all social oppressions, Chapter 4 will discuss examples of subjugation or persecution from the perspective of racially diverse people. Later, Chapter 5 will articulate ways in which various racial groups have provided leadership in the struggle for civil rights. It is through the advocacy work of many individuals and culturally diverse communities that progress toward equality moves forward in the United States.

To place Chapters 4 and 5 in context, examine the data from a New York Times/CBS News Poll about race and race relations. The telephone survey was conducted in July of 2015; it is a random sample of 1205 people chosen from 81,000 phone numbers from all over the country (Sack & Thee-Benan, 2015).

Following are some of the findings of the poll.

1. Do you think that race relations in the United States are generally good or generally bad?

	Generally Good	Generally Bad	DK/NA**
Blacks	67%	29%	4%
Whites	79%	17%	4%

2. Would you say there has been real progress getting rid of discrimination or hasn't there been much real progress?

	Progress	Lack of Progress	DK/NA
Blacks	56%	41%	3%
Whites	75%	21%	5%

3. In general, who do you think is more likely to encounter problems when trying to vote—White people, Black people, or there isn't much difference?

	Black people	White People	Not much difference	DK/NA
Blacks	50%	2%	47%	1%
Whites	24%	3%	71%	3%

4. In general, do you think the police in most communities are more likely to use deadly force against a Black person, or more likely to use it against a White person, or don't you think race affects police use of deadly force?*

	Most likely against a Black person	Most likely against a White person	Race does not affect	DK/NA
Blacks	74%	0%	22%	4%
White	34%	1%	58%	7%

*Percentages are reported.

**DK/NA (Don't Know, No Answer)

Though the poll only includes Blacks and Whites, it is still possible to assess the results and see that Blacks and Whites hold different perspectives about the state of race relations in the United States. Blacks are far more negative about issues of race. Racism is clearly an issue for more Black Americans than White Americans. Teachers must become aware of the perspectives of communities of color and other groups who have suffered extensive discrimination in society, to understand the experiences of non-Whites and to create more effective curricula. Cultural conflicts may occur because people have different views of the state of equality and freedom in this country. The results of the New York Times/CBS News poll show that Blacks believe police officers are more likely to use deadly force on Blacks compared to Whites. This is a major disagreement about everyday life.

The results of this survey demonstrate the importance of providing all Americans more information about the patterns of oppression in the United States. The poll does show that Black Americans have different views about racism and discrimination in society. Chapters 4 and 5 present information about social oppression to illustrate that discrimination is a major area of concern for many people of color. There are perennial issues in our history that have resulted in imperialism and exclusion. These chapters will give you the opportunity to think about not only oppression but also how numerous people within groups of color and White American communities challenge inequities and work toward freedom for all. There are also timelines that can be reviewed for patterns of oppression. Patterns are important to identify because they show that the issues of racism are perennial and continue to tear at our democratic foundation today. Ask yourself why social oppression is such a critical issue in our nation's history.

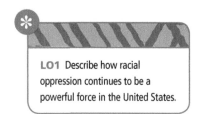

LO1 Describe how racial oppression continues to be a powerful force in the United States.

Racism is a legalized system of privileges and penalties based on the belief of the superiority of people or groups based on perceived racial differences. **Ethnocentrism** is a stage in Bennett's model of intercultural sensitivity in which a person's group culture shapes her or his view of the world and other cultures; does not consider the views of other cultural groups.

Racial Oppression and Our National Story

Have you thought about how race and racism have impacted our national history? This can be painful to think about because many people, both underrepresented and mainstream, have not been treated with respect and equality. Race is a sociopolitical construct in which people are identified by physical characteristics and divided into distinct groups; however, race is not a biological reality. And it is important to know when reviewing U.S. history that racism has been a powerful force. What is racism? **Racism** is a legalized and legitimate system of privileges and penalties based on the belief of the superiority of people or groups based on perceived racial differences. Often this leads to **ethnocentrism**. When people only consider their ethnic or racial group values and ideas, they are ethnocentric; people who are ethnocentric believe their group is superior to others.

There are numerous themes throughout our country's history, and three themes stand out. First, those who are seen as people of color and racially different are often considered to be outsiders or foreigners and therefore not eligible to be citizens. Second, these perceived outsiders are oppressed and treated as inferior and subordinate. Third, the outsiders must continually fight for civil rights because of their perceived image as not being members of the dominant culture. Fortunately, throughout the history of our nation, many individuals and groups have fought for equality and justice for all.

Can you think of how our nation would be if people from different ethnic groups had not fought for equality? Our lives as American citizens would be different. Without the fight for equality, women and people of color might not have had the opportunity to become teachers or principals or superintendents. The history discussed in this chapter demonstrates how social oppression in the form of colonialism, imperialism, slavery, and exclusion are

Consider this . . .

Social oppression is the result of the choices that people have made not to challenge inequalities. This can be seen throughout history, and that is why it is critical for teachers and their students to examine the influence these choices have had on the development of our nation.

Q What are some of the educational and societal inequities that you think teachers should address in their curriculum?

perennial patterns in U.S. society. Social oppression is the result of the choices that people have made not to challenge inequalities. This can be seen throughout our history. We need to learn from our history and move forward towards equality.

Our history shows that it is the responsibility of everyone to continually strive to make our foundational values of justice and freedom a reality. Take time to reflect upon the historical events presented about major racial groups in the United States—Native American, Hispanic American, African American, Asian American and Pacific Islander, and White American communities—so you have a more comprehensive knowledge of U.S. history. One of the major things to consider about history in the United States is the lens from which it is seen. Many of the events in this chapter reflect the views of members from communities of color. Often times their perspectives are not included. Remember African American history is U.S. history. Native American history is U.S. history. Latino/Hispanic history is U.S. history. Asian American and Pacific Islander history is U.S. history. We are all Americans.

The Integration of Literature, Sociology, Psychology, and History

Chapters 4 and 5 deal with the issue of racial oppression in the United States. Much of the content is about the history of diverse racial groups. Some teachers may ask themselves why they need to know this information; history is boring and not relevant today. However, it is critical that as teachers you have a strong knowledge of what has gone in the past to create the country we have today. This background will help you understand the roots of some events in today's society like the "Black Lives Matter" Movement. Knowing the historical roots of oppression can also be used to create lesson plans and connect with your students. See the Professional Resource Download section of the MindTap learning path for ideas about interdisciplinary teaching and integrating historical content into other disciplines.

If you teach English literature, sociology, or psychology, you will need to know about the history of the United States. For example, many tenth-grade classes throughout the nation read the book *To Kill a Mockingbird* by Harper Lee. This text has been taught for decades in high schools because it is seen as an important American novel. The book chronicles the work of Atticus Finch, a respected lawyer and father in the South. Finch is presented as the liberating lawyer who rises above racism and becomes an important role model for many against racism (Atkinson, 1999). However, the story is extremely complicated and includes discussion of deep racial discrimination in the community that Finch must deal with as he defends a Black man, Tom Robinson, who is accused of raping a White woman. Finch posits that equality before the law is one of our most important values; however, Atkinson believes that Finch sees himself as better than Robinson; there is an atmosphere of condescension and paternalism in this character.

In order to investigate this viewpoint, teachers and their students must review and know the history of slavery and social oppression against Blacks in the United States; otherwise, they will not understand or be able to interpret the views of ethnic minorities who have been subjected to continual racism. To fully analyze *To Kill a Mockingbird* and evaluate the role of society in the novel, knowing the history of racial oppression is necessary. When students have a historical context, they will be more able to evaluate the messages in the book and to investigate how accurate the novel is in presenting social mores.

Why else is history important to teachers? Knowing history gives citizens the opportunity to reflect upon our national values. What were the values of the country in the past, and what are they now? How have our values as a democracy changed? Why have they changed? For example, in the past history was primarily about the lives and views of European Americans who were thought to have settled and built this nation. However, as time has progressed, the history of all communities of color, women, low-income communities, people with disabilities, religious groups, and LGBT communities have been included and seen as U.S. history.

Why history? It has provided the following:

1. Foundation of who we are as a nation.
2. Different perspectives on issues.
3. Cultural and historical context for discussions of various disputes.
4. The big picture of human experiences.
5. Explanation for why societal values have changed and how society has changed.
6. Demonstration of how clarification of diversity and the value of equality continue to be at the base of our country.
7. Expanded knowledge of social change and communal beliefs.
8. Connections between student lives and lives of others from the past.

History is an element of culture; people's viewpoints can be highly influenced by the historical experiences of their racial and/or ethnic community. Individuals who share a culture may hold a sense of peoplehood and ethnic identity. To understand individuals from a culture may take extensive analysis and evaluation of knowledge from many sources, such as history.

Native Americans: Ethnic Diversity and Imperialism

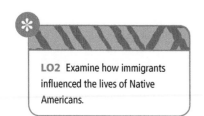

LO2 Examine how immigrants influenced the lives of Native Americans.

Some students have a one-dimensional view of Native Americans. They see them as the stereotypical "Indian" who wears feathers and buckskin and are often used as human mascots in society (Munson, 1999; Murphy, 2012; Pewewardy, n.d.). They are savages and uncivilized. One of the reasons that students may hold these images is that schools do not have enough visual representations of actual Native people today (Figure 4.1). It is important that various role models be included throughout your curriculum. Another way to eliminate the stereotype is to teach about the great diversity within the population known as Native Americans. For example, Native Americans who live in New England are different from those who live in Arizona. They wear different traditional clothing. Their shelters differ because the environments in these two areas of the United States are extremely different. The next section will provide some information about the diversity of Native Americans.

Figure 4.1: Students learning the Navajo language at a school in the Chinle Unified School District, Arizona.

Ethnic Diversity of Native Americans

When Christopher Columbus, an Italian explorer who sailed from Spain, landed at San Salvador in the Bahamas, some historians believe there were over 18 million people living in North America, speaking over 300 different languages (National Museum of the American Indian, 2007). The people were members of distinct ethnic groups. They had their own languages, histories, customs, and foods. Though Columbus misnamed the people he saw as "Indians" because he was searching for the country of India, there were numerous indigenous people who inhabited the Northern Hemisphere. The people were native to the land, though Columbus was not aware of this. As we know today, Columbus did not reach India. Instead he found himself in the Bahamas and later countries now known as Cuba and Haiti. The next section will discuss one of the most well-known events in U.S. history from the view of the Native people who were part of the first Thanksgiving.

Thanksgiving: A Wampanoag Perspective

Hundreds of Native people in the Wampanoag alliance lived in the area where the first colonial Thanksgiving was held. This area in Massachusetts was where the Pilgrims chose to settle. The Wampanoag were an extremely large and powerful confederation of Indian nations (National Museum of the American Indian, 2007). Relationships were eventually forged, and the Wampanoag soon taught the Pilgrims how to farm and take care of themselves in their new home land. The first Thanksgiving was probably a feast of three days, and much of the food was provided by the Wampanoag. Massasoit, their chief, brought deer to the celebration. It is a myth that Native people engage in a "Thanksgiving" once a year, as many Natives give thanks every day.

As part of the history of the Pilgrims and Wampanoag alliance, it is important to explain the view of many explorers and new settlers. They were often part of a movement toward imperialism. **Imperialism**, a major theme in U.S. and global history, is a systematic process by which countries accumulate territory, natural resources, cheap labor, and new markets to sell goods for financial gain. Countries like Spain, France, and

Imperialism is the political, economic, and cultural control over another country or territory; in the process a country takes control of the government and economic system by dominating the weaker population.

Great Britain, during the time of Christopher Columbus, sent explorers to what is now the United States and Canada to expand their imperialistic goals. You might not know that there were many explorers who had sailed to the Americas before Columbus, such as Leif Erickson, a Viking from Iceland, and that many colonizers, like Columbus, were financed by Spain (Loewen, 2007). At this time, Great Britain did not have the financial resources to establish colonies in what was referred to as the "New World," so the country encouraged adventurous individuals from trading companies to settle new found colonies. The oldest colonial business in the United States is the Hudson's Bay Company, which was incorporated by the British in 1670 (Weatherford, 1988). This company is still in business today and includes department stores such as Lord & Taylor and Saks Fifth Avenue. The British wanted the Hudson's Bay Company to challenge the expansion of French interests in the North. In addition, groups of individuals from other countries also found their way to the continental United States. Let's discuss the first Europeans to settle what we now know as New England.

Pilgrims Seek Religious Freedom in a New Colony

The Pilgrims were the first European community that voyaged to what is now Massachusetts, a state in New England. Why did the Pilgrims migrate to the new world? The Pilgrims, who were Protestants, were actually called Separatists during their time period, and wanted the opportunity to develop businesses outside of Europe (Weatherford, 1988). They already had found religious freedom in Holland, but were not able to create a strong financial foundation there. The Pilgrims took passage in 1620 on the *Mayflower*, a ship that traveled 66 days from Plymouth, England, to reach Massachusetts. They named their new colony after their home in England. When they landed in November, after a long and arduous journey, it was cold and the Pilgrims did not have much food. Life was extremely hard, and half of the original Pilgrims died during their first winter in this new land. Though they grew food the next spring, they still did not have enough to eat. The Wampanoag were wary of the Pilgrims when they first established camp because the immigrants had taken corn, beans, and other items from Indian graves (James, 1970). These food offerings had been left for the dead, but the Pilgrims might not have been aware of the damage they were causing when, in their own desperation, they took the food. The Locator Map shows where the Wampanoag tribe lived. The use of maps and pictures are essential teaching tools. A map helps students understand where people lived in comparison to others and provides important context.

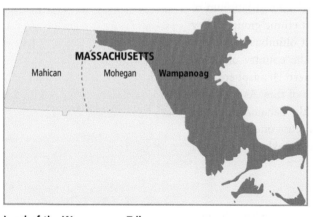

Land of the Wampanoag Tribe

Consider this . . .

When Columbus landed in San Salvador, Native American historians believe there were as many as 18 million people who lived in what is now the United States. They spoke over 300 languages. They were not known as Indians. They were known by their own names such as the Arawaks, Seneca, Yakima, Hopi, Cherokee, Wampanoag, and Blackfeet.

Q How can you help your students understand the great diversity within the community known as Native Americans?

The Wampanoag Alliance and Pilgrims

The Wampanoag people knew that Europeans could be a threat to their community. Before the Pilgrims had journeyed across the Atlantic Ocean, English explorers had kidnapped 24 people from the Patuxet and Nauset tribes, members of the Wampanoag confederation, and took them by ship to Spain. Several were sold as slaves; one was named Squanto. He later returned to the colonies and served as an interpreter because he had learned to speak English during his time abroad. Squanto returned to the area in about 1618. Tragically, in 1616 just before his return home, a terrible plague of small pox began to spread all along the coast of New England and many Native Americans died from the disease (National Museum of the American Indian, 2007). The European explorers and colonists had unknowingly brought new diseases like typhoid and small-pox to the area, and because the Native people had not yet developed needed immunity to fight these infections, they quickly perished. When Squanto returned to his village after being kidnapped to Spain, every member of the Patuxet village had died and his former way of life was gone. Through immigration from Europe and the result of disease, imperialism was pushed forward. In addition, Native groups like the Wampanoag became victims of **genocide**, the systematic eradication of a group of people and their cultures, values, and languages.

> **Genocide** is the elimination of a group of people and their way of life.

It is important that you understand that Native nations like the Patuxet were eliminated through disease. However, imperialism also contributed greatly to the demise of many native tribes. Imperialism is about gaining control and power over land, its people, and resources. Many other Wampanoag people were killed through conflicts with colonists who moved west by pushing Indians off of their lands. Later, the relocation of Native Americans during the Trail of Tears through forced marches from 1838–1839 also led to the death of many Native people. Numerous East Coast Indians, including members of the Cherokee, Chickasaw, Choctaw, Seminole, and Creek tribes, were forced from their territories to west of the Mississippi river so European settlers like Andrew Jackson could gain control of their lands. Researchers for the National Museum for the American Indian believe that by the end of the nineteenth century, there were only 250,000 Native people left in the United States (2007).

As more colonists moved into lands that were once settled by Native Americans, life became extremely difficult for the Natives, and their numbers dwindled. Therefore, some Native Americans do not celebrate Thanksgiving. In their view, the increased number of Europeans caused the death of tribes and ways of life. In November 1970, **Wamsutta Frank B. James**, the leader of the Wampanoag confederation, was asked to speak at the 350-year celebration of Thanksgiving in Plymouth, Massachusetts. James decided not to speak because his words reflecting Native American history from the point of view of the Wampanoag were going to be censored. Reflect upon his views of Native American history as a Wampanoag and a U.S. citizen.

> … A time of looking back, of reflection. It is with a heavy heart that I look back upon what happened to my People. Even before the Pilgrims landed it was common practice for explorers to capture Indians, take them to Europe and sell them as slaves for 220 shillings apiece. The Pilgrims had hardly explored the shores of Cape Cod for four days before they had robbed the graves of my ancestors and stolen their corn and beans… We, the Wampanoag, welcomed you, the white man, with open arms, little knowing that it was the beginning of the end; that before 50 years were to pass, the Wampanoag would no longer be a free people.
>
> History wants us to believe that the Indian was a savage, illiterate, uncivilized animal. A history that was written by an organized, disciplined people, to expose us as an unorganized and undisciplined entity. Two distinctly different cultures met. One thought they must control life; the other believed life was to be enjoyed, because nature decreed it. Let us remember, the Indian is and

My Journal

Reflecting on the Speech of Wamsutta Frank B. James, Wampanoag Leader

Wampanoags are people of today. *Teach* with this perspective.

Mr. James's 1970 speech about the first Thanksgiving gives a different perspective on the U.S. holiday. Go back to the speech and think about what he says.

Q *What did you learn from his words?*

Q *What were you surprised to learn?*

Q *How does this information assist you in understanding the Thanksgiving holiday?*

Q *Since we are a democracy, should the views of Native people be considered in our teaching? Why or why not?*

Q *Write a short 250-word letter to Mr. James.*

Q *How would you respond to his views about Thanksgiving?*

Q *What would you write?*

❯❯ Professional Resource Download

was just as human as the white man. The Indian feels pain, gets hurt, and becomes defensive, has dreams, bears tragedy and failure, suffers from loneliness, needs to cry as well as laugh. He, too, is often misunderstood...

What has happened cannot be changed, but today we must work towards a more humane America, a more Indian America, where men and nature once again are important; where the Indian values of honor, truth, and brotherhood prevail...

You the white man are celebrating an anniversary. We the Wampanoags will help you celebrate in the concept of a beginning. It was the beginning of a new life for the Pilgrims. Now, 350 years later it is a beginning of a new determination for the original American: the American Indian...

(From the Speech of Wamsutta Frank B. James, Wampanoag, 1970, Retrieved from http://www.uaine.org/suppressed _speech.htm)

TAKE A STAND CHRISTOPHER COLUMBUS

Hero, Villain, or a Man of His Times?

Read through this description of the work of Christopher Columbus.

Let's say a student asked you whether you thought Columbus was a hero, villain, or a man of his times. What would you say and what evidence would you give?

Discussion of Columbus

Columbus is seen by some historians as being a brave and courageous explorer who opened up many lands that people in Europe knew little about. Though he did not "discover" new lands, he did provide maps of new lands for other Europeans to explore. Many Americans see Columbus as an important hero because he opened up the exploration of the continental United States though he never landed there. He is an example of globalization in his time period (Bartozik-Veléz, 2006).

Columbus is believed to have been extremely courageous and an important Italian role model. He bravely traveled the seas in small

ships, not knowing where he might end up. He showed great leadership in bringing many explorers to the Caribbean. In 1968, Columbus Day became a federal holiday (Schuman, Schwartz, & D'Arcy, 2005). Some historians believe that Columbus represented the belief of many Europeans of his day and so should be judged by the lens of his times.

There are historians who believe that elite revisionists have changed accurate historical descriptions. The revisionist scholars are those whose voices were similar to those who called for minority rights after World War II (Schuman et al., 2005). This perspective often supports a Native American viewpoint, especially the history of those from the Caribbean Islands where Columbus actually landed. Columbus in this perspective is seen as part of Spanish imperialism. Imperialism is the political, economic, and cultural control over another country or territory; in the process a country takes control of the government and economic system by dominating the weaker population. However, others feel that

Table 4.1 The Six Periods of Native American History
1. Creation: 1492 (Beginning of time including creation stories to prior to European contact)
2. Contact Era: 1492–1800 (European contact with Native Peoples)
3. The Removal Era: 1800–1830
4. The Reservation Era: 1830–1929
5. The Reform Era: 1930–1969
6. Contemporary Resistance: 1970–present

It is critical to include photos of various diverse role models in the classroom because it gives students a stronger sense of individuals as people from diverse communities. If only portraits and photos of George Washington and Abraham Lincoln are shown in the classroom, then students do not get the opportunity to learn about other role models. Like it is said, "a picture is worth a thousand words." Frank B. James was a real person and contemporary leader of the Wampanoag.

The Complexities of Native American History

The history of Native Americans is extremely complex. It is not possible to comprehensively cover Native American history in this book. However, Native American historians have identified six important and specific periods of their history. The first period begins with creation, and the last period ends with contemporary times. Following is the list for the six periods (Almeida, 1997). Take time to identify events found in the Native Americans in the United States Timeline and the six periods of Native American History (Table 4.1).

Columbus was extremely ruthless and the actions of his men caused the genocide of the Arawaks.

After his landing, Columbus encountered many island people; they were known by their tribal names. Columbus misnamed many of the indigenous people on the islands and later in North America as "Indians." For example, the people who lived on San Salvador were Arawaks (Rea Salisbury, 1980). Some authors use the term Arawak Indians to describe the population, but that is like saying German Europeans. The Arawaks also included a group of people called Taino (Walker, 1992). The Arawaks had a long-established aristocracy with customs, specific tools, dress, and cultural beliefs. They were a peaceful and happy community. The Arawaks often partied and danced together. They treated everyone like family. They had developed their own tools for farming and fishing. They were a peaceful people (Rea Salisbury, 1980; Melendez, 2015).

However, Columbus and his crew needed to prove that their expedition was profitable. This led Columbus to gather various goods. For example, Columbus took gold from the Arawaks and when they did not bring more gold, their hands and feet were cut off; some died from their wounds. In a subsequent trip to the islands, he also enslaved Arawaks, taking the people to Spain. Many of the actions of Columbus's men resulted in genocide of this community because other Arawaks were hunted and killed or they died from diseases like small pox brought to the area by Europeans (Melendez, 2015).

How enduring has the work of Columbus been? First, the misnomer of "Indian" has been used for hundreds of years, though today individuals have chosen various terms to identify themselves, such as American Indian, Native American, Indian, Native people, indigenous American, or by their tribal name (National Museum of the American Indian, 2007).

TAKE A STAND . . .

▶ **Was Columbus a hero, a villain, or a man of his times? Give reasons for your answers.**

TIMELINE

NATIVE AMERICANS IN THE UNITED STATES

12,000 YEARS AGO (APPROXIMATELY) — Native people created vibrant civilizations.

9200 YEARS AGO (APPROXIMATELY) — The Kennewick Man lived in the area now called Kennewick, Washington.

1491 — 18 million Natives lived in North America.

1492 — Christopher Columbus, an Italian explorer, landed in what is now known as the Bahamas and calls the people "Indians."

1513 — Ponce De Leon, a Spanish explorer, landed in Florida near Charlotte Harbor and captured members of the Calusa tribe.

1539 — The Napituca Massacre occurred when Hernando de Soto, a Spanish explorer, landed near Tampa, Florida, and later captured Timucuan warriors and executed them.

1565 — In Florida, St. Augustine became the first permanent settlement established by Europeans from Spain.

1614 — Tisquantum—later known as Squanto—a member of the Wampanoag Confederation, was captured by an Englishman who took him as a slave to sell in Spain.

1618 — Beginning of a plague, possibly tuberculosis or small pox, that killed a whole village of Pautuxets, members of the Wampanoag Confederation.

1620 — Hungry Pilgrims found fresh corn in a Nauset graveyard; the corn was left there for the ancestors buried in the cemetery. Conflict arose between Indians and colonists.

1621 — Massasoit, chief of the Wampanoag confederation, signed a peace treaty with the Pilgrims in March. Later in the King Philips War, his son was killed. Many conflicts arose between colonists and various Indian nations. Many people died.

First Thanksgiving was held in Plymouth. Massasoit and people from his nation brought deer, corn, and shellfish to the feast.

1637 — The Pequot War between the Pequot tribe and English colonists in Connecticut; the Pequots, a powerful tribe in the area, lost their lands in the conflict.

1754–1763 — The French and Indian War was a series of wars between the French and English over lands in the colonies and west of the original colonies. The French and British both tried to align with various Indian tribes. The British defeated the French and took control of the lands in the Northeast.

1778 — The Continental Congress signed the first treaty with an Indian tribe, Delaware.

1812 — The United States and Great Britain fought over trade restrictions imposed on the United States. Another reason for their conflicts was that the British were aligning Indian tribes against the expansion of the United States.

1824 — The United States established the Bureau of Indian Affairs, which later became part of the War Department.

1830 — The Removal Act was passed by Congress, which allows for the removal of Indians from the East to lands west of the Mississippi River. This was part of Andrew Jackson's systematic strategy to take over Indian homelands.

1838–1839 — The "Trail of Tears" was the forced removal of Cherokee from Georgia to the barren lands of Oklahoma. Approximately 4000 out of 15,000 Cherokees died due to hunger, disease, and the physical journey.

1876 — In the Battle of Little Big Horn, Cheyenne, Sioux, and Arapahos under the direction of Sitting Bull fought George Custer and his soldiers to protect their way of life. Also known as Custer's Last Stand.

1879 — U.S. District Court ruled in favor of Standing Bear, a Ponca leader, who sued the federal government for relocating him. The judge ruled that Native Americans had the same rights as other citizens.

1887 — Dawes Severalty Act broke up Indian nation lands into individual allotments in order to assimilate Indians and to provide land to White settlers.

1890	Wounded Knee Occupation at the Pine Ridge Reservation in South Dakota.
1924	Native Americans became U.S. citizens with the passage of the Snyder Act.
1934	Wheeler-Howard Act gave control and self-government of reservation lands to Native American tribes.
1970	Native American Rights Fund was created in order to advocate for the legal rights of Native Americans. Wampanoag leader Frank James was invited to give a speech about Thanksgiving to the Commonwealth of Massachusetts but was later disinvited when officials learned what he was scheduled to talk about. This led to the first National Day of Mourning, which commemorates the oppression of Native Americans.

1973	Occupation of Wounded Knee by the American Indian Movement to bring attention to the plight of Native Americans.
1975	Indian Self-Determination and Education Act was passed to encourage Native Americans to take leadership in health, education, and other federal programs that serve them.
1990	Native American Languages Act was passed, which protects the use, preservation, and freedom to use Native American languages in their affairs, from schools to official business.
1996	President Clinton designated November of each year to be National Indian Heritage month.
2004	The Smithsonian National Museum of the American Indian was opened in Washington, DC, on the National Mall.

Latinos/Hispanics: Diversity and Manifest Destiny

Hispanics, Latino, or Chicano

CAEP InTASC naeyc

LO3 Examine How Latinos/Hispanics were caught in the U.S. policy of Manifest Destiny.

Like Native Americans, Hispanics are an extremely diverse community, and the term "Hispanic" is an umbrella designation that is used by the U.S. Census Bureau to denote many different ethnic and racial groups. Some individuals do not like the term Hispanic because it was chosen by the federal government for demographic data collection and not chosen by the people themselves. Others do not want to be identified as Latino because their roots may not be from a Latin country. A Latin American is often thought of as a person whose family can be traced to Central or South America and who speaks Spanish or Portuguese. In contrast, some people identify with the designation of Chicano. Historians Matt Meier and Feliciano Ribera view the term "Chicano" as one of pride for those of the late twentieth century, though its history can be traced back to the days of the Spanish conquistadors (1993). Often, the term Chicano was used as an identifier for people who advocated for the rights of Mexican Americans. In addition, sometimes the term "Chicana/o" or "Latina/o" is used to identify both females and males. For the purpose of this text general terms of Latino and Chicano will be included in the text.

There are other terms that people use to identify themselves, such as Latin American, Spanish-surnamed, Spanish-speaking, and hispanic (spelled with a lower case h) (Meier & Ribera, 1993). The word "mestizo" refers to people who are mixed. Many members of this community can trace their ancestry to Europe, Africa, and Native American communities.

Mexican Americans make up about 60 percent of today's Hispanic population in the United States. You may have heard the term *la raza*; this term refers to ethnic solidarity among Mexican Americans and other members of the Hispanic community. You also may see the terms *Nuevomeixanos*, *Californios*, or *Tejans* to identify Spanish-Mexican people who want to distinguish themselves from Anglos, Anglo Americans, or European Americans. Some individuals have decided to identify themselves with more specific terms such as Cuban, Cuban American, Puerto Rican, Puerto Rican American, Mexican, Mexican American, Venezuelan, or Venezuelan American.

In order for you, the teacher, to understand the ethnic identity of students, it is best to have students explain how they identify themselves. For the purpose of discussion in this book, the terms Latin American and Hispanic will be used interchangeably.

Treaty of Guadalupe Hidalgo

Many Latino Americans are indigenous people to lands that are now part of the United States, and many teachers may not realize that the ancestors of some of their Latino students may be native to the area. For example, Ed Rivera is 80 years old and his ancestors have always lived in what is now New Mexico. His family is indigenous to the region. However, many of his neighbors do not know his familial roots go back before the formation of the United States.

The Treaty of Guadalupe Territory

How did Ed's family become part of the United States? In 1848, the Treaty of Guadalupe Hidalgo was signed, ending the Mexican-American War. In that treaty, the United States acquired over 500,000 square miles of territory that was originally Mexico. This area is now known as California, Utah, Texas, and Nevada. Parts of Arizona, New Mexico, Wyoming, and Colorado were also obtained. If you had lived at that time, let's say in Nevada, you went from being a citizen of Mexico to being a resident in a territory of the United States. More about this treaty will be explained in a later section. The Treaty of Guadalupe Hidalgo resulted in the addition of 525,000 square miles to the United States.

Did you know there were advanced civilizations that developed in the Western Hemisphere years before Columbus arrived in the Bahamas? These civilizations were the Maya, Inca, and Aztec. When people do not know about a group, they may cultivate and promote beliefs that can eventually turn into stereotypes. As teachers, it is important you know about the historical roots of your students.

Mexican Americans: Indigenous People

Many Mexican Americans and other Latinos have strong indigenous roots. For example, the Maya had created an extensive and sophisticated civilization around 1000 B.C. They established four major cities, which are now part of Mexico and Central America: Uaxactún (Guatemala), Bonampak (Chiapas, Mexico), Copán (Honduras), and Tikal (Guatemala). Each was an important center for government, religion, trade, and education. A hierarchical system was put in place with religious leaders at the top and peasants at the bottom. The communities were linked by a system of roads and governments that were based on clans and tribes (Meier & Ribera, 1993).

According to Cornelius (1999), the Maya culture was primarily organized around the growing and cultivation of corn. In fact, the people honored a goddess of maize called Centeotl. The Maya had a special ceremony to give thanks for corn and were careful to make sure to harvest all the produce to avoid wasting any of the precious life that was shared with them. Social studies textbooks may indicate that corn was important, but they may not explain how the culture of people in this civilization centered on corn. A community's diet has revealed powerful philosophical and religious beliefs about the role and origin of corn in people's lives (Cornelius, 1999).

The Maya also used specialized agricultural techniques. For example, the Maya used a slash and burn strategy of harvesting along with the application of an irrigation system. They also terraced and fertilized their crops. Maya grew other products besides corn such as beans, peppers, tomatoes, and cacao. They became extremely successful in growing crops and were able to spend time developing other skills in mathematics, astronomy, and architecture. One of the most important concepts that the Maya discovered was the construct of zero, the use of zero in their counting and not as a placeholder (Mann, 2011). Have you ever thought of how we would count without a zero? How would we subtract and add without a zero? Our number system would be very different. The Maya also developed a place value system using a base of 20 unlike our base 10 system. The Maya civilization created a more precise calendar system 1000 years before the European Gregorian calendar (Meier & Ribera, 1993). Scientists are not sure what happened to the Maya civilization. There is evidence that extreme drought and over use of natural resources may have pushed the people from their homes in massive numbers (Mann, 2011).

Manifest Destiny

In the 1800s **Manifest Destiny**, the move to expand the United States from the Atlantic Ocean to the Pacific, was one of the most powerful forces within this nation. After France sold the Louisiana Territory to the United States in 1803, many Anglo American settlers also wanted to gain Texas. As the United States tried to acquire more land, conflicts with Mexico arose. During the same time period, people who lived in Texas wanted their independence, and Mexico sent armed troops to squash the rebellion. After many fierce battles between Anglo Americans, Tejanos (Mexicans who lived in Texas), and Mexican soldiers, the Treaty of Velasco between Mexico and Texas was signed. Texas gained its independence from Mexico in 1836 (Meier & Ribera, 1993).

> **Manifest Destiny** is the move to expand the United States from the Atlantic Ocean to the Pacific.

Texas requested to be annexed by the United States. Mexico and the United States had been in conflict over land for many years. However, this antagonism brought both countries to war when the United States annexed Texas in March of 1845. In 1847, the United States sent troops to Mexico City and occupied the capital. In a weakened position, Mexico was forced to sign the Treaty of Guadalupe Hidalgo on February 2, 1848.

Through the Treaty of Guadalupe Hidalgo, the United States acquired over half a million square miles of land. Our nation paid Mexico $15 million for a little over half a million square acres. The approximately 80,000 Mexican citizens became U.S. nationals. Most chose U.S. citizenship; they were assured property and religious rights. See the Locator Map for a comprehensive view of how much land was annexed by the United States.

Think about the history of Mexican Americans and the stereotypes that abound about their community. Many families have roots in what is now the United States hundreds of years prior to when they became citizens. There are many stereotypes around the idea that Mexican Americans are all undocumented migrants; however, this is obviously not true. One of the reasons that history is powerful is because it provides more information about the context of many of the issues that we are confronted with today. Understanding history and the context behind what is happening currently in your world is an important aspect of being a citizen. See the Latinos/Hispanics in the United States Timeline.

TIMELINE

LATINOS/HISPANICS IN THE UNITED STATES

1519 — Hernán Cortés, a Spanish conquistador, landed in what is now Mexico.

1521 — Cortés along with Indian allies took over the Aztec city of Tenochtitián, and the Aztec empire fell.

1598 — The first permanent Spanish settlement was established in New Mexico.

1700 — Spain began settling in what is now known as Arizona.

1716 — Spain began to establish settlements in what is now known as Texas.

1718 — The mission and presidio of San Diego was established by Father Junipero Serra.

1769 — Father Juniper Serra established the mission and presidio of San Diego.

1810 — Mexicans began their fight for independence from Spain on September 16. This is celebrated annually in communities especially in the Southwest.

1821 — Mexico won its independence from Spain.

1836 — Texas declared independence from Mexico and created the Republic of Texas after defeating Mexican troops at San Jacinto.

1845 — United States annexed Texas, which became the 28th state.

1846 — Beginning of the Mexican-American War over Texas and border issues.

1848 — Treaty of Guadalupe Hidalgo was signed between Mexico and the United States. The United States acquired over 500,000 square miles of territory (Texas, California, Nevada, and Utah, most of Arizona and New Mexico, and parts of Colorado and Oklahoma).

1890s — Mexican citizens migrated north seeking work.

1895 — Puerto Rican immigrants gathered in New York City pledging independence for Puerto Rico and Cuba.

1898 — During the Spanish-American War, New Mexicans joined the Rough Riders in Cuba. As a result of the Treaty of Paris, the United States received the territories of Guam, Puerto Rico, and the Philippines.

The United States began a period of "Americanization" of Puerto Rico.

1903 — Mexican Americans working in beet fields carried out a successful strike in Ventura, California.

1910 — Revolution in Mexico resulted in the migration of Mexican immigrants north to the United States in search of employment and safety. Francisco (Pancho) Villa and Emiliano Zapata were two leaders in the revolution.

1917 — Passage of the Jones Act, which allows Puerto Ricans to gain U.S. citizenship and gave the United States control over the immigration, defense, and other governmental affairs of Puerto Rico.

1929 — A group calling for assimilation and U.S. citizenship, the League of United Latin American Citizens, was established in Texas.

1930 — Lemon Grove Incident in which Roberto Alvarez, a 12-year-old student, was the main plaintiff in the first legal challenge to school segregation.

1939 — John Steinbeck published the novel, *Grapes of Wrath*, which tells the story of migrant workers.

| **1942–1964** | Mexico and the United States entered into an agreement, the Bracero Program (guest worker program), that allowed Mexican immigrants to enter the country and work on farms. They became the backbone of the farming industry in states like California, Arizona, and New Mexico. |

| **1942** | Sleepy Lagoon case regarding the murder of José Diaz; a group of Mexican American youth were convicted of the crime with little evidence. |

| **1943** | Zoot Suit Riots raged in Los Angeles for more than a week when Mexican American youth who wore zoot suits were beaten, their suits torn off their bodies by Whites. The Los Angeles police did little to stop the violence. |

| **1947** | In *Mendez* v. *Westminster School District*, Mexican Americans fought school segregation and won. The parents of Gonzalo and Felicitas Mendez claimed that they were being discriminated against based on national origin. |

| **1954** | Operation Wetback was a program of deportation implemented by the U.S. Immigration and Naturalization Service and targeted Mexican American immigrants. |

| **1959** | Cuba was taken over by Fidel Castro. |

| **1961** | President Dwight D. Eisenhower closed the embassy in Havana and severed diplomatic ties with Cuba (January 3). Due to the Cuban Missile crisis, all planes to the United States were stopped.

President Kennedy implemented the Cuban Refugee Program. Many unaccompanied children were sent to the United States by air and boat. |

| **1965** | César Chávez, Dolores Huerta, and Philip Vera Cruz established the United Farm Workers Association; they also led a grape strike in the Central Valley of California. |

| **1966** | The Cuban Refugee Adjustment Act granted legal status to Cuban nationals who entered or already resided in the United States for at least one year. |

| **1975** | Due to discrimination at polling places, the U.S. Voting Rights Act was expanded to require language assistance when voting. The original act of 1965 applied only to Blacks and Puerto Ricans. |

| **1980** | The first Cuban refugees left their country by boat in April. |

| **1986** | The Immigration and Reform Act of 1986 provided a pathway to citizenship for those who had entered the country without documentation since 1982 and also prohibited the hiring of undocumented immigrants. |

| **2003** | The newest U.S. Census data showed that Hispanics are the largest minority group with 37.1 million people. |

| **2006** | Many Hispanic, Latino American, and other individuals demonstrate in support of the rights of immigrants. |

| **2009** | The DREAM Act (Development, Relief, and Education of Alien Minors) was introduced in Congress to provide pathway to citizenship for students came to the United States before sixteen years of age, resided continuously for more than five years, and graduated from high school. The act did not pass and was reintroduced in 2011. |

CASE STUDY Puerto Rican Americans: Citizens

In the 1800s, Spain wanted to continue to hold onto Puerto Rico as a military base. As Eakin (2007) notes, during this time the country had a successful sugar plantation economy. There were also increasing revolts from local inhabitants, the Spanish born on Puerto Rico, as well as individuals who were captured as slaves from Africa and forced to work in the sugar plantations. There were several major slave rebellions in the nineteenth century, and these eventually led to Puerto Rico gaining its independence from Spain in 1898. However during the transition period, the United States took over Puerto Rico during the Spanish-American War and its status, to this day, is still in question, though, as Eakin points out it acts like a territory of the United States. The Jones Act of Puerto Rico in 1917 made Puerto Ricans official citizens of the United States. Puerto Ricans have a much different historical background than other Latinos. Puerto Rico continues to be controlled by the United States and though some would like it to become a state, this has not occurred. There are about four million Puerto Ricans who live on the island, and since they are citizens, the population can move freely between the island and the U.S. mainland. There are approximately three million Puerto Ricans living on the U.S. mainland. They are U.S. citizens and yet culturally and linguistically they are more like their neighbors who reside in Latin American countries like Panama, El Salvador, Honduras, Haiti, the Dominican Republic, Brazil, Venezuela, and Peru (Eakin, 2007). People in Puerto Rico speak both English and Spanish.

Puerto Rican Americans are part of the Hispanic/Latino community. Hispanics/Latinos are an extremely diverse population.

Reflection Questions

Q Are Puerto Ricans U.S. citizens?

Q Based on what you answered above, what does that mean about their movements between Puerto Rico and the mainland?

LO4 Investigate the slavery of African Americans as a legal and accepted practice in the United States.

Indentured servants are people who agree to a contract to work for another; in colonial times, the agreement was often for a period of about seven years.

African Americans: Explorers and Slavery

What do you know about African American experiences? You probably know African American role models such as Harriet Tubman, Rosa Parks, and Martin Luther King, Jr., but do you how their ancestors arrived in what is now the continental United States?

Many of the first African Americans came here as indentured servants in the early 1700s. An **indentured servant** is someone who agrees to a contract to work for another for a specified time, after which they gain their freedom. Initially Africans who migrated to the United States were not considered enslaved individuals, rather they were indentured servants. This is an important aspect of history. They had freedoms. However, this drastically changed.

African Explorers in the New World

Many Africans were explorers and members of Spanish and French expeditions. Franklin (1974) tells of Nuflo de Olano, an African explorer who accompanied the Spanish explorer, Balboa, when he identified the Pacific Ocean.

It is important for students to know that there were African explorers as well as Italian, Spanish, French, and English. Because history is often taught from the perspective of the victors, we do not learn about courageous people from underrepresented groups. Consider the story of Estevanico. According to Franklin, Estevanico, enslaved from Africa, was an explorer who opened up the lands now known as Arizona and New Mexico for Spanish control of the area. Estevanico is considered the first African to have set foot in what is now the United States.

Another African explorer in North America was Jean Baptiste Point du Sable who spoke French and is thought to have been from Haiti. In approximately 1790, he built the first building in what would be known as the city of Chicago (Franklin, 1974). Point du Sable is also thought to be the first non-Native resident of Chicago and had a trading post there.

It is difficult to find much information about these two explorers. Why might that be the case? Can you think of any other African explorers of that time? Have your students identify and investigate other African explorers and the contributions they made in establishing our nation.

Global Slavery

As Franklin notes, prior to the fifteenth century, slavery was common in Europe, the Middle East, Asia, and Africa. Enslaved people may have worked in the homes of wealthy landowners, but they were not always seen as intellectually inferior; many also had the opportunity to learn and develop new skills. Those who were slaves could be from any country. For example, Egyptians captured individuals from the Mediterranean to Nubia, and the people primarily worked as servants (Franklin, 1974).

Indentured Servant or Slave?

In order to earn their way on a ship to the East Coast of America, many individuals, both African and European, signed contracts as indentured servants. These contracts stipulated that after they worked, usually for a period of seven years, and repaid their passage to the United States, they became free people. These contracts provided a way for African immigrants to become free men in the colonies. The twenty African men who came off of a Dutch ship and helped establish Jamestown in 1619 were indentured servants and not slaves.

During the fourteenth and fifteenth centuries, many explorers from Spain and Portugal sailed to various places in Africa, especially along its coast. During those journeys, they often captured people who they took to Europe; they rationalized that it was a better life for the Africans because they would be taught Christianity and leave their "heathen" lives behind (Franklin, 1974). As time went by, European countries had fewer need for large numbers of slaves; however, there was an increasing need for labor in the colonies. Slavery became one of the largest and most profitable businesses in the New World; cheap labor was needed in the fields where cotton, tobacco, and sugarcane were grown.

Slavery began to develop in what is now the United States in the early 1500s around the beginning of the Renaissance period that was taking place in Europe. Around 1517, Bishop Bartolomeo de Las Casas, a Dominican friar, encouraged Spaniards to import African slaves and use them in the New World. Even though Las Casas advocated for anti-slavery and the rights of Native Americans in the New World, by doing so he in turn encouraged the capture of slaves from Africa. Because of La Casas's influence, Spain decided to lift its ban against enslaving Africans. During this time there were many countries engaged in the trading of African men as slaves. Powerful European countries such as Spain, England, France, Holland, and Portugal all engaged in the capture and bondage of men from the west coast of Africa (Franklin, 1974). Africans fought against being captured by throwing themselves off the ship while they could still see land, or developing a mutiny along the six month journey to the New World (Blassingame, 1979). As the colonies and their businesses grew stronger, there was a greater need for labor. During the eighteenth century, England was one of the most active countries in the slave trade.

Unfortunately, during the expansion of the colonies, the institution of slavery evolved into legitimate and legalized bondage and continued that way for several generations. In the early part of the twentieth century, W. E. B. Du Bois, a prominent African American scholar and co-founder of the NAACP, asserted that slavery developed as a lawful institution during the Renaissance, which roughly spanned a timeframe from the fifteenth century to the seventeenth century. During the Renaissance, Europeans began to believe that they had freedom to pursue what they wanted (Franklin, 1974). Du Bois believed that this shift in thinking enabled people to exploit and take away the rights of others.

Slavery Brought to the New World

Slave trade developed as one of the most profitable businesses in the New World (Goodheart, 2011). Colonists found that Native Americans were difficult to keep as slaves because the communities they were taken from were still close by and they could easily escape. However, the colonists soon realized that it made more sense to capture and enslave African men; these

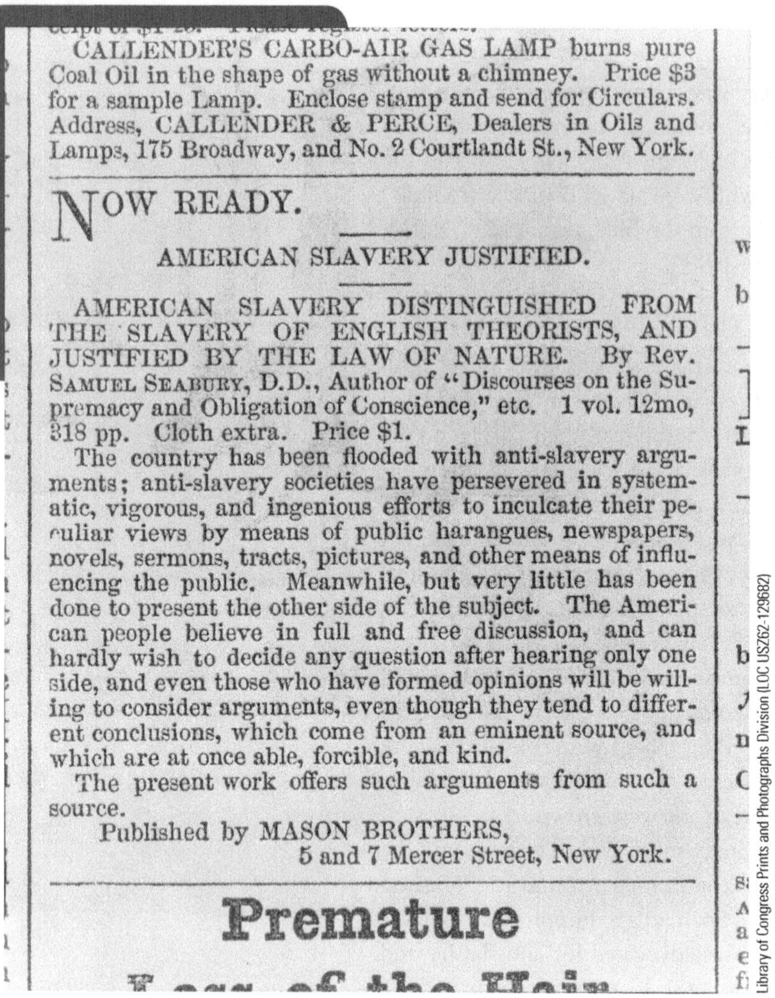

CALLENDER'S CARBO-AIR GAS LAMP burns pure Coal Oil in the shape of gas without a chimney. Price $3 for a sample Lamp. Enclose stamp and send for Circulars. Address, CALLENDER & PERCE, Dealers in Oils and Lamps, 175 Broadway, and No. 2 Courtlandt St., New York.

NOW READY.

AMERICAN SLAVERY JUSTIFIED.

AMERICAN SLAVERY DISTINGUISHED FROM THE SLAVERY OF ENGLISH THEORISTS, AND JUSTIFIED BY THE LAW OF NATURE. By Rev. SAMUEL SEABURY, D.D., Author of "Discourses on the Supremacy and Obligation of Conscience," etc. 1 vol. 12mo, 318 pp. Cloth extra. Price $1.

The country has been flooded with anti-slavery arguments; anti-slavery societies have persevered in systematic, vigorous, and ingenious efforts to inculcate their peculiar views by means of public harangues, newspapers, novels, sermons, tracts, pictures, and other means of influencing the public. Meanwhile, but very little has been done to present the other side of the subject. The American people believe in full and free discussion, and can hardly wish to decide any question after hearing only one side, and even those who have formed opinions will be willing to consider arguments, even though they tend to different conclusions, which come from an eminent source, and which are at once able, forcible, and kind.

The present work offers such arguments from such a source.

Published by MASON BROTHERS,
5 and 7 Mercer Street, New York.

Premature

Library of Congress Prints and Photographs Division (LOC USZ62-129682)

Figure 4.2: "American Slavery Justified" was published in 1861 by Samuel Seabury.

Middle passage is the name for the slave's journey to the Americas across the ocean.

men were a lot less likely to escape back to their families because they would need to find a way back across the vast Atlantic Ocean. In addition, they did not speak the local languages and were physically easy to identify. These factors made it extremely difficult for kidnapped Africans to escape. The language used is notable. When the term slave is used it seems to denote that a person was only a slave. His or her own views and beliefs were not important. However, this book uses men who were enslaved or enslaved people because this indicates that African Americans were more than slaves; they were humans first and then they were captured or enslaved by more powerful others. Slave owners developed specific strategies to maximize their profits. One of the critical values they held was that people who were enslaved were property and not humans.

There have been estimates that between 1701 and 1810 there were 6,051,700 men enslaved from Africa and taken to the New World. In addition, between 1810 and 1870, 1,898,400 individuals were captured and delivered. This indicates that between 1451 and 1870, approximately 9,566,100 people from Africa were sold in the New World (Franklin, 1974). It is also thought that many people died during the **middle passage**, the name for the slave's journey to the Americas, as well as when captured, so the numbers of men who were actually taken from Africa are much higher. Figure 4.2 shows and advertisement in the newspaper for a book that justifies slavery. The author believed that some people were superior to others. In Chapter 5 we will discuss abolitionist Frederick Douglass, who escaped slavery.

Ethnic Diversity

Most African Americans have roots in Western Africa. Their ancestors were kidnapped from countries now known as Ghana, The Republic of Congo, and Angola. Many families have been in the United States for hundreds of years. However, today there is an increase in African refugees fleeing persecution. Africans who come from Africa today bring different cultural backgrounds to this country.

The United States takes its cue from the United Nations High Commissioner for Refugees, which defines a refugee as someone who is unwilling or cannot return to their homeland because of fear of prosecution; their status is based on race, a social group, political orientation, religion, or national origin (American Immigration Council, 2014). Recently, there have been numerous African refugees who have migrated to the United States; they came from countries such as Liberia, Sudan, and Somalia. In 2015, the number of African immigrants, which includes refugees, was 3.8 million people—four times more than in 1980 (Anderson, 2015a). How are African immigrants and African Americans different? The median age of African immigrants is 42-years-old in comparison to 29 for African Americans (Anderson, 2015b). More immigrant Blacks are likely to be married and live in a household with a higher income.

See the African Americans in the United States Timeline for a general history of African Americans in the United States.

TIMELINE

AFRICAN AMERICANS IN THE UNITED STATES

1494	Free Africans were members of Christopher Columbus's crew who landed in San Salvador during several of his later trips.
1501	The King of Spain allowed Africans who were slaves to be taken to Spanish colonies in what is now the United States.
1518	The King of Spain allowed the capture of Africans from Africa to be used as slaves in the West Indies.
1526	First non-native settlement in the United States was established by Africans, who were initially enslaved by Spanish explorers, in present-day South Carolina near the Pee Dee River.
1565	African Americans along with Spanish colonists built the colony in St. Augustine, Florida.
1607	The English settlement, Jamestown, was established in Virginia.
1620	Pilgrims arrived from Europe to what is now Massachusetts.
1634	Slavery began in the colony of Maryland.
1641	Slavery was legalized in the colony of Massachusetts.
1662	In the Virginia colony, it was established that children born to a woman who was a slave would inherit her status and not their fathers'. This was called *Partus sequitur ventrem*. This ensured that children born of White fathers would continue to be born into slavery.
1667	The colony of Massachusetts legalized the sale of children from enslaved families.
1763	Emancipation Proclamation dismantled slavery in many states, primarily those in the North.
1831	Nat Turner, originally born a slave, led a revolt of slaves in Virginia.
1851	Sojourner Truth delivered a speech at the Women's Rights Convention in Ohio. Her speech entitled "Ain't I A Woman?" discusses the need for women's rights and Black rights.
1852	Harriet Beecher Snow published her novel, *Uncle Tom's Cabin*.
1857	Dred Scott decision. Supreme Court ruled that African Americans cannot become citizens of the United States.
1859	John Brown, a White abolitionist, raided Harpers Ferry in order to get arms to fight against slavery. He was captured and later hanged.
1862	The District of Columbia abolished slavery.
1863	Lincoln's Emancipation Proclamation took effect on January 1; people who were slaves were freed in rebellious states in the South.
1865	The Thirteenth Amendment was passed by Congress abolishing slavery.
1866	The Ku Klux Klan was established to intimidate African Americans and other ethnic groups; the group believed in White supremacy.
1870	The Fifteenth Amendment was passed by Congress, granting the right to vote to African Americans by stating that citizens cannot be prohibited from voting due to their race, color, or previous position as a slave.
1896	The Supreme Court decision of *Plessy* v. *Ferguson* ruled that "separate but equal" was constitutional.
1904	Mary McCleod Bethune established a school for African American girls, which later became Bethune-Cookman College in Daytona Beach.
1905	The Niagara Movement was organized by W. E. B. Du Bois. This movement brought together African American intellectuals who created a document identifying their principles of civil rights such as the belief in equal treatment in public facilities and equal economic opportunity.
1910	An interracial group of people came together to create the National Association for the Advancement of Colored People (NAACP) to fight racism against African Americans. Blacks such as W. E. B. Du Bois, Ida B. Wells-Barnett, and Mary Church Terrell along with White members such as John Dewey, Mary White Ovington, Oswald Garrison Villard, and Jane Addams worked together to establish the organization.
1917	Race riot in St. Louis, Illinois, resulted in the death of 39 African Americans.
1919	In Chicago, Illinois, a series of race riots occurred; 23 African American and 15 White Americans were killed.

(Continued)

AFRICAN AMERICANS IN THE UNITED STATES *continued*

1943	In Detroit, Michigan, during a riot against African Americans, 25 African Americans and 9 White Americans were killed.
1954	In the Supreme Court decision *Brown* v. *Board of Education*, the justices ruled that school segregation was inherently unequal.
1955	Rosa Parks refused to give up her seat on a bus to a White person. She was arrested. Her actions were the beginning of the Montgomery Bus Boycott that lasted 381 days. She is called the "mother of the Civil Rights Movement." The day after Rosa Parks was arrested, the Montgomery Bus Boycott began. The Supreme Court ruled in 1956 that Montgomery's segregation laws were unconstitutional.
1957	Martin Luther King, Jr., established the Southern Christian Leadership Conference (SCLS), a civil rights action group.
1960	Sit-in movement began in Greensboro, North Carolina, at a Woolworth lunch counter. African American teenagers from a local college, Franklin McCain, Joseph McNeil, Ezell Blair, Jr., and David Richmond, sat down at the counter and ordered coffee, donuts, and soda. They protested segregation of public facilities such as restaurants, drinking fountains, and bathrooms. SNCC (Student Nonviolent Coordinating Committee) was formed at Shaw University and became a powerful force in the Civil Rights Movement.
1961	Freedom Riders, both African American and White American, took buses to Alabama and Mississippi to desegregate interstate travel. They were beaten, their buses bombed, and police did not protect them.
1963	Martin Luther King, Jr., led a march in Birmingham, Alabama. The protesters were attacked by the police. Martin Luther King, Jr., spoke to 200,000 protesters who marched on Washington. He delivered his "I Have A Dream" speech.
1964	The Civil Rights Act of 1964 was passed by Congress and signed by President Lyndon B. Johnson.
1965	The Voting Rights Act was passed.

1967	The Supreme Court ruled against state interracial marriage bans in *Loving* v. *Virginia*.
1968	Martin Luther King, Jr., was assassinated. The first African American woman, Shirley Chisholm, was elected to U.S. Congress. The Kerner Report, written by the National Advisory Commission on Civil Disorders, reported that White racism, economic inequalities, and educational inequalities were major reasons for the violence and race riots that occurred throughout the nation.
1972	The Equal Opportunity Employment Act was passed and prohibited discrimination based on color, race, religion, gender, and national origin in employment.
1983	The federal holiday commemorating the life of Martin Luther King, Jr., the first named for an African American, was established by Ronald Reagan.
1990s	Somali refugees arrived in the United States.
1993	Toni Morrison was the first African American novelist to be honored with the Nobel Prize in literature.
1996	Rising racial strife led to the burning of 40 churches of African American communities.
2003	The Supreme Court in *Grutter* v. *Bollinger* upheld the University of Michigan Law School's admission policy, sustaining affirmative action.
2008	Barack Obama was elected the 44th President of the United States; he is the first African American President.
2013	The Black Lives Matter movement begins after George Zimmerman was acquitted of shooting Treyvon Martin, an unarmed African American young man.
2015	Dylann Roof killed nine African Americans in Charleston, SC, at the Emanuel African Methodist Episcopal Church. They had invited him to join their Bible study session.
2016	Smithsonian National Museum of African American History and Culture opens on the National Mall.

Asian Americans and Pacific Islanders

> **LO5** Assess the exclusion and internment of Asian Americans and Pacific Islanders in the United States..

How much do you know about the experiences of Asian Americans and Pacific Islanders? In many social studies and history textbooks, little is written about their history in the United States. Because of this omission, students do not know much about what happened to these groups and how hard they have worked to establish themselves in the United States. This extremely diverse community is almost invisible in much of the school curriculum.

Asian American and Pacific Islanders are an extremely diverse population. Many people think all Asians look the same or are all alike. This is a stereotypical view, Asian Americans and Pacific Islanders (AAPI) are a heterogeneous population, meaning that they are composed of unrelated or differing parts. The acronym of AAPI is used in today's research to show that Pacific Islanders have their own cultural orientations and history compared to Asian Americans.

Ethnic Diversity

According to the U.S. Census Bureau, in 2010, there were approximately 17.3 million Asian Americans and 1.2 million Pacific Islanders living in the United States; together these two distinct groups represented approximately 5.5 percent of the U.S. population. The states with the largest AAPI numbers are California, New York, and Hawaii. In fact, in Hawaii, AAPIs make up 57 percent of the state population. The AAPI population continues to grow at a record pace; their numbers have increased by over 40 percent in the past decade (U.S. Census Bureau, 2011). By 2050, it is estimated that AAPIs will number over 43 million people and account for almost 10 percent of the U.S. population.

It is important that you understand the diversity within the AAPI community. Listed here are a number of select American ethnic groups from the AAPI community:

- Asian Indian
- Bangladeshi
- Burmese
- Chinese
- Filipino
- Guamanian
- Hmong
- Indonesian
- Iwo Jiman
- Japanese
- Korean

- Laotian
- Malaysian
- Maldivian
- Marshallese
- Native Hawaiian
- Nepalese
- Okinawan
- Pakistani
- Palauan
- Singaporean
- Samoan
- Tahitian
- Taiwanese
- Thai
- Tibetan
- Vietnamese

These groups are not often studied and differ in many aspects; from their personal history in the United States to the languages they speak at home, as well as the cultural values that make up their groups. They also achieve at different levels in school (Pang, Han, & Pang, 2011). Keep in mind that there are many AAPIs who are members of more than one ethnic or racial group. For example, Asian Indians are one of the fastest growing Asian American communities. Their contributions to this country are numerous; Indra Nooyi is Chief Executive Officer of Pepsi and Satya Nadella is Chief Executive Officer of Microsoft. Both were born in India. According to Desilver (2014), in 2010, 87.2 percent of Asian Indian adults were immigrants and 70 percent of those over 25 had earned a college degree. Many have come on specialty occupation visas in science and engineering (Desilver, 2014).

The ancestors of AAPIs or they themselves moved to the United States from a variety of countries. Though AAPIs are often referred to as foreigners, many are native born and fifth- or sixth-generation American. As teachers, we must be careful not to treat students who may appear to be physically different or speak another language other than English as if they were foreigners (Pang, 2006). Like in the case of Hispanics/Latinos, this may not only be inaccurate but also hurtful because the implied message is that Asian American and Pacific Islander students do not belong in the United States.

Nativist Movement

Racism is also a dominant theme in AAPI history. The Nativist movement in California was one of the most powerful anti-immigrant forces in the United States. Nativism gathered force during the second half of the nineteenth century when jobs were at a minimum and many European American workers felt that Chinese labor drove down their wages. Nativists did not support immigration, and they often made the lives of immigrants more difficult by passing laws that were used against them. Nativists often believed that immigrants could not benefit the United States because they would not assimilate into the mainstream. Due to the political and social pressures exercised by Nativists, the Chinese Exclusion Act was passed by Congress in 1882 barring Chinese laborers from entering the United States for ten years. Chinese immigrants were the first ethnic group to be prohibited from migration. This legislation was extended for another ten years in 1892 and further renewed in 1902 until the exclusion became permanent in 1904 (Leong & Okazaki, 2009).

The pattern of recruiting Asian laborers continued after the 1882 Chinese Exclusion Act; Japanese immigrants were not only enlisted to labor in Hawaii, but also on the

West Coast. They found work in agricultural fields, railroad construction, and canneries (Takaki, 1993). Japanese children, along with their Korean immigrant peers, were also subjected to legal discrimination. In 1906, the San Francisco Board of Education ruled that the children of Japanese and Korean families had to attend segregated schools with Chinese American students; this ruling included students who were U.S. born Asian Americans.

There was a push and pull dynamic acting upon Asian immigrants. First, they were encouraged to move to the United States and Hawaii in order to provide cheap labor in the fields. However, when they became successful, many Nativists did not want them living in the United States any longer. As they worked the land, Japanese, Korean, and South Indian immigrants were able to clear some of the most difficult areas and develop profitable farms. Nevertheless, prejudice toward Asians grew and resulted in California passing the Alien Land Law of 1913, which prohibited Asians from purchasing property. This law was further expanded in 1920, and the Nativist movement continued to be strong, especially in the West. Legislation was passed so that Japanese American immigrants and their sons could not own land. With the outbreak of World War II and the bombing of Pearl Harbor, prejudice against Asian Americans and Japanese Americans in particular became much stronger.

Japanese Americans and Internment

Japanese Americans were subjected to serious discrimination after Japan's bombing of Pearl Harbor on December 7, 1941. Hawaii had been a territory of the United States since 1898, and its people were considered citizens. When the Japanese bombed Pearl Harbor, they also struck the Japanese Hawaiians and Pacific Islander American populations who were residents. People often do not consider that the Japanese American population was also bombed by the Japanese. These actions by the country of Japan had a ghastly impact on Japanese Americans. Several months later, on February 19, 1942, President Franklin D. Roosevelt signed Executive Order 9066; this document ordered all Japanese Americans who lived 100 miles inland from the West Coast to be taken away from their homes and property and placed into prison camps.

The order authorized the removal of all 120,000 Japanese Americans who lived on the West Coast from the state of Washington through Oregon and down California to the Mexican border. Though not one Japanese American was found to have committed espionage, all were evacuated, even children. Over 77,000 were American-born citizens of Japanese ancestry and 43,000 were Japanese American nationals who had become permanent residents (Japanese American Citizens League, 2011). (See Figure 4.3.) The Japanese Americans were incarcerated by their own government (Chan, 1991).

Most of the Japanese Americans were sent to 10 major concentration camps located in Idaho, California, Wyoming, Arizona, Colorado, Utah, and Arkansas. Children, teenagers, parents, and grandparents were sent from their homes to camps, which were often located in a desert (Figure 4.4). Many of the people in the Seattle area were taken by bus to the Puyallup Fairgrounds, for example. Some stayed in a horse stall for over three months. Later they boarded trains and were taken to Hunt, Idaho to live in the Minidoka camp. Why were they taken away? Because of their perceived physical differences and the extreme racism of the time. They were of Japanese ancestry. It did not matter that they were American citizens. The internment of Japanese Americans demonstrates how stereotypes, fear, and hatred can make one group turn on another based completely on looks and differences in so-called race.

After the Japanese attack on Pearl Harbor, many groups had called into question the loyalty of Japanese Americans. Even prior to and during World War II Americans from *The Los Angeles Times* to the Western Growers Protective Association had begun to scrutinize

Figure 4.3: Japanese American children reciting the Pledge of Allegiance, though taken away from their homes.

Japanese Americans' loyalty to the United States (Takaki, 1993). However, many incarcerated Japanese Americans wanted to prove their loyalty and demonstrate their belief in the importance of democracy, and so they volunteered for the armed services. While their families were imprisoned in internment camps, Japanese Americans comprised the 442nd regimental unit, a segregated Army unit.

Figure 4.4: Mananar was an internment camp where Japanese Americans were taken in the high desert of California. It was extremely hot in the summer and cold in the winter. The people shared barracks.

Table 4.2 Japanese Americans: Constitutional Rights Violated during World War II	
Constitutional Rights Violated	**Description**
Freedom of religion	Japanese Americans could not practice their religion, especially Buddhism and Shintoism. They were encouraged to practice Christianity.
Freedom of speech	Japanese Americans could not speak out on public issues or assemble together in internment camps.
Freedom of the press	Newspapers written in internment camps were censored and could not be written in Japanese.
Right to assemble	Large public meetings were not allowed. Speaking Japanese was also not allowed.
Freedom from unreasonable searches and seizures	The FBI searched many Japanese American homes without warrants. They confiscated radios and materials written in Japanese.
Right to an indictment or to be informed of charges	Japanese Americans were held without an indictment from a grand jury.
Right to life, liberty, and property	Japanese Americans were denied their property when they were forced to leave their homes and possessions.
Right to be confronted with accusatory witnesses	When Japanese Americans were taken away without due process and lived in internment camps, they could not confront those who accused them of crimes. They also were not told what their crimes were.
Right to call favorable witnesses	When Japanese Americans were taken away without due process and lived in internment camps, they could not call witnesses who would be favorable to them.
Right to legal counsel	Most Japanese Americans were denied the right to have a lawyer.
Right to a speedy and public trial	Japanese Americans were denied a speedy and public trial.
Right to reasonable bail	Japanese Americans did not have the opportunity to post bail.
Freedom from cruel and unusual punishment	Japanese Americans were subjected to deplorable treatment like living in horse stalls and taken to internment camps without adequate healthcare and food. Schools were of poor quality.
Right against involuntary servitude	Japanese Americans worked internment camps, from being cooks to acting as nurses; however, their pay was much lower than current wages.
Right to equal protection under the laws	Japanese Americans were not protected by the Bill of Rights. They were accused because of their Japanese ancestry, not provided compensation for their property losses, and deprived of freedom when held in prisons with armed guards, surrounded by barbed wire fences.
Right to vote	Japanese Americans were not allowed to vote, which is a fundamental right of citizens.
Right to habeas corpus (to be brought before a court)	Japanese Americans were denied being brought to court at a specific time and place. The government also tried to suspend the *writ of habeas corpus*.

*Information adapted from the Japanese American Citizens League's *The Japanese American Experience*, 2011.

The internment of Japanese Americans is important to all Americans because when the rights of citizens are taken, every citizen is in jeopardy. The constitutional rights of Japanese Americans that were violated during World War II are outlined in Table 4.2.

Many Japanese Americans and other citizens have pushed for redress of this issue. After extensive attempts at getting legislation passed, more than 40 years after Executive Order 9066 authorized the removal of Japanese Americans to concentration camps, President Reagan signed the Civil Liberties Act of 1988, which called for a national apology from the U.S. government and monetary compensation to survivors. This act is a milestone in U.S. history because it is the first time that the government gave redress to an entire group of citizens because their constitutional rights were taken away. These events plus many more are included in the Asian Americans and Pacific Islanders in the United States Timeline.

ASIAN AMERICANS AND PACIFIC ISLANDERS IN THE UNITED STATES

Native Hawaiians lived on the Hawaiian Islands for thousands of years prior to European contact.

1763 Filipinos jumped ship in the Louisiana bayous. They become the first Asians to settle in what is now known as the United States.

1776 Captain James Cook landed on Kauai, an island in the Hawaiian chain. His crew brought deadly diseases.

1810 King Kamehameha I established the Hawaiian kingdom and unified the people.

1820 Protestant missionaries arrived in Hawaii.

1835 King Kamehameha III allowed a mainland firm to purchase a long-term lease to establish a sugar plantation.

1848 Property rights were given out to various Hawaiian families. Later these lands were bought by European and mainland businesses. Gold was found in California; many Chinese immigrants traveled to work in the gold fields.

1850 The Foreign Miner's Tax was passed forcing Chinese miners to pay higher taxes than others.

1859 Chinese children were barred from attending San Francisco public schools.

1865 Chinese immigrants were recruited to work on the Central Pacific Railroad Company's transcontinental railroad.

1867 Chinese Worker Strike involved over 2000 Chinese immigrants working on the railroad; they struck against dangerous working conditions and lower pay.

1868 The Burlingame Treaty signed by the United States and China established the right of the Chinese to travel and live in the United States. U.S. citizens were allowed the right to trade and travel to China.

1869 Anti-Chinese riot occurred in San Francisco.

1882 Chinese Exclusion Act, also known as the Geary Act, barred the immigration of Chinese workers into the United States for 10 years. First group identified by ethnic/racial membership from immigration.

1884 Mamie Tape, a Chinese American child, born in the United States was not allowed to attend school in San Francisco. The district created an "Oriental school" for her. The Supreme Court ruled in her favor.

1885 Japanese recruited to Hawaii as contract workers for expanding agriculture.

1886 Anti-Chinese riot occurred in Tacoma, Washington.

1892 Chinese Exclusion Act was extended another 10 years, limiting the rights of Chinese immigrants.

1893 Queen Liliuokalani was overthrown by a group of mainland business people. The Republic of Hawaii was established and Sanford B. Dole became its first president.

1896 In the Supreme Court decision of *U.S. v. Wong Kim Ark*, the Court ruled that a child born in the United States was a citizen and could not be barred from returning to the country because he was protected by the Fourteenth Amendment.

1898 During the Spanish American War, Hawaii was annexed and used by the United States as a military installation. The United States was given 1.8 million acres of land of the Hawaiian kingdom.

1900 Japanese workers in Hawaii began moving to the United States (mainland).

1902 Chinese exclusion extended for 10 additional years.

1903 Korean workers recruited to work in Hawaii to break strike of Japanese labor.

1904 Chinese Exclusion Act of 1904 was extended indefinitely.

1905 San Francisco Schools barred Japanese children from attending school.

1907	Filipino workers were recruited as cheap labor to work in Hawaii.
1910	Angel Island Immigration Station began processing individuals before access into the United States.
1913	California Alien Land Law was aimed at Japanese; those ineligible for citizenship could not purchase land.
	The Anti-Korean riot in Hemet, California, took pace.
1922	In the Supreme Court decision of *Takao Ozawa* v. *U.S.*, the Court ruled that Japanese immigrants were not eligible for naturalized citizenship because they were neither "White" nor "free Blacks."
1924	Asian Exclusion Act, which was part of the Immigration Act of 1924, completely barred immigration from Asia.
1942	President Franklin D. Roosevelt signed Executive Order 9066, which authorized the removal of 120,000 Japanese Americans from their homes on the West Coast.
1952	McCarren-Walter Act allowed for a minimal number of Japanese immigrants.
1956	Dalip Singh Saund became the first Asian American and South Asian elected to Congress. He also served as a judge in Imperial County, California.
1959	Hawaii became the 50th state.
	Hiram Fong became the first Asian American U.S. senator.
1965	Philip Vera Cruz, one of the original founders of the Agricultural Workers Organizing Committee, joined with the United Farm Workers and worked as Vice President with César Chavez. The 1965 Immigration Act removed the "national origin" element, changing the way immigrants were allowed into this country. Before, immigrants from Europe made up the largest numbers. As more Asian immigrants were allowed into the country, this imbalance changed.
1974	The Supreme Court in *Lau* v. *Nichols* ruled that the San Francisco school district was not providing equal educational opportunity to Kinny Lau and other Chinese American children

because students who did not speak English could not participate in a meaningful education. Bilingual education was established with this decision.

1975	Approximately 130,000 refugees from Vietnam, Laos, and Cambodia were accepted into the United States following the Vietnam War.
1983	Three Japanese Americans, Fred Korematsu (born in California), Min Yasui (born in Oregon), and Gordon Hirabayashi (born in Washington) filed petitions to overturn their World War II convictions; they had been accused of violating curfew or refusing to evacuate during the forced internment of Japanese Americans.
1988	The Civil Liberties Act was signed by President Ronald Regan. It authorized an apology and payment to all Japanese Americans who were wrongly interned during WWII due to racism, wartime hysteria, and lack of leadership.
1993	The United States apologized for its role in the overthrow and oppression of the Native Hawaiian people with Public Law 103–150.
1996	Gary Locke was elected the first Asian American governor on the mainland; he served as governor of the state of Washington.
2000	Norman Mineta was the first Asian American appointed to a cabinet position as Secretary of Commerce by President Bill Clinton. He was interned as a boy when Japanese Americans were relocated during WWII. He and his family were taken to Heart Mountain, Wyoming.
2001	Elaine Chao was appointed Secretary of Labor and became first Asian American woman cabinet member.
	Norman Mineta, an American of Japanese descent, was appointed Secretary of Transportation.
2008	Gary Locke, an American of Chinese descent, was appointed Secretary of Commerce by President Barack Obama and later served as Ambassador to China.

Jewish Americans: Anti-Semitism

Many European American groups have also suffered social oppression. One example is the Jewish American community. Though they are not a racial group, they are a religious community in which many are considered Whites and can include a variety of ethnic groups such as Russians, Germans, Polish, and Spaniards. Jews have often been discriminated against due to their religion; they are not Christians. Some individuals have accused Jews of killing Jesus Christ. Jewish scholars like Michael Galchinsky (1994) believe that Jews have given up much of their religious freedom to be considered part of a diverse nation. Though they often were forced into cultural assimilation, they often suffer from a split personality of being White in public and then practicing Judaism in private. Unfortunately, there has become a rise of anti-Semitism in countries such as Germany, France, and Iran demonstrating that prejudice against Jews are still powerful social and political forces (Brooks, 2015).

Let's take a look at the life of Joachim Gans, the first Jewish settler in the colonies; he settled in what is now North Carolina (Grassl, 1998). He landed in the New England area about 35 years prior to the Pilgrims. He was a metallurgist—his job was to accompany explorers and locate valuable metal and minerals that could be sent back to England, Portugal, or Spain.

Gans was a German Jew from Prague. He lived several years in the New World. However, when Gans returned to London after his expedition, he was accused of not believing in Jesus Christ as God. He was Jewish and so explained to the authorities that he was not Christian. In the late 1590s he could be put to death for not believing in Jesus Christ. It is not clear what happened to him. Some historians believe he was deported rather than placed in prison, while others believe he escaped and lived out his life searching for metals near the German border north of Prague (Grassl, 1998).

It is difficult to identify one event or period during which social oppression was most rampant against Jews because anti-Semitism can be found all over the world at many different time periods. (See the Jewish Americans in the United States Timeline.) **Anti-Semitism** is prejudice and hostility against Jews as individuals or as a group; it may be due to their religious beliefs, seeing the people as being inferior, or related to the state of Israel (Galchinsky, 1994). According to the Holocaust Museum in Washington, DC, anti-Semitism has occurred for over 2000 years. The Holocaust during World War II is the most grievous example of anti-Semitism. There were about 14 to 20 million Jews held in concentration camps during the war, and of those about 6 million were murdered by the Nazis (Bennett, 1995).

After World War II, when people around the world saw the horrors of the Holocaust, anti-Semitism became more limited. However as time goes by, the memory of the Holocaust has begun to fade and there has been a recent rise in anti-Semitic activities in the United States (Anti-Defamation League, 2013). For example, according to the Anti-Defamation League (2015), in 2014 anti-Semitic incidents rose 21percent from the year before; the audit compiled 912 events. They ranged from fatal shootings at a Jewish community center in Kansas by White Supremacists to destruction of Jewish property to verbal harassment of Jews. Lately, Jewish organizations and synagogues have been targeted by international hackers (Anti-Defamation League, 2015). For example, Jewish websites have been ruined and vandalized. Online discrimination is also increasing. In Chapter 5, Jewish organizations that fight for equality and against anti-Semitism will be discussed.

Anti-Semitism is prejudice and hostility against Jews as individuals or as a group; it may be due to their religious beliefs, belief that they are inferior, or related to the state of Israel.

TIMELINE

JEWISH AMERICANS IN THE UNITED STATES TIMELINE*

1655	Jews established a settlement in the New World in New Amsterdam.
1600	The British took control of New Amsterdam and renamed it New York.
1730	Jews from New York built their first synagogue, Shearith Israel.
1788	Most states adopted the U.S. Constitution providing Jews with full rights.
1791	Bill of Rights, which includes freedom of religion, was accepted.
1830s	Large numbers of Jews from Germany migrated to the United States.
1843	B'nai B'rith, a humanitarian organization, was established to support Jewish community.
1863	Labor leader Samuel Gompers arrived in the United States and later established the American Federation of Labor.
1880	According to the Union of American Hebrew Congregations, there were about 250,000 Jews living in the United States.
1893	The National Council of Jewish Women was created.
1913	Anti-Defamation League of B'nai B'rith began fighting anti-Semitism.
1915	Anti-Semitic hatred led to the lynching of Leo Frank, a Jew, in Georgia.
1917	About 200,000 Jews became members of the armed forces of the United States.
1920s	Anti-Jewish activities increased. Henry Ford was one of the most well-known anti-Semitics.
1939–1946	Over 6 million Jews were killed during the Holocaust.
1948	Brandeis University was established and led by Jewish Americans. Israel announced its independence. The United States recognized this new country.
1964	Civil Rights Act was passed, insuring the rights of Jews.
1985–1990	The USSR faltered and many Jews migrated to the United States.
1993	The Holocaust Memorial Museum opened in Washington, DC.
2000	Jewish Senator Joseph Lieberman became the vice president candidate for the Democratic Party.

*Selected events taken from Jacob Rader Marcus Center of the American Jewish Archives at http://americanjewisharchives.org/education/timeline.php.

Professional Resource Download

TEACHING TIPS

Using the Library of Congress in Your Lessons

It is important for students to take charge of their own learning. National, state, and local curriculum standards emphasize the development of critical thinking and the use of nonfiction, which includes documents and primary sources. Teachers must help to organize learning so students have initial success in using nonfiction. Remember that success begets more success. You can create lessons that help students develop successful learning skills so that they will be more motivated to keep investigating and exploring.

One of the best ways is to teach students how to conduct research and to use primary documents, which can include the U.S. Constitution or photographs of the time.

The U.S. Library of Congress is an exceptional resource. The materials in the institution are free, and it houses many references. One of the areas that I suggest you teach your students to use is the Photos, Prints, Drawings section. Though students read about history in a text, visuals can have a more powerful effect on their learning. Here is a search about the Wampanoag tribe.

1. First go to https://www.loc.gov/.
2. On the main page, a variety of places will arise. There is a section called "Photos, Prints, Drawing."
3. In the search box towards the top, type in the issue that the class is interested in. For example, let's say it is Wampanoag because they are interested in finding out information about the Native American community.

(Continued)

TEACHING TIPS *(Continued)*

4. One of the first photos that comes up is King Philip, Sachem of Wampanoags, 1676. Students can read information found on the record. Students may need to look up what Sachem means. This can get students started to investigate.

5. Reviewing the photo, students can be asked: What do you notice that King Philip is wearing? Is he wearing clothing that is what you think an Indian might wear? How is it the same or different?

6. Students should record the title of the photo and photograph number, LC-USZ62-62742. LC refers to Library of Congress. That way if students want to look it up again, they have the location number.

7. There is little in the Library of Congress about King Philip. Let's try another search.

Second Search: Narratives of Blacks Who Were Enslaved

Sometimes students may not understand some of the historical events they are taught. Events and issues are often abstract. However, using the audio files from the Library of Congress may help students to appreciate the lives of other people if they hear their stories. They also may create a poster or essay about the person. Using a timeline of events, students may add the names of various people and include their contributions and narratives to the timeline.

1. First go to https://www.loc.gov/.

2. Click on Prints and Photographs Online

3. In the search box type "African American slaves." Remember that students must use terms that are used by the Library of Congress.

4. A variety of images come up. Choose Sarah Ashley, ex-slave. See the photo of her. It is LC-USZ62-125165.

5. Let's say your students are interested in hearing stories from Black folks who were enslaved in the United States.

6. Go to the top of the former page and see the arrow next to the phrase Photo, Prints, Drawings. Pull down the menu until you find Audio Recordings. Keep the phrase African American slaves in the search box.

7. When you click the search, many narratives are available. Each one is shown by a symbol of a microphone. Pick "My grandmother was a slave."

8. Listen to the story of Donna Choate. You can also read the transcript if you look further down on the page. Donna Choate's grandmother was a slave. She loved to read.

Professional Resource Download

Thinking about Intersectionality

All the experiences of the various racial groups discussed demonstrate that race is usually not the only issue that arises in patterns of oppression. The examples include not only oppression due to race, but also economic status. People were often subjugated because they were poor. African American communities of color were enslaved and members of the Wampanoag tribe had their land taken by European settlers. Japanese American land was taken away when they were interned. The Nativist movement attacked them due to differences in their ethnic background, language, and religion. Jews were also attacked because of their religious beliefs, ancestry, and often because they lived in tight-knit communities. Mexican Americans were oppressed because they spoke Spanish, lived on land that others wanted, and were often poor. Unfortunately, analyses of intersectionality demonstrate that most groups are persecuted for more than their "racial" membership. Often others want their land, hold stereotypes of immigrants, are fearful of immigrants, and feel superior.

Summary

1. **Describe how racial oppression continues to be a powerful force in the United States.**

   Racial oppression is a perennial issue in U.S. history. Many non-White communities have been discriminated against because of their racial membership. Recent surveys from the *New York Times* and CBS News poll have found that Blacks and Whites hold extremely different views about the discrimination that Blacks encounter in the United States. Blacks were more negative about social oppression toward African Americans compared to the perspective of Whites. The experiences of many communities of color, as well as White Americans like Jews, have identified a pattern of social oppression that is still evident to many today. Teachers must study and teach the experiences of various groups from their perspective. Though history textbooks often give the views of the victors, knowing the interpretations of subjugated populations can give teachers a more in-depth understanding of conflicts that arise between groups that may play out in the classroom.

2. **Examine how immigrants influenced the lives of Native Americans.**

   Native Americans are an extremely diverse community. At one time there were millions of different indigenous groups living in what is now North America and the Bahamas. Columbus landed on San Salvador, which is now known as the Bahamas. His goal was to establish colonies for Spain and to gather resources from gold to spices. He created various trade routes and named the people in the area "Indians." However, the people were part of the Arawak nation. They were a peaceful population that treated everyone as family. This was in contrast to the explorers who felt it was their right to gather metals, take over the land, and kidnap people who were then taken to Spain as slaves. In addition, Pilgrims sought religious freedom and sailed to the area that is now Massachusetts. They almost died the first winter because they lacked enough food. The Wampanoag taught them how to farm and shared food with them. However, diseases brought by Europeans killed many from the Wampanoag nation.

3. Examine how Latinos/Hispanics were caught in the U.S. policy of Manifest Destiny.

The Latino/Hispanic people are also an extremely diverse population. The people come from many parts of the globe such as Cuba, Puerto Rico, the Dominican Republic, and countries in Central America. Many U.S. citizens do not know that numerous Mexican Americans have ancestors who were indigenous to states such as California, Arizona, Colorado, and Utah. Due to the Treaty of Guadalupe Hidalgo, many of the Mexicans who lived in those areas became citizens because the United States took over those lands. They are original settlers of much of the Southwest.

4. Investigate the slavery of African Americans as a legal and accepted practice in the United States.

The first African Americans were not enslaved, they were indentured servants. Some sold their labor for passage to the New World. Others were important explorers. Slavery was a legalized and legitimate institution before the colonies were formed. Millions of people were kidnapped from Africa and taken on the middle passage to the New World where they were often sold. The enslaved people were considered property. They were considered inferior and treated as subordinates. Some of the social oppression and stereotypes of African Americans have their roots in slavery. African Americans were taken from many different countries in Africa and so spoke different languages and had diverse cultural backgrounds.

5. Assess the exclusion and internment of Asian Americans and Pacific Islanders in the United States.

Asian Americans and Pacific Islanders comprise an extremely diverse community. Though stereotypes reinforce the idea that all AAPIs are the same, this is not true. They speak different languages and hold diverse cultural backgrounds. Chinese immigrants were the first ethnic groups to be barred from entering the United States. Later, the Nativist movement became strong and pushed for the evacuation of Japanese Americans. This allowed their White neighbors to take their land during World War II. Wartime hysteria and fears led to the evacuation and imprisonment of over 120,000 Japanese Americans. Many had been born in the United States. Numerous constitutional rights were disregarded.

6. Explain the segregation of Jewish Americans and summarize their fight for economic and political equality.

Jewish Americans, though members of the White population, faced and continue to deal with anti-Semitism. They were used as scapegoats for civil and economic strife in Germany during World War II. Over 14 million Jews were placed in prison camps where over 6 million people were murdered by the Nazis. Persecution of Jews often arose because of their religion and because they are not Christians.

Check Your Cultural Knowledge

Reflective Essay Question

After studying the patterns of oppression in various groups, what do you see that at least three of the racial groups have in common? When students make judgments about the events and seek clarity, they are using the higher-order thinking skill of evaluation.

How can pattern of oppression be taught to fifth graders, for example, so that they understand that discrimination and domination of others are choices that people make? As a teacher, what are the insights you want your students to come away with after studying the issues in this chapter?

If you have students engage in debate about the issue of social oppression, then students will need to formulate positions about the racism that they have chosen to discuss.

Application

Know & Go Tools in the Classroom

Cooperative Learning

Students benefit from learning in cooperative groups. They learn communication, leadership, organizational, and collaborative skills if they are taught how to work together. Interdisciplinary units or projects are opportunities for students to develop higher-order thinking skills. Creating small groups also can address the cultural patterns that some children bring to school that deter them from participating in class discussions. Research on Native American and Hawaiian children has demonstrated that some students within these communities may bring different behavioral expectations to school (Delpit, 1995; Au, 1993). They prefer to talk in small groups rather than in whole classroom settings. They are more likely to participate when they are more comfortable with the context.

(Continued)

Communication skills that students should develop for successful group learning:

- Listen to each other.
- Ask questions when one does not understand a group member's comments.
- Each person contributes to the goal of the group.
- Make suggestions regarding the activities. Do not judge others.
- Be positive and encourage each other.

Teacher skills needed to mentor successful group work:

- Make sure the common goal for the group work is clear.
- Check to make sure each member of the group has specific responsibilities. These can include the group manager, group resource person, group editor, group photo editor, and technology consultant.
- Provide enough time for students to organize their projects.
- Create a checklist for the group to use to keep the project moving forward. This will ensure each member is on the same page.
- Monitor group activities to ensure that each member of the group has equal opportunities to learn and develop academic skills.

⌄⌄ Professional Resource Download

Many interdisciplinary units focus upon a question. This helps to direct student learning.

Here are samples of focal questions that might be used with the content of this chapter:

1. Why is race a powerful category that people use to classify others even though we know race is not a biological fact? Is there a more effective way to present social oppression?

2. How sensitive should we be to the terms we use such as "slaves"? Why? Can you provide other examples of ways we should consider how terms can be used to shape the way we think?

3. What are the commonalities that the experiences of all five groups discussed in this chapter? What does that say about social oppression?

4. Would you prefer to find out more about one of the events? If so, why? Create at least three questions to guide your expanded study.

Each group can pick one set of questions and then write a group essay that answers the queries.

CHAPTER

5

Race and the Struggle for Civil Rights

Learning Objectives

LO1 Explain how race and racism are issues that have many intersectional connections in various disciplines such as psychology, sociology, anthropology, history, and political science.

LO2 Explain how Native Americans pushed forward using the value of self-determination, and created schools that reflected Native values and taught Native languages and Native worldviews.

LO3 Examine how Latinos/Hispanics were leaders in the struggle for labor rights.

LO4 Assess how African Americans such as Frederick Douglass were leaders in the fight for civil rights.

LO5 Evaluate the fight for the constitutional rights of Asian Americans and Pacific Islanders with particular focus on Japanese Americans.

LO6 Assess the ability of Jewish Americans to fight social oppression by establishing organizations that fight hate crimes.

STANDARDS COVERED

INTASC 3, 4, 5, 6, 7, 8, 9, 10 **InTASC**

NAEYC 5, 6 **naeyc**

CAEP 1 **CAEP**

Overview

This chapter provides information about the knowledge and skills that members of various racial groups have used to fight the patterns of oppression discussed in Chapter 4. The domination of mainstream society over many racial groups has lessened over time because individuals and organizations have fought inequalities and provided leadership throughout society. This chapter will present information about various ways that individuals and groups have fought for civil rights. One of the important aspects of understanding racism and social oppression in the United States is to see patterns within our history. How can you as a teacher ensure that your students know that a democracy is made up of people who fight for equality and freedoms? Democracy does not happen on its own. This is one of the reasons why encouraging your students to get involved in their associated student body's activities and various offices of leadership is important. Students gain knowledge for a lifetime through participation in school clubs because they learn to work together to make the school a more compassionate, respectful, and fair place. To do this, it is vital for students to examine their own biases and recognize that individuals hold multiple perspectives, so they may not always agree on what should be done (Ross, 2014; Singer, 2014). Students also must learn that their actions are directed by their cultural perspectives, ethics and expectations. By reviewing and discussing their values with peers, the group can decide which beliefs are most important in a democracy.

Our students also need to develop communication and social skills so they will know how to bring people together in identifying collaborative solutions to social concerns. Developing listening, observation, conflict resolution, decision-making, and leadership skills are all important for citizens living in a democracy. This chapter also includes teaching strategies that provide students with opportunities to review and discuss racial issues such as the use of Native American human mascots in schools and how Title IX has influenced the opportunities for women in various aspects of education in addition to sports participation.

LO1 Explain how race and racism are issues that have many intersectional connections in various disciplines such as psychology, sociology, anthropology, history, and political science.

Race ambivalence recognizes that though race and racism are still forces that influence the way people think, believe, and act, race is becoming more and more difficult to describe and define.

Context: Race Ambivalence

The educational philosopher, Zeus Leonardo, believes the United States is in a stage of race ambivalence (2013). **Race ambivalence** is a construct that posits that though race and racism are still forces that influence the way people think, believe, and act, the significance of race is weakening in society. One of the reasons is that race is difficult to define and boundaries of the concept are not easily identified. For example, how should Middle Eastern Americans be classified? They are White but not Caucasian or European. The U.S. Census Bureau is wrestling with these issues (Krogstad, 2014). Some people are lobbying for a designation of Middle East/North African instead of White. Leonardo believes the conceptual nature of race is changing. Many people realize there are no biological roots for race, yet people continue to use the socially-constructed concept of race as a category of difference. However, Leonardo has hopes that in the future, racism will diminish and people will move toward a more humanizing orientation. This is similar to the philosophical beliefs of John Dewey; information about Dewey's work can be found in Chapter 1.

Today, race and racism continue to be complex issues that appear in a variety of disciplines. We may have abolished slavery in the United States through the passage of a Constitutional amendment, but we have yet to abolish beliefs in racial superiority from the minds of many people and institutions.

Intersectionality: History, Psychology, Sociology, and Political Science

This book has discussed intersectionality as it comes together within one student. A learner should not be seen only as a Mexican American or as a Chinese American, but a member of numerous cultural groups. Our students are complex, as is any discussion of race and racism. Intersectionality is also a construct across various disciplines when looking at race and racism. For example, investigation and assessment of how different systems of privilege and inequalities operate can be undertaken by several disciplines. Discussions of historical events can be found throughout this text; however, to see these incidents from only one discipline—history—limits teachers' understanding of racism as a social structure. For example, not only can racism be examined using a historical lens, but also the system of racism can be investigated in political science. This lays another level of structural analysis. For example, the Nineteenth Amendment of the U.S. Constitution guaranteed the right of women to vote in 1920. If students study the event only, without examining the complex social context of the issue, then they will not appreciate how difficult it was to get the amendment passed. By studying the event using a political science lens, students will examine the structural inequality of the voting issue and understand political policies and government. Women had fought for equality since colonial days; however, it was more difficult for them to secure voting rights because they lacked the ability to vote on the issue. The structural inequality in voting was an obstacle in their push for the right to vote.

In Chapter 4, the Treaty of Guadalupe Hidalgo is discussed because many Mexican American students have ancestors who are indigenous to California, New Mexico, Utah, Colorado, or Nevada. However, since the perspective of history is usually that of the victors and not the conquered (Wineburg, 2001; Ross, 2014; Singer, 2014), that information may not be included in nationally-written social studies textbooks. As scholars such as Wayne Ross, Alan Singer, and Jack L. Nelson explain, history has the capacity to humanize people; however, for this to occur we must provide a more comprehensive view of social issues and perspectives to students. Nel Noddings' ethic of care, discussed in Chapter 1, also focuses on the importance of developing a compassionate and just society. If the views of the conquered are not included, a teacher may not understand why a student in class is angry when a passage in the textbook does not include her family's historical perspective. She knows her ancestor's lands were taken away many years ago by the United States after the Treaty of Guadalupe Hidalgo was signed.

In addition to ensuring students understand the goals of imperialism and colonialism, Ross (2014) and Singer (2014) are adamant about teaching for social justice in a democracy. Teaching not only history but also about controversial issues provides students with opportunities to examine and make decisions on how to actively participate in the betterment of society. Students learn to see how the past can inform the present and future. Schools are not just for learning information; they are places where knowledge is debated and questioned. For example, students may discuss what would have happened if the Treaty of Guadalupe Hidalgo was not signed. How would life be different for many Mexican American students in our schools today? History and political science classes can provide students with the opportunity to challenge inequalities and injustices, and to identify new avenues for building community.

Wineburg and Singer also remind teachers that the collective memory of society may not be the same as historical memory. **Collective memory** is the memory that we share as members of society that has been shaped by the media, popular culture, movies, books, and other aspects of society. Sociologists also believe that the collective memory reflects the way people currently think (Wineburg, 2001). Wineburg has put forth the concept of collective occlusion to describe what happens. **Collective occlusion** refers to the parts of history and human experiences that have been forgotten or are not easily obtained. So if a more comprehensive knowledge of the views of people of color and other oppressed communities are not included in history or sociology texts, then this limits the understanding of our citizens.

In psychology, social cognition is an important area. Social cognition entails the development of learner ability to understand the views others. When teaching history

Collective memory is the memory that we share as members of society that has been shaped by the media, popular culture, movies, books, and other aspects of society. **Collective occlusion** refers to the parts of history and human experiences that have been forgotten or are not easily obtained.

Table 5.1 Intersectionality and Disciplines

Discipline	Nineteenth Amendment, 1920	Student Activities
History	Students read the legislation that explains that women are guaranteed the right to vote.	Identify and assess nondiscriminatory statements in the amendment.
Psychology	Students take the perspective of an African American woman in 1920.	Compare the views of African Americans and White Americans on the issue of women suffrage.
Political Science	Students explore political equality.	Decide why it took so long for women to get the right to vote. What U.S. policies were in place that served as obstacles to women voting?
Sociology	Students investigate social hierarchies.	Judge the gender roles of the time. If there was a lack of equality in society, why was that the case?

such as is previously described, this is critical. Social cognition includes the following skills:

1. **Perspective taking:** learners appreciate other perspectives and assessments.
2. **Putting oneself in someone else's shoes:** students get the opportunity to see an issue from multiple viewpoints—values and goals of a plantation owner, a person who is enslaved, a Wampanoag, and Pilgrim may all differ.
3. **Social information processing:** students observe others' behaviors and interpret their actions (Ormrod, 2006).

In anthropology understanding the worldview of others is also essential. Therefore in Chapter 2, culture and its impact on ethnic identity and group values were discussed extensively. In this chapter, you can see that the positions individuals and groups take on historical events reflect cultural values and belief systems. Political science is also one of the disciplines that researches and studies aspects of society such as Manifest Destiny, social oppression, colonialism, and imperialism.

To fully understand history, it is crucial that you understand how a historical event or experience can be seen through the lens of other disciplines such as anthropology, psychology, sociology, and political science. Intersectionality is about more than diverse categories a person holds such as race, social class, sexual orientation, gender, religion, exceptionalities, and age; intersectionality in the disciplines allows teachers to provide students with a deeper knowledge and abstract ability to understand the complexities of human experiences. See Table 5.1 for examples of how one event in history can be used to discuss equality from the lens of several disciplines. These investigations, discussions, and decisions can expand the knowledge and comprehension of students.

Native Americans: Fighting for Self-Determination

LO2 Explain how Native Americans pushed forward using the value of self-determination, and created schools that reflected Native values and taught Native languages and Native worldviews.

The discussion in Chapter 4 provided two examples of how imperialism and genocide have crushed many Native American tribes. Even today, Native researchers like Teresa McCarty believe that their ways of life are continually threatened. The education of Native Americans is an example of how the U.S. policy of total assimilation almost destroyed their communities and cultures (Szasz, 1977). Legally, the government had signed numerous treaties with various Native American nations, agreeing to provide services such as education. However, federal policies often were based on an assimilationist perspective whereby schools could be used to eliminate the values and beliefs of Native cultures and replace them with mainstream culture and English. These policies and practices reinforced imperialism and **cultural genocide**, the eradication of cultural backgrounds, including languages, way of life, values, and identity, of a group. These practices and policies did not support the self-determination or self-empowerment that Native people fought for throughout their history as citizens of the United States. **Self-determination** refers to the ability of Native people to make their own decisions and to have a voice in their self-government whether on Indian reservations or in regard to broader issues dealing with Native Americans.

Bureau of Indian Affairs: Assimilation

In 1824 the Bureau of Indian Affairs was established under the War Department and was used to assimilate Native people and their children. Indian Affairs policies often attempted the total annihilation of Indian culture; many students were taken from their homes and put in boarding schools away from their families and communities (Szasz, 1977). They were also pushed into acceptance of Christianity in many schools. For example, it was not unusual for a young boy of six years old to be taken from his family and placed in a Bureau of Indian Affairs (BIA) boarding school hundreds of miles away from his home (Hoerig, 2002). At the BIA school, he would have grown up in an environment where he could no longer speak his native language. In addition, the young man would be forced to cut his hair and all vestiges of being a Native person—from clothing to spiritual practices—would be taken away. How would you have felt being torn from your parents to live at a school thousands of miles away? Though there were some Indians who had positive experiences in BIA schools, many students found that these boarding schools were not well funded, served poor quality food, lacked quality teachers, and did not provide a caring community that nurtured young people (Hoerig, 2002). In schools that stressed cultural assimilation, students had difficulty maintaining Native culture because the values of mainstream culture were in direct opposition to what their tribal elders had taught them. To some young Native youth who had been taught to be collaborative and reticent, the idea of individual success and the importance of aggressive competition placed them in cultural conflict. In addition, many schools provided vocational education, but not much else. For example, girls were often taught cooking, sewing, and secretarial skills. It was believed the women would go back to the reservation and would not need additional skill development or education.

Historically, our nation's efforts have been to assimilate rather than to educate Native American students, and there is little evidence to show success (Almeida, 1997). In fact, scholars have found that Indian youth show the lowest levels of educational attainment (Machamer & Gruber, 1998). It is difficult to find information about the achievement of Native youth in mainstream educational journals and little attention or national concern has been shown to Native achievement, which has led to the invisibility of Indian students and their educational needs.

Researchers who have studied the achievement of some Native American students have identified disturbing findings. Machamer and Gruber (1998) found that Chippaqua and Sioux students from Minnesota were twice as likely as their Black peers and three times more likely than their White classmates to earn low grades such as Ds and Fs. Forty-four

Cultural genocide is the eradication of the cultural background, including the language, way of life, values, and identity, of a group.
Self-determination refers to the ability of Native people to make their own decisions and to have a voice in their self-government whether on Indian reservations or in regard to broader issues dealing with Native Americans.

Consider this . . .

Native Americans were not considered citizens of the United States until 1924 though they were indigenous to the continent.

Q Why do you think it took so long for the indigenous people to gain citizenship? List at least three reasons.

percent of the Indian students reported skipping school during the research. This figure was higher than that of Black students (38 percent skipped school) and White students (32 percent skipped school). In addition, they found that Indian students who lived off the reservation were less likely to be successful in school and felt less connected to their families. Next is a discussion of a school created and implemented by Native Americans for their children.

The Rough Rock Community School: Self-Determination

Many members of the Navajo community were aware of the negative impact of BIA schools on their children, so the community in Arizona decided to develop the Rough Rock Demonstration School in 1966, which became the Rough Rock Community School (McCarty, 2002). The Rough Rock community wanted high-quality education that was relevant and meaningful for their children. Parents, community members, and others also wanted to fight long-established policies of cultural extermination. The Rough Rock Community School, named *Diné Bíóltá*, was the first community school established by Native Americans. The school taught Navajo language and used literature written by Native people.

The school's curriculum evolved into a bilingual program called the Rough Rock English-Navajo Language Arts Program, or RRENLAP, and became a K–6 Navajo–English maintenance language program (McCarty, 2002). The Navajo language was used throughout the curriculum. For example, bulletin boards around the school featured students' writings describing their lives in both Navajo and English, and posters for holidays like Halloween shared space with the four sacred mountains of *Dinétah*, Navajo land. On these bulletin boards, students' writings in both languages told of traditional Navajo dyes and rugs. Students not only explored stereotypes of Indians but also examined historical events from the viewpoints of members of their community.

How effective has RRENLAP been? During the beginning of the twenty-first century, McCarty, an educational researcher, found that up to 60 percent of kindergartners from the

My Journal

Iroquois League, Representative Government

Q *Have you read about the representative government that the Iroquois nation had developed before Columbus sailed to the New World?*

If you have little knowledge or have not heard of this, why not?
Read below for more information.

The Iroquois League, one of the important Native communities in the Northern areas of what is known as the United States, was founded between 1000 A.D. and 1450 A.D. It included five nations: Mohawk, Oneida, Onondaga, Cayuga, and Seneca (Weatherford, 2010). Their alliance was established with a constitution called the Great Law of Peace (*Kaianerekowa*). In 1722, the Tuscarora nation also became members of the confederation. The league was one of the most orderly political organizations in North America. Before Columbus landed in the Bahamas, the Iroquois League had already established a working government. Each nation had to agree to the constitution and each sent representatives to the league meetings. The number of representatives each nation sent was dependent upon the number of members in their tribe. The representatives often engaged in a great deal of discussion before voting. However, in business dealings that involved the entire league, each nation had only one vote.

Each nation had its own council of representatives. For example, the Seneca Nation had eight elected representatives, or *sachems*, in its council. These individual councils governed their own specific territories but would come together to address common issues like the signing of treaties with other nations. This representative government was studied by Benjamin Franklin, one of the Founding Fathers of our country. Historians believe that many of the ideas that Franklin integrated into the new U.S. government structure came from aspects of the Iroquois League that he observed (Weatherford, 2010). Unfortunately, many of the early explorers and colonists did not know about the sophistication of many Native communities. The colonists were driven by the value of imperialism, which views others as inferior and as people to be subjugated.

Mascots are objects, people, or animals that are used as a group's representative, often presented as a caricature or cartoon.

TAKE A STAND: THE USE OF HUMAN MASCOTS

Fighting Inequalities

Questions that can be posed to teachers and students is: Should Native Americans be used as school mascots? Why or why not?

Have you ever thought about the use of Native Americans as mascots in schools, college teams, or national sports teams, or as costumes at Halloween? In Chapter 4 and this chapter, you have read about some of the inequities that Native Americans have experienced throughout their history. Treaties have been broken, BIA schools have forced students to assimilate, and many Native Americans have been moved from their lands.

In the United States there are thousands of elementary, middle, and high schools that have adopted Native American mascots (mascots are objects, people, or animals that are used as a group's representative, often presented as a caricature or cartoon). There are hundreds of schools with mascots based on Native American tribes that include: Apache, Braves, Comanches, Chieftains, Chiefs, Indians, Kiowas, Papooses, Red Raiders, Redskins, Tomahawks, Totems, and Warriors (National Congress of American Indians, 2013).

In Chapter 1, social justice, a foundational value of our democracy, was discussed. Scholars such as Pewewardy (n.d.) and Salamone (2013) continue to work against the use of stereotypes and Native mascots. Barbara Munson, an Oneida artist, has written extensively about the use of Native American, human mascots in schools. She explained:

> The logos, along with other societal abuses and stereotypes, separate, marginalize, confuse, intimidate and harm Native American children and create barriers to their learning throughout their school experience. Additionally, the logos teach non-Indian children that it's all right to participate in culturally abusive behavior. Children spend a great deal of their time in school, and schools have a very significant impact on their emotional, spiritual, physical and intellectual development. As long as such logos remain, both Native American and non-Indian children are learning to tolerate racism in our schools. (Undated, Common themes and questions about the use of "Indian logos")

Teachers have the most important role in providing safe and respectful educational environments where cross-cultural discussions and collaboration occur. Many individuals and organizations have fought to make schools places where students from all communities, regardless of gender, ethnicity, exceptionalities, religion, sexual orientation, and class, come together. The nondiscrimination policies that schools instituted after the Civil Rights Act of 1964 demonstrate our move toward an inclusive society of equality and justice. Students not only learn their academics at school but also through their social interactions with each other about issues of equity.

Consider these questions:

- Should anything be done about the Naive American mascots in schools? Why or why not?
- What is a mascot? What is the definition of a mascot?
- Why are mascots chosen?
- Why were Native American mascots chosen? When were they chosen? Who made the choice?
- What impact do mascots have on various student groups?

The table below shows that names commonly used for Native American mascots have possible parallel terms with other groups. This table has not been created to offend, but rather to make you think; it is a summary of a discussion that teachers had about the terms used in this feature. For example, many teachers did not believe the term *Redskins* was negative because it is a mascot for a national sports team and they had become accustomed to the term. However, when the same teachers read the name *Whiteskins* in the chart, they did not like the label. When teachers added to the discussion the term *Blackskins*, the educators felt very uncomfortable. Initially they were okay with the *Redskins* term, but as the discussion went on, they realized the mascot issue was really about power and authority. Many teachers came to believe that the term *Redskins* was unacceptable, especially after considering Native American history.

Mascots—Parallel Examples	
Existing Mascot Names	**Possible Parallel Names**
Apache	Germans, Chinese, Ethiopians, Cubans
Chiefs	Popes, Premiers
Chieftains	Presidents, Prime Ministers
Indians	Whites, Asians, Blacks, Latinos, Mexicans
Papooses	Infants, Babies, Toddlers
Red Raiders	White Raiders, Black Raiders
Redskins	Blackskins, Whiteskins
Tomahawks	Samurai Swords, Guns

Points of View: An Oneida Mother, Stanford University, and the State of Oregon

Do you think it is important to gather the views of different people when teaching about complex issues? Consider these two issues for discussion: (1) Why did the students at Stanford University change their mascot? (2) Barbara Munson's view: an educator and Oneida artist from Wisconsin.

Issue (1): In 1972, 55 Native American students and staff at Stanford University went to the school's president to petition that the mascot of a red-faced, large-nosed Indian in a Plains headdress of feathers be eliminated as the mascot. The university did not believe that Indian cultures should be used as a mascot.

The president of the university did decide to remove the mascot because he felt it was insensitive to the values of equality and justice. In 1975, the students were asked to vote on the reinstatement of the Native American mascot; the initiative failed.

Issue (2): Barbara Munson (1999) explained her perspective on the view that some people see the mascots as honoring Indians: "Native people are saying that they don't feel honored by this symbolism. We experience it as no less than a mockery of our cultures. We see objects sacred to us—such as the drum, eagle feathers, face painting and traditional dress—being used not in sacred ceremony, or in any cultural setting, but in another culture's *game*."

Take a Stand *continued*

Here is her response to the idea that many teachers believe strong warrior logos should be acceptable because they show strength in Native people:

> Both depictions uphold stereotypes [caricatures and warriors]. Both firmly place Indian people in the past, separate from our contemporary cultural experience. It is difficult, at best, to be heard in the present when someone is always suggesting that your real culture only exists in museums. The logos keep us marginalized and are a barrier to our contributing here and now.
>
> Depictions of mighty warriors of the past emphasize a tragic part of our history; focusing on wartime survival, they ignore the strength and beauty of our cultures during times of peace. Many Indian cultures view life as a spiritual journey filled with lessons to be learned from every experience and from every living being. Many cultures put high value on peace, right action and sharing. (Munson, 1999)

Have there been states that have decided to eliminate Indian mascots? Oregon became the second state to forbid the use of Native American mascots in schools, followed by Wisconsin (Murphy, 2012). In a vote of 5 to 1, the Oregon State Board of Education decided that a change was needed in schools to provide a nondiscriminatory education and to eliminate stereotypes. The new policy in Oregon prohibits the use of any names, symbols, or images that refer to Native American tribes, customs, or traditions as mascots (Murphy, 2012). Schools also cannot use Indian nicknames; the new policy identified names that are forbidden as: "Redskins," "Savages," "Indians," and "Braves." The term "Warriors" can be used if it is not done so in collaboration with Native Americans. Lots of communities gave their views about the positive nature of long-term relationships with Native American local tribes; however, the state board of education indicated that though they want schools to continue to honor Native Americans, the use of Native Americans as mascots in any way was demeaning.

TAKE A STAND...

▶ What do you think teachers, students, and communities should do to address the issue of Native American human mascots?

▶ What are your values as a teacher? Identify the three most important values and list why these are important.

▶ How can a mascot issue be resolved if you use a human mascot at your school? Give five reasons and evidence to support your viewpoints.

Students believe they hold values of social justice and equality; however, they may not have thought about how Native American human mascots denigrate people. Most of us believe in fairness, but it is not always easy to identify our own biases and make changes in our beliefs and actions.

program speak Navajo fluently. However, another study of 3300 Native five-year-olds from 110 Navajo schools found that only about 30 percent of kindergartners spoke Navajo proficiently (McCarty, 2002). Language loss is still a grave concern in Native American communities today. By teaching the language in school, a critical link to Navajo culture and ethnic identity is provided. Language is a powerful force in the community because it shapes students' worldviews and ethnic identities by using various cultural elements such as songs, prayers, greetings, blessings, stories, science, philosophy, geography, and history of the community. These components of culture, along with their oral tradition, were woven into the total curriculum.

The academic achievement of children who participated in RRENLAP has been strong. Children who arrived at school speaking Navajo and were involved in early literacy education demonstrated the greatest gains on national standardized tests. McCarty also found that children who learned to read in their first language, Navajo, learned how to read well in English. Another important outcome is described by Lomawaima and McCarty (2002):

> . . . the Native struggle for sovereignty and self-education is a powerful model for all U.S. citizens because public education in the United States was founded on the principle of local control . . . the lessons from Indigenous America . . . can illuminate and enrich the national debate surrounding educational issues that affect us all. American Indian education teaches us that nurturing "places of difference" within American society is a necessary component of a democracy. (p. 280)

The Rough Rock community was able to limit assimilation and emphasize biculturalism. I encourage you to read McCarty's book, *A Place to Be Navajo*, so that you can better understand not only the successes of the Navajo but also their lengthy struggle against an educational system that was extremely detrimental to their community and their children. Through self-determination, the Rough Rock community stood up and created a school to ensure that the civil rights of their children were protected.

Latinos/Hispanics: Fighting for Labor Unions

LO3 Examine how Latinos/Hispanics were leaders in the struggle for labor rights.

We cannot seek achievement for ourselves and forget about progress and prosperity for our community . . . Our ambitions must be broad enough to include the aspirations and needs of others, for their sakes and for our own. —César Chávez

As you read in Chapter 4, there are many indigenous Mexican American families in the United States. They can trace their heritage to hundreds of years in Mexico prior to the land becoming part of the United States. Like the Native Americans, they are native to many areas in our nation. There are also many Latino immigrants who, like most of us, have families who came to the United States in search of a better life.

One of the issues in Latino history was labor exploitation (Southern Poverty Law Center, 2016). In 1942, an agreement between the United States and Mexico allowed *braceros*, contract workers, to come to the United States temporarily. The program provided much-needed workers since most American laborers were serving as soldiers in the armed services during World War II. Meier and Ribera list a series of agreements that allowed for many workers to come into the United States under the Bracero Program (1993). It is important to note and understand that the United States invited and encouraged many people to come to this country to serve as cheap labor. Here are some examples of those efforts:

1. During World War II, in 1942, the first agreement was signed, and it ended in 1947.
2. The second agreement ran from February 1948 to 1951.
3. The third agreement ran from 1951 through December 1964 (Meier & Ribera, 1993, p. 172).

The agreements were continually authorized by the two governments.

For about 22 years, the United States requested workers from Mexico, and U.S. officials agreed upon the following provisions for the guest workers:

1. The United States would supervise the program.
2. The workers would not suffer from discrimination.
3. Transportation costs for the workers were to be provided.
4. Workers were to have clean and safe lodging.
5. Workers were to be provided the same health benefits as other workers.
6. Workers were to be paid wages without deductions.
7. Contracts would be written in Spanish so workers could read them.
8. No workers under 14 years of age would be allowed.
9. Mexican workers could not replace a domestic worker.

There were many complaints by the workers. Their food was substandard, and often they were placed in rooms where they slept in two-level bunks; they had little privacy or space. These workers were also exposed to extreme levels of pesticides without any protection. Between 1951 and 1965, 4.5 million people served in the **Bracero Program** (Meier & Ribera, 1993). The Bracero Program was a series of laws and agreements that began in 1942 and ended in 1964 providing manual labor between the United States and Mexico. The agreements provided Mexican laborers with human rights, sanitation, shelter, food, and a minimum wage of 30 cents an hour.

Frank Hurley/NY Daily News Archive/Getty Images

After years of low wages and lack of rights, civil rights leaders emerged from the Latino community. Two of these leaders were **César Estrada Chávez** and **Dolores Huerta** who felt it was their calling to organize farm workers. Together they founded the National Farm Workers Association in 1962.

In 1965, Filipino farm workers of the Agricultural Workers Organizing Committee (AWOC), led by Larry

The Bracero Program was a series of laws and agreements that began in 1942 and ended in 1964 providing manual labor between the United States and Mexico. The agreements provided Mexican laborers with human rights, sanitation, shelter, food, and a minimum wage of 30 cents an hour.

Itliong, called for a strike against the San Joaquin Valley table-grape growers in California (Meier & Ribera, 1993). Chávez and his organization joined with the AWOC, and their new union became the United Farm Workers. Philip Vera Cruz, a Filipino American, served as second vice president of the new union. Dolores Huerta, a long-time union activist, also co-founded the United Farm Workers (UFW). She believed in protecting the civil rights of workers in the fields. Their combined effort against the grape growers became known as the Delano grape strike. Chávez believed in nonviolence and thought this was the best time to strike because the Bracero Program had ended in 1964. The strike led to a national table-grape boycott, and finally the union was able to get the growers to agree to three-year contracts in 1970 that provided important concessions to farm workers. The Delano strike was over. Many Mexican Americans like Chávez have fought for the civil rights of farm workers, including fair pay and safe working conditions.

Is There a Connection Between the Bracero Program and Illegal Immigration?

The Bracero Program is an example of how the United States has encouraged immigrants to come to work in the United States. However, many Americans are concerned about unlawful immigration. A report written by Stuart Anderson, the executive director of the National Foundation for American Policy, discussed how to reduce the numbers of undocumented workers from Latin America who come to the United States in search of employment. The National Foundation for American Policy is a nonpartisan, nonprofit organization dedicated to examining policies dealing with issues such as trade, immigration, and education. Several members of the board served on Presidents Ronald Reagan's and George W. Bush's staffs.

The report is entitled *The Impact of Agricultural Guest Worker Programs on Illegal Immigration*. Though there is no room to include an extensive discussion of this issue, it is important to discuss a few findings. The foundation believes that illegal immigration can be greatly decreased with the implementation of a legal program. In other words, providing legal means for entry into the United States to provide labor is a more effective way to encourage and manage workers. They came to that conclusion by examining the number of workers who were legally admitted to our country to work and the number of people who were apprehended by Immigration and Naturalization Services (INS). Table 5.2 looks at the number of Bracero Program admissions and INS apprehensions, beginning with the year 1954. At that time, there was a movement by the United States called "Operation Wetback," to remove undocumented individuals, which resulted in increased numbers of people entering the United States illegally. The foundation explained that Operation Wetback used similar practices that are used today; it was not successful even in the 1950s, so the report suggests that using the same techniques will not be effective at this time. The term "Wetback" is also an extremely offensive term.

Following are the findings of the foundation:

1. Apprehension of adult Mexican males increased 600 percent from 1964 until 1970 after the Bracero Program ended.

2. Comparing the numbers from 1953 to 1959, after Operation Wetback ended, the numbers of INS apprehensions fell 95 percent.

3. The average number of legal entries from 1956–1959 increased to 437,643; the 1959 INS apprehensions were only 4.2 percent of 1954 total.

4. The number of U.S. Border Patrol agents increased from 3600 to 10,000 from 1990 to 2003, yet there were 5.5 million people who came into the United States without documents from 1990 to 2000 (Anderson, 2003).

Participant in the Bracero Program

Table 5.2 Selected Years, Bracero Program Admissions and INS Apprehensions from 1954–1966*		
Year	**Bracero Program Admissions**	**INS Apprehensions**
1954	309,033	1,089,583
1955	398,850	254,096
1956	445,197	87,696
1957	436,049	59,918
1958	432,857	53,474
1959	437,643	45,336
1960	315,846	70,684
1961	291,420	88,823
1962	194,978	92,758
1963	186,865	88,712
1964	177,736	86,597

Information taken from *The Impact of the Agricultural Guest Worker Programs on Illegal Immigration*, Stuart Anderson, 2003, Arlington, VA: National Foundation for American Policy.

How should the United States address the problem of undocumented workers? The foundation report and the United Farm Workers union (Gonzalez, 2016) recommend that the United States government should revise the temporary worker program that provides an H-2A visa. Unfortunately, the process as it stands now is a cumbersome one and few workers enter through this avenue (Anderson, 2003). The Southern Poverty Law Center (2007, 2013), a national civil rights organization, contends that the H-2 guest worker program is abusive to workers in that many employers pay lower wages to them, do not provide clean lodging, and do not arrange for medical care. This organization believes, along with the United Farm Workers, that temporary workers are treated like indentured servants, almost to the level of slaves. Approximately 120,000 individuals were granted H-2 visas from Mexico, Jamaica, and Guatemala in 2005 (Southern Poverty Law Center, 2007). The Southern Poverty Law Center recommends that the United States government make numerous changes in the H-2 programs. For example, the institution strongly suggests that the United States change the program so that workers are not tied to a single employer and are able to file complaints if their rights have been ignored. The issue of guest workers is an important issue in our nation today and is interwoven with concerns about legal and illegal immigration. To learn more about these issues, read *Close to Slavery: Guest Worker Programs in the United States* researched by the Southern Poverty Law Center at www.splcenter.org and *The Impact of Agricultural Guest Worker Programs on Illegal Immigration* written by the National Foundation on American Policy at www.nfap.com. The issues of temporary workers and immigration are extremely complex; as a teacher you will need to have knowledge of the many social concerns that may impact your students and their families.

Consider this . . .

The United States is often called a nation of immigrants; however, in addition to European immigrants, there are many generations of Native American, Pacific Islander, and Hispanic families who are indigenous to the area now known as the United States.

Q Why are many often called foreigners though they are not?

CASE STUDY   The Lemon Grove Incident: A Challenge to School Segregation

Many years before the 1954 Supreme Court case of *Brown* v. *Board of Education*, Roberto Alvarez, a 12-year-old student, was the main plaintiff in the first legal challenge to school segregation (Espinosa, 1986). This case is known as the Lemon Grove Incident. Alvarez was a student in school in Lemon Grove, California, a small city in San Diego County.* He was born in California and was therefore a U.S. citizen. He was part of a class-action suit that represented 75 Mexican American families who fought the segregation of their children in public schools.

Parents believed that their children would not receive quality education in a separate building that was a converted barn. The case came at a time when many mainstream residents were concerned with immigration from Mexico and Mexican Americans. Some individuals blamed Mexican immigrants for economic problems that the area was experiencing. The arguments are similar to ones that are present today.

There was a deep divide in the community about the importance of Americanizing all students through the schools. Some parents believed it was important that there be a transitional school where students would be culturally assimilated so they would become part of mainstream society. Anglo members of the community requested during a Lemon Grove School Board meeting that Mexican American children be separated from Anglo students because they brought various diseases and could not speak English. Prejudicial attitudes existed. The school board decided the best alternative was to create a school for Mexican American students on Olive Street.

Mexican American parents argued that they paid taxes like their Anglo neighbors, so they wanted the same quality of education for their children. They also wanted their children to continue to attend the neighborhood school. One morning when they were directed by their grammar school principal to go to the barn, the Mexican American children went home. Their parents continued to keep them home because they did not want their children segregated.

The parents created a social action association. Mexican American parents formed the Neighborhood Association of Lemon Grove. The association approached the Mexican consulate, which provided a lawyer. With the help of the lawyer, the parents sued the school district and won their suit. The judge agreed that although segregation laws allowed for the separation of Anglo students from Black, American Indian, and Asian Americans, Mexicans were considered to be Caucasians and so they could not be segregated from other Anglo students. The Mexican American children went back to Lemon Grove Grammar School.

There are many other examples of Mexican Americans who have fought school segregation (San Miguel, 2001). In 1947, *Mendez v. Westminster School District* ended segregation of Mexican Americans in schools in California. Sylvia Mendez was only eight years old when she, along with her aunt and brothers, attempted to register for school in Westminster, a city in Orange County, California. She and her brothers were turned away by school officials because of her dark skin and Mexican last name. At the time when Sylvia tried to register for school, Orange County had many segregated theaters, stores, and restaurants. Her parents, Gonzalo and Felicitas Mendez, fought inequality by organizing a group of parents who filed the petition that their children were being discriminated against based on national origin, an action that violated the U.S. Constitution. Briefs were also filed in support of the Mendez family by the NAACP, ACLU, Japanese American Citizens League, and the American Jewish Congress. The Ninth Circuit Court of Appeals ruled in their favor and outlawed the segregation of Mexican American children in schools in California. Thurgood Marshall, the lead lawyer in the 1954 *Brown*. v. *Board of Education* segregation case, used the Mendez decision in his arguments.

In these two examples, children were not only discriminated against but also were physically removed from attending their neighborhood schools. I believe that the two cases demonstrated more than simple discrimination; they were cases involving physical and intellectual exclusion. Social institutions were used to discriminate against children.

In 1954 the Supreme Court ruled in *Brown* v. *Board of Education* that separate schools were "inherently unequal." This decision has guided school policies for many years. However, does segregation continue to plague U.S. schools today? Unfortunately, we are seeing a trend toward the resegregation of students.

Today, segregation in schools is often a result of housing and other institutional policies (Frankenberg, Lee, & Orfield, 2003). Resegregation is the reverting back to patterns of segregation. In a recent report called *A Multiracial Society with Segregated Schools: Are We Losing the Dream?* authors Frankenberg, Lee, and Orfield (2003) relate that our schools are becoming more segregated. In fact, segregation is reaching levels found in the 1960s in some regions of the country. The two scholars suggest that we read the book by James B. Washington titled *A Testament of Hope: The Essential Writings and Speeches of Martin Luther King Jr.,* because they feel the goal of equality in schools has been lost.

Reflection Questions

Q Today resegregation is common in the largest school districts in the United States. Do you think educators should do something about this issue? Why or why not?

Q Remember that the Supreme Court decision of *Brown* v. *Board of Education* said that separate schools based on race were "inherently unequal." What should be done to ensure equal education?

*One of the best sources for information about the Lemon Grove court case is a one-hour video called "The Lemon Grove Incident." It was produced by Paul Espinosa, a writer and producer from the San Diego television station, KPBS. I recommend that you watch this film to better understand not only the impact of a young Latino child on your life but also how the Mexican American community fought against inequality and for the rights of their children to have access to equal education.

African Americans

African Americans have provided extensive leadership in the struggle for civil rights and freedom. One of the most effective leaders was Frederick Douglass. Take time to learn about how he challenged the system of oppression and advocated for civil rights for all.

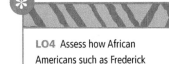

LO4 Assess how African Americans such as Frederick Douglass were leaders in the fight for civil rights.

Frederick Douglass: From Slavery to Freedom

One of the most powerful books about fighting for freedom that teachers and students can read is an autobiography entitled *Narrative of the Life of Frederick Douglass, an American Slave.* Though you may have read descriptions of the lives of those who were enslaved, it is much more personal to understand how slavery shaped the life of a single human being.

Library of Congress Prints and Photographs Division

Frederick Douglass was born Frederick Augustus Washington Bailey in Maryland around 1818. As a child born into slavery, he never had any official birth certificate, and the law at the time decreed that children born of slave mothers took the last name of their mothers and not their fathers. His mother was Harriet Bailey, and Douglass believed his father was a White man named Aaron Anthony, an overseer working for Colonel Edward Lloyd, a plantation owner. Harriet Bailey was sent to a farm to work as a laborer in the field 12 miles from where young Frederick grew up. He rarely saw his mother because she would have to walk 12 miles at night in order to see him and then had to get back to the other farm in order to be in the field in the morning. He did not remember what his mother looked like; as a baby and child, he was cared for by his grandmother.

One of the disturbing aspects of young Frederick's life was that he never got to know his mother because she died relatively young. Douglass didn't find out until years later that his mother had become ill and died when he was a young boy. As a child he was not told of her illness or allowed to visit her before she passed away. From the following passage, you can see how practices in slavery were designed so that mothers and their children did not bond. Members of families were sent away so that physical, emotional, and social connections could not be established. Slave owners believed that this practice made it easier to separate families who were treated as slaves at will. Later in his life Douglass wrote about his separation from his mother and her subsequent death:

> Frequently, before the child has reached its twelfth month, its mother is taken from it, and hired out on some farm a considerable distance off, and the child is placed under the care of an old woman, too old for field labor. For what this separation is done, I do not know, unless it be to hinder the development of the child's affection toward its mother, and to blunt and destroy the natural affection of the mother for the child . . . I was not allowed to be present during her illness, at her death, or burial. She was gone long before I knew anything about it. Never having enjoyed, to any considerable extent, her soothing presence, her tender and watchful care. . . . (Douglass, 2003, p. 18)

Fredrick Douglass believed his father was a White man. Here Douglass reflects on a subject he knows personally, the practice of selling off the interracial children who were the result of fornication between a White master and a slave:

> The master is frequently compelled to sell this class of his slaves [interracial children], out of deference to the feelings of his white [sic] wife; and, cruel, as the deed may strike any one to be, for a man to sell his own children to human flesh-mongers, it is often the dictate of humanity for him to do so; for, unless he does this, he must not only whip them himself, but must stand by and see one white son tie up his brother, of but a few shades darker complexion than himself, and ply the gory lash to his naked back; and if he lisp one word of disapproval, it is set down to his parental partiality, and only makes a bad matter worse, both for himself and the slave whom he would protect and defend. (Douglass, 2003, p. 19)

As a child growing up on the plantation, young Frederick did not have to work in the fields, but life was not easy. The type of food served to the children who were slaves was a corn mush placed in a wooden trough-like container; there were no utensils. He endured cold winters without proper clothing and had no shoes, pants, or socks. His only outfit was a thin linen shirt that draped to his knees. At night, Douglass did not have a bed and slept on a cold clay floor, occasionally finding a burlap sack to use as a blanket. Life for young Fredrick and the other slaves was miserable.

When Frederick Douglass was about seven years old, he was loaned out to live at a ship carpenter's home in Baltimore. Frederick was happy to leave the Lloyd plantation; he did not have strong emotional bonds with his two sisters and brother there. He saw Baltimore as a bright new beginning. His new mistress, Sophia Auld, taught Frederick how to read, starting with the alphabet. When her husband realized these lessons were taking place, he put a stop to them right away. Douglass recalls that Mrs. Auld's husband said:

> . . . if you teach that nigger (speaking of myself) how to read, there would be no keeping him. It would forever unfit him to be a slave. He would at once become unmanageable, and of no value to his master. As to himself it could do him no good, but a great deal of harm. It would make him discontented and unhappy. (Douglass, 2003, p. 41)

After he heard what Mr. Hugh Auld said, Frederick's heart stirred and he realized that the pathway from slavery to freedom was learning how to read. He realized that living in Baltimore might allow him to learn. Living as a slave in the city was different than being a slave in the country or on the plantation. Most slave owners in the city did not want to be seen as cruel and unreasonable, so they fed, clothed, and generally took care of the Blacks they owned. Douglass lived in the Auld household for about seven years, and during his time in Baltimore he was able to teach himself how to read and write.

How did Frederick Douglass learn how to read? Mr. and Mrs. Auld had put a stop to young Frederick's learning to read, and Mrs. Auld, taking her husband's words to heart, would turn into a tiger if she saw Frederick with a newspaper or book. However, sometimes Frederick was able to go outside of the house and play with young White boys in the street. There he would get them to act as his teachers by bribing them with bread. This bartering system worked because many White boys that he met in the streets had less to eat than he did. As he got older, he also had them teach him how to write.

Frederick was able to find books about human rights and the abolition of slavery. Just as Hugh Auld had predicted when reprimanding his wife, Douglass's new found knowledge was making him frustrated and depressed. He wrote, "In moments of agony, I envied my fellow slaves for their stupidity. I have often wished myself a beast... Anything [sic], no matter what, to get rid of thinking! It was this everlasting thinking of my condition that tormented me" (Douglass, 2003, pp. 45–46). Everything Douglass did, saw, and thought about reminded him of the freedom he so desired.

Douglas's time with Mr. and Mrs. Auld ended when he was 16 years old and was loaned out to work for one year with a man named Edward Covey. As Douglas's owner, Thomas Auld rented him to Covey because he was known as someone who could break a slave. Frederick found himself in the most horrible situation. Covey made Douglass work in the field, something he hadn't ever done because he had lived in the city most of his life. Covey was a terrible person to work for and whipped Frederick mercilessly, almost killing him once. Frederick later stood up to him and beat him back. This rebuttal scared Covey so much that in the remaining six months left on Douglass's time, Covey did not beat him again. Covey also did not accuse him of beating a White man because this probably would have hurt Covey's reputation as a "Negro breaker." From this experience Douglass learned that his own inner strength and his desire for freedom were as strong as ever. He wrote:

> I felt as I never felt before. It was a glorious resurrection, from the tomb of slavery, to the heaven of freedom. My long-crushed spirit rose, cowardice departed, bold defiance took its place; and I now resolved that, however long I might remain a slave in form, the day had passed forever when

I could be a slave in fact. I did not hesitate to let it be known of me, that the white man who expected to succeed in whipping, must also succeed in killing me. (Douglass, 2003, p. 69)

Douglass was never whipped again in his life.

One of the issues that Douglass wrote about in *Narrative* was that many of the Southern slave owners were religious. They would go to church on Sunday but beat people who were enslaved on Monday. Frederick found that often the most "religious" were the meanest slave owners. In the epilogue, Douglass carefully explained they did not act in a Christian way though they went to church. But he always considered this question: How could church-going people treat other human beings so savagely?

Later, when he was loaned out to work for Mr. William Freeland, who was fair and not like Covey, Douglass taught fellow slaves how to read on Sundays, their one day off. People from other farms would also come to attend his class. Those who were enslaved told their bosses that they were gathering to enjoy each other by boxing, wrestling, and drinking whiskey. They did not dare tell their owners about learning to read. When these gatherings were found out several slave owners brought sticks and other weapons and broke up the class.

In 1836, Douglass attempted an escape. He wrote permission slips—used by owners to allow enslaved people to go to another place during their free time—for all who were to go, but an informant told slave owners that they were attempting an escape to the North. They were put in jail and then sent back to their original farms; however, Douglass was returned to Hugh Auld in Baltimore. Auld then sent him to work building boats in a shipyard; he earned about a dollar and a half a day for Auld. One day while working at the shipyard, four White apprentice carpenters brutally beat up Frederick to the point where he almost lost an eye. Disturbed by what happened to Douglass, Hugh Auld complained to the authorities but was reminded that the testimony of an African American meant little. Unless a White carpenter would say something in Frederick's defense, legally nothing could be done. No one came forward.

After this incident, Douglass began planning his next escape. He did not believe in the **Underground Railroad**, a covert escape route for Blacks who were enslaved. He did not believe the hidden network would work for him. Frederick thought it best to hide in plain sight and so he would use the uppperground railroad where people could see him. He had to come up with an innovative plan of escape.

In Baltimore, Douglass, with the help of his fiancée, Anna Murray, who was a free Black, went first by train wearing a sailor's uniform and carrying paperwork from a free Black. Next, he traveled by ferry to Philadelphia and then by train to Delaware. Later Douglass traveled by steamboat to New York, a free state. He was finally free.

Later in his life, Frederick was actively involved in the Underground Railroad as a conductor at a station for people escaping to freedom. He changed his name from Bailey (his slave name) to Douglass so he could not be found and returned as a slave. He lived with his wife in New Bedford, Massachusetts. While living in New Bedford, Douglass read the *Liberator*, a newspaper written by William Lloyd Garrison, a popular and powerful White abolitionist. Douglass would go on to work with Garrison as an important proponent of the abolition of slavery. During these years as an abolitionist, he gave many speeches in Black churches and to anti-slavery organizations.

After publishing his autobiography in 1845, Frederick Douglass was forced to flee America to go to Europe because of the details of his life that were included in his narrative. He gave many lectures in England, Scotland, and Ireland against slavery and on the importance of civil rights. In 1847 he began publishing *The North Star*, a newspaper in which in which he wrote about the wrongs of slavery and not only encouraged the abolition of slavery but also supported the rights of women. In his later life, he worked with White feminists such as Susan B. Anthony and Elizabeth Stanton. His second wife was White and worked for the right of women to vote. Douglass also advocated the passing of the Fourteenth and Fifteenth Amendments. The Fourteenth Amendment called for the equal protection and citizenship rights to all individuals born or naturalized in the United States. Douglass lived to see these important changes.

The Underground Railroad was a covert escape route for Blacks who were enslaved.

Consider this . . .

Slavery did not exist in a vacuum; it was an integral part of life and business in the colonies and early history of the United States.

Q How should teachers relate the far reaching consequences of the past legal practice of slavery to issues in today's society?

The Racial Divide

Slavery has been a powerful force in the United States, and it continues to influence the lives of many in society today because it created a hierarchical system of economics and political position. Unfortunately, much of the early history of the United States centers on slavery (Loewen, 2007). The earliest recorded use of slaves in the United States dates back to 1501 on what is now the East Coast. Race has been one of the most divisive elements of our nation. The business of selling people as property continued for many hundreds of years until the Emancipation Proclamation of 1863. The **Emancipation Proclamation** was an executive order signed by President Abraham Lincoln to set free only the slaves who lived in states that were members of the Confederacy; it did not provide citizenship rights to slaves or provide freedom to all African Americans (Foner, 2010). After the Emancipation Proclamation was signed, there were still over 800,000 slaves who were not freed. African Americans enslaved in the following parts of the country were not included in the order: Missouri, Kentucky, Maryland, Delaware, West Virginia, "seven counties in Tidewater Virginia . . ., thirteen parishes in southern Louisiana, and the entire state of Tennessee" (Foner, 2010, p. 242). From a military standpoint, Lincoln freed many slaves in the South so that the Confederacy could not force Blacks to fight as soldiers for them.

A teacher can discuss the racial divide in our nation today through cooperative learning. Here is a suggestion using the jigsaw method in which different groups contribute to the knowledge base of students by working on different aspects of an issue.

1. Have students together as a class decide on which event they will discuss:
   a. The Dred Scott Supreme Court decision
   b. The Emancipation Proclamation
   c. The Thirteenth Amendment
   d. The Fourteenth Amendment
2. Divide students into small groups of four.
3. Explain to students that each issue can be viewed from a variety of disciplines (Figure 5.1).

> **The Emancipation Proclamation** was an executive order signed by President Abraham Lincoln to set free the slaves who lived in states that were members of the Confederacy; it did not provide citizenship rights to slaves or provide freedom to all African Americans.

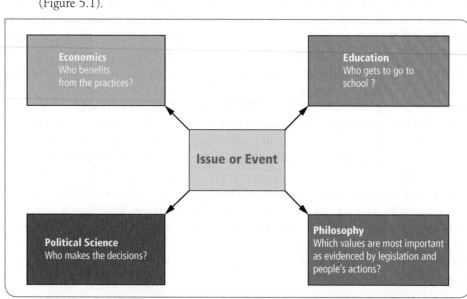

Economics
Who benefits from the practices?

Education
Who gets to go to school ?

Issue or Event

Political Science
Who makes the decisions?

Philosophy
Which values are most important as evidenced by legislation and people's actions?

Figure 5.1: The right to go to school often depended on the color of one's skin.

Figure 5.2: Equal educational opportunities are important in building a strong democratic nation. This is a photo of a diverse group of students who work collaboratively to learn and solve problems.

4. Each group can create a concept web for their work. The concept web will give the group important directions and identify the information the small group is seeking. By creating the web, each member can also be given a portion of the task and see how their information will add to a comprehensive view of the issue or event.
5. Each group shares their findings with the entire class in short presentations.
6. Groups come together to identify the patterns of human behavior and impact of the legislation, values, and actions of people on the nation.

When there is a long-term issue like slavery, it is critical for students to view it from various disciplines or ethnic perspectives. Teachers can change the concept web and change the disciplines to perspectives from racial communities. For example, four small groups could identify and investigate the views of former enslaved African Americans, Mexican Americans, Anglo-Saxon Americans, and Chinese immigrants. Their views may have some similarities but also great differences based on their experiences and histories. It's important to remember that civil rights must be fought for and maintained, and should never be taken for granted.

We don't write about and discuss our nation's history of slavery to make anyone feel guilty. No one today is directly responsible for the horrendous practices and policies of slavery. But it is important for everyone in the United States to understand our history and how slavery has fueled racism. Historical events are extremely important teaching tools; remembering and analyzing past actions and results help students and teachers to navigate our country's past and future. It is our responsibility to fight for equality in society today; as teachers we must be committed to providing every student with equal opportunities to excel and develop her or his potential (Figure 5.2).

Asian Americans and Pacific Islanders Fighting the Internment

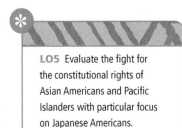

LO5 Evaluate the fight for the constitutional rights of Asian Americans and Pacific Islanders with particular focus on Japanese Americans.

The internment of Japanese Americans during World War II demonstrated that the Constitutional rights of citizens should not be taken for granted. American-born Japanese were denied constitutional rights during the internment, as follows:

- Freedom of religion
- Freedom of speech
- Freedom of the press
- Right to assemble
- Freedom from unreasonable searches and seizures
- Right to an indictment or to be informed of charges
- Right to life, liberty, and property
- Right to be confronted with accusatory witnesses
- Right to call favorable witnesses
- Right to legal counsel
- Right to a speedy and public trial
- Right to reasonable bail
- Freedom from cruel and unusual punishment
- Right against involuntary servitude
- Right to equal protection under the laws
- Right to vote
- Right to habeas corpus (to be brought before a court) (JACL, 2011)

Japanese Americans did fight back (JACL, 2011; Lyon, 2012). They knew that as U.S. citizens, their rights were protected by the U.S. Constitution. However, they learned that during wartime, constitutional rights can be taken away.

Some interned Japanese Americans fought curfew restrictions, evacuation from their homes, and their imprisonment in internment camps. These court cases were important because race and ethnicity were being used as the criteria for the removal of thousands of people. There were four major Supreme Court cases brought by Japanese Americans challenging the denial of their civil rights during World War II. Three cases were brought to the Supreme Court by men: Gordon Hirabayashi, who was born in Seattle, Washington; Fred Korematsu, who was born in Oakland, California; and Min Yasui, who was born in Hood River, Oregon (Goldstein, 2012; Korematsu Institute for Civil Rights and Education, 2015; Lyon, 2012). There was one woman who also fought for the civil rights of Japanese Americans through the courts named Mitsuye Endo (Nakano, 1990).

Mitsuye Endo: An Asian Woman Fights the Internment

Mitsuye Endo, the only woman to challenge the internment, was born in Sacramento, California. She was a second-generation Japanese American and grew up as a Methodist (Ng, 2002). Endo did not speak or read the Japanese language. She had never traveled to Japan in her life. She worked as a California state employee in the Department of Motor Vehicles. Endo was first questioned regarding her loyalties and then fired from her job solely because of her Japanese ancestry (Nakano, 1990; Ng, 2002; Asakawa, 2015).

Endo was taken to Tanforan Assembly Center in the San Francisco area. She challenged the constitutionality of the evacuation through her attorney, James Purcell, a White American. He was appalled at the conditions in which Endo lived. Purcell knew she was being held in a prison-like environment with watchtowers and guards. Endo lived with her family in horse stalls that smelled terribly (Ng, 2002). Later she was moved to the Tule Lake internment camp in northern California and then to Topaz in Utah.

One of the most compelling aspects of her case was that she did answer the orders to be evacuated and was a model citizen. Purcell filed a writ of habeas corpus, which was a petition that argued she was being held arbitrarily (Ng, 2002). Most often in cases of this type, a person can post bail and then get out of prison until the case is decided; however, the judge would not allow her to leave the internment camp.

Endo's case went to the Supreme Court, and the justices unanimously ruled to let her leave the internment camp because she was a loyal citizen, and loyal citizens could not be held by the War Relocation Authority, a civilian organization. However the Supreme Court ruling came one day after President Roosevelt issued a proclamation to rescind the evacuation orders (Ng, 2002). Endo had been held for over two years in internment camps despite the fact that her brother was serving in the military during the war and her parents had not gone back to Japan, which demonstrated her strong American heritage (Ng, 2002). The proclamation rescinding evacuation orders would affect the lives of many thousands of other Japanese Americans who were also loyal citizens. In the 1940s, it was extremely unusual for a woman, especially an Asian American woman, to speak out against any political or community decision. Endo was truly a courageous individual, and her story can be used as a teaching tool. Ask your students what it would have been like for a woman to challenge the U.S. government during a time when women were not supposed to speak out. How would existing gender roles have made it more difficult for Endo to challenge President Roosevelt's executive order? Have students investigate what it was like for women in the 1940s. What types of jobs did most women have? Did they have leadership positions? Why or why not? Also, students could examine the cultural values of the Japanese American community of the 1940s. At that time, women usually did not work outside the home, and families were primarily directed by fathers, grandfathers, uncles, and sons. The voices of mothers, grandmothers, aunts, and daughters were not as strong because of the patriarchal orientation of the culture (Takaki, 1998).

Japanese Americans: Three Challenged Curfew, Evacuation, and Incarceration

Many citizens do not know that there were Japanese Americans like Mitsuye Endo who stood up for the rights of citizens during World War II when the mass incarceration and internment of Japanese Americans took place. There were three other citizens who also believed that the United States government should not take away their civil rights. Gordon Hirabayashi, Fred Korematsu, and Minoru Yasui took their cases to all the way to the Supreme Court. The experiences of these citizens show that we must challenge inequities in society, even if they come from our government.

The Major Supreme Court Cases of Japanese Americans Timeline shows the court cases for Yasui, Hirabayashi, and Korematsu. It gives the reader a sense of how difficult it was to fight discrimination and racism when it comes from our federal government. Executive Order 9066, which was signed by President Roosevelt, called for the evacuation and internment of "all persons of Japanese ancestry." Flyers with this phrase were posted all over the Japanese American community along the West Coast.

Consider this . . .

Asian Americans and Pacific Islanders were often invisible in the fight for civil rights. Four Japanese Americans went all the way to the Supreme Court to fight for their constitutional rights as citizens during World War II. They were Mitsuye Endo, Minoru Yasui, Gordon Hirabayashi, and Fred Korematsu.

Q How would you teach about these American citizens to the students in your class? What insights would you like them to learn from their research? How might this relate to events happening today?

MAJOR SUPREME COURT CASES OF JAPANESE AMERICANS

1942

Minoru Yasui defied curfew placed against Japanese Americans because he felt it deprived him of his constitutional rights. Born in Oregon, he became a civil rights lawyer and the first Japanese American to graduate from the University of Oregon Law School in 1939. After he graduated, however, no one would hire him.

- After Executive Order 9066 was signed, curfew on the West Coast was implemented. Japanese Americans could not be out of their homes from 8 p.m. until 6 a.m.

- Yasui challenged this by being out in Portland after 8 p.m. on March 28, 1942. He was put in jail for nine months and later incarcerated at Minidoka, an internment prison in Idaho.

- The Supreme Court upheld the decision that put him in jail in June of 1943, ruling that the rights of citizens could be suspended during wartime.

- Yasui served almost a year in solitary confinement in prison and then was sent to Minidoka, one of the 10 large internment camps used until the war ended. He did not stop fighting to show that the Supreme Court decision was wrong.

- It wasn't until 1987 that his court decision was overturned.

1942

Gordon Hirabayashi defied evacuation orders. He was born in Seattle, Washington.

- Hirabayashi challenged the curfew and evacuation orders. He was a student at the University of Washington when Executive Order 9066 was signed in February, 1942.

- He was found guilty of curfew and evacuation violations and served a total of seven months in a local jail.

- The Supreme Court ruled in 1944 that the internment was constitutional.

- In 1987 his court decision was overturned.

1944

Fred Korematsu defied curfew and evacuation orders. He was born in Oakland, California.

- Korematsu was arrested in May of 1942 for not evacuating and staying in California with his Italian girlfriend.

- Korematsu was sent to jail and later to Topaz, Utah, one of the internment camps. He went to court to fight the evacuation orders.

- He lost in 1944 because the court ruled that war powers allowed the government to put him in an internment camp.

- He had trouble securing work after WWII because he was labeled a felon.

- In 1983, the courts ruled that the government was not justified in removing people from their homes.

LO6 Assess the ability of Jewish Americans to fight social oppression by establishing organizations that fight hate crimes.

White and Jewish Americans: Anti-Defamation League and Southern Poverty Law Center

Like other groups, White Americans including Jewish Americans have fought for civil rights. They not only fought anti-Semitism, but they also spoke out against inequalities and hate crimes against all people. Two of the most active organizations that fight hate crimes are the Anti-Defamation League, which was founded by Jewish lawyers, and the Southern Poverty Law Center. You should be familiar with these two organizations not only because they fight for civil rights but also because they provide many free materials that teachers can use in the classroom to eliminate prejudice and discrimination in schools and their classrooms.

Anti-Defamation League

The Anti-Defamation League (ADL) has worked to protect the rights of all people since 1913. It was created to fight anti-Semitism and hate toward all groups. The organization is dedicated to ensure equality throughout society. **Sigmund Livingston**, a lawyer from Chicago, led a group of Jewish ground breakers and established the organization in collaboration with B'nai B'rith, a Jewish association in New York. B'nai B'rith established the first Jewish public library and was extremely active in other humanitarian efforts. Like B'nai B'rith, ADL's leaders were concerned about the bigotry and discrimination they witnessed in society (ADL, 2014). Their mission was to eliminate the defamation not only of Jews but of all marginalized groups.

Livingston started with only two desks in a law office. Today the organization has branches throughout the world. One of their current slogans is "Imagine a World without Hate." One of the services that ADL provides is to monitor hate crimes throughout the world. They also maintain of a database of hate crime symbols. These symbols are often worn by White Supremacists, anti-Semitic individuals, and prejudiced groups.

ADL has created the A World of Difference curriculum project for teachers and has trained thousands of educators (ADL, 2014). The organization provides many lesson plans for teachers to use in their classrooms to assist students in identifying prejudice and teach them to develop communication skills that help to break down bias and stereotypes. Several years ago, ADL published a series of posters with current sports stars that were entitled "Prejudice is Foul Play!" These were effective materials to use in the classroom and especially attractive in this day of media and popular culture.

Southern Poverty Law Center and Teaching Tolerance

In 1971, two lawyers from Alabama, Morris Dees and Joe Levin, felt a great need to establish a law center that fought for equality in the southern portion of the United States. Dees and Levin saw that there was much inequality throughout the country. They took on cases that dealt with segregation of recreational facilities and the integration of state troopers in Alabama (SPLC, undated). Not only were so many African Americans without employment or housing, but there were numerous hate groups that harassed and discriminated against people of color (SPLC, undated).

In 1971 Julian Bond, a well-known African American civil-rights activist, became president of the center. SPLC has become a prominent institution that monitors White supremacy activities and hate crimes. They maintain the Hate Map. This map is a digital, interactive service that allows you to identify hate groups in your state. The map will identify many discriminatory groups such as White Supremacists, anti-immigrant, anti-LGBT, anti-Muslim, Black Separatist, and neo-Nazi. The organization also monitors hate crimes. There are approximately 260,000 hate crimes committed each year.

Their educational arm is called Teaching Tolerance. You can sign up for their free magazine, which is published three times a year. The organization also provides videos that can be shown in the classroom depending on the grade level you teach. They provide materials that help teachers include multiple perspectives in their lessons. This program is called "Perspectives for a Diverse America." Students develop higher-order thinking and writing skills that align with the Common Core. They are also involved in community inquiry. This is a great resource for teachers, allowing us to fight prejudice and discrimination when we teach spelling, language arts, math, science, and other disciplines.

Thinking about Intersectionality

As explained in Chapter 4, intersectionality as it pertains to historical oppression is complex. Though there are many examples of social oppression due to racial or ethnic membership, other characteristics such as social economic status, religion, age, disability, and sexual orientation are often woven in with racial/ethnic persecution and discrimination. For example, Langston Hughes was discriminated against not only because he was African American but also because he was poor, working as a busboy sometimes, and gay. He experienced severe cruelty from society and individuals. Another example is the Native American community. The use of Native American stereotypes as mascots shows that as a community, they are still being subjected to domination and discrimination. This may be due to their lack of economic, military, and political power. In addition, historians have documented the continual subjugation of many Native Americans by various countries such as Spain, Italy, France, and Britain before the United States was established as a nation.

The purpose of this chapter is to show that many people and organizations have worked to fight inequalities and to provide examples to be used in the classroom. Members of every racial group have pushed for civil rights. It is the responsibility of everyone to work toward equality in a democracy, beginning with the classroom.

Summary

1. **Explain how race and racism are issues that have many intersectional connections in various disciplines such as psychology, sociology, anthropology, history, and political science.**

   Intersectionality of various disciplines is important to include in our teaching. When we see a historical event only as a historical element, then we miss the opportunity to engage our students in much deeper research about the issue or concept. For example, presenting multiple perspectives gives students the opportunity to see an event or issue from other people's viewpoints. Developing this skill can enhance a students' knowledge of an issue. Collective memory is not the same as historical memory. Often as society changes, popular culture shapes what is remembered as important.

2. **Explain how Native Americans pushed forward using the value of self-determination, and created schools that reflected Native values and taught Native languages and Native worldviews.**

   Native Americans fought injustice with self-determination. After years of being forced into cultural assimilation by mainstream society and the federal government, many Native Americans now make their own choices. Instead of sending their children to Bureau of Indian Affairs schools, some Natives have created schools and implemented their own skills that teach and use Native languages and content. The Rough Rock Community School in Arizona is an example of self-determination, and students who attend the school are academically successful.

3. **Examine how Latinos/Hispanics were leaders in the struggle for labor rights.**

   César Estrada Chávez and Dolores Huerta established the United Farm Workers Union to fight for the right of farm workers. Many poor laborers did not have rights as they worked in the fields. They lacked proper sanitation, bathrooms, living quarters, healthcare, and nutrition. The United Farm Workers became a powerful force in Central Valley, California, challenging growers who did not pay fair wages to their laborers.

4. **Assess how African Americans such as Frederick Douglass were leaders in the fight for civil rights.**

   There are numerous civil rights activists who have come from the African American community. One of the most notable is Frederick Douglass. He was born to an enslaved mother. His story is one of self-confidence, belief in equality, and perseverance. Though physically beaten, he is a role model of someone who dedicated his entire life to fighting for civil rights. One of the ways he challenged inequalities is through literacy; he learned how to read and write despite many obstacles.

5. **Evaluate the fight for the constitutional rights of Asian Americans and Pacific Islanders with particular focus on Japanese Americans.**

   Mitsuye Endo, Minoru Yasuie, Gordon Hirabayashi, and Fred Korematsu fought for their constitutional rights during World War II. All four were born in the United States but were of Japanese ancestry. Due to the fear and strong Nativism of the times, they were sent to internment camps during World War II; however, they challenged their incarceration because they were native-born citizens. Constitutional rights are not always given; sometimes they must be fought for.

6. **Assess the ability of Jewish Americans to fight social oppression by establishing organizations that fight hate crimes.**

   White Americans and Jewish Americans have also provided leadership and built organizations that fight hate and bigotry. Jewish American lawyer, Sigmund Livingston, brought together a team of Jewish lawyers to fight discrimination including anti-Semitism, which was extremely prevalent during the early 1900s. They created the Anti-Defamation League. Two other White lawyers, Morris Dees and Joe Levin, established the Southern Poverty Law Center to fight White Supremacy, hate crimes, neo-Nazis, and discrimination against all groups.

Check Your Cultural Knowledge

Reflective Essay Question

There are numerous civil rights activists who have fought for our constitutional and civil rights. Pick two civil rights activists—either from this chapter or others that you know about—and write an essay that examines what their values were/are, why they chose to be civil rights advocates, and who they helped.

You might consider giving a presentation to your students about the two people you have chosen and discuss the following questions:

1. Why did you pick this civil rights activist to study?
2. Do you have anything in common with this person? If so, what?
3. What values did the activist hold? Define their values.
4. Explain what contributions the person made to our nation. What is different because of what the individual did?
5. How can you extend the work of this activist in your own life? Explain why you think this is important to you?

Application

Know and Go Tools for the Classroom

Heroes: Helping Others

In Chapter 4, we talked about whether Columbus was a hero, villain, or person of his times. Now students should have the opportunity to more fully think about what the concept of hero means to them.

In many classrooms teachers or their textbooks have chosen heroes for students to emulate and study. However, these heroes are often not people of color, women, or people who fight for the rights of poor or LGBT populations. Today's students are far more knowledgeable about their world, and teachers can build on their awareness.

One of the most important ways for students to find meaning in the curriculum is by learning how to make their own choices. They can choose heroes they want to study, which pushes them to use higher-order thinking skills such as analysis, synthesis, evaluation, and creativity.

Teachers also need to provide students opportunities to work together in groups. For example, students could talk about who they think is a hero. In this way, students will create criteria together and identify a hero. Those discussions can be extremely rich if students are really engaged in their study.

Heroes are made, they are not born.

Children can be heroes too.

Following are some questions that get students to use higher-order thinking skills like evaluation and building concepts and ideas. Open-ended questions get students to think more comprehensively about the issue of who are heroes.

Lesson 1

1. How would you define a hero?
2. What do heroes do?
3. What are the values of the hero?
4. What are the characteristics of a hero?
   a. Is a hero brave? Why or why not?
   b. Is a hero kind? Why or why not?
   c. Is a hero rich or poor? Explain.
   d. Is a hero smarter than the average person? Why or why not?
5. Why did the hero help someone else?

Lesson 2

1. Who is your hero?
2. What did the person do?
3. What are the values of this person?
4. Interview the person and ask them why they acted in the way they did.
5. Was there an event in his or her life that really made a difference to her or him? If so, describe what happened.
6. Who influenced her or him?
7. Could you be a hero? Why or why not?

Lesson 3

1. Write down the sequence of what the hero did.
2. Make the person's life into a story. If you cannot remember what his or her life was like, draw little pictures that show what the person did along his or her lifeline. You can call the person's history a lifeline. Create a poster of the lifeline. It should include important events that taught the person what a hero does.
3. What did the person accomplish? Place that paragraph at the end of the lifeline.
4. When writing the story, make sure you think of the beginning, middle, and end. Otherwise you may not really provide an accurate retelling of the person's life.

David Grossman/Alamy Stock Photo

Social Oppression: Classism and Sexism

Learning Objectives

LO1 Define classism, income, wealth, and sexism.

LO2 Describe classism and poverty rates and their impact on children and low-income individuals.

LO3 Evaluate how school stratification acts as an obstacle to equal educational opportunities.

LO4 Explain how poverty is a global issue.

LO5 Describe how traditional gender roles can conflict with values of equality.

LO6 Summarize how Title IX has assisted women in gaining equity in schools and society.

LO7 Examine how stereotype threat can undermine the self-confidence and performance of women.

LO8 Analyze the way women have been presented in the school curriculum.

Classism and Sexism

LO1 Define classism, income, wealth, and sexism.

Any discussion of human diversity includes the topics of class and women's rights. The purpose of this chapter is to get you to think about classism and sexism. These are two large categories in society in which people are not always treated equally. Let's define each concept so that we have a common starting point.

Classism is a complex construct that is defined as prejudice or discrimination of people and groups based on their social class, which is often defined as "lower" class.

Discrimination can also target people who are considered wealthy. For example, a teacher may believe that it is not important to give much feedback to a student from a wealthy family because that family can afford to hire tutors and put their children in many academic after school programs. Let's move to other terms about financial stability and earnings.

Social class refers to an individual's or group's economic level of income and/or wealth. Income is different from wealth. **Income** is defined as what one is paid for services or work that has been completed as in the case of earnings from a job answering the phone for a business. However, **wealth** is much more than income; it includes financial resources that might be income from a job along with property owned, stocks invested, and savings held. As a new teacher, you will have an income but may not have much wealth. Your wealth may only consist of the income you make from a school district and the car you own. This makes a difference in life because if you got sick and could not work, you may not have any backup financial resources to help you. However, if you owned real estate in the form of a house, you could sell it if you had no money in the bank and couldn't pay your mortgage or buy groceries. Real estate is considered part of wealth.

Another common form of social discrimination that is often interwoven with classism is sexism, also known as gender bias. **Sexism** is "the belief that females and males have distinctive characteristics and that one gender has the right to more power and resources than the other; it is policies and practices based on those beliefs" (Schniedewind & Davidson, 1998, p. 8). Sadker and Sadker also think sexism includes the belief that "one sex is superior to the other" (2000, p. 568). Sexism has powerful implications in our schools too. Teachers may have lower educational expectations of girls or girls from poor families. In addition, educators may find many single mothers raising children by themselves; they struggle with providing their children with the basics such as food, shelter, and medical care. This chapter is devoted to presenting you with information about classism and sexism and emphasizing that teachers need to review their own biases about students from lower-income families as well as gender biases. The next section will bring forth information about classism.

Social Context—Classism and Teacher Beliefs

Teachers, like other people, may hold negative beliefs about students who come from low-income families. Due to classism, teachers may not have high expectations for students who are homeless or come to school hungry. This results in inequity in education because educators who are prejudiced do not expect or provide low-income students with the same level of education as students from middle or upper class families.

Jean Anyon was one of the first qualitative researchers to show that poverty and social inequalities are related (Anderson, 2005). She studied the beliefs, skills, and attitudes of teachers and schools in low-income neighborhoods. Anyon found that social stratification

Classism is a complex construct that is defined as prejudice or discrimination of people and groups based on their social class, which is often defined as "lower" class.

Social class refers to an individual's or group's economic level of income and/or wealth. Income is different from wealth. **Income** is defined as what one is paid for services or work that has been completed as in the case of earnings from a job. **Wealth** refers to a person's financial resources, which might be income from a job along with property owned, stocks invested, and savings held. It is much more than income.

Sexism is "the belief that females and males have distinctive characteristics and that one gender has the right to more power and resources than the other; it is policies and practices based on those beliefs" (Schniedewind & Davidson, 1998, p. 8). In other words, women are inferior to men. Also known as gender bias.

Social stratification is defined as a systematic hierarchy based on group membership characteristics such as class, race, or political status.

of society was reproduced in classrooms (Anyon, 1981). **Social stratification** is defined as a systematic hierarchy based on group membership characteristics such as class, race, or political status. Researchers have found that many low-income students attend schools that have the least qualified teachers and do not have the same materials and other resources as higher-income neighborhood schools. This impacts the quality of education that many poor students receive in school (Anyon, 1995, 2005a; Boser, Wilhelm, & Hanna, 2014).

Teachers have a powerful influence on students. A recent study sponsored by the Center for American Progress looked at tenth grade students who were part of the 2002 through 2012 data of the National Center for Education Statistics' Education Longitudinal Study. Following students for 10 years, Boser, Wilhelm, and Hanna (2014) found that secondary teachers believed that African Americans were 47 percent less likely and Latinos were 42 percent less likely than their White counterparts to graduate from college. In addition, teachers also felt that students from poor families were 53 percent less likely to graduate from college in comparison to their more well-off classmates. They also discovered that tenth-grade teacher expectations are one of the most reliable predictors of students going to college and graduating.

The Pygmalion effect is the influence of teacher expectations on student performance.

The stereotypes about race and social class were found to have powerful effects on students and have been referred to in education as the Pygmalion effect. **The Pygmalion effect** is the influence of teacher expectations on student performance. Robert Rosenthal and Lenore Jacobson put forth this idea in education (Postman, 2013). They found that if teachers were told a random sample of students were smarter than the others, then the teachers treated these children differently and the students did better in school. Rosenthal and Jacobson believe that teacher expectations can be used to advance student performance or can be used to lower student achievement. This is a concern especially if students of color and poor students are going to school and repeatedly receiving messages from their teachers that they are not as smart or capable as their peers (Good & Nichols, 2001; Natanovich & Eden, 2008). In addition, low teacher expectations can result in less feedback to children, calling on them less, and expecting lower quality work from students.

Classism and Poverty Rates

LO 2 Discuss classism and poverty and their impact on children and low-income individuals.

Classism, poverty, and ethnic/racial membership often come together as explained in this book as an example of intersectionality. It is important that teachers understand how poverty and race/ethnicity come together in ways that are damaging to children and their parents. Educators must learn how race and poverty do not occur separately (Larke & Larke, 2009). Unfortunately, because of historical prejudice and issues of economic insecurity in our nation, there are many students of color who live in families who may be hungry, may not have shelter, or may not have health insurance. (See Figure 6.1.)

Lareau, a sociologist who studies families, believes that a child's socioeconomic status, family influence, and family prestige in a community are powerful influences in shaping her or his future possibilities. For example, she found that parents in middle-class families worked hard to develop their children's potentials and skills through organized activities such as sports, music lessons, and after-school enrichment programs. They wanted children to develop their language and thinking skills. This process, called **concerted cultivation**, means that young people develop skills and knowledge that are valued in society and they become socialized to expect equality. Middle-class children learn how to question and engage in dialogue with adults almost as equals. This is in part because their parents spend time discussing issues with them. In contrast, lower-income parents were concerned with providing for daily needs such as food, shelter, and the ability to negotiate safely in the

Concerted cultivation refers to the process in which people, including young students, develop skills and knowledge that are valued in society and become socialized to expect equality.

Figure 6.1: Severe economic inequality has led to many families becoming homeless.

neighborhood or go to the doctor when sick (Lareau, 2011). Lower-income parents do not have the financial resources to place their children in private violin or swimming lessons; instead, their children may have more opportunities to interact with other members of their extended family. Working-class and poor parents believe in the natural growth of young people where children may have more time to play or engage in leisure activities (Lareau, 2011). Working-class parents may be more directive and not use reasoning in order to explain what they would like their children to do.

Let's take an example of how differences in child rearing practices may help or hinder the future opportunities of young people. In middle-class families, babies, children, and adolescents are taught to greet others by shaking their hands and looking people in the eye when talking (Lareau, 2011). These are important skills in an interview situation. However in some neighborhoods, looking at someone in the eyes may act as a challenge to another and can result in serious conflict. Middle-class students often have more **cultural capital**; Bourdieu, a French sociologist, defined the concept as knowledge, behaviors, values, and skills of how society works and the ability to use them in increasing one's economic status. They know which behaviors are expected in society and understand how to respond to others. So in other words, there are students who come to your class who may know what is expected of them because their parents have socialized them; however, there are others who may not really understand the system of achievement and schools. Bourdieu also discussed the importance of **social capital** which is the social network that parents and families may have. Sometimes a person is able to find a job because she has an extensive network of people she knows. Have you heard the saying, "It's not what you know, but who you know"?

Poverty rates differ based on the racial background of children. In Figure 6.2, you can see that overall, the national average poverty rate of children in 2014 was 21 percent; however, 38 percent of African American and 35 percent of Native American children live in poverty. These are huge numbers. Huge numbers of students in African American and Native American families live in poor situations. There are 32 percent of Hispanic students who live in poverty; this is almost a third of the children. So many students come to school with inadequate financial resources and may not even have the basic needs of food, shelter, and healthcare.

> **Cultural capital** refers to the knowledge, behaviors, values, and skills of a social group; when a child has learned elements of cultural capital, they are able to function and know what is expected of them in the community.
> **Social capital** is the social network that parents and families have developed and can tap into.

Mario Tama/Reportage Archive/Getty Images

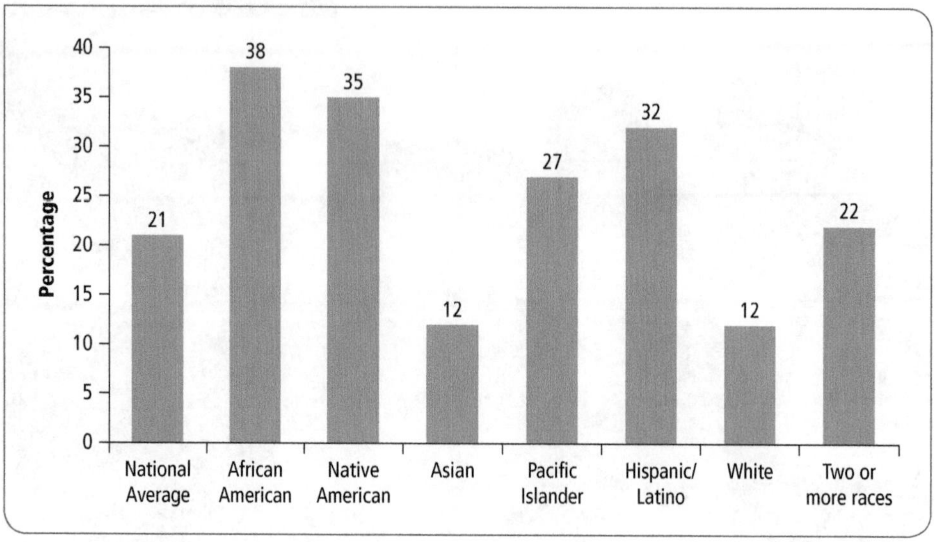

Figure 6.2: 2014 National Poverty Rates for Children Under 18 Years Old Based on Racial Membership
Source: U.S. Department of Commerce, Census Bureau, American Community Survey (ACS), 2009 and 2014.

Note: These rates represent the percentage of children in each identified category who are living in poverty. The percentages have been rounded.

Increasing Poverty Rates in the United States

America may be the land of opportunity, but it is also a land of inequality. (Lareau, 2011, p. 3)

The poverty rates for children and their families continue to rise in the United States. This has to do with the increase in unemployment due to recent recessions. The United States has found itself in recession in the early 2000s and again in 2008. Our recovery has been slow, and many people have not been able to secure a job or find a position with health and dental insurance that children need. The Patient Protection and Affordable Care Act legislation signed in 2010 is one of the most comprehensive changes in healthcare in the United States. One of the goals is to provide children without healthcare with immediate coverage. When the legislation was put into place, millions of children were not insured because their parents could not afford health insurance. Below are some of the general rates of increasing poverty.

- For African American children, the poverty rate in 2014 was 38 percent. The poverty rate for African American children in 2014 was 7.6 percentage points higher than the low in 2001.
- For Hispanic children, the poverty rate in 2014 was 32 percent. The poverty rate for Hispanic children in 2014 was 5.1 percentage points higher than the recent low in 2006.
- For non-Hispanic White children, the poverty rate was 13 percent in 2014. The poverty rate for non-Hispanic White children in 2010 was 3 percentage points higher than the recent low in 2000.

Another way to view childhood poverty is via a chart that runs from 2000–2014. You can see in Figure 6.3 that the rates continue to increase and that many more African American and Hispanic students live in poverty.

To more fully under understand how poverty in families occurs, Figure 6.4 reports the percentage of parents who did not have a full-time job year round in 2011. It is easier to understand that if parents are jobless, there will be fewer funds for the family and children end up living in poverty. Child poverty is serious, and every group has numerous children living in poverty. This impacts our nation and the future of many children. Can you imagine how difficult it must be for parents and children when they live in poverty or have a low family income? For example, not having much money can impact the ability of parents to provide wholesome food and a safe living environment. Poverty has led to an increase in the number of homeless children (Figure 6.5). Many families live with extreme stress.

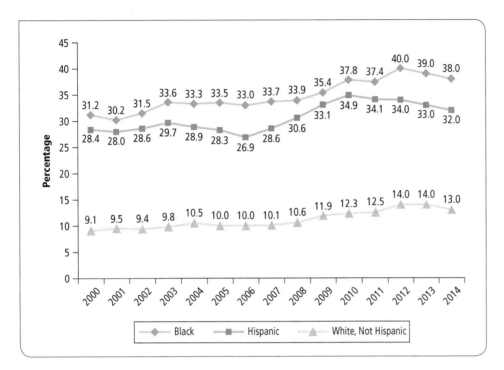

Figure 6.3: Child Poverty by Race and Ethnicity, 2000–2014

Source: 2012 and earlier Current Population Survey Annual Social and Economic Supplements (CPS ASEC) conducted by the Census Bureau. Cited statistics for 2012–2014 are based on information from *Kids Count, Children in Poverty by Race and Ethnicity*, September 2015.

Note: Hispanic includes children of all races. White, Non-Hispanic does not include any Hispanic children. Black or African-American includes Hispanic children and starting in 2002 includes Black or African-American children reporting multiple race categories.
Cited statistics include median household income in 2011, the number and rate of all persons in poverty, children in poverty, all persons and children under 50 percent of the poverty threshold, and African American and Hispanic children in poverty from 2000 to 2011.

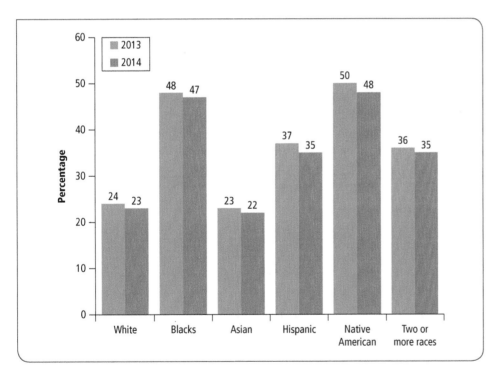

Figure 6.4: Percentage of Children with Parents Who Do Not Have Full-Time Work, 2013–2014

Source: *Kids Count, Children in Poverty by Race and Ethnicity*, September 2015.

Note: These rates represent the percentage of children in each identified category who are members of a household where parents do not have a year round, full-time job.

Sometimes the data do not provide as accurate of a picture as educators need. When large groups are put into one category, such as Asian Americans and Pacific Islanders, teachers may not know that there are some students who are extremely poor while others are middle class. When students are placed into a large total group, also known as an **aggregate**, the data may be used to stereotype individuals within a community. For example, nationally in 2007, researchers reported that Asian American and Pacific Islander students had an 11.1 percent poverty rate. However, if we were to investigate a little more deeply and look at the data based on disaggregates and specific ethnic groups, we would find there is a great range of poverty rates within the Asian American and Pacific Islander population.

> **Aggregate** refers to data placed in a large general category.

Table 6.1	Asian American and Pacific Islander Child Poverty Rates in the United States for Children under 18, 2007	
Population	**Specific Ethnic Population**	**Poverty Rate**
Asian American		11.1%
	Asian Indian	7.5%
	Chinese	10.5%
	Filipino	5.0%
	Japanese	9.9%
	Korean	10.8%
	Vietnamese	15.2%
	Other Asian	19.9%
Native Hawaiian/Pacific Islander		25.6%

Status and Trends in the Education of Racial and Ethnic Groups, by National Center for Education Statistics, 2007, Table 4, Percentage of Children Under age 18 Living in Poverty, by Living Arrangements and Race/Ethnicity with Hispanic and Asian Subgroups, p. 16.

> **Disaggregate** refers to dividing a large group into smaller components.

(See Table 6.1.) **Disaggregate** refers to dividing a large group into smaller components. In this text data may be presented by ethnic group membership or social class. Table 6.2 presents information based on specific ethnic group membership within the Hispanic community. Read through the tables carefully so you can see how an aggregate does not provide enough information about the needs of specific ethnic groups. During 2007, White children had a poverty rate of 10.1 percent.

Reading through the table on Asian American and Pacific Islander children, which community had the highest poverty rate? How different was it from the general Asian American and Pacific Islander rate? Which group had the lowest child poverty rate? How did the general Asian American and Pacific Islander child poverty compare with the rate for White children? How does the use of the aggregate (placing all groups into one large grouping) give a false impression about poverty in the Asian American community?

Let's now go to the table on poverty in the Hispanic community. Reading through Table 6.2 when the data was disaggregated, which specific ethnic community had the

Figure 6.5: Many students in schools are homeless.

Visions of America, LLC/Alamy Stock Photo

Population	Specific Ethnic Population	Poverty Rates
Table 6.2 Poverty Rates in Hispanic Communities		
Hispanic		27.1%
	Mexican	28.6%
	Puerto Rican	31.6%
	Cuban	12.7%
	Dominican	34.1%
	Salvadoran	19.8%
	Other Central American	25.1%
	South American	14.3%
	Other Hispanic or Latino	20.9%

Status and Trends in the Education of Racial and Ethnic Groups, by National Center for Education Statistics, 2007, Table 4, Percentage of Children Under age 18 Living in Poverty, by Living Arrangements and Race/Ethnicity with Hispanic and Asian Subgroups, p. 16.

highest child poverty rate? How different was it from the aggregate Hispanic rate? Which group had the lowest child poverty rate? How did the general Hispanic child poverty compare with the rate for White children? How does the use of the aggregate give a false impression about poverty in the Hispanic community? Though the rates of all Hispanic groups were higher than Whites, the poverty rates ranged from 12.7 percent for Cuban American children to 34.1 percent for Dominican American children.

The poverty rates listed on Table 6.2 for all children are high. Millions of children are at risk and growing up without adequate nutrition, shelter, healthcare, and education. Parents may be extremely frustrated because of the lack of pay for their efforts. They may not have time to help their children with their homework because they have more than one job. The Annie E. Casey Foundation's report, 2014 *KIDS COUNT Data Book*, provides evidence that poverty impacts children in many other ways too. Here are several of the major effects:

1. Children are not attending preschool and so are not prepared to enter kindergarten.
2. Fourth graders are not proficient in reading.
3. Eighth graders are not proficient in math.
4. Many high school students are not graduating.

The next section gives information about how difficult it is to earn enough to pay one's bills if a person only makes minimum wage.

Consider this . . .

"Show by your actions that you choose peace over war, freedom over oppression, voice over silence, service over self-interest, respect over advantage, courage over fear, cooperation over competition, action over passivity, diversity over uniformity, and justice over all."

Anthony J. Marsella, Psychologist

Q What actions can you take in your personal and professional lives to support these beliefs? If you cannot, why not?

Nickel and Dimed: A Study of Classism

A book that describes the impact of classism is *Nickel and Dimed: On (Not) Getting By in America* by Barbara Ehrenreich (2001). The book shows the intersectionality of class and gender. The author of the book is a professional writer interested in looking at the impact of welfare reform on individuals in our society. She found out what it meant to live on meager wages. She also noted that as a White woman who was a native speaker of English, she had advantages because she was more likely to be hired than others who were from underrepresented groups and spoke with a Spanish accent. As a service worker, Ehrenreich was forced to work at least two jobs and an average of eleven hours a day in order to earn enough money to pay for food and housing. In addition, there was never the possibility of getting benefits like health, dental, or vision insurance, so medical bills could push a person into homelessness.

Ehrenreich met many people who are often labeled "the working poor," not because they did not work hard, but because they worked full-time and did not make enough money to rent safe, clean housing and were not able to buy enough to eat (Figure 6.6). Ehrenreich worked as a Wal-Mart clerk, nursing home aide, house cleaner, hotel maid, and waitress. One of her jobs as a waitress paid $2.43 an hour and tips. She did note in her book that the Fair Labor Standards Act requires employers to pay a restaurant server at least $5.15 if the server has not made up the difference in tips. However, Ehrenreich explained that neither employer at two restaurants ever informed her of this law (Ehrenreich, 2001, p. 16). Later most of her jobs paid $6 to $7 an hour, but even with this increase she could barely afford nutritious food. The most difficult aspect of living was finding affordable, safe housing. Most service workers do not make enough money to save first and last month's rent, so they end up renting hotel rooms by the week or living in their cars. When people live in hotels with no kitchen facilities, they usually end up eating fast food such as hot dogs or hamburgers.

When Ehrenreich began her journey into the life of service workers, she wondered why they did not just move to another job when they were mistreated. She thought, why don't

Figure 6.6: Many women have low paying jobs that do not provide a living wage.

David Grossman/Alamy Stock photo

they just quit? However, the reality of the lives of many she met was sobering. Many did not own a car, so they could not just change from one job to another. They needed to be close enough to ride a bike, walk, or catch a bus. Also, the workers knew the problems of one place, but a new job would have a whole new set of issues to cope with. It was sometimes easier to stick with what one knew even if it wasn't the best situation.

One of the most difficult aspects of the lives of service workers is the humiliation and disrespect they are often subjected to at their jobs. Ehrenreich said that the boss could search her purse at any time looking for stolen food or salt shakers. In addition, many jobs required a drug test even though some people see this as a violation of the Fourth Amendment freedom from unreasonable searches. Sometimes a service worker must urinate in a cup while a technician watches.

From Ehrenreich's work, one can see that people working in service professions 11 to 12 hours a day for $6 or $8 an hour will only be able to minimally survive. This is even more complicated for the millions of single mothers with young children who need day care in order to go to work. Ehrenreich calls for business reform in a country where some folks make hundreds of millions of dollars a year as chairpersons of corporations while others barely make $15,000 a year working full-time jobs. Many people, including Ehrenreich, are calling for a living wage, and there is a movement to pay a minimum of $15 an hour. In fact, Governor Andrew M. Cuomo announced that the state of New York would pay a minimum of $15 for all positions in New York (McKinley, 2015).

Ehrenreich further discovered that a social hierarchy was in place and still continues to be (Ehrenreich, 2014). Some consider those who have a job rather than a profession as inferior, not only in regard to a lack of financial resources but also intellectually. Many waitresses and other clerks are subjected to humiliation and belittling because others believe less of them. The hierarchical system is based on the belief that a service position, such as secretary, waitress, security guard, or gardener, is not as desirable as a professional position. **Meritocracy**, a core value in the United States, is affirmed; those who work hard make the most money. In effect, those who hold lower-paying positions are seen as not working hard or not smart; therefore, they do not merit higher-paying positions or careers. The United States is a democracy, and it is important for us to raise questions about issues of equity (Pryun, 2013). When we are a fully functioning community in which we care for others, we are more likely to examine severe inequities, as pointed out by Ehrenreich. When we feel connections with and care for others, we cultivate humanity through an inclusive society (Noddings, 2002; Nussbaum, 1997). When we acknowledge the contribution of all constituent groups—including service workers and other full-time people who cannot make a decent living, but who contribute to the wealth and stability of our nation—we create a community built on ethics (Noddings, 2002; Nussbaum, 1997). The issue of social class is a major obstacle to the creation and maintenance of a just society.

As Socrates suggested, an examined life is one worth living. Sometimes we may not understand the lives of others. I hope that this information helps teachers understand that there are many parents who may not come to class picnics, class assemblies, and other school activities, not because they don't want to be there, but because they literally can't afford to take the time off from their jobs because they would lose valuable income. In addition, in our country, power and money are intimately intertwined. Wealthy individuals

> **Meritocracy** refers to the belief that those who work hard make the most money; therefore, those who do not make much money must not work hard or are not smart.

Consider this . . .

Q How has the work of low-paid workers made a contribution to your life? What is our responsibility to ensuring people who work full time earn enough to live?

may have more political and social power because they have the time and resources to be active in local or national politics. We see this even in our schools. *Savage Inequalities*, a book written by Jonathan Kozol, documents how poor, ethnically diverse communities often had schools in which the textbooks were outdated and buildings were crumbling and dangerous to students.

Income Inequality

Income inequality refers to the fact that there are some Americans with great wealth and others who do not earn a living wage, resulting in a huge economic imbalance. It refers not only to income, but also to wealth. So some people earn a large income and have many assets, while others have little income and no assets. This is income and wealth inequality.

Many legislators and citizens are grappling with income inequality because the level of poverty continues to grow in the United States (Annie E. Casey Foundation, 2014). Cities (Seattle, Tacoma, and SeaTac) in many states, like in the state of Washington, have voted to raise the minimum wage to $15 an hour. (See Table 1.2.) Many see the large gap between rich and poor as being created by the policies that the country puts into place to support large businesses such car manufacturing companies, international banks, and other huge corporations.

Food Insecurity

You may find yourself teaching in a school where almost every student qualifies for reduced-cost or free lunch. The federal government classifies those who are not able to

> **Income inequality** refers to the fact that there are some Americans with great wealth and others who do not earn a living wage, resulting in a huge economic imbalance.

★ TEACHING TIPS

Class and Poverty

Here are some ideas to effectively teach every student.

1. Have high expectations for educational success for all of your students. Class, race, gender, and other human diversity aspects should not serve as obstacles to your belief in each student!

2. Develop relationships by listening and providing consistent feedback to your students. Taking time to talk with students is a way to show that you care. Emailing and texting them about their work can be another way to develop relationships. You may be one of the few people who learners interact with on a regular basis. In reality, most students would like to develop trusting and positive relationships with you, the teacher. As a teacher, you might be one of the most important role models in their lives.

3. All learners do better when they understand the material, so explain the content in various ways. Also use lots of different examples. One example may resonate with one student while another may mean more to a different child.

4. Affirm students' ethnic or cultural identities. All students need to know they are accepted for who they are. Maybe you share a story about a famous Puerto Rican who has contributed to our nation, such as Lin-Manuel Miranda, Tony award–winning composer and playwright on Broadway. He is from a low-income family. His story is one way to affirm a student's ethnic background. The story could also be about a local role model who has been a leader in the area's Boys & Girls Clubs. It may be someone who is the mayor. Many children may grow up in a family with few financial resources, but their social class should not be used to define them or their potentials. Sharing positive successful role models from the local community can not only affirm their identities but also show that every person should have goals and can achieve them.

5. Integrate experiences from students' lives in lessons as bridges between concepts they know and new knowledge. Let's say a student has shared with you his or her work in the community. The student has helped to sign up new voters or collected money for research in childhood leukemia. These stories about your students can be the content that you use to teach concepts like citizenship. In addition, many students may not know that leukemia is a cancer of the blood. Your learners may know that having leukemia is not a good thing, but they may not understand it is a type of cancer. By building on students' experiences, teachers not only affirm student experiences but also help students create their own meanings of the material being taught. They are more likely to remember the new knowledge because it "makes sense to them."

6. Acknowledge every student as they come into the classroom. Greet and shake their hands. This is one way that teachers can build a community of learners and show that they really care.

7. Know each student's name and how to spell it correctly. This is another way to show that you care. Call on each student every day if you can. Have your class roster in front of you so you learn student names quickly.

provide healthy and nutritious food in safe and socially acceptable ways for themselves and their families as being food insecure. **Food insecurity** is the lack of proper nutrition and safe foods; people often may not be able to obtain food in socially acceptable ways (some may have to beg, go to food banks, steal, and eat from garbage cans).

When children are members of food insecure families, they may be hungry. **Hunger** is defined as the condition in which a person does not have enough food; this need causes bodily discomfort and pain. After a period of time, this can result in malnutrition. Following is a summary of data about food insecurity in the United States in 2012:

- 49.0 million people lived in food insecure households.
- 15.9 million children were food insecure.
- 8.8 percent of seniors who lived alone were food insecure.
- In every county in the United States, there are food insecure people.
- 36.4 percent of households headed by women with children were food insecure.
- 24.5 percent of households headed by men with children were food insecure
- 24.6 percent of Black and 23.3 percent of Hispanic households were food insecure (Coleman-Jensen, Nord, & Singh, 2013).

If you have students coming to class hungry, they may exhibit a variety of symptoms, such as falling asleep at their desks, daydreaming more, having trouble concentrating, being angry and frustrated, or showing other learning problems. They also may get sick more often than their peers and may suffer from developmental delays from lack of proper nutrition.

What have some communities done to assist families with child hunger? Feeding America, a nonprofit organization dedicated to eliminating hunger, has created a program called Kids Cafe (Figure 6.7). It began in 1989 when two brothers broke into a kitchen in a housing community because they were hungry. The Second Harvest Food Bank of Coastal Georgia established the first Kids Cafe. Now there are about 1500 Kids Cafes across the nation in schools and organizations where kids can go after school to eat a healthy meal. The cafes are also safe places where young people can do their homework. Many cafes are housed in Boys & Girls Clubs. Go to their website and find out how you can participate in the Kids Cafe program or send your students to them at www.feedingamerica.org.

> **Food insecurity** is the lack of proper nutrition and safe foods; people often may not be able to obtain food in socially acceptable ways (some may have to beg, go to food banks, steal, and eat from garbage cans).
>
> **Hunger** is defined as the condition in which a person does not have enough food; this need causes bodily discomfort and pain.

Taro Yamasaki/The LIFE Images Collection/Getty Images

Figure 6.7: The Kids Cafe is a safe place that provides healthy food for children.

CASE STUDY Kristen and Bill Missed School

As mentioned previously, some teachers may believe that there is a relationship between low income and lower intelligence. The beliefs teachers hold about the financial resources a child has can influence their expectations of what the child can do in school. In addition, sometimes teachers may not understand how lack of money can affect the life of a child.

Kristen

One of my students, a young second-grade girl named Kristen, was not attending school. I thought maybe her parents didn't care about school or perhaps she didn't care about school. After I did some checking, I found I was the one who had a problem. I held prejudicial misconceptions.

When Kristen arrived at school, I curtly began asking her why she didn't come to school. Kristen said, "I was too embarrassed to come."

Since I wasn't sure what she meant, I said, "You must not care about learning because you didn't come to school."

Finally, Kristen looked up into my eyes and said, "I didn't come to school because I lost my socks. I was too embarrassed and cold to come to school with shoes and no socks."

I thought about the snowy playground and felt about two inches tall. I had doubted Kristen without really listening to her. I had assumed many things that weren't true.

"My mom had to wait until she got paid on the fifteenth before I could get socks," Kristen said quietly.

Although I had thoroughly embarrassed her, I had embarrassed myself, too.

Bill

Later in the year, I also found out that Bill missed school because he didn't have a pair of underwear that fit. After numerous situations like the ones Kristen and Bill found themselves in, parents in our school began a small clothing bank for students. I know of a clothing bank in a high school that is just as important for older students. They can purchase a pair of pants or a blouse for a dollar or less.

Pauline Lipman, an educator (1998, pp. 236–237) also discovered the impact of not having enough money on parent involvement in two schools she studied. Teachers wanted parents to get involved. Many of the students were African Americans from working-class families. At first the educators thought parents weren't involved because they didn't care about education; then the teachers found out that many parents worked during the day and couldn't take off from their jobs without reprisal. Also, because most did not have cars, they didn't have transportation to attend meetings at night. Unfortunately, the parents were not able to advocate for their children as other middle-class parents in the school could. So many ethnically diverse students from low-income families often found themselves at the margins of the school, concentrated in remedial or nonacademic classes (Lipman, 1998).

Reflection Question

Q What can a school do to ensure that children/students do have the basic clothing they need so they can regularly go to school?

Q What can schools do to encourage and collaborate with parents who work and cannot volunteer at school during the day?

The Development of Poverty in the United States

Jean Anyon (2005), an educational researcher, believed that federal policies in the United States led to the increase in a huge underclass of people. She described how the tax burden has been moved from the wealthy to a decreasing middle class. For example, corporations, which in the 1940s contributed about 40 percent of the federal income tax, now pay about 9.2 percent (Anderson, 2005). Anyon writes that in order for the economic needs of children to be addressed, the distribution of wealth has to be more equitable (Anderson, 2005; Anyon, 2005). Over 23 percent of children 18 years or younger in the United States lived in poverty in 2013, which adds up to over 16.4 million teenagers, adolescents, and young children (Annie E. Casey Foundation, 2014, p. 14). In 2012, the U.S. government defined living in poverty as a family of four, which includes two adults and two children, subsiding on $23,283 or less for the year (Coleman-Jenson, Nord, & Singh, 2013).

Our country suffered from severe economic recessions at the beginning of the twenty-first century. A difficult recession began in December 2007 when the housing bubble burst and the stock market fell. The price of houses drastically dropped. Many banks had invested in numerous poor mortgage loans and were over leveraged (Lewis, 2010). The banks could not pay on the mortgages that they held; they found themselves in deep debt. When this occurred, the economy of the nation fell into a recession and the U.S. federal government stepped in with financial resources to guarantee that many of these banks were secure. Billions of dollars were supplied by the U.S. Treasury to save the banks deemed "too big to fail." The houses that many people had bought were not worth as much as their home loans. This became known as being "underwater." During this time, individuals also lost much of their wealth if they had invested in the stock market. Many people lost their jobs as industries and corporations were forced to lay off workers. So, increasing numbers of individuals went bankrupt and lost their homes. It was and continues to be challenging to find another job or position. Many people continue to be unemployed or underemployed because of these events.

Poverty has now greatly increased as a result of the two recent recessions, which has led to the increase of children living in poverty. However, even before these events occurred, many workers were not being paid a living wage, as discussed in the earlier section on Barbara Ehrenreich's work. A **living wage** is a level of income that is enough to pay for one's housing, food, utilities, and other necessities. If a person is not being paid a living wage, the individual may fall through the cracks of society even with a job. Anyon wrote that "a typical job of the future is retail sales at Walmart. The average pay at Walmart which employs over a million people and is the largest private employer in the world, was $20,030 in 2000. According to Business Week, half of Walmart's full-time employees are eligible for food stamps" (Anyon, 2005, p. 21). Many children are members of families whose parents are not being paid a living wage. Unfortunately, economic well-being and class come together. There are many African Americans, Cambodian Americans, Hmong Americans, Latinos, and Native Americans who not only suffer from poverty but are also discriminated against because of their ethnic/racial background. This can make it more difficult for people to find employment and jobs that pay a living wage. When parents cannot find positions that pay adequately, children suffer along with their mothers and fathers. They may suffer from hunger (some call this food insecurity, but I think hunger is a more accurate description), lack of shelter, lack of healthcare, lack of dental care, and lack of medicine. There are over 50 million children who live in poverty in the United States.

> **Living wage** is a level of income that is enough to pay for one's housing, food, utilities, and other necessities.

Classism and Poverty Influence Equal Education

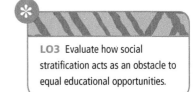

> **LO3** Evaluate how social stratification acts as an obstacle to equal educational opportunities.

School stratification based on class and race often reflects societal stratification. **School stratification** refers to a systematic hierarchy in which the best schools and educational opportunities are found in high-income neighborhoods and the poorest schools are found in low-income communities (Kozol, 1991). The best schools have exceptional science and technology labs. The opposite is true in poor schools; these institutions may not have a basic chemistry lab or even textbooks. Therefore, many students do not receive equitable education, especially those in our largest school districts, which are comprised of a majority of poor students of color. Educators have called for more financial resources for school computer labs, science labs, and libraries. In addition, some states such as California have implemented smaller class sizes in K–3 classrooms to address the lack of academic equality in schools.

> **School stratification** refers to a systematic hierarchy in which the best schools and educational opportunities are found in high-income neighborhoods and the poorest schools are found in low-income communities.

Researchers have found that more poor students and students of color are found in low-tracked classes and not in college preparation courses. This can result in academic segregation (Anyon, 2005; Oakes, 1992, 2005), though our nation supports the value of equal education. Therefore, teachers have pushed for common curriculum so that all students have access to the same discipline content, no matter if the school serves low-income or wealthy neighborhoods. In addition, algebra is now required of most high school students and not just those who are preparing for admission to college. Poor students and poor students of color have been marginalized in schools (Anyon, 1995, 2005); this often results in the placement of students in lower quality schools or less effective classrooms.

Academic tracking, identified by educational researcher Jeannie Oakes (1992, 2005) is one of the most damaging school practices to impact the education of our students. In her research, Oakes found that poor students and students of color were often tracked. **Tracking** refers to placing students by perceived abilities into different ability-groups, classes, or career paths (Oakes, 1992, 2005). In elementary school, tracking can be seen in various reading levels; students of color are most likely found in lower-level reading groups. This results in many poor and students of color being placed in classes where basic or remedial skills and knowledge are taught. In high school, many students of color will also not be found in most advanced placement or honors classes. This can have an impact on student opportunities for college admissions.

> **Tracking** refers to placing students by perceived abilities into different ability-groups, classes, or career paths.

How can this be damaging? Have you ever been placed in a low reading group in grade school though you knew you had more advanced skills? Students know if they are members of a weak group. In grade school, learners who are in the brown sparrow group may want to be a beautiful bluebird, which is a more advanced unit. Though it is acceptable to have changing tutored groups, when students are stuck in one academic group for the entire year, they become labeled. They do not have access to the most advanced knowledge or skills of the grade level, and they find that the teacher and their peers do not hold high expectations for them. Some teachers have developed flexible groupings that change depending on the skills and knowledge being taught. However, this is not a usual practice. Gaps between higher and lower achieving elementary-grade students continue to increase (Oakes, 1992). In secondary schools, there was no benefit to placing perceived low-ability students in advanced-placement or honors classes. However, students in high-tracked classes were provided more opportunities for learning, so their achievement increased (Oakes, 1992). Their teachers often have more experience teaching and provide more feedback to students. Researchers have also found that students develop friendships with those in their classes; therefore, high-tracked learners are surrounded with high-achieving peers in these environments, which fosters more self-confidence. Low-tracked students often feel isolated or alienated from other students. However, research on detracking has shown that the use of differentiation in a classroom where heterogeneous learners are classmates is the most effective environment (Burris & Garrity, 2008). There is more about differentiation and learning in Chapter 8.

Lower Teacher Expectations and Overreaching

As discussed, when schools are stratified, teachers often hold lower expectations for poor students and students of color. Sometimes teachers do not even realize that they have low expectations for various groups of learners. Here are two comments made by different educators about students:

> Just do your best. If they [students] learn to add and subtract, that's a bonus. If not, don't worry about it.

> What these children need is the basics … The three Rs—simple skills … They're lazy. I hate to categorize them, but they're lazy. (Anyon, 1995, p. 7)

Often poor students and students of color are placed in remedial classes and so have not passed classes that are needed for college admissions, such as algebra.

Having low student expectations can lead teachers to avoid teaching high-level subject area content. Educators may think that poor students and students of color are not prepared to work with and learn academic knowledge of certain disciplines such as mathematics

TAKE A STAND HOMELESS STUDENTS

Analyze this photo.

Halfpoint/Shutterstock.com

TAKE A STAND...

▶ What issues of class does the photo bring up? Write a list of at least five.

▶ What are the two most important issues that it conveys?

▶ What information do you need to gather in order to discuss the realities of the photo?

▶ As a teacher, what are your responsibilities to the homeless children and their families? Do you have any role in solving this problem? Why or Why not? What if one of the children is in your class?

or history. The following is a comment made by a fifth-grade teacher about why it was not important to work hard with poor students:

> You can't teach these kids anything. Their parents don't take care about them, and they're not interested. (Anyon, 1995, p. 7)

However, research by Anyon has found that many urban poor schools are disorganized, do not have strong educational faculty, and are not well led. So children are blamed for the lack of increase in achievement, though it is the adults in the school who are not co-ordinated and do not have an operational plan. For example, many schools suffer from what Michael Fullan, an educational leadership expert, calls **overreaching**. This means that schools that need improvement may bring in numerous programs as part of school reform; however, these programs do not build on each other (Anyon, 1995). Twenty different programs can be brought into the school and are going in many directions. There is no overarching vision and school mission that coordinates the programs. This creates tension and confusion throughout the school. An administrator of a school going through reform where this was happening said, "It's like Animal House [the movie]: We're making one last futile attempt to get even with the town" (Anyon, 1995, p. 62).

Poor schools have little chance of improving. They lack the financial resources, the leadership, effective teachers, successful instructional strategies, a well-developed strategic plan, and a way to integrate high-level subject area content into the curriculum for all students (Anyon, 1995, 2005; Oakes, 1992, 2005). The ultimate losers in these scenarios are the students.

> **Overreaching** in education means that schools that need improvement may bring in numerous programs as part of school reform; however, these programs do not build on each other.

Poverty in Global Context

> **LO4** Explain how poverty is a global issue.

> Being poor, doesn't mean poor quality. —Dr. Muhammad Yunus

Poverty and the lack of educational opportunities are global issues. There are many, many children and their parents who are food insecure and do not have a consistent income. This section of the chapter will talk about efforts around the globe that have been developed

Gerry Pang

Muhammed Yunus, a devout Muslim, was born in what is now known as Bangladesh. A serious student, he earned both a BA and MA from Dhaka University. Later a Fulbright scholarship provided Yunus the opportunity to study at Vanderbilt University in Nashville, Tennessee. He was surprised by the strong vestiges of segregation in the South when he studied at the university from 1965 to 1969. He earned a Ph.D. in economics there and studied under Nicholas Georgescu-Roegen, a respected economist (Yunus, 2003). Later Yunus taught at Middle Tennessee State University. As an ardent supporter of the independence of Bangladesh, he returned back home after it won its independence in 1971.

Social Context of Yunus's Development of Microfinancing

Along with political unrest, the country has also faced many problems, from cyclones to severe famine. Yunus, as a professor of economics at Chittagong University, began to study poverty in the rural area adjacent to the school. In 1974 there was famine and people were dying of hunger (Yunus, 2007b). He did not understand why grand economic theories were not relevant to saving people from hunger. Malnutrition was not a disease (Yunus, 2007b). Why were so many starving when the country had 21 million acres of fertile land that could be farmed (Yunus, 2003)? He believed that as a professor of economics, it was important for him to discern why there was so much poverty, especially in rural areas. In addition, he saw many acres of land near Chittagong University not being farmed. People were starving, yet these lands were not being used to grow food.

During his research of the area called Jobra, Yunus realized that there were different levels of poverty. In order to learn more, he made

the village his university, and he studied the economy and what people did to earn money (Yunus, 2007b). One of the key insights that Yunus came to was that farmers did not necessarily represent the poorest level of individuals. While many owned land and could grow crops, there were numerous others who had less. For example, he witnessed women who labored to separate the rice from the chaff for ten hours a day and earned only forty cents. These women were some of the poorest individuals he encountered in his research. From his findings, Yunus decided to focus on those who did not own land because they had fewer assets and had a more difficult time earning a living.

Microcredit: A Basic Human Right

From his training as an economist, Yunus created a philosophy based upon a belief in the self-empowerment of each individual. His philosophy runs opposite of most bankers. Banks loan funds to individuals with financial resources. Yunus believed banks should be loaning money to the poorest segment of society. Banks ask for collateral. Yunus did not believe his borrowers should provide collateral because he knew that the poor did not have resources. From this novel viewpoint, he saw credit as a human right. His economic belief system was based on the potential he saw in the poor of many villages in Bangladesh. In a speech he made in San Diego in 2007, Yunus said, "Being poor doesn't make you poor quality." Since he met with so much resistance from commercial banks and governmental authorities, Yunus himself created the Grameen Bank, Bank of Villages. It is through the Grameen Bank that he began actualizing his practice of microcredit.

In accepting the Nobel Peace Prize in 2006, Yunus stated, "Poverty is the absence of all human rights." His views are similar to those of the United Nations Universal Declaration of Human Rights that includes the following: "*Whereas* recognition of the inherent dignity and of the equal and inalienable rights of all members of the human family is the foundation of freedom, justice and peace in the world" (United Nations, 1949). Yunus did not believe that most economic theories had direct impact

on the poor in his country. These theories were not practical and supported those who already had financial resources, not those with the most need.

Yunus does believe in the free market. Members of the Grameen Bank participate in the free market and use capitalistic tools. However, Yunus does not believe that capitalism's sole goal should be maximum profit. He believes capitalism should be used to strengthen the community as a whole. It is important for members of society to examine the social, political, and emotional areas of the community and work to build a society where the dignity and rights of each person are respected. It is critical for people not to use capitalism so that only a few have control over the financial resources of a country. Yunus believes in simultaneously creating financial resources and also addressing poverty. Each individual should have the opportunity to create a life of dignity. The free market can provide opportunities for many more people to engage in and become self-sustaining by creating a business (Yunus, 2006). He believes in the strong spirit and creativity of each person to develop a business that brings self-respect and financial sustainability.

In his Nobel Lecture, Yunus clearly identifies economic and political structures and belief systems that create the underclass:

Poverty is created because we built our theoretical framework on assumptions which under-estimates human capacity, by designing concepts, which are too narrow (such as concept of business, credit-worthiness, entrepreneurship, employment) or developing institutions, which remain half-done (such as financial institutions, where poor are left out). Poverty is caused by the failure at the conceptual level, rather than any lack of capability on the part of people. (Yunus, 2006)

Reflection Questions

Q Do you use credit? Why or why not?

Q Why do you think Dr. Yunus believes credit is a human right?

Q What difference does it make in many people's lives?

Figure 6.8: The Grameen Bank has provided millions of dollars of micro-loans. In this photo, Dr. Yunus talks with members of the Grameen Bank.

to address poverty and to provide people with the opportunity to get themselves out of poverty. It is through their own actions that they are able to earn enough money for their families. One way is through the use of microcredit. This strategy was implemented by economist Muhammad Yunus.

Grameen Bank: Bank of the Villages

Grameen Bank has assisted more than 20 million women with their microcredit program (Yunus, 2007a; Grameen Bank, 2016). (See Figure 6.8.) Most of the clients are women because Yunus found that when women were given loans, the money they earned went primarily to pay for the needs of the family. Many men would use their funds on liquor and other nonproductive things. Approximately $6.5 billion has been loaned since the bank began in 1976. The loan repayment rate is 98.40 percent (Yunus, 2007a). The bank is owned by all those who have participated in the microcredit loan process of Dr. Yunus. His principles and banking methods have been used all over the world, and there are numerous microfinancing programs worldwide that have extended the work of Yunus and the Grameen Bank. There are microcredit programs in the Philippines, India, Arkansas, and Illinois. Yunus has also expanded his microcredit to providing the poor with loans for homes and education.

Grameen Bank and the Education of Children

Social class and poverty are powerful elements of human diversity. Many children who come from families with little financial security or who are hungry find themselves in schools where teachers often hold low expectations of them. However, most of the individuals who are members of the Grameen Bank invest in their children's education. Since the majority of borrowers are mothers, these women use their profits to put their children through school. This has broken the cycle of poverty because many of the children are preparing for various careers and vocations. The Grameen Bank also gives out scholarships to deserving children including girls so their families can afford for them to go to school. In addition, the Grameen Bank has created the Higher Education Loan Program so that members can borrow funds to send their children to college and later graduate school (Grameen Bank, 2016). The microcredit system is providing many parents with basic human rights, including the right of credit, and this has resulted in successful entrepreneurial projects. As Dr. Yunus, Nobel Peace Laureate said, "Poverty is the absence of human rights."

Sexism and Gender Roles

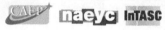

Though it is not possible to discuss all aspects of gender role discrimination and sexism in one chapter, it is possible to provide you with sociological, psychological, and historical information about the experiences of many women. **Traditional gender roles** refer to the ways in which women and men are expected to behave and are often based on patriarchal social norms. Women were and are often seen as the weaker sex who could not and should not compete with men (Collins, 2009). This underlying belief was and is a common view in society, and it has taken women many decades to fight the consequences of this covert and damaging view. Traditional gender role expectations have strongly influenced the way individuals believe women and men should behave and in the United States are based on a patriarchal orientation that men should be dominant in society. For example, women should support men, while men should be the leaders because they are smarter and emotionally stronger. Today this viewpoint is seen as being biased and oppressive. Collins identifies the leadership of activist women such as Betty Friedan, Gloria Steinem, Bella Abzug, and Robin Morgan who pushed for women's rights.

A common form of social discrimination is sexism. Historically, the terms sex and gender were often used as if they were practically the same expressions, and most people believed a person was either a female or male; in today's society, this is not accurate for many people. Sex refers to the biological nature of a person based on the physical characteristics and hormonal and biological aspects of an individual (Henry, 2015). However, some researchers believe there is a continuum of sexes (Fausto-Sterling, 2000). For example, some individuals have androgen insensitivity syndrome; this means they have biological elements of both females and males; however, only one sex may develop (Fausto-Sterling, 2000). On the other hand, gender is a socially constructed concept (Henry, 2015). For example, individuals who appear to be women are expected to be more domestic and often subservient to males. These are gender roles that have been taught through toys, books, and modeling in society. Have you ever seen a letter addressed to Mr. and Mrs. So and So? Why is the Mr. first? Why is the Mrs. second? These practices reinforce the patriarchal society we live in.

Education of Women in the United States

Do you think women and men have always attended school together? In fact, in our country's past, girls were prohibited from going to school. For example, Sadker and Sadker (2000) found that in 1687 the town council of Farmington, Connecticut, wrote that all children would learn to read and write, but that the phrase "all children" meant males only. Coeducation did not become a reality until the early nineteenth century (Tyack & Hansot, 1990). As Tyack and Hansot wrote:

> Gender is a basic organizing principle in society, but the importance of gender distinctions may vary between societies ... We see gender as a social construct, a set of cultural meanings attached to the biological division of the sexes. (1990, p. 2)

Shortly after the American Revolution, there were discussions about the possibility of creating a public grammar school for girls in Massachusetts. Civic leaders and business owners wanted their daughters to have the opportunity to read, write, and compute. However, there were many men who objected. They argued that the female mind was inferior to those of males and if women went to school, the relationships between men and women

LO5 Describe how traditional gender roles can conflict with values of equality.

Traditional gender roles refer to the ways in which women and men are expected to behave and are often based on patriarchal social norms.

would be undermined (Tyack & Hansot, 1990). Some also argued that girls would ignore their work and write love letters instead. These examples certainly provide some indication of underlying beliefs people held about the role and abilities of women in society.

Those who did believe in educating women thought that schooling would make women more efficient wives and mothers; they did not believe that women would challenge the authority of men (Tyack & Hansot, 1990). Remember, at this time women could not vote, but they were seen as important in raising children to become good citizens. There were women who worked for women's right to an education during the mid-eighteenth century. For example, Judith Sargent Murray believed women should get a good education. She fought against those who said that women were not as intellectually able as men. She believed that women should develop skills for a profession and that education should not just be oriented toward duties for the family. Soon private schools for women were established. However, many schools did not provide the same level of education for females as was provided males in public schools. There is a long history showing that women have been excluded from important aspects of society such as schooling and voting.

Consider this . . .

Many teachers do not know much about the history of women. They may know that women did not get the right to vote until 1920, but have not considered the obstacles that women have faced.

Below is a list of selected events from the Women in the United States Timeline. Read through the timeline and think about the expectations that most people had for women at the time?

Selected Events

1769 In many cases, women could not own property in the colonies.

1836 Sarah Grimké, an abolitionist and women's rights advocate, was told by male abolitionists not to speak in public because they felt she would hurt their cause.

1837 Mount Holyoke College was founded for women by Mary Lyon. Later Vassar College opened in 1861 and Wellesley and Smith in 1875.

1848 The Seneca Falls Convention for Women's Rights was first held and became a regular meeting.

1866 American Equal Rights Association was founded by Elizabeth Cady Stanton and Susan B. Anthony. The organization fought for universal suffrage and included White women, Black women, and men.

1868 Fourteenth Amendment, which protects the rights of citizens against unfair state laws, was ratified. This amendment guarantees citizens equal protection under the law and the right of due process. This amendment identifies citizens and voters as male.

1870 Fifteenth Amendment, giving Black men the right to vote, was ratified.

1893 National Council of Jewish Women was founded by Hannah Greenbaum Solomon in Illinois.

1896 A group of Black women's organizations came together to establish the National Association of Colored Women's Clubs.

1920 Women earned the right to vote with the ratification of the Nineteenth Amendment. The core of the National American Woman Suffrage Association became the League of Women Voters.

Q In what ways have women not been treated as equals to men? Why did it take women so long to secure the right to vote? Give three reasons.

As a teacher it is important for you to more fully understand how patriarchy shaped our nation and acted as an obstacle to women's rights. Take time to read the book *Learning Together* by David Tyack and Elisabeth Hansot so that you will more fully understand the changes we have made as a society in regard to gender roles. See the Women's Suffrage Timeline in the Professional Resource section for Chapter 6 in MindTap. A shorter list of events in the struggle for women's rights is shown in the Consider this ... feature. Use the list and think about the obstacles that many women and men fought in order to get more equality in society in a variety of areas such as in voting, career opportunities, financial parity, and as leaders.

Consider the fact that women did not get the right to vote until 1920 when the Nineteenth Amendment was passed. That was less than a hundred years ago and fifty years after African Americans were granted voting rights with the passage of the Fifteenth Amendment in 1870. However, it is important to note that many African Americans were not able to vote in many Southern states until the Voting Rights Act of 1965. Change takes time, and many people committed time and energy to fight against the status quo and inequalities. Is it finally time for women to be accepted more fully as leaders? Do you think that women have made it?

Stereotypes: Old Fashioned and Modern Racism and Sexism

Swim and her colleagues conducted three studies in 1995, 2004, and 2012 about historic sexism and racism and modern sexism and racism. They wanted to see if modern racism and sexism were present in people today. They first used old-fashioned racist and sexist assertions with their subjects. The statements were strong and blatantly prejudicial. Most of us would cringe if we heard these things today. For example, statements like the following showed powerful biases in the past:

"Women are generally not as smart as men."
"Black people are generally not as smart as Whites."
"It is a bad idea for Blacks and Whites to marry one another."
"It is more important to encourage boys than to encourage girls to participate in athletics."

Swim, Aikin, Hall, and Hunter (1995) wanted to know if people today had moved away from such narrow views of others. In order to examine modern racism and sexism, they used the following statements in their research and asked participants to select between two statements:

"Discrimination against women is no longer a problem in the United States."
"It is rare to see women treated in a sexist manner on television."
"Blacks have more influence on school desegregation plans than they ought to have."
"Blacks are getting too demanding in their push for equal rights."

These statements represent old and new racism and sexism, and many statements place blame on people of color and women for the lack of movement toward equality. Can you tell the subtle differences between the two types of oppression in the statements? Swim and her colleagues found that participants who were more individualistic and did not believe in equality in their personal lives were more likely to show old-fashioned and modern prejudices. The researchers also discovered that strong individualism and inequitable values correlated with racism and sexism. Individualistic values focus upon individual merit, effort, and achievement. Many people who believe in individualism believe that inequalities in society are due to deficiencies in women and people of color. It is almost as if inequalities are their fault.

Think back to the work of Barbara Ehrenreich and how hard the people she met worked. They were not slackers, but the jobs they held were sometimes stereotypically viewed by others. Are they to blame for the inequalities in society? Recall that Ehrenreich found that some individuals believe that many waiters, waitresses, house cleaners, and clerks deserve to be in lower-earning positions. They view those jobs as not having high social status. They feel a sense of entitlement that they are better than others with lower-status jobs.

In contrast, Swim and her colleagues found that people who held egalitarian values think everyone should have equal access to opportunities. They recognize that in today's society, some people have special privileges and entitlements because of their economic, gender, or racial status. People who hold social justice as one of their prime values believe that until equal opportunity is a reality, society must develop ways to address these inequalities. One of the most powerful findings in the Swim research is that many Americans do not believe that discrimination is a current problem in the United States. They believe that racism and sexism are patterns of the past and that the Civil Rights Movement of the 1960s and subsequent legislation healed our nation. However, evidence points to the contrary. The 2013 data show that women earn only about 80 percent of a man's dollar. This is disturbing considering that many people believe that our country is founded on equality and that value is being upheld in society.

Swim, a psychologist, along with her colleagues, Mallett, and Stangor (2004) extended their research on modern sexism and used a scale that included statements such as "Discrimination against women is no longer a problem in the United States" and "It is easy to understand the anger of women's groups in America." They found that individuals who held modern sexism beliefs used more sexist language. For example, a person who scored higher on the modern sexism scale used the term "he" for both women and men. They also were more likely to use the term "she" when referring to certain roles such as nurses, but "he" for most other responsibilities. Their research is a way to examine gender prejudices, and it indicates the importance of teaching students about sexism. The bias can manifest itself in subtle ways.

Following up on discrimination due to sexism, Swim along with her colleague, Becker (2012), found that many women also participate in subtle sexism. They found that females and males did not think that minimal sexism was destructive and inequitable. However, when they were presented with the theory that stereotypes of women can impact their competence and abilities, people moved away from modern sexist beliefs (Becker & Swim, 2012).

Prejudice still exists against the advancement of women and people of color in financial and career opportunities. Although there are many more women in the workforce today, they still fight prejudice about their intellectual ability and emotional stability. Though there are also many more people of color who have moved into the middle class, they continue to struggle against long-term biases and subsequent subtle and overt discrimination.

Lean In: Gender Roles and Sheryl Sandberg's Book

Examine the question of who leads Fortune 500 companies. There are far more men CEOs than women. Why is that? Of course there are numerous thoughts on that imbalance.

Sheryl Sandberg, the Chief Operations Officer (COO) for Facebook, created a social network platform that includes over a billion users. That's one out of seven people in the world! She published a book in 2013 called *Lean In: Women, Work, and the Will to Lead*. It created quite a stir in the nation. The book was on the *New York Times* best seller list for many weeks and later made the *New York Times* 100 Notable Books for the 2013 collection. The book was widely read, and it spawned a website where people could also join discussion circles. Many readers wanted to know how Sheryl Sandberg become so successful and how they could use her advice to also do well in the corporate world of work, while simultaneously balancing motherhood.

Before discussing the messages in her book, you should know that Sandberg did not grow up in a low-income community such as Bedford Stuyvesant, a neighborhood in New York City, or Back of the Yards, a neighborhood in the south side of Chicago. She grew up in North Miami Beach. Her father was an ophthalmologist and her mother was a housewife who had started a Ph.D. program before she had children. Both parents were college graduates. Sandberg graduated with a Bachelor of Arts degree in Economics and later earned a Master of Arts in Business from Harvard University. Sandberg was an excellent student and earned honors of distinction for both degrees. After earning her bachelor's degree, she went to work at the World Bank for Lawrence Summers who was one of her professors at Harvard. Later, she worked for him as his chief of staff when he was U.S. Secretary of Treasury under President Clinton (Sandberg, 2013). So you can see, she graduated from an Ivy League university and has had opportunities to work for some of the most powerful individuals in the world. Most people do not have the experiences that she has had; nor do they have sizeable financial resources. Sandberg is said to be worth hundreds of millions of dollars. This does not take away from her intelligence and accomplishments.

Though you may not have had the opportunities that Sandburg had, you can still use some of her advice. It is important to teach women to be self-confident and give them the chance to make decisions on their own. So though there are women who make 59 cents to a male's dollar, it is still important to encourage women to stand up for themselves.

Bell Hooks: Unpacking Lean In

The issues of gender bias and women's rights are complex. To talk about the issue of new sexism or what now is referred to as gender bias, we must include discussion of a society where patriarchal beliefs are strong and structural obstacles exist to maintain the status quo (Pomerantz, Raby, & Stefanik, 2013). It must be pointed out that Sandberg's experiences are most likely different from yours, whether you are a female or male. She earned degrees from one the country's of the most prestigious universities, and she grew up in an upper-middle class family.

Feminist bell hooks, who is also African American, has read Sandberg's book using the lenses of race, gender, and class. She looks at sexism from a much different perspective than Sandberg. Her work focuses on institutional and societal structures that serve as obstacles to equality in society. Though much of Sandberg's discussion is about gender bias, hooks believes there are other social forces at work. The issues of gender equality in corporations and society are another example of intersectionality because issues of patriarchy, class, White privilege, and race come together in oppressive ways. For example, hooks explains that race and class mobility are intimately tied. About 95 percent of Fortune 500 companies are led by men, and most are White men. The concept of patriarchal authority can be seen in how many women are CEOs. There are five African American males—or 1.2 percent—and one African American female heading Fortune 500 organizations (Catalyst, 2016). Her name is Ursual Burns and she is head of the Xerox Corporation. There are also 10 Latino CEOs, but no Latinas who lead a Fortunate 500 corporation. There are eight Asian males who are on the list, such as Satya Nadella, CEO of Microsoft, but only one Asian woman, Indra Nooyi of Pepsi. These are examples of the kind of class and gender mobility issues that hooks points out in her many essays. In fact, one of the metaphors used to explain the obstacles that women face in career advancements is called the **glass ceiling**. The concept refers to social and institutional obstacles—not based on merit or abilities—which serve as barriers to the advancement of women and people of color in financial and career opportunities.

Glass ceiling refers to obstacles—not based on merit or abilities—which serve as barriers to the advancement of women and people of color in financial, career, and other opportunities.

TAKE A STAND STEREOTYPES OF WOMEN AND MEN

Let's say a friend just quickly gave off descriptive words about people. What would be your first impression? Do they describe women or men?

Read through them as fast as you can and just check the box for women or men.

Don't think, just respond.

Check one box only.

TAKE A STAND...

> How did you do?

> Were you honest and did not think about the terms, but just reacted?

> What did you learn about yourself? Where did you learn these associations?

> Most people do hold a few biased beliefs about women and men. Do you agree? Why or why not?

In general the term describes...	Men	Women
Assertive		
Emotional		
Decisive		
Indecisive		
Gentle		
Confident		
Leader		
Unemotional		
Ambitious		
Competent		
Caring		

 Professional Resource Download

Title IX: Implications in Schools

CAEP naeyc InTASC

LO6 Summarize how Title IX has assisted women in gaining equity in schools and society.

The next section is about **Title IX** of the Education Amendments of 1972 stated that women and men could not be discriminated against in "any educational program or activity receiving federal aid." Although this law was passed over 40 years ago, there are some individuals who would like to make changes to it. Read through the section carefully. What would you want for your daughters and sons?

Title IX of the Education Amendments of 1972 stated that women and men could not be discriminated against in "any educational program or activity receiving federal aid."

Title IX: "Wrestling" with Gender Inequity

As a nation, one of our most cherished values is equality. But what does equality mean in an area such as school sports? It has been over 40 years since the federal government passed Title IX of the Education Amendments (1972), which stated that women and men could not be "excluded from participation in, or denied benefits of, or be subjected to discrimination under any educational program or activity receiving federal aid" (Preamble to Title IX of the Education Amendments of 1972). This law protected the rights of women and men, from grade school through graduate school, from inequities in areas such as sports, scholarships and financial aid, employment, counseling, health benefits, and admissions. Sports programs need to be in compliance with Title IX; schools must have roughly the same percentage of female athletes and male athletes as their percentage enrollment in the institution (Ziegler, 2003). Nationally, colleges are comprised of about 55 percent women and 45 percent men, so a college with 55 percent female students should have an athletic participation of 55 percent women and 45 percent men. What has happened in schools as a result of Title IX? In middle schools, gender-separated physical education was eliminated. In the past, some schools allowed boys to engage in basketball skills, while women were taught dancing steps. Having both genders in the same class is thought to discourage the difference in physical education curriculum.

Complaints continually arise about women's sports and the proportion of funding that schools and colleges must provide to women's athletics. For example, many men's wrestling and gymnastic coaches contend that the Title IX's structure of proportionality is like a quota system that is unfair to male students (Ziegler, 2003). They are concerned that many sports programs for men have been eliminated to accommodate more funding of sports for women, and that this has been unreasonable to male athletes. They believe that although not as many women are interested in participating in school sports, many schools have still done away with some men's programs like wrestling. However the research of Walker and Melton (2015) shows that the participation and funds for men's sports in college have actually increased since the implementation of Title IX. It is a myth to think that participation in men's sports has decreased over the past 40 years.

In 1972 when Title IX was passed, only 1 out of 27 women participated in collegiate sports. By comparison, in 2012 two out of every five females participated in sports (Dusenbery & Lee, 2012). Though the participation of women in collegiate sports has increased 600 percent, they have 60,000 fewer opportunities to play than their male peers. Women make up more than half the college population, but their sports do not receive as much funding as male sports.

It is important to note that women, after the passage of Title IX, have advanced in formerly male-dominated careers such as law and medicine. Table 6.4 shows progress that women have made in these areas.

Table 6.4 Percentage of Degrees Earned By Women in Law and Medicine			
	1972	1994	2010
Percent of Medical Degrees Awarded to Women	9%	38%	48%
Percent of Law Degrees Awarded to Women	7%	43%	47%

Data retrieved from Catalyst Knowledge Center at http://www.catalyst.org/knowledge/women-medicine and http://www.catalyst.org/knowledge/women-law-us

Another important aspect of Title IX is the protection of women and men against sexual harassment. This includes harassment against gay and lesbian students. Sexual harassment continues to be an issue in schools and colleges. The federal government takes the position that instances of sexual harassment serve as obstacles to the freedom to learn in a nonthreatening environment.

In July of 2003, the Bush administration sent a letter to colleges and high schools that reaffirmed the basic provisions of Title IX (Litsky, 2003). The letter, signed by the assistant secretary of education for civil rights, Gerald Reynolds, also stressed that men's teams should not be eliminated in order to ensure equality. There are three ways that universities, colleges, and high schools could comply with Title IX:

1. The percentage of female students should be in line with the percentage of female athletes.
2. Expand the number of women's teams and/or rosters.
3. Provide women's sports that are most popular in that area (Litsky, 2003).

Marcia Greenberger, the co-president of the National Women's Law Center indicated that their organization was pleased with the guidelines described, while she also noted that support for women still lags behind men. For example, there is $50 million less in athletic scholarships awarded to women compared to men (Litsky, 2003). In contrast, Eric Pearson, chair of the College Sports Council, an organization that represents coaches and sports groups, was concerned that opportunities for men would lessen in order to comply with Title IX (Litsky, 2003). This is a complex issue.

Going back to the initial issue presented by coaches regarding the loss of wrestling programs in colleges for the past 20 years, what do we find regarding the status of athletic programs in high schools compared to colleges? Following are some examples of the status of women in sports.

1. High schools:
   - In 1972, 295,000 girls participated in sports in high school compared to 3.67 million boys. By 2010–2011, the number of girls who played in a sport was 3.2 million, while 4.5 million boys participated (National Women's Law Center, 2012).
   - In the school year 2010–2011, girls had 1.3 fewer opportunities to play high school sports (National Women's Law Center, 2012).
   - During 2010–2011, high school girls of color did not participate in school sports as much as White girls. For example, 76 percent of White girls played in a sport compared to 64 percent of African American and Latino girls and 53 percent of Asian American females (National Women's Law Center, 2012).
2. College sports:
   - Men received 70 percent of sports scholarships in 1993 (Fagan & Cyphers, 2012).
   - In women's college sports from 1992 to 1997, expenditures for athletic programs grew only 89 percent while men's programs grew by 139 percent (Riley & Cantú, 1997).
   - In 2012, an NCAA report found that in the Division I Football Bowl Subdivision, colleges spent a median of over $20 million on men's sports in general in comparison to $8 million on women's sports (Fagan & Cyphers, 2012).
3. Sports experts believe that because Title IX has been in effect since 1972 and more women have participated in sports, this has led to many more Olympic medals won by women in the 2016 games in Rio de Janeiro. In 1976, about 21 percent of those who participated were women in comparison to 45 percent in 2016. For example, Simone Manuel is the first African American woman to win a gold medal in an individual swimming event (Farrell & Scott, 2016).

People cannot seem to agree on solutions to the issue. Many argue that since a sport like football usually makes money and provides resources for both women's and men's sports, football should be exempt from Title IX requirements. Others say that 85 scholarships for male football and basketball teams are proportionately too many and therefore result in a minimum of scholarships for women athletes.

What should be done about inequities in sports? There are few easy solutions to these issues when college sports are an important business that can generate dollars that an institution needs. Sporting events can be a critical aspect of building loyal alumni and a college or high school presence in the community. But underlying all of the arguments, many believe schools and universities are there to provide equal educational opportunities for students, and one avenue for individuals to fund their college education is through athletic scholarships, which are more numerous for men than women (Fagan & Cyphers, 2012). For high school students, women who participate in sports are less likely to develop obesity and more likely to stay in school rather than dropping out (National Women's Law Center, 2012). In the United States, where democracy is one of our basic values, we as educators must provide all students, women and men, the opportunity to develop physical skills within a team situation. Participation in sports not only encourages physical fitness but also self-discipline, goal setting, and working collaboratively with others in a community.

Many people feel that they have moved away from sexism and racism. However, in the following section, research is described explaining how people's perceptions of racism and sexism still exist but are more hidden than in the past. The work of Swim, Aikin, Hall, and Hunter (1995) found that negative attitudes about women and people of color are more subtle than in the past and that there is continual denial that discrimination is a force in society.

New Sexism: Girl Power and Successful Girls

Today, sexism has evolved, and new terms are being used. There are new programs such as Girl Power and Successful Girls (Baker, 2010; Pomerantz et al., 2013), where young women

Consider this . . .

This is a photo of the first Latina astronaut. Who is she?

Ellen Ochoa

This astronaut earned a bachelor's degree from San Diego State University and a Ph.D. in physics from Stanford University.

Q How can teachers add more female role models in the curriculum?

Q Would you choose this scientist? Why or why not?

are told they can do anything and be anyone they choose to be today. One of the underlying messages is that gender inequities do not exist. This message has been clearly conveyed in the media with songs written by well-known artists such as Beyoncé. Her hit song and video called "Grown Woman" has phrases such as "I'm a grown woman, I can do whatever I want." Beyoncé is an extremely powerful role model for many, especially young women, who listen to her music and watch her on television. Indirectly she is saying in her music that girls and women can be anyone they want to be. Do you think that each girl can become another Beyoncé? Probably not. Though it is great to be motivating and hopeful, girls, women, and others must learn skills and knowledge to achieve their personal and professional goals.

What is Girl Power? In the late 1990s it was a term that was often used to describe girls who were assertive, strong, and intelligent. It is a concept that often communicated that sexism was no longer an issue in society because women had "made it." Women no longer needed support from the government and were able to rise above social oppression because of the higher levels of education they were attaining and the many who were graduating from college (Pomerantz et al., 2013). Women and girls must work hard, but the belief was that social obstacles were no longer an issue. Pomerantz and her colleagues believe that this construct is dangerous to young women because the covert messages are untrue:

There are no social inequities.
There is no sexual harassment.
There is no sexual violence.
There is no domestic abuse.
There is no objectification of women.
There are no double-standards.

Sexism in this case was seen as a problem for individuals and not women in general (Pomerantz et al., 2013). However, as Pomerantz and her colleagues, researchers in sociology

TEACHING TIPS

Inclusion of Women Into the Curriculum

It is crucial that teachers provide curriculum that gives an accurate view of the contributions and abilities of women. Here are some teaching tips.

All Grades

⯈ Celebrate the passage of important historical events like the Nineteenth Amendment, which states that every citizen has the right to vote, including women. It was ratified on August 18, 1920, when the state of Tennessee voted for the amendment. Thirty-six states were needed to ratify the amendment. Have students create posters identifying various dates such as this one and the first women's suffrage convention in Seneca Falls, NY.

⯈ Play "Who am I?" This is a fun activity to have students engage in. Each student picks a different role model such as Elizabeth Cady Stanton, Harriet Tubman, or Mary McLeod Bethune. The students can dress in appropriate costumes and then give a series of hints so other classmates can guess who they are. This activity gives students the opportunity to learn about the contributions of women along with sharing that information with others.

High School

⯈ Read autobiographies, biographies, or memoirs of strong women. These books should be appropriate for the reading and developmental level of students. They could include books such as *I Know Why A Caged Bird Sings* by Maya Angelou (for high school, mature material),

The Diary of a Young Girl by Anne Frank (middle school and higher), *Woman Warrior* by Maxine Hong Kingston (high school), *Thinking in Pictures: My Life With Autism* by Temple Grandin (high school), *Narrative of Sojourner Truth* by Sojourner Truth (upper elementary), and *My Beloved World* by Sonia Sotomayor (high school).

Middle and High School

⯈ Take time to learn how to review curriculum materials for gender bias. It is important that women are shown as leaders; women can also be shown as problem solvers, and women should be seen as strong and decisive. Drawings of women with aprons and brooms are considered stereotypical by many, especially if there is not a balance of gender roles. If women are presented that way, then men should also be presented with an apron. For example, men should not be portrayed as chefs at fancy restaurants while women are presented only as cooks only at home. Do you see the bias?

Upper Elementary, Middle, and High School

⯈ Another excellent activity for children and students to engage in is to have them count how many women are pictured in the sports section of the newspaper. It is often extremely unbalanced. Children and high school students may be surprised by the lack of representation of women in sports. This activity can be undertaken when students are studying the implications of Title IX.

⯆ Professional Resource Download

and cultural studies, have explained, there are many societal obstacles that girls and women must deal with including being assertive; some find that when they are strong minded, others see them as being offensive and call them "bitches." At the same time, assertive men are called "go getters" (Pomerantz et al., 2013). Do you hear the difference?

As the concept of Girl Power gained favor, there arose a new interpretation of meritocracy, which said that women who worked hard enough and had high levels of self-confidence could be successful. However, Baker (2010), a researcher in gender studies, found that in reality girls have fewer career options. There are gender parameters. Most women can be found in people-oriented and service-oriented positions, which do not necessarily include being CEO or directors of organizations.

Another concept that became much more accepted was known as Successful Girls. This refers to the belief that girls are much more successful in school than boys. This belief also led to the "Failing Boy" idea. However, data from the report, "The Facts about Gender Equity in Education," published by the American Association of University Women demonstrate that boys are not failing in comparison to girls (Corbett, Hill, & St. Rose, 2008). There has been much talk about girls surpassing boys in achievement performance and therefore are at social parity; however, Corbett and her colleagues found that when NAEP (National Assessment of Educational Progress) data was disaggregated, both girls and boys were doing better in reading and math performance. Therefore, the success of girls did not come at the expense of boys (Corbett et al., 2008). In fact, boys performed higher on the SAT (Stanford Achievement Test) in both reading and math. However, the SAT scores of female and male Hispanic and African Americans are much lower than Whites. Consider the charts showing academic achievement of girls and boys in reading on the SAT. Girls do show a slight increase in achievement in

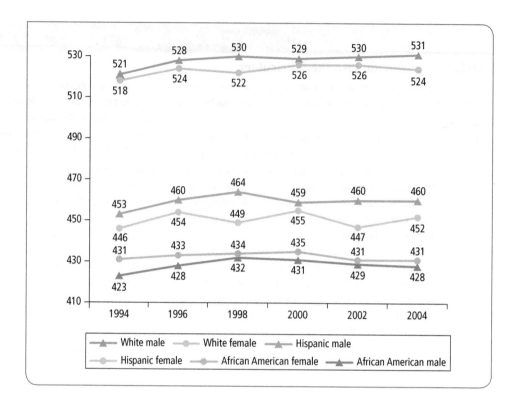

Figure 6.9: SAT, Reading Mean Score, By Gender and Race/Ethnicity, 1994–2004

Source: Adapted from *Where the Girls Are*, AAUW, 2008, p. 41.

reading scores over time. However, Figure 6.9 shows that White boys perform better in reading than White girls. And examining reading performance by ethnic/racial groups, Hispanic males consistently did better than Hispanic females from 1994 to 2004. Black females did better than Black males in reading during the same decade. In Figure 6.10, you will also see that income levels make a big difference in achievement performance of girls and boys; both females and males who were members of the high-income group did statistically better in reading than middle-income and low-income students. Again the intersectionality of gender and class is powerful.

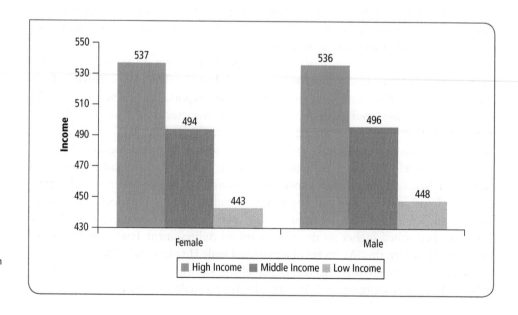

Figure 6.10: Stanford Achievement Test, Reading Mean Score by Gender and Family Income, 2004

Adapted from *Where the Girls Are*, AAUW, 2008, p. 42.

Note: Low-income families are those whose annual family income is less than $30,000. Middle-income families are those whose income is between $30,000 and $70,000. High income is defined as families who report an annual income of more than $70,000.

Consider this . . .

"According to *The Economist*'s 2013 'Glass ceiling index,' a study that ranked countries' efforts to give women the best chance of equal treatment in the workplace, America came in 12th, behind France and Denmark. That's right; the United States didn't even make it in the top 10."

Senator Kirsten Gillibrand, *The Shriver Report* (2014), p. 368.

Q Do you think that the United States should take actions to ensure that women are treated fairly in society? Why or why not?

Stereotype Threat: The Case of Women and Girls

LO7 Examine how stereotype threat can undermine the self-confidence and performance of women.

Swim and her colleagues clearly believe that the new sexism has arisen because many people, including women, believe that sexism or gender bias has largely been eliminated. However, there is evidence that this is not true. For example, Maria Shriver's Shriver Report (2014) clearly shows that women do not get paid the same as men who do the same type of work. And as we've discussed, there are few women CEOs in Fortune 500 corporations.

So will the threat of a stereotype being true influence the test performance of women? There continue to be structures and practices that place women and girls at risk. For example, *stereotype threat* has been found to influence the performance of females and African Americans (Steele, 1997; Steele & Aronson, 1995; Temple & Neumann, 2014).

Research was first conducted with African American college students to measure the influence of stereotype threat on their achievement on tests (Steele & Aronson, 1995). The students in this racial group were vulnerable to the suggestion that African Americans did not do well on intelligence exams. One way that stereotype threat can be put into place is if an instructor or teacher talks about how African American students do not do well on standardized tests. This type of stereotyping can be an obstacle to African American students who believe they can perform well on intellectual examinations. Stereotype threat can also arise when students of color fill out demographic questionnaires where racial membership is highlighted because this can trigger in their minds stereotypes about the low performance of African Americans.

Stereotype threat has also been found to influence the performance of women and girls on examinations (Temple & Neumann, 2014; Tomasetto & Appoloni, 2013). For example, when female college freshmen psychology students were asked to read a one-page summary of a study saying that stereotype threat made a difference in the performance of women, they subsequently did not do as well on a math test as their male counterparts (Temple & Neumann, 2014). The researchers believed that the math test results were not due to intellectual ability, but rather heavily influenced by the stereotype that women do not do as well as men in math.

What do these studies have to do with teachers? It is important for educators to understand how emotion can have an adverse effect on how women and girls perform on math and other tests. It is also important for teachers to watch how they discuss issues such as stereotype threat so as not to introduce or increase any negative feelings women may have regarding the chosen task or assignment. Researchers also explained

TEACHING TIPS

Strategies for Inclusion of Women in the Curriculum

Elementary Grades

▶ Teachers can read picture books about role models such as Amelia Earhart, Eleanor Roosevelt, and Harriet Tubman.
  - *Amelia and Eleanor Go For A Ride* by Pam Munoz Ryan, 1999, Scholastic Books
  - *Aunt Harriet's Underground Railroad in the Sky*, by Faith Ringgold, Dragonfly Books

▶ Students can write short stories about chosen women role models like their moms, grandmothers, aunts, or family friends.

▶ Students can also write short biographies and then practice public speaking skills or using cue cards and dressing in costumes. The clothing can be something that their mother has worn or a piece of clothing that represents the career of that woman.

Middle and High School Grades

▶ Students can choose female CEOs of Fortune 500 companies and write stories that explain where the CEO was born, how she grew up, and identify issues she has had to deal with in her career.

▶ High-school students can interview chosen role models. They can ask questions about their career goals, mentors, and their advice for women in the class.

▶ Middle and high school students, both women and men, could put on an all-school assembly honoring several local mothers who have contributed to the school. Students could give a short biography of each mother and introduce them.

▶ Students can write reports collecting data that discusses the participation of girls in high school and middle school sports.

▶ High school students can write extensive biographies about important role models like Mary McLeod Bethune, who not only fought for the rights of Black women but who also established a college so women could earn an education.

▶ Have students read the book, *Headstrong: 52 Women Who Changed Science-and the World*, by Rachel Swaby, Broadway Books, 2015. This is an excellent book about the contributions that women have made to science and to the world.

≫ Professional Resource Download

that stereotype threat can negatively influence the performance of students of color, so teachers again must be prudent when they discuss stereotypes and the abilities of individuals who are from oppressed groups. There are a variety of strategies that teachers can integrate into their teaching provided in the Teaching Tips. The characteristics of strong women can be powerful knowledge for women and men to learn in schools.

Women's Rights History: Equality, Suffrage, and Education

The fight for women's rights has gone on many, many years, and the struggle continues today. As you will read later in this section, women make much less than men for the same job. Equality is still an issue that faces women in a variety of areas such as employment, suffrage, and education. **Suffrage** is defined as the right to vote. When this nation was founded, women could not inherit land, vote, participate in a jury, and enter a college (National Park Service, 2015). They were barred from many aspects of society that we take for granted today.

> **Suffrage** is defined as the right to vote. This term is often associated with women's fight for the vote.

When the U.S. Constitution was first drafted, the only individuals who could vote were White males who owned property. It was not until 1920 when women got the right to vote in the United States. At that time 36 states were needed to pass the amendment, and the Nineteenth Amendment was ratified by three-fourths of states in August of 1920. Interestingly, some of the states did not ratify the amendment until much later. For example, Mississippi did not ratify the Amendment until 1984. You did read that correctly, 1984. Though the state of Mississippi denied ratification in 1920, legislators did change their minds later. Some were embarrassed.

One of the most important events in the fight for women's suffrage was the Seneca Falls Convention of 1848. Elizabeth Cady Stanton and Lucretia Mott started working together, and their efforts led to the convention. Many others in the planning group were Quakers and became an important force in the movement for women's right to vote (National Park Service, 2015). The community modeled equality among women and men and had representatives at the convention in 1848. The women's suffrage movement had its roots in the fight against racism and the abolition of slavery. Thomas and Mary M'Clintock, a Quaker couple, helped to write the initial draft of their major document, *Declaration of Sentiments*, to include the statement, "All men and women are created equal" (National Park Service, 2015). This document was patterned after the U.S. Declaration of Independence (National Portrait Gallery, 2015). Frederick Douglass, the abolitionist, also supported the *Declaration of Sentiments* and lobbied for its passage at the convention. It seems odd today that women were not able to vote for almost 150 years after the birth of the nation in 1776. This is an important issue for teachers and students to think about.

This leads us to the ERA proposition. The Equal Rights Amendment was first proposed in 1923 and every year in Congress until 1972 (Freeman, 1988). It initially was proposed several years after the Nineteenth Amendment was passed to give women the vote. The ERA proposes that women have equal rights as men that are protected by the Constitution. When legislation is passed, laws can be changed; however, the Constitution is a document that is difficult to change. The ERA was passed by 35 states at different times, but three more were needed to ratify the amendment by the 1982 deadline. The ERA has been introduced in Congress every year since then, but there continue to be states that will not ratify it (National Council of Women's Organizations, 2013).

Some women have also opposed the ERA because they thought it would place women in male roles. For example, Phyllis Schlafly, a strong voice in the Republican Party, organized the Stop ERA campaign. She was concerned that women would be drafted into the military and that the passage of the ERA might lead to sex-neutral bathrooms. There are states such as California and Wyoming that have included protection of citizens by sex; however, there are other states where there are no guarantees for women, many of which did not ratify the ERA. These include Florida, Louisiana, Missouri, Nevada, North Carolina, and Oklahoma.

Education is another aspect of society that women did not participate in for many years as this country grew and developed. The previous section on gender roles explained how women in general were taught to stay at home and take care of the home; they were generally not encouraged to go to school. Their role was to cook, have children, take care of them, and keep the house clean. However, in poor families, women were also expected to work alongside their husbands in the fields if needed.

In the history of women, women have had to work hard over years to establish their civil and human rights. Recall that Title IX was a law to ensure equal rights for women, and was not passed by the federal government until 1972. To put this in perspective, consider that our nation was founded in 1776 and it took 196 years to put these rights for women in place. Obtaining voting, property, and reproductive rights have all been major problems for women since before the United States was established.

Women are continually subjected to subordination by men because in many countries around the world, including the United States, a patriarchal social system shapes and dominates many perceptions and limits opportunities of women (Crocco, 2007). Not only men but also women perpetuate the patriarchal system and subordination of females in society (Crocco, 2007). Some researchers believe that the fight for women's rights is similar to the struggle for human rights. Crocco (2007) has researched how the United Nations Declaration of Human Rights passed in 1948 helped to promote women's rights in the United States. She cites the work of Eleanor Roosevelt in promoting equal dignity, equal opportunity, and equal justice for women. As you can see, civil and human rights only come when people fight for social justice.

TIMELINE

WOMEN IN THE UNITED STATES

1776 — Abigail Adams conveyed to her husband, John Adams, that as a member of the Continental Congress in Philadelphia, he should remember women when making the laws of the new nation. However, her wish was not acknowledged. The Declaration of Independence drawn up by the Continental Congress famously states that "all men are created equal."

1836 — Sarah Grimké, an abolitionist and women's rights advocate, was told by male abolitionists not to speak in public because they felt she would hurt their cause.

1837 — The National Female Anti-Slavery convention was first held in New York City with 81 delegates from 12 states.

Mount Holyoke College was founded for women by Mary Lyon. Later Vassar College opened in 1861 and Wellesley and Smith in 1875.

1848 — The Seneca Falls Convention for Women's Rights was first held and became a regular meeting. This was an important event in the women's movement. Attending were Elizabeth Cady Stanton and Lucretia Mott. During the convention the *Declaration of Sentiments and Resolution* was accepted, which uses wording similar to the U.S. Declaration of Independence.

1866 — The American Equal Rights Association was founded by Elizabeth Cady Stanton and Susan B. Anthony. The organization fought for universal suffrage and included White women, Black women, and men.

1868 — The Fourteenth Amendment was ratified, protecting the rights of citizens against unfair state laws. This amendment guarantees citizens equal protection under the law and the right of due process. This amendment identifies citizens and voters as male.

1870 — The Fifteenth Amendment was ratified, giving Black men the right to vote. Women such as Susan B. Anthony and Elizabeth Cady Stanton did not agree with Frederick Douglass on this issue because they wanted universal suffrage.

1893 — The National Council of Jewish Women was founded by Hannah Greenbaum Solomon in Illinois.

1896 — Two Black women's organizations came together to establish the National Association of Colored Women's Clubs. This organization brought together the National Federation of Afro-American Women and the Colored Women's League of Washington. Mary Church Terrell was the first president of the collaborative organization.

Representatives of the National Association of Colored Women's Clubs came together to meet with Harriet Tubman in Washington, DC. They included Mary Church Terrell, Ida B. Wells Harper, Charlotte Forten Grinké, and Harriet Tubman, hero of the Underground Railroad.

1915 — The first woman elected to the U.S. Congress, Jeannette Rankin, served in the House of Representatives for the state of Montana. Though women generally could not vote in many states, Rankin voted in Congress

1920 — Women earned the right to vote with the ratification of the Nineteenth Amendment. The core of the National American Woman Suffrage Association became the League of Women Voters.

1921 — Margaret Sanger established the American Birth Control League, which later became Planned Parenthood Federation of America in 1942. Birth control continues to be an issue that polarizes many citizens.

1923 — The Equal Rights Amendment was first proposed to eliminate discrimination based on gender. Because not enough states ratified the amendment, it has never passed. The ERA has been introduced in Congress every year since 1982; however, 38 states have not ratified it.

1931 — Jane Addams became the first U.S. woman to be awarded the Nobel Peace Prize.

1963 — The Equal Pay Act was passed to require employers to pay women and men equally.

1972	Title IX was passed, which legislates that schools receiving federal funds could be at risk of losing them if the school does not provide equal access to women and men. The law has made a difference in the hiring, employment statistics, and academic scholarships for women. Women and men shaped and wrote the Title IX legislation, including Patsy T. Mink, Edith Louise Starrett Green, Birch Bayh, and Bernice R. Sandler.
1973	The U.S. Supreme Court decision in *Roe v. Wade* stated that the privacy rights of "Jane Roe" (Norma L. McCorvey) were violated when the state of Texas banned abortion.
1974	"Norma Rae" (Crystal Lee Sutton) organized a labor union that won the right to represent textile workers. The movie *Norma Rae* was based on her work and advocacy.

1981	Sandra Day O'Connor became the first woman on the U.S. Supreme Court.
2014	Maria Shriver, along with the Center for American Progress, published *The Shriver Report: A Woman's Nation Pushes Back From the Brink*. The document reported that 42 million women along with 28 million children live close to or in poverty.
2016	U.S. women win 61 medals at the Summer Olympics at Rio de Janeiro. Men won 55. At the 1972 games in Munich, women won 23, while men won 71.

*Adapted from "One Hundred Years Toward Suffrage: An Overview," by Susan Barber, *National American Women's Suffrage Association Collection 1848–1921*, Library of Congress; and *Women's Rights Timeline*, Annenberg Institute for Civics. Retrieved from http://www.annenbergclassroom.org/Files/Documents/Timelines /WomensRightstimeline.pdf

❯❯ Professional Resource Download

Refer to the Women in the United States Timeline (a more extensive timeline is available online in the Professional Resource Download section of MindTap). Identify the five most important events that you consider to have been pivotal in the history of women. What is your rationale for picking these events? Your reasons will be based upon your values as a teacher and person.

Fighting Sexism in Schools and Society

LO8 Analyze the way women have been presented in the school curriculum.

Presenting women in positive and nonstereotypical roles is not only important to their development but also to changing all people's attitudes about the accomplishments and abilities of women. What will you do in your classroom to make sure that you are showing the abilities and accomplishments of women? Various women from all groups must be presented in schools to fight stereotypical images that are often present. In this next section, take time to read about some of the accomplishments of women and think about how you might integrate the information into your curriculum. One way is to teach about U.S. senators and representatives who have recently been elected to Congress. These names may be more current and identifiable by students. For information on several women active in our government today, see the Professional Resource Download section in MindTap.

Portrayal of Women in Textbooks: Teaching Students to Analyze

The portrayal of women in U.S. history textbooks (Kirby & Julian, 1981; Schocker & Woyshner, 2013) and introductory sociology textbooks (Puentes & Gougherty, 2011) shows significant gaps and presents women in the context of a patriarchal orientation in society. It is important for students to analyze and evaluate how women are portrayed in the books they read in their classes.

Table 6.5 Images of Women and Men in Textbooks*					
Text	Total Number of Women and Percent of Total	Number of Black Women and Percent of Total	Number of White Women and Percent of Total	Number of Men and Percent of Total	Total Images Women and Men, 100%
African American History Textbook	156 (14%)	132 (12%)	24 (2%)	926 (86%)	1082
Two General U.S. History Textbooks	544* (28%)	103 (5%)	389 (20%)	1368 (71.5%)	1912

*Original numbers included Asian Americans, Latinos, and Native American women.

Adaptation of *Textbook Numbers of Presentation of Black Women, White Women, and Men*, by Schocker and Woyshner, 2011, table, p. 24.

The contributions of women are often not included. In addition, they are sometimes presented as being in subservient positions to men. See Table 6.5 for the findings of a pictorial analysis of three textbooks, one of which was for an African American history class used in Philadelphia schools and the other two were general U.S. history textbooks (Schocker & Woyshner, 2013). You can see that the images of women are not represented equally in the textbooks compared with men. There is a huge disparity. In the African American history textbook, only about 14 percent of the presentations are women, of which a majority of the images were African American women. This surprised Schocker and Woyshner because they thought a text about African Americans would be more sensitive to the inclusion of women. However, examining the two general U.S. history textbooks, the researchers found women are portrayed in 28 percent of the total number of images. Again, there were many more men shown. What messages does that send children? Why are so many more men shown in these textbooks?

As you read through your various textbooks, check to see if you find similar aspects about women in the materials you are using in your training or college education:

1. Stratification of women, which refers to inequalities that women face such as not earning as much as men, not having similar positions of authority, and the stereotyping of women as being too emotional or not able to lead. These are often structural aspects of society.

2. Intersectionality should be included in your textbooks where women are shown to have more than one identity. The connection of the three social categories of race, class, and gender can demonstrate that people do not experience life in one dimension only, say as a Black woman. A more comprehensive way to view the person may be as Black, a woman, and middle-class. Looking at another example, teachers often ask a student of color to speak for an entire ethnic or racial community. A teacher may ask a female student to give her view of an issue only as a Mexican American. Of course, she may understand that she cannot speak for everyone in the ethnic community to which she belongs to, but the teacher's orientation serves to also deny other aspects of her life such as her gender, her social class, and her religious background.

3. Sometimes women are presented as supporting men but not involved in developing their own personal goals. Abigail Adams is often quoted as reminding John Adams, a member of the Continental Congress, that women should be included in the laws of the new nation. However, few textbooks talk about her role as an abolitionist and women's rights advocate.

Teaching Students to Write a Persuasive Essay

Teach your students how to write a persuasive essay. Let's say the assignment is to write a convincing essay about the contributions of a woman to society.

⟩ Gather information about the person who the student has chosen to write about.

⟩ The purpose of this essay is to present an interesting report about the contributions she made to the community.

⟩ The author is to identify the points she is going to make in the essay. She can list them on a piece of paper to organize her thoughts.

⟩ The author should gather further evidence to support her point of view.

⟩ The author should rank the points she wants to make.

⟩ The author should identify her conclusion and explain why the contribution this person made to society was important.

4. Students need to know about the contributions of women in society. Some textbooks do not include women who may be seen as controversial like Margaret Sanger who promoted birth control, a term that she coined. She founded Planned Parenthood, and the organization provides birth control and is dedicated to women's health. The discussion of women's contributions should be presented within the historical context of the times, discussing the obstacles that they had to overcome. In addition, passages should not be limited to a sentence or paragraph, but may need a full page to explain the contribution.

5. The leadership that many women have provided to our society should also be discussed in our textbooks. Women have led as abolitionists like Harriet Tubman, as founders of colleges for women like Mary McLeod Bethune, or in organizations like Dolores Huerta, who cofounded the United Farm Workers with Cesar Chavez.

Male and female students will benefit from knowing the rich history and contributions of women in society. They will learn that many individuals and organizations have also fought for equal rights for all. As the teacher, you may need to integrate and bring in materials that are not provided. The Common Core emphasizes critical thinking skills and the importance of reading nonfiction such as historical documents. The Common Core also encourages teachers to instruct students how to use evidence and to investigate issues. Students can write arguments to support their positions and viewpoints. Integrating the portrayal of women in the curriculum is another way to get students to consider the contributions and leadership of women from various ethnic groups and social classes.

Consider this . . .

Tammy Baldwin (D-Wisconsin) was the first openly-gay woman elected to the Senate and Mazie Hirono (D-Hawaii) is the first Asian American female and Buddhist senator.

The first two women with military combat experience in Congress were Tulsi Gabbard and Tammy Baldwin.

Q Why do you think it took so long for more women to be elected to Congress?

See the Professional Resource Download section of MindTap for more information about Senators Baldwin and Hirono and Representative Gabbard.

You could also develop an issues-centered lesson. For example, do you think women should be allowed in combat positions in the armed services? In 2013, Secretary of State Leon Panetta agreed that women should be allowed to serve in combat. Some soldiers are concerned because most women are not as physically strong as their male peers. However, others believe in gender-neutral opportunities in combat. Women are already serving in war zones and being effective as drivers and medics. In the past, the front line of battle was important as the boundary for the inclusion of women. Today the border of war can be almost anywhere with the use of many types of military warfare such as improvised explosive devices (IEDs), missiles, and drones. Women, as well as men, can operate these technologies.

Another issue is the lower percentage of wages women earn compared to men, as illustrated in Table 6.6.

Table 6.6 Women's Earnings as a Percentage of Men's Wages, Ages 25 Years and Older	
Year	Women's Earnings as a Percent of Men's
1980	62.8
1981	62.6
1982	64.9
1983	65.8
1984	67.1
1985	66.8
1986	66.5
1987	67.3
1988	68.8
1989	70.2
1990	72.1
1991	74.0
1992	74.6
1993	74.8
1994	73.1
1995	72.8
1996	74.1
1997	75.1
1998	75.9
1999	74.4
2000	74.5
2001	75.4
2002	77.6
2003	78.5
2004	78.6
2005	79.4
2006	78.7
2007	78.5
2008	78.2
2009	78.7
2010	80.5

Source: U.S. Bureau of Labor Statistics, July 2011. "Highlights of Women's Earnings in 2010," Report 1031. Retrieved from http://www.bls.gov /cps/cpswom2010.pdf

Consider this . . .

Read through the Table 6.6.

Q How would you explain that in the 2010s, women earn about 80 cents to a man's dollar?

Q What do you think that women must do to gain parity with men in earnings?

Q How do gender and class come together in the area of income and earning possibilities?

Q If you had a daughter, what would you tell her about the economics associated with being a woman within the context of our democracy?

Thinking about Intersectionality

This chapter focuses on class and oppression toward women and girls. There are two main reasons for this focus. First, it is important for teachers to understand that women have had to struggle against stereotypes for many years. The suffrage movement is a good example of how women have not been treated equally with men because we live in a patriarchal society that has led to the subordination of women. Second, many teachers have not had the opportunity to really reflect on issues that may influence the achievement of women and girls in their classrooms.

Legislation such as Title IX has had a powerful effect on the growing opportunities for women. However, gender bias continues to plague our nation. For example, teachers should understand how stereotypes about women can serve as obstacles for girls in developing confidence and self-regulation skills in disciplines such as math, science, technology, and engineering. Teachers can be important role models and supporters of girls and women who choose these fields and should encourage them to develop their confidence and abilities.

Summary

1. **Define classism, income, wealth, and sexism.**

   Classism and gender bias refer to two different types of discrimination. Classism is a complex construct that is defined as prejudice or discrimination of people and groups based on their social class, which is often defined as "lower" class. Gender bias is the belief that women and men have different characteristics and these differences are based on the right of males having more resources and power than women. Though different in definition, these two concepts have often been linked. Class refers to the social-economic status of people, which can include income and wealth. Often students from low-income families do not get the same opportunities in society because they do not have the cultural capital or social capital which tells them what is expected and the behaviors they need to do well in life.

   Wealth is different from income. Income is the money one earns at a job. However, wealth is much broader because it refers to financial resources beyond one's salary. It includes one's car, house, stocks, bonds, other real estate investments, and bank accounts.

2. **Describe classism and poverty rates and their impact on children and low-income individuals.**

   Classism, poverty, and social stratification can hinder the opportunities that children will have as they go through school and life. The rates of child poverty for African Americans and Latinos are much higher than for White students. This is partly due to the low wages that parents earn. Almost half of African Americans and Latino parents do not have full-time jobs, which leads to food insecurity and lack of housing. Children also may not have healthcare and dental care.

3. **Evaluate how school stratification acts as an obstacle to equal educational opportunities.**

   Social stratification refers to a systematic hierarchy based on aspects of class, race, sex, and other social categories. Oftentimes, students who are from low-income families live in the poorest neighborhoods with the least qualified and least experienced teachers. This can limit their access to quality education and equal educational opportunities.

(Continued)

Summary *(Continued)*

4. Explain how poverty is a global issue.

The story of Dr. Yunus demonstrates how poverty is a global issue. The Nobel Peace Prize Laureate believed that credit is a human right and that being poor does not make people of poor quality. He thought that many people were poor because they did not have credit, so he created the Grameen Bank and lent out millions of dollars to people with little money in Bangladesh. Many of the people who created businesses were women. The repayment rate for loans given by the Grameen Bank is about 95 percent.

5. Describe how traditional gender roles can conflict with values of equality.

Society has reinforced many traditional gender roles. Gender roles in the United States often have a patriarchal orientation. Historically, men were expected to go to work outside of the home and women were to stay home and take care of the children. In colonial times, most women were not allowed to go to school. Education was provided primarily for men. Some felt that education would be wasted on women who took care of the family. Gender roles are reinforced in many ways in society so that it is expected that women would not become leaders in large corporations or businesses. Today, however, some business people like Sheryl Sandberg believe that women can be leaders and take care of their families if they have supportive spouses or partners. Women must be more confident. However, bell hooks cautions women, explaining that the issues of race, social class, and other areas of oppression influence the opportunities that many women may have.

6. Summarize how Title IX has assisted women in gaining equity in schools and society.

Title IX is legislation that was passed in 1972. The goal of the law was to protect the rights of women and to ensure that they were given the same opportunities as men in sports, education, and careers. In the past, few women participated in sports in high school or college; however, after Title IX was passed, many more women were actively involved in sports. In addition, the law required that universities, colleges, and high schools had to provide equal opportunities for women. Some colleges instituted women's tennis and volleyball teams to provide females with the chance to play these sports. Due to Title IX, many women's locker rooms were greatly improved since their accommodations were to be as well built as their male counterparts'. After the law was put in place, many more women graduated in selective fields such as medicine and the law.

7. Examine how stereotype threat can undermine the self-confidence and performance of women.

Stereotype threat has been found to impede the performance of women. When stereotypes of inabilities of women are pointed out prior to an assessment, women and girls may not do well. Teachers should be careful to present positive role models that can be used to enhance the view women have about their abilities to succeed.

8. Analyze the way women have been presented in the school curriculum.

The history of women in the United States illustrates the perennial issues of suffrage, education, employment, childcare costs, and wages. Women have had to fight for equal rights and continue to do so because they have not met parity with men. Many women make about 80 cents of a man's dollar for the same job. This shows a lack of equality in the United States. Women also had to fight to get an education. Women were not allowed to attend most colleges during colonial days. It is imperative that teachers present strong female role models throughout the year in their classrooms. They can have students bring photos of the chosen women or make drawings of their role models. Everyone can benefit from learning about a woman who has made a contribution to our nation. In addition, teachers should analyze the presentation of women in their textbooks and consider how to integrate more knowledge about the leadership of women. Role models are important for women so girls know they can achieve their dreams, no matter how difficult. Males also learn from female role models. They learn that women can be self-confident leaders who make major contributions to our nation.

Check Your Cultural Knowledge

Reflective Essay Question

What are the two most powerful challenges that women must deal with before they are integrated into all aspects of society, from being the CEO of a Fortunate 500 company to becoming a soldier in war time?

Know and Go Tools in the Classroom

Activity 1: Women's Contribution to the War Effort

Present this photo to the students in your class.

The Vietnam Women's Memorial in Washington, DC

Women Soldiers in the Armed Services of the United States

Elementary-Grade Classroom

Women, like men, serve as soldiers during war time. This memorial honors the 265,000 women who volunteered during the Vietnam War. The woman sculptor who created this monument is Glenna Goodacre. The memorial shows three women soldiers, one nursing a male soldier. This monument is the first to celebrate women soldiers.

For more information go to http://www.vietnamwomensmemorial.org/history.php.

Ask students the following questions about the memorial:

1. What is this monument about? Have you seen it?
2. One woman is holding another armed service person. What is she doing?
3. Have you ever seen a monument dedicated to women in war?
4. Write down five reasons the sculptor created this monument. What are the messages?
5. Who is Glenna Goodacre? What does she have to do with the Vietnam Women's Memorial?
6. Is it important to have a monument about women in Washington, DC? Why or why not?
7. How does the memorial show courage?

High School Classroom

Use the questions above and then ask middle/high school students about the characteristics of women who serve in the war.

1. What characteristics must the women possess?
2. Are they treated equally with men in society? If so, why? If not, why not?

Activity 2: Women as Role Models

To show women as role models, have students make posters of women leaders from around the world. The list could include:

- Mother Teresa (religious leader)
- Angela Merkel (chancellor of Germany)
- Mary Robinson (president of Ireland)
- Malala Yousafzai (Nobel Laureate)
- Aung San Suu Kyi (leader of prodemocracy movement in Burma and Nobel Laureate)

Elementary Grades

Divide students into small groups. Each group can develop a biography for the person they select and then find a photo of that woman. They might answer questions such as the following:

1. Why did you choose this woman as a role model?
2. What characteristics does she possess that you admire?
3. What did she do that was important to our community, state, nation, or world?
4. What title will you have on the poster that will interest your friends to read the poster and that identifies what this woman did?

High School Classrooms

Use the same directions and then add the following:

Have students create a website that includes the person's biography, picture, description of what they have done to contribute to society, characteristics, a title for the, and a report that includes the person's lifeline (history of her life).

Hang the posters all over the room and school library. It might be okay to hang some posters in the school cafeteria if students will be respectful and not write on them.

Middle School and High School Classrooms

For older learners, teachers can have students create a wiki about the female role models. They could also be part of a classroom blog. These are digital methods that students can use to distribute their information to their peers. One website that tells how to create a wiki is http://www.wikihow.com/Start-a-Wiki. A wiki is a webpage with information that can be changed. One example is Wikipedia, the free encyclopedia on the Web. The term "wiki, wiki" is Hawaiian for hurry up or fast. Students can create a place where they write an essay describing an important female. Because it is a wiki, the information is easy and fast to access.

Pekic/Getty Images

Human Diversity: Sexual Orientation and Gender Identity

Learning Objectives

LO1 Describe how elements of human diversity have changed.

LO2 Define and discuss concepts of gay culture, sexual orientation, and gender identity.

LO3 Identify bullying and homophobia issues and discuss strategies to eliminate discrimination in schools.

LO4 Interpret and justify the importance of presenting role models from the LGBTQ community.

STANDARDS COVERED

NAEYC 1, 2, 6
naeyc

CAEP 1 **CAEP**

INTASC 1, 2, 3, 4, 5, 6, 7, 8, 9, 10 **InTASC**

How Has the View of Diversity Evolved?

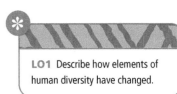

LO1 Describe how elements of human diversity have changed.

Humans continually change their beliefs about life, and so their views of the term *cultural diversity* also change. About 40 years ago, the term *diversity* was not a common one. In fact when people talked about human difference, it was mainly about race and the categorization of people by the color of someone's skin. Many individuals saw race as an accurate reflection of people. However, today more people know that race is not a biological truth. Race is a sociopolitical construct.

In the middle of the twentieth century, role models were primarily from mainstream culture. For example, there were many White news anchors who were seen in homes every night, commentators such as David Brinkley, Chet Huntley, and Walter Cronkite. At that time, there were few people of color or women anchors or reporters. This is how society was structured in those days, though today many people would say this was not right. This orientation began to change as the Civil Rights Movement and the issue of equality moved into mainstream life during the 1960s.

By the time the civil rights and women's movements had been fully established in the 1970s and 1980s, the faces on TV began to be more diverse. Maybe you remember watching *The Cosby Show* when it first appeared on television in 1984 or in reruns. The series was about the Huxtable family; they were Black and lived in an upper middle-class neighborhood in Brooklyn, New York. The mother, Claire, was a lawyer and her husband, Cliff, was an obstetrician. The show continued until the eighth season came to a close in 1992. This was one of the few TV series that featured an affluent Black family. At the time, the program was considered unusual. However, today there are several sitcoms and dramas on TV that include issues of ethnic, linguistic, gender, and sexual-orientation diversity.

As new television shows developed for the twenty-first century, many diverse actors were included. For example, *Modern Family* began in the fall of 2009, approximately 25 years after *The Cosby Show* debuted. The series is about the extended family of Jay Pritchett. Jay's second wife is originally from Colombia and Spanish-speaking. Jay's daughter, her husband, and their three children are part of the ensemble cast. In addition, Jay's son is gay and he and his partner have adopted a Vietnamese daughter. The series is very funny and has won the Emmy award for best comedy several times. Some of the funniest parts of the show happen when the writers tie in humor with stereotypes. The series uses humor to make fun of bias. Initially, there was some criticism from the LGBTQ community because the gay couple portrayed did not show much affection toward each other. **LGBTQ** refers to lesbian, gay, bisexual, transgender, and questioning or queer individuals. The show took note and addressed the criticism later in the season when the couple kissed. *Modern Family* was honored in 2010 by GLSEN (Gay, Lesbian and Straight Education Network) for its portrayal of a gay couple.

LGBTQ refers to lesbian, gay, bisexual, transgender, and questioning or queer individuals.

The show was also criticized over the fact that Jay's wife and his daughter are both stay-at-home moms. However, there are episodes in which the women are in control of what goes on, too. For example, Jay's daughter, Claire, ran for a local public office because she wanted to make her community a better place. Though she lost, Claire then went to work for her dad's company and deals with being a woman in the workplace. This television program brings to the forefront many issues that are found in everyday life. As time moves forward, changes in attitudes, opinions, and stereotypes are seen in how characters cope with different problems. *Modern Family* often sheds light on how society has progressed forward and moved away from damaging stereotypes of the past (Figure 7.1).

Another television program that worked to break down stereotypes is *Glee*. *Glee* wove together the lives of students and teachers in a high school glee club. The series included a wide variety of characters showing the cultural diversity of our society. For example,

Figure 7.1: The cast of *Modern Family* includes individuals from various culturally diverse communities. For example, Jesse Tyler Ferguson and Eric Stonestreet play a gay couple with a daughter.

Arnie is a wonderful singer, and he uses a wheelchair. He can be seen singing and dancing just like any other character on the show. Several of the main characters are gay, and the series presented them as any other high school students struggling with relationship issues. The character Unique is transgender, and the writers also included aspects of her life such as challenges with self-esteem and friendships. Another main character is Becky, who has Down syndrome. Becky is an important member of the cheer club, and she also struggles with issues of belonging and coming of age, which is common among high school students. Marley is one of the main characters and has a boyfriend named Jake. Marley comes from a poor single-parent family, and the students at school tease her mother because she is obese. One of the stories in the series showed how Jake stood up for Marley's mom when she was being discriminated against because of her size. The series won numerous awards such as a Golden Globe for the best television musical or comedy show (Figure 7.2).

There is also a television show that includes a transgender character. A transgender individual is a person whose gender identity differs from the sex the physician

Figure 7.2: The TV show *Glee* included characters who represented diverse communities; the individuals represented diversity in race, ethnicity, ability/disability, sexual orientation, gender identity, and social class.

wrote on their birth certificate (GLAAD, n.d.). In the series *Orange is the New Black*, Laverne Cox is the actress who plays Sophia Burset. Cox is transgender and plays a transgender female in this adult-oriented television series. Through her character, Cox explains some of the issues that she must deal with as someone who has gone through reassignment surgery and must takes hormone pills to complete her change to a transgender woman. Her character experiences a crisis when the prison will not give her the number of hormone pills she needs. Cox also wants others to understand that trans women are often discriminated against. Her character is a powerful way to educate viewers about issues that the transgender community must deal with and how many people have little understanding

Figure 7.3: Sophia Burset, on the TV program *Orange Is the New Black*, is played by Laverne Cox, a transgender actress. She also plays a transgender inmate in the program.

of the inner gender identity conflicts and sexual orientation struggles of transgender citizens (Figure 7.3).

These highly visible, award-winning television series illustrate and contribute to the popular culture; this includes music, foods, brands, media, video games, and language that people use. So it is possible to see how cultural diversity has expanded. The term *diversity* is much more than race, which was the common definition during the early twentieth century. Now the term has expanded in its designations and includes differences due to language, sexual orientation, exceptionality, religion, gender roles, gender identity, age, and social class. Just a note, sometimes individuals and groups identify themselves as queer. **Queer** has a variety of definitions. For some individuals, it has been repossessed from being used negatively against gays and lesbians to one of self-pride. The term is also used to generally identify lesbians, gays, bisexuals, and transgender people. Some individuals still see the term as offensive.

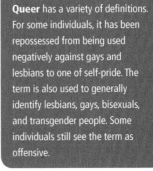

Queer has a variety of definitions. For some individuals, it has been repossessed from being used negatively against gays and lesbians to one of self-pride. The term is also used to generally identify lesbians, gays, bisexuals, and transgender people. Some individuals still see the term as offensive.

Sexual Orientation: Lesbian, Gay, Bisexual, Transgender, and Queer

Sexual orientation is a complex construct. Some LGBTQ students tell teachers that when they were extremely young they knew they had different views about their sexual orientation. However, they did not want to say anything to their teachers for fear of being rejected or ignored. Many scholars believe that LGBTQ communities have created and sustained various subcultures, which include gender identity and gay politics.

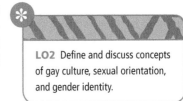

LO2 Define and discuss concepts of gay culture, sexual orientation, and gender identity.

Alfred C. Kinsey: Much Has Changed Since the Kinsey Report

In the early twentieth century, zoologist Alfred Kinsey was one of few researchers who studied sex and sexuality. Many scholars studied sex from a medical orientation and not through interviewing or gathering data about human behavior (Bullough, 1998). In fact, during the late nineteenth century and early years of the twentieth century, physicians labeled people who were gay as being immoral and unnatural. Heterosexual behavior was seen as being common and expected. At the time, it was also difficult to gather data on

CASE STUDY Patrick: Five Years Old and Gay

Patrick is a five-year-old kindergartener. He enjoys playing with his friends outside. They run throughout the playground at recess and the teacher can hear them laughing together. When he goes into the classroom, his teacher says, "Valentine's Day is coming this week. We need to make our Valentine cards." The teacher continues and says, "I want you to make a Valentine's card for someone. There is red and white paper in the cupboard and lots of different markers."

As Patrick gathers his art supplies, the teacher whispers," Patrick, which girl are you going to make a Valentine for?"

Patrick freezes. He wants to make a card for his friend, Neil. He doesn't want the teacher to know, so he smiles and says, "I am still deciding."

The teacher nods and walks away.

Patrick heaves a sigh of relief. He is worried that his teacher might find out that he likes another boy. He picks a friend who is a girl and writes her name at the top of his card. No one will know if he just does what his teacher tells him to do.

Reflection Questions

Q How would you feel if you had to hide who you are?

Q What would you say to Patrick if he was a student in your class? What would be the most appropriate?

people's sexual behaviors because people did not talk about what they did in their private lives. Therefore, the topics that Kinsey studied were considered extremely taboo (Capshew, Adamson, Buchanan, Murray, & Wake, 2003).

In the beginning Kinsey conducted many interviews of young people, gathering information about the age at which they engaged in sexual behaviors and premarital sex, and asked them to identify the number of sex partners they had had. Some of his original research was funded by the Committee for Research in the Problems of Sex (CRPS) because the committee believed that the information that Kinsey collected would help young people stay married (Bullough, 1998). Kinsey was always walking difficult lines of morality in the social context of the day.

Because Kinsey was a scientist, he believed in gathering data, and his institute on sexuality gathered a total of more than 18,000 files (Winkler, 2005). Initially, Kinsey's work in sexuality focused primarily on women and their sexual issues (Capshew et al., 2003). Two of his most well-known books are *Sexual Behavior in the Human Male* published in 1948 and *Sexual Behavior in the Human Female* published in 1953. One of his goals was to provide women more sexual freedom. Women were presented as individuals who had their own sexual desires and were not there for the pleasure of men. In addition, Kinsey believed that sexual behavior could be described by a continuum (Capshew et al., 2003; Winkler, 2005). Kinsey refuted the binary belief in sexuality, heterosexuality and homosexuality (Kirby, 2007). In his 1948 Kinsey Report, the researcher reported that about one third of men his research team interviewed had feelings for other men and/or had participated in a gay experience (Kirby, 2007). Some researchers believe that due to Kinsey's research, the issue of homosexuality became more acceptable, while others think that Kinsey's research was methodologically flawed and based on his own insecurities (Capshew et al., 2003; Kirby, 2007; Monaghan, 2015). Later in this chapter, there is discussion of new research on gay identity development that uses a psychological orientation. In addition, many scholars see LBGTQ individuals as members of a culture that is similar to an ethnic or racial background with its own language, history, role models, values, customs, and beliefs. Unlike Kinsey's Heterosexual/Homosexual Rating Scale, it is more about lifestyle than the sexual behaviors of a person.

What Is Sexual Orientation?

Unlike Alfred Kinsey, researchers today see sexual orientation as a complex construct that includes gender identity, culture, history, political advocacy, social community, and psychological changes. Individuals who identify as gay, lesbian, bisexual, transgender, and queer have a rich background and should not be looked at only through a sexual lens. Even as young as five years old, many children like Patrick who are gay or transsexual know that their sexual orientation is not like most others in their classes. They know they do not have the same feelings for their opposite-sex classmates. However, children and young people may not have a term to explain their emotions for same-gender friends. They also may sense that others do not support their feelings for same-gender individuals. To address the needs of LGBTQ students, it is important that educators use the same definition of sexual orientation. Because sexual orientation may mean different things to many people, for the purpose of this text, the definition from the American Psychological Association (2011) is used:

> **Sexual orientation** refers to the sex of those [to] whom one is sexually and romantically attracted. Categories of sexual orientation typically have included attraction to members of one's own sex (gay men or lesbians), attraction to members of the other sex (heterosexuals), and attraction to members of both sexes (bisexuals). While these categories continue to be widely used, research has suggested that sexual orientation does not always appear in such definable categories and instead occurs on a continuum… In addition, some research indicates that sexual orientation is fluid for some people; this may be especially true for women…

So as you can see, the American Psychological Association believes, as did Kinsey, that there is a continuum regarding sexual orientation though the identified categories do not have rigid boundaries. For example, individuals do not need to be either gay or heterosexual. Some people may be attracted to both sexes. However, there are individuals who do not identify as being gay, heterosexual, bisexual, transgender, or lesbian; they may identify as being queer, which they see as a more general term (Jover, 2014). This has led to the designation of LGBTQ. It is important for teachers to know that Q can also refer to persons who are questioning their heterosexuality (Jover, 2014).

Though in the past some researchers believed that LGBTQ identity and orientations were indications of mental health issues, this view has been found to be erroneous and stopped. The American Psychological Association (2008) believes that being LGBTQ is not a mental illness. The organization has written that LGBTQ are common aspects of humanity.

Sexual orientation and gender identity are complex issues that many people find difficult to talk about. The ability of individuals to talk about their sexual orientation and gender may have to do with how sex and gender identities were discussed in their families as they grew up.

The American Psychological Association says that sex represents a person's biological status, which is often grouped as male, female, or intersex (a person may have features of both females and males). This indicates that gender identity can be extremely complex, especially if one's gender identity is not consistent with their biological sex. According to the American Psychological Association, **transgender** is an overarching term used to recognize those whose internal gender identity does not collaborate with their biological sex. Transgender can be used to describe people with atypical genitalia (Case, Stewart, & Tittsworth, 2009). In addition, there are students with **intersex conditions**, which means that they have various irregularities that may involve "external genitals, internal reproductive organs, sex chromosomes, or sex-related hormones" (American Psychological Association, 2011). For example, a baby might be born with ambiguous genitals; the baby does not have expected female or male genitalia. This can be challenging for the child and parents.

Sexual orientation refers to the sex of those to whom one is sexually and romantically attracted. Categories of sexual orientation typically have included attraction to members of one's own sex (gay men or lesbians), attraction to members of the other sex (heterosexuals), and attraction to members of both sexes (bisexuals). While these categories continue to be widely used, research has suggested that sexual orientation does not always appear in such definable categories and instead occurs on a continuum. This definition comes from the American Psychological Association.

Transgender is an overarching term used to recognize those whose internal gender identity does not collaborate with their biological sex. Transgender can be used to describe people with atypical genitalia.

Intersex conditions refers to individuals who have various abnormalities that may involve various aspects of the body such as external genitals, internal reproductive organs, and sex chromosomes.

For the purpose of this book, terms such as homosexuals, homosexuality, and homosexual community are generally not used. Though these terms are acceptable in some contexts, I believe that the expressions are associated with extremely negative misconceptions and so usually do not employ them. However, when titles of materials such as books and research instruments use these terms, they will be repeated here.

Educators may not see gay, lesbian, bisexual, and transgender communities as cultural groups; rather, they may see people whose identities are primarily rooted in deviant sexual intimacy. However, there are many scholars who believe LGBTQ individuals are members of cultural communities. For example, the American Psychological Association believes that LGBTQ communities are diverse cultural groups that have histories, identities, languages, attitudes, and viewpoints; their lives are much more than about sexual intimacy.

Gay and Lesbian Subcultures

Gays and lesbians have developed their own subcultures, which reside within the general, dominant culture. Some people refer to the concepts as gay culture and lesbian culture. It is not possible to describe one gay or lesbian subculture; however, Valle's model of culture (1997) can help you understand that LGBTQ youth are members of subcultures. Let's look at the three levels of culture as identified by Valle:

1. First in his model, Valle identifies cultural aspects of culture that can be easily seen or heard. For example, you can observe what people wear, the language they use, the places they go, and the music they listen to. Though many gay and lesbian individuals may like the music of Cher and Barbra Streisand, others like the music of the Beatles, U2, and Coldplay. However, there are some general symbols LGBTQ communities use to represent themselves. For example, marching in a PRIDE parade reinforces and celebrates LGBTQ communities. LGBTQ individuals and others may wear a rainbow t-shirt. The rainbow is often used as a symbol of the LGBTQ community and represents the inclusion of the diversity of the LGBTQ population.

2. The second level of culture has to do with interactional patterns and behaviors. With the legalization of same-sex marriage, LGBTQ couples are adopting different ways of celebrating their marriages. During wedding ceremonies, couples may choose to have a justice of the peace or ask a friend to marry them versus a religious cleric (Reynolds, 2014). Only 38 percent of respondents to a survey conducted by The Knot (a wedding media company) and *The Advocate* (LGBTQ news organization) would include some type of religious aspect to their celebration. The couple may also not walk down the aisle and most likely will spend much less than straight couples. In the survey, 82 percent of the lesbian and gay couples called their celebrations a marriage and not a civil union (Reynolds, 2014). These are all aspects of level 2 of culture behaviors and interactional patterns in regard to weddings and civil unions.

3. The third and most important level of culture includes the values that LGBTQ individuals hold dear. Like many U.S. citizens, LGBTQs value equality, freedom, democracy, and civil rights. These values are apparent throughout the history of LGBTQ communities. Review the historical events in the LGBTQ in the United States Timeline. The timeline shows how the theme of civil rights and equality are core themes in the LGBTQ community. Members have rioted, protested, organized, marched, and fought against institutional and social inequalities. You can see from the events outlined in the timeline that there have been many people who have fought for civil rights for LGBTQ individuals for many years.

Which one of these events are you aware of? If you do not know any of them, why do you think that is the case? Should teachers include LGBTQ history in schools? Why or why not?

TIMELINE

LGBTQ IN THE UNITED STATES

1924 The Society for Human Rights was established by Henry Gerber. It was the first gay rights organization. However, after much political pressure, it was disbanded soon after it was started.

1948 The Kinsey report was published explaining that homosexuality in men was much more common than originally thought.

1950 The Mattachine Society was founded to fight discrimination and prejudice toward gays. In addition, one of the organization's goals was to assimilate gays into society.

1952 The American Psychiatric Association identified homosexuality as a personality malady in its publication, *Diagnostic and Statistical Manual of Mental Disorders*. The organization was criticized for not having evidence for their assertions.

1953 Executive Order 10450 was signed by President Eisenhower; it barred the hiring of gays in federal positions.

1955 Daughters of Bilitis was established. It was the first lesbian rights organization.

1962 Illinois was the first state to decriminalize homosexual acts between consenting adults.

1966 The first transgender organization, the National Transsexual Counseling Unit, was established in San Francisco.

The Mattachine Society held a "sip in" at a bar in Greenwich Village, New York, because gays were not allowed to be served at bars.

1969 On June 28, the New York City police raided a gay bar, the Stonewall Inn. The patrons at the bar felt that the police were harassing them, so they rioted for three days. This event is considered to be one of the most important events in the history of gay civil rights in the United States and is widely considered the beginning of the LGBTQ movement.

1970 On June 28, the first Pride Parade was held in New York City. It was a civil rights protest, highlighting the struggle for equal rights at the Stonewall Inn.

1973 The American Psychiatric Association altered its position and took homosexuality off of its list of mental disorders.

Harvey Milk sought public office in San Francisco, and his platform opposed the government's intervention in the personal, sexual lives of people.

1976 Harvey Milk was appointed by San Francisco Mayor George Moscone to the Board of Permit Appeals. Milk became the first openly gay city commissioner in the nation.

1977 Legislation was passed that outlawed discrimination based on sexual orientation in Dade County, Florida. This ordinance was overturned by a vote of the people led by the campaign of a Christian fundamentalist group and singer Anita Bryant.

1978 Harvey Milk was voted in as a member of the San Francisco Board of Supervisors and later sponsored a civil rights bill forbidding discrimination based on sexual orientation. This legislation became law when Mayor Moscone signed the document.

Dan White, a former San Francisco supervisor, murdered Harvey Milk, a city supervisor, and Mayor George Moscone.

1979 The Supreme Court of California ruled that public utility companies could not discriminate against gays in hiring or refuse to allow them to participate in gay organizations in *Gay Law Students* v. *Pacific Telephone and Telegraph Company.*

1980 The Democratic National Convention took a strong stand on gay rights with the statement, "All groups must be protected from discrimination based on race, color, religion, national origin, language, age, sex or sexual orientation."

1982 Wisconsin was the first state to forbid discrimination based on sexual orientation.

1984 Berkeley, California, became the first city to approve domestic-partnership benefits to employees.

(Continued)

LGBTQ IN THE UNITED STATES *continued*

1991 Three gay couples in Hawaii believed that defining marriage as between one woman and one man is constitutionally limiting. They sued the director of health who would not issue them a marriage license.

1993 "Don't Ask, Don't Tell" became a policy in the U.S. military.

The Supreme Court in Hawaii ruled in favor of same-sex marriage.

The U.S. Congress passed the Defense of Marriage Act (DOMA), limiting marriage—and its federal benefits—to heterosexual couples.

1997 TV host and comedian Ellen DeGeneres announced that she is gay and later her show, *Ellen*, was cancelled by ABC Television.

2000 The Vermont Supreme Court ruled that the current definition of marriage discriminates against same-sex couples.

The Vermont legislature voted for the first civil-union law in the United States.

2004–06 Eleven states passed legislation or constitutional amendments banning gay marriage.

2008 Courts in California and Connecticut ruled in favor of gay marriage. However, the people of California voted for Proposition 8, opposing same-sex marriages. This popular vote rendered the court decision moot.

2015 Thirty-seven states (Alaska, Arizona, California, Colorado, Connecticut, Delaware, Florida, Hawaii, Idaho, Illinois, Indiana, Iowa, Kansas, Maine, Maryland, Massachusetts, Minnesota, Missouri, Montana, Nevada, New Hampshire, New Jersey, New Mexico, New York, North Carolina, Oklahoma, Oregon, Pennsylvania, Rhode Island, South Carolina, Utah, Vermont, Virginia, Washington, West Virginia, Wisconsin, and Wyoming) and the District of Columbia recognized same-sex marriage. The issue of gay marriage was argued in the U.S. Supreme Court.

2015, June 26 U.S. Supreme Court ruled in *Obergefell v. Hodges* that same-sex marriage is a constitutional right.

Professional Resource Download

Consider this . . .

GLSEN, Gay Lesbian and Straight Education Network, suggests that students, teachers, parents, and community members Take the Ally* Pledge.

"I believe all students, regardless of sexual orientation or gender identity/expression, deserve to feel safe and supported. That means I pledge to:

- Not use anti-LGBTQ (lesbian, gay, bisexual, transgender, queer) language or slurs.
- Intervene, if I safely can, in situations where students are being harassed or tell an adult.
- Support efforts to end bullying and harassment.
- Encourage others to be Allies."

To find out more about the pledge go to http://www.allyweek.org/about/.

Q How can you incorporate this pledge into your classroom?

*An ally is a person who is a member of a privileged group and fights against social oppression. This person advocates for social change and not oppression. (GLSEN, n.d.).

Gender Identity

Cultural identity is discussed in this book, and it is also important for teachers to be familiar with the concept of gender identity. Gender identity is often difficult for many LGBTQ youth to develop because society teaches primarily about gender-conforming identities. Gender deals with one's given biological sex; however, gender identity is the identity that a person identifies with, and it may not be associated with his or her biological sex (American Psychological Association, 2011). The American Psychological Association (APA) provides the following definitions about gender and gender identity from their website under, "Definition of Terms: Sex, Gender, Gender Identity, Sexual Orientation."

Gender "refers to the attitudes, feelings, and behaviors that a given culture associates with a person's biological sex. Behavior that is compatible with cultural expectations is referred to as gender normative, behaviors that are viewed as incompatible with these expectations constitute gender non-conformative…" (American Psychological Association, 2011). Gender is socially constructed and is identified with beliefs such as "she throws like a girl."

Gender identity "refers to 'one's sense of oneself as male, female, or transgender' (American Psychological Association, 2011). When one's gender identity and biological sex are not corresponding, then the person may identify as transsexual or as another transgender category (Gainor, 2000). Later in this chapter, the contrast between gender identity and sexual identity will be discussed.

One of the most difficult aspects of many LGBTQ individuals is coming out. **Coming out** "refers to the process in which one acknowledges and accepts one's own sexual orientation. It also encompasses the process in which one discloses one's sexual orientation to others. The term closeted refers to a state of secrecy or cautious privacy regarding one's sexual orientation" (American Psychological Association, 2011). Many times LGBTQ individuals may not want to let others know what their sexual orientation is because they think they will be looked down upon or feel shame.

Sexual Identity and Gender Identity

Sexual identity and gender identity are not the same. Sex has two meanings (Arundel, 2015). First, sex is about intimate relationships. Second, sex is also about biology, physical body parts, and chromosomes. Gender comes from our minds and how we see ourselves (Ehrensaft, 2011). However, in the general society, the concepts of sex and gender are often intertwined; therefore, many people consider the two terms to be interchangeable. However, this is not true for individuals whose sexual identity is not the same as their gender identity.

Let's talk about how the ideas of gender and sex are presented in society and what is considered "normal." In the delivery room when you were born, your parents probably asked the doctor, "Is the baby a girl or a boy?" The doctor looked at your body parts as you were "arriving" and then answered. The idea of gender in most families has been socially constructed around body parts. The social construction of gender is so strong that many times when baby gifts are picked out for girls, the presents may be pink lace baby blankets and little knit tops. If the baby is a boy, then blue clothes are given that may have trucks or dinosaurs printed on them. As they grow, boys are taught to climb trees, while girls are expected to play with dolls. Boys wear pants and not dresses. Girls wear dresses and pants. Boys play football and girls play tennis. Girls like to cook, while boys fix cars. Can you see how sex and gender are intertwined? Also can you see how young people can be pressured into specific gender roles that may differ from their gender identities?

Gender identity is about one's sense of self and who a person believes that she or he is (Egan & Perry, 2001; Arundel, 2015). Gender identity may not match one's biological parts. A person who was born with so-called male body parts may identify with being a woman.

Gender refers to the social attitudes, behaviors, and feelings that are associated with an individual's biological sex. It also denotes the cultural behavioral expectations that are seen as normative.

Gender identity is when a person identifies as being male, female, or transgender. Sometimes one's gender identity is not congruent with his or her biological sex.

Coming out refers to a person telling others about his or her sexual orientation. Sometimes the term also is described as "coming out of the closet," which means that someone is no longer keeping her or his sexual orientation a secret.

Figure 7.4: A girl is playing a traditional female role of feeding her baby (left), while a boy is playing with traditional male toys (right).

Her gender identity is female. She must then challenge the expectations of gender conformity that is found in so many ways in society. One of the most important periods when numerous girls and boys confirm their heterosexual gender identity of being a female or male is during elementary school (Ehrensaft, 2011). (See Figure 7.4.) And, as they grow older, socially constructed gender expectations grow. In this society, young people also learn what is expected of them such as getting married, having children, and establishing families.

Gender Identity: Gay, Lesbian, and Bisexual

Each of us must develop our identity as a human being. Some of us have strong ethnic identities that are tied to cultural or racial group memberships. Others identify strongly with their gender as a woman or man or both or neither; this includes transgender individuals. Gender identity scholars have moved away from a binary perspective of gender as being female or male. Gender identity is extremely personal, and during adolescence, individuals may be investigating this part of who they are. Gender identity may also be difficult to develop when one's sexual orientation is not heterosexual since heterosexuality is seen as legitimate and expected (Blackburn & Smith, 2010). Dealing with gender identify can also be difficult because of peer pressure and the expectations of what is considered "normal" (Egan & Perry, 2001). In contrast to this expectation, many gay individuals grow up hiding feelings of shame (Downs, 2012). They may feel that they have a deep secret that most people would not understand and if others did know, they would exhibit hostility toward them. Shame leads to the belief that they are unlovable (Downs, 2012). Alan Downs, a clinical psychologist, wrote about the lack of acceptance of being gay by a gay person and how society sends destructive messages:

> Knowing they were different in such a significant way led them [gays] to internalize the beliefs of shame. The statistics continue to bear out that gay men in their early twenties are increasingly likely to struggle with addiction, depression, and even suicide—all symptoms of the man who bears the pain of feeling unlovable. (2012, p. xiii)

Like ethnic/racial identity formation, gender identity is an important aspect of development for LGBTQs. Cass (1984) identified six stages of gender identity development for gay, lesbian, and bisexual individuals, which moves them from confusion to pride and authenticity. Downs (2012) believes that within this social and psychological process, gay men are overwhelmed by shame and have a need to be validated by others. As they move away from the feeling of shame, Cass and Downs believe that gay and bisexual persons move through various stages of self-acceptance and find meaning in life.

Cass's model of gay identity development begins with the initial stage of having negative feelings about one's sexual orientation. This often leads to inner conflict when a gay, lesbian, or bisexual person sees how others respond negatively to him or her. As individuals go through all six stages, they understand that their sexual orientation is only one aspect of their overall identity and learn to accept themselves. The person could be bisexual, but also a Black American who sings opera, speaks Mandarin, and is a father of three children. The linear model is a continuum and does not mean there are rigid boundaries between each stage. In addition, a person may not journey through all six stages.

Read through Cass's six stages of gay identity development that follow. In addition, the work of psychologists Halpin and Allen (2004) provides more explanations about each stage. They studied 425 males, and their findings demonstrated that the six stages could be grouped into three larger dimensions of gay identity development. Examples of statements from individuals in each stage are described in the next section.

Gay Identity Development Stages by Cass

The researcher Vivian Cass (1984) developed a psychosocial-identity development model for gays and lesbians. This model is about the psychological changes that a person goes through in his or her identity process. The process arises as an individual decides to come out to others about his or her sexual orientation. Cass's model is not at all like the model developed by Alfred Kinsey. The Kinsey model is based primarily on sexual experiences. Cass's model encourages individuals to ask themselves who they are and which community they identify with as they tell their family members or friends who they are. There are also models that describe bisexual identity development (Bilodeau & Renn, 2005); however, binary models do not take into account the complex elements of social class, race, and disabilities within the paradigm.

1. **Initial Dimension:** This dimension includes stages 1 and 2 in which individuals may not have a deep awareness of sexual identity and continue to be closeted (Halpin & Allen, 2004); however, there are also those in these stages who may begin to realize that they may be gay (Eliason & Schope, 2007).

   a. **Stage 1—Identity Confusion:** A person may perceive that their feelings, behaviors, and thoughts may be gay in nature (Cass, 1984).
      i. "Who am I?" (p. 152).
      ii. "Where do I belong?" (p. 152).

   b. **Stage 2—Identity Comparison:** The individual who is questioning his or her sexuality begins to seek out others who are gay, lesbian, or bisexual (Cass, 1984).

      i. "I probably am a homosexual" (p. 151).

     ii. "I am 14, gay, and I can't tell my parents I'm gay cause (sic) I know they hate gays. I have never met another gay person. I want a gay friend who understands me more than anything in the world. . . being gay does make you feel bad about yourself sometimes. Gay people are really looked down upon in society" (Halpin & Allen, 2004, p. 121).

2. **Middle-Stage Dimension:** Stages 3 and 4 make up this dimension and indicate that individuals reluctantly adopt a gay, lesbian, or bisexual identity; however, they continue to fear the responses of others to being gay. Those in stages 3 and 4 develop a "second" life in the gay community (Eliason & Schope, 2007). These stages are more difficult for people to move through because they must cope with feelings of isolation and rejection as they learn who they are in this process (Halpin & Allen, 2004).

    a. **Stage 3—Identity Tolerance:** A person realizes and tolerates that she or he is gay and in the process seeks out other gay, lesbian, and bisexual individuals; however, the person projects two separate images. The image is gay within the gay community, while the public persona may be heterosexual (Cass, 1984).

      i. "I may be gay, but I may not be in the future" (based on Cass's stage 3 description, p. 156).

    b. **Stage 4—Identity Acceptance:** An individual slowly accepts her or his gay identity but still pretends to be heterosexual in some contexts, while becoming more peaceful in who he or she is (Cass, 1984).

      i. "I accept but am not proud of being gay… that would be like saying I am proud to be white. It makes no sense. But I am proud of myself for coming to terms with being gay when it is a hard thing to accept yourself. Especially feeling so different during puberty, adolescent hell" (Halpin & Allen, 2004, p. 121).

3. **Final Stages:** Stages 5 and 6 comprise the dimension where a person becomes more open with others and resolves his or her sense of self as being gay, lesbian, or bisexual (Eliason & Schope, 2007). Those in these stages develop strong self-esteem, become happier, and are satisfied with life (Halpin & Allen, 2004).

    a. **Stage 5—Identity Pride:** The individual is proud of who he or she is as a gay, lesbian, or bisexual person and extremely loyal to the community. He or she may have deep anger toward the heterosexual community and may promote equality for gays (Cass, 1984).

      i. "I refuse to be molded into a group… I am just me"; "Labels restrict and limit the soul… I am happy and content being who I am: a productive, intelligent and healthy human being" (Halpin & Allen, p. 121).

    b. **Stage 6—Identity Synthesis:** The person sees that the world cannot be divided into "good" gay community and "bad" heterosexual world. Individuals understand that who they are is much more complicated than their gay identity, and disclosure of their sexual orientation is not an issue any more. Those in this stage are at peace with themselves and others (Cass, 1984).

      i. "I have been 'married' to the man of my dreams for seven years now. Although habitation is illegal in the state of Arizona, we own a house together and live our lives as 'normal' people…" and "My parents are the best! They are why I have been able to be more comfortable than other gay people I know."

Addressing Homophobia

Q *What should I do about homophobia in my classroom and school?*

Other important questions to think about:

Q *How can I address discrimination toward students with disabilities who are also dealing with issues of gender identity?*

Q *Which strategies can I use in my classroom and school that will ensure inclusion of all students?*

Think about the possibility of having your students respond to the question "Who am I?" They might talk about their ethnic background and favorite hobbies. They may also talk about the prejudice they feel from others.

❯❯ Professional Resource Download

Take time to read through this section carefully. It is a long journey for most LGBTQ students because they have few role models and they are members of a community that is often ignored or seen as atypical and therefore face extreme societal hostility. The process of discovering one's gender identity may be difficult, and if so, can create great psychological stress. Adolescence is already a tough time of life because young people are trying to figure out who they are and where they belong. Being LGBTQ places another layer of confusion onto a student when the society the person lives in does not generally support gay, lesbian, bisexual, transgender, or queer communities. Researchers have demonstrated that LGBTQ students can thrive in schools and environments that are supportive; however, many school personnel and peers are hostile. In these cases, young people can become extremely angry, distrustful, disappointed, and reject members of oppressive groups (Eliason & Schope, 2007).

In understanding the needs of LGBTQ students, educators must be careful not to over-generalize. LGBTQ individuals may identify more strongly with their racial or ethnic membership rather than sexual orientation. In conclusion, it is important for teachers to understand that many LGBTQ students are trying to develop their gender identity and may begin in the stage of confusion and hide their feelings, believing they cannot safely express themselves. For some, the journey takes many years before an authentic self emerges. (See Table 7.1.)

Table 7.1 Cass's Gay Identity Development Stages

Stage	Description
1. Identity Confusion	Person may be confused about who she or he is.
2. Identity Tolerance	Person accepts that he or she may be gay, though will act heterosexual in some situations.
3. Identity Comparison	Person seeks out others to privately discuss confusion and concerns.
4. Identity Tolerance	Person is more comfortable being gay but still may act heterosexual in certain circumstances.
5. Identity Pride	Person is proud being gay but due to lack of equality may hold anger toward heterosexuals.
6. Identity Synthesis	Person is proud being gay and does not divide people into being good gays and bad heterosexuals.

Source: Cass, 1984.

LGBTQ Issues in Society and Education

The issue of same-sex marriage for LGBTQ individuals is a prevailing matter. Though the U.S. Supreme Court decision of *Obergefell* v. *Hodges* in 2015 ruled that same-sex couples have the constitutional right to marry, there are some states that do not honor the federal decision. The Supreme Court decision is an example of how there is a social shift to include same-sex marriage as a civil right (Liptak, 2015).

DOMA and Same-Sex Marriage

The subject of same-sex marriage has become one of the most powerful issues in the nation. In 1996, the Defense of Marriage Act (DOMA) was passed in the United States defining marriage as a civil union between one woman and one man. The bill was signed by President Bill Clinton, and it identified a spouse as a person of the opposite sex. The legislation also reinforced the power of states to decide on same-sex marriages. Along with this federal law, Proposition 8 was voted on in the state of California, with a majority of voters not in support of same-sex marriage.

In opposition to this position, others believe that marriage is a fundamental right of citizens in the United States. There have been numerous Supreme Court decisions that have supported the right of the individual to marry. For example, in *Loving* v. *Virginia* (1967), the Supreme Court ruled that interracial marriage between a Black and Native American woman, Mildred Loving, and a White male, Richard Loving, was legal; the decision overruled the state of Virginia's anti-miscegenation law. This ruling also supported the fundamental right of citizens to marry.

In March 2013, the Supreme Court heard arguments questioning whether Proposition 8 in California violates the equal protection rights of gay individuals who would like to have the ability to get married. The Court ruled in 2013 by a 5 to 4 vote that DOMA is unconstitutional because it violates the Fifth Amendment of the U.S. Constitution (Reilly & Siddiqui, 2013). However, more people surveyed throughout the United States agreed that members of the gay community should be able to get married and receive health, retirement, and death benefits from their partners. For example, a CBS news poll was conducted in 2013 and 53 percent of the people interviewed felt that same-sex marriage should be legal. This compared with 39 percent who disagreed. Why did people change their minds from years prior? About 20 percent of those surveyed stated that they knew someone who was gay or lesbian and that has made a difference in their opinion. Those who favored DOMA were extremely disappointed; however, by 2015, 37 states and the District of Columbia have legalized same-sex marriages.

On June 26, 2015, the United States Supreme Court's 5–4 decision in *Obergefell* v. *Hodges* ruled in favor of same-sex marriage (Liptak, 2015). Same-sex marriage became a constitutional right of all people. Jim Obergefell married his partner John Arthur in 2013; they had been together for twenty years (Rosenwald, 2015). Ohio did not allow for same-sex marriage at the time, so Obergefell and Arthur flew to Maryland to be married because Arthur was terribly sick with ALS (Amyotrophic Lateral Sclerosis), also known as Lou Gehrig's disease. When Arthur died several months later, Jim filed the death certificate as Arthur's surviving spouse (Rosenwald, 2015). The state of Ohio wanted a new death certificate so that Obergefell would not be listed as Arthur's spouse. Jim took his case to the Supreme Court. Richard Hodges was the respondent and director of the Ohio Department of Health

Justice Anthony Kennedy wrote the majority opinion and he stated that the union of two people in love and fidelity creates a stronger bond and he acknowledged that marriage "is a keystone of our social order" (Liptak, 2015). Anthony based the decision on the Due Process Clause and Equal Protection Clause of the Fourteenth Amendment. The majority of Supreme Court justices believed that same-sex marriage is a fundamental right protected

Table 7.2	Same-Sex Marriages Legalized: Nations
Year	**Country**
2001	Netherlands
2003	Belgium
2005	Canada and Spain
2006	South Africa
2009	Norway and Sweden
2010	Argentina, Iceland, and Portugal
2012	Denmark
2013	Brazil, England and Wales, France, New Zealand, and Uruguay
2014	Luxembourg and Scotland
2015	Ireland and the United States
2017	Finland

"Ireland Votes to Approve Gay Marriage, Putting Country in Vangard," by Danny Hakim & Douglas Dalby, May 23, 2015, *New York Times*.

by the Constitution. There are still some counties in the United States that will not issue a marriage license to same-sex couples. The struggle for right of same-sex marriage is also a struggle throughout the world.

Ireland: First Country to Vote for Same-Sex Marriage

In May 2015, the country of Ireland became the first nation to pass same-sex marriage legislation by popular vote. This was surprising considering the strong Catholic origins of the country and that the Catholic Church opposed the legislation (Hakim & Dalby, 2015). The final vote was 62 percent for same-sex marriages, with 38 percent of the voters against the new law. This law was passed by voters, making this vote historic. Though the church is a powerful force in Ireland, people, who may have differed in gender and age, voted for the legislation because they believed in the value of equality. The grassroots movement is credited for passing the new law (Hakim & Dalby, 2015).

There are other countries that have legalized same-sex marriages, as listed in Table 7.2.

Transgender Individuals

In 1976, Bruce Jenner won the gold medal in the men's decathlon at the Olympic Games held in Canada. The decathlon is one of the most grueling sports because an athlete must participate in 10 different track and field events. They include: 100 meters (sprint), long jump, shot put, high jump, 400 meters (1/4 miles), 110 meter hurdles, discus throw,

Consider this . . .

Gender identity is not the same concept as sexual identity. Teachers need to know the difference so that they will more fully understand how their students see themselves. Students may be in various states of identity confusion.

Q What is the difference between sexual identity and gender identity? How would you define these identities?

Figure 7.5: Caitlyn Jenner identifies as a transgender woman.

pole vault, javelin throw, and 1500 meters (almost a mile).

Recently, however, Bruce Jenner identified himself as transgender and chose the name of Caitlyn Jenner. (See Figure 7.5.) Denise Norris, director of the Institute for Transgender Economic Advancement, believes that Caitlyn Jenner's public announcement about her sexual orientation creates opportunities for others to learn more about the transgender community (Lyall & Bernstein, 2015). Jenner's photograph first appeared in an issue of *Vanity Fair*, a popular women's magazine, in 2015 (Somaiya, 2015). The article was titled "Call Me Caitlyn." Jenner was pictured as a celebrity of the 1950s with long curled hair and beautiful flowing dresses. Caitlyn is much more comfortable as a woman and is relieved to be able to present herself as a female (Somaiya, 2015).

There are other celebrities who have shared their transgender change such as Chaz Bono, son of Sonny and Cher, and Richard Raskins, a successful tennis player, who became Renee Richards. Scholars like Marcia Ochoa, chairwoman of feminist studies at UC, Santa Cruz, believe that by sharing her personal changes, Jenner is showing the courage to stand up for herself and present her real self.

TAKE A STAND · TRANSGENDER FIRST GRADER

In February 2013, the Transgender Legal Defense and Education Fund* filed a complaint with the Colorado Civil Rights Division to support the rights of a 6-year-old girl who will no longer be able to use the girls' bathrooms in her school. The first grader has been using the girls' bathrooms for the past year. However, the Fountain-Fort Carson School District 8 let her parents know that she must now use the boys' bathrooms, a staff bathroom, or the nurse's bathroom.

Though the first grader was identified as a male at birth, she has expressed the belief of being a girl since she was 18 months old. In kindergarten, the young person wore girls' clothing to school. The teacher and her peers have referred to her with female pronouns for more than a year.

Her mother wants the first grader to be treated like everyone else and not to be singled out because she is a transgender individual. The young student's lawyers have argued that by forcing her to use different bathrooms, the school is making her a target for bullying and harassment. The child is being homeschooled until the situation is resolved.

TAKE A STAND . . .

▶ If you were the child's teachers and principal, what would you say to the little girl? What stand would you take? Do you think she should use the boys' bathrooms or girls' bathrooms? Why?

▶ The first grader's gender identity is as a girl. What is the best resolution of this issue for the student? For the school? For the other children?

*For more information on the issue, go to http://transgenderlegal.org/.

Bullying in Schools

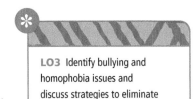

Bullying, which is harassment causing fear in others, is unfortunately a powerful force in our schools today (Bickmore, 2011). Many LGBTQ students are often bullied; even when school officials are told, many do nothing to address the hostility and physical abuse that LGBTQ students encounter daily (Kosciw, Greytak, Palmer, & Boesen, 2014). Sometimes bullying is a result of **homophobia**, which is the fear of gay, lesbian, bisexual, transgender, and queer people. However, other times discrimination can come from people or students who are self-centered and do not have any compassion or empathy for others. Some bullies strike out at others because of stress they are feeling. In other situations, students intimidate because they want to feel power and control over those around them, and bullying makes them feel more valued. If you went to a school and interviewed students, you would probably find many anecdotal stories of bullying on the playground, at recess, in the classroom, in the cafeteria, and after school. However, it is also important for teachers to become familiar with actual evidence or data regarding bullying. The information from the National School Climate Survey provides teachers with specific areas that schools can improve to create an environment of trust and respect for all students.

The results of the 2013 National School Climate Survey reported extensive bullying in schools by LGBT students. GLSEN (Gay and Lesbian and Straight Education Network) conducted the survey of K–12 schools, and information about the survey can be found at www.glsen.org. The organization has been gathering data for almost two decades.

Here are sample findings for 2013:

Harassment and bullying due to sexual orientation
- 71.4% of LBGT students have been verbally harassed.
- 36.2% of LGBT students have been physically harassed.
- 16.5% of LGBT students have been physically assaulted due to their sexual orientation.
- 49.0% of LGBT students have been electronically harassed (Facebook, texting).

Negative use of the term "gay" or other terms, such as "that's so gay"
- 71.4% of LGBT students have heard the use of "gay" in a negative way.
- 64.5% of LGBT students have heard the use of homophobic remarks such as "dyke" and "faggot" at school.
- 33.3% of LGBT students have heard negative remarks about transgender people (like "tranny").
- 51.4% of LGBT students have heard teachers or staff make homophobic remarks.
- 55.5% of LGBT students have heard teachers or staff make negative remarks about gender expression.

Felt unsafe at school because of their sexual orientation and gender expression
- 55.5% of LGBT students did not feel safe at school because of their sexual orientation.
- 37.8% of LGBT students did not feel safe because of their gender expression.

Felt unsafe in specific school spaces
- 36.2% of LGBT students were physically harassed (shoved, pushed) because of their sexual orientation.
- 35.3% of LGBT students felt unsafe in locker rooms.
- 35.4% of LGBT students felt unsafe in bathrooms.
- 31.9% of LGBT students felt unsafe in physical education/gym classes.

Homophobia is the fear of gay, lesbian, bisexual, transgender, and queer people.

Skipping school because of safety concerns

- 61.1% of LGBT students skipped class at least once in the past month because of safety concerns.
- 30.3% of LGBT students skipped an entire day of school in the past month because of safety concerns.

Never reported an incident of harassment or assault to school personnel

- 56.7% of LGBT students never reported an incident of harassment or assault to school personnel.

Academic achievement

- LGBT students who had been harassed had an average GPA of 3.0 in comparison to 3.3, the average GPA of others who had not been harassed.

Note: The report used LGBT to denote the population that was studied.

The report is sponsored by GLSEN. The organization has been gathering data every two years about school climate for LGBT students since 1999. These findings are extremely disturbing; the report provides evidence that teachers and administrators need to come together in each school and develop strategies and policies to address the issues that are described. Go to the website and read the report. Take time to reflect upon the data.

Addressing Bullying and Harassment of LGBTQ Students in Schools

LGBTQ students often are subjected to bullying and intimidation in schools as noted in the above report. Martin Luther King, Jr., taught that when one of us is bullied, we all suffer. It is important that schools are safe places that respect the rights of all students no matter their sexual orientation or race or social class or many other differences. We must all work to ensure that our students are treated equally and respectfully. Teachers and student teachers need to develop a plan for addressing bullying prior to working in the classroom so that they are prepared to deal with harassment (Sadowski, 2010; Bickmore, 2011; Clift, 2015). GLSEN provides suggestions as to what can be done at schools to support and encourage LGBTQ students. The following are GLSEN strategies that garnered positive results when implemented in schools:

1. When a high school establishes a Gay-Straight Alliance, a collaborative club where students can come together and discuss issues in a safe place, there usually is a decrease in bullying and abuse. For example, fewer homophobic remarks such as "that's so gay," "queer," or "fairies" are heard in school. There is also less victimization due to sexual orientation and gender expression because a strong community of LGBTQT and straight students is created. These clubs may speak out against about homophobia, sexual orientation, and **transphobia** (fear of transgender people). Straight students who support gender equality and civil rights are known as allies; they also challenge homophobia and transphobia.

Transphobia is the fear of transgender people.

Consider this . . .

Take time to read through the 2013 National School Climate Survey and identify what you think are the most important issues that teachers, parents, and students should come together to address in your school. The report can be found at: www.glsen.org.

Q What do you think are the three most pressing issues that you found in the report?

2. Having an LGBTQ curriculum with history and positive role models resulted in more acceptance throughout the school. The next section of this chapter includes a lengthy list of LGBTQ individuals who have advocated for equal rights.

3. When school personnel become more supportive of LGBTQ students, fewer students miss school because they feel that schools are increasingly safe.

4. Schools with particular policies against bullying due to sexual orientation and gender identity and expression have more respectful school environments. Fewer homophobic remarks are made and more staff and faculty intervene when harassment and assaults occur.

Prejudice reduction strategies include:

Policies
- Create and implement policies against discrimination and bullying due to sexual orientation and gender identity and expression.
- Train all teachers, staff, and administrators in prejudice reduction strategies.
- Develop a Gay-Straight Alliance.

Curriculum
- Integrate positive LGBTQ role models in the school curriculum at all levels.
- Integrate case studies of students who support each other against discrimination and bullying in the classroom and on the playground.

Other researchers also suggest strategies that can be integrated into a school environment to support educational equality and inclusiveness. These particular strategies can be used at all levels, from elementary school through high school.

1. Do not have students line up for the bathroom by gender with one line for females and one line for males, otherwise students may learn that the two roles are unquestionable. This can create an uncomfortable situation for transgender students (Blackburn & Smith, 2010).

2. Have a variety of gender role models in schools, for example, women coaches, male nurses, and male secretaries (Blackburn & Smith, 2010).

3. During homecoming festivities, a school might move from having a king and a queen to a homecoming court with a king and a king or a queen and a queen (Blackburn & Smith, 2010).

4. The curriculum can be reviewed for heterosexual bias. For example, some schools have moved from teaching Shakespeare's *Romeo and Juliet*, which teaches heterosexual love and marriage, to the use of the screen play, *Brokeback Mountain*. The story has protagonists who are gay and provides students with additional viewpoints on relationships (Blackburn & Smith, 2010).

5. Heterosexual privilege needs to be addressed in school so that students understand how heterosexualism is presented as common or natural in the school curriculum, but other perspectives are often not provided (Macgillivray & Jennings, 2008).

6. Gender role language can be used to provide rigid views on gender identity, especially when name-calling terms such as "sissy," "tomboy," "queer," and "gay" are not challenged in schools. Teachers need to consider how they model heterosexual views through vocabulary or lack of addressing hurtful labels (Macgillivray & Jennings, 2008).

7. Include LGBTQ civil rights history in the curriculum, such as the Stonewall Riots during which drag queens of color in New York City fought against harassment from the police. It is considered one of the most important historical events in LGBTQ history (Renn, 2010).

8. Teachers can include discussion of LGBTQ issues in sex education classes rather than ignoring or stigmatizing the lives of LGBTQ students (McGarry, 2013).

Table 7.3 Dos and Don'ts: Fighting Homophobia in Schools

Do	Don't
Include LBGTQ civil rights history and the fight for equality.	Present LBGTQ people as victims.
Discuss LGBTQ issues in sex education.	Ignore LGBTQ issues in sex education. Stigmatizes LGBTQ concerns.
Challenge gender identity name calling like "sissy," "tranny," "queer," "gay."	Allow name calling without confronting it.
Include a queen and queen or king and king or queen and king at homecoming.	Allow only a queen and king at homecoming.
Include not only the play *Romeo and Juliet* but also the love story of two gay individuals.	Only include the play of *Romeo and Juliet* with no readings that include gay, bisexual, or transgender characters.
Present a variety of role models from many diverse groups: racial, LGBTTQ, women, poor, religious.	Include primarily European American, male role models.
Allow students to go to the bathroom of their choice. It may mean that bathrooms are not gender specific. For example, there are individual doors for restrooms that have unisex symbols.	Line up students for the bathroom based on sex.

❯❯ Professional Resource Download

9. The curriculum in English and social studies must include the real-life experiences of LGBT families, identities, relationships, and inequalities (Bickmore, 2011; Souto-Manning, 2008). Many parents have found that teachers have a policy in their classrooms of "don't ask, don't tell" when related to LGBTQ issues (Souto-Manning, 2008).

See Table 7.3 for the dos and don'ts of fighting homophobia in schools.

All of these suggestions are important in building a more inclusive and caring school environment for all students. Which ones could you implement right away in your classroom? Which ones would take a review by the principal and teachers in your school? Do you think it is important that all of the recommendations be discussed at faculty meetings? Even if it is not possible to integrate all suggestions, the ideas will provide teachers with opportunities to think about issues from the view of LGBTQ students. And remember, not all LGBTQ students think alike. There is no one LGBTQ viewpoint.

LGBTQ Issues and Inequalities

Educators Ian Macgillivray and Todd Jennings (2008) have provided new insights into LGBTQ issues. The researchers found that when school discussions of LGBTQ students occur only in light of suicides or data on AIDS/HIV, that this results in the stereotyping of the LGBTQ community. They believe that while bullying statistics and other issues are important, it is more crucial to provide guidelines for teachers to make the school community more inclusive and caring. For example, they recommend that power relationships among LGBTQ and heterosexual students in schools can be discussed whether in English or civics class; otherwise, a process of silencing will occur. Silencing happens when LGBTQ or other students do not feel safe to discuss social issues. When this happens, inequalities often follow because no one is willing to challenge discrimination and harassment. They also suggest that gay role models should be provided for all students. Presenting positive role models provides information regarding the contributions of LGBTQ individuals and communities to learners. It also demonstrates the abilities of LGBTQ people to advocate and fight for civil rights rather than portray them as victims. This leads to the next section, which includes a list of many LGBT individuals who have made contributions to our nation and the world.

In order to understand the worldview of a group of people, it is often necessary for teachers to read and reflect on the historical experiences of people in the group. Refer back to the LGBTQ in the United States Timeline, ask yourself:

What are the themes in LGBTQ history?
How much of the LGBTQ history did I know? Why or why not?
How much of LGBTQ history is taught in schools? Why or why not?
How has LGBTQ history changed the way I think about many LGBTQ issues?

Curriculum: Using Role Models

LO4 Interpret and justify the importance of presenting role models from the LGBTQ community.

Role models are important examples of how students can advocate for social justice and freedom in our nation. Barbara Deming, a lesbian, fought for women's rights and civil rights for all. She was also an anti-war protester. She believed in nonviolent change (Duberman, 2011). In addition, Harvey Milk and James Baldwin were fearless advocates for civil rights for LGBTQ individuals and communities. They did so even though they were harassed. In fact Milk was murdered by someone who was not only concerned about Milk's politics but also his sexual orientation.

James Baldwin

Ullstein bild/Getty Images

James Baldwin was a celebrated novelist and civil rights activist in the 1950s through the 1980s. His life is an example of intersectionality and resilience. Baldwin is an excellent role model. His works can be read in English and social science classes because they provide a diverse perspective regarding the history of his times.

Originally from Harlem in New York, he wrote a great deal about discrimination against poor Blacks. Baldwin lived some of his life in France where he wrote about how White Americans did not understand that their entitlements led to the unconscious exclusion of African Americans through institutional racism and segregation (Miller, 2008). He believed that many White Americans lived in a romanticized world where prejudice did not play much of a role in life. Though he struggled with his African American identity, Baldwin was able to take a step back from the racism that he deeply felt in the United States and figure out who he was by living in Paris. Baldwin optimistically believed during that time that White America would welcome the contributions of African Americans.

Baldwin also included gay characters in his novels. For example, two major characters in his novel, *Tell Me How Long the Train's Been Gone*, were gay. In an interview he gave in 1982, Baldwin shared that he did not like the terms such as gay, homosexual, or bisexual (Field, 2004), so he did not use them in his writing. Though Baldwin did not talk much about his personal sexual orientation, he also included gay characters in other works such as *Just Above My Head* (Field, 2004).

Baldwin was discriminated against in life not only because he was Black but also because he was from a poor family and gay. In fact, his role in the civil rights movement was sometimes discounted because he was gay (Field, 2004). He is known for his collection of essays, which discusses the intersectionality of issues of race, sexuality, and class, *No One Knows My Name: More Notes of a Native Son*.

Baldwin also wrote nonfiction essays. One of the most important essays that he wrote about the purpose of schools is called, "A Talk to Teachers." This was originally a speech that Baldwin gave in 1963 to a group of teachers in New York City. Baldwin talked about how schools could be used to indoctrinate students, similar to what was done by Hitler and the Third Reich in Germany, or schools could be institutions of social and individual revolution for social justice. Baldwin believed most societies want schools and teachers to guide students to support the status quo rather than to teach their learners how to critically think about injustices and advocate for civil rights. This piece could be given to teachers today to discuss the lack of opportunities for students of color and how schools in poor neighborhoods are different from those in high-income areas. Baldwin believed that schools need to present an accurate history of the roots of the United States, not so many myths, especially about African Americans. Teachers should facilitate the ethical development of citizens who are dedicated to social change with equality at its core.

Harvey Milk

Harvey Milk was one of the first openly-gay politicians elected to a public office (Milk Foundation, 2015). Though there was severe discrimination against the LGBTQ community, Milk became a San Francisco County Supervisor in 1977 and continued to fight for LGBTQ civil rights. Milk was born into a Jewish family in New York. As a young person, Milk served in the Navy and then later worked as a teacher and stock analyst.

Milk established the Castro Village Association, which became one of the earliest LGBTQ business organizations. The Castro area of San Francisco became a visible and exciting place for people to visit. One of Milk's closest allies was Mayor George Moscone, who appointed him to San Francisco's Board of Permit Appeals in 1976, making him the first openly gay city commissioner (Milk Foundation, 2015).

Milk ran for San Francisco City/County Supervisor in 1977. He easily won. Milk was well known because he was a visible advocate for the LGBTQ community and the community at large. Milk had worked for the creation of daycare centers for families; he also lobbied for the conversion of military buildings into low-income housing. He believed in building strong neighborhoods where public libraries and public safety agencies were members of the community. In order to accomplish many of these goals, Milk brought together representatives from many ethnic communities, people with disabilities, women, and teamsters. He was a hard-working supporter of community. Unfortunately, in November 1978, Dan White, a former city supervisor, murdered Harvey Milk and Mayor Moscone at the San Francisco City Hall. They had ongoing conflicts about city politics regarding the increase in crime and the growth of the gay population in the city.

Milk is an important civil rights role model. He was posthumously awarded the Presidential Medal of Freedom in 2009. In addition, May 22 was named Harvey Milk day in California by the legislature and signed into law by Governor Arnold Schwarzenegger. Milk exemplified Stage 6 of Cass's identity development because he was an excellent role model, someone who was proud of being gay and worked for equity for many different groups.

Barbara Deming

How does an activist begin? **Barbara Deming** was born in New York City in 1917 to Harold and Katherine Deming. Barbara grew up in an upper-middle-class Manhattan family with her parents and three brothers (Duberman, 2011). Barbara believed her mother was self-absorbed, while her father was rather traditional and expected her to find a good husband. As a young kindergartener, she entered a Quaker school and continued through high school graduation. When Barbara was 16, she began a relationship with Norma Millay, an older neighbor and sister of the famous poet, Edna St. Vincent Millay (Duberman, 2011). Barbara told her mother of her bond with Norma and that she was a lesbian as a teenager.

In the 1950s she wrote stories about being a lesbian, but because of the negative social views about her lifestyle, she used third person in the essays. Several were sold and appeared in the *New Yorker* magazine. During those early days Barbara was not political, though she took trips around the world. For example, Barbara studied Ghandi's nonviolent work in India and later joined the Committee for Non-Violent Action and worked for racial civil rights, nuclear disarmament, feminism, and gay rights. Deming was a pacifist who believed that nonviolence was androgynous in nature; it combined both a male orientation and a female focus. Masculinity was the push to be self-assertive, while the feminine denoted sympathy for the other who had a different viewpoint, so this was an important amalgamation (Duberman, 2011). The first time she was arrested was when she, along with other women, protested in front of the Atomic Energy Commission building in New York City. The police took them away, and they were arraigned.

As part of her work for peace, Barbara also protested the treatment of African Americans. She believed that the movement toward nuclear disarmament and Black civil rights should be combined. She was part of a march that included African Americans and Whites. Barbara marched in a civil rights protest in Birmingham against segregation. She wore a sign in the march, "All Men Are Brothers." Barbara was arrested. After six days, she was released. She witnessed the illegal treatment of protesting Blacks. When she returned to Birmingham, she saw how the public safety commissioner "Bull" Connor ordered the use of fire hoses on young African Americans. The force of the hoses was so powerful that the clothes of protesters were ripped off of their bodies along with the bark of nearby trees (Duberman, 2011). Initially Barbara was scared, but she was encouraged by Blacks in various nonviolent protests and became more involved in the struggle for Black civil rights. During her life, she served various terms in jail with her colleagues, and they sometimes went on hunger strikes to protest their poor treatment and lack of rights as citizens.

Barbara saw how the struggle for justice and peace included many different groups: Blacks, gays, lesbians, welfare mothers, veterans, and prisoners. As a pacificst, she acknowledged human anger but believed people should not strike out at others. Rather, they should gather together, guiding their anger into collective determination. Her belief in the civil rights of Blacks also included the rights of gays and lesbians.

Barbara Deming is a powerful role model who believed that nonviolence was the avenue for peace in our lives. Barbara saw herself not only as a lesbian, but as a member of the human race who worked against social oppression. She worked against inequalities and power inequities in the hopes of creating a more peaceful and respectful world.

Role Models from the LGBTQ Community

Role models are important people in our lives. There are many LGBT individuals who have enriched our lives, from Langston Hughes to Sally Ride. The list in Table 7.4 is a beginning from which teachers may begin their search for role models from the LGBTQ community who have contributed to the development of our nation and world. Maybe the person contributed new scientific knowledge, fought for civil rights, or established a community organization.

Table 7.4 Role Models from the LGBTQ Community

Alvin Ailey, dancer, choreographer, and African American activist, established the Alvin Ailey Dance Theater

John Amaechi, NBA star, an African American who played for the Cleveland Cavaliers, Orlando Magic, and Houston Rockets

Josephine Baker, dancer, actor, and African American activist

James Baldwin, U.S. author, wrote *Notes of a Native Son*, *Giovanni's Room*, *Go Tell It To the Mountain*, and *Another Country*

Tammy Baldwin, first openly gay U.S. senator from Wisconsin

Truman Capote, U.S. author, wrote *In Cold Blood* and *Breakfast at Tiffany's*

Pamela Ki Mai Chen, first gay Asian American woman to serve as a federal judge in the U.S. District Court

Countee Cullen, African American poet of the Harlem Renaissance period

Emily Dickinson, U.S. poet whose work was primarily published after her death

Alan Downs, U.S. clinical psychologist and writer, wrote *The Velvet Rage: Overcoming the Rage of Growing Up Gay in a Straight Man's World* and *The Half-Empty Heart*

Michel Foucault, French philosopher, wrote *Madness and Civilization*, *The Birth of the Clinic*, *The Archeology of Knowledge*, *Discipline and Punish*, *The History of Sexuality*, and *The Order of Things*; he influenced critical theorists and their discussion of oppression

Barnett "Barney" Frank, first openly-gay U.S. Congressman

Lady Gaga, bisexual, singer and songwriter of "Born This Way"

Rudy Galindo, Latino figure skater, won 1989 and 1990 U.S. National Championships

Allen Ginsberg, U.S. poet, published poem "Howl," which describes gay and straight sexuality

bell hooks, U.S. author and African American activist, wrote *Teaching to Transgress: Education as the Practice of Freedom*

Langston Hughes, U.S. poet and author, wrote "A Dream Deferred"

John Maynard Keynes, British economist whose Keynesian theories discuss the importance of federal stimulation during economic depressions and recessions

D. H. Lawrence, English author, wrote *Lady Chatterley's Lover*

Michael Levine, Stonewall Riots, civil rights activist

Margaret Mead, U.S. anthropologist, bisexual/lesbian, wrote *Coming of Age in Samoa* and *Sex and Temperament in Three Primitive Societies*

Michelangelo, Italian painter, sculptor, and poet; sculpted David and Pietà; painted the Sistine Chapel

Harvey Milk, politician and activist, first openly gay city supervisor in the country

Enrique "Ricky" Martin Morales, Puerto Rican singer, made famous by song, "Livin' La Vida Loca"

Rudolph Nureyev, Russian dancer who later became a U.S. citizen

Camille Paglia, U.S. feminist, wrote *Sexual Personae: Art and Decadence from Nefertiti to Emily Dickinson*

Sally Ride, U.S. astronaut and physicist, first U.S. woman in space

Susan Sontag, U.S. author and activist, wrote *On Photography*, *Illness As Metaphor*, and *In America*

Gertrude Stein, U.S. author and painter, wrote *The Autobiography of Alice B. Toklas*

Mark Takano, first openly gay Asian American elected to Congress in 2012

Walt Whitman, U.S. poet

David Wilson and Rob Compton, sued Massachusetts for same-sex benefits

Virginia Woolf, English author

TEACHING TIPS

Research a Role Model

It is important that students have the opportunity to investigate and explore the lives of many diverse people. Use higher order learning objectives to guide your students to assess the lives of others. For example, you could have your students pick a person and research his or her contributions to society. Here are several learning objectives:

❯ Student will gather information about the lives of a person on the list.

❯ Student will evaluate how the person's life experiences shaped their value of equality.

❯ Student will create a monologue where she or he presents the life of the role model chosen. Your student could participate in an activity called "Who Am I?" Students would come up one by one to the front of the class. The student might want to wear a lab coat (if the person is a scientist) or hold an important novel during his or her presentation if the person was a writer like James Baldwin. The student gives clues as to who the person is. Other students in class volunteer to guess the person's identity. This is a fun activity during which everyone works together.

Professional Resource Download

For future lessons, consider the following Bloom's taxonomy, which will help you to create higher order lessons for your students. The levels on the left of the chart move students toward critical thinking.

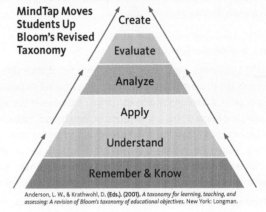

Anderson, L. W., & Krathwohl, D. (Eds.). (2001). *A taxonomy for learning, teaching, and assessing: A revision of Bloom's taxonomy of educational objectives.* New York: Longman.

Bloom's Taxonomy

Thinking about Intersectionality

The work of James Baldwin provides many examples of essays and novels examining the intersection and interweaving of issues of race, class, and sexuality. He questioned the oppression of individuals and communities and saw that societal and individual discrimination was often linked to various types of harassment. Baldwin felt the far-reaching persecution as a Black man, a gay individual, someone from a poor family, and a person who was born in a poor community, Harlem.

Had you ever heard of James Baldwin before reading this chapter? Why or why not? He is an important civil rights figure and author. His life is an excellent example of how intersectionality impacts our world. His life is a model of how socially constructed identities can put a person in an inferior position in our society. The social hierarchy in which he lived influenced his opportunities. Baldwin was placed in many social boxes that oppressed him: he was in placed in a racial box by being Black, a sexual orientation box by being gay,

an economic box by being poor, and a neighborhood box by being from Harlem. These boxes placed James Baldwin in continual inferior social status. He was oppressed because of numerous social categories, from homophobia to racism to classism. Intersectionality shows how these various identities are socially constructed and created a life of inferiority.

How can you teach about intersectionality using the life and works of James Baldwin? You may want to ask your students to build a tower of boxes to show the oppression that Baldwin faced throughout his life.

Teaching Tolerance, an arm of the Southern Poverty Law Center, has created a set of lessons on James Baldwin and how racial and gay rights are connected. The curriculum unit is called "James Baldwin: Art, Sexuality and Civil Rights." Take time to review the unit at the following website: http://www.tolerance.org/lesson/james-baldwin-art-sexuality-and-civil-rights.

Summary

1. **Describe how elements of human diversity have changed.**

   The concept of human diversity has expanded. Human diversity includes many different human characteristics such as sexual orientation, race, culture, gender, social class, religion, age, language, and exceptionalities. It is important that people accept others though they may belong to a variety of culturally diverse communities.

2. **Define and discuss concepts of gay culture, sexual orientation, and gender identity.**

   LGBTQ communities are complex and are comprised of many different elements. LGBTQ communities represent subcultures that include language, history, political action, neighborhoods, customs, and values of civil rights, equality, and education. The subcultures include three layers of culture from artifacts and history to customs and interactional patterns to values and beliefs. LGBTQ refers to lesbian, gay, bisexual, transgender, and questioning/queer individuals/communities. Sexual orientation is not binary—many researchers today believe that sexual orientation represents a continuum.

   Gender identity and sexual identity can be different in a person. Sexual identity is about one's body parts; however, gender identity deals with how a person sees her- or himself. Gender and sexual identities are vital aspects of one's self-concept. Teachers need to understand the powerful influences these characteristics have on the self-image and self-esteem of students. Alfred Kinsey's research demonstrated that the binary view of sexual orientation was not accurate. Today, gay identity is seen as a psychological and social orientation rather than a sexual one. The Cass model of gay identity recognizes six stages of development. They are as follows: Identity Confusion; Identity Comparison; Identity Tolerance; Identity Acceptance; Identity Pride; and Identity Synthesis.

3. **Identify bullying and homophobia issues and discuss strategies to eliminate discrimination in schools.**

   Many LGBTQ students are bullied in schools and society. They are harassed verbally, physically, psychologically, and through cyber methods. This has made going to school difficult for many students. It impacts their academic achievement. One way for teachers to fight LGBTQ discrimination is to teach all students about the history of LGBTQ communities and emphasize how LGBTQ organizations and individuals fight for civil rights. Another strategy that can be instituted in a school is to establish a Gay-Straight Alliance. This way all students can participate in working toward equality and respect in the school. An additional strategy is to provide teachers with professional development on issues of gender identity, sexual orientation, and bullying. Teachers must be part of the whole-school efforts to move the school climate and learning environment toward equity and collaboration.

4. **Interpret and justify the importance of presenting role models from the LGBTQ community.**

   LGBTQ role models are important for all students. There are numerous individuals and groups who have fought for equality for all citizens throughout our history. Have students create posters, book clubs, and discussion groups to discuss the contributions of individuals such as James Baldwin, Sally Ride, Walt Whitman, George Takei, Susan Sontag, Virginia Wolf, Langston Hughes, and Tammy Baldwin. Students can examine the lives and struggles of their role models and identify how they were able to become successful and contribute to society despite the many obstacles they faced in society.

Check your Cultural Knowledge

Reflective Essay Question

Sexual orientation is a subject about which there is much controversy. What would you do in your classroom if a parent came to you saying that he or she was against presenting LGBTQ role models in the curriculum? What would you say to that parent? What values would you use as the foundation for your answer?

Application

Know and Go Tools for the Classroom

Writing to Prepare for Class Discussions

Teachers often have students discuss various topics or issues in class. Sometimes students know what to say and will volunteer their thoughts, while others need more time to think before they join a discussion. For example, you ask the question, "What can we do to make our classroom more inclusive?" This can be an emotional issue for some students who have been bullied. This can also be hard for students who are painfully shy. Even for the students who may be leaders in associated student body activities may not want to be put "on the spot" to respond.

How can teachers get students to be more comfortable about sharing their views? One way is to integrate writing skills with their discussion skills. When you have students practice their writing skills, you can also help them become more prepared to participate in class discussions.

When students have had time to think about an issue or topic, they may be more willing to share their ideas out loud with the class. They also may present a more nuanced view of the issue. Their reflection through writing will assist them in examining a subject in a more comprehensive way. Writing and discussion skills are important for students to develop because they can use both throughout their lives.

Have students take 15 minutes to write a paragraph about the issue. This gives students time to reflect. If your students have trouble with writing, you may want to start with a prompt such as:

1. I believe that teachers could make the classroom a safe place by...
2. Students can help each other by...
3. If I could work with others to stop bullying in the classroom, I would suggest...
4. One of the most difficult aspects about sexual orientation to understand is...

Social Biases: Discrimination Based on Religion, Immigrant Status, and Exceptionalities

Learning Objectives

LO1 Analyze how religious freedom was one of the first core freedoms in the United States and describe the diversity of religious groups.

LO2 Describe how to teach religion in public schools and identify stereotypes about Muslims.

LO3 Challenge bias and prejudices about Muslim American students.

LO4 Differentiate among indigenous persons, immigrants, migrants, and refugees and describe how Nativism, global migration, and immigrant students impact the United States.

LO5 Evaluate the challenges that immigrant students face in achieving in schools.

LO6 Compare disability studies with special education within the context of ableism.

LO7 Explain how traditional special education groups students into various categories based on their exceptionalities.

LO8 Describe how labeling of students can be destructive and lead to increased oppression of learners with disabilities in schools.

STANDARDS COVERED

NAEYC 1, 5, 6
naeyc

CAEP 1 CAEP

INTASC 1, 2, 3, 4, 5, 6, 7, 8, 9, 10
InTASC

Freedoms are not free; we must fight for them.

People are often discriminated against because they participate in a specific religion, are learners with exceptionalities, and/or are an immigrant, migrant, or refugee. They are diverse cultural groups. This chapter will present demographic data and attitudes that are commonly found in society about these three social areas. First, a discussion of religion is presented. Freedom of religion, included in the First Amendment in the Constitution's Bill of Rights, is a vital right for many people in the United Sates. There is a great diversity of faiths even within a group such as Protestant. You should think about how you would teach religion. This does not mean that teachers instruct students on dogma; rather, educators should teach learners that one of our important rights is religious freedom and there is religious diversity in the United States (Subedi, 2006). In addition, misconceptions about Muslims continue to proliferate. Much of this occurs because people have little knowledge about Islam, and this has led to Islamophobia.

Teachers must also know about immigration and migration. What are the differences between the two terms and the concept of refugee? The second section contrasts the concepts of immigrants, migrants, refugees, and indigenous people. New immigrant students come to the United States every day; some have chosen to move to the United States, while others are refugees who have fled persecution in their homelands. In addition, several case studies are presented of actual high school students who must decide if they will continue their studies at a college and seek the American dream.

Finally, the last section in the chapter is about disability studies and special education. As a nation, we are committed to providing services to all students; this includes youth and adults with exceptionalities. Teachers need to carefully articulate the instructional and psychological interventions they deliver to students. It is also important for you to compare how disability studies and special education are similar and different. This will help you understand the foundational values you choose in providing interventions for students with disabilities and exceptionalities.

Religious Freedom in the United States

Religious freedom guaranteed in the First Amendment of the U.S. Constitution and gives Americans the freedom to worship as they choose. This was one of the most important rights the nation was founded upon. The thirteen colonies were established to ensure that individuals did not have to follow the Church of England. Religious diversity developed. One of the originators of our country, Thomas Jefferson, believed in the separation of church and state, though privately he was a strong Christian (Ragosta, 2013). In regard to government, Jefferson believed that by keeping religion independent, religious thought would more fully develop. In addition, he also believed that a nation founded on religious dogma could divide it; Jefferson wanted a governmental structure that encouraged diverse people to create and unite around common goals (Ragosta, 2013). However, within this orientation, most colonists were Protestant and members of religious organizations such as Baptists, Methodists, Quakers, Puritans, and Unitarians.

Religious illiteracy often shaped the way early colonists treated Native Americans with regard to their own religions, and they did not always support Native American religions. In fact, Native Americans were often persecuted for their religious beliefs and practices. **Religious illiteracy** is lack of knowledge about the values, beliefs, and history of various religions throughout the world. This also refers to the absence of understanding how religions can overlap with political and cultural aspects of societies.

Though our nation was founded on the belief of religious freedom, there are numerous examples of social oppression around the world. For example, **anti-Semitism**, which is

> **LO1** Analyze how religious freedom was one of the first core freedoms in the United States and describe the diversity of religious groups.

> **Religious illiteracy** is the lack of knowledge about the values, beliefs, and history of various religions throughout the world and how religion overlaps with political and cultural aspects of societies.

> **Anti-Semitism** is prejudice against Jews and their religion, Judaism.

prejudice against Jews and Judaism, existed in the colonies, but was more prevalent in the United States after World War I. Discrimination against Jews was extremely severe during the Holocaust in Europe during World War II, when at least 6 million were exterminated at the hands of the Nazi party and Adolph Hitler. Jews were blamed for the civil and economic unrest in Germany and used as scapegoats for the country's problems.

One Jewish organization, created in 1913 to fight bigotry and racism against Jews and other groups, is the Anti-Defamation League. They continue their work today. The organization has developed a prejudice reduction program for use in schools called "A World of Difference." The curriculum teaches students how to identify stereotypes and scapegoating, which are critical elements of prejudice. The organization also includes teacher training so educators know how to use the lessons they provide on events like *Kristallnacht* (Crystal Night), attacks on Jews on November 9–10, 1938, by members of the Nazi party. Many businesses were broken into, leaving much glass on the streets and sidewalks. This was part of mob violence against the Jews known as **pogroms**. A World of Difference includes a lesson on *Kristallnacht* and gets students to talk about the behaviors of Jewish citizens' Russian, Polish, and German neighbors who participated in the destruction.

Fortunately, many Jewish immigrants migrated to the United States to escape persecution and created strong multicultural communities. One well-known synagogue is Sixth and I Historic Synagogue in Washington, DC, serving many different Jewish denominations and other community groups in the city (Figure 8.1).

When the early colonies were established, there were Catholic immigrants already living in the area from Germany, Ireland, and England (Gordon, 1964). Later, after the Louisiana Purchase, Catholics who spoke French and others from Spain became part of the United States. Many early Catholics were from poor Irish, Italian, and Slavic families and were mostly manual laborers (Gordon, 1964). As time progressed, a few Catholics were able to create successful businesses and establish a network of parochial schools and academies. There seems to be an intersection between class and religion in regard to Catholics. During

> **Pogroms** were riots, destruction, and persecution aimed at Jews during the nineteenth and twentieth centuries.

Gerry Pang

Figure 8.1: The Star of David can be seen on the front of this nondenominational Jewish synagogue. The synagogue is one of the oldest in the city. The building also holds cultural events.

the early years of this country, being Catholic was almost synonymous with being poor. However, when John F. Kennedy ran for president of the United States in 1960, the Kennedy family raised the visibility of Catholics in the United States. At that time, there were many voters, Protestant and others, who were concerned that John F. Kennedy might get direction from the pope if he was elected president. Kennedy stressed to the voters that he was the Democratic candidate and believed in the separation of church and state.

Religious Diversity in the United States

Religious diversity is extensive in the United States (Subedi, 2006). There are numerous religious institutions, including Christian, Jewish, Muslim, Buddhist, and Hindu. There are also many Americans who are agnostic or atheists. The religion with the greatest number of members in the United States is Protestant. See Table 8.1 for the largest 15 Protestant organizations and the percentage of Americans who are members of each religion. The largest Protestant group is the Southern Baptist Convention, which includes 6.7 percent of the U.S. population. The second largest is the United Methodist Church (mainline), comprising 5.1 percent of adults. Did you realize there were so many different Protestant churches?

Table 8.2 provides you with an overall view of religious group membership in the United States. Christians are the largest community and make up about 70 percent of the members in the nation. There are many other religious communities, such as Hindu, Sikh, Buddhist, and Jewish.

Table 8.3 shows the percentage of college graduates who are members of each religious group. This table shows more of the diversity within the nation. Hindus and Jews have the largest proportion of members who have earned a college degree. In 2014, the Pew Research Center reported that 77 percent of Hindus have a college degree while 59 percent of Jews

Table 8.1 Largest Protestant Denominations in the United States, Among All U.S. Adults, Percentages, 2014*

Religious Denomination	2007 in %	2014 in %	% Change
Southern Baptist Convention (evangelical tradition)*	6.7	5.3	−1.4
United Methodist Church (mainstream** tradition)	5.1	3.6	−1.5
American Baptist Churches USA (mainstream)	1.2	1.5	+0.3
Church of Christ (evangelical)	1.5	1.5	0.0
Evangelical Lutheran Church in America (mainstream)	2.9	1.4	−0.6
National Baptist Convention (historically Black tradition)	1.8	1.4	−0.4
Assemblies of God (evangelical)	1.4	1.4	0.0
Lutheran Church—Missouri Synod (evangelical)	1.4	1.1	−0.3
Presbyterian Church USA (mainstream)	1.1	0.9	−0.2
Episcopal Church (mainstream)	1.0	0.9	−0.1
Church of God in Christ (historically Black)	0.6	0.6	0.0
Seventh-day Adventist (evangelical)	0.4	0.5	+0.1
United Church of Christ (mainstream)	0.5	0.4	−0.1
Presbyterian Church in America (evangelical)	0.4	0.4	0.0
Church of God (Cleveland, TN.) (evangelical)	0.4	0.4	0.0

Adapted from Pew Research Center, May 12, 2015, *America's Changing Religious Landscape; Christians Decline Sharply as Share of Population; Unaffiliated and Other Faiths Continue to Grow*, Washington, DC, p. 27.

*Evangelical refers to people who believe they are to preach about and convert others to believing that Jesus Christ is the only way to eternal salvation.

**Mainstream refers to older, traditional religious communities that also believe in Jesus Christ but do not try to convert others.

Table 8.2 Religious Membership in the United States, Percentage of Population, 2014

Religious Group	Percentage
Christians	**70.6%**
Protestant	46.5
Evangelical	25.4
Mainstream	14.7
Historically Black	6.5
Catholic	20.8
Orthodox Christian	0.5
Mormon	1.6
Jehovah's Witness	0.8
Other Christians	0.4
Non-Christian Faiths	**5.9**
Jewish	1.9
Muslim	0.9
Buddhist	0.7
Hindu	0.7
Other world religions*	0.3
Other faiths**	1.5
Unaffiliated	**22.8**
Atheist	3.1
Agnostic	4.0
Nothing in particular	15.8
Don't Know/Refused to Answer	**0.6**

Adapted from Pew Research Center, May 12, 2015, *America's Changing Religious Landscape; Christians Decline Sharply as Share of Population; Unaffiliated and Other Faiths Continue to Grow*, Washington, DC, p. 4.

*Other world religions include Sikhs, Baha'is, Taoists, and Jains, among others.

**Other faiths include Unitarians, New Age religions, Native American religions, and other non-Christian faiths.

Numbers may not add up to 100% due to rounding.

Table 8.3 Percent of Religious Groups Reporting a College Degree

Group	% in 2007	% in 2014
All Americans	27	27
Christian	25	25
Protestant	24	24
Evangelical	20	21
Mainline	34	33
Historically Black	16	15
Catholic	26	26
Orthodox Christian	46	40
Mormon	29	33
Jehovah's Witness	8	12

(Continued)

Table 8.3 Percent of Religious Groups Reporting a College Degree *(Continued)*

Group	% in 2007	% in 2014
Non-Christian Faiths	51	50
Jewish	59	59
Muslim	40	39
Buddhist	48	47
Hindu	74	77
Unaffiliated	29	29
Atheist	42	43
Agnostic	43	42
Nothing in Particular	24	24
Religion not important	31	30
Religion important	17	16

Adapted from Pew Research Center, May 12, 2015, *America's Changing Religious Landscape; Christians Decline Sharply as Share of Population; Unaffiliated and Other Faiths Continue to Grow,* Washington, DC, p. 56.

also reported earning a college degree. These numbers are in comparison to 27 percent of people in general in the United States who have a college degree.

Assess the three tables. Did you learn something about the names of different religions? Are you surprised at the number of religious institutions? Why or why not? If you have never heard of several of the religions, take time to search for information about them so you will be more fully prepared to teach students from many different religious communities.

Fighting Islamophobia

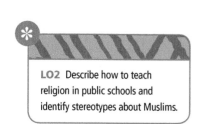

LO2 Describe how to teach religion in public schools and identify stereotypes about Muslims.

As discussed previously, there are numerous Protestant religions and many different faiths. Islam is a religion that has been in the news lately; with the many news articles and TV shows about Muslims, it would seem that there are a large number of Americans who are members of Islam. As shown in Table 8.2, the Pew Research Center reported that 0.9 percent of Americans are Muslims. Are you surprised the percentage is so small?

Since this book cannot cover all of the religions in the United States and because there are many misconceptions about Islam, this text presents information that might help teachers to review what they know about Islam.

Current events have deeply affected religious intolerance (Subedi, 2006). An example of how religion has influenced views in the United States is the prejudice that arose after the September 11 attacks on New York City and Washington, DC. Many people associated the terrorist attacked with Islam and blamed Muslim Americans for the deaths of people in the Twin Towers, the Pentagon, and the airplanes that were hijacked that day. In addition, when the United States went into Iraq to overthrow Saddam Hussein, prejudice against Muslim Americans increased. There also have been repeated instances in which Muslims in the Middle East, Europe, and Asia have demonstrated against the United States due to our military presence throughout the world, including Iraq and Afghanistan. There is growing dissatisfaction with the United States in some countries. This has resulted in numerous instances of **Islamophobia** in schools and society, which is defined as unproven fear and/or hostility toward Muslims.

Islamophobia is defined as unproven fear and/or hostility toward Muslims.

After the September 11 attacks, there were people who went to local mosques to demonstrate support for Muslim Americans. Individuals stood outside mosques with signs reading "Peace" or "United for Peace." Unfortunately, some people drove by giving the supporters the middle finger and yelled "rag head lovers." Only a few cars honked in support of the demonstrations. Islamophobia is real and it cuts at our core values of equality and freedom. Muslim Americans continue to be objects of harassment and discrimination. It is up to citizens to work toward the reduction of prejudice and hate. As part of multicultural education, teachers can integrate accurate information about Islam and Islamophobia in the curriculum so that students learn about similarities and differences with Christianity (Moore, 2009).

Generally, teachers know little about Islam or Muslims. Stereotypes develop and expand when people and groups do not have much knowledge of others. The media often is one of the most influential sources of information about Muslims and has tended to sensationalize news dealing with Islam (Jackson, 2010; Moore, 2009). For example educators and students may see on television Muslims celebrating the bombings of September 11 or the violence in London subways (Sewall, 2008). Movies and other entertainment media may depict Muslims as being rich Arab men who have large harems of women. The stereotypes of Muslims as anti-American and anti-Semitic are also common in the media (Moore, 2009). In addition, middle school and high school social studies textbooks do not adequately cover the history, beliefs, and values of Islam, and how Islam interacts with political and cultural events (Sewall, 2008). Providing information does not mean indoctrinating students. Teaching higher-ordering thinking skills such as evaluation, analysis, and judgment can guide students to reflect on what they know about Islam and the stereotypes they see in their lives.

Gilbert Sewall, an educator, believes that history textbooks should include the following concepts in their content and that teachers should follow up with discussions in class (2008):

- European policy was directed at containment of Islam from Tours to Vienna, and there were numerous battles in the eighth century through the seventeenth century (p. 37).
- Napoleon led an invasion of Egypt in 1798 and continued to drive into Islamic lands for both strategic and economic reasons (p. 37).
- Modern Islam is diverse, and Islamic unity suffers from power struggles from within; there are a variety of power centers—Egypt, Saudi Arabia, Iraq, Iran, Pakistan, and Indonesia (p. 37).
- Islam may not be able to incorporate modern change within a secular society because as a religion it does not have a way to facilitate religious liberty (p. 38).

These are vital issues in world history and today.

Four Myths about Islam

There are numerous misconceptions about Islam. Here are four of the most prevalent beliefs (Rauf, 2011). Do you believe in these myths?

1. Muslim Americans are foreigners.
   When Blacks from Africa were kidnapped and enslaved, about 30 percent were Muslim. Muslims have lived in the United States before it became a nation (Rauf, 2011). American Muslim soldiers fought in the Revolutionary War, Civil War, World War I, World War II, and Vietnam War, and have served in the War on Terror in Afghanistan and Iraq. In addition, 37 percent of the Muslim population are native-born Americans, while 70 percent of those who migrated to the United States became naturalized citizens (Pew Research Center, 2011).
2. Muslim Americans are ethnically, culturally, and politically monolithic.
   Muslims in America are extremely diverse. Some are members of the Republican Party; others are members of the Democratic Party. Most are not Arab American; they come from over 77 different ethnic groups (Pew Research Center, 2011).

Consider this . . .

Teachers can address religious illiteracy that is fueling Islamophobia by centering their discussions on our Constitutional values of freedom, equality, and rights.

Q Should Muslim Americans be protected by our Constitution? Why or why not? Provide evidence.

Q Do we truly believe in equality and freedom for all Americans?

3. Muslim Americans oppress women.
   American Muslim women have earned higher levels of education than most Americans. They are highly educated and work outside of the home (Rauf, 2011). The Pew Research Center conducted a survey in 2011 and found that 90 percent of Muslim Americans believe women should be able to work outside of the home. In addition, the same study found that 68 percent of women and men did not believe there were differences in the abilities between the two groups. More information about Muslim women will be presented later in this chapter.
4. Muslim Americans are terrorists.
   Many more non-Muslims were involved in terrorist activities than Muslim Americans in the United States (Rauf, 2011). Over 80 percent of Muslim Americans expressed the belief that there is no justification for suicide bombers (Pew Research Center, 2011). More Muslim Americans than other Americans have worked with authorities to thwart terrorist activities (Rauf, 2011).

Prejudice and stereotypes easily take root in people's minds when individuals do not have much information about a group. Seeking and reflecting on accurate information is one of the ways to eliminate prejudice and discrimination.

Teaching about Religion in Schools

It is important for schools to include information about various religions in the curriculum to help students understand their diversities and that people hold many different religious identities (Subedi, 2006). For example, information about Islam can be included in school by having upper-elementary, middle- and high-school students read the text, *The American Muslim Teenager's Handbook* by Dilarza Hafiz (Barack, 2010). One of the most controversial issues in religion in the United States is the teaching of the Bible. In Georgia, Texas, Tennessee, and South Carolina, state legislatures have passed laws to encourage the teaching of Bible courses as electives for high school students (Haynes, 2008). This is controversial because it grays the line between church and state. Others would argue that it flat out breaks the law to teach the Bible in a public school. Religion is a complex issue in a democracy, and religious groups should work to find common ground (Haynes, 2008). Charles C. Haynes of the First Amendment Center believes religion should be taught in schools, and following are several of his recommendations:

1. Schools have constitutional "safe harbor" agreements regarding religion with numerous groups. These can be used as foundations to the discussion of First Amendment issues.
2. Schools can develop sound policies about the First Amendment. Religious freedom is an exceptional opportunity to bring school boards, superintendents, and community representatives together to develop these issues.
3. Include all constituent groups, such as people from the community, parents, teachers, the school board, and students, in dialogue and decision making regarding religion.

4. Continue to have the dialogue among various groups so that school policies continue to be updated.

5. Ongoing professional development can be offered regarding religious conflicts in schools to ensure that religious liberty is addressed in the most effective ways.

6. Religious education should also be addressed in pre-service training. Novice teachers need to know about First Amendment issues.

Being Muslim in the United States

LO3 Challenge bias and prejudices about Muslim American students.

ISIS, which stands for the Islamic State of Iraq and Syria, is a terrorist group.

It can be difficult for a young person to be a Muslim in the United States today because of the many stereotypes people have about Muslims. For example, there are those who think that all Muslims are members of **ISIS (Islamic State of Iraq and Syria)**, considered a terrorist organization, which is absolutely not true. ISIS is a fundamentalist and extremist Islamic group, and they are very different from moderate Muslims who believe in peace. In 2011, 1 percent of Muslim Americans believed that violence or suicide bombers were often justified, while 7 percent say sometimes violence is defensible; in comparison 86 percent of Muslim Americans say violence is rarely or never justified (Pew Research Center, 2011). The word "Islam" can be translated as either "submission," which means to submit to God, or as "peace." Is this different from what you thought you knew about Islam?

Islam is the second largest religion in the world after Christianity; there are approximately 1.3 billion Islamic followers and there are about 2.3 billion Christians in the world (Hafiz, Hafiz, & Hafiz, 2009). Islam began about 1400 years ago and has many commonalities with Judaism and Christianity. All three religions are centered on the belief in one God and have a core document. Jews read the Torah. Christians have the Bible. Muslims read the Quran. Muslims believe in charity, faith, goodness, and community just like members of other religions. How is Islam different? Muslims believe that the Prophet Muhammad acted as a messenger for God, though he was not divine like God (Hafiz et al., 2009). Muhammad was human, and so he made mistakes like other humans.

Dilara Hafiz and her children Yasmine and Imran wrote a good reference book on Muslims for teachers and students at about the fifth-grade level and older. It is called *The American Muslim Teenager's Handbook*. This book provides information from a Muslim American viewpoint and answers questions teachers and young people, who are Muslim and non-Muslim, hold about being a member of the Islamic religion. Let's pick one of the issues they discuss. Some students may be late for school because they have been praying. Many Muslims pray five times a day: before sunrise, when the sun is at its highest, as the sun begins to drop in the sky, after the sun sets, and in the middle of the night. Muslims believe praying five times daily is an important aspect of their spiritual life. In contrast to Catholic Christians and Jews, Muslims do not believe in an intermediary or someone who acts on their behalf to God, such as a priest or rabbi; they pray directly to God themselves (Hafiz et al., 2009).

It is also important for all students in a democracy where religious rights are an important freedom to understand the different aspects of various religions. When conflicts arise, it is important for us to identify commonalities and then address differences. What are some of the similarities among Judaism, Christianity, and Islam? Jews, Christians, and Muslims believe in God. In Judaism, Abraham is known as a patriarch. Christians believe Jesus Christ was the son of God. In Islam, Muhammad is seen as a prophet. These three religions all teach the importance of community, peace, and charity. It is important for students to carefully think about the content taught in sixth-grade social studies education about world civilizations and religions. Students also can take world history in high school. These courses can provide students with accurate knowledge about various religions and help squash stereotypes that are perpetuated in the media.

Peer Pressure and Muslim American Youth

It is common for people to feel excluded from a group because of religion. Teenagers generally want to feel as if they belong to the school community. Dilara, Yasmine, and Imran Hafiz suggest that a Muslim student who is feeling like an outsider should find strength in her or his religion, but they also realize that most adolescents feel isolated from peers at one time or another. It's important to show students that what they are feeling may not be that different from others. Teachers can also suggest that sometimes it is best for students to walk away if someone is pressuring them. If you have Muslim students who do not participate in a specific group, suggest that they search for a sports team or club that they are interested in (Hafiz et al., 2009). Dilara, Yasmine, and Imran Hafiz recommend that teachers can assist students in dealing with peer pressure by suggesting their students consider the following:

1. Find a mentor, who may be a teacher, counselor, or another student.
2. Research internships and find an opportunity to learn about a field one is interested in.
3. Locate a part-time job and learn new skills.
4. Volunteer at a local community center.
5. Volunteer at a local humane society.

All of these strategies are ways that young Muslim youth can participate in and feel a sense of belonging in a variety of community settings. (See Figure 8.2.)

Common Stereotypes about Muslim Women and Men

There are many stereotypical images about Muslim women and men in the media. Some show Muslims with camels. Others depict Muslim men and women as terrorists with bombs. They are also seen as foreigners and not members of the American democracy. These are overt stereotypes that can be easily identified; however, there are more complex images that have surfaced especially after the September 11, 2001, attacks. For example, women are often presented in three ways:

1. Muslim young women are veiled, silent, and unknown.
2. Muslim young women who wear veils are oppressed.

Figure 8.2: Muslim students working together on a school project.

pistolseven/Shutterstock.com

3. Muslim young women and adult females need to be saved by Westerners (Özlem and Marshall, 2009–2010).

In all of these stereotypes, Muslim women are seen as voiceless individuals who are oppressed by their religion. The metaphor of young Muslim or Middle Eastern girls as veiled is a common symbol of their silence and lack of freedom (Özlem & Marshall, 2009–2010). Therefore, they end up being described by the veil that covers their mouths and bodies; their entire being is tied up with the veil, which may be a cultural or religious tradition. (See Figure 8.3.) These overgeneralized images can have a huge impact on the attitudes of others about young Muslim females.

Hijab   **Chador**   **Niqab**   **Burka**

Figure 8.3: Shown are various veils worn by Muslim women. Should students in the United States be allowed to wear scarves in schools? Why or why not?

Özlem and Marshall argue that women in general often are silenced by their gender. This is a concern of women throughout the world. Women in many teen novels about Muslim or Middle Eastern girls show the vulnerability of young females within Muslim communities. However, in countries like Turkey, a predominantly Muslim country, Muslim women and girls have made a choice to wear veils as an act of resistance in order to challenge what they see as Western imperialism (Özlem & Marshall, 2009–2010).

Stereotypes about Muslim men abound. After September 11, the media often reinforced the generalization that portrayed all Muslim males as extremists like Osama Bin Laden. One of the major misconceptions is that all Muslim men oppress Muslim women. To counter that viewpoint, a Muslim fraternity at the University of Texas at Dallas, Alif Laah Meem, demonstrated against domestic violence with signs that read "Muslims Say Yes to Women's Rights" and "Real Men Do Not Hit Women" (Durey, 2013). A majority of Muslim American men are in favor of building peace, creating strong, peaceful communities, and supporting women's rights. There are many misconceptions about the behaviors of Muslim Americans, especially men. For example, Ambassador Akbar Ahmed, professor at American University in Washington DC, explained that though the word "jihad" has been used to describe an assault on Westerners, in reality it means "struggle." He described that the struggle for all Christians, Jews, Buddhists, and Muslims is to make oneself a better person and to grow spiritually.

Because teaching about Muslims can be complex, Özlem and Marshall recommend that when using any novel about Muslims, teachers should ask students these questions as part of their literary analysis:

1. How are Muslims depicted on the cover and in the other illustrations of the novel? Provide descriptions of the drawings. How accurate are the images? How do these images refer to the relationships within the story?
2. Which aspects of the story are accurate? How do you know? What are the sources of your information?
3. Who is the author of the novel? What background does the person have to write about the issues? Whose viewpoint is the author providing? Who benefits from that perspective?
4. Whose perspective is missing? Are there other aspects of the protagonist and other characters that could be discussed such as class, race, gender, and education? How could these elements provide a richer description of the characters? Where could you find more information?

LO4 Differentiate among indigenous persons, immigrants, migrants, and refugees and describe how Nativism, global migration, and immigrant students impact the United States.

The United States: A Nation of Many People, Including Immigrants, Migrants, and Refugees

naeyc *CALD* **InTASC**

The United States is a nation of many people, including numerous immigrants. The United States also includes many indigenous people such as the Wapanoag and Iroquois nations. Along with Native groups, immigrant, migrant, and refugee children and their families came and continue to come to the United States from around the world for a variety of reasons, including genocide in Somalia; suppression of Christianity in Iraq; severe poverty, unemployment, and hunger in Mexico; civil strife in the Philippines; reunification with family members; desire for quality education; and the search for reliable employment (Stratton, Pang, Madueño, Park, Atlas, Page, & Oliger, 2009). The Pew Research Center states that more than half of the existing 12 million undocumented immigrants entered the country legally on student, business, or tourist visas and simply remained in the United States past their visa expiration dates (Kochhar, 2006).

How are immigrant, migrant, refugee, and indigenous individuals different? First of all, an **indigenous person** has ancestors who are original people of a particular land. The person also shares in a sense of peoplehood with his or her tribe's cultural background and history, and may speak the indigenous language. In the United States, Native Americans are the indigenous people of the country, and they continue to fight for their economic well-being and cultural integrity in comparison to the dominant society (Corntassell, 2003). Do you know someone who has Native American roots? Their status is extremely different from immigrants or migrants. Everyone else who is not indigenous migrated or their ancestors moved to this country that we now call the United States.

An **immigrant** is someone who has decided to move to the United States from another country and is planning to stay. Many Americans fall into this category. This person does not want to work a temporary job and then later move back to their home nation. This individual wants to stay here and make the United States their new homeland. Do you know someone who moved, let's say from Russia? The mother and father have chosen the United States as their new country. However, there are others who are migrants. A **migrant** is an individual who moves to the United States but who hopes to go back to his or her native land in the future. There are people who work for international companies who may come to Boston to live for five years and then return to Singapore. These people are migrants. There are also many seasonal workers who are migrants; they come from other countries and work during specific growing seasons and then return to their home countries.

In comparison, a **refugee** is a person who moves to a new country because they fear persecution due to their racial, political, or religious views. When a person migrates to another country without official documents and permission, that person is called an undocumented or unauthorized immigrant or migrant. Therefore, you can see that refugees are a subset under migrants; however, not all migrants are refugees. Many refugees become immigrants because they are fleeing unsafe situations and may never be able to return to their native countries.

Refugees in the World and United States

There are many refugees in the world. The United Nations definition of a refugee is a person who willingly or unwillingly cannot return to his or her home country due to fear of prosecution because of race, religion, nationality, political views, or membership in a specific social group (American Immigration Council, 2014). Approximately 45,000 to

Indigenous person Is one who has ancestors who are original people of a particular land, shares in a sense of peoplehood with his or her tribe's cultural background and history, may speak the indigenous language, and struggles to maintain the tribe's cultural integrity and self-determination.

Immigrant refers to someone who has decided to move to the United States from another country and is planning to stay.
Migrant refers to an individual who moves to the United States but who hopes to go back to his or her native land in the future.

Refugee is defined by the United Nations as a person who willingly or unwillingly cannot return to his or her home country due to fear of prosecution because of race, religion, nationality, political views, or membership in a specific social group.

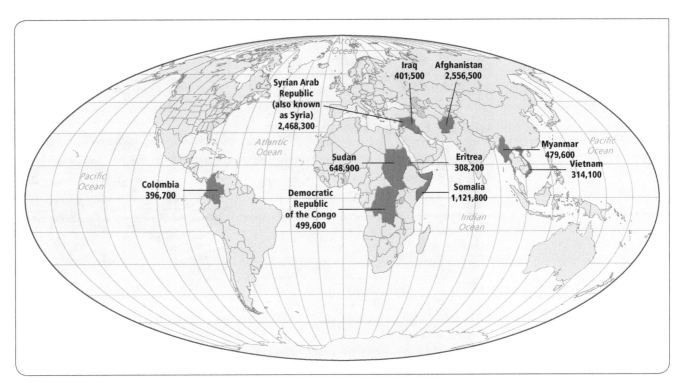

70,000 refugees enter the United States each year. The United Nations High Commission for Refugees reported that there were about 60 million refugees and internally displaced persons in the world in 2014 (Graham, 2015). Internally displaced people (IDPs) are defined by the United Nations High Commission for Refugees as individuals who do not cross foreign borders in search of safety; they remain in their home country. Not all IDPs have moved because of war; some have had to move to other areas in their countries because of natural disasters like hurricanes and earthquakes. Today, the refugee situation is the worst it has been since World War II. One in every 122 people in the world have been forced out of their homes due to armed conflict, general violence, human rights violations, war, and persecution. For example, 9.5 million Syrians have left their homes; that is about 43 percent of the total population (Graham, 2015). In 2014, almost half of the refugees were children who were 18 years of age or less (American Immigration Council, 2014). Though it is difficult to gather accurate numbers on refugees, read through Figure 8.4 to find out where refugees who are under the care of the United Nations High Commission of Refugees and Displaced Persons (2013) originated. You can see which countries had the largest numbers of refugees. The UNHCR do not have the funds to take care of all refugees.

Figure 8.4 shows the number of refugees from selected countries of the world with the highest number of refugees. Where do these refugees go? During 2015, for example, the United States had a limit of 70,000 refugees it would allow into the country. The president declared that people from countries such as Cuba, Iraq, Honduras, Guatemala, and El Salvador could also be considered for entrance into the United States. People come to the United States to seek asylum, which is a specific immigration status (Figure 8.5). Individuals and families who seek **asylum** can do so if they need protection because of persecution due to religion, race, nationality, membership in a specific social group, and political opinion. (See Table 8.4.)

Do you think that allowing 70,000 refugees each year into the United States is too much, not enough, or just right? The United States Census Bureau continues to estimate the population in the United States. The bureau estimated that on January 1, 2015, there were 320,090,957 people living in the United States (U.S. Census Bureau, 2014). If 70,000 people were to be accepted for refugee status in the United States in 2015, that would add .0003 percent to our population.

Figure 8.4: Refugees from Selected Countries Worldwide Served by the UNHCR, 2013

Asylum refers to when a person asks a nation to allow him or her to enter its country for protection because of persecution due to religion, race, nationality, membership in a specific social group, and political opinion.

Figure 8.5: Refugees, asylum seekers, and other immigrants become new citizens in the United States at the U.S. Holocaust Museum, where they recite the Pledge of Allegiance.

Table 8.4 Refugee Allocations for 2015 for Entrance into the United States*	
Area	Number of Refugees
Near East and South Asia	33,000
Africa	17,000
East Asia	13,000
Latin America and Caribbean	4000
Europe and Central Asia	1000
Unallocated Reserve (some ceilings can be higher)	2000

*Presidential Memorandum—FY 2015 Refugee Allocations (September 2014). Retrieved from https://www.whitehouse.gov/the-press-office/2014/09/30/presidential-memorandum-fy-2015-refugee-admissions

Nativism is a term used to describe an anti-immigrant attitude and actions aimed at people who have migrated or immigrated to the United States; Nativists are concerned that their way of life—including jobs, education, housing, and other opportunities—will be lost. **Xenophobia** refers to prejudice and fear of individuals and groups from other countries.

Bicultural refers to a person who is able to function in both mainstream and subcultural environments; they understand the values, norms, and behaviors of either community.

Nativism

Though our nation is considered primarily a nation of immigrants, there has been and continues to be strong nativist attitudes among citizens. In Chapter 4, the text discussed how Nativism led to the internment of 120,000 Japanese Americans during World War II, so fears of people who do not look mainstream or who come speaking a language other than English can have a powerful influence on our political and legal policies (Pang, 2006). **Nativism** is an anti-immigrant attitude and results in actions aimed at people or their descendants who have migrated or immigrated to the United States. Nativists are concerned that their way of life—including jobs, education, housing, culture, and other opportunities—will be lost. Nativism is also a part of **xenophobia**, which refers to prejudice and fear of individuals and groups from other countries.

There is often a belief that new immigrants and migrants must take on the culture of mainstream society, which also means they must rid themselves of cultural traditions and behaviors of their native countries. Others understand that new people can become bicultural. A **bicultural** person is able to function in both mainstream and subcultural environments; they understand the values, norms, and behaviors of either community.

Consider this . . .

How is Nativism a threat to the values in the U.S. Constitution? How would you describe Nativism? Nativism is not patriotism. It is a set of beliefs that terrorizes and excludes immigrants, migrants, refugees, religious groups, and people of color in general.

Q Have your students create a chart listing "U.S. Constitutional Values" and "Values of Nativism." In this way, students can assess and evaluate how these orientations are different.

Cultural sustainability, the maintenance of culture, can occur when multiculturalism is accepted. In Chapter 1, multiculturalism was discussed, including how teachers can affirm children's subcultures while students are also taught citizenship skills and community unity.

> **Cultural sustainability** is the maintenance of culture.

One of the issues that arises with immigration and migration is social cohesion. As discussed above, Nativists often are concerned that new immigrants or migrants will not become an integral part of society. They want to be sure that new immigrants are participants in the social cohesion of the community. **Social cohesion** in this case refers to strong social ties where participants agree with community decisions, conform to social expectations, and have a strong commitment to the country. It can be a positive force; however, Nativists are afraid that new migrants will not conform to American ideals, so some people, such as members of the Ku Klux Klan, may threaten those they see as outsiders to conform. The KKK, for example, feared the eradication of slavery would lead to the equality of African Americans. They worked hard to ensure that did not happen by lynching, bombing, and threatening people so that Black citizens were prevented from holding the same position in society as Whites. This organization is an example of Nativism at its extreme.

> **Social cohesion** refers to strong social ties where participants agree with community decisions, conform to social expectations, and have a strong commitment to the country.

Transborder Identity

Many immigrants and native-born Americans have transborder identities. Teachers also need to understand that numerous students in their classes may have transborder cultures. **Transborder** refers to experiencing and knowing two or more cultures and the border culture. For example, many Mexican American students who live in San Diego may often cross the border to visit with their grandparents and cousin who live in Tijuana. They feel comfortable in Mexico, California, and at the border. They speak Spanish and English. They know how to get around in both countries. They know how to cross the border. They have a transborder identity. Students who attend schools in San Diego, Chula Vista, Escondido, La Jolla, or Los Angeles schools may hold strong attachments to and understandings of both countries. Their lives are not made up of separate experiences in either California or Tijuana. Their way of life comes from both cultures. It is more than being bicultural because they also understand the physical, sociological, and psychological borders between the United States and Mexico. If a teacher was to ask them about being Mexican or American, students may not be able to choose either one. They may choose to identify as being a person with a transborder identity. There is a blend of the three cultures that cannot be separated (Ramirez, 2010). The borders of identity are more flexible and dynamic.

> **Transborder** refers to experiencing and knowing two or more cultures and the border culture.

Students with transborder identities—whether they are migrants, immigrants, refugees, or indigenous people—are contributing to new conceptions of democracy (Ramirez, 2010). They are assisting in expanding the borders of people's minds to examine and challenge cultural and economic inequalities that continue to weaken our nation. For example, students who move freely between the United States and other countries will bring new ideas to commerce. They will bring together people who have cross-cultural knowledge, which can result in setting up a business that is culturally sensitive to several nations. One example is James Gosling, who is known as the father of JAVA, a computer programming language used throughout the world. He is originally from Canada and worked with two American colleagues to expand his original version of the language.

Individuals who are comfortable in several countries and cultural environments also are pushing for stronger relationships and networks with people who are not as different as first thought, individuals and groups within the United States and in other nations. There is a fluidity to transborder identities and relationships that can contribute to enlarging the possibilities of our democracy. New Americans can assist in opening up the way people think about what the common good is and expanding egalitarianism.

Benefits Immigrant Families Bring

Immigrant families bring to the United States many traditional values, such as a strong-work ethic, the strength of family and community ties, and a belief in education (Stratton et. al., 2009). Marjorie Orellana (2001) studied the contributions of immigrant children. She found that because immigrant students were family orientated, they were more likely to volunteer with classroom duties, offer to assist in the library, and tutor younger students.

Often, immigrant children serve as bridges between the family and others. Because children learn English in school and therefore can communicate not only with peers and teachers but also with the community outside their immediate neighborhood, they take on the role of interpreter. For example, it is not unusual for our students from elementary through high school to accompany their parents to the Department of Motor Vehicles or the USCIS (United States Citizenship and Immigration Services) Office to translate (Stratton et al., 2009; Pang, Stratton, Park, Madueño, Atlas, Page, and Oliger, 2010). However, being the family translator at school can be difficult because older children are sometimes asked to translate teachers' concerns about themselves or their siblings. In this case, it may be best to ask for a district translator to attend parent–teacher conferences. It should be noted that some children's rapid acculturation and acquisition of the local language can come with a cost: it often leads to an even larger divide between their generation and that of their parents, causing even greater social and emotional hardship for our immigrant families. Teachers can help students whose parents do not speak English by inviting them to volunteer in the classroom so they learn what the school system is about and in the process learn more English. Parents then also become important members of the school community.

An orientation toward the community provides young people with a solid foundation for citizenship. Many also become important role models for younger siblings. The younger children watch their older successful brothers and sisters and learn English more rapidly and develop strong helping skills in schools. Taking on many family responsibilities transfers into self-reliance and hard work, which are important skills linked to successful achievement. These abilities then transfer to the development of careers as professionals (Gándara, 1994).

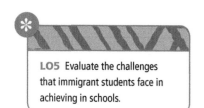

LO5 Evaluate the challenges that immigrant students face in achieving in schools.

The American Dream and Immigrant Students in Schools

Read through the three case studies, which are based on real people (Stratton et al., 2009). Identify the similarities and differences. Do you agree with their decisions about college?

TAKE A STAND: CONTRIBUTIONS OF IMMIGRANTS AND REFUGEES

Identify the pros and cons of having immigrant, migrant, and refugee students in schools. What do new immigrant students bring to schools that can benefit other students in becoming global citizens? Cross-cultural translators? How can immigrant students help others see issues from many viewpoints?

	Pros	Cons	References
Immigrants	1. 2. 3. 4. 5.	1. 2. 3. 4. 5.	
Migrants	1. 2. 3. 4. 5.	1. 2. 3. 4. 5.	
Refugees	1. 2. 3. 4. 5.	1. 2. 3. 4. 5.	

▶ Write at least five pros and cons for each group. List your references in the table. Would you vote for immigrants and refugees to come to the United States? Why or why not? What values would you use as foundational to your decision?

Middle-School Students

Answer these questions:

▶ How can we as citizens of the world help our new immigrant or refugee students feel more comfortable in our schools? In our classrooms? On the playground? Completing homework?

High-School Students

Answer these questions:

▶ What should the United States do when a group of people such as Syrians or Somalis are being slaughtered in their country and have nowhere to go? What responsibilities does the United States have toward refugees?

▶ Find a partner and then each share your position.

▶ Find two other people who disagree with your position.

▶ Find common ground with each other. What did you learn from this discussion?

⌄ Professional Resource Download

As a teacher, you will meet many young immigrants such as the ones described. The students have had to make difficult decisions about their lives. You may have students in your classes who also must make hard choices. How will you help them achieve their career goals?

The values that culturally diverse students have may not be the same as yours or other teachers in the school. As an educator, you need to reflect on how your values may differ from your students' and how much you should interject your beliefs into their lives. This can be extremely difficult because we want the best for our students; however, families may not understand the importance of going to college or why the type of university can enrich a student's education more than another. Values people hold may represent the level of their cultural assimilation. You need to know your students and their parents well enough to give the best advice that *they* would want.

Use one or all of the three scenarios in the Case Study as beginning points for class discussions. Teachers and other members of the class can learn from their immigrant and refugee peers by having them create a discussion group. Nonimmigrant students can make the outer circle and listen to the discussion about how to solve the problem of going to college. This would provide an opportunity for immigrant and refugee students to express their views while other members of the group also learn different views. Many times we do not know there are so many ways to look at an issue. The next section is also important for teachers to reflect on because educators may not understand the needs or views of students with disabilities.

CASE STUDY Young Immigrants Deciding on College

On graduation day, the members of a class await their opportunity to cross the stage and receive their diplomas. The large auditorium is filled with culturally diverse families. The urban high school from which these students graduate is home to an array of immigrants from Mexico to Somalia, Vietnam to Peru. The ceremony is conducted in English, Spanish, Arabic, Vietnamese, and Cambodian. The hope of the American dream can be seen shining on the faces of the high school graduates.

Case Study 1: Renee*

Renee sits in the front row wearing a white cap and gown with gold cords draped around her shoulders signifying graduation with highest honors. Somewhere in the audience, Renee's family sits proudly awaiting her turn to walk across the stage and accept her diploma. This will be the first step in her journey from adolescence to adulthood and the opportunity she has worked toward since immigrating to this country only seven years earlier. It has taken time, stacks of paperwork, and sacrifice to bring the family together for this momentous occasion. Her family came piece by piece over the course of 15 years through legal channels. The most recent addition is her father, a former auto dealer in Peru who is now starting over as a dishwasher in a downtown hotel. Virtually all of Renee's adolescence was spent anxiously hoping for his arrival and helping her mother with the paperwork so her father could emigrate. Graduation day is here and attending college is not just a pipe dream for Renee. She has been accepted to several top universities including UC Berkley, UC Santa Barbara, and UC San Diego. It's a great accomplishment—one made of sacrifice and hard work, built over a lifetime of making difficult choices. She is struggling over yet another tough decision—stay in the city and attend a local university as her parents wish, or go away to a highly competitive university, leaving just when her dream of a reunited family has finally been realized.

Renee has waited 15 years to have her entire family together, yet she also believes it is important for her future to attend the best university she can. "When I came, I had all these beliefs from my parents, but I now have the values that I have learned in American schools also." In the end, Renee's choice combines the best of both worlds; she is somewhere in the middle. She now lives in a dormitory at a highly respected university, close enough to travel home on the weekends to enjoy family dinners.

Reflection Question

Q What role did teachers and classmates play in the education of Renee?

Case Study 2: Mohamed

Mohamed is also dressed in white, but he is sitting on the stage. He is translating the greeting for the other Somalis in the audience. Mohamed has a green card because he is a refugee from Somalia. His family fled across the border to a refugee camp in Kenya; they waited for 10 years to emigrate from Kenya to the United States. They originally lived in Mogadishu but had to flee on foot. It was a difficult existence, yet Mohammed always dreamed of an education. It has not always been easy for his parents in the United States either. In the evenings and after school, Mohamed worked at a local theme park to help his family financially.

Mohammed's parents are proud of his achievements; he is graduating with honors even though he worked throughout high school.

Mohamed has opted for the path of least resistance and is attending the state university 40 miles from his home. His major is criminal justice. He was honored with an AVID scholarship, so most of his tuition and books are paid for at the state university. Still, he wonders how his life might have been different if he had followed his heart and gone to UC Berkeley instead of staying with his family.

Reflection Question

Q The value of family can be a huge influence in the choices a high school graduate makes. What would you say to Mohamed if you had been his counselor?

Case Study 3: Maria

Like the other students in the front row, Maria is graduating with honors. Maria is the associated student body vice president and has been instrumental in planning the class graduation celebration. However, for her, this day is bittersweet. Today marks the end of Maria's educational opportunities in America. Maria is undocumented; her mother, a single parent, migrated to the United States from Mexico when Maria was a toddler. Many years ago her mother was admitted into the United States with a visa; she found a job at a fast food restaurant and never left. Her employment allowed the family to survive. Maria, now an accomplished high school student, wishes to become a nurse. In order to pursue her career goals, she has to make a decision. Her mother has found a young man who has agreed to become her husband so that she can pursue a path to citizenship and her educational dreams. Initially, Maria considered joining the armed forces, but her mother needs her help with her younger sisters so marriage seems to be the best option. Although Maria cannot discuss her predicament without tearing up, she knows that this is what she must do to remain in this country.

Maria has decided to follow through with the marriage. In spite of several college acceptances, Maria will be attending a community college because she cannot afford even state college tuition. By the time she is ready to transfer to a four-year university, she will have finalized all of the paperwork and earned her legal residency. However, she will need to put her personal career goal on hold at this time in order to support a family.

Reflection Question

Q As one of Maria's teachers, do you think it is appropriate for you to talk with Maria and her mother about this decision? Why or why not?

*These are case studies of graduating seniors from high school who are immigrants from around the world.

Disability Studies and Special Education: Similarities and Differences

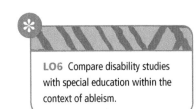

LO6 Compare disability studies with special education within the context of ableism.

Teachers need to address the social oppression of ableism to ensure that students are treated respectfully and have the opportunity to learn. **Ableism** is the systematic exclusion and discrimination against people with physical, intellectual, or developmental disabilities. There are two major orientations that address ableism. Special education is a field that seeks interventions for individuals with disabilities. In contrast, disability studies is the field that does not agree with attempts of some educators to make people with disabilities "normal" or "fixed." Rather, this orientation sees individuals with disabilities as a cultural group like a racial or ethnic community. This section of the book may be somewhat challenging to understand because you probably grew up learning about the special education perspective on disabilities and exceptionalities and not a disability studies viewpoint.

> **Ableism** is the systematic exclusion and discrimination against people with physical, intellectual, or developmental disabilities.

Disability Studies: A Cultural Model of Disabilities

Disability studies uses a social model approach to disabilities (Danforth, 2008a; Erevells and Minear, 2010; Siebers, 2008). This field of education contrasts with special education, which uses a medical model orientation.

How is disability studies different from special education? In disability studies, a student is not seen as someone who is "abnormal" or needs to be "fixed" as in the case of the medical model orientation. Rather, a person with a disability is seen as a person first. His or her disability is not the main characteristic that defines the person. So a disability is viewed as a cultural characteristic somewhat like race (Danforth, 2008a). A person is born Black or Asian. A person is born with a disability; this does not diminish the individual.

Let's take a look at how some folks think about disabilities. Many teachers believe in the ideology of ability in which the value as a person is defined by one's physical and intellectual abilities. Tobin Siebers (2008) has identified viewpoints that relate to the belief in the **ideology of ability**:

- A person's value is defined by their ability: physical, intellectual, emotional, and social.
- A disability is an individual characteristic, whereas ability is common.
- A disability can be eliminated if one works hard enough.
- "It is better to be dead than disabled" (p. 10).
- The value of a person with a disability is not the same as an individual without a disability.
- People with disabilities are sad, frustrated, and unhappy in comparison to able-bodied persons.

Siebers believes that the ideology of ability has been used to shape the view of people with disabilities. In opposition, he explained the following:

- A person's value is defined by who they are as a person.
- A disability does not name a person.
- A disability is not something to be eliminated; just like one's gender or ethnicity, it is not something to be removed.
- A person with a disability is not worth less than another person.
- People with disabilities are happy, productive, and collaborative individuals.

> **Ideology of ability** is the belief that a person's value is defined by his or her physical, intellectual, emotional, and social abilities. A disability can be eliminated if a person works hard enough. A person who has a disability is not as valuable as a person without a disability. People with disabilities are sad, frustrated, and ego-centric.

In contrast to the ideology of ability, disability studies view disabilities as cultural characteristics with political elements. Siebers sees disability as similar to being a person of color in society. A person of color cannot change who they are and yet have been oppressed

My Journal

Addressing Discrimination Toward Students with Exceptionalities

Q *What should I do about discrimination against students with exceptionalities in my classroom and school?*

Students with disabilities are often discriminated against and bullied.

Q *What can you do in your classroom to address this issue of ableism?*

Also ask yourself:

Q *Will my attitudes about students with disabilities lead to their isolation in my classroom?*

Q *Which strategies can I use in my classroom and school to ensure inclusion? Describe your year-long goal to eliminate ableism in your classroom.*

because of their physical differences. This orientation is in sync with multiculturalism and encourages teachers to addresses ableism. How are people with disabilities similar to other groups that have been oppressed?

- Disabilities are identifiable. Often disabilities are linked to physical differences such as behavioral diversity, body shapes, and gender traits.
- Disabilities are linked to social oppression. People with disabilities have less political and cultural power.
- People with disabilities are often treated unfairly and discriminated against. Therefore they often come together with common goals.

Siebers believes that if a cultural and political orientation toward disabilities is taken, then people with disabilities can develop a positive identity. In other words, like many people of color, women, and poor individuals, they take ownership of who they are. Disabilities studies scholars recognize that some individuals have disabilities, but they see these individuals as members of society just like anyone else.

How can teachers respect the needs of students with disabilities and not isolate them in schools? Scot Danforth (2015a), an educational researcher, described programs in which teachers develop opportunities for all students to engage in a class project. For example, what if a teacher created a gardening club and invited two students with disabilities? The two students then also invited other peers to come along. They picked a variety of children, and now there is a garden club. The teacher has identified goals of following directions and focusing for longer periods of time on a task. In addition, all the children work together in designing, implementing, and caring for their garden. All of the children have many chances to learn about gardening, and the students with disabilities are working on their academic and behavioral needs within the gardening context. In this scenario students are not pulled out of class or labeled (Danforth, 2015a).

Legal Support for Disability Services

Providing equality for all in education is a foundational value in the United States. This belief was extended to all students in 1974 with the passage of the Education for All Handicapped Children Act (Public Law 94-142); Congress wanted to ensure that children with disabilities would obtain an education just like other students. The law was revised in 1990, 1997, and 2004 and is identified by the acronym **IDEA (Individuals with Disabilities Education Act)** (Koch, 2014). IDEA is based on the value of a free and appropriate education for students with disabilities (Hardman, Drew, & Egan, 2011). Students with disabilities also must be provided with the least restrictive environment. This means that children with disabilities must be placed in a classroom where they can be successful and have the opportunity to participate with other students without being separated; students with disabilities are included in regular

Individuals with Disabilities Act (IDEA) is the legislation that ensures that all children with disabilities are provided an effective, high-quality education.

classrooms as much as possible. The students are not segregated or pulled out of a general education classroom unless for targeted instruction for individual learners or if they have severe behavioral difficulties (Hardman et al., 2011).

As part of this movement, the Americans with Disabilities Act (ADA) of 1990 called for the civil rights of individuals with disabilities with regard to employment, public services, public accommodations, telecommunications, and transportation. This is why you might see that sidewalks in many neighborhoods have been altered at the corner to allow for wheelchairs. In addition, when you cross the street at a light, do you hear a beeping or other sound? This is to alert someone who is blind that pedestrians can walk.

In schools these laws and others have pushed for the **inclusion** of students with disabilities to be included as members of a classroom. Inclusion is a term that describes the process by which students with disabilities are included in the general education classroom with educational supports that are developed for the individual learner. For example, there is a program called Positive Behavioral Interventions & Supports for high school students, especially those with behavioral difficulties. See their website at https://www.pbis.org/school. Teachers and students identify positive goals and ways to create a positive school climate. Students can have discussions about their problems such as parents yelling at them for poor report cards. Teachers, students, and parents work together to include all students in this educational environment. The teachers who are involved in this system of inclusion do not believe that students should be pushed out of school for bad behavior; rather they believe every student is worthy of being in the school. They do not have a punitive view of students. Teachers bring in parents to contribute because by high school, parents often think their children are too old for them to need to participate in school activities. However, teachers get parents to work in the schools, and together they help their students solve problems they are facing from alcoholism to anger management. The teachers never give up on students; they care about them. Students see that teachers are genuine and also learn to care about themselves. Students may have come to school drunk before or tried to hurt themselves; however, they are made to feel they belong and are accepted no matter what problems they have at home.

> **Inclusion** refers to students with disabilities being included as members of a general education classroom.

Individualized Education Program (IEP)

Because of IDEA, each student with disabilities must be assessed by an Individualized Education Program (IEP) team. Since there are so many different types of disabilities, each qualifying student must be given an IEP (Koch, 2014). This team includes the student's parents, the classroom teacher, a special education teacher, a representative from the school district, and a principal or school psychologist who acts as a liaison for parents (Hardman et al., 2011). The team can also include the student if she or he is old enough to participate. This process includes the following:

1. Identify student's present levels of performance
2. Develop annual and measurable goals for the student
3. Identify skills the student needs to develop
4. Document student progress
5. Assess the student using appropriate measures
6. Identify a process to inform parents of the student's progress (Hardman et al., 2011)

Various elements of student development are documented and identified in the IEP process. For example, social development is an important area. How does the student relate to his or her peers and teachers (Koch, 2014)? How are students developing fine motor and large motor skills?

One of the interventions that teachers use in order to prevent the placement of students into special education classes is **Response to Intervention (RTI)**. RTI is a program that has a three-level process of intervention (Koch, 2014). The first level of the program examines whether students are meeting the standards for that grade level. In the second

> **Response to Intervention (RTI)** is a preventive program that teachers can implement. Educators develop programs that will prevent students from falling so far behind that they must be placed in special education classes.

level, students who are not achieving at the grade level receive instructional support, which has been agreed upon by the general education teacher and the special education teacher. Assessments are made about every three months in order to determine if students are making progress in the core program. Students from level 2 who need additional instruction are placed into the third level. Teachers make assessments as to why this student continually needs extra supports in order to learn and continue to address their educational difficulties. Students may be placed in special education classes or other instructional programs. Some researchers believe that RTI can help to prevent the overrepresentation of African American students in special education (Proctor, Graves, & Esch, 2012). The strategies used in RTI move away from the use of standardized testing and take a broader view of assessment.

Types of Inclusion

There are two types of inclusion:

1. **Full inclusion** refers to students with disabilities receiving all of their instruction within the general education classroom. This refers to the type of school discussed above in which students, teachers, and parents work to include everyone in the school. Another type of full inclusion is where special services are provided within the classroom; students do not leave the classroom and are not isolated from their peers. (See Figure 8.6.)

2. **Partial inclusion** is the process in which students with disabilities continue to work part of the time in the classroom while receiving additional services in another learning environment (Hardman et al., 2011).

In the past many teachers talked about the importance of mainstreaming. Unlike inclusion, **mainstreaming** is a process in which students are placed into the regular classroom without supports (Danforth, 2008a). The term has been around since the 1960s and has also been referred to as "main dumping" because some educators felt students with disabilities were "dumped" into general classrooms so that extra services would not be needed, saving financial resources (Hardman et al., 2011). Some scholars believe the process of mainstreaming is negative and do not advocate it. The next section discusses advanced learners, sometimes referred to gifted and talented students, which is considered an area within special education.

> **Mainstreaming** refers to the placement of students with disabilities into the general education classroom so they have the opportunity to learn the same curriculum as their peers and become part of a regular learning environment. To many teachers, this has come to be known as the "dumping" of students with disabilities into the general education classroom without support for students or teachers.

Figure 8.6: Students with varying abilities are participating together in a collaborative choral presentation.

Alex Farnsworth/The Image Works

Exceptionalities

The term **exceptionalities** includes students who are advanced learners with special talents and gifts (Tuckman & Monetti, 2013). Though IDEA does not include financing for advanced learners, the Jacob Jarvits Gifted and Talented Students Education Act, also known as Gifted and Talented Education (GATE), passed in 1988 as part of the Elementary and Secondary Education Act, provides funds for the needs of advanced students.

Many other learners can benefit from various aspects of schooling for students with exceptionalities. One of the strategies is the use of technology in the learning process, called universal design for learning (UDL). The concept of **universal design for learning** is a framework with the goal of providing the most flexible environment to increase the accessibility of students to learning. UDL has three main principles (Snowman & McCown, 2013):

1. Multiple methods can be used to teach content, including lecture, cooperative learning, singing, field trips, hands on demonstrations, and other learning style avenues from using photographs to music (Figure 8.7).
2. Multiple methods can be used to teach the "how" of learning, such as asking guiding questions, teaching students how to identify main ideas, using examples from students' lives, and teaching them how to write essays.
3. Using multiple methods, students are engaged in the "why" of learning, and they may engage in researching a personal interest or cultural topic. Learning can be a result of a personal goal.

Different types of learners need knowledge presented to them in various ways. One way technology can be used in schools is by presenting lectures through closed captions, just like they are used on television. A student who has hearing loss will be able to read what has been said and this can keep him or her involved in the learning process. In addition, students who are visual learners will be reinforced by the display of text. Speech synthesizers, software that can translate text as if someone is talking, can also be used for visually impaired students. There are programs in which a learner can have materials presented

> **Exceptionalities** broadens the concept of disabilities and includes students who are advanced learners.

> **Universal design for learning** (UDL) is a framework with the goal of providing the most flexible environment to increase the accessibility of students to learning.

(a)

Lee Snider Photo Images/Shutterstock.com

(b)

SpeedKing./Shutterstock.com

(c)

Figure 8.7: (a) Students are learning by engaging in hands-on lessons with a variety of objects. (b) Students here are on a field trip to Washington, DC. (c) Students pictured are actively involved in expressing a song.

orally. Students with orthopedic impairments can control their learning by using pointers attached to a head device or held in their mouths that interact with a computer (Snowman & McCown, 2013). Another advantage of UDL is that many students benefit from visualization. The teacher can use computers to show various geometric figures while she is verbally explaining shapes. The teacher can show how a right triangle can be found in real world situations and assist students in seeing how two right triangles can be identified within a rectangle (Hardman et al., 2011). There are many ways that technology can assist learners and create instruction that is more effective for all students, from providing pie graphs of economic data to using videos to show what happens when baking soda (sodium bicarbonate) and vinegar (acetic acid) mix to create a gas made of carbon dioxide, water, and other ions.

Special Education: Human Diversities

LO7 Explain how traditional special education groups students into various categories based on their exceptionalities.

There are numerous areas within special education that categorize the needs of students with physical, emotional, and mental needs. Special education is based on the medical model; for example, a student may have a learning disability such as dyslexia, which is a cognitive information processing issue in which the brain is not able to distinguish between specific parts of a word. It is important for teachers to present the entire word and then break it down in to parts so the learner understands how to look at various parts of the word. As part of this instruction, teachers can use word families so students see patterns within words such as cake, bake, lake, and take. The student will learn to identify the common root of ake and how to build words.

Learning Disabilities

There are many types of learning disabilities. The Learning Disabilities Association of America explains that students with learning disabilities have problems storing, processing, and producing information. Students with learning disabilities are generally those who have trouble with reading, language, and math skills. This also includes difficulties with listening, speaking, writing, spelling, and reasoning (Koch, 2014).

Learning disabilities is a broad term. For example, dyslexia is when students have trouble reading due to neurological issues and may not be able to take small chunks of words and sound them out. Other students may have short attention spans. There are students who have selective attention in that they focus on what is happening on the peripheral in the classroom rather than what the teacher is teaching. Other children may have memory issues, making it challenging for them to remember words they learned from one day to another. Another student may have trouble with visual perception and so does not see all the aspects of a letter (Hardman et al., 2011). Some students have problems with figure–ground discrimination. This means that they cannot see individual words within a page of words. Often students with learning disabilities become frustrated with learning and have low self-esteem. However, learning disabilities are not necessarily connected to emotional and social characteristics such as **attention deficit/hyperactivity disorder (ADHD)**, which is described as impulsive behaviors, excessive activity, and difficulty paying attention (Hardman et al., 2011). Sometimes children do not have learning disabilities but may need more time to develop their skills, so it is important to have students assessed by professionals. See Table 8.5 for a list of various learning disabilities.

Students arrive at school with a complexity of situations. It is important for teachers to identify and then create learning environments that are shaped for their success.

Attention deficit/ hyperactivity disorder (ADHD) is described as impulsive behaviors, excessive activity, and difficulty paying attention. Though often associated with learning disabilities, ADHD is not considered a learning disability.

Table 8.5 List of Selected Learning Disabilities

- Dyslexia: problems reading, writing, spelling
- Dyscalculia: problems with math, telling time, understanding the use of money
- Dysgraphia: problems writing, managing ideas, spelling
- Dyspraxia: problems with hand-eye coordination and balance
- Dysphasia/Aphasia: problems understanding and comprehending language
- Auditory Processing: problems with hearing different sounds
- Visual Processing: problems with reading charts, symbols, letters, numbers

Hearing, Visual, and Other Physical Disabilities

There are numerous students who have a variety of hearing, visual, and other physical impairments. It is imperative that teachers observe carefully their students learning. For example, if students do not follow verbal directions right away, learners may not hear the teacher. When students cannot hear well, there is a lag between the time the teacher talks and when they hear the information. Students with hearing disabilities may not hear at all or hear at a minimum due to partial hearing loss. They may not feel they are a part of a conversation or fail to understand what is being taught. It can be embarrassing not hearing the conversation of a group. Students who do not hear well may pretend to hear a comment and laugh when everyone else does, but in reality they may not know what they're laughing at. Most people want to belong, so sometimes we do things to be part of a community. A hearing loss makes it extremely hard to learn language or learn how to read because students may not hear the proper sounds when sounding out words. Students with hearing loss should sit in the front of the classroom near the teacher where the sound may be louder and they can see the lips of the instructor. The teacher should face a hearing impaired student when talking; it may take a student longer to respond because the learner needs more time to make sense of what the teacher has said. So a teacher should count 1001, 1002, 1003, 1004, and 1005 to make sure enough processing moments have passed, and then the student should be able to respond to the question. In addition, the instructor can write the information on the board so learners can visually follow along though there may be a hearing lag. English learners are at a further disadvantage because it is harder to acquire English when one has a hearing loss.

Students with visual disabilities may not see at all, function with minimal sight, or have low levels of vision. Young people who have a hard time learning academic content may have trouble socializing and may have difficulties interacting with others. When students cannot see they also may have trouble with motor development (Tuckman & Monetti, 2013).

Individuals with physical disabilities have trouble with mobility. They may have difficulty because of the following (Tuckman & Monetti, 2013):

- Congenital issues may have resulted in the lack of a limb
- Diseases, such as polio, may make mobility and motor development limited
- Health issues, like cerebral palsy or fractures, make it difficult for students to do well in schools because of medications or due to missing school when seeking medical treatments

There are many people who have physical disabilities. In 2012, CNN News reported that there are almost 2 million individuals who have had amputations (Siek, 2012). People may have had a leg crushed in a car accident. Others have suffered from diabetes and lost a foot. With the recent wars in Afghanistan and Iraq, many soldiers have lost limbs in battle and to improvised explosive devices (IEDs). Because of this, more and more people have been fitted with prosthetic devices. Having more attention placed on adults with physical disabilities may also help children in schools to feel that there are many others with physical difficulties. There seems to be more of an acceptance in society of physical differences as a result of the public discussion of war injuries.

CASE STUDY: Trilingual Student Identified with Asperger's Syndrome: Juan

Juan was a third grader who spoke three languages. His mother originally was from Colombia and his father was born in Japan. When Juan was a second grader, his teacher realized that his first languages were Spanish and Japanese. His third language was English. The first-grade teacher thought something was "wrong" with him because he did not talk much. What she did not know was that Juan was trilingual. The teacher did ask the bilingual resource teacher to work with him, but Juan and this resource teacher did not seem to get along. Juan often ignored her and she also ignored him. Sending him to the bilingual specialist did not help him.

Juan's teacher had talked with the second-grade teacher before third grade began and realized that Juan would need specialized instruction. Juan did not want to be taken out of the classroom because he would be labeled and might miss something fun that the other students were doing. The teacher also did not want Juan to be labeled and felt that Juan had fun in her classroom.

She could have had him tested and placed in a resource room where special needs students spent their entire day in the separated environment. However, the teacher did not think this was the best for Juan. So the third-grade teacher got a volunteer to work with Juan weekly in her classroom. Inclusion was one of the goals of the third-grade educator.

The volunteer was a former teacher and had taught primary grades. The third-grade teacher asked this person to volunteer because she had some knowledge of Japanese and thought that

Juan might warm to her because she was also Japanese American. There was some diversity in his class of 20 students; for example, Kris was Filipino American and Alan was Black American.

The volunteer used four tactics in her work with him:

- Situational factors
- Linguistic input
- Culturally relevant teaching
- Modeling conversation skills

First the volunteer thought Juan was extremely shy. He would sit in his chair, curl up with his knees up to his chin, and rock back and forth. The volunteer would remind him that it was best to sit up in his desk. She used situational information to help show there was another way to act.

Sometimes Juan would place his head on the desk during seatwork time. However, when Juan would go outside for recess, the volunteer would see him holding out his arms like an airplane and running around the playground. This was one of his common play behaviors. The volunteer asked the teacher if she had thought to have him tested for autism. The teacher said she had but felt that if Juan was identified with Asperger's syndrome, then he would end up in the full-day resource room; she did not think Juan would like that. The teacher was still thinking about what she should do and was going to have a conference with his parents.

The volunteer worked with Juan every week for a school year. She would bring him different things to do at home. For example, because Juan had trouble with reading comprehension, she had him work on his sight words. Next, because he

did not understand more advanced vocabulary in social studies, she had him look up terms like the food chain, animal kingdom, and lush vegetation.

One day when Juan was not being cooperative, the volunteer spoke to him in Japanese. Juan looked up and was surprised. He began to do his seatwork. He understood what she had said and that it was time to work. She provided appropriate linguistic input, and it was a strong link to his cultural background.

To motivate Juan to do his vocabulary work, the volunteer would bring plastic cartoon action figures for him to play with after his homework was completed. He liked specific Japanese cartoons. This was a way to integrate what Juan liked into the curriculum using culturally relevant materials. She would also ask him to tell stories about the characters because developing social skills was one of her goals in working with him.

At the beginning of the year, he was not able to have a conversation with the volunteer. He would ask questions in rapid fire like:

Juan: "Do you like South Park?"
Volunteer: "No, I do not like South Park."
Juan: "Do you like Rugrats?"
Volunteer: "Yes, I like Rugrats."
Juan: "Beavis and Butthead?"
Volunteer shakes her head: "No, I do like them."
Volunteer: "What cartoon do you like?"
Juan doesn't answer.
Volunteer asks him again and Juan says: "Rugrats."
Juan continues: "Do you like Powerpuff Girls?"
Volunteer: "Yes, and my daughter likes the character, Blossom."

Autism Syndrome Disorder (ASD)

Many students who participate in special education fall within the autism spectrum. Autism and autism spectrum disorder are complex disorders dealing with brain development. The Centers for Disease Control and Prevention (CDC) report that 1 in 68 students are on the spectrum. This is about a 30 percent increase from 2008, and the numbers continue to rise. Boys are five times more likely to be identified with ASD than their female counterparts (CDC, 2014). About half of the children also have an average IQ. Autism spectrum disorder (ASD) is a developmental disability that is lifelong and may cause students to have issues with social communication, social interactions, repetitive behaviors, and repetitive interests (CDC, 2014; Morris, Foster, Parsons, Falkner, Flakner, & Rosalie, 2015). For

CASE STUDY *continued*

Volunteer: "Do you like Powerpuff Girls?"
Juan, looking down at the desk: "No."

The volunteer modeled full sentences to help Juan develop conversational skills so he interacted rather than just asking question after question.

By the middle of the year, after modeling conversational skills, Juan was able to have a conversation with the volunteer:

The volunteer pulled out a blond wig from a brown-grocery bag.

Juan, enthusiastically and reaching with his arms up in the air: "A wig!"
Volunteer: "Yes, my sister bought it after Halloween for 75 percent off."
Juan, very excited about the wig, says: "Please, can I keep it!"
The volunteer smiles. Juan jumps out of his desk.
Volunteer: "What is a wig?"

Juan puts on the wig, his head low to the table. He seems shy, but at the same time likes having the wig on. He is somewhat embarrassed to have the wig on his head, but likes it at the same time.

Juan: "Fake hair."
Volunteer: "That's a good answer. So why do people wear wigs?"
Juan: "Because no one wants to see the hair. They would laugh at them."
Volunteer: "Who wore a wig?"
Juan: "Abraham Lincoln?"
Volunteer: "How about Beethoven? Did you find a picture of Beethoven wearing a wig?" (Juan had read several books about Beethoven with the volunteer.)
Juan: "Yes, he's [Beethoven] with a wig."
Juan: "It is distracting to the kids? I better take it off." His tone of voice shows he is asking a question. Juan removes the wig.

Volunteer: "Yes, it is distracting to the other kids. They are working quietly at their desks."

The following is what Jun wrote about the wig. Juan was working on his comprehension and writing skills.

The Wig
The wig is fake hair.
The wig feels itchy.
The wig can stick in my hair.
People wear wigs when they sing music.

Juan was tested later in the year and the psychologist found him to fall within the autism spectrum for AS. The third-grade teacher and fourth-grade teacher had talked with Juan's parents, who were against having him attend the special-day class in the next year because Juan wanted to go to the fourth grade with his friends. Culturally, Juan's father did not want his son to be part of special education. This is a common issue with some Asian American parents. Juan's mother attempted to talk his father into letting him attend the special-day class.

Juan was not only trilingual but he also had strong artistic talent.

Here is a drawing of himself that he drew during one of the sessions with the volunteer when he did not want to do his seatwork.

The young student drew a picture of himself not wanting to do his homework.

The second drawing below is of Vivaldi, the composer, who Juan read about in his study of musicians. He liked the biography that he read of Vivaldi. Juan often drew cartoons when he finished his work.

The student drew a picture of Vivaldi, the composer.

Before the summer ended and the educational decision was made, Juan and his family moved away. About four years later, his third-grade teacher received an email from Juan; he was happy and in the seventh grade.

Reflection Questions

Q Do you agree with the teacher's decision to use a disabilities studies approach rather than a strict special education one with Juan? Why or why not?

Q What approaches would you use if you were the teacher? How would you have reached Juan?

example, a child who falls within the autism spectrum may lack nonverbal and verbal communication, causing issues such as:

- Little face-to-face interactions with others
- Lack of eye contact with another individual
- Does not share a toy with another
- Does not point in referring to another individual
- Does not gesture in the process of communicating
- Does not readily respond to an adult's interaction (Mundy, Sigman, Ungerer, & Sherman, 1986)

ASD was thought to be an umbrella term for distinct disorders, but at this time all are considered on the same spectrum, including Asperger syndrome (AS) (Robinson, York, Rothenberg, & Bissell, 2015). Individuals who are identified with AS fall within the high end of the autism spectrum. Students with AS are often identified around the age of 11 years; however, interventions can be more effective if AS is addressed when they are younger (Robinson et al., 2015). Students often demonstrate problems in talking with others and are not able to set academic goals. They also may not be able to develop social interactive skills. In addition, they may have heightened sense of touch, sound, and taste and so may react more strongly than their classmates to loud noises (Robinson et al., 2015). For a discussion of a student with Asperger syndrome, see the Case Study called "Trilingual Student Identified with Asperger's Syndrome: Juan."

Advanced Learners

There is no one criterion for students with special gifts and talents. Various researchers and organizations have identified guidelines for assessing students who are advanced learners. Here are some of the characteristics of advanced learners (Tuckman & Monetti, 2013):

- Has high general intellectual abilities
- Uses creative and innovative thinking
- Has leadership abilities
- Is able to solve problems
- Shows high levels of imagination
- Acquires skills without training

How are these abilities assessed? A variety of methods are used by teachers to identify advanced learners (Tuckman & Monetti, 2013), including:

- Intelligence tests
- Comprehensive projects
- Portfolios of materials developed by students
- Nominations from teachers, parents, peers, and/or self
- Participation in extracurricular activities

One of the reasons that the term "gifted" is not used is because definitions of the term may differ among cultures.

Emotional/Behavioral, Intellectual, and Developmental Disabilities

Students come to school with many different types of disabilities. Though learning disabilities are most often addressed in the classroom, there are also students who may have emotional/behavioral, intellectual, and developmental disabilities. Students may also be advanced learners.

Emotional and Behavioral Disabilities

There are students who come to school with emotional and behavioral disabilities. Examples of some behaviors that teachers may see in children are:

- Being irritable
- Fighting with others
- Not telling the truth
- Arguing
- Having temper tantrums
- Yelling
- Not completing their homework and seatwork

These students often demonstrate continual negative behaviors rather than prosocial actions. **Prosocial behaviors** include working collaboratively, following rules, waiting in

Prosocial behaviors include working collaboratively, following rules, waiting in line, and inviting others to participate.

line, and inviting others to participate. These actions are often modeled and taught by teachers. IDEA has also identified criteria for students with emotional disabilities, which include the following elements (Tuckman & Monetti, 2013):

- Unable to learn, but not due to intellectual, sensory, or physical well-being
- Unable to develop interpersonal relationships with others such as peers and teachers
- Exhibit behaviors that are out of place
- May be depressed
- May also develop fears about school and peer problems

Young people are also evaluated based on the number of times they demonstrate negative behaviors.

Students with emotional and behavioral disabilities often do not do well in their academic learning and are more apt to drop out of school (Tuckman & Monetti, 2013). When helping students with these types of disabilities, one of the most effective strategies that teachers can develop is to create strong and trusting relationships with learners. For example, educators can take five minutes to talk with a student with disabilities prior to the start of class so he or she knows that the teacher believes in him or her and will provide the support he or she needs. The teacher can also send home weekly notes to the learner's parents to keep them informed about the student's progress. Students benefit when teachers and parents work collaboratively. In addition, when teachers model positive behaviors and are fair, students often develop more self-control.

Intellectual Disability

Intellectual disability has also been known as mental disability. Like other aspects of exceptionalities, it includes a wide range of abilities (Hardman et al., 2011). Many people believe the term retardation, which was often used in the past, is extremely offensive; therefore for the purpose of this book we will use "intellectual disability." This term may include children who have developmental delays along with those students with severe intellectual disabilities. The criteria for those who are seen as having intellectual disabilities arose

TAKE A STAND   MYTHS ABOUT CHILDREN WITH DOWN SYNDROME

Denis Kuvaev/Shutterstock.com

About 3000 to 5000 children are born with Down syndrome every year. Down syndrome is caused by an extra or part of an extra chromosome. Some teachers hold misconceptions about students with Down syndrome.

Create a plan for a 30-minute teacher training workshop on the misconceptions.

How can you help teachers remedy their lack of knowledge and lose their misconceptions that may serve as obstacles to the articulation of effective instruction for students with Down syndrome?

Myth: Most children with Down syndrome are born to older parents.
Fact: Approximately 80 percent of children with Down syndrome are born to women who are 35 years old and younger.
Myth: Individuals with Down syndrome are severely disabled.

Fact: Most people with Down syndrome are in the moderate range of an intellectual disability. They can learn, and it is not known how extensive their potential can be.
Myth: Most students with Down syndrome must be placed in segregated school settings.
Fact: Many students with Down syndrome function well in general education classrooms. The inclusion of students often depends on the ability of the teacher and the skills of students.
Myth: Adults with Down syndrome are not able to work.
Fact: Many adults with Down syndrome can be found working in banks, corporations, nursing homes, hotels, restaurants, and offices.

TAKE A STAND . . .

▶ **What if you saw another teacher treat a student with Down syndrome in a mean and unjust way? What would you do? Nothing? If you would act, what actions would you take?**

Source: Adaptation of "Myths and Truths about Down Syndrome," Hardman, Drew, & Egan, 2011, p. 239.

out of IDEA and the work of the American Association on Intellectual and Developmental Disabilities (Tuckman et al., 2013):

- Intellectual functioning is below average and children have difficulties in memory retention, learning rate, attention, and competencies to use skills in new settings.
- May have problems with competencies in self-care, home living, academics, work, and free time.
- Inabilities arise during development and maturation prior to becoming 18 years old.
- Different measures are utilized to identify intellectual disabilities. Sometimes children are tested using intelligence tests and/or academic measures to identify this exceptionality.

Developmental Disabilities

Developmental disabilities are chronic mental and physical impairments that keep people from taking care of themselves (Hardman et al., 2011). The term **developmentally disabled** refers to individuals with intellectual or physical impairments that inhibit their ability to take care of themselves and limit their ability to develop conceptual, social, and practical skills. People with developmental disabilities have a lack of skills in conceptual (language, reading, money concepts), social (interpersonal skills, self-responsibility, self-esteem, gullibility), and practical (eating, toileting, dressing, occupational skills, transportation, taking medication, money management) areas (Hardman et al., 2011). Individuals who are not able to care for themselves may have been born with cerebral palsy, spina bifida, Down syndrome, or autism. Teachers can make sure that each student has the opportunity to work with a student partner. Educators can also speak to students at eye level to show their care and support. Learners also may need additional time to finish an assignment. Some learners may need tables and chairs that are created especially for their needs. This furniture will help students to be more comfortable in the classroom. Parents may also have knowledge of what works best for their children. Ask them for suggestions. There are many ways that teachers can make the classroom a more effective environment that encourages inclusion.

> **Developmentally disabled** refers to individuals with intellectual or physical impairments that inhibit their ability to take care of themselves and limit their ability to develop conceptual, social, and practical skills.

Labeling and Stereotyping

> **LO8** Describe how labeling of students can be destructive and lead to increased oppression of learners with disabilities in schools.

Labeling and stereotyping is common in referring to students with disabilities. Teachers should avoid using language to label and exclude people, young and older. In today's diverse classroom, teachers need to treat everyone with respect. One of the most well-known organizations devoted to the needs of students with disabilities is the Council for Exceptional Children. You can access many of their resources at https://www.cec.sped.org/. For example, there are blogs, books, conferences, and teacher training that educators can tap into. There is also the Society for Disability Studies at https://disstudies.org/. This organization also offers publications, books, and conferences. In 2015, a special issue of *Disability Studies Quarterly* was published, which covers the twenty-fifth anniversary of the Americans with Disabilities Act (ADA).

Let's think about what it means to be "typical." In much of the literature on special education, there is an implied view of typical. Some educators use the term "normal" to refer to people who do not have a disability. This would mean those who are of average intelligence and are able-bodied. However, this is an overgeneralized view of life. Language has shaped our political and cultural views of disabilities (Danforth, 2008b).

As described in the Case Study, labeling focuses on deficits or defects (Danforth, 2008a). In fact, some students with hearing losses are treated as intellectually disabled. For example, they may not volunteer in class, but the reason is because they cannot always hear what is going on. Check to see if there are students who consistently do not volunteer to give answers in class. Having a hearing loss might be one of the reasons. We are all complicated beings who represent many cultural characteristics. One student may have Down syndrome and another student may have dyslexia. Labeling often results after the

CASE STUDY

Having Hearing Loss: Elementary Grade

I remember when I was in the fourth grade, the teacher took my class to the auditorium. There were several long tables with headsets on them. A group of eight students would sit down at the table. Then each child put the head set on and waited for the teacher. She told us to raise our hands when we heard a beep.

I slightly opened my eyes so that I could see when my friends raised their hands. I did not hear anything, but I wanted to be like everyone else. I did not want to be seen as any less of a person. I did not want to be thought less of. I wanted to belong.

Holding large group assessments was probably not the best strategy to evaluate our hearing. It would have been harder for me to "cheat" if I had been evaluated independently.

My sisters would tease me when I couldn't hear things as a child. They would yell at me and laugh. Even as we grew older, adult family members would joke about my hearing loss. It is hard on one's self esteem because my siblings would be cross and say mean things like "Huh?????" with sarcasm. Sometimes I would not ask that particular person many questions to avoid these interactions.

Now I have hearing aids, but it took many years before I was willing to come to terms with my hearing. Much of this was due to labeling and poor treatment from others. Hearing impairment as defined by IDEA means that a student's academic performance is negatively affected.

Reflection Questions

Q Why don't others (peers, students, parents) understand when students have trouble hearing and label or say mean things?

Q What are appropriate things to say? Teachers can model positive behaviors and ways to address this disability.

assessment process when students are placed in segregated situations; this can result in lower self-esteem and lower teacher expectations of students. If you are a new teacher and do not know what to do about the issue, ask a seasoned teacher who others respect for advice. Most will be more than willing to provide suggestions.

Research has shown that the special talents label is seen positively by many young people, but most often labels like mentally handicapped or learning disabled have negative attitudes associated with them (Hardman et al., 2011). Labeling also is an overgeneralization of the characteristics of individuals, which can lead to stereotyping and discrimination and the exclusion of students in schools.

The Deficit Viewpoint

Race coupled with disabilities has been used to track and segregate many students of color in special education classrooms (Erevelles & Minear, 2010). Let's look at another example of how a deficit viewpoint can be used as a rationale for exclusion. Danforth (2008b) explains that there is an overrepresentation of African American males and males from low-income families labeled as emotionally/behaviorally disabled. Though African American children make up 17 percent of the school population, over 33 percent have been categorized as "mentally retarded" (Erevelles & Minear, 2010). Danforth contends that there may be political and economic reasons for their active behaviors apart from the individual. Instead of looking at the behaviors of young males in isolation of society, it is imperative for educators to look at how their actions have developed within the political and economic contexts of their lives. Educators tend to blame the children; however, the most critical reasons for inappropriate behaviors may lie within the political space that African American males and poor males find themselves. By refusing to consider the social context, the responsibility of behaviors is moved to individuals and families. They are seen as "less than" and as deficit members of society, so their social and political exclusion is acceptable (Danforth, 2008a and 2008b; Erevelles & Minear, 2010; Siebers, 2008).

Why is labeling so prevalent in schools? Educational services are often provided based on assessments that lead to labeling (Hardman et al., 2011). Teachers and special educators may assess learner language abilities, cognitive competencies, social skills, appropriate classroom behaviors, and subject-area knowledge. Depending on the results, students may be pulled out of class and taken to a "special" class. This practice can result in students' peers developing negative attitudes about learners with disabilities (Hardman et al., 2011). However, federal legislation mandates that careful evaluations are conducted, and these categories do provide for extra services and programs for students too. We are members of a nation that prides itself on social justice and equality. Therefore, it is important for teachers to think about how students with disabilities are taught within schools. For example, because African American students are over represented in special education, it is critical for teachers to review their own biases about student behaviors (Rebora, 2011). Maybe a student may have learned different ways to address conflict that may not be the same as the teacher's (Rebora, 2011). Some children come to school with the view that they must not allow other students to "push them around." This can be a source of conflict within the classroom. The teacher should ask students why they are behaving in a specific manner. This may give an educator a more comprehensive understanding of how a student has been taught to address an issue.

Social justice can be about providing equality of instruction, but what does that mean with regard to the education of students with disabilities? Is it possible to deliver social justice in education to students with disabilities and exceptionalities if the assessed categories are often used to exclude students from regular classrooms? These are complex issues. And within a social justice orientation, it is crucial for teachers to realize that *students are not their disability or exceptionality*. Students are students; they bring a multiplicity of characteristics with them to the classroom—from race, gender, social class, culture, hobbies, families, and interests. Students are much more than their disability. They are human beings who should be respected and cherished.

Differentiated Instruction and Inclusion

Disability studies and special education are fields in education that are dedicated to educating each student in the most effective ways possible. Inclusion refers to the policy of teaching students with disabilities in the regular classroom. At the heart of inclusion is social justice, furnishing effective academic programs for all students (Danforth, 2014, 2015a, 2015b).

One of the approaches developed to address the needs of students in the same classroom with diverse abilities is differentiated instruction. Today inclusion has become a valuable strategy for students with disabilities. Some states are attempting to ensure that students with disabilities spend at least 80 percent of their day in the general classroom (Danforth, 2015b). However, there seem to be many teachers who challenge this orientation because they feel that inclusion has become a top-down directive (Danforth 2015b). **Differentiated instruction** is an approach that can be successfully used in inclusive classrooms; it is the use of diverse instructional strategies so that the needs of various students can be addressed in the same lesson or unit (Hardman et al., 2011). Maybe several students work with only the story problems of a fractions worksheet because they need more practice in logical and verbal thinking. However, others are asked to create additional story problems as they work with the concept of fractions.

Differentiated instruction is addressing the needs of students according to their needs. Instruction does not have to be given to each student in the same way (Thousand, Villa, & Nevin, 2015). Differentiating instruction starts with students are and teachers working to maximize their growth. One strategy is that teachers can plan instruction using Howard Gardner's multiple intelligences. Some students learn more effectively when teachers tap into one or a combination of several multiple intelligences (Thousand et al., 2015). The eight multiple intelligences identified by Gardner are as follows:

1. Verbal/Linguistic: uses language to express oneself and is sensitive to learning when using phrases, jokes, riddles, and rhymes
2. Kinesthetic/Physical: integrates movement, dance, acting, and touch to explain one's viewpoints

> **Differentiated instruction** is the use of diverse instructional strategies so that the needs of various students can be addressed in the same lesson or unit.

3. Logical/Mathematics: uses reasoning, looks for logical patterns, and implements computer skills

4. Visual/Spatial: uses images in one's mind; is sensitive to color, drawings, and photos; may be extremely creative or inventive

5. Musical/Rhythmic: uses rhythm, melody, songs, rhymes, mnemonics, and patterns to learn and express oneself

6. Intrapersonal: prefers to learn alone, has clear personal goals, writes out notes and summarizes information

7. Interpersonal: prefers group learning, shares ideas, and encourages group goals, teaches others, is motivated by group work

8. Naturalist: learns through knowledge of the natural world and can see patterns in nature.

Students come to school with various intelligences. Teachers can use them to effectively reach each student. In differentiated instruction, teachers may have different groups engage in diverse learning activities in order to access their intelligence strengths. Some delivery methods may meet the instructional needs of several intelligences. For example, use of a graphic organizer like a concept map may assist visual, logical, and verbal ability groups.

Another approach to differentiated instruction is for teachers to integrate various levels of Bloom's taxonomy into student instructional behaviors. Table 8.6 lists the levels of Bloom's taxonomy.

Teachers can use both Bloom's taxonomy and Garner's multiple intelligence theory to enhance student instruction. For example, one student may need more time to develop her vocabulary skills and may be asked to write in her personal dictionary vocabulary words, their meanings, and a sentence using the word. The vocabulary may be for a lesson on the U.S. Constitution, rights, freedom, equality, and citizens. She may also be asked to draw a picture of the word if it is a noun or verb that can be visually represented, like the U.S. Constitution. The student is working at the remember level of Bloom's taxonomy and is also accessing her verbal and artistic abilities. Three other students, on the other hand, may be asked to create a play that describes a discussion among George Washington, James Madison, and Benjamin Franklin, signers of the U.S. Constitution, about which rights should be included in the Bill of Rights. This requires the small group to engage in the create level of Bloom's taxonomy along with using their verbal, kinesthetic, and interpersonal abilities. The first student had to develop her level of knowledge about the U.S. document by retrieving and recalling information, while the second group of students engaged in the highest level of Bloom's taxonomy by bringing together information into a play and creating a new product in collaboration with other students. While all the students are in the same classroom, the teacher created different lessons for each student depending on their individual level of knowledge, using different intelligences.

Table 8.6 Levels of Bloom's Taxonomy	
Thinking Category	**Cognitive Process**
Remember	Recall, retrieve, record
Understand	Compare, outline, estimate, exemplify, express
Apply	Organize, demonstrate, illustrate, classify
Analyze	Examine, categorize, contrast, investigate, infer, differentiate
Evaluate	Assess, judge, defend, evaluate, improve
Create	Create, compose, plan, generate, hypothesize

TEACHING TIPS

Strategies to Use with Students with Learning Disabilities

Here are some teaching tips that can be used in your classroom in dealing with students with various abilities as well as students who learn at different rates.

▶ Think about how the classroom could be modified so that students with learning disabilities can be successful in school. For example, if a student has trouble seeing two-dimensional print, allow her to use a felt board where letters can be felt and moved by hand or use computers where the font of letters are made larger or outlined in a darker color so they are easier to distinguish.

▶ Make sure your directions are clear and simple. Have students with disabilities repeat them back to you and the class to ensure un-

derstanding. If the student does not understand, try to explain the directions in different words.

▶ Provide for shorter sections of time for instruction and practice so students will be able to attend to what is being taught. Make instructional adjustments so children will be successful and less frustrated.

▶ Make sure to use examples from students' lives so they can see connections between what is taught and their experiences. Use photos and drawings to give the examples more depth.

Encourage older students to use a planner or organizer for all assignments so they will remember what is due and when. Teach them organization skills like how to list due dates for different subjects on the calendar.

 Professional Resource Download

Consider this . . .
Students with disabilities are not their disability.

Thinking about Intersectionality

The case study about Juan is a good example of how layers of difference can create huge obstacles to providing equity in education due to language diversity, racial diversity, and disabilities. Intersectionality refers to how various aspects of oppression come together and are interrelated. First, Juan was different because he spoke three languages. For some reason the bilingual resource teacher who spoke Spanish and English saw this as a weakness rather than a strength. The resource teacher seemed to have negative feelings about Juan. She would not work with the third-grade teacher in creating an instructional plan for him and would return him to the classroom after 10 minutes rather than work with him for 25 minutes. Juan believed the woman did not like him so he would curl his body into a ball and not respond to her.

Juan also was interracial in that he was Colombian and Japanese American. As an Asian American, it was also more difficult for the third-grade teacher to secure educational services for him. For example, the principal at the school did not think Juan needed extra assistance, and though there are laws about not providing equal education to all students, the process needed to prove this takes much time to document. His physical appearance was Asian. The third-grade teacher fought with the principal to get Juan tested by a school psychologist who identified students with disabilities for the

district. Finally, he gave his approval for the testing. Juan's parents by that time had also agreed also to have a professional make an assessment. Juan later was found to fall within the spectrum for autism with Asperger syndrome.

Juan exhibited some behaviors that were considered "different" such as rocking at his desk and not making eye-to-eye contact during conversations. Though the bilingual resource teacher was extremely negative toward him, his third-grade teacher did not see his behaviors as negative. She accepted Juan and believed that this was just the way he was; she cared for him and enjoyed having him in class. She saw his beautiful smile every morning and was happy he was in her third-grade class. This made a big difference in Juan's life. His third-grade teacher liked him and thought he was smart!

The fields of disability studies and special education differ in the methods that the disciplines suggest. In this case, because Juan's third-grade teacher realized that she needed to have someone work with him early in the year, she was able to get a volunteer teacher who stayed in the classroom. Juan did not want to be taken to another room for an hour a day. He preferred inclusion. The teacher believed that Juan needed to be with his friends in class because while Juan initially had trouble getting to know other students, he had many friends. The teacher made sure the children knew she valued the creation of a caring and respectful classroom family. The students saw that though Juan had learning issues, he also was an exceptional artist and a kind person.

The teacher used differentiated instruction so Juan would be exposed to the same curriculum content as his peers.

Sometimes Juan did do the same work as his classmates, and other times he worked on specific vocabulary of the discipline because he had not learned some abstract discipline content such as what is a rain forest. Unfortunately, Juan was subjected to many levels of prejudice because of his language diversity, special needs, and racial backgrounds.

Summary

1. **Analyze how religious freedom was one of the first core freedoms in the United States and describe the diversity of religious groups.**

   Religious freedom is guaranteed by the First Amendment of the U.S. Constitution. It is the major reason that immigrants from Britain took the harrowing trip across the Atlantic Ocean to start a new life in what is now the United States. There are many different faiths in this country. Religious diversity is an important fabric of this nation. Though Protestants make up the largest religious organization, there are numerous other Christians who comprise this group, such as Mormons, Seventh Day Adventists, and Jehovah's Witnesses. There are also other denominations that include Catholics, Buddhists, Hindus, Jews, and Muslims. In addition, atheists and agnostics are members of the United States. Currently, Islamophobia is one of the most prevalent religious biases in the United States, though Muslim Americans make up less than 1 percent of the population.

2. **Describe how to teach religion in public schools and identify stereotypes about Muslims.**

   Teachers should teach about religion in public schools, but not dogma. Religious freedom should be an issue presented in teacher staff development so that educators know how to address prejudice and discrimination that is found in society and schools. Conflicts have arisen among various religious communities, and teachers should know how to present various viewpoints but also know how to help students sort through them in an objective way.

3. **Challenge bias and prejudices about Muslim American students.**

   Currently, there is a great deal of prejudice about Muslims and Islam following several terrorist attacks. Fear of Muslims is called Islamophobia. There are many misconceptions about Muslims, which has led to the increase of discrimination. For example, Muslim American males are often portrayed in the media as terrorists. The women are also presented as not having equal rights with their husbands, which is not true in many Muslim families. In addition, Muslim Americans have lived as members of U.S. society since Africans were brought to our lands. Therefore, many Muslims are native-born citizens. They are not foreigners. They are not immigrants.

4. **Differentiate among indigenous persons, immigrants, migrants, and refugees and describe how Nativism, global migration, and immigrant students impact the United States.**

   There are differences among immigrants, migrants, refugees, and indigenous people. Immigrants move to another country to live and to establish a new homeland. Migrants are people who move because of economic, religious, and other strife; however, they hope to return to their homeland. Refugees are individuals and groups who willingly or unwillingly cannot return to their home country for fear of prosecution because of race, religion, nationality, political views, or membership in a specific social group. Refugees are also migrants.

5. **Evaluate the challenges that immigrant students face in achieving in schools.**

   Students who migrate to the United States can have an extremely difficult time. They not only often must learn conversational English but also academic English, which is used in schools. Their parents may not speak English and do not understand the educational system in the United States. This makes it challenging for immigrant students because they must find their own way through schooling. When students graduate from high school, they may want to go to college but their parents may not feel comfortable for the young people to move away and live far from home. This is a common cultural conflict that college applicants must face. Many immigrant students have high hopes of the American dream, but it can be a struggle to balance family values and personal goals.

6. **Compare disability studies with special education within the context of ableism.**

   Ableism is the systematic exclusion and discrimination against people with physical, intellectual, or developmental disabilities. There are two different fields in education that address the needs of people with disabilities. First is disability studies; second is special education. Disability studies uses a social model in which people with disabilities are seen as members of an underrepresented group like those with racial differences seeking equality. Special education is a medical model in which students are in need of interventions in order to address their differences.

7. **Explain how traditional special education groups students into various categories based on their disabilities and exceptionalities.**

   In traditional special education, there are numerous categories in which students with disabilities are placed. The groupings are based on developmental, physical, and intellectual disabilities. One of the groupings is Autism spectrum disorder where students may have social communication and social interaction limitations. Differentiated instruction is an approach used by teachers for the inclusion of all students in the regular classroom.

8. Describe how labeling of students can be destructive and lead to increased oppression of learners with disabilities in schools.

Labeling of students with disabilities is a difficult issue in schools. Teachers want to address the needs of students with disabilities. However, the segregation of students into special education classes can give the message that a child is not "typical." This occurred in the case study of Juan. Though he had many skills, such as the ability to speak three languages, Juan became defined by his disability. Terms change over time. For example many educators prefer the use of the term "exceptionalities" to identify students with disabilities or special talents.

Check Your Cultural Knowledge

Reflective Essay Questions

In this chapter, discrimination based on religion, immigrant status, and disabilities is discussed. Identify five ways in which prejudices in these areas are similar and jeopardize our democracy.

Does our Bill of Rights protect citizens from prejudice and discrimination in schools? Why or why not? What evidence can you share to support your point of view?

What strategies would you use in your classroom to eliminate bias due to religion, immigrant status, and/or disabilities/exceptionalities? How would you get your students to work together to support each other? Remember that it takes time to build caring and collaborative communities of learners. This must start on the first day of school. You are the most important model of this orientation.

Application

Know and Go Tools in the Classroom

Many teachers believe in inclusion, where students with disabilities are included and taught in the regular classroom. Many students do not want to be separated from their classmates and pulled out every day to go to another room for interventions. Therefore, many teachers use differentiation to make sure every child is included in the instruction of the classroom.

What would you do?

Suggestions for Classrooms

1. As discussed in this chapter, universal design for learning is one way to incorporate strategies so that students with various learning disabilities are able to stay in the classroom and are not pulled out. Students may enjoy listening to a story that has been recorded by the teacher on the computer. In this way, if a learner needs to work on comprehension, he or she can review the materials more than once.

2. In your teaching, you can give whole-class short presentations that include a lot of visuals, such as maps, photos, and graphs, along with verbal discussion. In this way, you will address several student modalities in your lesson.

3. Start your lesson with concrete examples. If you are teaching about grouping in math, use objects such as blocks, stuffed animals, or pencils. Then later move to abstract representations.

Older students may have developed negative views about themselves and school because of continuous failures. Find out what the students are good at and then ask them to help you to solve a problem. For example, maybe a student is great at using the computer. Ask for his or her help when the computer is stuck or PowerPoint is not working. That student can become the computer consultant. This can help you, and it gives a student an important role in the classroom. Hurray!

PeopleImages.com/DigitalVision/Getty Images

Prejudice and Bullying

Learning Objectives

LO1 Explain how most people have prejudices against others based on social categories such as race, ethnicity, gender, age, class, religion, sexual orientation, exceptionalities, language spoken, and/or appearance.

LO2 Define the stages of prejudice development and levels of prejudice that can be found in society, schools, and individuals.

LO3 Assess how White privilege has been used to keep the dominant group in power.

LO4 Evaluate what bullying is and why it occurs.

LO5 Suggest ways that teachers can move students from ethnocentrism to working together to eliminate prejudice and bullying.

STANDARDS COVERED

NAEYC 1, 5, 6
naeyc

CAEP 1

National School
Climate Standards
1, 2, 3, 4, 5 NSCS

INTASC 1, 2, 3, 4,
5, 6, 7, 8, 9, 10
InTASC

Hidden Hurdles of Prejudice

Most people experience hidden hurdles. Individuals and groups of people hold biases about financial status, languages, accents, gender, age, class, religion, sexual orientation, disabilities, body shapes, height, and many other aspects of life. Their beliefs may act as barriers to making connections with other people. Do your beliefs influence the way you interact with or see others? Personal biases may act as barriers to your caring for others. Looking at oneself can be difficult, but it is part of our own development and of creating more authentic and trusting relationships with others (Figure 9.1). Teachers, especially, must review their biases as important elements of the ethic of care and education for democracy, theories presented in Chapter 1.

If, as you begin to "unpack" your own biases, guilt creeps in, move it aside; guilt is not an effective motivator. Rather, most people need a chance to think about their own prejudices that are due to ethnicity, age, or gender in order to purge them from their minds. They must consider the person they heard these stereotypes or biases from and if the information is accurate. Reflection about the biases is important because most people do not realize they have them. It is not as easy as removing old software from a computer. Getting rid of personal prejudice takes hard work because one must challenge oneself. Caring teachers persist at being open-minded and refrain from labeling others. As one teacher put it, "Biases are hurtful."

We are all connected in many ways; when one of us succeeds, in a way we all succeed. The opposite is also true: when a person is treated unfairly, in a way we are all being treated that way because the act and intention to exclude one person can jeopardize the building of compassion, respect, and equality in our community. The field of multicultural education holds the long-term aim of creating a caring society that affirms cultural diversity, and emphasizes our common values of democracy, justice, equality, and freedom. Martin Luther King, Jr. believed that we all are connected and to create a strong community based on equality we must work together.

If you are like many teachers, you may think the most important task in learning about multicultural education is to understand more about the cultural customs, holidays, and

Figure 9.1: We all have personal biases such as those in relation to financial status and/or appearance. We must work hard to identify and eliminate them from our minds.

history of your diverse students. Yes, educators need cultural knowledge. However, the biggest hurdle many teachers face is to challenge and rid themselves of personal biases and prejudices and to view others with new eyes. This can be a painful and lifelong process, and it is helpful when we support each other through this undertaking. When asked about the obstacles they must address, a couple of teachers acknowledged the need to look at their own attitudes, and responded as follows:

- "How can I go into a classroom and not just give my narrow-minded White perspective on subjects?"
- "I want to limit my prejudices and biases."

Everyone has unconscious hurdles or prejudices. For example, many people may have been conditioned by society over years to see others as either "we" or "they." For teachers, these hurdles can act as obstacles to seeing the ability of some students. It can take numerous years to understand how a person's biases have worked as powerful filters that shape the information she or he gathers about others every day. It is hard work to recognize one's biases; no one wants to think she or he is a prejudiced person.

Most of us have been influenced by cues and messages we received growing up, from friends, parents, siblings, aunts, uncles, grandparents, family friends, and others. This is part of how we learn about our culture. However, today, besides people in our family and neighborhood, another influential force is the media, especially television. If you were a child who watched a lot of television, by the time you entered school, you probably watched as many hours of television as it takes to get a four-year college degree. The messages you saw on television were continual, visual, and uncensored. While some of the messages were helpful, other messages should probably have been talked about with an older adult who could have explained the context behind the message. On the computer, for example, we can easily use the delete key and, in less than a second, those thoughts and ideas are gone. Unfortunately, it isn't as easy to delete beliefs and attitudes from our minds as it is to erase words from a computer document.

You may believe that you are not a prejudiced person because you are fair and have strong morals; this may be very true. You probably didn't decide to get an education degree or be a teacher in order to make money—most people know that teachers do not make megabucks. Rather, you are most likely an educator, or want to become one, because you are committed to making a difference in young people's minds. As a society, we need you! Yet, ethnic and cultural prejudices are often carefully hidden in the nooks and crannies of our minds, and you may hold some attitudes that could limit how you view your students. The truth is that many education students, as well as practicing teachers, take multicultural education classes believing that they do not need any instruction in personal biases because they are not prejudiced (Stephan, 1999; Dessel, 2010; Nelson & Pang, 2013).

Biases Are Like Weeds

Biases and prejudicial attitudes often have deep roots similar to weeds. If you cut off the top portion of the weed and leave several tiny roots, there's a possibility that the weed will sprout again (Figure 9.2). People are socialized by society, and most have heard stereotypical comments, seen stereotypical images, and have probably taken on stereotypical beliefs about others. In our society there are many examples of stereotypes. African American males are often seen as athletic and therefore expected to be great football and basketball players, while some stereotypes are harsh, like when people call children from European American families who have little money "poor White trash." Because of this type of label, others assume students with parents who are low income can't read well and aren't motivated.

Figure 9.2: Prejudice is like weeds such as these dandelions. Even when the surface aspects of bias have been eliminated, there are still deep roots to address and get rid of. Prejudice reduction takes time and much effort.

Business people with a great deal of money are viewed as greedy and selfish. Asian American, Pacific Islander American, and Mexican American women are often seen as weak and subservient rather than competent leaders. Native Americans are stereotyped as people who live on reservations, although most Native Americans live in cities. Women are sometimes portrayed as emotional rather than logical, and men are seen as macho instead of gentle. The list could go on and on!

How do prejudices look in society? On a television news program in 1991, ABC's *Primetime*, a news team conducted an experiment in which they sent out two men, one African American and one European American, into the community. Both had comparable bachelor's degrees in business; in fact, they were college buddies. First, the men went out to buy a car. Although both men showed interest in the same car, the African American man was quoted a price several hundred dollars higher than his White friend. The two were sure that this was just an isolated incident of prejudice, so they found an ad for an apartment and called on its owner. The European American male went to see an apartment and was given the keys to the apartment and the master key so he could look at the dwelling. Next, the African American male went to the same person renting the apartment and was told that all the apartments were already rented. The manager told the European American that an apartment was available and could be rented on the spot. The news team had a television camera and filmed each incident. When the experiences of the two were compared, it was sadly obvious that the Black male faced a great deal of discrimination. The two friends were shocked by their experiences because the year was 1991—more than 25 years since the Civil Rights Acts of 1964 had been passed.

Another experiment was shown in 2009 on the ABC program, *What Would You Do?* John Quinones, the reporter, hired three young White male actors around 14–15 years old to vandalize a car in a park that was located in a White neighborhood. In the several hours that ABC filmed the young people jumping on the car, spray painting it, hitting the car with large tools, and using a large piece of metal in the window trying to get into the car, only one person called the police. Most people, many who were taking walks in the park, did not say anything to the young men and ignored what was happening. However, then John Quinones had three young Black male actors around 14–15 years old do the same thing. During the same amount of time, 10 calls were made to the police. There was much more willingness to treat the young people as "outsiders" and to call the authorities. What would you have done?

Do you think if these experiments were conducted today the results would be different? How much progress do you think we have made as a society toward breaking down prejudice and stereotypes since the Civil Rights Acts of 1964?

Prejudice Development

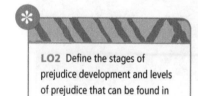

Prejudice is not always easy to detect or understand. When prejudicial attitudes are all around, we may not notice the negative beliefs about others. Prejudice may be hard to see unless it is directed at you. In the *Primetime* example, the White American male was shocked when he viewed the videos showing the high levels of prejudice aimed at his friend. The African American male knew that racial discrimination still occurs, but he was also surprised at how much he encountered in such a short time. The people who would not rent to the African American male had no apparent reason to reject him. He had the same qualifications as his friend. It was clear they were reacting to his physical and perceived racial differences.

Sociologist Gordon Allport defined **prejudice** as a feeling, favorable or unfavorable, toward a person or thing prior to, and not based on, actual experience (Allport, 1954). Allport believed that most ethnic prejudice is primarily negative. Why? When people use

LO2 Define the stages of prejudice development and levels of prejudice that can be found in society, schools, and individuals.

Prejudice is a feeling, favorable or unfavorable, toward a person or thing prior to, and not based on, actual experience.

over generalizations in looking at others, they do not see the real person. For example, let's say that someone meets you for the first time at a school board meeting. During the course of the meeting, you provide excellent reasons why a new math series should be adopted. You answer questions professionally and effectively. Unfortunately, by the end of the meeting, that person maintains that since you are a female and a kindergarten teacher, he or she is unsure of your professional judgment.

A prejudiced person will use selective memory in her or his judgment and continue to hold on to overgeneralizations about members of a group (Stephan, 1999; Mio, Barker, & Rodriguez, 2016). Prejudice can act as a filter that prejudges people and can cause us to hear or see only the information that reinforces what we already believe about others in a category. Our minds automatically use categories to sort the millions of pieces of information that we take in every day.

Allport believed that an individual can prejudge a person without being prejudiced when he or she is open to new information about a group or person. However, ethnic and cultural prejudices are often difficult to get rid of and can contribute to the inequitable treatment of people. Allport defined **ethnic prejudice** as hostility based upon a faulty and inflexible generalization. It may be felt or expressed. It may be directed toward a group as a whole or toward an individual because he or she is a member of that group (Allport, 1954). (See Figure 9.3.)

> **Ethnic prejudice** is hostility based upon a faulty and inflexible generalization. It may be felt or expressed. It may be directed toward a group as a whole or toward an individual because he or she is a member of that group

Prejudice and Bullying: Levels of Prejudice

Allport believed that there are various stages when children develop prejudice and when it becomes permanent. Assess Table 9.1 and think about how you may see students in your classes forming prejudices and how their behavior shows the level of their biases.

As you read through the table, think of how all of these types of behaviors are also linked to bullying. Often a victim is targeted because the person is perceived as being different. Many times teachers do not realize that prejudice is often a core ingredient in bullying. The perpetrator may see someone as being weaker, atypical, uncommon, unusual, or a threat

Figure 9.3: Prejudice based on categories such as race, culture, gender, and age can lead to hurtful and damaging injustices.

Table 9.1 Gordon Allport's Five Levels of Prejudice	
Level of Prejudice	**Description**
1. Antilocution	Negative comments made about someone in private conversations that reinforces the "our group" and/or "those people" orientation.
2. Avoidance	Avoiding a person or group of people because of a social category. People make comments such as, "Don't play with 'those' people."
3. Discrimination	Treating someone unfairly or inequitably because of a social category.
4. Physical Attack	Prejudice turns into aggressive physical behavior. Organized institutions like the Ku Klux Klan may actively lobby, write, and organize events that are aimed at discriminating against people of color.
5. Genocide	Most extreme form of prejudice is genocide, or extermination. This is the elimination of a people. This has happened in the Holocaust and destruction of Native American tribes. Contemporary examples have occurred in Cambodia, Iraq, Rwanda, and Bosnia.

and so targets that person. The perpetrator then avoids, spreads rumors, discriminates, excludes, or hits the targeted victim. One of the goals may be to make the student so uncomfortable and threatened that the victim feels he or she must move to another school. In the most extreme case, a student may feel hopeless and attempt suicide. This is similar to the Allport level of genocide. The victim feels driven enough to act in drastic ways. According to Bullying Statistics (www.bullyingstatistics.org), an organization devoted to the elimination of bullying, bullied victims are two to nine times more likely to attempt suicide. More than 14 percent of high school students have thought about committing suicide. Prejudice results in extremely damaging circumstances that perpetrators often do not consider. Teachers must stop bullying immediately when they see it in their classroom or school. Our schools are supposed to be places of equality, respect, and community.

Stereotypes: Forms of Bias

Many people realize that stereotypes can be harmful, but it is difficult to be aware of one's own stereotypical thoughts (Stephan, 1999; Mio et al., 2016). Let's say you are driving down the freeway and a blue car cuts you off. Immediately a thought comes to your mind, "Those women drivers!" However, what if you are woman and have studied sexism and know there are numerous stereotypes about females in society? Oftentimes it is easy to fall back into old patterns of thinking, even if you have worked to rid yourself of stereotypes about women (Stephen, 1999). Labeling all women is overgeneralizing. Gordon Allport

Consider this . . .

Many teachers believe all Asian American students are good in math, and that may come from a stereotype about Asian Americans. However, there are Asian American students who are not good at mathematics, but their teachers expect them to excel. They, like other students, may need extra help.

In addition, many Asian American children are pushed by parents, teachers, and even themselves toward math, science, and computer careers. Yet they may be more interested in careers in drama, politics, or law enforcement. Sometimes students feel the burden of fitting the stereotype of Asian Americans (Pang, Han, & Pang, 2011), as do students in other groups.

Q How can stereotypes which seem positive hurt students? Can you come up with another example?

would say that the driver held "a fixed idea." He defined a **stereotype** as a favorable or unfavorable exaggerated belief associated with a category whose function is to defend a person's conduct as it relates to the category (Allport, 1954). A stereotype is an untrue, fixed picture or idea or an inaccurate caricature that has a value judgment attached to it (Ormrod, 2013; Mio et al., 2016). For example, the woman driver stereotype promotes the belief that all women are incompetent drivers who can't be expected to drive carefully and correctly. Stereotypes are used as a screening measure in accepting or rejecting a person or group. Many stereotypes are based on a variety of reasons such as:

- Fear of the group
- Lack of knowledge of the group
- Differences in beliefs and practices
- Misconceptions

Stereotypes are destructive because these overgeneralized images act as filters about how a person views others based on group membership. Most of us belong to various groups that may hold stereotypes about other groups. We all need to continue to challenge our perceptions of others throughout life and remember that groups are comprised of individuals who may be extremely different from each other.

Discrimination Hurts!

Prejudice often results in **discrimination**. Discrimination is characterized as being excluded because of one's group membership; this often means not being treated equally. How does it feel when someone discriminates against you? What impact does it have on you? Unfortunately, students are also discriminated against, and it makes them feel bad.

Most of us have felt hurt, frustration, embarrassment, humiliation, and anger over discrimination, whether we are Irish, Muckleshoot, African American, Filipino American, Cuban American, or Swedish. Discrimination not only hurts but can also be deadly. After the terrorist attack of September 11, 2001, hate crimes directed toward Arab Americans and other Middle Eastern Americans increased. Many people and students were called "rag heads" or "dot heads." Clergy at mosques received threatening telephone calls and messages. This continues today as new terrorist attacks have occurred in places like Paris, France; San Bernardino, California; and Orlando, Florida. Though terrorism is more than discrimination because it involves violence with a political goal, the root of many acts of terrorism is prejudice and genocide. Prejudice is harmful because it leads to discrimination and more serious acts such as physical violence and extermination.

Teachers have also felt discrimination. Many teachers are from a variety of cultural communities and have been hurt by prejudicial comments or discriminatory actions within the institutions that they work. It is important that educators and other service providers understand the pain and destructive nature of discrimination to more fully understand how difficult it is for children in classrooms to cope with discrimination.

Prejudice can severely harm the spirit and self-image of a person. It is especially important for teachers to examine the force of their own and others' prejudice and discrimination because these influences can limit our ability to create caring relationships in classrooms and schools. Educators often witness students being excluded either on the playground, in the classroom, or in the cafeteria. They see the hurt and loneliness that exclusion creates. When teachers and students discuss their experiences in small groups, they begin to understand each other more fully and, through dialogue, build bridges with others. This is a vital discussion that must be undertaken especially as our nation grapples with issues of racism.

These discussions often help to establish compassion within themselves and others. In addition, all teachers, pre-service and in-service, need to gain a better understanding of how **individual racism**, **institutional racism**, and **cultural racism** can shape the experiences of people of color. Many people do not believe acts of discrimination

Stereotype is defined as a favorable or unfavorable exaggerated belief associated with a category whose function is to defend a person's conduct as it relates to the category.

Discrimination is characterized as being excluded because of one's group membership; this often means not being treated equally.

Individual racism refers to the attitudes, beliefs, and behaviors of someone who believes that she or he is superior to another because of her or his race.
Institutional racism is a system of legalized privileges, practices, and penalties designed to keep the dominant group in power.
Cultural racism refers to beliefs found within a community that perceives elements of another group's culture as being inferior.

CASE STUDY | Institutional, Cultural, and Individual Prejudice

Krystal Rodriguez, Mexican American Female

There have been many times in which I have felt discrimination. . . . People would verbally tell me such things as, "Are you sure you're in the right place? You look like you don't belong here." But the words and the looks did not hurt as much as my fourth grade teacher did . . . In the fourth grade, my teacher was Mrs. McGeorge (pseudonym). I will never forget her name. The very first day I started to notice things about her that I never noticed about other teachers. I started to notice that she spoke to the White students with a softer tone and with more passion. She spoke to the rest of us in a voice that was sterner. The first day she also put the class into reading groups. There were three reading groups: The robins, the blue jays, and the black birds. Everyone wanted to be in the robin group because we all knew that they were the group

that could read the best and that the black birds were the "dumb" group. As Mrs. McGeorge was placing people into the groups, I remember thinking that my third grade teacher said I read very well for a third grader so I knew that I was at least going to go into the blue jays. But I was wrong. I was placed into the black birds.

The next day it was reading time, so the class had to separate into their reading groups. As I was in my reading group, I remember looking around at all three reading groups. That is when I noticed something else. The robins were all White. The blue jays had two minorities and the rest were White. And the black birds were all minorities.

Even though I noticed many things that year, I just thought that that was the way it was supposed to be. I never questioned the teacher or told anyone about the things I noticed. . . . It was time again, in the fifth grade, to get put into our reading groups. Most of the same students that

were in my fourth grade class were now in my fifth grade class, so the teacher just had us go into the same groups. . . . The teacher heard me read. After we were finished the teacher came up to several students in our group, including myself, and told us that she did not know why we were put in the lower group. We read very well. I was then moved up to the robins.

Ronnie Daniels, African American Female

I am a woman, Black, short in stature, thick in build, with kinky hair. I began my life in a small diverse California city, but as I neared the age of eleven, my family and I migrated to a small town in the Mojave Desert . . . There are people of a variety of ethnicities such as Hispanic, African American, and Asian, but they are still in the minority. I attended both private and public schools during my years in the desert, and I was often the only or one of the few African Americans in

are isolated events. These discussions also assist teachers from underrepresented groups because they often do not realize that White Americans also have been targets of prejudice (Figure 9.4).

As discussions progress, new and experienced educators begin to become aware of the negative impact prejudice can have on the self-esteem and the aspirations of their

Figure 9.4: Discrimination can be aimed at anyone no matter their cultural background.

wavebreakmedia/Shutterstock.com

CASE STUDY *continued*

my classes. By this point in my life, race was a well-known factor to me, and I also knew that I was considered to be a minority. . . . I was never taught to be anyone other than myself, which in a large sense is Black.

About two weeks ago, my friend K and I were sitting in the living room with a mutual friend. During our conversation, she told me that I was not "Black." I was not majorly affected by it because it came from a friend, but what did she mean by saying that I'm not Black? She told me that I was not really Black. I suppose she meant to say that I was not "ghetto" or like the "other Black" people she sees on campus because I express my Blackness and my culture to her quite often.

How did she discriminate against me if she was not truly harsh? She discriminated against me because she put Blackness in a small little category and she excluded me from it. By doing this she is claiming that I do not know my culture, that I do not accept my culture, or

that I have no part of my culture. Could this be true? No. I believe that she made this judgment based on clothing, hairstyles, and other outward appearances. She knows that I grew up with horses and off-road vehicles, which in California is typically termed as White.

Due to the color of my skin I was separated. I had to read the words "GO BACK TO AFRICA NIGGERS" spray painted on the walls of my high school cafeteria one morning. In addition, I had to endure racial jokes at our local public pool, and I had to realize as I grew up that no one looked quite like me in many of my classrooms . . . As I mentioned before, my home life was very Afro-centric . . . It is sad that I am considered to be non-Black because of my interests and hobbies.

Patty Mason, Middle Eastern American Female

I am Muslim and so are all of the members of my family. I have light skin and do not wear a hijab (veil or head covering). However my sister wears a hijab every place she goes. What I notice is

that at the airport, I place my small suitcase onto the TSA rubber belt and my things are quickly screened. Then I walk through the security gate without any problems. However, my sister who wears a hijab is always stopped and searched. I do not know how they can say that people are randomly searched when she is searched every time she goes through the security checkpoint on her way to the airplane. I believe that she is being targeted because of our religion. I do not think it is right.

These case studies may represent more than one type of racism. Take some time to think about the judgment questions below.

Reflection Questions

Q Which case study is about institutional racism? Why?

Q Which case study is about individual racism? Why?

Q Which case study is about cultural racism? Why?

students. They gain more understandings of how the commitment to care for children includes knowing how prejudice and discrimination develop and become part of our everyday lives.

Why Do People Discriminate or Bully?

There are many different reasons why people discriminate against or bully each other, as presented in the Case Study. Here are some reasons:

1. Peer acceptance
2. To secure prestige with peers
3. To secure a high status in a peer group
4. To feel superior
5. To be accepted in a particular group
6. To be seen as popular
7. To scare or intimidate another person
8. To make another person feel inferior
9. To strike out at others because of shame and/or guilt
10. Is ignorant or given erroneous information
11. To have social control and dominance

Many of the teacher examples show how discrimination can be found in school. Prejudice and discrimination can be as destructive to a 10-year-old fifth grader as to a 70-year-old grandfather because they may question themselves. Thoughts like "What's wrong with me?" and "Why don't people like me?" may surface. Yet people may not realize that discrimination says more about the oppressor than the victim. A former principal, Mako Nakagawa, reminds teachers, "When a person points a finger at you, she has three fingers and her thumb pointing back at herself." In many cases, the person who is oppressing someone else is trying to create a separation and show he or she is superior (Daniels & Kitano, 1970).

Blaming the Victim

As previously discussed, people can be treated unfairly for many reasons. First, we may have been taught that people from another group are not as capable or as good as people in "our" group. The "our" group represents an ingroup affiliation and a sense of belonging. As members of specific ingroups, we may learn that to be part of this group, we are expected to think of other groups unfavorably. People who are members of the outgroup are often seen as less desirable. When people feel insecure about themselves, they may want to believe that their way of doing something is the one right way. Believing that others are not as smart or virtuous may make one feel better, but it is often a hollow feeling that comes from putting others down without reason.

Another example of discrimination is **scapegoating**. This involves shifting the blame for a problem to a victim or targeted group. I have heard comments such as, "All those Mexicans are taking our jobs" or "Our economy is so bad here in the United States because those Japanese are flooding the market with cheap cars." These are examples of scapegoating.

Scapegoating is shifting the blame of a problem to a victim

Historically there have been numerous examples of scapegoating all over the world. Prior to and during World War II, the Nazis continually condemned the Jewish community. The Jews were used as scapegoats for the economic and political problems in Germany. Another group that has been used as a scapegoat in the United States is Native Americans. Many people have grown up believing Native Americans were obstacles to progress during the early years of this nation. People do not see that Native Americans were victims of our nation's belief in Manifest Destiny; their land was taken away and their way of life was destroyed as settlers moved westward. Also Manifest Destiny was a movement that advanced the interests of the elite, especially large land speculators and owners. This was in contrast to common settlers who wanted to coexist with Native Americans.

Blaming the victim is a societal strategy that has been commonly used against people of color, women, poor Americans, and other disenfranchised groups (Ryan, 1976; King, 1991; Sleeter, 1994; Thornberg, 2015). Children who come from poor or low-income families have often been blamed for mediocre achievement in schools. Educators can be heard saying, "Those [poor] parents don't care about their kids. I know they don't care because they never come to parent–teacher conferences. I call parents and they are never home. Heaven knows where they are while their kids are roaming the streets. Those kids come to school speaking Spanish or Black dialect and they don't have any manners. I think it is horrible that we have to put up with these kids." Comments like this one show that this teacher has a strong underlying prejudicial attitude against children who do not speak Standard English or who live in a low income household.

Students who bully others often scapegoat their victims. They make up excuses that the victims were targeted because they are not as smart, they are Black, they are poor, they do not have friends, they have big teeth, and many more reasons. Bullies often will blame the victim for their aggressive and unwanted threatening behaviors.

When teachers blame the victim, they are engaging in a complex psychological system of beliefs (Ryan, 1976; Thornberg, 2015). Prejudice represents a complicated social and personal phenomenon because it includes personal and group values. Robert Thornberg (2015), an educational researcher in bullying and social psychology, found that students will create a negative portrait of someone based upon their differences and focus on dehumanizing them. In this process, the victim may also become to believe the harmful views that others project on him or her.

Ryan and Thornberg think that many prejudiced people hold conflicting beliefs. For example educators may blame students based on the beliefs of their own group membership's philosophy, but as individuals they also want to make a difference in the lives of their learners. These teachers are aware that racism and poverty are barriers in the lives of many students. And they realize that categories such as race, class, gender, exceptionalities, sexual orientation, religious discrimination, age, culture, and language have been used to discriminate against or

TEACHING TIPS

Teaching Definitions: Prejudice and Stereotypes

It is often difficult to explain to students, especially young students, what words such as prejudice and stereotypes mean. Most teachers do not realize they must have definitions ready to share when they discuss these issues. Often children may not be able to provide definitions themselves.

Read through the chart below. Notice how the definitions become more abstract the older the student. This chart will help with teaching English language learners too because it provides progressively more complicated definitions and will add to their vocabulary development.

Classroom Discussions: Possible Definitions for the Terms Prejudice and Stereotype		
Term	**Prejudice**	**Stereotype**
Grades K–3	• Not liking something different just because it's different from what you're used to. • Having bad feelings about someone based on what you've been told by others. • Disliking someone without knowing him or her.	• A wrong idea of a person based on what a person thinks of a whole group. • A negative picture based on one bad experience.
Grades 4–6	• To think people are a certain way before you know them. • To treat others unfairly because of their appearance or beliefs.	• False image of someone not based on experience with the person. • An overgeneralization.
Middle School	• A feeling about someone or something before you know anything about him or her or it. • To prejudge a person, place, or thing.	• Categorization of people based on appearance. • Labeling a person based on a generalization.
High School	• A preconceived judgment without prior knowledge of the person or thing. • An unfounded belief about someone before any actual experience with him or her. • Untrue picture of a person or a group.	• Overgeneralized opinion held about another person, group, or its values. • Oversimplified, standardized image held about a person or a group.

Another way to allow students to develop a comprehensive understanding of concepts such as prejudice and stereotypes is to have them list similes. A simile shows a comparison between two different things using the words "as" or "like." Oftentimes this activity can provide students with more examples. Take a look at the chart below; similes are listed that teachers have suggested. Some examples are better than others. Can you come up with definitions for the younger grades that are more accurate and easier to understand than what are listed in the two columns?

Similes: Prejudice, Stereotypes, Stereotyping	
Prejudice	**Stereotypes, Stereotyping**
• Prejudice is like a filter that prejudges people. • Prejudice is like having tunnel vision. • Prejudice is like judging a book by its cover.	• A stereotype is like a trap. • A stereotype is like a straitjacket. • Stereotyping is like finding one rotten apple and assuming the whole bushel is rotten.

exclude African Americans, Asian American/Pacific Islander Americans, Native Americans, Latinos, women, White Americans, and those living in poverty. These reflective but conflicted teachers may find themselves with a dilemma. In the words of an old Yiddish proverb, they are trying to dance at two weddings. They are old friends of both brides and fond of both kinds of dancing, and they want to accept both invitations. They cannot bring themselves to challenge the system that has been so good to them, but they want so badly to be helpful to the victims of racism and economic injustice (Ryan, 1976, p. 27). These issues of equity are difficult ethical ones and are not easily solved.

How Children Learn Prejudicial Attitudes: From Parents and Others

Many people learn prejudice toward others as they are growing up. Robert Coles, a child psychiatrist, found in his research that many children were aware of racial differences as young as two or three years old. In interviews with first- and second-grade children, Coles also discovered that children were extremely aware of class differences. Although adults may believe children do not know much about social class, gender, and race, the fact is that children have learned that these things should not be talked about because they are embarrassing matters (Teaching Tolerance, 1992). Coles discovered that children were very savvy about how people are treated differentially because of race and class. A teacher relayed a story about his young neighbor. He was in the yard talking with a White mother and her child, who was almost three years old. An African American child who lived several houses away asked to play with the younger child. The mother politely said, "She needs to take her nap now, so she won't be able to play." When the mother took her daughter inside to the porch, her tone changed dramatically. She said harshly, "I don't want you playing with any of those ugly children. Don't let me catch you with them." The young daughter's eyes opened wide as she carefully listened to her mother. The little girl didn't say anything. The teacher, who overheard the conversation, was shocked by the comments of his neighbor. He couldn't believe what he had heard. He knew that this young person could grow up thinking negatively about African Americans.

Here is another example. A Japanese American young woman was dating a Latino. Her parents never said anything directly to oppose the young man; however, one summer her parents suggested that she go to cultural activities at the Buddhist church. The young woman asked, "Why do you want me to go with you?" Her father said, "I want you to learn about Buddhism and Japanese American history. It will be a wonderful experience." He paused, then said, "You might find another boyfriend too, one who is more like you." Prejudice can be taught by people whom we trust and care for; some may be members of our family.

TAKE A STAND BOYS WILL BE BOYS

You are a teacher at Washington Middle School. When you have hall duty, you notice that one student is pushing a taller student against a locker. The shorter student yells, "You're Jewish and I know some Skinheads. They are going to bomb your house. Get out of my way." You go over and stop the bullying. The two students go to class.

As part of your hall duties, you note the altercation. You also tell the principal that the shorter boy continues to push the taller boy against a locker.

When you bring up the incidents again to the principal, she says, "Boys will be boys. The shorter kid will grow out of it and the other student will learn to stand up for himself."

TAKE A STAND...

▶ **What should you do? Should you do nothing? If so, why?**

▶ **If you choose to do something, what will it be and why?**

Children Learn about Others by Learning about Themselves

Children begin to make sense of the world by understanding themselves first. They know their names and who are members of their family. Later they begin to distinguish that those who are uncles, aunts, and cousins are relatives, while neighbors and others are friends. Children also show fear of strangers at about six to nine months of age (Allport, 1954). These strangers may wear different colored clothes or talk to children in an unfamiliar way. As children grow, they develop a sense of who they are while they are learning prejudicial attitudes from their environment. As children come into contact with others, they learn about people and make generalizations about life. Gordon Allport (1954) believes that children adopt the prejudices of others and develop prejudices as part of their life experiences. When children adopt prejudices, they are accepting and taking in the attitudes and stereotypes of the important or immediate people in their lives.

Children learn who they are as they learn who they are not. It is important to remember that prejudice and identity formation are integrally linked. The prejudice children learn may be due to physical characteristics, ethnicity, culture, class, gender, language, exceptionalities, and other social categories. Many children develop other ideas of who they are, and this involves the integration of a cultural or ethnic identity, religious identity, national identity, and family identity. These are complex constructs, yet they are often developing simultaneously. Children try to figure out where they fit in with their families, as persons with particular physical characteristics, as members of a family that has ties with an ancestral country other than the United States, and as members of a nation called the United States.

Allport believes that children who grow up in a highly authoritarian and disciplined family are sensitive to the approval and disapproval of their parents. Oftentimes, they are taught that authority and power, rather than trust and care, are key aspects of interpersonal relationships. Allport believes that children who are brought up in these types of family environments are more likely to be fearful or suspicious of others. If children are criticized a great deal, they will develop personalities that are more critical of others (Sleeter & Grant, 1987). On the other hand, children who grow up in families where love is unconditionally given are more likely to acquire higher levels of self-esteem and confidence (Derman-Sparks & Edwards, 2012). They are also more likely to accept others because their parents or guardians have accepted them (Figure 9.5). Think about the information in Table 9.2 on how children learn prejudices. Do you notice things that children and students say that show they are thinking about prejudice and stereotypes?

Andy Dean Photography/Shutterstock.com

Figure 9.5: Interracial families are important in the social growth of our nation as a multicultural society.

Table 9.2 How Children Learn Prejudice: Stages*		
Stage	**Description**	**Example**
Curious of Others	Children as young as 2 years old are curious about differences in others. They notice skin color, hair texture, or name differences (Goodman, 1964).	Children ask: "Why are there Black people?… Is Mexican my color?… Why am I called Black if my skin is brown?… Why is my skin called yellow? It's not yellow; it's tan (Derman-Sparks, Higa, & Sparks, 1980, p. 8). "You can't be the princess! Princesses have blond hair!" announces a White 4-year-old to an African American friend (Derman-Sparks & Edwards, 2012, p. 1).
Emotional Language	Children notice that words used to describe others may have strong emotional connotations. Also, children are trying to understand their various ethnic, gender, and national identities.	Children may hear parents, peers, and teachers call others by negative names that refer to their color, race, gender, exceptionality, class, and sexual orientation. Children try to understand who they should like and who they should avoid (Park, 2010).
Rejection of Others	Children begin to reject the people their parents, friends, and important role models do not like. This occurs around ages 7 to 11. They accept their parents' values without question.	A student was heard saying, "What was the name of the child I was supposed to hate?" (Allport, 1954, p. 292) "I don't like them either."
Prejudice Becomes Permanent	Children's prejudicial attitudes become fixed or permanent in teenage years. Children know social categories such as race, ethnicity, language, class, gender, sexual orientation, and disabilities. Teens make exceptions for friends.	Teenagers may be heard saying, "I believe in democracy. I'm not prejudiced. My best friend is Black. However, Blacks scare me."

*Allport's identified stages.

LO3 Assess how White privilege has been used to keep the dominant group in power.

White Privilege

This section describes research about White racial identity formation. Racism impacts not only people of color, but also White people who are members of the majority. Prejudice is difficult to get rid of because it includes not only a set of beliefs about others but also our emotional reactions, which can include feelings of goodness, morality, and ethics (Brislin, 1993, 2008). This section also describes the stages that European Americans may find themselves going through as they become more aware of racism.

Emotions are an integral part of prejudice. People know intellectually that stereotypes are harmful, but feelings are not as easy to change. These feelings can get in the way of real communication and personal change. Achieving lasting change is difficult for everyone, and it is only natural to feel somewhat threatened when we are asked to rethink our views of the world. It takes courage to change and a strong commitment to care for others and for oneself in order to address these complex beliefs. In addition, sometimes people feel uncertain when they are asked to build bridges with new people and examine different ideas. In order to encourage a broader view of society, teachers have been asked to assess their knowledge of U.S. history. As already discussed in Chapters 4 and 5 of this book, teachers need to have a full understanding of the nation's complex history.

White Privilege: Difficult To Think and Talk About

A complex issue for European Americans to understand is that they are members of a collective often referred to as White, White American, Caucasian, European American, or Euro-American. Although they may not identify with being European American or White, others may place them into those categories because race is a powerful **sociopolitical construct** in society; this refers to an idea or theory that deals with both social and political contexts such as race, class, or gender. Though all humans are members of one race, the human race, people often operate as if race is an accurate differentiation among people (Nelson & Pang, 2013). Many majority teachers have found it difficult to understand the issue of White privilege. As part of the majority, they usually are not confronted with

Sociopolitical construct refers to an idea or theory that deals with both social and political contexts such as race, class, or gender.

their racial membership. "I am an individual," said one teacher. However, Peggy McIntosh (1992) believes that European Americans are members of a community that has advantages, although many Caucasians do not understand that it is a privilege to be able to see their lives as morally neutral, normative, average, and ideal—lives that others should adopt.

White Privilege Defined

McIntosh, a feminist and antiracist activist, wrote an important piece about **White privilege**. Her insights have had a powerful influence in the area of diversity. She defined White privilege as "an invisible package of unearned assets" that can be cashed "…in each day, but …was 'meant' to remain oblivious. White privilege is like an invisible weightless knapsack of special provisions, maps, passports, codebooks, visas, clothes, tools, and blank checks" (McIntosh, 1992, p. 33). Through accepted social practices, White privilege has shaped elements of our culture such as our government's legalizing of slavery and Jim Crow legislation (Scheurich, 2002) and certain educational practices (Sleeter, 1994; Manglitz, 2003). For example, during the twentieth century there were numerous instances of the U.S. government, through the Bureau of Indian Affairs, taking Native American children from their homes and sending them to boarding schools in order to assimilate them into mainstream society. These practices demonstrated a deep belief in the inherent inferiority of Native cultures and languages and, in contrast, the superiority of the values of the White mainstream society.

Sometimes White teachers may expect their students to behave in a specific way. They may not understand that not all students speak in a straightforward manner (Brislin, 2008). Some learners may come from cultures where they hold respect for a teacher's position and so feel that they would be rude to speak in a forceful manner. These students may provide a "softer" version of their perspective (Brislin, 2008).

One of the privileges that White teachers have is the ability to take on the color-blind approach (Johnson, 2002). **Color blindness** refers to not considering or recognizing a person's racial or ethnic characteristics, though inequities and prejudice continue to be major forces in society. (See Figure 9.6.) Many White educators do not have to address race because they are part of the majority community and are not continually discriminated against or profiled by race. This sense of color blindness is a freedom that many people of color do not have. In McIntosh's article "Unpacking the Invisible Knapsack: White Privilege" (1992), she describes some of the privileges that she and her peers have as members of the European community. The following are several that she identified for White Americans to consider:

"I can, if I wish, arrange to be in the company of people of my race most of the time."

"I can turn on the television or open to the front page of the paper and see people of my race widely represented."

"I can be sure that my children will be given curricular materials that testify to the existence of their race."

"Whether I use checks, credit cards, or cash, I can count on my skin color not to work against the appearance of financial reliability."

"I can speak in public to a powerful male group without putting my race on trial."

"I am never asked to speak for all the people of my racial group."

"I can criticize our government and talk about how much I fear its policies and behavior without being seen as a cultural outsider" (McIntosh, 1992, p. 34).

White Educators Talk about White Privilege

To continue the discussion about White privilege, a teacher educator asked educators the question, "What does it mean to be White?" This was challenging for many teachers because they are rarely asked about their group membership. Some felt defensive. However, after several class sessions discussing this issue, many European American teachers began to realize that they had privileges that others did not, yet they did not feel privileged.

White privilege, as defined by Peggy McIntosh, is "an invisible package of unearned assets" that can be cashed "in each day, but . . . was 'meant' to remain oblivious. White privilege is like an invisible weightless knapsack of special provisions, maps, passports, codebooks, visas, clothes, tools, and blank checks."

Color blindness refers to not considering or recognizing a person's racial or ethnic characteristics, though inequities and prejudice continue to be major forces in society.

Figure 9.6: White privilege can include ignoring, silencing, and discriminating against people of color. White privilege is a way that some students get in favorable positions and "trim" away the views and rights of people of color. They often do not know they are acting in this way.

Here are a few of the comments the teachers shared:

Teacher Educator: What does it mean to be White? How do Whites view racism?

Tammi (European American): I never thought about what it means to be White until today.

Dawn (European American): I never thought much about being White either. It just wasn't an issue I thought about. I didn't have to think about being White because I am part of the majority.

Sally (European American): I think White people should start looking at their ancestors. White is so vague. I don't know much about my family and maybe if we did we would be more understanding.

Bruce (African American): We are being so nice. Yet Whites have little information about African Americans. They gave us the shortest month [February] to celebrate Black history. We aren't all the same. People say we are but we aren't. Why can't I feel good about myself? I've taken White history. How many classes in African American or Latino history have you taken?

Michael (European American): None.

Bruce: I go into a store and a cashier follows me around. My White roommates are beginning to see it when they come with me. They are shocked by how I am treated.

Kathy (Japanese/European American): There's also a lot of racism between groups of color, too.

Tammi: I didn't realize how deep-rooted racism is. I have taken for granted my privileges. I only think of racism in its extreme forms like the Ku Klux Klan. But many of us are "innocently" racist because we are ignorant of the racism within our institutions.

Joe (European American): White racism does exist and it is completely intertwined within our society. I think most of us in the White society do not want to jeopardize our "position" so we don't talk about racism.

Tim (European American): I agree. We don't want to discuss racism because we don't want to give up our lifestyle, privileges, and resources that we took from others. Basically I believe I must stop pointing fingers and look at myself first. We must also look at our institutions like schools and government for examples of White privilege.

Joyce (European American): I know that we are racist, but I don't think it is right to over generalize about White racism. I don't think we stick together about issues of race. I have a Black brother-in-law and though it took a while for my family to accept him, we have. So people can move ahead.

After listening to the teacher's discussion, White teachers in this class began to think about issues of race and how their Whiteness has protected them from these conversations. They learned that like teachers of color, in order to move forward and to eliminate racism from their lives, they also must examine racial issues and consider what impact White privilege has on their lives and those of people of color.

White Racial Identity Formation

What process do many European Americans go through in their awareness of their own racial identity? In the past three decades, some individuals have become more open about discussing issues of race. Within that context, many European Americans have become more aware that they are members of a racial group and sometimes referred to as White. Just as people from underrepresented groups deal with racial identity, European Americans also pass through different states of awareness and development about who they are. Beverly Tatum, a psychologist at Mount Holyoke College, says that **racial identity formation** is the process of identifying oneself and the personal significance of being part of a specific racial group (2003). Tatum has studied the development of racial identification and believes individuals pass through the stages of White racial identity described by Janet Helms (1990). These stages are:

Racial identity formation is the process of identifying oneself and the personal significance of being part of a specific racial group.

1. Contact
2. Disintegration
3. Reintegration
4. Pseudo-independence
5. Immersion/emersion
6. Autonomy

Table 9.3 is an adaptation of the work of Helms and Tatum. Many European American teachers go through a process of understanding who they are and must struggle with racial identity when they are confronted with the issue of White privilege. Read through Table 9.3 carefully and assess the various stages.

Racial Identity Formation: People of Color

Just as White teachers go through a process of understanding their racial identity, students and faculty of color go through a process of racial identity formation because society has created categories based on perceived physical characteristics, though genetically, humans are 99.9 percent the same. Both children and teachers of color often must deal with the social stigmas of being thought of as physically different. In addition, people of color are often members of groups that have less political, financial, personal, institutional, and social capital than majority ethnic communities (Tatum, 2003). The model presented is an adaptation of the work of William Cross (1991), Janet Helms, and Beverly Tatum, and was originally developed to explain how African

Table 9.3 White Racial Identity Formation: Stages

1. Acceptance of Status Quo
- Little knowledge of culture and racism, individual and institutional
- Does not see cultural differences in students or other people
- Accepts dominant culture as standard
- Does not question learned stereotypes of others

2. It's Not My Fault: Uncomfortable
- Feels guilty and defensive
- Avoids discussion of racism
- Wants acceptance of peers
- Sees some inconsistencies in society and a little of one's own racism

3. Denial: I'm an Individual
- Begins to look at inequalities in society
- Angry and upset toward those who question racial inequities
- Believes strongly in individual merit, and White privilege reflects that merit
- "I don't feel I have any advantage because I am White"

4. Clarification of Whiteness
- Examines racial self-identity and rejects White superiority
- Seeks historical information about other groups
- Begins to understand how White privilege is perpetuated in society
- Feels ashamed for being White and not sure what to do

5. Acceptance of Self and Group
- Accepts membership in White collective
- Realizes being White does not make a person racist
- Accepts positive and negative aspects of own group
- Studies White antiracist role models

6. White Antiracism: Change Agents
- Sees role of White Americans in fighting racism
- Forms alliances with people of color
- Dedicated to changing society

Sources: Adapted from "Decentering Whiteness: In search of a revolutionary multiculturalism," by Peter McLaren, 1997, *Multicultural Education, 5*(1), 4–11.

Table 9.4 Racial Identity Formation: An Adaptation of Cross, Helms, and Tatum

1. Acceptance of the Status Quo
- Learns a Eurocentric world view from the media, school, peers, and activities
- Learns that Whites are the standard for success
- Does not think much about own racial identity

2. Initial Conflict Begins to Arise
- Begins to encounter conflict based on race from peers and others
- May have been excluded from participating due to race
- Interracial dating becomes a sensitive issue

3. Exploration
- Begins to explore and learn about her or his racial and ethnic communities
- Becomes involved in organizations in the ethnic or racial community
- May feel more affiliated with ethnic or racial organizations

4. Internalization
- Begins to identify with a racial/ethnic community
- Actively involved in coalition building with students from other ethnic/racial communities

5. Commitment
- Secure in racial identity
- Committed to equality and justice for all

American children developed their racial identity. Compare the model of racial identity formation in Table 9.4 with the process Whites go through. There are many similarities.

White Privilege Unpacked: Thinking about Prejudice in Schools

One aspect of White privilege is that many don't think about practices and policies in schools that might be inequitable or oppressive. There are many, many examples in schools every day that can be identified. Allport's model of the five levels of prejudice in society was used to examine schools. Table 9.5 outlines a few that teachers have detected and listed. Read through them and decide if you have seen these behaviors in schools too. Maybe you have seen other biases that you think should be eliminated.

Fill in the blank form with examples of prejudice that you find in schools (Figure 9.7). Work with a partner or small group of educators. Thinking about these levels of prejudice at school can help you understand that some types of social oppression and inequalities have been institutionalized in schools. The examples may come from your own experiences or working in the schools as a teacher, aide, or volunteer.

	EXAMPLES		
Levels of Predudice Found in Schools	Race	Class	Gender
1. Antilocution: Saying things in private that show prejudice			
2. Avoidance: Prejudice is shown through avoidance of students			
3. Discrimination: Overt discrimination is evident by not giving feedback or including only certain students in classroom activities			
4. Physical Attack: Acts of violence can be seen in hallways, classrooms, and school yards			
5. Genocide of educational opportunity for students: Not providing equal opportunities to learners based on their group memberships			

Note: Students may fill in intersectional examples that include all three categories.

Figure 9.7: Teacher Prejudice Form ❯❯ Professional Resource Download

Table 9.5 Examples: Five Levels of Prejudice Found in Schools			
Level of Prejudice	Race	Class	Gender
1. Antilocution: Saying things that show prejudice	Teachers talk about children in the teacher's lounge, by saying, "My Black students always…"	Teachers name children by social class with comments like "Those kids from the projects are troublemakers. They'll never make it, so I do not want to waste my time with them."	A sixth-grade teacher describes his female students as "beautiful," "Playboy centerfold material."
2. Avoidance: Prejudice is shown through avoidance of students	Teachers stand near mainstream students and do not seat students of color near their desks.	Teachers avoid home visits to students who live in the inner city and only go to suburban homes.	Teachers call on males more often than females.
3. Discrimination: Overt discrimination is evident by not giving feedback or including only certain students in classroom activities	Teachers do not call on students who speak limited English because they take longer to talk.	Teachers isolate students who wear baggy pants and seat them in the back of the class. Yet parents may have bought baggy pants because several kids can wear them.	Teachers divide physical education into girls' sports and boys' sports.
4. Physical Attack: Acts of violence can be seen in hallways, classrooms, and school yards	Teachers are more physical with African American students when breaking up a fight than with White students.	Teachers believe poor students need to be physically restrained because they do not have manners.	A teacher loses her temper and yells at a male student saying he needs to get himself under control.
5. Genocide of educational opportunity for students	Students of color are over represented in special education classes, which can have extensive detrimental effects on their educational opportunity. They can be labeled and held back from access to regular classrooms and subject area content.	Poor students are placed in lower tracked classes, and this labeling follows students throughout their schooling. They are not encouraged to seek college degrees and advanced careers.	Women of color are denied opportunities to participate in sports, which can result in fewer women going to college.

White Antiracist Role Models Are Important

Role models are extremely important in teaching students and teachers what can be possible in life. A role model exemplifies not only a set of beliefs but also a person who has acted on those beliefs and made a difference in society. This is one of the most powerful ways to get teachers and students to explore the issue of racism.

When the question about White antiracist role models is posed, teachers and students must decide what the criteria are. In schools, we often discuss the issue of racism but not of antiracists, especially those who are White. Because many students are White, having White role models who stand out is extremely powerful in the classroom. Otherwise, students do not have a real vision of how a White person who is antiracist would act in life. Students begin to realize that an antiracist isn't just a person who does not like prejudice or someone who is against racism—an antiracist is a person who takes actions that require great courage and commitment. These people care about others. Their actions are usually directed at institutional practices of prejudice because they know that unless power relationships are changed, people from underrepresented groups will continually find themselves in oppressed positions.

It is also important for students from underrepresented groups to know about White people who see it as their responsibility to eliminate racism and who act on that responsibility. Students may then see the importance of creating cross-cultural coalitions that include Whites. Change will not occur if people only from communities of color fight against racism. Because racism is so pervasive, it will take everyone to make any substantial changes in institutions such as schools, businesses, and government institutions.

The following questions are important for teachers to consider:

- Whom would you teach as a White antiracist role model?
- What criteria would you use to choose a role model?

Table 9.6 lists numerous White antiracists that you might consider studying.

Table 9.6 White Antiracist Role Models	
Role Model	**Area of Influence**
Eleanor Roosevelt	Women's Rights Activist, Civil Rights Activist
Elizabeth Cady Stanton	Women's Rights Activist, Suffragist
Lucy Stone	Women's Rights Activist, Suffragist
John Brown	Abolitionist
Levi Coffin	Abolitionist
Lloyd Garrison	Abolitionist
Tim Wise	Civil Rights Activist, Columnist
Morris Dees	Civil Rights Activist, Lawyer
Sigmund Livingston	Civil Rights Activist, Lawyer
Peter Irons	Civil Rights Activist, Lawyer

LO4 Evaluate what bullying is and why it occurs.

Bullying is defined as repeated, unwanted, aggressive behavior that threatens, humiliates, isolates, and/or excludes an individual where there is a perceived or real power imbalance.

Cyberbullying is bullying using electronic devices and social media. This includes apparatuses such as cell phones, computers, and tablets, and can involve the use of chat rooms, text messaging, and websites.

Bullying

Bullying is one of the major social issues that face our students today. Bullying is an act of social oppression. It is often based on marginalized, social categories such as race, class, gender, sexual orientation, religion, exceptionality, neighborhood, language, accent, ethnicity, appearance, or a combination of several groupings (Poteat & Russell, 2013). Many students are hurt by prejudice and discrimination, which arises as bullying on the way to, during, and after school as well as electronically. **Bullying** is defined as repeated, unwanted, aggressive behavior that threatens, humiliates, isolates, and/or excludes an individual where there is a perceived or real power imbalance (Teaching Tolerance, n.d.; Salmivalli, 2015). **Cyberbullying** is bullying using electronic devices and social media. This includes apparatuses such as cell phones, computers, and tablets, and can involve the use of chat rooms, text messaging, and websites (U.S. Department of Health and Human Services, n.d.).

Bullying is a complicated action that represents the back-and-forth connections between individual and social group factors (Menesini, Palladino, & Nocentini, 2015; Thornberg, 2015). Bullying can arise from several categories such as being a student of color and having a disability and being gay (Poteat & Russell, 2013). This makes underlying reasons for bullying complex. However, bullies are often able to separate themselves from moral orientations. For example, a student may not feel a social responsibility to others; bullies often do not experience shame or guilt. They also may be egocentric and have a strong social goal of being seen as popular and powerful (Salmivalli, 2015). In addition, students often do not think of the consequences of their bullying behaviors; they are often able to distance themselves from feelings of remorse.

Researchers believe that bullying is a group activity; therefore, many psychologists and educators address bullying from a group level of intervention (Salmivalli, 2015). Though many bystanders do not condone bullying, they may have a difficult time deciding on what to do. Just as in cases of social oppression, people often do not stand up and speak out against discrimination that they know is wrong (Thornberg, 2015). They do not want to become the target of the group, so they do not stand up. They also want to belong to the group and do not want to jeopardize their membership.

Bullying and Discrimination Are Similar

Bullying and discrimination are related actions. However, psychologist Irina Parkins and her research team believe that discrimination differs from bullying. Bullying is intimidation using verbal, physical, psychological, or technological means to create fear in victims (Parkins, Fishbein, & Ritchey, 2006). Discrimination as has been previously defined as treating others unfairly because of group membership. Though both involve oppression and target others who are not socially desirable, discrimination is connected to stereotypes a perpetrator holds about the group membership of a victim, such as ethnicity or sexual orientation. Many perpetrators operate on underlying and unconscious bias they have learned. Those stereotypes are societal in origin. Parkins found that adults who discriminated were more likely to believe their group should be dominant over others and treat victims unfairly because they are seen as members of a specific group that is seen as inferior. Sometimes differences between discrimination and bullying are subtle. According to stopbullying.gov, if bullying is defined as harassing behaviors based on race, gender, class, sexual orientation, or religion, then federal funds provided to institutions where bullying takes place can be taken away. Aggressive behaviors based on the identified social categories create a hostile environment, and victims can seek protection using federal civil rights laws (U.S. Department of Health and Human Services, 2014).

Many teachers believe that bullying is a group process (Coloroso, 2011; Thornberg, 2015). They think bystanders play a strong role in bullying. They are usually not innocent spectators. Bystanders can be complicit in repeated aggressions because they want to continue to belong to the group. They also participate by saying things like "He's such a cry baby" to each other and excluding the isolated student (Coloroso, 2011). Often they join the bullying by spreading rumors about the victim and may leave nasty notes in his or her school locker or as a text message. This way teachers and administrators do not realize that bullying is occurring every day on campus. Therefore, to eliminate bullying, educators must work with both bullies and bystanders. In addition, a victim in one situation may be the perpetrator in another incident. Bullying is an issue that all school members—faculty and students—need to address.

One of the ways to get a group of students to create a safe space is to be an ally to others (GLSEN, 2013). An **ally** as defined by GLSEN is a person who does not identify with being LGBTQ and is from a privileged group; the person advocates for social change and works to stop bullying and harassment of LGBTQ young people in schools and society. Bystanders can be active supporters rather than complicit bullies. The Gay, Lesbian and Straight Education Network developed an approach in which people can become allies to LGBTQ students. This idea can be used to support anyone who is being bullied and discriminated against. A community of people come together to create a safe place for each other. They become allies and know this safe space is free from prejudice and harassment. It is a place of healing and trust where name calling and bullying is replaced with working together to create programs of acceptance and belonging for all students.

Ally refers to a person who does not identify with being LGBTQ and is from a privileged group; the person advocates for social change and works to stop bullying and harassment of LGBTQ young people in schools and society.

Because research indicates that teaching social and self-esteem skills can be effective in addressing bullying (Parkins et al., 2006), teachers can use the following strategies from www.stopbullying.gov to address this issue in schools:

1. Intercede right away.
2. Make sure all students are safe.
3. Do not minimize the event.
4. Get the facts from all students involved in the incident.
5. Listen without criticizing.
6. Keep the dialogue open with students.
7. Display respect for all.
8. Allow victim and perpetrator to talk individually with you.

9. Do not expect students to make up right then.
10. Determine if the situation involved bullying.
11. Ascertain if there is a power imbalance.
12. Suggest victims develop allies.
13. Explain to perpetrator the importance of accountability.
14. Teach conflict resolution.
15. Prevention is the best avenue; institute an antibullying program.

LO5 Suggest ways teachers can move students from ethnocentrism to working together to eliminate prejudice and bullying.

Moving Students from Bullying to Coalition Building: Teaching the Intercultural Sensitivity Model

One of the major goals of this book is to help teachers move their students away from inequality and toward cross-cultural understanding and intercultural perceptions. Milton Bennett created a developmental model for cross-cultural and human understanding. His work goes beyond describing stages of identity to suggesting strategies to eliminate prejudice and discrimination. Since culturally relevant teaching is a core component of multicultural education, it is important for educators to understand the worldview of their students. Because bullying and prejudice are often part of group processes, teachers can guide students toward the building of coalitions and encourage them to take on the frame of reference of others who may be culturally different from themselves. This is in opposition to what happens in the bullying process. Though Milton Bennett's (1998) model of intercultural sensitivity is primarily about bringing culturally different groups together, its method and means of bringing people together can be used to combat prejudice and bullying. Researchers have shown that an inclusive school culture and climate are powerful strategies against bullying (Dessel, 2010). Bennett's model can be used to change schools' climates of exclusion to inclusion.

Following are Bennett's assumptions:

1. People from different cultures and groups may respond differently to the same events and/or conditions.
2. People can move from seeing reality ethnocentrically. They understand that there is no universal response to what happens in life and can see the situation from various cultural views.
3. Ethical choices are important in intercultural sensitivity; however, there could be various ethical choices for the same issue. There are no universal or absolute principles.
4. It is vital to highlight the importance of equal status among participants and groups. This is created by developing communities and moving toward ethnorelativism.

Bennett has created a complex and dynamic model to describe how individuals can developmentally move from **ethnocentrism** and **egocentrism** to **ethnorelativsm**. Bennett's model moves people away from seeing life only from specific group culture and personal views (ethnocentric and egocentric). The model guides people and groups toward ethnorelativism, in which people reflect on and move toward understanding other worldviews and come together as a community. He also noted that people from oppressed cultural groups may find their way through the model differently. Their experiences are often controlled by the mainstream that forces them to conform to the status quo even though this may mean exclusion. See Table 9.7, which explains that Bennett's developmental

Ethnocentrism is a stage in Bennett's model of intercultural sensitivity in which a person's group culture shapes her or his view of the world and other cultures; does not consider the views of other cultural groups.
Egocentrism is a state in which a person can only see from his or her perspective.
Ethnorelativism is a stage in Bennett's model of intercultural sensitivity in which people learn about the values and views of others within the context of their cultures. In this stage, individuals are open to new viewpoints and perspectives.

Table 9.7 Bennett's Developmental Model of Intercultural Sensitivity
Ethnocentric Stages: Sees life through group and personal lens. Does not try to view issues from the perspective of others.
1. Denial: Ethnocentric individuals do not see that there are other cultural viewpoints in their society and community. **These individuals only see their own cultural realities and deny the existence of other cultural perspectives.** One reason for this ethnocentric viewpoint may be physical isolation. Maybe there are three African American students in the local high school while most are European American; the population at the school seems to be homogeneous. There is no move to try to see issues from the view of culturally diverse people.
2. Defense: Individuals in this stage are threatened by another's reality, and cultural differences are seen in a negative light. **Members believe their culture is the only viable and superior one.** They may try to protect their social privileges and not want others to have similar opportunities (Bennett, 1998). The most common defense is through denigration. Broad, negative stereotyping based on social categories such as race, cultural group, age, gender, religion, and other characteristics is used to discredit others. This can be seen in comments of hostility toward a group. One of the most powerful examples of this was the stereotypical, untrue, and extreme comments made by Nazis about the Jewish community in Germany and other European countries during the Second World War. This can result in extreme nationalism.
3. Minimization: People in this stage minimize differences and focus on our shared humanity. Although this seems to be a good position, Bennett cautions that people can continue to hold ethnocentric beliefs and not deal with cultural differences. For example, when people feel there are universal values that all share, those values usually come from their own cultures. Bennett cautions that people of color may be somewhat wary of the "assumption of common humanity. Too often, the assumption has meant 'be like me'" (1993, p. 42). In this stage people often cite the basic needs of humans as being common shared characteristics that support the feeling that all individuals can understand each other. **Cultural differences are marginalized.**
Ethnorelative Stages: Movement toward an understanding of behaviors based upon the cultural context in which they are used. That the behaviors may be different is neither "good" nor "bad." One person's culture is not better or more desirable than those of others; they are just different. How is this phase of development different from the ethnocentric stages? People do not feel threatened or become defensive. Instead, people see cultural differences as new ways of thinking and acting, and they are not trying to continue to maintain their own.
4. Acceptance: Respect cultural differences. Starting to move from ethnocentrism towards ethnorelativism. One of the forms of acceptance is respect for behavioral differences. **Individuals begin to understand that unfamiliar behaviors may arise from cultural differences.** One of the cultural differences that can easily be identified is language. In addition, people from various cultures may show diverse verbal and nonverbal communication styles and use different customs, tones, and nonverbal gestures.
5. Adaptation: People do not assimilate into the new culture. Ethnorelative individuals do not take on the new culture and abandon their own. Rather, people develop new skills and add them to their knowledge base. Culture is understood as a process and not an object. In this stage, **people move from their own cultural frame of reference to that of others, and their knowledge of perspectives expand.** The first step of this stage is empathy, seeing another person's viewpoint, feelings, and experiences.
6. Integration: When people understand diverse worldviews, they engage in a process of clarifying who they are. Through this process of self-identification, individuals no longer identify with any one culture. They see themselves as multiculturalists or interculturalists and are able to use a variety of worldviews in their lives. **They move from their viewpoint to others and build a community dedicated to respect, peace, and equality.**

model includes two different orientations, ethnocentric and ethnorelative stages. Basically, Bennett has individuals and groups identify their values and emphasize the importance of community. By providing a foundation of ethics and beliefs that focus on equality and fairness, people adopt the goal of cooperation and unity. This model is one that shows how to move students from an egocentric and ethnocentric orientation, which often is present in bullies who have little regard for others, toward belonging to a community with equality and respect at its core.

The first set of stages is called ethnocentric because the stages describe a worldview in which individuals see their reality as central to all experiences. In other words, individuals in these stages believe others see reality the way they do. Racism and outsider/ insider positions come from this ethnocentric perspective (Bennett, 1993).

Consider this . . .

"Ethical choices are important in intercultural sensitivity. There are no universal or absolute principles."
—Milton Bennett

Q Ask your students what their ethical values are and how those values should guide their everyday actions with regard to diversity and equality. Have students identify their values and give definitions and examples of each belief.

Teaching an Antibias Curriculum

An important component of multicultural education is reducing prejudice and discrimination in students. The intercultural sensitivity model not only moves people toward respecting others who may be different but also develops coalitions with diverse people. It is important to integrate this model into your classroom antibias curriculum.

If you teach preschool or the primary grades, the book *Anti-Bias Curriculum: Tools for Empowering Young Children* by Derman-Sparks and her colleagues is an excellent resource (1980, 2012). The reference may answer your questions about how to guide children away from prejudicial attitudes and discriminatory behavior. For example, if a child says, "John looks like chocolate," you can say to that child, "John has beautiful brown skin." In this way, you do not critique the child who is making an observation, but at the same time, you can take the moment to teach a better way to view John and reinforce his skin color and ethnic background. The book covers issues of race and gender and also has a chapter aimed at helping youngsters develop antibias attitudes toward children with learning and developmental differences. A continual thread throughout the book is that children need to learn to accept each other in a safe and respectful environment. This setting must also provide children with new ways of interacting with each other. Just placing children together does not necessarily build bridges of communication among students.

Derman-Sparks and her colleagues (2012) have identified several important goals for learning about culture that will help all children develop a positive sense of self while learning to foster healthy social interactions. These goals can help you create a classroom that cultivates equity and cultural diversity. The following is an adaptation of their goals:

1. A teacher affirms and fosters children's knowledge and pride, not superiority, in their cultural identity.
2. A teacher fosters children's curiosity, enjoyment, and empathetic awareness of cultural differences and similarities.
3. A teacher expands children's concept of fairness and feelings of empathy for others.
4. A teacher helps children change uncomfortable and inappropriate responses to differences into respectful and comfortable interactions.
5. A teacher helps children think critically about stereotyping.
6. A teacher helps children develop the tools and self-confidence to stand up for themselves and others against prejudice and discriminatory behavior.

Young Children: Teaching Positive Behaviors

How can you help children become aware of racist, gender-biased, or classist behaviors? As a teacher, you can help children see that when their behavior excludes others, they are discriminating against someone or bullying. Students may be treating others in an uncaring way. For example, when name-calling occurs, teachers should talk with their students right away. It is important that children realize that racist, gender-biased, and classist terms are unacceptable. Like adults, children need to understand that when someone is called a name, it threatens justice for all of us. Help children understand the "we" of a community. Even though they may not be the perpetrator or victim of a particular situation, when the dignity of one person is threatened, our communal values of justice and equality are also being questioned. Relating prejudice to children's notions of fairness helps young students realize they can eliminate prejudice.

The following example shows how a young child can question his or her own perceptions.

When D. was about seven, he began dancing one day to a record of Navajo music we have. All of a sudden he stopped himself, looked at us and said, "You know, I don't know how they dance. I'm just making it up." Another day, he told us, after seeing a movie, "I know one way that movie was racist. It only had white people in it." (Derman-Sparks et al., 1980, p. 7)

We can help children learn to respect each other's cultural ways and understand how powerful messages about cultural differences are given in society all the time. Suzanne, a principal in Laramie, Wyoming, shared with a group of teachers a public way she dealt with name-calling on the playground. She witnessed some serious name-calling one morning when several first graders used a racial slur at a peer. At first, she was stunned to see and hear the interchange. Then she walked up to the small group of children, looked at the child who had been treated disrespectfully, and said, "I am sorry this happened to you at our school. We will work harder to make sure this doesn't happen again to you or anyone else." Suzanne was providing a powerful message for all the children. She, as an administrator, did not take the situation lightly and modeled that it is the responsibility of all members of the school to eliminate prejudice and discrimination.

Suzanne is not only a competent administrator who directs the school, but she is also a good institutional role model, showing her students the ownership they can take in the fight against racism. Name-calling and other bullying behaviors may relate to race, but they may also relate to sexual orientation, gender, size, religion, or exceptionality.

Lourdes, a teacher in North Miami, Florida, shared another important strategy to deal with conflict (Teaching Tolerance, 1999). As a kindergarten grade teacher, she believes that peace and caring should be at the core of her classroom. As a teacher involved in the Peace Education Foundation, she adopted the "I Care Rules." These rules are as follows:

1. We listen to each other.
2. Hands are for helping, not hurting.
3. We use "I care" language.
4. We care about each other's feelings.
5. We are responsible for what we say and do (Teaching Tolerance, 1999, p. 143).

In addition to these general guidelines, Lourdes has instituted an important place in the classroom. When children have conflicts with each other, she sends them to the "Peace Table," a place where children feel safe and accepted. Lourdes helps her children role-play various situations that might arise during the year and teaches them how to focus on a solution.

The following are guidelines for the Peace Table; place a poster with the six steps on it so students can refer to the process:

1. Identify the problem.
2. Focus on the problem.
3. Attack the problem, not the person.
4. Listen with an open mind.
5. Treat a person's feelings with respect.
6. Take responsibility for your actions.

Students in this classroom are learning how to solve their own problems. They do not ignore them. The classroom becomes a place where children want to be because they know their feelings and perspectives will be respected. Children also affirm their own values of fairness and develop a strong sense of themselves. The Peace Table strategy is also often used in Montessori classrooms where young students engage in conflict resolution. The Peace Table can also be used as a place where students have the opportunity for quiet time. This method can be used to eliminate bullying and other forms of

My Journal

Bullying in School

Teachers may not know about the bullying that is occurring in a school. Often students bully in the bathroom, hallway corners, or far out on the playground where teachers do not see. It is important for teachers to gather data about how students see bullying in their school.

The following questions can be used as a survey that students fill out or as interview questions that a teacher or aide employs to get a sense of how much bullying is occurring in your school.

The responses of students should be kept confidential and anonymous. When you interview students, let them do most of the talking. Write down comments they provide if they volunteer additional information. This will provide additional context to your research.

How Safe Do You Feel At School?

Answers can show how safe the children feel.

		Agree	Do Not Agree
1.	Students at this school get along well together.		
2.	Students play with (interact with) everyone.		
3.	Students play with (interact with) people most like them.		
4.	Students are comfortable reporting bullying right away.		
5.	Students are comfortable reporting when someone calls them a name right away.		
6.	Teachers create a safe place for me.		
7.	Teachers create a safe place for all students.		
8.	Everyone feels like they belong at the school.		
9.	I look forward to coming to school every day.		

In the past month…

	True	False
I have heard someone use a racial slur or called a "bad" name.		
I have heard one student use a put-down toward another student.		
I have heard a grown up say something negative about another student.		
I have seen a grown up not do anything when someone was bullied.		

Q *What other questions could you add to this survey?*

Q *Are there other ways you could gather data about bullying at school besides using a survey or conducting interviews? If so, what are they and why would you do so?*

Source: Teaching Tolerance School Climate Questionnaire, Teaching Tolerance.
Retrieved from http://www.tolerance.org/sites/default/files/files/general/School%20Climate%20Questionnaire.pdf

≫ Professional Resource Download

discrimination and bias. It is important for teachers to have a clear vision of why they integrate an antibias curriculum and instructional strategies in their classrooms.

Helping Older Students Deal with Prejudice

Many students talk about how much it hurts when someone throws a racial slur at them. It is almost as if the hurt goes down to their souls. Their sense of self can be seriously damaged, especially in the adolescent years. For some very young children, the impact may not be as hurtful to their self-esteem because they are not as oriented toward their peers, and oftentimes they make up quickly after a conflict. However, for older students the role of prejudice may be much more disturbing and long lasting. As students grow older, they may find that they must deal with more severe aspects of prejudice. The comments may be more cutting and the actions of peers may be more deliberate. When students feel like their "arms have been tied behind their back" due to an act of prejudice, then that feeling can lead to further feelings of helplessness. Students also may feel that they cannot be themselves; for example, they may not feel comfortable speaking Spanish or identifying as Mexican American. The prejudice may be even more destructive because students feel victimized. In addition, when prejudice is felt at this age, the experiences tend to

Consider this . . .

Teachers can send out the message of "we can work together" or "you are a bad kid." Teacher language is a critical model. Teachers can use upbeat statements to create a positive classroom climate. Here are some examples.

"I liked how you gave the student your full attention when she spoke. That was an act of respect."

"If someone makes a mistake, it is important to think about how we would want someone to respond to us. We will treat others the way we would want to be treated."

"There are no dumb questions. We all can gain from your questions." (Hollomon & Yates, 2012)

Q What other affirming statements can you use with students? Make a list of 10 possible statements.

reinforce stereotypes they were forming about members of a particular group. For example, although Mary intellectually knows that it was only three [name of an ethnic group] girls who pushed and terrorized her in the bathroom, she may transfer this image to all young women in the group and not feel comfortable making friends or talking with other students in her classes from the same ethnic community as the perpetrators.

Because the incident in the bathroom can be characterized as bullying, older students may be participating in a group process of bullying (Salmivalli, 2015).

Discussing Bullying With Older Students

One way to get students to talk about bullying is to talk about incidents somewhere other than their campus. They may feel that if they say anything about bullying in their own school, they will become a target too. Group dynamics can prevent students from feeling safe discussing this topic. However, sharing national statistics with middle- and high-school students can get them to safely discuss the issue from a distance. Table 9.8 provides the number of incidents and the types of bullying behavior that students around the country reported in 2010–2011.

Table 9.8 National Center for Statistics, Bullying Statistics, 2010–2011*

Type of Bullying	Number of Students	Percentage of Total Reporting This Type of Bullying	Percentage of Type of Bullied Activity
Total Students, Bullied or Not Bullied	24,456,000	100%	
Bullied**	6,809,000	27.8%	
Made fun of, called names or insulted	4,303,000	17.6%	29%
Subject of rumors	4,469,000	18.3%	30%
Threatened with harm	1,232,000	5.0%	8%
Pushed, shoved, tripped, or spit on	1,923,000	7.9%	13%
Tried to make do things they did not want to do	804,000	3.3%	5%
Excluded from activities on purpose	1,365,000	5.5%	9%
Property destroyed on purpose	689,000	2.8%	6%
Total Number of Bullied Activities	14,785,000		100%
Total Students, Cyberbullied** or Not Cyberbullied	24,411,000	100.0	

(Continued)

Table 9.8 National Center for Statistics, Bullying Statistics, 2010–2011* *(Continued)*

Type of Bullying	Number of Students	Percentage of Total Reporting This Type of Bullying	Percentage of Type of Bullied Activity
Cyberbullied	2,198,000	9%	
Hurtful information on Internet	884,000	3.6%	23%
Purposely shared private information	263,000	1.1%	7%
Unwanted contact via email	454,000	1.9%	11%
Unwanted contact via instant messaging	659,000	2.7%	17%
Unwanted contact via text messaging	1,073,000	4.4%	26%
Unwanted contact via online gaming	356,000	1.5%	9%
Purposeful exclusion from an online community	286,000	1.2%	7%
Total Number of Cyberbullying activities	**3,975,000**		100%

*Students ages 12–18, bullied at school or cyberbullied.

**In interviews students could identify up to five types of bullying. Bullying occurred either on the way to school, on the school bus, at school, or on the way home.

Source: U.S. Department of Justice, Bureau of Justice Statistics, School Crime Supplement (SCS) to the National Crime Victimization Survey (NCVS), 2011.

National Center for Education Statistics, Retrieved from http://nces.ed.gov/pubs2013/2013329.pdf

If you have developed a caring community as discussed in Chapter 1, it will be possible to talk about bullying and how to eliminate it at school because you have created a trusting environment. In addition, using Bennett's model of intercultural sensitivity, students will be mentored to move from an ethnocentric viewpoint to one that is ethnorelative, in which learners hear and consider other perspectives and build a trusting and respectful community. Within this context, it is key that when students go to a teacher to report bullying or discrimination that the teacher acts. If students find out that a teacher will not do anything, they will feel that the teacher cannot be trusted.

It is critical that you as the teacher model consistent caring, respect, and equality in the classroom and school and stop the bullying or discrimination immediately. These values will be at the core of changing behaviors of bullies and bystanders. Elimination of bullying is a community responsibility.

TEACHING TIPS

Discussing Bullying

Before class discussion begins, give students a checklist of the following questions. Divide students into pairs and ask them to discuss the questions first and then to write their answers together. By using the checklist of questions, learners get familiar with the data and types of situations that are considered bullying.

▶ What is Table 9.8 about?

▶ Define bullying. Refer to www.stopbullying.gov.

▶ Who did the researchers survey?

▶ How many bullied activities were recorded that year?

▶ Which bullying activity was the most prevalent?

▶ What behaviors are considered bullying?

▶ Define cyberbullying. Look up the definition at www.stopbullying.gov

▶ How many cyberbulling activities were reported that year?

▶ Which cyberbullying was the most prevalent?

▶ What can we do as a community to stop bullying? List five suggestions.

It is important to let students get comfortable with the issue and statistics first. The real discussion will come later.

Have students come back together and report what they found. This may take some time. Discuss the different types of bullying. Ask: Have you ever witnessed any of the listed bullying? What happened? How did you feel?

⋙ Professional Resource Download

Thinking about Intersectionality

In this chapter, you have learned that students may be discriminated against for a variety of reasons. When there are numerous layers of prejudice based on more than one social category, intersectionality occurs. In many cases, educators may have blinders on and not see the bullying or discrimination that is occurring on the playground, in the cafeteria, or hallways. Teachers need to understand that though it may seem as if a victim is being bulled because he is a student of color or gay, the bullying may actually be based on several types of differences. Maybe the child is small in stature and comes from a low-income family and so seems to be more easily intimidated. Sometimes the root of the prejudice is not always immediately visible. For example, a teacher may notice that a student is being taunted on the playground because she is overweight, and then the teacher realizes that other students are also picking on her because she is Mexican American and has a hard time speaking in English. Often, bullying occurs because of a variety of differences (Parkins et al., 2006; Mio et al., 2016; Thornberg, 2015). Someone who is bullied may have low self-esteem, be depressed, and feel isolated. Numerous power imbalances may exist in relation to not only the listed social categories but also popularity and status in the classroom. This shows how prejudice and bullying come together in many different layers of discrimination.

Summary

1. **Explain how most people have prejudices against others based on social categories such as race, ethnicity, gender, age, class, religion, sexual orientation, disabilities, language spoken, and/or appearance.**

   Many people hold prejudices and stereotypes about others based on social categories such as race, ethnicity, gender, class, religion, LGBT orientation, language, appearance, age, and disabilities. Prejudices are favorable or unfavorable feelings about others based on a category without knowing a person or group. This happens often in society. Many times people do not even realize they hold prejudicial feelings against others because they learned the beliefs as a child or covertly. Teachers need to reflect upon terms like prejudice, discrimination, and stereotypes and identify definitions before talking about them in the classroom. Definitions of these terms can be difficult to explain, so teachers need to have age-appropriate descriptions at their fingertips"

2. **Define the stages of prejudice development and levels of prejudice that can be found in society, schools, and individuals.**

   Sociologist Gordon Allport developed a model that helps to explain how prejudice can continue to expand if a person does nothing to reflect upon their biases. The five levels of prejudice are antilocution, avoidance, discrimination, physical attack, and genocide. Prejudice and bullying can be connected depending on the type of harassment and if it is repeated. Bullying is aggressive, unwanted, repeated hostilities. Acts of bullying often have roots in social categories such as race, social class, gender, sexual orientation, language, culture, disabilities, exceptionalities, age, and/or religion.

3. **Assess how White privilege has been used to keep the dominant group in power.**

   White privilege is about the unearned assets that Whites may have based upon their membership in the dominant population. Though many Whites do not feel they are privileged, they need to take time to reflect upon how they are able to move through society without having to identify their racial background or justify their group. One of the views many majority people have is that society is color blind. However, numerous people of color disagree, noting that they are often confronted with their racial background whether at the grocery store writing a check or as a parent in a parent–teacher conference. Color blindness implies that one's racial background is neutral, which is not the reality for many people.

4. **Evaluate what bullying is and why it occurs.**

   Bullying is highly linked with prejudice. Bullying is repeated, unwanted, aggressive behavior that is used to threaten, exclude, isolate, or hurt another. There is usually a power imbalance, and it often includes a group of students. An incidence of bullying may be connected to social categories such as race, LGBTQ membership, exceptionalities, gender, and religion, which can be considered civil rights violations. Cyberbullying—the use of electronic devices to bully or the usage of social media sites, text messaging and other digital arenas—also continues to increase. Bullying often occurs because a person wants to feel more in control, increase social status, become accepted in a group, and/or exert dominance. Bullying can result from prejudicial beliefs and attitudes.

5. **Suggest ways that teachers can move students from ethnocentrism to working together to eliminate prejudice and bullying.**

   Teachers can use Milton Bennett's intercultural sensitivity model, which guides people from ethnocentrism to ethnorelativism. The model also stresses the importance of teaching ethics or values of equality, compassion, respect, and community. These values are critical for the creation of a classroom with a positive climate. Research has found that bullies are able to disassociate themselves from moral foundations; however, in classrooms where teachers model trust and respect for others, students are more likely to support positive behaviors. Bullying is not only an individual act but usually part of a group process in which students understand that bullying is taking place and may be complicit in the progression of intimidation. Therefore to thwart bullying in schools, it is critical for all members of the school community—from teachers to cafeteria workers—along with students to work toward challenging bully behaviors and to model positive, collaborative interactions.

Check Your Cultural Knowledge

Reflective Essay Question

Bullying has become a social epidemic in society. As a teacher in the classroom, what are the five most important rules that you could share with your students to address bullying? Ask students to add five more rules to prevent bullying. This way both you and the students address the issue. This gives students responsibility to act, and it also provides an opportunity for you to have them talk about the issue in the classroom. You can reinforce that bullying of any kind—verbal, physical, and nonverbal—is not acceptable in their school.

Application

Know and Go Tools in the Classroom

Five Ways to Teach Prejudice Reduction

1. Teach about positive role models who have fought for fairness and equality. Ask students to identify what they could do in their own lives to reflect the work of their hero. Be sure to ask students about heroes from many different groups such as individuals who are poor, younger, living in an inner-city neighborhood, or disabled.
2. Role play a situation students witnessed on the playground or lunch room when someone was excluded from participating. The teacher and students can discuss what the most appropriate responses would be and how to deal with prejudice.
3. Read children's literature to your students that brings up issues of prejudice and bullying. Situations discussed in these stories can provide a starting point for classroom conversations. Consider using literature such as the following:

Young Children

➤ *Chrysanthemum* by Kevin Henkes

Elementary Students

➤ *My Dream of Martin Luther King* by Faith Ringold
➤ *Moses: When Harriet Tubman Led Her People to Freedom* by Carole Boston Weatherford
➤ *The Story of Ruby Bridges* by Robert Coles

Middle School Students

➤ *Stargirl* by Jerry Spinelli

High School Students

➤ *The Absolutely True Diary of a Part-Time Indian* by Sherman Alexie (sophomores)
➤ *The Immortal Life of Henrietta Lacks* by Rebecca Skloot (seniors)
➤ *To Kill A Mockingbird* by Harper Lee
➤ *No-No Boy* by John Okada

Discuss the issue of prejudice and discrimination from the viewpoint of the main characters in the books.

4. Identify a problem in your classroom that deals with a stereotype. Do not name or pick out any particular person as the victim or perpetrator. It is the behavior that the community works to eliminate. Have the class brainstorm what could be done. Then have students vote on the appropriate solution. The class should also develop a plan of action about bullying. Make sure each member of the class has a responsibility in the plan.
5. Use cooperative learning in your classroom on a regular basis so students learn how to work with a variety of individuals. Make sure the projects have clear social and academic goals. Also monitor the progress of the group to ensure success.

⌄⌄ Professional Resource Download

Como hacer una piel de animal:

1. Cut out a rectangular shape
   the brown, grocery bag.

Hay que cortar una sección
forma de un rect

Bob Daemmrich/PhotoEdit

Language Development and Acquisition

Learning Objectives

LO1 Describe the demographics of English learners in U.S. schools.

LO2 Explain first language skills that babies develop, such as syntax, phonology, metalinguistic awareness, and morphology.

LO3 Analyze second-language acquisition models and theories.

LO4 Analyze how language levels such as BICS and CALP are linked to cognition and other literacy skills.

LO5 Assess differences among bilingual education programs.

STANDARDS COVERED

NAEYC 1, 5, 6
naeyc

CAEP 1 CAEP

INTASC 1, 2, 3, 4, 5, 6, 7, 8, 9, 10 InTASC

307

Overview

Many students arrive at school knowing how to speak a first language other than English, so it is important for teachers to understand how students learn their home language and a second language. Teachers need to learn how they can use language acquisition theories and models to implement various English language learner (ELL) teaching strategies. There are numerous links between learning language and the development of cognition. Language learning is not only important so that students can communicate with each other, but also language is a critical tool in the development of higher-order thinking, cognitive, and writing skills. The next section discusses the fact that many students arrive in the classroom speaking languages other than English.

Social Context: Demographics

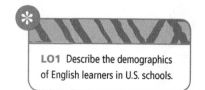

LO1 Describe the demographics of English learners in U.S. schools.

In the United States, numerous students come to school speaking a language other than English at home. The Migration Policy Institute (2015) reported that students ages 6 to 18 who attended school and had a home language other than English were recognized as English language learners (ELLs). The information was taken from the 2013 American Community Survey (ACS). Nationally, 71 percent of ELLs speak Spanish. In addition, the following nine languages and the percentage of students who speak a language other than English are included in Table 10.1. In reviewing the table, it is interesting to note that five of the languages are not based on the Latin alphabet; they are Chinese, Arabic, Yiddish, Korean, and Hmong. Immigrants are migrating to the United States from Asian, European, and Middle Eastern countries. Though many new Americans are from Central America, South America, and Mexico, there are numerous others who arrived in the United States from around the world.

Home languages vary from state to state. This is one of the reasons that teachers need to get to know their students. Spanish is not the top language spoken by ELLs in all states. Consider the examples in Table 10.2. You may not even know of some of the languages, such as Cushitic, Ilocano, or Yupik. Do you know their countries of origin? If not, take time to look them up. If you were teaching in areas where these languages were common, it would be important for you not only to learn about the country of origin but also a few phrases in each language so you could make your students feel

Table 10.1 Ten Languages Other Than English Spoken at Home	
Language Spoken at Home	**Percent**
Spanish	71%
Chinese (Includes Cantonese and Mandarin)	4%
Vietnamese	3%
French/Haitian Creole (Includes French, French Creole, Haitian Creole)	2%
Arabic	2%
Yiddish, Jewish	1%
Korean	1%
Filipino, Tagalog	1%
German	1%
Hmong	1%

Source: Migration Policy Institute, ELL Information Center Fact Sheet Series, Number 4, 2015.

State	ELL Populations
Table 10.2 States and Top Language Spoken by ELLs, Not Spanish	
Alaska	Yupik 40%
	Spanish 12%
	Inupiaq 9%
	Filipino 9%
	Hmong 8%
Hawaii	Ilokano 21%
	Chuukese 12%
	Marshallese 10%
	Tagalog 9 %
	Spanish 6%
Vermont	Nepali 17%
	Chushitic 10%
	Spanish 9%
	Chinese 7%
	Somali 6%
Maine	Somali 33%
	Arabic 11%
	Spanish 10%
	French 7%
	Chinese 4%

Source: Migration Policy Institute, ELL Information Center Fact Sheet Series, Number 4, 2015.

Phonology is the study of sounds.

LO2 Explain first language skills that babies develop, such as syntax, phonology, metalinguistic awareness, and morphology.

comfortable. By saying "how are you" in Yupik to students, you indirectly affirm their linguistic heritage.

Early Language Skills: Babies

When a baby hears language, she or he must make sense of the sounds. Although the baby is probably not aware of it, she or he is seeking answers to questions such as the following:

- What is the sound my father is making?
- How can I make the same sound?
- Is that the right sound?

The baby initially does not know what the sounds that her or his parents make mean but will often practice making the same sounds by trying to imitate the sounds she or he hears. When a baby learns how to put different sounds together into words, she or he is actually learning **phonology**, meaning she or he is studying sounds of language. Some people call this level of language "baby talk," but in actuality babies are learning how to put vowels and consonants together when saying something such as "da da." A baby is also learning patterns of language through the 16,000 plus examples of what her or his parents and others around them say in the first several months of life (Hotz, 2002). (See Figure 10.1.) When parents and other adults play, read stories, and model new vocabulary, babies

Marion Lopez/Shutterstock.com

Figure 10.1: Babies imitate parents in making their first sounds.

quickly develop more extensive language skills (Weisberg, Zosh, Hirsh-Pasek, & Golinkoff, 2013).

People who speak different languages may learn different sounds as well. For example, English speakers spend more time learning the sounds of consonants, while Spanish speakers focus on vowels (E. Garcia, 2002). Parents often sing songs to their children to teach them various sounds and patterns of a language. Not every language has the same sounds or phonemes. For example, in Japanese, people do not say the name Valerie as in English. In Japanese there are no sounds exactly like the English sound for *V* and *L*, so the person may say something like Bararie, in which the *r*'s are rolled. Therefore when students in your class are learning the sounds of English, some may be more difficult for them to master than others.

Vocabulary Development, Lexicon, and Syntax

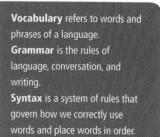

> **Vocabulary** refers to words and phrases of a language.
> **Grammar** is the rules of language, conversation, and writing.
> **Syntax** is a system of rules that govern how we correctly use words and place words in order.

While babies are learning the sounds of a language, they are also learning **vocabulary**, words and phrases of a language. Much of what they initially learn includes names of people they interact with or names of objects. Many youngsters, not much older than one year old, often ask for a "cookie" or "treat." A treat may have more than one meaning. It may mean a cookie, but it can also be candy or crackers depending on what country you're in. These babies are developing their vocabulary skills. Much later, children learn the appropriate use of terms within specific contexts, such as geographical location and dialect. In addition, once they are able to pronounce the words and know how to use them in grammatically correct sentences, they are considered skilled in the lexicon. Lexicon is complicated and is all meanings that are accumulated, the association of these meanings with the correct context, the ability to say the word correctly, the capacity to use the word grammatically in a sentence, and the knowledge of which morphemes are appropriately connected with the word. This knowledge is acquired as the brain absorbs and interacts with meaning in context (Díaz-Rico & Weed, 2010).

Toddlers are able to put words together into sentences by learning grammar and word order, known as syntax (Figure 10.2). **Grammar** is the rules of language, conversation, and writing. **Syntax** is a system of rules that govern how we correctly use words and place words in order. When learning how to create a complete sentence and convey a thought a child may say, "Ann and I is going to school tomorrow." She knows to place the subject first and then the verb in her sentence so that the word order is correct; however, the child still needs to learn about the grammatical rules regarding the use of a verb that denotes a plural subject. Amazingly, babies can do this at only one-year old.

Valerie Ooka Pang

Figure 10.2: This toddler smiles as a way of communicating with others.

Morphology and Pragmatics: Putting Words Together Within a Context

> **Morphology** is the study of the basic meaning units in language.

How do toddlers and young students build up their developing vocabulary? Can they begin to see that words have parts to them? This leads to **morphology**, which is the study of the basic meaning units in language (Díaz-Rico & Weed, 2010). Children begin to learn that words can be broken up into parts and those parts have different meanings. For example, children learn that the ending *er* added to a root of a word can mean "a person who does something." For example, a baker is someone who bakes and a runner is someone who runs. Another term that children can become familiar with is the word teacher; teacher is one who teaches. In Spanish, adding the ending *iendo* to some words is like adding *ing* in English. For example, corriendo means running and comiendo refers to eating.

One of the most difficult aspects of language to learn is context, otherwise known as pragmatics. A great deal of cultural knowledge is packed into this casual expression. **Pragmatics** is the complex understanding of context, which includes not only how language is used within specific situations but also which sentences are most appropriate within the flow of a conversation and inferences made by word choices (Díaz-Rico & Weed, 2010; Cook, 2012).

How does a child know how to use language in a specific context? Would the child use the same language at a baseball game with peers as he or she would at a formal dinner of adults in black-tie attire? The answer is: probably not. Context can be challenging for second-language learners because they need to understand the culture of the community in order to develop this skill. For example, maybe a friend says, "I've got to go catch a bus." This statement does not mean that the friend is going to actually catch a bus with a fishing pole or rope; it means she has to hurry so that she is not late when the bus arrives at her stop. Just think of all of the information we know about language due to the cultural context that we have learned.

Not being in the know regarding cultural meanings that surround a term can sometimes cause disagreements between people. For example, linguist Jiyon Cook (2012) explained how a Korean speaker might not understand the phrase "you're kidding." Many Koreans learning English have found the phrase to be rude, and they don't understand why it would be used within the context of a conversation. A Korean speaker may not understand that when a native English speaker says "You're kidding," it may be said in jest and not meant to infer that other person is joking or telling an untruth. The meaning, which may be lost on a non-native English speaker, can also be, "I don't understand why" or "I can't believe it." However, someone who is learning English as a second language may not understand the additional meanings of a phrase based on the social context of the term, which can lead to confusion.

There is an exhaustive amount of research available on language learning; however, the purpose of this chapter is to explain that it is important for teachers and other service providers to understand linguistics and language learning. In addition, the chapter will discuss how student-language levels can impact instructional strategies used in the classroom. Learning a new language represents many complex skills. Babies, children, and others must build millions of networks in their brains and develop social understandings in order to relate verbal language and gestures as they communicate with others. They must also learn about written language to become fluent and participating members of a society. Observing babies, one can see that they are quick language learners. They must use many language skills simultaneously, such as vocabulary retention, putting together correct words into sentences, understanding the social contexts of what is being said, and using proper grammar as they communicate with others. This is a lot of work!

Metalinguistic Awareness

As toddlers mature into four-year-olds, they begin to better understand underlying principles of language and the syllables of words. For example, linguist Ofelia Garcia described how children at this age easily figure out words that rhyme because they hold **metalinguistic awareness**. This means they are aware of underlying principles of language, such as the fact that rhyming words may have the same endings and how two words may sound the same but the context gives information about which spelling of the term is correct. At this age, students have learned that some words have a common final segment, and children have learned to replace the beginning consonant to create new words like *cat*, *mat*, and *sat*.

Another aspect of phonology has to do with pitch or tone. A parent who sees a baby reaching to touch a hot stove may say loudly and in an emphatic tone that denotes danger,

Pragmatics is the complex understanding of context, which includes not only how language is used within specific situations but also which sentences are most appropriate within the flow of a conversation and inferences made by word choices.

Metalinguistic awareness refers to understanding underlying principles of language, such as the fact that rhyming words may have the same endings and how two words may sound the same but the context gives information about which spelling of the term is correct.

"No!" The emphasis in tone the parent places on words also adds to the meaning of words. An example of this would be a teacher in her classroom whispering to her or his students to show quieter talking.

In some languages, it is the tone used in conjunction with a word that distinguishes it from different words. For example, in tonal languages such as Chinese and Vietnamese, words may be spelled the same but have different sounds. These words differ in their tones and therefore their meanings. In Vietnamese, there are six tones; for example, the word and pronunciation of *ma* means ghost, while the pronunciation of a word with the same spelling, *má*, means cheek. People who speak Vietnamese understand words by hearing their different intonations and accent (Tran, 1998). Native Vietnamese speakers who arrive in the United States and do not know English may have difficulty understanding that English is not a tonal language. They may be looking for phonological patterns that do not exist, which can hinder their learning process. However, as you teach ELL students, you can build on their knowledge of their first language skills. Students may already know to listen for specific sounds and to place the pattern of sounds together to make a word. Table 10.3 summarizes information about language learning. Take time to read through it so you more fully understand how complicated learning a new language is. Also remember that when students come to your class, they have already learned these skills in their home language. You can make connections between the languages they speak at home with English. Also, many English words come from other languages that your students may know.

Table 10.3 Learning a Language: Key Concepts		
Concept	**Definition**	**Example**
Grammar	The rules of language, conversation, and writing.	Able to create sentences that are accurate.
Lexicon	The complex combination of knowing how to pronounce words, understand the meaning of words, and grammatically use words.	Can refer to a dictionary, but in its more comprehensive meaning, lexicon refers to the vocabulary of a language.
Metalinguistic Awareness	Understanding the underlying principles of language.	One example is that a child may see a pattern in words like *make*, *take*, and *lake* by realizing the root is *ake*.
Morphology	The study of how words are formed.	For example, plurals are often made by adding an *s* to a word.
Phonology	Learning how to put different sounds together to form words.	For example, a diphthong is usually made of two vowels to create one syllable such as *oi* in words like *boy* or *coin*, or *ou* as in *dough*.
Pragmatics	How language is used in context.	"When are we going?" This is an example of a question that has a specific context.
Syntax	The rules used to put words together correctly.	Words are units of grammar. Run is a word. Runs is a word. *S* is not a word.
Vocabulary	Words and phrases of a language.	Words are used within a language to form phrases. For example, students might learn the word *eye* and know that it is a feature of the face and found on a person's head.

Have Fun with Language!

Do you know that many words in the English language came from other languages? Though you may know that English has borrowed from many languages, we do not usually give due credit to the linguistic origins of words from other cultures or language groups for many of our concepts and vocabulary. Various cultures may claim the same word because different languages may have roots in another; words may have developed into totally different meanings.

We may feel that we are separate from other nations, cultures, and regions in the world, but we may not be that distinct. What do you think?

For more information about various English words and their origins, take a look at this lecture: http://msuweb.montclair.edu/~franker/week11Africa4words.pdf. Because there are so many words commonly used in English that come from a variety of American Indian languages, read the article from the Oxford Dictionary website: http://blog.oxforddictionaries.com/2011/11/american-indian-words-in-english/, and another piece at http://nativeamericannetroots.net/diary/1223.

Write in your journal what you learned from this activity.

Words	Language Origin	Can you add more words?
Admiral, alcohol, cotton, couscous, gauze, genie, ghoul, hummus, mohair, muslin, ream	Arabic	
Alligator, bronco, cafeteria, cargo, cigarette, jaguar, mosquito, mustang, patio, renegade, salsa, tornado, tuna, vanilla	Spanish	
Chow, chow mein, feng shui, gung ho, ketchup, kowtow, silk, tycoon, wok	Chinese-Mandarin, Cantonese, Old Chines)	
Beluga, Bolshevik, gulag, intelligentsia, mammoth, Molotov cocktail, pogrom, Sputnik, steppe, troika, vodka	Russian	
Banjo, boogie woogie, chimpanzee, diddle, goober, gumbo, hullabaloo, jazz, jiffy, jive, jumbo, ruckus, Ubuntu, zebra, zombie	Bantu-group of African languages	
Bad, balcony, beggar, brother, calendar, candy, cash, caviar, cow, devil, God, gizzard, good, khaki, lemon, mother, mouse, name, paradise, rank, shame, sugar, thunder	Farsi (also known as Persian or Iranian)	
Caribou, chipmunk, hickory, husky, moccasin, muskrat, papoose, pokeweed, Quonset hut, raccoon, skunk, squash, tomahawk, totem	Algonquin languages	

Second-Language Acquisition Development Model

LO3 Analyze second-language acquisition models and theories.

What happens when a child or adult begins to learn another language? Is it easy? To a few it is, but to others learning to speak a second language is a challenge. For example, say you have a new student named Ana Maria in your seventh-grade social studies class. She migrated with her family from Colombia in Central America and speaks only Spanish. How do you think Ana Maria feels when she comes to school on the first day? She doesn't know anyone in the class. She has just been brought to the door by the principal and looks down at the floor.

Ana Maria makes some eye contact with you, the teacher, and with a friendly face you motion her to come into the classroom. She slowly walks in and looks blankly at the other students. You smile and then she smiles. You ask Carrie to come to the front of the room and take Ana Maria to a desk next to her. Ana Maria seems to be watching everything. She also seems to be listening and trying to figure out what is being said. She may be thinking the following:

- What is going on? I can't understand anything.
- Who will help me?
- Will someone make fun of me? What will they say?
- Oh, no. I need to go to the bathroom. How can I tell the teacher?
- Maybe I should go home.

Ana Maria constantly observes the nonverbal actions of you and her peers. Do the students smile at her? Do the students smile at you? Do you smile and joke with your students? Ana Maria follows what the other students do. Carrie takes out a blue book, so Ana Maria does the same.

Stages of Second-Language Acquisition

There are many stages that a student who is acquiring or learning English goes through. Teachers should understand and recognize the different phases that the learner must pass through in order to develop strong language skills, both conversational and abstract or academic. The next sections discuss the stages that two linguists, Stephen Krashen and Tracy Terrell, identified as part of the **natural approach**. This approach is based on the belief that in order for learners to acquire a language, it must be meaningful and comprehensible rather than just teaching grammar and language rules.

Preproduction Stage

In the natural approach, Krashen and Terrell (1983) believe it is important for teachers to assist students in developing comprehension and not to target their mistakes or language structure. Students should become more comfortable with the language and use gestures to communicate rather than to verbally respond. In this phase, Ana Maria is listening very carefully. She is trying to make sense of the sounds she is hearing. The first phase in this approach is called the **preproduction stage** (Krashen, 1981, 1982, 1993). In this stage, Ana is quiet; she is paying close attention to the sounds she hears because she knows they represent words. She is also sensitive to what her peers are doing and may try to imitate them. She sees them get out a specific book from their desks and then she does the same. Ana may be anxious because she is unsure of herself, but she is listening for patterns of sounds and trying to learn new words.

Early Production

As Ana Maria becomes more confident of herself and understands some of the conversation she hears around her, she is able to respond with a single word such as *yes*, *teacher*, or *no*. This is considered the **early production stage**, in which a person begins to use language in a limited way. She might say, "Don't know," or "What?" Ana Maria is also able to participate in classroom routines. For example, she can recite parts of the Pledge of Allegiance with her peers, even if she may not be saying each word correctly. In this stage of language development, Ana Maria is becoming familiar with English and begins to feel more confident.

Speech Emergence

In time Ana Maria moves forward into the **speech emergence stage**, in which she is able to respond to questions more naturally. She can create simple sentences, and often they are grammatically correct. Ana may say to the teacher, "I don't understand" or "I am confused." She is beginning to have control of her pronunciations and the level of voice sound that she uses when speaking in different situations. Ana Marie can read

Natural approach refers to a naturalistic strategy in teaching language. It refers to building on what is meaningful to students with less emphasis on direct instruction.

Preproduction stage is the silent period when the second-language learner is paying close attention to the sounds she hears because she knows they represent words.

Early production stage refers to the phase in which the language learner is becoming more comfortable and can provide short answers in the communication process.

Speech emergence stage refers to the period in which the second language learner is able to speak in short sentences.

short passages or easy picture books. She tries to sound out words and is familiar with approximately 3000 terms.

Intermediate Fluency

In the **intermediate fluency stage**, Ana Maria is able to participate comfortably in a conversation with others. She can self-correct some of her syntax errors. She is able to speak smoothly and is confident in expressing herself in school and with her friends. Ana Maria understands much of the vocabulary that she hears because people use it in her neighborhood. She knows almost double the amount of words that she did in the previous stage and can understand much more abstract content in various subjects, such as literature and history.

Advanced Fluency

Ana Maria continues to progress and has matured language skills; she is able to perform like a native speaker. This is referred to as the **advanced fluency stage**. Though arriving at this stage can take a person anywhere from 4 to 10 years, the individual is able to understand abstract vocabulary and concepts in disciplines such as social studies and science. See the summary of the language acquisition stages in Table 10.4.

> **Intermediate fluency stage** refers to the stage in which the second-language learner is able to communicate with others with ease.

> **Advanced fluency stage** refers to the stage in which the second-language learner has developed both conversational and academic language. These abilities can take from 4 to 10 years to acquire.

Table 10.4 Stages of Language Acquisition, Learner Characteristics, and Teaching Strategies

Stage	Learner Characteristics	Teaching Strategies
Preproduction	Listens to sounds. Listens to how people put words together. Is relatively silent and so does not speak much. May be able to say "yes" or "no." Uses many gestures. May draw a picture to communicate.	Use photos and other visuals. Use objects and other realia (concrete objects that act as a bridge in language learning) to convey ideas. Use gestures. Speak in short sentences Model correct sentences. Be positive rather than correcting student grammar.
Early Production	Has limited understanding. Primarily uses present tense. Can provide one- to two-word responses to questions. Memorizes familiar phrases or words like "okay."	Continue to use realia. Ask questions of ELLs that need only one- or two-word answers. Model short answers and have students repeat the phrases.
Speech Emergence	Feels more comfortable speaking. Speaks in sentences. Does not understand cultural context of everyday jargon. Makes many grammatical mistakes.	Prod students to participate. Ask questions using words such as "why" or "how." Use more abstract/conceptual vocabulary. Do not extensively correct student grammar. Ask students to explain concepts using their own lives.
Intermediate Fluency	Has strong comprehension skills. Makes fewer grammatical mistakes. Speaks naturally. Has trouble creating long sentences. Still needs help in language development.	Model prompts like "The story began…" and "I think the most important character is…" Have students make short presentations. Explain how cultural context may influence the meaning of a phrase.
Advanced Fluency	Speaks like a native speaker. Has strong, discipline-based vocabulary and conceptual understanding. Is doing well.	Understand that student is able to accomplish what native speakers can do. Provide guidance about grammar and writing. Realize that though students can speak naturally, they may still need guidance in abstract language development.

Sources: *Principles and practice in second language acquisition*, by Stephen Krashen, 1982, Oxford: Pergamon; *The natural approach: Language acquisition in the classroom*, by Stephen Krashen and Tracy Terrell, 1983, London: Prentice Hall Europe.

❯❯ Professional Resource Download

Second Language Acquisition Theories

As Ana Maria learns English, she can also be influenced by outside forces. Ana Maria sometimes has her feelings hurt by her classmates, teachers, and others as she tries to communicate in English. Her self-esteem suffers once in a while when a child in class laughs at her responses or her accent. As Ana Maria progresses through the stages of language development, two forces act to slow her learning of English—anxiety and worry. Ana Maria does not want to be humiliated in class. She worries about being excluded and laughed at because of her pronunciation and grammar. Stephen Krashen (1993) has developed a framework of linguistic principles to explain language acquisition, which deals with these types of issues. A **framework** is a set of interrelated principles.

> **Framework** is a set of educational principles, beliefs, policies, and practices.

Affective Filter Hypothesis

English learners such as Ana Maria must deal not only with learning a language but also with the affective component of communication. When Ana Maria makes mistakes in oral language, her classmates laugh. This situation can impact her self-esteem. Stephen Krashen (2011) calls this the **affective filter hypothesis**; this refers to his belief that language learning will be enhanced when students build up their self-confidence and motivation to acquire the second language. In other words, anxiety and worry will be obstacles to language learning. It is important for teachers to be positive and encouraging while guiding their students through the second-language acquisition process.

> **Affective filter hypothesis** is the belief that language learning will be enhanced when students build up their self-confidence and motivation to acquire the second language.

Some of the problems that English learners have identified are poor attitudes in teachers and peers. For example, some elementary school second-language students reported that they spent much of their class time watching movies, coloring, and drawing (Krashen, 2011). In this atmosphere, they weren't learning much language, and the students knew that the teacher was not truly committed to teaching them. In other classrooms, ELLs encountered teachers who were not pleasant and commonly called them "stupid." As a result, some of these students spent much of their class time in the bathroom. The affective filter, as Krashen has noted, can have a major influence on language learning, whether the student speaks Navaho, French, Mandarin, Arabic, Yup'ik, or Hawaiian. Krashen has shown that when students feel threatened or defensive, language learning will be limited; therefore he believes it is more advantageous for second language learners to use language and not worry about mistakes. The climate of the classroom should be supportive and encouraging so students will use the second language and not feel afraid. Any teacher can provide a positive environment from math to language arts by fostering a caring and trusting classroom. The more the students naturally use English, the more language they will acquire (Figure 10.3).

Figure 10.3: This young student is thinking how to respond.

Valerie Ooka Pang

Language learning occurs more rapidly when it makes sense and is meaningful to students. However, ELLs face a difficult process because second-language learning entails the integration of linguistic components such as social context, cultural language, and nonverbal cues, as well as everyday conversation skills and abstract formal language (the type of language we use to write research papers or give high-level speeches). When they enter U.S. schools, English learners are exposed to many new things. This doesn't include the content being taught in subjects such as history, geography, art, and health education and can be very overwhelming for the learner.

The Monitor Model and Acquisition-Learning Model

What do the experts say about how a student learns a second language? There are several theories about second language acquisition. First, the behaviorist B. F. Skinner believed that language is learned by constant reinforcement and drills. This theory views our minds as empty vessels into which teachers pour important information. Others, such as linguist Noam Chomsky, believed that people have innate or natural abilities to create sentences and understand linguistic rules (Díaz-Rico & Weed, 2010). Linguist Stephen Krashen, building on Chomsky's theories, developed the **monitor model**, which includes the affective filter hypothesis that was described earlier (Díaz-Rico & Weed, 2010; Smith, 2005; Krashen, 2011).

Krashen's monitor model is complex. In a speech to educators, he explained that he believed most people acquire language in similar ways. Krashen makes it clear that there are two different avenues for people to learn a second language. He believes that students can either acquire or learn language, and that acquisition is the process by which students naturally or involuntarily understand and use language in various conversational settings, such as on the playground or at lunch. He believes that it is more effective for students to *acquire* language through everyday conversations and being involved in fun activities with a low affective filter. However, schools often teach a second language by having students learn grammar and memorizing vocabulary. This approach is not the most efficient way that children *learn* because teachers present content without context. For example, if a teacher has students memorize words like bananas, oranges, lemons, and avocados without having the actual fruits in the classroom, the learner may not know which fruits they are and so can't remember the vocabulary. However, if a teacher has students try a lemon and experience the sour taste, students are more likely to remember the fruit because they have engaged with the concrete object. The students may also learn adjectives such as sour and yellow because of their experiences with the lemon. Krashen does not recommend teaching grammar rules, spelling, and vocabulary through formal instruction without a context as this makes learning a second language more difficult (Díaz-Rico & Weed, 2010). Krashen calls the difference between acquiring language and learning language the **acquisition-learning hypothesis**.

> **Monitor model** is the belief that people become more fluent in a language by using it. Minimal monitoring should occur so that the students feels comfortable acquiring the language through practice.

Input Hypothesis and Natural Order Hypothesis

Is it easier to learn a language by giving students an everyday problem to solve or teaching them how to conjugate verbs? Krashen would say that you would acquire language more rapidly if you needed to know how to use the subway to get to a new job rather than by making a chart of verbs like *ride* and *buy* in isolation. In order to get to your job, you would need to know vocabulary relating to the subway, such as *ticket*, and how to ask which way to go. In which situation would you be more likely to remember the new language? The language input must be meaningful to the learner. Oftentimes context is a critical aspect of language learning. Krashen believes students who read materials they are interested in or need to understand develop not only comprehension skills but also decoding skills such as how to sound out words and sight words (Krashen, 2011). How do you get students to learn to read? You get students reading! That's why having time in class for voluntary reading encourages language development. The natural order hypothesis involves people learning to respond in short answers using a "yes" or "no" situation. Later as the second language abilities of a person develop, the individual can answer questions dealing with who, why, or when, which are more complex and require additional skills in using grammar. The next section discusses how language acquisition is different from language learning.

> **Acquisition-learning hypothesis** refers to students acquiring language rather than learning language.

CASE STUDY

Stephen Krashen Teaches a Lesson in Language Learning to Nervous Educators

I was in the audience listening to Professor Krashen speak to educators about the importance of language acquisition over language learning (Krashen, 1993). Krashen, an extremely skilled teacher, began teaching a language lesson. The audience of deans and professors of education became quiet because, just like students in a classroom, some began to get anxious. Would he call on them to answer? What if they made an error in front of all their colleagues and bosses?

The lecture began with Krashen speaking German to his audience. No one knew what he was talking about, and there was a lot of nervous laughter. He spoke German for about one minute, but it seemed like ten minutes. Then he said in English, "Is this a good lesson so far?" Everyone laughed because of course no one had understood a word he said.

In English he then said, "What if I repeated it? Would that help?" Everyone laughed again because that wouldn't help at all. Yet teachers do this all over the country with English learners in their classes. They repeat the same phrases or questions to their Russian, Spanish, Farsi, or Vietnamese speakers and wonder why the students shake their heads or look down.

Continuing to speak German, Krashen then stopped and said in English, "What if I wrote the words on the board? Would that help?" Everyone laughed because they still wouldn't know what the lesson was about. He then said in English, "What if I talked louder?" Of course, the professors laughed again because some realized that this was a common mistake teachers made. He then held up his hand and said a word in German and pointed to his head. He repeated the German word again as he pointed

to his forehead. The audience began repeating after him. Then he drew a face on a piece of paper and again pointed to the forehead. He then said the word *stirn*, which means *forehead* in German.

Next, when the audience pronounced the word correctly, he answered, *ja*, which means *yes* in German and nodded his head and smiled. Then the audience repeated the German word for *yes*. An audible sigh of relief could be heard in the room. Krashen smiled.

Krashen proceeded to teach six features on the face by pointing to his own face and drawing it on a piece of paper. Why could we understand what he was saying? He used *comprehensible input*, gestures and drawings to explain the German words he taught. This is what Krashen (1981, 1982) calls the natural approach. Students first understand what is being taught; then they learn how to pronounce the language. With this approach, there is a low level of anxiety, and instruction is active and rich. This approach builds on what students know and affirms them as learners. The low-anxiety atmosphere is also a component of the caring-centered approach. By using this approach, teachers create classrooms of care and affirm students so that they are then encouraged to learn.

There are commonalities between Noddings' ethic of care philosophy discussed in Chapter 1 and Krashen's approach. Together with students, teachers who care are committed to academic excellence create a meaningful curriculum (Noddings, 1984, 1992, 2013). Krashen also emphasized a caring and respectful classroom atmosphere in which the content is understandable. He further explained: "We

acquire language in one way—when we understand messages. Comprehensible input." He also explained that language acquisition, as opposed to learning, should be effortless. When the input that children receive is comprehensible, they acquire the language involuntarily.

Krashen later explained that language classes can be helpful to explain aspects that students must learn, such as grammar, but that language isn't first taught by pointing out mistakes. Children acquire literacy when anxiety is low. The following is another quote from Krashen (1993) that is important to remember: "If the child believes the language class is a place where his weaknesses will be revealed, he may understand the input, but it won't penetrate. It won't reach the parts of the brain where Chomsky says there is the language acquisition device. Our job is to get input into the language device."

An excellent speaker, Krashen can be seen teaching German at http://www.sk.com.br /sk-krash.html. He explains why grammar alone or teaching vocabulary alone does not result in language learning. He believes that unless the information we convey to students is understandable and meaningful, they will not learn the second or new language because it will make no sense. See Table 10.5 for a summary of Krashen's theory of second language acquisition.

Reflection Questions

Q Do you agree with Krashen's approach to teaching language? Why or why not?

Q What does Krashen mean when he says the information conveyed to students must be comprehensible?

Consider this . . .

"Free reading is comprehensible input with a low-affective filter."
Stephen Krashen, 1993

Q Why do you think free reading helps students learn English?

Q How could you use this strategy in your classroom?

Table 10.5 Stephen Krashen's Language-Acquisition Theory

Theory	Discussion
Acquisition-Learning Hypothesis	Second language learners learn in two ways: 1. Students *acquire* language and context when the process is natural and meaningful. 2. Students formally *learn* language elements such as grammar and rules of language. This can be a struggle if the learning process is not meaningful.
Monitor Hypothesis	The English learner develops fluency in using the language. Minimal monitoring should be used so a student develops more language abilities.
Natural Order Hypothesis	The language learner looks for patterns and learns when language usage is meaningful. Grammar should be taught only minimally.
Affective Filter Hypothesis	Fear and ridicule limit the language development of learners, so less emphasis should be placed on mistakes. More emphasis is placed on creating a low-anxiety atmosphere.
Input Hypothesis	More language learning occurs when input is comprehensible and meaningful. Learner does better when he or she has high self-esteem and is part of a low-anxiety atmosphere. Krashen recommends teachers move away from memorization and drill approaches.

My Journal

Teaching Math and Language

Let's say you are teaching fifth grade and students must learn fractions. About half of your students are English language learners. How can you use Krashen's theories about language acquisition in your lessons? Come up with a topic for the lesson on fractions and decide how you would engage the students so they are not afraid to use their English skills or math skills.

Finish the following sentences:

Low affective filter: I would....

Monitor hypothesis: I would make sure I did not criticize my students because...

Instead I would make sure that my students were successful by...

Acquisition hypothesis: Students must be engaged in a problem that they are interested in. I would create the lesson around...

Input hypothesis: Whatever the students are studying must be meaningful. The input must be comprehensible, so I would...

 Professional Resource Download

Language and Cognitive Development: Moving from Conversational English to Academic English

 naeyc CAEP InTASC

> **LO4** Analyze how language levels such as BICS and CALP are linked to cognition and other literacy skills.

Have you ever spoken with a student who learned English as a second language and could carry on a good conversation? Didn't he seem ready to take on anything in school? Teachers often mistake conversational skills for academic language skill development. It takes a child approximately two years to develop conversational language. However, as linguist Jim Cummins believes, there is a great difference in language levels between mastery of conversational English and the mastery of academic English that is needed in content areas (2000). Cummins developed a theory that centers upon two concepts, one of which is **CALP**, which stands for cognitive academic language proficiency. These are skills and knowledge that students need in learning higher-level discipline content. For example,

> **CALP** stands for cognitive academic language proficiency and includes skills and knowledge that students need in learning higher-level discipline content.

Table 10.6 Comparing BICS and CALP	
BICS (Basic Interpersonal Communication Skills)	**CALP (Cognitive Academic Language Proficiency)**
The language that people use every day. Takes students one to two years to learn BICS. The language is informal. This includes gestures, tone of voice, and social context. Students can communicate well with others with basic skills; however, this ability is not enough for abstract, subject-specific school work.	High-level scholarly language that includes abstract concepts of subject areas. Takes students from five to seven years to learn CALP. Language of business, schools, and politics, which may include more complex language. Disciplines like social studies, mathematics, literature, and physics contain high-level abstract concepts that are part of academic English.
Individuals use slang such as "stuff," "cool," and "awesome." Individuals repeat words.	Individuals use more abstract words and do not use slang. Individuals use more high level and advanced vocabulary such as cultural pluralism, imperialism, acculturation, comprehensible input, etc.

> **BICS** stands for basic interpersonal communication skills and is the level of language that people use to talk with each other every day.

> **Academic English** is a broad category that includes many language skills and refers to the ability to use English on an abstract level, such as in writing.

students will have mastered social studies vocabulary in order to discuss concepts like democracy or social justice. The other, **BICS**, stands for basic interpersonal communication skills and is the level of language that people use to talk every day with each other (Cummins, 1996, 2000, 2011). CALP is a much more abstract set of cognitive skills and requires a higher level vocabulary of specific subjects; it can take another five to seven years to develop higher-order conceptual language.

Table 10.6 lists differences between BICS and CALP. Though Cummins believes they are connected skills, in order for second language learners to do well in subject areas, they need cognitive academic language.

Academic English is a broad category that includes many language skills. It is the ability to use English on an abstract level, such as in writing. Higher-order literacy skills enhance cognitive development in the areas of reasoning and decision making. Students construct meaning and make linkages between various facts and knowledge in these processes (Tharp & Gallimore, 1988). Often students work together in the creation of stories or nonfiction passages. In that activity, students contribute different points of view and challenge each other, which can enhance cognition and understanding.

Several skills that have been identified in academic English by linguists Fillmore and Snow are:

- Summarizes texts, using linguistic cues to interpret and infer the writer's intentions and messages
- Analyzes texts, assessing the writer's use of language for rhetorical and aesthetic purposes and to express perspective and mood
- Extracts meaning from texts and relates it to other ideas and information
- Evaluates evidence and arguments presented in texts and critiques the logic of arguments made in them
- Uses grammatical devices for combining sentences into concise and more effective new ones, and uses various devices—such as colons—to combine sentences into coherent and cohesive texts (Fillmore & Snow, 2000, p. 21)

This list includes all high-level language abilities. These skills are often not only difficult for English language learners (ELL) to master but also challenging for many native speakers and must be learned in school (Fillmore & Snow, 2000). Students need to be taught the complicated and sophisticated use of academic English to demonstrate the skills listed. Being able to master these skills will be critical for later academic learning and career opportunities.

One of the most difficult second-language skills is academic writing. For example, high school students need to be able to write a research report, which can include discipline-based vocabulary, theories, and an analysis of an issue (Figure 10.4). This is difficult for students who do not have high levels of subject area content and who may not think in a sequential manner (Nisbett, 2003). English language learners come to school with languages that have different structures and with different language experiences. Some languages have a linear manner of expression and their writings reflect that orientation. This approach is logical and formal. Other languages may support a more descriptive way of expressing ideas, so language learners may not understand the manner in which writing is expected. For example, a student's first language may not support the use of a topic sentence, which is the initial sentence that presents the main idea of the paragraph, and a second-language learner may not have "broad knowledge of words, phraseology, grammar, and pragmatic conventions for expression, understanding, and interpretation" (Fillmore & Snow, 2000, p. 20).

Figure 10.4: The young woman is looking up vocabulary and discipline-based concepts at the library.

g-stockstudio/Shutterstock.com

Common Grammatical Errors: Teacher Awareness

Educators can learn from the research findings of second-language experts. For example, second-language expert Robin Scarcella (2000) has identified common grammatical errors that she finds in the writings of Asian English learners. A consistent error deals with verb form: Asian students find it difficult to understand the difference in time reference. Here are two illustrations she provided:

- I always *remembered* when my friend died.
- I *study* English since 1986 (Scarcella, 2000, p. 2).

Another common error is the incorrect use or lack of prepositions. Because some Asian languages do not use prepositions in the same way as they are used in English, students may find them difficult to incorporate. Two examples of this are:

- The nucleus is *on* the cell.
- He discriminate *me* (Scarcella, 2000, p. 2).

Students also make errors because they do not know English vocabulary; when verbal statements are made, they may not understand the concepts being conveyed. For example, one student misinterpreted a title of a book because he didn't understand the vocabulary: "The book I read for my book report was *Catch Her in the Right* (Scarcella, 2000, p. 3). (The book was *Catcher in the Rye*.)

When educators understand that students make consistent errors based upon the structure of their home languages, they are better able to assist learners in understanding the mistakes they make and how to eliminate them. Second-language experts, such as Garcia (2002) and Scarcella (1999, 2013), believe that academic English and basic conversational skills are not separate language skills. In fact, they consider the two to be highly linked and to work collaboratively in helping a person to achieve better communication. In addition, they view academic English more narrowly than Cummins in that this level of language competence means that students will be able to do the following (E. Garcia, 2002):

- Analyze
- Compare

- Contrast
- Classify
- Hypothesize
- Persuade
- Evaluate
- Predict
- Generalize
- Infer
- Communicate

These are the higher-level thinking skills. Cummins has acknowledged the continuum between BICS and CALP and that there is overlap between the skills areas (2000).

Scarcella (2011) explained how CALP can be taught to English learners in disciplines through her presentation for *¡Colorín colorado*!, a popular bilingual education website. Here are examples that she suggests for teaching students how to use the vocabulary in various subject areas:

1. Students are shown how to write a lab report in biology.
2. Students are taught how to write a persuasive essay in social studies.
3. Students can practice writing in math by writing word problems.

English learners need many opportunities to practice language. Teachers can provide tasks for students that apply the use of academic vocabulary and writing skills in context, such as in a lab report. Not only is the purpose of the assignment given, but also learners are taught the format, terminology, and proper way to fill in the report. In addition, English learners can partner with others and explain vocabulary to each other. It is important that English learners use language in situations where they understand the goal of the task; in this way they acquire language and the contextual meaning simultaneously.

Teaching Cognitive Academic Language

As most teachers have found, it is easier to teach everyday English or BICS than academic English or CALP. This leads us to the question: How do I teach in content areas? Suppose English learners in your tenth-grade writing class can speak fluently but are having trouble following a sequence of directions that you verbally give. This might be due to your use of specific terms in the discipline, such as metaphor and irony, and your students may not have learned these concepts in Spanish, for example, and are not already familiar with them. Therefore it is important for teachers to build on the prior knowledge of students and use many prompts to guide student learning. Teachers may give examples of metaphors so that their modeling assists student comprehension of the vocabulary. Do you know these metaphors that are often used in society?

Time is money.
Love is blind.
Honesty is the best policy.
Life is a journey.

When teaching, instructors also need to be careful to use short sentences rather than long complex ones to ensure that students understand the discussion and instructions being modeled.

Sheltered English and SDAIE Approaches

Some educators say, "I use the *sheltered* method." What does that mean? **Sheltered English** and the **SDAIE** approaches to teaching are methods that teach both subject area content and language skills in an English-only classroom. Sheltered refers to providing supports when students are learning discipline content. This might mean building on vocabulary that leaners may already know in the subject area. Maybe students have put water or soup

Sheltered English is a method that is supportive of English learners so that they learn both subject area content and language skills.

SDAIE refers to specially designed academic instruction in English. This method is like sheltered English in which both language skills and subject area content are taught.

in a pan and heated the liquid on the stove. The learners may have seen bubbles rise out of the water or soup. The teacher can use student knowledge to explain the concept of boiling, that when the water reaches the temperature of 212 degrees Fahrenheit or 100 degrees Celsius, then the liquid will boil. A cook can tell when the soup is boiling because of all of the bubbles and movement in the pan.

How do you pronounce *SDAIE*? It sounds like *su* in *supper* and *die,* as in "not living." It means specially designed academic instruction in English. It is "su-die." SDAIE, sheltered English strategies, and other content-centered approaches to instruction are based on the beliefs that a second language and content are best learned when the material has meaning for students as discussed above (Crandall, 1994; Krashen, 2011). Language skills can be taught while students focus on academic content from basic disciplines such as geography, mathematics, science, and social studies.

There are three major goals in these classrooms:

1. English language learners need to be taught the same subject area content as their native speaker peers are learning. Equal educational opportunity is important for all students.
2. English language learners also need to continue to work on developing their English language skills and becoming mature in their use of academic content in their writing and verbal communication.
3. Students must learn the behaviors that are expected in the classroom, such as responding appropriately when a teacher calls on them.

Crandall (1994, p. 1) suggests that the following conditions must be present for effective sheltered learning to occur:

- Learning focuses on "meaning rather than on form."
- Language is at or a little above the expertise of learners.
- Creation of a stress-free classroom.
- Creation of many opportunities to use language in ways that are relevant and understandable to learners.

In addition to these components, the SDAIE model is most effective when teachers bring to the classroom positive beliefs about the ability of their English language learners (Díaz-Rico & Weed, 2010).

> **CALLA (cognitive academic language learning approach)** focuses on teaching academic content to intermediate English learners.

CALLA: Cognitive Academic Language Approach

Another content-based approach, for those students who are intermediate or advanced English learners, is the **cognitive academic language learning approach**, or **CALLA** (Chamot & O'Mally, 1994; Chamot, 1995). This approach focuses on developing higher-level thinking skills in discipline areas while enhancing language skills. The theoretical foundation is the sociocultural theory of learning where language and social interaction are key tools for instruction.

CALLA is often used in disciplines such as science, math, language arts, social studies, and literature and composition. For example, students may learn about the gold rush in California from about 1848 to 1853 via hands-on learning (Figure 10.5). Upper-elementary and middle-school students learn about territories, immigrants, mining, and panning for gold. In addition, English-language learners develop *metacognitive* strategies. These strategies are skills

Figure 10.5: This educator is teaching about the California gold rush through a hands-on, interactive activity: panning for gold.

that students can use in various subject areas such as vocabulary strategies for new or confusing words, finding the key ideas in the text, using photos for cognitive clues, and figuring out what information is most important to remember (Díaz-Rico & Weed, 2010). Although some researchers believe CALLA and SDAIE are to be used only when students are at the intermediate fluency and advanced levels of English-language development, Chamot and O'Malley (1994) believe it is important to use content-based CALLA approaches even with early language learners because these strategies can make content concepts more understandable.

The following is an example of a CALLA lesson. In their social studies class, high-school students studied issues brought up by the September 11, 2001, terrorist attack on the United States (Pang & Jones, 2004). The class focused on issues of terrorism for the week. Students tackled such questions as:

- What is terrorism?
- Who is a terrorist?
- Why do terrorists commit acts of violence against innocent people?
- What civil liberties, if any, are we willing to give up for greater security?

Students wrote definitions for terms such as *terrorism*, providing important characteristics of the word. They consulted the Internet for information about other countries that were dealing with terrorism. Students used atlases to find the locations of various countries on the globe. In addition, they were asked to write an essay describing their feelings about the day. Rosa, a native Spanish-speaking high school student wrote, "I have mixed feelings about this day. I feel depress when I think about all the people that die that day." Rosa's two sentences contained errors that she had made consistently in her papers during the week. The teacher noted that the student did not understand the proper use of the past

TEACHING TIPS

Teaching Writing to English Language Learners

The following are cognitive strategies used to teach students how to write in the California Writing Project (Olson & Land, 2007). This chart is an adaptation for teachers to use with their students.

Planning and Goal Setting

1. Set a writing goal.
2. Identify one's writing purpose.
3. Identify audience of piece.
4. Identify the practical order of investigation.

Use Prior Knowledge

1. Get together knowledge of the topic/issue.
2. Explore knowledge of topic/issue.
3. Analyze what knowledge is needed before writing piece.

Ask Questions and Formulate Predictions

1. Create questions about the topic/issue/insights/purpose.
2. Identify a focus of the piece.

Build the Message

1. Reflect on the message.
2. Look for patterns or linkages among one's knowledge.
3. Identify the main idea.
4. Gather and organize information.
5. Develop the sequence of how ideas are to be presented.

Monitor

1. Teachers monitor student progress.
2. Teachers give feedback about purpose and organization of ideas.
3. Teachers suggest if students should go back to a previous step.

Revise

1. Reflect on writing or author's purpose.
2. Assess literary tools used by author.
3. Assess flow of piece.
4. Judge effectiveness of transitions.

Reflect

1. Take time to reflect on major messages conveyed.
2. Ensure interpretations are clear and accurate.
3. Evaluate the quality of the ideas and writing.
4. Judge effectiveness

If your students have trouble writing an essay, choose a topic or issue that they are interested in. For example, you can have your students interview their grandmother, grandfather, uncle, aunt, mother, or father and choose one of these topics to discuss:

- A time when she or he was young and a mentor helped her or him to learn a life lesson
- Something funny that happened in his or her life
- The most fun family event that he or she remembers

⌄ Professional Resource Download

tense. The word *depress* should have been *depressed* and the term *die* should have been *died*. The teacher gave this student a lesson about rules regarding the past tense verb form. In addition, Rosa needed to think about the use of pronouns in her writing. Because the word *that* in the second sentence referred back to the word *people*, Rosa needed to think about using the pronoun *who*.

Although Rosa was able to write about a more abstract concept such as "Call of Duty" because she was extremely interested in the work of firefighters, she was not aware of grammatical mistakes in her writing. The teacher noted that her errors were consistent and suggested that Rosa read her written work aloud because that might help her hear some of the mistakes she was making. In social studies lessons, the teacher was able to teach about various issues related to September 11 and also focus on English language skills. Language was a vehicle for Rosa to learn about her world and to understand the complexities in it.

Length of Time to Teach English Skills

The length of time it takes for an English language learner to become proficient varies depending on many factors, such as the extent of instruction the student has had in her or his first language, whether the student was schooled previously in a home country, the social and economic status of the family, the amount of English heard in the family and neighborhood, and the age of the individual (G. Garcia, 2000; Crawford & Krashen, 2015).

Linguists Thomas and Collier (1997) found that students who were in bilingual programs and doing well in their native language (L1—first language) performed at the fiftieth percentile in English (L2—second language) after approximately 4 to 7 years of schooling. However, in the same study the researchers found that it may take 7 to 10 years for students who have had little instruction in their native language (L1) and most of their years of schooling in English (L2). (See Figure 10.6.) What accounts for this difference in achievement? Historian Gilbert Garcia (2000) explained that when students have been schooled in their first language, they acquire important language skills, such as syntax, vocabulary, discourse, and pragmatics— features of language that students can use to learn English. That is why Thomas and Collier suggest that each English language learner be enrolled in a bilingual program for at least the first several years of school.

Another factor that influences a student's ability to acquire English is the attitude of teachers. Castañeda and Ríos (2002) found that teachers resisted learning about languages and cultures different from their own. In fact, some teachers were hostile to language acquisition staff development. Here is a comment of one of the teachers Castañeda and Ríos had in their classes: "I don't like it [diversity], really, because it seems to pose more problems than we previously had. We all wish for students who speak our language, are part of American culture and don't require special provisions; it makes our job easier" (2002, p. 10).

Castañeda and Ríos recommended that teachers be guided through deep self-reflection about their own values and biases. It is imperative that teachers have a good understanding of the power of culture and language in learning; otherwise, they may not be able to provide nurturing and effective instruction. Learning English may take longer in classrooms where students face negative attitudes about their home languages or schools where they are isolated and marginalized and therefore not learning enough content or language. Teacher prejudice can have

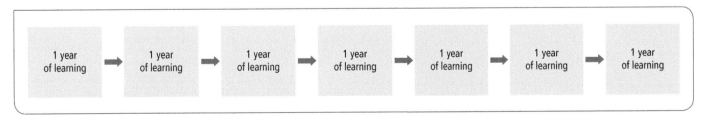

Figure 10.6: It can take students up to seven years of instruction in order for them to learn abstract and discipline-based language.

a powerful effect on student learning. Sometimes, teachers do not even realize that they hold biased views about a specific language or English learners and their families.

Bilingual Education Programs

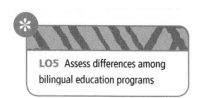

Having a good understanding of how language is learned and taught will help you see why bilingual education is so important. The following section provides a discussion of various programs in bilingual education. Language researchers such as Kenji Hakuta, Stephen Krashen, Lilly Wong Fillmore, and Jim Cummins believe that when children receive a strong foundation in their home language, they can learn English more efficiently and quickly. When instruction is initially provided in their native language (e.g., Spanish), then children can build on what they already know. They know Spanish—the sounds, the rhythm of the language, sentence structure, vocabulary, pragmatics, and many other aspects of language—and can build upon their language skills. If schools have bilingual education programs that focus on maintaining Spanish, then children will have the time to learn the same subject area content that their peers are also receiving in regular classrooms. When students' knowledge of Spanish is strong, learning the skills in English becomes easier. In other words, when students have developed cognitive language skills in their home language, then students can use those abilities to learn English. Students who already know how language is put together can use those skills to more easily learn a second language.

Evangelina Bustamante Jones taught high school English learners. She learned that students may already understand specific linguistic rules such as what a noun and verb are. Therefore, when those skills are taught in English, the teacher doesn't have to translate vocabulary and language concepts at the same time. Because Professor Jones's Spanish-speaking students already understood the rules of Spanish, she used their knowledge to teach the syntax and context of English. Krashen provides an example of two children who speak Spanish. Suppose both have a good background in math and one has been in a bilingual classroom for three years. The second child is in a regular classroom. Their language resources are still in the early stages of developing CALP or academic language. Who is going to do better? The first student will understand more math and English because these subjects are more comprehensible. His teachers are able to build on his knowledge of Spanish to teach in English. The other child will not understand either because he does not have much background information about Spanish or English.

Krashen believes skills from first languages transfer to the acquisition of a second language. Other researchers have echoed what he has said. Why then is there so much resistance to bilingual education? James Crawford and Stephen Krashen (2015) found that people believed several fallacies:

1. Bilingual education is far more costly than English-language instruction.
2. Research is inconclusive on the benefits of bilingual education.
3. The best way to learn a language is through "total immersion."

Take time to read the text by Crawford and Krashen (2015). They refute each of these fallacies and discusses many more.

Let's examine the three fallacies listed above.

1. Is bilingual education far more costly than English-language instruction? A study commissioned by the California legislature found that bilingual and English-only approaches cost about the same each year per pupil. In many ESL (English as a second language) classrooms, additional teachers had to be hired for these pull-out programs. This is quite expensive, so hiring bilingual teachers in the first place does not necessarily cost more.

2. Research by scholars such as Collier, Fillmore, Hakuta, Ramirez, Krashen, Tomas, Garcia, Cummins, and Snow has shown that students who have been in well-designed and well-implemented bilingual education generally do better than their second-language peers who have not had any bilingual instruction. These gains are found not only in elementary school but also later in secondary school.

3. Why don't students who are thrown into submersion situations do well? One of the major reasons is that students are neither learning English nor the grade-level content. The culture of the students is not being affirmed. Students' knowledge is not being built on because limited communication occurs between teachers and students. In the early grades, ESL students may do quite well, but when they are placed in a regular classroom with little language support, they tend to fall behind native English speakers. This usually happens in the fourth grade, when instruction becomes more text-driven and the content areas are taught in more formal ways. If children have not been exposed to the academic language of the content areas in earlier grades, and they have not learned them through primary language instruction, they may have more difficulties in junior and senior high school.

Bilingual Education and Other Language Programs

What is bilingual education? This is not an easy question to answer. The term *bilingual education* has many connotations and means different things in various schools and districts. However, generally **bilingual education** refers to students receiving instruction in their native language and English. (See Figure 10.7.)

The goal of bilingual education is **biliteracy**, which is the ability to read and write in two languages. This approach includes various types of programs in which students are first taught in a classroom where almost 100 percent of instruction is given in a heritage/home language, and then placed in other classrooms where the environment uses various levels of English. To be clear, bilingual education differs from pull-out ESL programs (teaching English as a second language) in which a child may get 20 minutes of English language instruction a day.

Bilingual education carries some controversy. There has been opposition to bilingual education in the United States (Krashen, 1996). One example is Proposition 227 that was passed in California in 1998. This proposition banned bilingual education unless parents

> **Bilingual education** refers to students receiving instruction in their native language and English. **Biliteracy** is the ability to read and write in two languages.

Andrew Rich/Getty Images

Figure 10.7: This student enjoys learning a second language and is proud of his accomplishment.

requested that their children be placed in bilingual programs. Proponents of this law believed that students should learn English in school. Proponents also believed that parents should teach their children a heritage language at home and that teachers should be using research-based sheltered methods in the classroom rather than bilingual programs.

Transitional Bilingual Education (Early Exit and Late Exit)

Colin Baker, a bilingual education expert, has carefully explained that in transitional bilingual education (TBE), the primary goals are to assimilate students into American society and to teach them English. He uses a swimming pool analogy: The student is taught the free stroke and backstroke before being asked to swim in the larger pool; in other words, the student does have some English-language skills. Early exit refers to situations in which students have instruction for a maximum of two years, during which the first language is used part of the time and English is used for the other portion. Unfortunately, the curriculum may center on BICS only and not CALP because two years is not long enough for English learners to develop complex cognition and conceptual skills (Díaz-Rico & Weed, 2010).

In the transitional bilingual education (Late Exit) program, the student is kept in the bilingual program until the sixth grade and may receive 40 percent of instruction in the home/heritage language (Baker, 2006). Students in these programs can speak and read in both languages. Cultural relevancy is an important aspect of this approach. The teacher is a cultural mediator and usually has some ties to the native language community. However, some implementations of this approach are seen as weak because the focus is assimilation, similar to the submersion models of English-language development (Baker, 2006). However, late transitional programs do afford students more opportunity to retain their primary language.

Developmental Bilingual Education

In maintenance or MBE, which stands for maintenance bilingual education programs, two languages, cultures, and viewpoints are maintained and developed. Bilingualism is seen as an important benefit and skill. The goal of MBE is to help a student become fully proficient in both languages (Baker, 2006). Because language is a dynamic element of life where new vocabulary and history are being added to the cultural group, it is important that teachers guide students in developing academic concepts and terms (Figure 10.8); this is the reason that maintenance bilingual education does not go far enough (O. Garcia, 2009). This approach also emphasizes the importance of students developing a strong ethnic and linguistic identity.

Dual-Language Programs

The goal of dual language programs (also known as two-way dual language programs) is to teach students so they are skilled and able to function well in two languages. Language brings agency and self-identification, how a child identifies and sees him- or herself as

Figure 10.8: This bilingual poster lets parents know that students will be investigating science concepts.

Valerie Ooka Pang

being part of a cultural/linguistic community. Both English learners and native speakers of English are members of the program. Bilingualism and biliteracy are major goals of this program (Baker, 2006). In these programs, both cultures and languages of students are affirmed and used in instruction. Most dual-language programs feature Spanish and English, although Mandarin or Japanese and English can be found where there are large numbers of Asian speakers. Garcia (2009) also points out that because the term "bilingual education" is seen by some as a politically loaded, the term "dual language" is used.

Baker (2006) and Garcia (2009) have identified four characteristics of two-way bilingual programs:

1. A language other than English maybe used from 50 percent to about 90 percent of instruction in early grades. Move to the 50/50 model of instruction in upper grades (50 percent home language and 50 percent English is used in class).
2. In each instructional period, only one language is used.
3. The numbers of non-English and English-speaking students are approximately the same so that there is a language balance in the classroom.
4. Both English learners and native English speakers are participants in all lessons.

As dual language programs have increased, the Center for Applied Linguistics published a well-developed document identifying essential principles. The principles stress the importance of developing curriculum that:

- Supports assessment and accountability of student progress
- Is standards-based and teaches bilingual, biliterate, and multicultural competencies
- Is instruction research based
- Has high quality dual language educators as faculty
- Supports an equitable program
- Builds strong networks with parents and community members
- Provides strong financial resources

One of the goals of the program is student integration. For example, in order to encourage the cross-mixing of classmates, students who are native Spanish speakers may help their English-speaking peers with their homework in Spanish, while English speakers assist Spanish-speaking students with their English seatwork. It is critical that our students have the opportunity to develop not only English but also other languages. Language brings power, control in one's community, and self-identity.

Language Programs: Other Programs for English Language Learners

There are several types of language programs. The first two are those that provide little support for native language, progressing to programs in which both native and second languages are nurtured and therefore would not be considered bilingual education programs.

Submersion

Submersion is one approach to teaching English learners and should not be confused with bilingual education. In this program, students who do not speak English are placed in an all-English–speaking classroom and expected to learn English while they learn grade-level academic content. This approach is often called the "sink or swim" method since the home/heritage language is not used at all.

The program is **subtractive** in that teachers ignore the first language of their students. The goal is learning English, and these classrooms, for the most part, have an assimilationist orientation. Assimilation in this context means that the child is expected to learn the culture, language, behaviors, and so forth of the majority group, while the culture and language of her or his group is placed in the background, becomes secondary, or is forgotten altogether in the learning process.

Submersion is an approach to teaching English learners and should not be confused with bilingual education; students are expected to learn English while they learn grade-level academic content. This approach is often called the "sink or swim" method. **Subtractive** bilingualism approach is one in which teachers ignore the first language and culture of their students.

TAKE A STAND

WHICH APPROACH IS BEST FOR A BILINGUAL STUDENT?

English Submersion	Dual Language
Many immigrants have done well with the submersion approach because they learned English quickly and became Americanized so that they fit in well with others. New immigrants need English in order to survive economically and socially.	Immigrant and other bilingual individuals can act as important linguistic and cultural mediators in our global society because they are bilingual and bicultural. This is especially important in the area of economics.
Bilingual education programs are extremely costly because specially trained teachers must be found for many language groups. It can be difficult and expensive to hire bilingual teachers who can speak Farsi, Russian, Lao, Cambodian, Vietnamese, Spanish, Somali, or Arabic.	Bilingual education programs do not cost more than English as second language pull-out programs. Schools have hired many dual language teachers to address the needs of English learners. Dual language teachers do not cost any more than bilingual teachers.
It is not advisable to have children segregated into classrooms only for Spanish-speaking, Cantonese speaking, or other non-English groups. We should encourage integration.	Many bilingual programs are dual language ones so that students who are native language speakers are also learning a second language, are affirmed as diverse language speakers, and develop biliteracy skills.
There are Latino parents who want their children in English-only classrooms and feel that without this approach their children will not learn English. Some children who have participated in bilingual programs have not learned either English or Spanish well.	Many language diverse parents have requested bilingual education programs for their children because they and other elders want to be able to continue to communicate with their children. Language is an important vehicle in the preservation and the teaching of cultural values.
In English-only classrooms, test scores for second-grade Latino students in California rose on the STAR assessments from 1998 to 2001.	The most difficult time for English learners is after fourth grade when students are expected to use academic language and engage in higher order thinking skills and concepts. Hakuta's research demonstrated that districts that banned bilingual education did not see their school test scores rise for English-language learners (http://www.stanford.edu/~hakuta/Publications/index.html).

TAKE A STAND...

▶ **Take time to think of both positions. Write down other reasons for each one. Then find a partner and discuss this issue.**

Suppose you were a 13-year-old from a country where there was civil strife and your family has refugee status. You find yourself in a classroom where no one looks like you, no one speaks your native language, and you don't know what is going on. Your parents didn't want to leave their home country but knew that their family would have been killed if they stayed, so they reluctantly left and came to the United States. You are happy to be out of danger, but now you face a new type of uncertainty: How do you survive in another country, especially when you can't speak the language?

You end up in a middle school where you feel isolated. You are quiet and try not to do anything that would bring unwanted attention. As you become more accustomed to the school, you begin to pick up words and then phrases in English, but you are behind in your schoolwork. The teachers are extremely kind; however, few teachers or students ask about your background. You wish for the day when you don't seem so different. Your desire to be considered an American grows every day.

Many teachers would argue that this is best for students. They believe that it is important for English language learners to learn English as fast as possible so that they will be able to cope with and participate in their new country, while other teachers argue that they can help students to preserve their native language and culture while learning English and mainstream culture. It could be to our advantage as a society to have students who speak English as well as Spanish, Arabic, Farsi, or Russian. As a nation, we will need students who as adults can build relationships with global partners, and who understand and are comfortable in various cultural settings.

English as a Second Language (ESL)

There are also programs that have ESL components and are not bilingual education approaches. Many of these programs are "pull-out classes" (also called withdraw classes) (Baker, 2006). This means that students leave their main classroom and work with a specialist for 20 to 30 minutes a day or several times a week. The focus is only on English skills such as vocabulary, spelling, grammar, and conversational skills. Unfortunately, students have difficulty learning the material while they are pulled out because the curriculum of the ESL teacher usually does not include the missed classroom content (Díaz-Rico & Weed, 2010).

These programs have limited success for a variety of reasons (Baker, 2006). Following are several reasons for their nominal effectiveness:

1. English instruction is only for a short period several times a week. Students do not have the opportunity to practice language skills consistently.
2. The programs do not build on the cultural knowledge of students because one of the major goals is to assimilate English learners into society.
3. The home culture and language of English learners are not affirmed.
4. Because the teacher is not familiar with the students' heritage languages, they do not have the ability to develop biliteracy or transfer language skills from the home language (L1) to English (L2).
5. It is costly to hire resource ESL teachers in addition to providing regular educators.
6. Students pulled out feel stigmas of needing remediation and of not being smart.

I once tutored a third grader with a disability in his classroom; he was trilingual, and English was his third language. He felt unintelligent because of his lower language skills. However, because of his fear of leaving the classroom, the teacher asked me to work with him in the back of the room. The young student thought that the other kids would think he was going to "special ed" if we went out of the classroom. For a year, we sat in the back corner working on the complex vocabulary and abstract concepts that he did not understand in his social studies and science texts. This approach worked effectively because I could observe for an hour prior to our sessions what the teacher was covering and then help the student with his class seatwork.

In contrast to ESL instructional programs that do not foster content area instruction, sheltered instruction such as CALLA or SDAIE provide both language skill and content development. (For a further description, see the sections titled "CALLA: Cognitive Academic Learning Approach" and "Sheltered English and SDAIE Approaches.") There is little use of the primary language in ESL classrooms where these approaches are implemented (Díaz-Rico & Weed, 2010).

English Dialects: African American English or Ebonics

Because this chapter is about language, it is critical for teachers to understand that Ebonics or African American English (AAE) is a language in its own right. The Center for Applied Linguistics (CAL), a resource on language instruction and culture located in Washington, DC, notes that the term has changed over the years from Black English to Ebonics to African American English.

Teachers should know that many scholars believe **African American English**, also called **Ebonics**, is "a legitimate, rule-based, systematic language, and this language is the primary language of many African-American children" (Perry & Delpit, 1998, p. 3). Others believe it is a dialect of English. Dialect differences may refer to pronunciation and vocabulary and also include syntax or the word order and way that words are used (Rickford, 1998; E. Garcia, 2002).

Is Ebonics a real language? Should it be respected as a language? The Linguistic Society of America passed a resolution recognizing Ebonics as a "systematic and rule-governed" language and affirmed that it should not be described as "lazy," "slang," or "defective" (E. Garcia, 2002). Educational researchers, Perry and Delpit (1998) believe that some educators fall into a category of teachers who do not value African Americans and do not want to legitimize Ebonics as a language because of racist or negative beliefs toward African Americans. I highly recommend reading their book *The Real Ebonics Debate* because it takes a comprehensive

> **African American English,** also called Ebonics, is a rule-governed language that arose out of African American culture.

CASE STUDY: Teaching Math and Science Education to English Language Learners

The integration of Spanish and Latino culture into math and science education, as well as research on strategies for English learners, is growing in this country. This is good news for native Spanish speakers who make up approximately 17 percent of the U.S. population. The following case describes the work of Rochelle Gutiérrez (2002), who observed several successful high school mathematics teachers who worked with English dominant Latino students. These students did not attend bilingual education classes. The teachers supported bilingual education for their students, but were not bilingual themselves.

The teachers that Gutiérrez studied understood that access and retention of Latino students in mathematics classes needs to be addressed, although many Latino students still find themselves on the sidelines when it comes to their learning experience. Unlike elementary grade subjects, high school math content is more abstract and often more challenging to teach. Gutiérrez found that many math teachers believe that mathematics is a "culture free" content area.

The High School Math Classroom: Recommendations

Gutiérrez clearly explained that language, culture, and ethnic identity are intimately tied together for many students. For example, if Spanish is used at home, the language represents family, home, and national cultures,

along with a sense of community with others whose ancestors may have come from diverse countries such as Puerto Rico, Mexico, Cuba, and Guatemala.

Spanish as a language can be at the heart of students' identity, although their levels of proficiency will vary. Gutiérrez found in math classes that although students might be fluent in conversational Spanish, they might not have an academic background in the language. Many students were not familiar with high-level mathematical concepts and vocabulary in Spanish. Therefore, some students who come with a home language of Spanish need to study math in both languages in order to become bilingual (Gutiérrez, 2002).

In the same classrooms, there were also second- and third-generation Latinos who did not speak Spanish, although some of their teachers believed they were English-deficient (Gutiérrez, 2002). This view resulted from stereotypes that teachers believed and associated with ethnicity. Also, students come to school with cultural knowledge and experiences that may be different from their teachers. It is important for teachers to build on the prior resources, information, and languages that their students possess. When teachers include the cultural knowledge of students, it honors them and their families.

According to Gutiérrez, learning for bilingual students is complex because students must

grasp new mathematical concepts while at the same time learning new English vocabulary. In these classes, students helped each other make mathematical connections using both English and Spanish. This enhanced the English skills of English learners and the Spanish skills of students whose primary language was English. The bilingual process can include three levels of learning:

- Math concepts
- Spanish vocabulary
- English vocabulary

Teaching the Language of Mathematics

Mathematics has its own language, and when students are told to plot a series of points or calculate differentials, they must understand the vocabulary and constructs of this language in order to carry out these functions. It is critical for educators to teach the language of mathematics and, as one teacher explained, children need to understand both the forest and the trees (Gutiérrez, 2002). The forest represents the "big picture" and math concepts that students learn. The trees are the details or particular examples of a concept. Mathematicians expect people to express themselves in the language of mathematics. One way to do this is to provide several ways to explain the same situation; this might include the use of visuals, role-playing, stories, charts, and group work.

look at the Ebonics controversy. For some educators, African American English has been a hot button topic, and it is important for teachers to investigate both sides of the issue.

Within this discussion, it should be noted that the Oakland (California) School District school board passed a resolution in 1996 to participate in the Standard English Proficiency Program, also known as SEP, that used Ebonics as a link in teaching literacy in the only all-Black school district in California. As linguist Mary Rhodes Hoover (1998) explained, Ebonics emphasizes the teaching of Standard English skills and African American culture, and has the added advantage of affirming speakers of Ebonics. African American English is used as a bridge to teaching Standard English (Secret, 1998).

When teaching Ebonics, educator Carrie Secret recommends that African and African American cultures are used to demonstrate literacy skills because cultural background is seen as the foundation for learning. Secret also emphasizes that Ebonics is not taught because the children already know the language; rather, she uses beauty and cultural images found in literature written in Ebonics by African American authors such as Maya Angelou, Toni Morrison, and Alice Walker. These writers use the style and rhetorical

CASE STUDY *continued*

How effective is group work? Another strategy for teachers is to encourage students to use mathematical language with their classmates in small-group discussions. Many research studies indicate that students who work as partners or in small groups learn more effectively (Gutiérrez, 2002). Researchers believe that some students act as cultural mediators or interpreters for students having trouble following their teacher and can help in solving problems by explaining the content in several ways. Sometimes in small groups, individual students are more likely to make the content their own by taking ownership of the material. In fact, one of the teachers whom Gutiérrez interviewed explained how a student used Spanish in a small group to help two bilingual peers.

Teaching the Language of Additive Bilingualism

James Shulman is a White teacher who did not believe Latino students were deficient but instead that he should value and affirm their native language. He did not speak Spanish himself; however, he believed in incorporating his students and their cultures into the learning process. In his classroom he practiced additive bilingualism, an approach in which students were encouraged to use both their native language and English in the learning process. He believed that encouraging students to use Spanish was an asset in class because students could help their bilingual classmates more fully understand complex math concepts.

In her research, Gutiérrez found that effective teachers were those who took time to know their students by observing and interacting informally with them. In taking this approach, teachers developed strategies that addressed their individual and group needs. Caring and personal reciprocal relationships provide the foundation for a community of learners to thrive. Teachers need to embrace the fact that all students should have the opportunity to participate in high-level quality math education and realize that by doing so they are participating in liberatory education and the belief that teaching is a political act.

Gutiérrez found the following characteristics in her study of mono-English math teachers of Latino students:

1. Teachers believed in their students and saw teaching as a political act in providing education that liberated students rather than oppressed them.
2. Teachers wanted students to make mathematics their own and nurtured them in developing high-level problem solving skills. This in turn gave students access to higher math level classes, with many taking calculus courses.
3. Teachers created a learning community by encouraging group work and getting to know students informally. Teachers honored and affirmed the cultural and linguistic background of their students by observing their needs and developing caring, reciprocal relationships with them.
4. Teachers taught students the language of the content area, in this case, the language of mathematics. The educators believed that in order for young people to participate in building their own understandings of the mathematical concepts being taught, they needed to know the language of mathematics.
5. When students did not understand the mathematical concepts fully, bilingual students were encouraged to use Spanish to help their peers more completely grasp the constructs. They not only learned the concepts more fully, but their mentors also took control and made the content their own.
6. Teachers realized that there are many ways of knowing.
7. Gutiérrez found that monolingual English-speaking teachers could incorporate strategies that are often recommended to bilingual educators. These methods were also effective with English-dominant Latino students, monolingual English students, and bilingual (Spanish/English) youth.

Think about the strategies that Gutiérrez identified. They could be helpful in your classroom also.

Reflection Questions:

Q Do you think bilingual students should help translate for their peers if they cannot understand the content? Why or why not?

Q Why did Gutiérrez see teaching as a political act?

---

characteristics of Black language and culture to create strong and memorable characters and settings (Meier, 1998).

Since the SEP program has been implemented, Secret has found parents to be more willing to come to school and not feel embarrassed when they speak Ebonics. Another teacher noticed that African American students are seeking out literature written by Africans or African Americans at the library (Meier, 1998). In SEP, Standard English is taught because teachers believe that all students need to be proficient in its use in order to survive in mainstream society. For example, being able to write using Standard English will be a necessary skill for both higher education and career opportunities. Students learn Standard English and integrate aspects of Ebonics, such as cultural images, culturally based analogies, rhythm, proverbs, and vocabulary in their own writings (Meier, 1998).

African American English speakers, even young children, know that there are different words that people use that have specific cultural meanings or contexts. Children often understand the cultural roots of language expressions (Delpit, 2002). When high school students are asked to speak in Standard English, they know what teachers are referring to; however, they also may be

> **Additive bilingualism** is an approach in which students are encouraged to use both their native language and English in the learning process.

> **Consider this . . .**
>
> "Human relationships are at the heart of schooling . . . devaluation of identity played out in the interactions between educators and students convinces many students that academic effort is futile."
>
> —Jim Cummins, 1996, pp. 1, 3.
>
> **Q** What do teachers say that may devalue the ethnic or linguistic backgrounds of students? List five examples.
>
> **Q** Also list five things that teachers can say affirming ethnic and linguistic backgrounds of students.

sensitive to the tone, vocabulary, and verbal style that individuals use. Delpit shared a story of a young student who said to her teacher, "Teacher, how come you talking like a White person? You talkin' just like my momma talk when she get on the phone!" (2002, p. 154). The young girl knew by the words chosen, the tone, and the style that the teacher was using a different dialect. She was aware that social acceptance differed based on what language was used. In addition, she may also be learning about how she identifies with the language that *she* uses. As you have read, language can often be an integral aspect of a student's cultural/ethnic identity, whether they speak Ebonics, Spanish, or Polish. The marginal statement in the Consider this… feature can be applied to children whose African American English is devalued in schools.

Thinking about Intersectionality

Intersectionality is about the layering of power differentials. When students arrive at school speaking a home language other than English and the language is one that is considered of lesser status than English, then students can be subjected to social oppression from peers and teachers. This can result in students abandoning their language and cultures. Intersectionality in regard to language can also deal with cultural backgrounds. Often English language learners feel tremendous social pressure to stop speaking their home language.

As time progresses, many begin speaking only English not only at school but also at home. The pressure to assimilate, linguistically and culturally, are powerful social forces, and teachers must affirm the cultural and linguistic backgrounds of their students in all subject areas so that they retain who they are (Nasir, Cabana, Shreve, Woodbury, & Louie, 2014). By acknowledging a student's diverse language and cultural background, the teacher reaffirms the student's identity and can use this to build English language and cultural skills.

Summary

1. **Describe the demographics of English learners in U.S. schools.**

   There are many English language learners in schools. Though 71 percent of ELLs are Spanish-speaking, there are also many students who speak a home language such as Mandarin, Vietnamese, Yupik, Russian, Yiddish, Arabic, Urdu, Crow, Hmong, Somali, and Tagalog. Each state has different languages in schools that it must address. The states with the largest number of ELL students in 2012–2013 were California with 1,521,772, Texas with 773,732, Florida with 277, 802, and New York with 237,499.

2. **Explain first language skills that babies develop, such as syntax, phonology, metalinguistic awareness, and morphology.**

   Babies learn their first language by developing linguistic skills such as phonology, which is the putting together of different sounds to create

   words, lexicon, which is the complex knowledge of how to put words together within the correct context, and metacognition, which is knowing the underlying principles of language. Metacognition is thinking about thinking.

3. **Analyze second-language acquisition models and theories.**

   There are many second-language acquisition theories, from having low-affective filter in the classroom so students are not worried about making mistakes to the acquisition theory in which students acquire language through engaging in a problem that they are interested in solving. This is in comparison to students acquiring language by learning grammar, the rules of language. Often when students focus on grammar and rule-based characteristics of language, they are more likely to take a long time to learn because there is a lack of real-world purpose in the use of the language. Consider using acquisition strategies in your teaching rather than integrating more formal learning techniques.

4. **Analyze how language levels such as BICS and CALP are linked to cognition such and other literacy skills.**

Language is closely tied to the development of cognition. It is through language that individuals learn to think, develop comprehension skills, find patterns in language, learn to question, and learn how to write (Tharp & Gallimore, 1988). Language also teaches individuals to use analogies and comparisons, which expands cognition. Asking questions also encourages the mind to extend understanding and perspectives. There is a developmental process in which students acquire a second language. This process includes preproduction, early production, speech emergence, and intermediate fluency. It is important for teachers to understand that a student may have excellent command of conversational English or BICS and not have mastered CALP (academic language). In order for students to do well in school, they must acquire CALP because these are the skills needed for abstract critical thinking and writing. These skills include categorizing, comparing, analyzing, evaluating, and synthesizing.

5. **Assess differences among bilingual education programs.**

There are numerous bilingual programs from dual language programs in which students learn the second language. Dual language programs have become successful in the United States, but there is not enough research to show that it is the best approach for most students (Crawford & Krashen, 2015). There are also English-only approaches such as CALLA, SDAIE, and sheltered English. These approaches encourage the development of content area knowledge while teaching language skills to English language learners. Ebonics, or African American English, is considered by linguists to be a language with its own phonology, lexicon, syntax, and vocabulary.

Check Your Cultural Knowledge

Reflective Essay Question

There have been several case studies presented in this chapter. How would you integrate the recommendations of the teachers discussed to enhance the teaching of English learners in your classroom? List at least three of the most important strategies you would use and explain why. Provide evidence for the strategies you select, not just your opinion.

Consider going back to review the case study that presented the research conducted by Gutiérrez, who studied the approach of teaching math to Spanish-speaking high school students.

Application

Know and Go Tools in the Classroom

Teaching English language learners can be extremely challenging. One of the most effective ways to get across ideas and teach words is through the use of pictures, photographs, or realia (concrete items).

1. Teach concepts about foods. One of the best ways to teach concepts such as sweet, sour, smooth, rough, savory, or salty is to bring actual foods to class for students to taste. For example, teachers can bring snacks like pretzels, popcorn, or small packages of beef jerky. This way the educator can ask students what taste do all of these foods have in common. If someone says salt, then the teacher can write the word salt on the board. Then to increase student knowledge of language, she can also write "Lots of salty pretzels. Lots of salty jerky. Lots of salty popcorn." This way students also learn a phrase along with new vocabulary words.

2. Place students in groups. Then have a basket of words with pictures of items. Maybe if the lesson is on food, there are these words: oranges, sour, lemons, sweet, cherries, smooth, yellow, limes, apples, and firm. Then a person for each group runs up to the basket, finds the name of a fruit, and then picks a word that describes an attribute of the fruit. They tape their choices on the board. The group that gets the right match first gets a point. This can be done over and over until all words have been chosen.

3. Teaching students songs where there are repeated patterns of words is also another way to teach English. For example, you can teach songs like "Old Mac Donald Had a Farm" to help students learn sentences. Then they will also learn the sounds animals make in English, such as "moo" for a cow and "oink" for a pig. This can be a fun song that students act out as they sing.

4. Create a poster that lists tools students can use to aid them in their comprehension of a nonfiction story. The poster can list the following terms:

   a. Title and Author
   b. Maps
   c. Graphs
   d. Drawings
   e. Figures/Models
   f. Photos
   g. Sidebars
   h. Section heads
   i. Terms listed

Have students work in groups in which each member picks one of the terms and independently identifies the information. The student may have to make inferences. Each student brings the information back to the group, and the group discusses the information together in order to identify the main points, events, and context of the story.

Miami Herald/Getty Images

CHAPTER
11

Diversity and the Achievement Gap

Learning Objectives

LO1 Discuss why diversity is a fundamental principle in life.

LO2 Analyze and address the achievement gap between students of color and their White peers.

LO3 Demonstrate how to integrate technology to address the achievement gap found in schools.

LO4 Reflect upon and discuss moving from teacher-centered to student-centered education applying a framework that integrates the ethic of care (relationships), sociocultural theory of learning (culture and cognition), and education for democracy (community).

STANDARDS COVERED

NAEYC 1, 5, 6
naeyc

CAEP 1 *CAEP*

INTASC 1, 2, 3, 4, 5, 6, 7, 8, 9, 10 **InTASC**

Diversity: Fundamental Life Principle

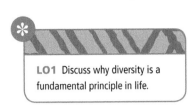

LO1 Discuss why diversity is a fundamental principle in life.

As you have learned while reading this text, diversity is much more than skin color or differences in gender, class, race, religion, sexual orientation, exceptionalities, ethnicity, and age. Making sure you include diversity in your life can help you lead a happy, healthy, and balanced existence. Here are some examples of how diversity can enrich your life outside of education.

Diversity Is Great for the Body

This first example demonstrates how diversity is great for our bodies. Do you go to the gym and exercise? Many people are members of fitness centers. They want to keep their muscles working, vascular system healthy, and ensure that they are physically fit. However, to keep physically healthy, humans need to be involved in diverse activities. There is greater benefit in varying one's workout. If you take Zumba classes (aerobic dancing) twice a week, it would be good for your physical health to also take a spinning class (aerobic activity on bikes) another day. Though both can keep the heart healthy and increase the blood flow throughout the body, the body can get used to these physical activities and after a while will not be challenged. To help mix things up, a person can also add interval training. This means, for example, that instead of just walking on the treadmill at 3.5 miles per hour, the workout may be mixed with a run at 4.7 miles per hour for 20 seconds and then walk at 3.5 mph for the next minute.

Diversity Is Important to the Human Gene Pool

The second example of why diversity is important has to do with genetics. Humans have learned that it is best not to marry and reproduce with someone who is in their immediate family, which is also known as **consanguineous mating** (Alvarez, Quinteiro, & Ceballos, 2011). In some communities, a person may marry their first cousin or second cousin. In animals, such as cheetahs, inbreeding can result in more susceptibility to diseases. Why is genetic diversity important in humans? Genetic diversity in people is found to strengthen the gene pool of individuals, helping humans more easily adapt to changing conditions in their environment, such as food supply and weather.

> **Consanguineous mating** is reproducing between people who are close relatives.

One of the most famous examples of the importance of diversity in biology is the "Royal Disease" of hemophilia. Queen Victoria of England, who lived during the nineteenth century, is believed to have passed on the genetic disease hemophilia, in which the blood is not able to clot, to members of her family. According to some scholars such as Price (2008), Victoria and other members of her family passed on hemophilia because they shared close genetic heritage. Many researchers also believe that consanguineous unions have resulted in individuals who may have higher rates of hypertension, bipolar depression, cancer, and diabetes (Alvarez et al., 2011). When related individuals have children there is a higher chance that recessive genes will become active, which can result in birth defects or other issues. This is why some societies have banned marriage between blood related relatives.

Diversity Is Important to Your Financial Health

The third example of diversity regards your finances, or rather your investments. If you listen to the people on television discussing financial wealth, they may say that the key to financial security is diversity. What do they mean?

Let's say you had $10,000 to invest. Should you put it all into a real estate investment? Should you put all of it into bonds? What about stocks? Many financial planners would probably tell you to pick different types of investments. They may suggest putting $3,000 in the bank for a "rainy day." Or $2,000 in a real estate trust, $3,000 into a mutual fund

My Journal

Genetic Variation within the One Human Race

AAAS (American Association for the Advancement of Science) has provided a comprehensive unit on teaching genetic variation and the construct of race. The organization is highly respected and an excellent resource for educators. Concepts that are discussed include natural selection, genes, genetic variation, race, and migration. The following questions are addressed:

- How do researchers move beyond the simplistic conceptualizations of race or ethnicity?
- How does genetics assist them to do so?

This unit can be found at the following link and includes not only background information about genetics but also has attached student worksheets: http://sciencenetlinks .com/lessons/genetic-variation-within-one-human-race/

It is important that you understand genetics and how the knowledge of genetics has changed the way many people think about race. Race is not a biological concept but rather a cultural and political construct (Pang & Valle, 2004).

Answer the following questions in your journal:

Q *Why is there the most human diversity on the continent of Africa?*

Q *Do individuals who are indigenous to Africa have genetic variations that other places in the world do not have?*

Q *Are there variations in Asians and Europeans that are not found among indigenous Africans?*

Q *How can you explain to others that race is not a biological concept? What would you tell them?*

Answers from AAAS Website: 1. Because the human species first arose in Africa, there is more diversity in humans. 2. Yes because only a section of the African population moved from the continent and so only some of the variations have been taken to other parts of the world. 3. Yes. Genetic mutations and new combinations developed after individuals migrated out of Africa. 4. Answers may vary.

⌄ Professional Resource Download

Humans are genetically similar though there are variations, as in the characteristic of height.

Tribune News Service/Orlando Sentinel/Getty Images

of stocks, and $2,000 in a conservative bond fund. Many financial planners believe in diversification.

Why would you diversify when it comes to your money? Sometimes real estate is hot and goes up; however, the worth of real estate also drops in a recession. At other times when real estate is not worth as much, the stock market may go up. Though bonds do not yield that much in interest, bonds are a steady investment and usually do not fall quickly. No one knows for sure which investment will do well, so it is best to place your money into several types of assets.

These three examples regarding physical health, gene pool, and financial investments show that diversity is a powerful principle in life and not only in education. Diversity means much more than "racial" categories. It is important for teachers to guide their students in understanding the importance of diversity in their lives too. Doing so can mentor students in developing higher-order thinking skills and thinking outside the box. However, sometimes there are misconceptions about diversity. Though we represent many different social differences, the next section discusses the fact that humans are biologically more alike than different.

The Myth of Race: We Are More Alike

Before going to the next section, it is important for teachers to examine their views of race carefully. Some people think of the concept of diversity as meaning race. And many of us have been taught that the construct of race is real. Remember that racism is real, but race is not. We are not members of diverse races. We are members of one race, the human race. This is a key belief that teachers need to review and understand.

Teachers must review their understanding of the biological concept of race and how the belief in "racial" categories has created misconceptions (Pang & Valle, 2004). Today's use of race is like a placeholder to indicate that physical characteristics between groups have important meanings (Gould, 1995, 2002). With the new data on DNA, biologists know that race is an artificial construct (Gould, 1996, 2002; Olson, 2002).

If "racial" groups were real, how would they be defined? Would we look at the shape of our nose or texture of our hair? If skin color was one of the measures, how would skin color differences be quantified? Would there be a chart that indicated different skin tones and their corresponding "racial" categories? For example, how light is light? Or what is an olive skin tone? Today, people often use skin color and other physical characteristics to define a "race." These categories often have social connotations attached to them. However, few people may understand that there is much within-group variance with regard to physical characteristics.

Physical Characteristics: Adaptations to Climates

Physical characteristics are adaptations from living in specific climates. As Jablonski and Chaplin (2002) have demonstrated, skin color patterns in the world are due to natural selection. In this process the body regulates the impact of ultraviolet radiation. "Throughout the world, human skin color has evolved to be dark enough to prevent sunlight from destroying the nutrient folate but light enough to foster the production of vitamin D" (Jablonski & Chaplin, 2002, p. 75). Many of our physical adaptations are due to environmental factors (Dar-Nimrod & Heine, 2011). The earliest *homo sapiens* evolved from Africa approximately 120,000–150,000 years ago, and their skin adapted to the conditions of ultraviolet radiation and heat. Melanin acted as a natural sunscreen to protect humans from the damaging effects of UV radiation (Jablonski & Chaplin, 2002). As people moved to northern areas of the world, they lost their skin pigmentation. Therefore, skin color is an adaptation of the body to survive in various types of geographical environments and is not an indication of any level of intelligence or abilities.

Many researchers believe that modern humans evolved from eastern Africa. Scholars (Gould, 2002; Olson, 2002; King & Motulsky; 2002; Cann & Wilson, 2003) have reported that there is little doubt that the origin of *homo sapiens* is a small group of humans in Africa. Olson wrote about this belief: "Everyone alive today is either an African or a descendant of Africans" (Olson, 2002, p. 38). The evidence points to an origin in eastern Africa, where *homo sapiens* lived in lush savannas in countries now known as Kenya and Tanzania. Bryan Sykes, a genetics professor from Oxford University, wrote about the beginnings of humans: "…we need only go back in time as far as Mitochondrial Eve. The genetics tells us very clearly that modern humans had their origins in Africa within the last hundred and fifty thousand years. At some point, about a hundred thousand years ago, modern humans began to spread out of Africa to begin the eventual colonization of the rest of the world. Incredible as it may seem, we can tell from the genetic reconstructions that this settlement of the rest of the world involved only one of the thirteen African clans" (2001, p. 277).

How can scientists say that we descended from the same mother? In the late 1980's a group of scientists studied the mitochondria DNA of human cells (Sykes, 2001). The mitochondria in our cells are passed down from our mothers through the egg cells.

The Eve, whose mitochondria is found in all of us, most likely lived about 150,000 years ago in eastern Africa (Olson, 2002). There were other women who lived at the same time of the "woman who produced all the mitochondrial DNA on the planet today; the mitochondria DNA from those women are extinct" (Olson, 2002). Mitochondria are elements in cells that provide the energy needed to conduct various chemical reactions. The subsequent genetic and paleontological science that has been directed from that point in time has consistently verified that we, the modern humans, are descendants from this Eve (Sykes, 2001). It is important to note that Sykes brought up the importance of cultural orientation in the naming of the woman as Eve. The use of Eve denotes a distinctly Judeo-Christian orientation because it does not seem to be an African name. This is another indication of how science used a powerful Western civilization orientation.

The Achievement Gap

LO2 Analyze and address the achievement gap between students of color and their White peers.

The **achievement gap** refers to the difference between students of color and their White peers in various subject areas.

Since we are all the same species, *homo sapiens* (humans), it is essential for teachers to raise questions about why the achievement of some groups of students is substantially lower than their peers even though many of our social characteristics such as gender, sexual orientation, and cultures cannot be traced to any single genetic attribute (Dar-Nimrod et al., 2011). This points to the importance of our main, student-learning environment, schools.

The results of the National Assessment of Educational Progress (NAEP) present student academic performance. The 2001 federal legislation No Child Left Behind was enacted to close the achievement gap. Educational statistics are used to show if equal outcomes for students from different ethnic groups is occurring. The **achievement gap** refers to the difference between students of color and their White peers in various subject areas. Test results show that in 2009 and 2011, Black and Hispanic students continued to lag behind Whites in reading and math. In fact, they performed more than 20 points lower at the fourth and eighth grades in both areas. The data showed that many Black and Hispanic students are performing two grades lower than Whites in math and reading (Education Week, 2011). However, there is also much evidence that positive changes can be made so students achieve at higher levels. Research shows that the implementation of home visits, creating access to strong preschool programs, and providing high-quality, integrated schools are various ways to address the achievement gap (Shelton, 2015).

Unfortunately, the data show that many students of color continue to be left out from attending integrated schools with the same or equal educational opportunities as Whites (Frankenberg & Orfield, 2012). On top of this, they are not performing as well as Whites in important core areas such as reading and math. If we really believe in equality as a value in education, students in all racial groups should show about the same levels of achievement. What does 40 years of data tell us? Figures 11.1 and 11.2 show data that NAEP gathered regarding the reading performance of 17-year-olds from Black, Hispanic, and White populations from 1972 to 2012 (National Center for Education Statistics, 2013). The numbers represent averages of reading achievement. Unfortunately, the figures show that African Americans scored 26 points lower than Whites in reading in 2012. Hispanic students show a similar gap; Latinos scored 21 points lower than White students in reading in 2012. The graphs show that we as teachers have a lot of work to do. What do the graphs tell you?

Model Minority: Stereotyping Asian American and Pacific Islander Students

Some teachers may want to know how Asian Americans and Pacific Islander students perform in reading. NAEP does not always gather data on Asian Americans and Pacific Islander youth, so additional research was conducted on seventh-graders from the state

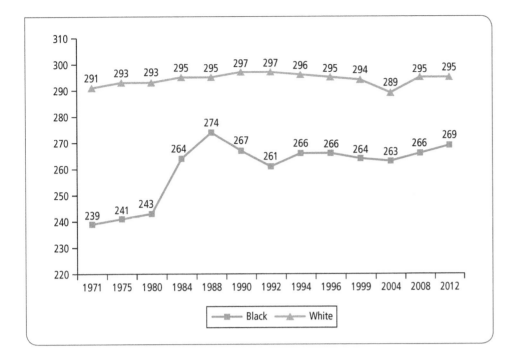

Figure 11.1: **17-Year-Old Students, Reading Achievement Means, Black and White, 1971–2012**

Source: *NAEP 2012 Trends in Academic Progress Reading 1971–2012 Mathematics 1973–2012*, National Center for Education Statistics, 2013.

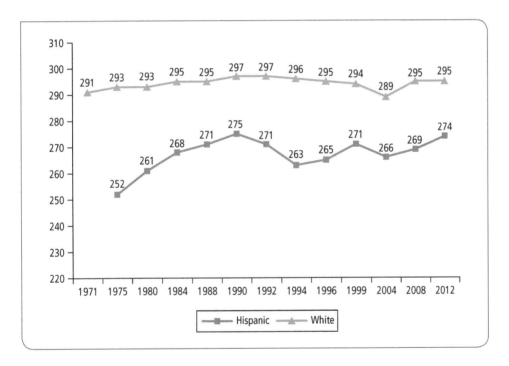

Figure 11.2: **17-Year-Old Students, Reading Achievement Means, Hispanic and White, 1971–2012**

Source: *NAEP 2012 Trends in Academic Progress Reading 1971–2012 Mathematics 1973–2012*, National Center for Education Statistics, 2013. Note: 1971 reading achievement means data not available for Hispanics.

of California. One of the reasons that data were gathered from California is because the state not only collected ethnic information on Asian Americans and Pacific Islanders from 2003 to 2008, but also the state used a standardized test, the California Achievement Test Survey 6, to measure the knowledge of all seventh graders (Pang, Han, & Pang, 2011). The data challenged the model minority myth that many teachers previously believed about Asian American and Pacific Islander students. The **model minority myth** is a stereotypical, racist belief that Asian American and Pacific Islander students do not need help in schools because they are all high achievers in math and reading. (See Figure 11.3.)

Model minority myth is a stereotypical belief that Asian American and Pacific Islander students do not need help in schools because they are all high achievers.

Figure 11.3: Teachers need to understand that the model minority stereotype is an example of racism.

Figure 11.4 shows that Asian American and Pacific Islander students, depending on their ethnicity, performed differently in reading. Ten Asian American and Pacific Islander groups scored lower than their White peers. Most often when data on Asian American and Pacific Islander students are reported, educators use the aggregate score, a combined score. When the scores of Asian American and Pacific Islander students are reported together, the students who do well bring up the scores of those who do not. When this method is used, educators are not able to identify the needs of specific groups. The research by Pan, Han, and Pang demonstrated that teachers need to address the reading skills of students from the following groups: Asian Indian, Vietnamese, Filipino, Other Asians (including Bangladeshi, Burmese, Nepalese, Thai), Guamanian, Hawaiian, Other Pacific Islanders (including Tahitian, Fijian, Palauan, Marshallese), Cambodian, Laotian, and Samoan. You can see in Figure 11.4 that these groups scored lower than Whites (represented in purple). That means there is an achievement gap between *many* Asian American and Pacific Islander (AAPI) groups and their White peers. So why are Asian Americans and Pacific Islanders treated as if they are one big group of highly successful students? Teachers believe the model minority to be true. However, this belief was proven to be false, a myth (Pang et al., 2011). Few teachers have revised their thinking. Not all AAPI students do well and some need extensive skill development to improve their reading skills. If their needs are not being met, then this again points to the lack of equity in education.

Figure 11.4: **Asian American and Pacific Islander American Ethnic Groups, Reading Means, State of California, 2003–2008**

Source: Asian American and Pacific Islander Students: Equity and the Achievement Gap, by Valerie Ooka Pang, Peggy P. Han, and Jennifer M. Pang, 2011, *Educational Researcher, 40* (7), 378–389.

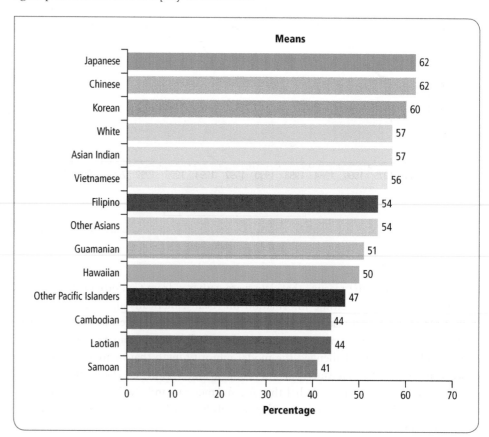

Common Core State Standards (CCSS)

The governors and the commissioners of education from each state throughout the nation were the prime forces in the creation of standards that all teachers in every state would follow. They felt that Common Core State Standards (CCSS) (National Governors Association Center for Best Practices, 2010) would provide students with a high quality, aligned K–12 curriculum. Their efforts began in 2009, and some teachers were involved in the development process. The Common Core Standards allow for assessment of learners across the nation. By implementing CCSS, the curriculum would be similar in the seventh grade in Nevada and the seventh grade in Virginia. Therefore, when a seventh-grade student moved from Georgia to Montana, the young person would have had similar content and not be behind after a move. Doesn't that make sense? Have you ever moved and then found that the kids in the new place learned a totally different curriculum than you did? The hope was that the Common Core State Standards would make the content and skills students are learning consistent within the nation. At this point, 45 states and four U.S. territories have adopted the CCSS.

The standards focus on curriculum alignment in grades K–12 English language arts and mathematics. They also include standards for grades 6–12 literacy in history/social studies, science, and technical subjects. In addition, the National Research Council, the National Science Teachers Association, and the American Association for the Advancement of Science have developed the Next Generation Science Standards (NGSS). The National Coalition for Core Arts Standards directs the standards for arts education. The American Council on the Teaching of Foreign Languages has also developed national standards for learning languages with the ELA Common Core State Standards. Many of the CCSS are devoted to making sure English learners develop needed skills and knowledge more fully, especially in reading and writing. As you can see, there is a national movement in various subject areas to standardize the content and skills being taught throughout the country.

Another reason for the Common Core State Standards is to make sure that students are preparing for college. Having uniform standards across the nation may assist young people

My Journal

Common Core State Standards

It is important for every teacher to become familiar with Common Core State Standards (CCSS).
    Begin your adventure into the CCSS by reading through their website at http://www.corestandards.org/.
    Answer these questions in your journal. You should become familiar with the CCSS in order to be able to plan your class curriculum.

Q *Which subject areas does the CCSS include?*

Q *Why was the CCSS developed? Give at least three reasons.*

Q *What kind of testing will result from this initiative?*

Q *Identify two standards in language arts and explain how a teacher can address each in his or her curriculum.*

Q *Take time to get familiar with the Next Generation Science Standards at http://www.nextgenscience .org/next-generation-science-standards. These standards focus on students engaging in critical thinking processes. There is a stronger focus on literacy in science. For example, teachers are directed to provide more opportunities for students to read nonfiction trade books and to write about their observations. Give one example of how you would integrate a science standard into your teaching.*

in being ready to move from K–12 to university settings. It is important for each student to have the opportunity to be prepared to go to college whether they choose that path or not.

Teachers must have a clear understanding of the CCSS because they provide direction for instruction. Teacher and researcher, Mariana Souto-Manning (2013) explained that teaching biographies in the second grade is an important standard; she chose to use the biographies of Sojourner Truth or Gandhi in her classroom. Students learn not only literacy skills regarding the creation of biographies, but they are also exposed to historical information about important role models who fought for civil rights. The Common Core State Standards must include additional discussion of critical thinking skills that include activities the involve students in examining controversial public issues that affect all of us.

There has been some pushback on the CCSS because the focus of the standards leads to extensive testing of students. Many educators, parents, and community members do not believe that schools should be preparing students primarily for assessment and that the CCSS are moving students away from developing critical thinking and citizenship skills (Au & Ferrare, 2015). In fact, the Gates Foundation has invested over $2.3 billion into supporting projects that contributed to the development and implementation of the CCSS (Hursh & Martina, 2016). Educators such as David Hursh and Camille Anne Martina are concerned that the CCSS represent a strong presence of business corporations in education. Through the funding of foundations like the Gates Foundation and Broad Foundation, business interests are powerful forces in schools moving them toward continual testing and giving corporations control over what is taught in the curriculum (Au & Ferrare, 2015; Hursh & Martina, 2016). In addition, some educators do not believe there is adequate integration of knowledge and viewpoints from communities of color throughout the standards and included in the curriculum (Au & Ferrare, 2015; Hursh & Martina, 2016). Who should determine what is taught in schools? What should be our goals as teachers? Is it to prepare students for the working world? Is it to prepare students to be contributing members of a democracy based on social justice?

Decreasing or Eliminating the Achievement Gap: Comprehensive Programs

There are successful educational programs that address the achievement gap and have proven their ability to decrease the disparity for many students of color or students from lower-income families. It is exciting to read that we as teachers can make a difference. Many of these programs are made up of teachers who have a strong educational philosophy of caring, culture, and community with social justice at its core. In these programs, teachers often work collaboratively to ensure that there are carefully articulated skills and knowledge taught to students as they move through their school years. In Chapter 2, the Puente Project and Lemon Grove Academy for the Humanities and Sciences were presented, while in Chapter 3 the Algebra Project was discussed. All of the programs focus on student success and guide participants not only to do well in school but also to give back to the community.

The Puente Project is a mentoring and writing program preparing students to do well in school with a strong foundation of affirming culture and integrating the importance of community. Students in the high school program are mentored to finish high school and to set college admissions and graduation goals. In addition, Puente programs in colleges provide guidance and tutoring to ensure students success in the university. Puente is dedicated to mentoring students to become leaders in their communities and to not only graduate from college but also to become mentors to other students after they earn their degrees.

The Algebra Project is a civil rights and culturally relevant curriculum program. Bob Moses and Charles Cobb (2002) wrote about the Algebra Program and explained how it not only taught algebra and other math skills to students, but also included building caring and citizenship skills within the communities it serves. Students and parents are involved in leadership training with the goal of fighting for civil rights in education. Moses created a curriculum that is based on the principles of culturally relevant education where the instructional methods and content arise from the experiences of students. The curriculum has used the teaching of math through experiences such as riding the subway, making lemonade, and building African drums. Moses connected math concepts to the everyday lives of students. Moses tied student successes in math to civil rights. He did not believe students were attaining equal educational opportunities if they did not pass algebra, which is one of the admissions requirements into college. Prior to the Algebra Project, many African American high school students were not placed in algebra or did not pass algebra so were not able to get admitted to college. Algebra was a gatekeeper class keeping many students from attaining college degrees.

The Lemon Grove Academy for the Humanities and Sciences is a comprehensive wellness program founded on strong values of social justice, community, and caring, focusing on the whole student (Oser, Beck, Alvarado, & Pang, 2014). The goals include academic excellence and equal education by providing health and dental programs for students and their families. This is an all-inclusive academic program. There is a free health and dental clinic for students and their families in the school because a majority of students need healthcare. The school has become the center of the local community. This school went from having some of the lowest achievement measures to the highest in its district. This was done by placing emphasis on civil rights and equal education through wellness. The food that students receive in the cafeteria is healthy and contains many fruits and vegetables. To celebrate Halloween, teachers bring erasers and pencils and small toys rather than chocolate candies. In addition, the school parent association has established a farmer's market where organic fruits and vegetables are sold at a discount at the school to parents. Grade-level teams also work together to address the instructional needs of students who are not doing well. Everyone pitches in to help the school, from creating school vegetable gardens to painting inspirational murals throughout the school grounds. One of the role models in this program is Martin Luther King, Jr., because he believed in educational excellence and fighting for civil rights for all students (Figure 11.5).

Figure 11.5: The Martin Luther King, Jr., Memorial is an inspirational monument about courage, hard work, equality, and freedom for all students, faculty, and staff.

Gerry Pang

TEACHING TIPS

Strategies to Address the Achievement Gap

1. Carefully assess student knowledge and skills.
2. Develop goals to address specific gaps in student knowledge and skills.
3. Identify culturally relevant strategies and create a list that will be used to guide students toward acquiring target knowledge and skills and engage students in the learning process.
4. Create partnerships with other teachers or grade-level teams so that you can get feedback from other educators regarding most effective culturally relevant instructional strategies and content to use with students not doing well.
5. Listen for culturally relevant examples that students share about their experiences and write them in your teacher log so that you can refer to them in your teaching to build bridges between what you are teaching and what students are asked to learn.
6. Make learning relevant and meaningful to your students by clearly stipulating what is being taught and why.
7. Identify cultural models that can be used as analogies to build upon your students' knowledge.
8. Affirm student identity and cultural backgrounds.
9. Continually seek ways to integrate cultural knowledge and cultural modes of delivery in the learning process using opportunities for participation in plays, use of hip-hop and rap, and integration of other creative avenues for expression.
10. Engage parents and develop partnerships with them to enhance the learning of their children.

Professional Resource Download

Consider this . . .

Teachers are significant people in the lives of most students.
You are important to your students. What are you going to do with their trust?

These exceptional programs have clear goals, develop strong academic policies, include parents in the learning process, provide many opportunities for students to excel, and employ teachers who hold extremely high expectations for both students and themselves.

Three major characteristics that these programs share are parent engagement, culturally relevant education, and caring throughout the school. They are founded on the integration of student cultures into all aspects of learning from the curriculum, instructional strategies, parent involvement, school policies, drama activities, sports programs, and counseling techniques. The programs encourage parent inclusion by having them participate in tutoring, act as guest lecturers, and help with student homework; parents, faculty, and staff share the value of high expectations for students. Parents also join in school activities, from holiday events to reading-oriented slumber parties. Also, students support each other with

TAKE A STAND
WHAT SHOULD TEACHERS DO ABOUT THE ACHIEVEMENT GAP?

This section of the book included information about the achievement gap between Whites and Latinos, Whites and Blacks, and Whites and Asian Americans and Pacific Islander students.

TAKE A STAND . . .

- What did you learn about the achievement gap? How long has it been documented?
- Write several paragraphs describing the achievement gap.

- What do you think are the responsibilities of teachers to address the gaps?
- If you think teachers should do something, list five recommendations of how teachers can address this issue. Rank order them.
- With a partner, discuss what teachers should do about the achievement gap issue. Who is responsible? Why?

compassion and caring, building a strong community of learners. As you read through this last chapter, think about the programs that are successful with low-income students of color. What makes them different? What makes them successful? What could you add to your own classroom to ensure student success?

The Use of Technology: Providing Additional Instructional Avenues to Address the Achievement Gap

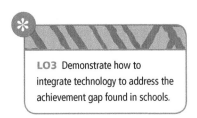

LO3 Demonstrate how to integrate technology to address the achievement gap found in schools.

Computers and other technological devices have become important tools for educating all students and can be used to address the achievement gap. It is important for school districts to provide all learners with access to technology. Some districts partner with companies like Apple or Alphabet (Google) to secure their students the opportunities to use various devices and the Internet.

Teachers and students can use many technological devices:

Computers: Students can use them to research many topics and work on collaborative reports.

Cell phones: Students can respond to a teacher's presentation in the classroom, then teachers can engage all students in the lesson.

Tablets/iPads: Students can create weblogs to share information about a topic or issue with others.

Promethean boards: Teachers can use flipcharts and interactive pens to draw, write, and erase. Students can go up to the board and write their answers.

These tools can assist in providing extra opportunities and support for all students. The use of technology has exploded in the past 25 years and can also be used for students with special needs and students who may need more time to learn or investigate knowledge. For example, you can teach using a hybrid format. **Hybrid** is an approach that combines online teaching and face-to-face instruction. Both types of teaching formats have their advantages. For example, students learning online have the flexibility of doing their work at a time that is convenient for them. However, the down side is that they do not receive immediate feedback as they would in class. In a face-to-face session, students have the opportunity to ask questions of the teacher and get instant answers. Teachers can also ask students about the readings or the issues being discussed. The use of hybrid instruction and the pros and cons of the format makes for interesting conversations and keeps students and teachers accountable for their work.

For some elementary, middle, and high school teachers, using computers can help them to provide individual instruction. The teachers can deliver additional examples of concepts and identify video segments that can teach the vocabulary or skills being taught. Online teaching can also be an innovative way to create modules through which students learn new vocabulary, discuss issues with their classmates, view interesting videos, and research new ideas. There is no limit to the range of online tools. However, immediate teacher feedback is not always possible.

When teaching online, be sure to first introduce new vocabulary and the ideas that the module or lesson is centered around. As students get engaged in the online module, they will begin to use new ideas and concepts. For example, let's say a teacher wants to use an issues-centered model of teaching in which students will take a stand at the end of the unit. Students will have to decide if they agree with the actions of the civil rights leader

Hybrid is an approach that combines online teaching and face-to-face instruction.

TEACHING TIPS

Teaching Online

Following are some suggestions to consider when you teach online.

▶ It is challenging to teach online effectively. Even if you only know the students through an online class, you should learn their names and have some synchronous sessions. These are sessions when everyone logs into the class at the same time. If you use Skype, you can see the student and they can see you.

▶ Each student creates their student page where each member of the class describes his or her favorite hobby, musician, trip, and theme park. Then you can have a class scavenger hunt, where you have a sheet with questions and students must find whose student page has the answer. For example, who has a pet turtle named Mandy or whose favorite theme park is Disney World.

▶ Have consistent office hours so that whoever needs extra help can go online and talk or write their questions in a chat box that you answer immediately. This is an exceptional way to connect with your students. If your students are not keeping on task, then you can make some of the office hour sessions required.

▶ Tutoring online is also a good way to connect with and provide after school education for students who may need a little extra time with you.

▶ Be sure to have examples of completed assignments so that your students will know what is expected of them on the platform. Sometimes having an assignment rubric may not be enough direction.

▶ Use announcements as another way to instruct your students. After correcting an assignment, discuss some of the features of the best work. You can identify student names with passages from their assignments. Be sure to use the work of all your students throughout the year. Everyone wants to be recognized for great work. Many teachers use the announcement section primarily as a teaching tool rather than only giving housekeeping messages.

▶ Be positive. For example, you can write something like "I really like the assignments everyone turned in. The work shows great insights. It is fun for me to read your ideas." Sometimes students only get criticism and so use the announcement or email features from your class to give positive comments.

▶ Lastly, a personal email to a student once in a while can be a way for you to develop a trusting and caring relationship with each student. The student can read and save your messages. This is another way to encourage students and teach the content.

⌄ Professional Resource Download

they chose to research, for example. Teachers in this unit will first have students grapple with defining concepts like civil rights, social justice, and freedom. These are extremely complicated terms. Have you ever been in a class where the professor says she believes in social justice? Does she ever describe what she means? Without this discussion, you may not understand what she means. However, it is essential in your teaching that students understand what you mean and learn to define complex ideas. The World Wide Web provides many resources for students to investigate and evaluate how various individuals define social justice. This in itself could be one lesson in a unit on civil rights. Your students can follow up this discussion by analyzing and evaluating the behaviors and work of civil rights activists such as Rosa Parks, Cesar Chavez, Frederick Douglass, Eleanor Roosevelt, Fred Korematsu, and Malcolm X.

Advantages of Using Technology for Students

Technology has provided distinct advantages to students. For example, students who must purchase their books can now purchase less expensive digital copies of texts. This also gives students access to many more resources than before. It is much easier for them to carry their books and references around. Do you remember the huge backpacks of heavy books that students hauled around from classroom to classroom? Many students now use Kindles, Nooks, iPads, computers, or tablets and can download numerous textbooks on one device. Learners can also make notes on their digital textbooks and underline sections that are important. Many middle schools, high schools, and colleges now use e-books.

Another aspect of technology in the classroom is that your students can store their work on the cloud. This way, they can work on their assignments anytime they have access to Wi-Fi connections. So students may go to coffee shops or the library and work on projects using their own computers. It is also surprising that some students complete their work on their smartphones and then upload the homework for the teacher to grade. One problem with using a cell phone is that most have small screens, which make them difficult to use for something such as writing a paper. However, some students do not find this hard to do.

Using computers and phones to pass work between student and teacher also is convenient in that teachers do not have to provide paper. With all this new technology, it is possible to go paperless; this is good for our environment and shrinking school budgets. Can you think of some other ways that technology can be used in the classroom?

Provide Mini-Lectures Online for Review

Teachers have also found that some students need additional explanations of a concept or skill, so they may create short five-minute lectures and place them online for learners to review. In these mini-lectures, instructors can discuss issues in more depth. For example, the teacher might explain how DNA, deoxyribonucleic acid, forms a double helix. The genetic material is in every human. A drawing can be included in the mini-lecture. In addition, the instructor can talk about Rosalind Franklin, whose work on the structure of DNA was the foundation for the identification of the double helix; however, though she was a scientist, as a woman in the 1940s and 1950s, she was considered second class. Her photograph can be included in the lecture. Visuals can be extremely powerful. Discussing the intersectionality of science with gender discrimination could add an additional dimension to the lecture on DNA. Another lecture might be about the importance of ethnic identity with explanations as to why we have them. Ethnic identities can be a part of the personal ways an individual considers her- or himself to belong. The individual relates to the ethnic identity(ties) and communities he or she has chosen. These lessons can be reviewed by students in class whenever they want to watch them and can be viewed more than once. PowerPoint slides can also be used in mini-lectures. These materials are a visual way to reinforce concepts being discussed.

Online PowerPoint lectures can also include study notes that either students share with each other and/or the teacher provides. These notes give students the opportunity to review important ideas and information of the lectures (Cennamo, Ross & Ertmer, 2014).

Provide Online Tutoring and Open Office Hours

Teachers can also use online sessions to provide further instruction during open office hours and tutoring sessions. Educators will schedule specific times when students can also participate online. During these sessions, students can ask questions about concepts or homework they do not understand. Another aspect that can be provided is using the time for specific tutoring. Several students might have asked about writing techniques. Teachers can give short, small group tutoring sessions on specific aspects of writing such as the use of commas and semicolons to create clearer essays. By using technology, instructors have the opportunity to respond one-on-one or to small groups of students; technology can give teachers the opportunity to provide extra instruction. This is especially important in high school as some teachers have almost 200 students a day and often do not have time to provide quality feedback during class time. Teachers may also use Skype or Facetime in order to speak directly to students. With this type of software, students can then see their teachers and instructors can see them. This makes the tutoring session more personal.

Universal Design for All Learners

There are many students in class who may need teachers to provide additional support in their learning. Maybe they need specific visual and audio materials and services. Other students may benefit from visual clues when learning new knowledge and skills. Universal design (UDL) refers to creating a learning environment that the largest number of learners can use. UDL also includes the use of different ways to engage students, provides diverse means to explain a model such as showing a video, and makes the learning more meaningful by building on what students know. For example, a teacher may be lecturing online and include captions on each PowerPoint slide. The captions reflect the exact script that the

Synchronous means that everyone meets online together at a particular time for instruction. **Asynchronous** refers to online teaching where the members of the class access the session at a time they choose; there is no set time when all students attend class online together.

Differentiated instruction refers to offering students opportunities to learn materials on different levels using various methods or strategies.

teacher uses to discuss each picture. Therefore students who are deaf can also follow the lesson. Students who are visually impaired will be able to hear the lesson though they cannot see the slides. However, they can always ask questions, either through the chat room if the class is **synchronous**, which means that everyone meets online together at a particular time, or email the instructor if the class is **asynchronous**, meaning the members of the class access the session at a time they choose. One of the ways this particular textbook has been created to serve various populations is that the entire book is provided electronically with an audio app (ReadSpeaker) so those who are visually impaired can still learn from the materials, and people who learn best through an audio format can listen to the material in the car or at the beach!

In elementary and secondary schools, some teachers provide UDL for students who may also have specific disabilities. In this way differential instruction can be provided. **Differentiated instruction** refers to offering students opportunities to learn materials on different levels using various methods or strategies. Students learn in different ways such as through engaging with materials, learning by the use of visuals and/or audio sources, via reading, from teacher demonstrations, and many other avenues. Not all students learn in the same way or understand the same examples that a teacher may provide. Therefore, some students may need additional time and lessons to reinforce a concept or skill. Teachers in general education, special education, and English as a second language classes often use differentiated instruction. For example, maybe a student needs to learn her or his fractions but is having a difficult time. With technology, a teacher may use graphic organizers and other visuals along with actual hands-on material, such as a pizza.

Universal design involves creating a learning environment that uses many different instructional strategies and various digital devices to engage culturally different students and address the achievement gap. Following are samples of what a teacher may choose to do:

1. Use many visual materials, from flip charts to physical props such as toys to video clips that include sign language. As these materials are used, vary the pacing, include lots of color to emphasize various ideas, and make sure that the pitch and tone of voice are easy for students to hear in face-to-face and online teaching (Brand, Favazza, & Dalton, 2012).

2. Self-regulation can be an important strategy. Students identify a personal learning goal. In order to succeed, they may use a checklist, chart, stop watch, photographs, and/or tape recorder or cell phone to record their observations (Brand et al., 2012). When students learn to use various tools, they become more adept at gathering data, analyzing, synthesizing, and creating new ideas.

3. Not all assessments need to be paper and pencil evaluations such as essays and multiple choice exams. Maybe students can create plays, engage in debates with their classmates, develop a set of questions to ask other learners, or produce and design journals (Brand et al., 2012). Students also may rather do their writing using a keyboard, which for some learners is more accessible (Courey, Tappe, Siker, & LePage, 2012). Students might work together to solve an issue or identify possible alternatives to a problem. Though this process, they create posters, charts, blogs, videos, or wikis instead of writing a research paper. Additionally, students might take photographs to describe specific vocabulary or to document community issues and create a photography gallery in the classroom.

4. Teachers can use peer tutoring as a strategy in the learning process. Maybe the tutors also have access to 3D models of science concepts such as an atom; this could be used in describing the abstract nature of atoms (Courey et al., 2012).

5. Teachers include hands-on activities to involve students. One student had difficulty understanding the process of growing, so a teacher had her plant several different types of herbs. In this process, the learning became more meaningful and the

student became more engaged in understanding the process by recording the plant growth using graphs from various computer software (Courey et al., 2012).

6. Teachers can provide an outline so students know what to expect and learn the big picture of the concepts being taught. The big picture orientation will assist students, especially English learners and those who may have cognitive processing needs, with what to listen and watch for. It will be easier for them to know what notes to take and what to pay attention to (Danforth, 2013).

7. Materials can be provided on websites in ways that give additional examples to students who may need more time to process the information being taught. Also, teachers can have available different reading levels of the abstract concept being taught. Technology can be an exceptional avenue by which differentiated instruction can be delivered (Danforth, 2013).

Using UDL and technology with students can assist all learners to more fully understand the knowledge and skills being taught and helps teachers to expand their repertoire of instructional strategies. Students enjoy learning from the variety of methods used, and teachers can engage students in becoming more directed and empowered learners.

Consider this . . .

What obstacles stand in the way of using technology in the classroom? How can this be overcome?

Q If your classroom does not have computers, tablets, or other devices, how can you secure funding to provide them to your students?

TEACHING TIPS

Five Ways to Use Technology in Your Teaching

1. One of the best uses of technology in your classroom is to provide additional information for your students. You might want to have a document section where you add items and readings that students can use in their homework assignments. These documents can range from timelines to articles to photographs.

2. Many students like to work in groups. As a teacher, you can organize various groups to create a wiki, research paper, or video all through the use of an online platform. Maybe the project describes a social issue that affects a local neighborhood. For example, many students themselves may be hurt by racial profiling, so they may choose to research what can be done about this issue. Place the members of each group into a section online where only the group participants can access the project. Also you could create a link where the emails of all members can be found so students can update each other and ask questions as they develop their work.

3. Use links to short videos that explain specific concepts. Students can watch them over and over in order to remember the vocabulary being taught. This is especially helpful to students who are English learners or who have trouble learning vocabulary. Each subject area includes discipline-based vocabulary that students must learn and understand. Short videos can reinforce and make the definitions more meaningful.

4. One of the most fun projects for students is to create short videos. These videos can be a role play of an historical event, such as George Washington crossing the Delaware River during the Revolutionary War or a video that shows high school students acting out how to deal with a bully. Videos can be powerful learning tools not only for those who create them, but also for students who watch them. Students can also create public service announcements to address bullying, which can be placed on the school website. Some students may also want to put their work onto YouTube. Students like to see their work viewed and enjoyed.

5. One way to affirm students is through email. Teachers should use email and other technological devices to praise learners for an insightful comment they made during the class discussion or to give feedback on a particular written project. The emails are private, and it is an opportunity for teachers to develop trusting relationships with students. The students enjoy getting positive and affirming messages. Most often the messages students receive are negative, so if you provide praise, students are often delighted and feel encouraged.

⌄ Professional Resource Download

LO4 Reflect upon moving from teacher-centered to student-centered education applying a framework that integrates the ethic of care (relationships), sociocultural theory of learning (culture and cognition), and education for democracy (community).

Paradigm Shift to Student-Centered, Culture-Centered, Caring Schools

naeyc CAEP InTASC

In Chapter 1, the importance of a combined philosophy of the ethic of care, sociocultural theory of learning, and education for democracy was discussed. By using this framework, schools become places of learning that are **student-centered, relationship-centered, and culture-centered** based on the values of social justice and democracy (Pang, Rivera, & Mora, 1999; Pang, 2005). As explained in Chapter 1, this framework is founded upon a cultural-assets–based orientation with a cognitive psychology base. Teachers build on and use student knowledge as a key component in the learning process. In addition, students become self-empowered learners who are dedicated to building a trusting and respectful community. Students take charge in their learning and work together to develop meaning in what they are learning. Both teachers and students are people who believe in themselves and create compassionate relationships with each other. They also must address their own prejudices. Research has shown that teacher bias toward students of color leads to lower teacher expectations of learners (Ferguson, 1991; Nasir, Cabana, Shreve, Woodbury, & Louie, 2014; Pang & Park, 2003; Pang & Sablan, 1998). Table 11.1 presents many of the essential characteristics of a successful student and a successful teacher.

The profiles of successful students and teachers are quite similar. Are you surprised? What would you add to the profiles? Are there aspects that should be added to the chart?

There is a great deal of scholarship that shows education must be meaningful and empowering for students to effectively learn. It should not be primarily about testing. The characteristics in Table 11.1 are key to school reform, moving teachers from a cultural deficit viewpoint to seeing student cultures as an asset. School reform and policy changes should not be shaped and pushed by large corporations and wealthy donors (Au & Ferrare, 2015). Schools are about local community empowerment and educating students so they become critical thinkers and active participants in our democracy who challenge social inequities. Students are encouraged to take charge of their learning. It is almost like teachers and students get an "Ah ha!" view of life. There is a transformation, a huge paradigm shift like a Big Bang (Figure 11.6). Exceptional teachers encourage their students to become empowered active learners; they use clear objectives, distinct feedback, caring motivation, and genuine support. Student-centered learning is where students take control of their education and work hard as collaborative citizens of a democracy.

Educational researchers Wayne Au and Joseph Ferrare found that some of the largest movements in education such as the charter movement are being funded disproportionately

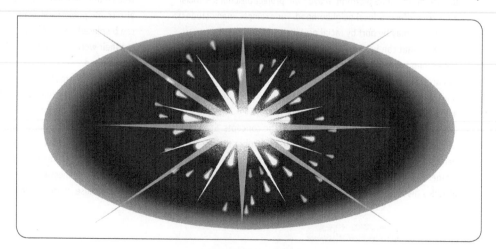

Figure 11.6: Big Bang: Paradigm Shift to Student-Centered, Relationship-Centered, and Culture-Centered Teaching

Table 11.1 Characteristics of a Successful Student and Successful Teacher in a Caring-Centered, Culture-Centered, and Relationship-Centered Multicultural School

Successful Student	Successful Teacher
• Believes in self and teacher	• Believes in each child/student and self
• Self-directed learner	• Self-directed teacher
• Happy, fulfilled person	• Happy, fulfilled person
• Caring toward others and self	• Caring toward others and self
• Empowered, contributes to the community	• Self-empowered, contributes to the community
• Cooperative, community oriented; makes connections with peers and others	• Cooperative, community oriented; makes connections with parents, students, colleagues, and others
• Supportive of classmates, friends, family, and teacher	• Supportive of colleagues, students, parents, family, and others
• Open minded, flexible	• Open minded, flexible
• Knows when to keep on task and when to provide assistance to classmates	• Knows when to step in to assist students and when to step back and encourage students to direct their own learning
• Affirms the worth of self and classmates (includes culture, gender, language, social class, religion, etc.)	• Affirms each child's/student's worth (includes culture, gender, language, social class, religion, etc.)
• Listens without criticism; accepts others' ideas; gives helpful feedback	• Listens without criticism; accepts others' ideas; gives constructive suggestions
• Reflects on own learning	• Reflects on own teaching and learning
• Is comfortable and can function within a variety of cultural contexts (culture, race, language, religion, etc.)	• Is comfortable and can function within a variety of cultural contexts (culture, race, language, religion, etc.)
• Has high expectations for self and teacher	• Has high expectations for self and all students
• Enjoys and is enthusiastic about learning	• Uses a variety of instructional approaches to teach information and skills, monitor student progress, and provide feedback
• Understands and works toward identified learning objectives	• Has clear learning objectives and conveys them to students
• Sees connection between school learning and real life	• Conveys connection and meaning between school knowledge and skills and lives of students
• Shares cultural background with others	• Integrates the cultural background of children naturally into all aspects of the classroom, from bulletin boards to teaching basic skills to use of cultural tools and models and believes in a cultural-asset orientation of student knowledge
• Develops a "voice" and speaks out on public issues; works to make society and the community a more just and compassionate place	• Encourages students to develop their own value orientation and "voice"; supports students in learning to make their own decisions and to become active in directing their own education; speaks out on public issues and works to make society a more just and compassionate place
• Desires to be part of and works toward a strong collaborative community in the classroom and school; sees self as part of a team	• Has goal of creating a learning community in the classroom and school that is collaborative and affirming for all participants—students, parents, community members, and administrators
• Disciplined and successful learner	• Disciplined and successful learner and professional
• Develops into a cultural mediator and change agent of our democracy	• Develops into a cultural mediator and change agent of our democracy

The author wishes to thank Maria Marshall for her input to this chart.

by wealthy companies and foundations. For example, they examined Initiative 1240 in the state of Washington, which proposed a system of charter schools that would have little oversight. Though opposed by the League of Women Voters, the Washington Education Association, and the National Association for the Advancement of Colored People (NAACP), the initiative passed. It was heavily funded by many wealthy individuals and corporations such as the Gates Foundation, Alice Walton (Walmart), Vulcan Inc. (Paul Allen, Microsoft co-founder), Mike Bezos (father of Jeff Bezos, Amazon), and Eli Broad. Research conducted by Au and Ferrare found that student achievement in charter schools was either at the same level or lower than other public schools and often charter schools are able to selectively admit students. Though the purpose of many charter schools is to provide for working-class students, there was little participation of working-class parents who advocated for the initiative. When this happens charter schools have little oversight from established educational organizations such as the National Education Association, parent-teacher organizations, and local governmental associations (Au & Ferrare, 2015). Schools are not for advancing the corporate agenda of businesses. Schools are places of learning. But more than that, they are, as John Dewey explained, laboratories for democracies where students are empowered to work together to solve social problems. Therefore, high test scores should not be the key goals of schools.

Meaning In Life and Grit

This entire book is about ways that teachers can make schooling more relevant and effective. They can examine their own biases and develop culturally relevant competencies (Pang, Stein, Gomez, Matas, & Shimogori, 2011). Teachers need to know that social oppression is real and continues to obstruct equity in society (Alexander, 2012). The strategies and values discussed in this text can contribute to minimizing the achievement gap. As Berliner and Glass (2014) have written there are many aspects of life that are not in control of teachers. For example, students need stable living environments, healthcare, parents with jobs, and the elimination of racial bias (Berliner & Glass, 2014). However, we also must address the personal needs of our students. Life for learners can be chaotic and complex. Many students are not connected to a community, whether a school, religious community, or family. Many students hunger for communal caring (Beck, 2004; Fulghum, 1988; Pang, 2005; Oser, et al., 2014). Students also seek acceptance and belonging. They want their teachers to believe in them and see their potential. Individuals like your students also need meaning in their lives (Frankl, 2006). Some ways they find meaning is through excelling in school or participating in various clubs such as being a reporter for the school newspaper or a member of MECHA, (Movimiento Estudiantil Chicanx de Aztlán, an organization that encourages Chicano unity). Others may be members of the Gay-Straight Alliance or an artists' organization. Students need to know they have choices in life and they have opportunities to develop their potentials. Life can be difficult; however, students can dig deep into themselves and find their character and dignity.

Students in your classes need to know that what they are learning has relevance to their lives. The goal of learning is to get learners to think and to use information to help them to understand the world or problem solve; the goal of schooling is not to answer questions on standardized tests (Berliner & Glass, 2014). Teachers need to guide students to understand how the information being taught can be used in life. For example, the Shakespeare play of *Romeo and Juliet* can be applied to situations that students find themselves in today. One of the messages of the play is to remind readers not to make rash and quick decisions; they need to take time to think through their choices.

Poor and rich students have different obstacles. Students from poor families may have more stress because of the lack of economic resources (Tough, 2012). Students from wealthy families may not have the guidance that they need because their parents are not home. There are so many elements that make a difference in academic success. However, students may know how to persevere, but our learners also need to identify personal and career goals and work towards them with grit. **Grit** is defined as the inclination to work towards goals with perseverance and passion (Duckworth, Kirby, Tsukayama, & Ericsson, 2011). Teachers can mentor their students so they can pinpoint current and future career goals applying their grit. In this way, students can also understand how their academic successes will assist them in reaching their future career goals.

The framework presented in this text is founded upon the belief that we are all equal and worthy people. All students need to feel they are valuable and can achieve valued life goals. Teachers can mentor and guide their students to identify their grit and character. Many students are survivors, but they do not know that. You as the teacher can help students reach down and find their grit and passions.

As teachers and students, whether one is 6 or 86 years old, we can encourage each other and build a supportive, caring community based on equality and social justice. The successful

Grit is the inclination to work toward goals with perseverance and passion.

Figure 11.7: These caring teachers believe in engaging students and building on their interests to teach a health unit on the muscles.

teacher and successful student mirror and support each other. Their goals, values, and behaviors are similar and work in tandem with each other. Teachers work hard to motivate, teach, and support their students. (See Figure 11.7.)

Have you asked your students what their future career goals are? How about their weekly goals? If your students do not have many goals, start small. Have them fill out a sheet of paper on which they write one academic goal per day and place on their desk. Students have a reminder and then are able to check off each goal when it is completed. Later you might ask students what they do that gives meaning to their lives.

Consider this . . .

The integration of the theoretical framework that brings together the ethic of care, the sociocultural theory of learning, and education for democracy builds student-centered, relationship-centered, and culture-centered schools; learners are at the core of the mission of schools.

Q How do you build relationships with your students?

Q What can you do to ensure that the learning environment in your classroom is student centered?

Q How do you integrate student culture into the curriculum of your class?

The Changing School Landscape: Whose Views Should Teachers Teach?

We must work hard to develop student-centered, relationship-centered, and culture-centered classrooms. Though there are some changes in life, those changes are minimal. For example, there are still desks in most classrooms; however, these desks may allow students to stand while they do their work. Classroom walkways may accommodate wheelchairs. Twenty years ago, there was no such thing as an iPad. Today new technologies used by teachers and students in their personal lives are also commonly found in classrooms. New ideas address issues in schools; for example, issues of sexual orientation are now included in many school curricula and sex education classes. Racial issues have also shifted in society, and the term "Black Lives Matter" has become a part of our lexicon. Another issue that has become much more upfront is Islamaphobia. Though Muslims have lived in what we know as the United States since before the Revolutionary War, there are now larger numbers because of immigration. However, it is critical that our mainstream curriculum be restructured so that issues of social oppression and power are covered throughout all areas of the school curriculum (Au, Brown, & Calderon, 2016). This must be part of any educational reform—diversity and social justice must be core values in structuring our schools.

Conclusion

The students who come to your classroom **believe in you** and your ability to teach them. **Teachers are significant people in the lives of most students.** Even a student who says skeptical things to you is hoping that you will see her or his abilities and help her or him to develop and learn. As educators, we know that teaching is more than just conveying information; we must come to know the whole person. We can understand our students' dreams and hopes, guide them through their weaknesses, and enhance their strengths. When students care for others, they contribute to the creation of a community and build stronger human bonds with others. In the process, their own self-worth increases. Some students will find a cure for cancer. Some students will become great teachers and teach other students how to be peacemakers. Some learners will provide important services to others as plumbers, librarians, and mail carriers. We have one of the most exciting and important careers that impacts all avenues of society. Your students want to be dressed and ready for future success (Figure 11.8).

Teachers must get to know students well in order to create a caring environment built on trusting relationships. When educators know their students, they can more naturally integrate student experiences, expectations, goals, and knowledge into the curriculum and instructional strategies of the classroom using culturally relevant teaching. They also do their best to eliminate social oppression in the classroom and school. See the Teaching Tips: Culturally Relevant Teaching in Science feature which lists some of the principles of culturally relevant teaching. How can you add to the table? Student-centered teachers know their students and consistently encourage them. They also are effective teachers!

Caring and sharing are keys to effective teaching. Remember the first grader named Eugene who used a pick instead of a brush to fix his hair? Eugene could have asked the teacher why she didn't know about his life. Instead, he patiently explained to her what a pick was. Eugene did not think less of her; rather, he respected and cared for the teacher enough to share his knowledge without criticism. This is what it means to develop a trusting relationship.

Students bring a wealth of knowledge to school. Their understandings and the knowledge that is taught in schools may represent different perspectives on life. Neither is better than the other—their perspectives and knowledge bases are just different. In order to survive in this society, students will need general societal knowledge and skills to get a job and earn a living. However, students can live a bicultural or multicultural life where they are able to code switch according to the cultural context in which they find themselves. Diverse students will enrich your life and help you to become a more effective teacher.

When you are surrounded by people who say it isn't possible to reach all students, find others you can talk to who know teaching isn't always easy, but who are committed to making a difference. Build up your professional libraries. Read the work of dedicated educators like Ramón Valle, Jennifer M. Pang, Mario Garrett, Joe Melendez, Geneva Gay, Pat Larke, Jackie Jordan Irvine, Jose Luis Alvarado, E. Wayne Ross, Joyce King, Alan Singer, Yoon Pak, Kevin Vinson, Luke Duesbery, Jason Naranjo, David Hursh, Herbert Kohl, Cinthia Salinas, Kohl, Rick Oser, Ellen Beck, Julian Helig-Valesquez, Jose Lara, Alfie Kohn, Frank Smith, Merry Merryfield, Binaya Subedi, Scot Danforth, Yuji Shimogori, Francisco Rios, Clift Tanabe, Ron Rochon, Marc Pruyn, William Ayers, Robert Rueda, Nel Noddings,

Jennifer M. Pang

Figure 11.8: Students who graduate are dressed for success!

CASE STUDY: Not Just the Dead Guys: Focusing on 21st-Century Arts in the Art Room

Don Masse is an artist and K–5 visual arts teacher at Zamorano Fine Arts Academy in San Diego. He ties in the artwork of his students with their own interests and what is happening in the world. As a teacher, Masse integrates the cultural and local interests of students into their artwork. The diversity ideas and imagination that art provides to students is unlimited. Masse presents many ways that teachers can use to integrate cultural student experiences in their art. Here are adaptations of his suggestions:

1. **Make Content Real.** Use work of current artists such as Frank Romero, Mexican American muralist; CYJO, Korean American photographer; Jeffrey Gibson, Cherokee/Choctaw mixed-media artist; Awol Eriku, African American photographer; and Jennifer Packer, African American painter. This strengthens student connections and understanding of the content.
2. **Artist Feedback.** When your students use an artist's work as an inspiration for their art, contact the artist via email or their blog. They often respond and write letters or emails back to the teacher and students. This is another great way to engage with individuals who are members of various ethnic communities.
3. **Student Writing Opportunities.** Students may send questions to contemporary artists and then write essays based on the artists' responses. This inserts authenticity into the English and language arts standards and ties in with art. Mario Quezada, a painter, and Dalek, a graffiti artist/painter, have written to students.
4. **Publishing Opportunities.** The teacher often shares the artwork of students on social media such as Twitter, Instagram, and Facebook. Also, student work has been placed on blogs. Artists such as Lisa Congdon, artist/illustrator/author, and Geninne Zlatkis, artist/illustrator/graphic designer, have placed students' work on their websites. This gives the school and young people more visibility.
5. **Swag!** The school has also auctioned off student work at special events raising funds for the school's art program. This is extremely exciting for students and their parents. In addition, the school has a "get caught doing something good" program. When a child gets this award, he or she puts their reward slip in the art jar; he or she may get the opportunity to pick an art piece from an artist who has donated work to the school.

Reflection Questions

Q Could you choose to integrate one of these art strategies into your teaching? If so, which one would you choose and why?

Q Think about working with a teacher partner. Maybe it would be possible to begin creating art for the school museum room.

TEACHING TIPS

Culturally Relevant Teaching in Science: Getting All Students Engaged in Science

Following is an extensive table that suggests ways you can integrate culture into science, which can lead to addressing the achievement gap.

Read through the table carefully and familiarize yourself with each of the principles.

Culturally Relevant Principles	Instruction	Curriculum	Visuals/Tables/Graphs
Affirm Student and Family Cultural Backgrounds	Learn students' names and their correct spellings. Call on children by name so they are active participants in the learning process. This also helps to build trusting relationships.	Integrate information about a local neighborhood garden or creek in a life science activity. Students draw a plan to reveal invisible features of a system such as flows and interactions (Crosscutting concept of Systems and System Models). Integrate examples from student-lived experiences.	Use bilingual posters that present science core ideas to familiarize parents with concepts being taught in science class for school events. Students can share their science logs with parents, explaining various scientific concepts, models, and principles of environmental science and life science.
Affirm Student Ethnic Identities	Parents act as guest speakers who talk about how they use science at home, such as the use of a thermometer in the oven during baking or the use of a tape measure and level putting up a picture frame.	Include a science role model from the children's neighborhood or ethnic group. This could be a grandmother, aunt, uncle, neighbor, friend, or national/international person.	Create posters with photos of science role models students have chosen. Students create biography boards that include information about the person's career and contributions. Posters can be hung in the school library.

(Continued)

TEACHING TIPS (Continued)

Culturally Relevant Principles	Instruction	Curriculum	Visuals/Tables/Graphs
Insert Cultural Tools or Models into Science	Teachers have students each take a different day to draw in the life cycle of a chicken in an egg (which is about 21 days). The life cycle of the chicken is a cultural model that many students know.	Teachers can use the chicken in the egg and its birth as an example of how students can change and develop new skills. Learning new skills can be like breaking out of the shell of not knowing.	Teachers use video that shows a chick hatching from an egg.
Activate Students' Prior Knowledge and Connect Learning to Their Experiences	Prompt students to bring household objects to school that can be used in investigations with magnets such as toilet paper rolls, pens, stuffed animals, model cars, *Ebony* magazines, Mexican coins, and U.S. coins.	Ask students to predict if U.S. coins will be attracted to the magnet and ask for an explanation. Ask students to predict if Mexican coins will be attracted to magnets. Explain the results. (Measurements of a variety of observable properties can be used to identify particular substances—Physical Science 1.A)	Encourage students to create tables and graphs that predict which objects are attracted to a magnet. Students develop a game called "Myth or Truth?" for other students to consider magnetic properties of objects.
Engage Students in Subject-Area Discourse	Student groups can plan and carry out an investigation on friction. Groups engage in discussions based on evidence gathered about the speed of an object (Physical Science 2.A and PS2.B). Use small toy cars and various surfaces from plush carpet to sandpaper.	Ask students to give examples of how friction influences their lives, from walking to riding a bicycle; include a discussion of the force of gravity. (Pushes and pulls have different strengths and directions—PS2.A and PS2.B)	Have students create tables or posters that describe and explain the force of friction using examples from their lives. Discussion of forces and interactions should be included. Students communicate core ideas via the poster/table.
Provide Higher Order Thinking and Decision-Making Opportunities	Develop class criteria that students use to identify which bubble is the "best bubble." Students bring an object from home that is generally not used as a bubble toy wand. (Planning investigations—Science and Engineering Practices)	Ask students to create a bubble using what they brought from home and a Dawn dish detergent mixture. Teachers can bring items such as a potato masher, plastic hanger, rope loop, and tennis racket for students to use in the investigation. Students rate their bubbles based on the class criteria. (Carrying out investigations—Science and Engineering Practices)	Students plan, design, and create charts that identify items from home that may or may not make bubbles. Have students ask their peers to predict which object makes the "best bubble." Students use the evidence to draw conclusions on why particular items make bubbles. Photos of students and their bubbles can be taken and added to tables.
Teachers Develop Trusting Relationships with Students and Their Families	Invite parents to participate in science activities at school. Ask them to predict what they think will happen in various lessons. Also encourage parents to volunteer as a small group leader during science activities in the classroom.	Listen to students and learn about what is important to learners such as values, beliefs, and people. Students interview adults in the community on specific subjects and report back to class. Teachers keep a journal of stories students share about their experiences and can then integrate that information into science lessons.	Encourage students and parents to check out science library books that parents can read with their children. Teachers teach parents how to ask children about crosscutting concepts such as patterns and identifying cause and effect.

Reflection Questions

Q How can you take these principles and ideas and integrate them into the grade level or subject area that you are preparing to teach, even if it is a subject area other than science?

Q What can you add to the chart that comes from the cultural experiences of your students?

Adapted from "Culture Matters in Science: Culturally Relevant Teaching," by V. O. Pang, K. E. Lafferty, J. M. Pang, J. Griswold, and R. Oser, 2014, *Science and Children*.

James Banks, Jack Nelson, Patricia Larke, Gregory Cajete, Lisa Delpit, John Palmer, Carl Grant, Cherry A. Banks, James A. Banks, Pauline Lipman, Jessica Gordon Nembhard, A. Lin Goodwin, José Lara, Wayne Au, Joseph Ferrare, Peter McLaren, Bob Peterson, Jesse Hagopian, Martha Nussbaum, James D. Anderson, Diane Ravitch, and Jean Anyon. They say, "Yes, all children have great potential and yes, all teachers can be effective," and they provide ideas on how to reach even the most distant and disenfranchised students.

Through effective teaching, you are sharing not only discipline content, but also important aspects of life with others. When students are learning, they are living the fullness of life. Their minds and sense of selves are growing. Learning is meaningful to them. There are many students who can't wait to get to school because their teachers make it is a place of success and belonging (Figure 11.9). This occurs most frequently within the context of trusting, respectful, and caring relationships. Students and teachers form a family, a community of learners who care about each other, care for themselves, and care for ideas. However, caring teaching is not always easy. General John Stanford, the former superintendent of Seattle Public Schools, wrote:

> Loving and leading doesn't mean going easy on people no matter what they do; it means coaching people to do their best, it means pushing them farther than they want to go, it means letting them know when you think they can do more. Love and leading can mean giving tough love. We often assume, when people disappoint us, that they can do no better. But that's rarely true . . . Often, their problem is really our problem; the person isn't performing because we weren't clear in our directions . . . America, our children are waiting and we must not disappoint them. Let's all love them and lead them. (Stanford & Simons, 1999, pp. 206, 213)

Enjoy all the precious moments that your students share with you. Learning can be very joyous and exciting. Schools can become places of care where active learning brings people together. Remember that *you* and your *students* are precious gifts of life. As Robert Fulghum wrote in his book, *All I Really Need to Know I Learned in Kindergarten*, "no matter how old you are—when you go out into the world, it is best to hold hands and stick together."

Figure 11.9: In a successful school, students support each other as members of a community of learners. They are encouraged to be courageous and resilient in their lives.

Thinking about Intersectionality

Teachers must address the achievement gap in schools. Some researchers believe it is, in part, to a participation gap where students of color and poor learners do not have the same opportunity to engage in higher order content and skills (Carter & Welner, 2013; Nasir et al., 2014). Some researchers believe causes of the achievement gap are varied and include many social characteristics from poverty, race, gender, culture, language proficiencies, and neighborhood. Teachers realize that to address the achievement gap, schools must consider many how these elements, as different aspects of intersectionality, compound to make equality in education difficult.

One aspect of schools is economics, both of students and schools. Many poor students of color are at a disadvantage in society because they attend less quality schools; students who are poor often live in poor neighborhoods. Many schools are dependent on local property taxes, so low-income schools do not have the same financial resource foundation as schools located in rich neighborhoods. Poor neighborhoods repeatedly have schools with limited resources (Ferguson, 1991). For example, many poor students attend schools that do not have high quality teachers, small class sizes, well-funded science labs, up-to-date textbooks, and computer labs. Disadvantaged students attend disadvantaged schools (Ferguson, 1991; Berry, 2013). However, the most important element in the classroom is the teacher; research has shown this to be the vital facet (Berry, 2013).

Poor schools in neighborhoods of color are often staffed by the most inexperienced teachers. Though there are many exceptional educators, they are not always found in poor schools (Berry, 2013). Isn't this the opposite of what would be expected? Wouldn't the most experienced and successful teachers work in the most challenging schools? Why isn't this the case? Teachers need to know about the cultural, living, and social conditions of their students and families (Pang et al., 2014). Educators can then build upon student knowledge as they teach grade-level and subject-area content. The integration of culturally relevant education connects what students know with the curriculum of schools. Well-trained teachers know of the cultural worldviews and experiences of their students.

Teachers can do the following:

Examine how intersectionality reinforces inequalities in the classroom.

Have high expectations of all students.

Give quality feedback to all students.

Provide lessons that are engaging.

Create lessons that build on student knowledge.

Affirm student cultural identities and home languages.

Provide students with opportunities to explore future careers.

The best teachers know that their teaching must be meaningful in order for students to learn. Effective educators have strong relationships with students always encouraging and motivating them. Learners know their teachers believe in them. You, the teacher, are the most important element in the learning process!

Summary

1. **Discuss why diversity is a fundamental principle in life.**

Diversity is more than identifying cultural and linguistic differences in students. Diversity is an important element of our lives; for example, humans need to engage in a variety of physical activities to challenge the body and keep it healthy. The body will adjust to the same physical actions, so to test one's form, one must add other behaviors. In addition, diversity in our financial savings is critical. To save for retirement, a person should invest in different types of investments and not just one. Diversity is part of life. However, we also must realize that biologically, we are all more alike than different. We may represent many cultural differences, but we also need to work collaboratively to ensure we build a strong democracy.

2. **Analyze and address the achievement gap between students of color and their White peers.**

The achievement gap must be examined and attended to in schools. Though there are many strategies that teachers can employ, it is also important for educators to be aware of comprehensive programs that include revision of policies, goals, curriculum, teacher attitudes, and teacher practices. Three such programs are the Puente Program, which involves counseling, writing, and mentoring, the Algebra Project, which is founded on educational opportunity in math education, and the Lemon Grove Academy of Humanities and the Sciences' Wellness program. These educators analyzed the needs of students and designed exceptional academic, social, and emotional courses of study to address those essentials.

Summary (Continued)

3. **Demonstrate how to integrate technology to address the achievement gap found in schools.**

   Teachers can use technology to provide differentiation in the classroom and individualized tutoring to students. Use of digital devices can also result in students collaborating with each other using Google Docs or the creation of a wiki. In addition, technology can be used to assess student knowledge and skills. Students can engage in research on various topics and/or issues in social studies, environmental studies, government, history, literature, science, and economics. Technology is another avenue that teachers can implement in their classroom to address the wide-ranging interests and academic needs of their students.

4. **Reflect upon and discuss moving from teacher-centered to student-centered education applying a framework that** integrates the ethic of care (relationships), sociocultural theory of learning (culture and cognition), and education for democracy (community).

   The caring-centered framework provides a foundation for teachers that emphasizes the importance of democratic values, critical thinking, inquiry education, collaboration, and cognitive theory. This framework integrates caring, culture, community, and social justice and moves teachers from a teacher-centered philosophy about education to a student-centered one. It is a paradigm shift; like a chick coming out of an egg, the student becomes an empowered and engaged learner. Instead of teachers being the "sage on stage," they become the "guide on the side." In other words, students take ownership of their learning. They set goals and work toward them. They also make decisions on their own by choosing issues or topics they will study. Students are encouraged to take charge of their learning.

Check Your Cultural Knowledge

Reflective Essay Question

As you reach the end of this text, what do you think are the most important insights you have learned? Identify 10 and rank them in order from 1 being important to 10 being most important. What philosophical foundation and or theories would you include in your list? The list should include theories, curriculum approaches, teacher attitudes, and information about culture.

Application

Know and Go Tools in the Classroom

Here are some ideas to consider when you teach:

1. Before you go into the classroom, outline your game plan. This includes the rules that you absolutely think students must adhere to. Have several activities in which you can engage students; the lesson you planned may not take as long as you thought. Be sure to have a list of student names. This is critical in order to maintain order. You won't be that effective if you have to say, "You, in the red sweater, sit down."

2. No matter who you are teaching, appear as if you are in charge even if you are scared. Students want teachers who are confident and fair.

3. Once your students are able to follow the rules and know you are genuinely interested in them, create caring relationships among your students. Have students write a story of the funniest thing they ever did and then have them share in pairs. It is easier to keep students on task in pairs than in groups of four learners.

4. Praise, praise, praise. As soon as the students come into the classroom, praise them. Start the day on a positive foot. Even with the student who seems to NEVER do anything right, try to identify something good that student is doing at the beginning of the day and give praise. Some students do not like being praised in front of others, so you may find other ways to do so quietly like having a card taped to their desk so you can stamp it with a special seal.

5. Be sure the bulletin boards include great work from every student. Affirm each student whether a second grader or a tenth grader; they all want to be respected and do well in school.

6. Encourage students to work together. Do you think that sharing is cheating? If so, then you might want to rethink that position. In life, students will go out into the world of work and will be evaluated on how well they collaborate with others on their jobs. If you think some students are not doing their fair share of an assignment, talk about what it means to be responsible to each other.

7. Most students want their teacher to care about them. They also want their teacher to be fair and respect their cultural and linguistic backgrounds. Look at your own biases and get rid of them. If you make a mistake, tell the student you are sorry. If said sincerely, students will see your apology as a strength and not a weakness.

8. Get to know your parents. Most parents want their children to do well in school. Remember to call parents when students are doing well. Your most powerful ally can be a parent.

9. Don't beat yourself up when you make a mistake. We all make mistakes. Reviewing our own mistakes can be the source of our most growth.

10. Care for your students by being fair and respectful. They will treat themselves, you, and others in the way you treat them. When you care, you will be fair.

Teachers are the most important element in the classroom. Do great things with your students! They are waiting!

Glossary

A

Ableism is the systematic exclusion and discrimination against people with physical, intellectual, or developmental disabilities.

Academic English is a broad category that includes many language skills and refers to the ability to use English on an abstract level, such as in writing.

Acculturation refers to the process in which people learn about and feel comfortable with the practices and cultural ways of life of the dominant culture, but still retain their home/native cultures. It can also refer to the exchange of cultural elements such as food, art, and other aspects of culture among people from diverse groups.

Achievement gap refers to the achievement difference between students of color and their White peers in various subject areas.

Acquisition-learning hypothesis refers to students acquiring language rather than learning language.

Additive bilingualism is an approach in which students are encouraged to use both their native language and English in the learning process.

Advanced fluency stage refers to the stage in which the second-language learner has developed both conversational and academic language. These abilities can take from 4 to 10 years to acquire.

Affective filter hypothesis is the belief that language learning will be enhanced when students build up their self-confidence and motivation to acquire the second language.

African American English, also called **Ebonics** is a rule-governed language that arose out of African American culture.

Aggregate refers to data placed in a large general category.

Algebra Project is a culturally relevant curriculum program in math that integrates community action and math instruction. It uses an inquiry approach and was created by Robert Moses.

Ally refers to a person who does not identify with being LGBTQ and is from a privileged group; the person advocates for social change and works to stop bullying and harassment of LGBTQ young people in schools and society.

American dream is a belief in individualism and meritocracy: if you work hard enough and get an education, you can become economically successful because this nation is founded upon the belief in equal opportunities for all.

Anti-Semitism is prejudice and hostility against Jews as individuals or as a group; it may be due to their religious beliefs, belief that they are inferior, or related to the state of Israel.

Asian American and Pacific Islander students are placed into a large general group and denoted by AAPI. The AAPI community includes over 50 groups such as Chinese Americans, Japanese Americans, Korean Americans, Samoan Americans, Guamanian Americans, Hawaiian Americans, Hmong Americans, Taiwanese Americans, Cambodian Americans, Laotian Americans, Vietnamese Americans, South Indian Americans, Thai Americans, and others.

Assimilationists identify with mainstream society and take on mainstream views, behaviors, values, and ways of thinking. They do not relate to their ethnic or racial communities.

Asylum refers to when a person asks a nation to allow him or her to enter its country for protection because of persecution due to religion, race, nationality, membership in a specific social group, and political opinion.

Asynchronous refers to online teaching where the members of the class access the session at a time they choose; there is no set time when all students attend class online together.

Attention deficit/hyperactivity disorder (ADHD) is described as impulsive behaviors, excessive activity, and difficulty paying attention. Though often associated with learning disabilities, ADHD is not considered a learning disability.

B

BICS stands for basic interpersonal communication skills and is the level of language that people use to talk with each other every day.

Bicultural refers to a person who is able to function in both mainstream and subcultural environments; they understand the values, norms, and behaviors of either community.

Bicultural identity refers to members of a group who retain cultural values, customs, and ways of seeing life, yet they have adopted practices and beliefs of the mainstream culture.

Bilingual education refers to students receiving instruction in their native language and English.

Biliteracy is the ability to read and write in two languages.

Bracero Program was a series of laws and agreements that began in 1942 and ended in 1964 providing manual labor between the United States and Mexico. The agreements provided Mexican laborers with human rights, sanitation, shelter, food, and a minimum wage of 30 cents an hour.

Bullying is defined as repeated, unwanted, aggressive behavior that threatens, humiliates, isolates, and/or excludes an individual where there is a perceived or real power imbalance.

C

CALLA (cognitive academic language learning approach) focuses on teaching academic content to intermediate English learners.

CALP stands for cognitive academic language proficiency and includes skills and knowledge that students need in learning higher-level discipline content.

Capitalism refers to an economic system of production resulting in profit for private owners.

Chunking refers to creating smaller pieces of knowledge so that the information being taught is not overwhelming to students.

Classism is a complex construct that is defined as prejudice or discrimination of people and groups based on their social class, which is often defined as "lower" class.

Collective memory is the memory that we share as members of society that has been shaped by the media, popular culture, movies, books, and other aspects of society.

Collective occlusion refers to the parts of history and human experiences that have been forgotten or are not easily obtained.

Collectivism refers to the identification of a person with a group or collective and its goals, behaviors, values, and general way of life.

Color blindness refers to not considering or recognizing a person's racial or ethnic characteristics, though inequities and prejudice continue to be major forces in society.

Coming out refers to a person telling others about his or her sexual orientation. Sometimes the term also is described as "coming out of the closet," which means that someone is no longer keeping her or his sexual orientation a secret.

Complex instruction is a collaborative approach to instruction that uses group work activities.

Concerted cultivation refers to the process in which people, including young students, develop skills and knowledge that are valued in society and become socialized to expect equality.

Consanguineous mating is reproducing between people who are close relatives.

Cultural asset-based orientation recognizes the cultural strengths and benefits of what a child and his family add to the school community.

Cultural assimilation is the process by which an individual adopts language, behaviors, values, and a way of life from the dominant culture while letting go of home or heritage cultures.

Cultural capital refers to the knowledge, behaviors, values, and skills of a social group; when a child has learned elements of cultural capital, they are able to function and know what is expected of them in the community.

Cultural deficit viewpoint is the belief that students from underrepresented groups come with cultures and languages that place them at risk of failing in school; intellectual inferiority is often an underlying belief that links cultural differences with cultural deficiency.

Cultural difference viewpoint is the belief that students from underrepresented communities come with cultures that are not deficient from the dominant culture, rather they are different.

Cultural diversity is a broad term and includes subcultures such as race, ethnicity, social class, gender, religion, neighborhoods, families, language, exceptionalities, and sexual orientation.

Cultural genocide is the eradication of the cultural background, including the language, way of life, values, and identity, of a group.

Cultural identity refers to the identity a person can develop based on affiliations with various subgroup communities. Cultural identities can be personal or public. Sometimes outsiders may adopt a cultural identity of others that can be in conflict with the person's chosen cultural identity.

Cultural models are systems of interconnected ideas.

Cultural pluralism refers to respecting people from diverse cultures and their ways of life.

Cultural racism refers to beliefs found within a community that perceives elements of another group's culture as being inferior.

Cultural sustainability is the maintenance of culture.

Cultural traditionalists follow the ways, beliefs, and patterns of the cultural group much of the time and may continue to speak the native or home language.

Cultural worldview or perspective refers to a holistic orientation based upon the history, values, and beliefs of a cultural group.

Culturally relevant, culturally responsive or **culturally appropriate** teaching refers to education that builds on the cultural knowledge, values, and experiences that students bring to school.

Culturally relevant education is an approach that incorporates student-lived experiences and cultural modes of delivery into the curriculum and instructional methods of teaching. Culturally relevant teaching can also be referred to as meaningful teaching where instruction is relevant, interesting, and purposeful to all students.

Culturally relevant elements that can be integrated into lessons: student personal experiences, role models, culturally relevant stories/legends/folktales/songs, photos/pictures, linguistic expressions, multiple perspectives, formal subject content, and community issues.

Culturally relevant teaching (CRT) is an approach to instruction founded on the belief in equity education that responds to the sociocultural context of students and seeks to integrate their cultural and social capital.

Culture is a dynamic, shared social system of human components such as language, dress, customs, history, philosophies, behaviors, institutions, norms, and values; it also can include geographical influences.

Culture of power refers to the beliefs, behaviors, standards, and expectations for success in U.S. society as defined by mainstream culture.

Cyberbullying is bullying using electronic devices and social media. This includes apparatuses such as cell phones, computers, and tablets, and can involve the use of chat rooms, text messaging, and websites.

D

Detracking refers to not placing students in stereotypical ability groups.

Developmentally disabled refers to individuals with intellectual or physical impairments that inhibit their ability to take care of themselves and limit their ability to develop conceptual, social, and practical skills.

Differentiated instruction is the use of diverse instructional strategies so that the needs of various students can be addressed in the same lesson or unit.

Disaggregate refers to dividing a large group into smaller components.

Discrimination is characterized as being excluded because of one's group membership; this often means not being treated equally.

E

Early production stage refers to the phase in which the language learner is becoming more comfortable and can provide short answers in the communication process.

Education for democracy is a theory developed primarily by John Dewey that identifies the values of democracy, equality, community, and justice as core values of schools.

Egocentrism is a state in which a person can only see from his or her perspective.

Emancipation Proclamation was an executive order signed by President Abraham Lincoln to set free the slaves who lived in states that were members of the Confederacy; it did not provide citizenship rights to slaves or provide freedom to all African Americans.

Equality in education is defined as providing students with the same instruction, curriculum, counseling approaches, and other activities in school; it is about fair and equal treatment.

Equity refers to providing students with what they need in order to excel and demonstrate equality of outcome.

Ethic of Care is a theory developed primarily by Nel Noddings which focuses on the importance of developing trusting, reciprocal relationships in schools.

Ethnic prejudice is hostility based upon a faulty and inflexible generalization. It may be felt or expressed. It may be directed toward a group as a whole or toward an individual because he or she is a member of that group.

Ethnicity refers to a place of family-national origin such as Ireland, Japan, Croatia, Nigeria, or Mexico.

Ethnocentrism is a stage in Bennett's model of intercultural sensitivity in which a person's group culture shapes her or his view of the world and other cultures; does not consider the views of other cultural groups.

Ethnorelativism is a stage in Bennett's model of intercultural sensitivity in which people learn about the values and views of others within the context of their cultures. In this stage, individuals are open to new viewpoints and perspectives.

Exceptionalities broadens the concept of disabilities and includes students who are advanced learners.

Explicit culture refers to tangible and visible cultural elements, including food, dress, holidays, governmental systems, country of origin, history, and language.

F

Food insecurity is the lack of proper nutrition and safe foods; people often may not be able to obtain food in socially acceptable ways (some may have to beg, go to food banks, steal, and eat from garbage cans).

Framework is a set of educational principles, beliefs, policies, and practices.

Funds of Knowledge is a culturally relevant program that teaches the whole child and builds upon the knowledge that students bring to school, brings parents into the classroom, and affirms student identity and family knowledge.

G

Gender refers to the social attitudes, behaviors, and feelings that are associated with an individual's biological sex. It also denotes the cultural behavioral expectations that are seen as normative.

Gender bias is "the belief that females and males have distinctive characteristics and that one gender has the right to more power and resources than the other; it is policies and practices based on those beliefs" (Schniedewind & Davidson, 1998, p. 8). In other words, women are inferior to men. Also known as sexism.

Gender identity is when a person identifies as being male, female, or transgender. Sometimes one's gender identity is not congruent with his or her biological sex.

Genocide is the elimination of a group of people and their way of life.

Glass ceiling refers to obstacles—not based on merit or abilities—which serve as barriers to the advancement of women and people of color in financial, career, and other opportunities.

Grammar is the rules of language, conversation, and writing.

Grit is the inclination to work toward goals with perseverance and passion.

H

Harlem Renaissance refers to the period during the 1920s and 1930s where there was a great burst of outstanding work from artists, musicians, and writers from the Black American community. Langston Hughes was one of the great writers of the time.

Hidden curriculum is the implicit set of values that exist but may be found mostly by looking at behaviors and unstated practices and content.

Homophobia is the fear of gay, lesbian, bisexual, transgender, and queer people.

Hunger is defined as the condition in which a person does not have enough food; this need causes bodily discomfort and pain.

Hybrid is an approach that combines online teaching and face-to-face instruction.

I

Ideology of ability is the belief that a person's value is defined by his or her physical, intellectual, emotional, and social abilities. A disability can be eliminated if a person works hard enough. A person who has a disability is not as valuable as a person without a disability. People with disabilities are sad, frustrated, and egocentric.

Immigrant refers to someone who has decided to move to the United States from another country and is planning to stay.

Imperialism is the political, economic, and cultural control over another country or territory; in the process a country takes control of the government and economic system by dominating the weaker population.

Implicit culture is made up of elements that are often hidden: the values, assumptions, beliefs, and philosophies of a group. Implicit cultural aspects are harder to identify because they include expectations and worldviews.

Inclusion refers to students with disabilities being included as members of a general education classroom.

Income is defined as what one is paid for services or work that has been completed as in the case of earnings from a job.

Income inequality refers to the fact that there are some Americans with great wealth and others who do not earn a living wage, resulting in a huge economic imbalance.

Indentured servants are people who agree to a contract to work for another; in colonial times, the agreement was often for a period of about seven years.

Indigenous person Is one who has ancestors who are original people of a particular land, shares in a sense of peoplehood with his or her tribe's cultural background and history, may speak the indigenous language, and struggles to maintain the tribe's cultural integrity and self-determination.

Individual racism refers to the attitudes, beliefs, and behaviors of someone who believes that she or he is superior to another because of her or his race.

Individuals with Disabilities Act (IDEA) is the legislation that ensures that all children with disabilities are provided an effective, high-quality education.

Individualism is an important value in the United States and refers to the ability and perseverance of the individual to generate his or her own success.

Institutional racism is a system of legalized practices designed to keep the dominant group in power.

International Reading Association along with the National Council of Teachers of English have identified K–12 standards in language arts that compliment local, state, and district standards.

Intersectionality refers to how various aspects of oppression come together and are interrelated.

Intersex conditions refers to individuals who have various abnormalities that may involve various aspects of the body such as external genitals, internal reproductive organs, and sex chromosomes.

ISIS, which stands for the Islamic State of Iraq and Syria, is a terrorist group.

Islamophobia is defined as unproven fear and/or hostility toward Muslims.

Issues-centered approach is a method that is taught to students so they develop skills to make important decisions in their personal lives and as citizens of a democracy and the world.

Intermediate fluency stage refers to the stage in which the second-language learner is able to communicate with others with ease.

L

LGBTQ refers to lesbian, gay, bisexual, transgender, and questioning or queer individuals.

Living wage refers to a level of income that is enough to pay for one's housing, food, utilities, and other necessities.

M

Macroculture refers to the larger cultural group, which includes expectations, symbols, and behaviors.

Mainstream or **dominant culture** arises out of the experiences and values of middle-class, Protestant Caucasians who live in the U.S. democracy.

Mainstreaming refers to the placement of students with disabilities into the general education classroom so they have the opportunity to learn the same curriculum as their peers and become part of a regular learning environment. To many teachers, this has come to be known as the "dumping" of students with disabilities into the general education classroom without support for students or teachers.

Manifest Destiny is the move to expand the United States from the Atlantic Ocean to the Pacific.

Mascots are objects, people, or animals that are used as a group's representative, often presented as a caricature or cartoon.

Meritocracy refers to the belief that those who work hard make the most money; therefore, those who do not make much money must not work hard or are not smart.

Metalinguistic awareness refers to understanding underlying principles of language, such as the fact that rhyming words may have the same endings and how two words may sound the same but the context gives information about which spelling of the term is correct.

Middle passage is the name for the slave's journey to the Americas across the ocean.

Migrant refers to an individual who moves to the United States but who hopes to go back to his or her native land in the future.

Model minority myth is a stereotypical belief that Asian American and Pacific Islander students do not need help in schools because they are all high achievers.

Model of culture consists of three levels: Level 1, artifacts, explicit elements; Level 2, interactional patterns; and Level 3, values, beliefs, and norms.

Monitor model is the belief that people become more fluent in a language by using it. Minimal monitoring should occur so that the students feels comfortable acquiring the language through practice.

Morphology is the study of the basic meaning units in language.

Multicultural education is defined as a field in education that calls for total school reform and is based on the belief that education is an intellectual and ethical endeavor where students are provided equity in schools.

N

National Council for the Social Studies, National Curriculum Standards for the Social Studies is a document that identifies standards for social studies from K–12.

National Council of Teachers of English along with the International Reading Association have identified K–12 standards in language arts that complement local, state, and district standards.

Nativism is a term used to describe an anti-immigrant attitude and actions aimed at people who have migrated or immigrated to the United States; Nativists are concerned that their way of life—including jobs, education, housing, and other opportunities—will be lost.

Natural approach refers to a naturalistic strategy in teaching language. It refers to building on what is meaningful to students with less emphasis on direct instruction.

O

Overreaching in education means that schools that need improvement may bring in numerous programs as part of school reform; however, these programs do not build on each other.

P

Phenotype refers to the use of outward physical characteristics to identify someone. This could be the labeling of a person as Native American or Black.

Phonology is the study of sounds.

Pogroms were riots, destruction, and persecution aimed at Jews during the nineteenth and twentieth centuries.

Pragmatics is the complex understanding of context, which includes not only how language is used within specific situations but also which sentences are most appropriate within the flow of a conversation and inferences made by word choices.

Prejudice is a feeling, favorable or unfavorable, toward a person or thing prior to, and not based on, actual experience.

Preproduction stage is the silent period when the second-language learner is paying close attention to the sounds she hears because she knows they represent words.

Prosocial behaviors include working collaboratively, following rules, waiting in line, and inviting others to participate.

Pygmalion effect is the influence of teacher expectations on student performance.

Q

Queer has a variety of definitions. For some individuals, it has been repossessed from being used negatively against gays and lesbians to one of self-pride. The term is also used to generally identify lesbians, gays, bisexuals, and transgender people. Some individuals still see the term as offensive.

R

Race is a political and social construct that refers to categorizing people based on perceived physical differences such as skin color; there is no basis for race in biology.

Race ambivalence recognizes that though race and racism are still forces that influence the way people think, believe, and act, race is becoming more and more difficult to describe and define.

Racial identity formation is the process of identifying oneself and the personal significance of being part of a specific racial group.

Racism is a legalized system of privileges and penalties based on the belief of the superiority of people or groups based on perceived racial differences.

Refugee is defined by the United Nations as a person who willingly or unwillingly cannot return to his or her home country due to fear of prosecution because of race, religion, nationality, political views, or membership in a specific social group.

Religious illiteracy is the lack of knowledge about the values, beliefs, and history of various religions throughout the world and how religion overlaps with political and cultural aspects of societies.

Resegregation refers to the practice of continual segregation of students of color even after many legal and social practices aimed at desegregation, from busing to court-ordered remedies.

Response to Intervention (RTI) is a preventive program that teachers can implement. Educators develop programs that will prevent students from falling so far behind that they must be placed in special education classes.

S

Scaffolding refers to instructional strategies that a teacher uses to facilitate the learning of a student such as providing visuals, explaining how to think about a concept, modeling a skill, asking pertinent questions, and giving students feedback.

Scapegoating is shifting the blame of a problem to a victim.

School stratification refers to a systematic hierarchy in which the best schools and educational opportunities are found in high-income neighborhoods and the poorest schools are found in low-income communities.

SDAIE refers to specially designed academic instruction in English. This method is like sheltered English in which both language skills and subject area content are taught.

Self-determination refers to the ability of Native people to make their own decisions and to have a voice in their self-government whether on Indian reservations or in regard to broader issues dealing with Native Americans.

Self-regulation refers to a process in which an individual or student identifies a goal and then works towards achieving or accomplishing the goal.

Sexism is "the belief that females and males have distinctive characteristics and that one gender has the right to more power and resources than the other; it is policies and practices based on those beliefs" (Schniedewind & Davidson, 1998, p. 8). In other words, women are inferior to men. Also known as gender bias.

Sexual orientation refers to the sex of those to whom one is sexually and romantically attracted. Categories of sexual orientation typically have included attraction to members of one's own sex (gay men or lesbians), attraction to members of the other sex (heterosexuals), and attraction to members of both sexes (bisexuals). While these categories continue to be widely used, research has suggested that sexual orientation does not always appear in such definable categories and instead occurs on a continuum. This definition comes from the American Psychological Association.

Sheltered English is a method that is supportive of English learners so that they learn both subject area content and language skills.

Social capital is the social network that parents and families have developed and can tap into.

Social class refers to an individual's or group's economic level of income and/or wealth. Income is different from wealth.

Social cohesion refers to strong social ties where participants agree with community decisions, conform to social expectations, and have a strong commitment to the country.

Social stratification is defined as a systematic hierarchy based on group membership characteristics such as class, race, or political status.

Socialization is a process whereby individuals learn the values, expectations, and behaviors of a group.

Sociocultural theory of learning is a theory developed primarily by Lev Vygotsky where social interactions and language are seen as the vehicles of learning.

Sociopolitical construct refers to an idea or theory that deals with both social and political contexts such as race, class, or gender.

Speech emergence stage refers to the period in which the second language learner is able to speak in short sentences.

Stereotype is defined as a favorable or unfavorable exaggerated belief associated with a category whose function is to defend a person's conduct as it relates to the category.

Subculture is a smaller community that has shared features that distinguish it from a larger social group.

Submersion is an approach to teaching English learners and should not be confused with bilingual education; students are expected to learn English while they learn grade-level academic content. This approach is often called the "sink or swim" method.

Subtractive bilingualism approach is one in which teachers ignore the first language and culture of their students.

Suffrage is defined as the right to vote. This term is often associated with women's fight for the vote.

Synchronous means that everyone meets online together at a particular time for instruction.

Syntax is a system of rules that govern how we correctly use words and place words in order.

T

Title IX of the Education Amendments of 1972 stated that women and men could not be discriminated against in "any educational program or activity receiving federal aid."

Tracking refers to placing students by perceived abilities into different ability-groups, classes, or career paths.

Traditional gender roles refer to the ways in which women and men are expected to behave and are often based on patriarchal social norms.

Transborder refers to experiencing and knowing two or more cultures and the border culture.

Transgender is an overarching term used to recognize those whose internal gender identity does not collaborate with their biological sex. Transgender can be used to describe people with atypical genitalia.

Transphobia is the fear of transgender people.

U

Underground Railroad was a covert escape route for Blacks who were enslaved.

Underrepresented refers to non-White people, including African Americans, American Indians, Alaska Natives, Asian Americans, Hispanic/Latinos, and Pacific Islanders.

Universal design for learning (UDL) is a framework with the goal of providing the most flexible environment to increase the accessibility of students to learning.

V

Vocabulary refers to words and phrases of a language.

W

Wealth refers to a person's financial resources, which might be income from a job along with property owned, stocks invested, and savings held. It is much more than income.

White privilege, as defined by Peggy McIntosh, is "an invisible package of unearned assets" that can be cashed "in each day, but . . . was 'meant' to remain oblivious. White privilege is like an invisible weightless knapsack of special provisions, maps, passports, codebooks, visas, clothes, tools, and blank checks."

X

Xenophobia refers to prejudice and fear of individuals and groups from other countries.

Z

Zone of proximal development is an extended range of a child's learning, from the actual developmental level to the potential level achieved through the guidance of an adult or collaboration with a more knowledgeable peer.

References

Alexander, Michelle. (2012). *The new Jim Crow: Mass incarceration in the age of colorblindness.* New York: The New Press.

Allen, J. (1999). Pancho Villa: An issues-centered lesson plan. Unpublished manuscript.

Allport, Gordon W. (1954). *The nature of prejudice.* Reading, MA: Addison-Wesley.

Almeida, Deidre A. (1997). The hidden half: A history of Native American education. *Harvard Educational Review, 67*(4), 757–771.

Alvarez, Gonzalo. Quinteiro, Celsa, Ceballos, Francisco C. (2011). Inbreeding and genetic disorder. In Kenji Ikahara (Ed.), *Advances in the Study of Genetic Disorders* (pp. 21–44). New York: Intech.

Amanti, Cathy. (1995). Teachers doing research: Beyond classroom walls. *Practicing Anthropology, 17*(3), 7–9.

American Immigration Council. (2014). *Refugees: Fact sheet.* Retrieved from http://www.immigrationpolicy.org/sites/default/files/docs/refugeefactsheet2014.pdf.

American Psychological Association. (2008). Answers to your questions: For a better understanding of sexual orientation and homosexuality. Washington, DC: Author. Retrieved from www.apa.org/topics/sorientation.pdf

American Psychological Association. (2011). Definition of terms: Sex, gender, gender identity, sexual orientation. American Psychological Association. Retrieved at https://www.apa.org/pi/lgbt/resources/sexuality-definitions.pdf

Anderson, Gary L. (2005). Academia and activism: An essay review of Jean Anyon's radical possibilities. *Education Review, 8*(1). Retrieved from http://www.edrev.info/essays/v8n1index.html.

Anderson, Monica. (2015a, April 9). A rising share of the U.S. Black Population is foreign born. Washington, DC: Pew Research Center. Retrieved from http://www.pewsocialtrends.org/2015/04/09/a-rising-share-of-the-u-s-black-population-is-foreign-born/

Anderson, Monica. (2015b, April 9). Six findings about Black immigration to the U.S. Washington, DC: Pew Research Center. Retrieved from http://www.pewresearch.org/fact-tank/2015/04/09/6-key-findings-about-black-immigration/

Anderson, Stuart. (2003). *The impact of the agricultural guest worker programs on illegal immigration.* Arlington, VA: National Foundation for American Policy. Retrieved from http://www.nfap.com/researchactivities/studies/Nov_study1.pdf

Anti-Defamation League. (2013). A brief history of anti-Semitism. Retrieved from http://www.adl.org/assets/pdf/education-outreach/Brief-History-on-Anti-Semitism-A.pdf

Anti-Defamation League. (2014). *A world of difference.* New York: Anti-Defamation League. Retrieved from http://www.adl.org/education-outreach/anti-bias-education/c/a-world-of-difference.html

Anti-Defamation League. (2015). Audit: In 2014 anti-Semitic incidents rose 21 percent across the U.S. in a particular violent year for Jews. Retrieved from http://www.adl.org/press-center/press-releases/anti-semitism-usa/adl-audit-in-2014-anti-semitic-inicidents.html#.VfexRpcXW7Q

Annenberg Institute for Civics. (n.d.). *Women's rights timeline.* Retrieved from http://www.annenbergclassroom.org/Files/Documents/Timelines/WomensRightstimeline.pdf

Annie E. Casey Foundation. (2014). *Kids count: 2014 data book state trends in child well-being.* Baltimore, MD: The Annie E. Casey Foundation.

Anyon, Jean. (1981). Social class and school knowledge. *Curriculum Inquiry, 11*(1), 3–42.

Anyon, Jean. (1995). Inner city school reform: Toward useful theory. *Urban Education, 30*(1), 56–70.

Anyon, Jean. (1997). *Ghetto schooling: A political economy of urban educational reform.* New York: Teachers College Press.

Anyon, Jean. (2005a). *Radical Possibilities: Public policy, urban education, and a new social movement.* New York: Routledge.

Anyon, Jean. (2005b). What counts as educational policy? Notes towards a new paradigm. *Harvard Educational Review, 75*(1), 65–88.

Arundel, Rikki. (2015). Why is gender identity so important? TED Talk. Retrieved from https://www.youtube.com/watch?v=IFBU7h7fqLc

Asakawa, Gil. (2015). *Being Japanese American: A JA sourcebook for Nikkei, Hapa…& their friends.* Berkeley, CA: Stone Bridge Press.

Ashton-Warner, Sylvia. (1986). *Teacher.* New York: Touchstone.

Atkinson, Rob. (1999). Liberating lawyers: Divergent parallels in *Intruder in the Dust* and *To Kill a Mockingbird. Duke Law Journal, 49*(3), 601–748.

Au, Kathryn H . (1993). *Literacy instruction in multilingual settings.* Fort Worth, TX: Harcourt.

Au, Kathryn H., & Kawakami, Alice J. (1994). Cultural congruence in instruction. In Etta R. Hollins, Joyce E. King, and Warren C. Haymans (Eds.), *Teaching diverse populations: Formulating a knowledge base* (pp. 5–24). Albany, NY: SUNY Press.

Au, Wayne, Brown, Anthony L., & Calderon, Dolores. (2016). *Reclaiming the multicultural roots of the U.S. curriculum: Communities of color and official knowledge in education.* New York: Teachers College Press.

Au, Wayne, & Ferrare, Joseph J. (2015). *Mapping corporate education reform: Power and policy networks in the neoliberal state.* New York: Routledge.

Baker, Colin. (2006). *Foundations of bilingual education and bilingualism.* United Kingdom: Multilingual Matters.

Baker, Joanne. (2010). Claiming volition and evading victim-hood: Post-feminist obligations for young women. *Feminism and Psychology, 20*, 186–204.

Banks, Cherry A. M. (2005). *Improving multicultural education: Lessons from the intergroup education movement.* New York: Teachers College Press.

Banks, James A. (1984). *Teaching strategies for ethnic studies.* Boston, MA: Allyn & Bacon.

Banks, James A. (1993). Multicultural education: Development, dimensions, and challenges. *Phi Delta Kappan, 75*(1), 22–28.

Banks, James A. (2014). *Introduction to multicultural education.* New York: Pearson Education.

Banks, James A., & Banks, Cherry A. M. (Eds.), (1997). *Multicultural education: Issues and perspectives* (3rd ed.). Boston: Allyn and Bacon.

Barack, Lauren. (2010). Islam in the classroom: It's never been more important. *School Library Journal, 56*(10), 34–37.

Barber, B. (1993). Global multiculturalism and the American experiment. *World Policy Journal, 10*(1), 47–55.

Barber, E. Susan. (n.d.). One hundred years toward suffrage: An overview. *National American Women's Suffrage Association Collection 1848–1921.* Library of Congress.

Bartozik-Veléz, Elise. (2006). Globalism and Cristopher Columbus in the Americas. *CLC Web: Comparative Literature and Culture, 8*(4), 1–10.

Beck, E. (2004, Fall). Integrating the art and science of medicine—A humanistic approach. *California Family Physician,* 22–24.

Beck, E. (2005). The UCSD student-run free clinic project: Transdisciplinary health professional education. *Journal of Health Care for the Poor and Underserved, 16*(2), 2007–2219.

Becker, Julia C., & Swim, Janet K. (2012). Reducing endorsement of benevolent and modern sexist beliefs: Differential effects of addressing harm versus pervasiveness of benevolent sexism. *Social Psychology, 43*, 127–137.

Bell, Duncan. (2014). Before the democratic peace: Racial utopianism, empire and the abolition of war. *European Journal of International Relations, 20*(3), 647–670.

Bennett, Christine. (1995). *Comprehensive multicultural education: Theory and practice.* (3rd ed.). Boston, MA: Allyn and Bacon.

Bennett, Milton J. (1993). Towards ethnorelativism: A developmental model of intercultural sensitivity. In R. Michael Paige (Ed.), *Education for intercultural experience* (pp. 21–71). Yarmouth, ME: Intercultural Press.

Bennett, Milton J. (1998). *Basic concepts of intercultural communication: Selected readings.* Yarmouth, ME: Intercultural Press.

Berliner, David C., & Glass, Gene V. (2014). *50 myths & lies that threaten America's public schools: The real crisis in education.* New York: Teachers College Press.

Bernard-Powers, Jane. (1999). Composing her life: Hilda Taba and social studies history. In Margaret Smith Crocco and Orzo Luke Davis, Jr. (Eds.). *Bending the future to their will: Civic women, social education, and democracy* (pp. 185–206). Boulder, CO: Rowman and Littlefield.

Berry, Barnett. (2013). Good schools and teachers for all students: Dispelling myths, facing evidence, and pursuing the right strategies. In Prudence L. Carter and Kevin G. Welner (Eds.), *Closing the opportunity gap, what American must do to give every child an even chance* (pp. 181–192). New York: Oxford Press.

Bickmore, Kathy. (2011). Policies and programming for safer schools: Are "anti-bullying" approaches impeding education for peacebuilding? *Educational Policy, 25*(4), 648–687.

Bilodeau, Brent L., & Renn, Kristen A. (2005). Analysis of LGBT identity development models and implications for practice. *New Directions for Student Services, 111*, 25–39.

Blackburn, Mollie, & Smith, Jill M. (2010). Moving beyond the inclusion of LGBT-themed literature in English language arts classrooms: Interrogating heteronormativity and exploring intersectionality. *Journal of Adolescent & Adult Literacy, 53*(8), 625–634.

Blake, Márcia de Toledo, Drezett, Jackson, Vertamatti, Maria Auxilladora, Adami, Fernando, Valenti, Vitor E., Paiva, Adriana Costa, Viana, Joseval Martins, Pedroso, Daniela, & de Abreu, Luis Carlos. (2014). Characteristics of sexual violence against adolescent girls and adult women. *BMC Women's Health, 14*(15). Retrieved from http://bmcwomenshealth.biomedcentral.com/articles/10.1186/1472-6874-14-15

Blassingame, John W. (1979). *The slave community: Plantation life in the antebellum south.* New York: Oxford University Press.

Bohan, Chara Hauessler. (2007). A rebellious Jersey girl: Rachel Davis DuBois: Intercultural education pioneer. In Sam Totten and Jon Pedersen (Eds.), *Addressing social issues in the classroom and beyond* (pp. 99–115). Charlotte, NC: Information Age.

Boser, Ulrich, Wilhelm, Megan, & Hanna, Robert. (2014). *The power of the Pygmalion effect: Teachers expectations strongly predict college completion.* Washington, DC: Center for American Progress.

Brand, Susan Trostle, Favazza, Antoinette E., & Dalton, Elizabeth M. (2012). Universal design for learning: A blueprint for success for all learners. *Kappa Delta Pi Record, 48*, 134–139.

Brislin, Richard. (1993). *Understanding culture's influence on behavior.* New York: Harcourt Brace College Publishers.

Brislin, Richard. (2008). *Working with cultural differences: Dealing effectively with diversity in the workplace.* Westport, CT: Praeger.

Brooks, David. (2015). How to fight anti-Semitism. *New York Times.* Retrieved from http://www.nytimes.com/2015/03/24/opinion/david-brooks-how-to-fight-anti-semitism.html?_r=0

Brown, Ann L. (1992). Design experiments: Theoretical and methodological challenges in creating complex interventions in classroom settings. *Journal of the Learning Sciences, 2*(2), 141–178.

Bruner, Jerome. (1990). *Acts of meaning.* Cambridge, MA: Harvard University Press.

Bullough. Vern L. (1998). Alfred Kinsey and the Kinsey Report: Historical overview and lasting contributions. *Journal of Sex Research, 35*(2), 127–131.

Bullying Statistics. (2015). Bullying and suicide. Retrieved from http://www.bullyingstatistics.org/content/bullying-and-suicide.html

Burris, Carol Corbett, & Garrity, Delia T. (2008). *Detracking for excellence and equity.* Alexandria, VA: Association for Supervision and Curriculum Development.

Cann, Rebecca. L., & Wilson, Allan C. (2003). The recent African genesis of humans. *Scientific American, 13*(2), 54–61.

Capshew, James H., Adamson, Mathew H., Buchanan, Patricia A., Murray, Narisara, & Wake, Naoka. (2003). Kinsey's biographers: A historical reconnaissance. *Journal of the History of Sexuality, 12*(3), 465–486.

Carbado, Devon W. (2013). Colorblind intersectionality. *Signs, 38*(4), 811–845.

Caraballo, Limarys. (2009). Interest convergence in intergroup education and beyond: Rethinking agendas in multicultural education. *International Journal of Multicultural Education, 11*(1), 15.

Carter, Prudence L., & Welner, Kevin G. (2013). *Closing the opportunity gap: What America must do to give every child an even chance.* New York: Oxford University Press.

Case, Kim A., Stewart, Briana, & Tittsworth, Josephine. (2009). Transgender across the curriculum: A psychology of inclusion. *Teaching Psychology, 36,* 117–121.

Cass, Vivienne C. (1984). Homosexual identity formation: Testing a theoretical model. *Journal of Sex Research, 20*(2), 143–167.

Castañeda, Lillian Vega, & Ríos, Francisco. (2002). Teachers as students: Resistance to diversity. In P. Larke and N. Carter (Eds.), *Examining practices in multicultural education,* College Station, TX: JOY Publishing.

Catalyst. (2016). Women CEOs of the S&P 500. Retrieved from http://www.catalyst.org/knowledge/women-ceos-sp-500

Cennamo, Katherine, Ross, John, & Ertmer, Peggy. (2014). *Technology integration for meaningful classroom use: A standards-based approach* (2nd ed.). Belmont, CA: Wadsworth.

Centers for Disease Control and Prevention. (2014). Prevalence of autism spectrum disorder among children aged 8 years—Autism and Developmental Disabilities Monitoring Network, 11 Sites, United States, 2010. *Surveillance Summaries.* Retrieved from http://www.cdc.gov/mmwr/preview/mmwrhtml/ss6302a1.htm?s_cid=ss6302a1_w

Chamot, Ana Uhl. (1995, Summer/Fall). Implementing the cognitive academic language learning approach: *CALLA* in Arlington, Virginia. *The Bilingual Research Journal, 19*(374), 379–394.

Chamot, Anna U., & O'Malley, J. M. (1994). *The CALLA handbook: Implementing the cognitive academic language learning approach.* Reading, MA: Addison-Wesley.

Chan, Sucheng. (1991). *Asian Americans: An interpretive history.* Boston, MA: Twayne Publishers.

Chandler, Adam. (2015, June 15). A woman on the sawbuck. The Atlantic.com. Retrieved from http://www.theatlantic.com/politics/archive/2015/06/a-woman-on-the-sawbuck/396203/

Chaskin, R., & Rauner, Diana M. (1995). Youth and caring. *Phi Delta Kappan, 70*(9), 667–674.

Chen, C. (2011). *Public elementary and secondary school student enrollment and staff counts from the common core of data: School year 2009–10* (NCES 2011-347). U.S. Department of Education, National Center for Education Statistics. Washington, DC: National Center for Education Statistics. Retrieved from http://nces.ed.gov/pubsearch

Cheng, Li-rong Lilly. (1998). Language assessment and instructional strategies for limited English students. In Valerie Ooka Pang and Li-rong Lilly Cheng (Eds.), *Struggling to be heard: The unmet needs of Asian Pacific American children* (pp. 181–195). Albany, NY: SUNY Press.

Choi, Candice. (2015, April 15). Fight for $15 wage expand for low-wage workers. *Seattle PI.* Retrieved from http://www.seattlepi.com/news/us/article/Fight-for-15-protests-planned-over-McJobs-6200554.php

Clift, Forrest. (2015). Beyond bullying: The LGBT student experience. *Colleagues, 11,* 1–5. Retrieved from http://scholarworks.gvsu.edu/cgi/viewcontent.cgi?article=1216&context=colleagues

Cole, Michael. (1996). *Cultural psychology: A once and future discipline.* Cambridge, MA: Belknap Press of Harvard University.

Cole, Michael. (2005). Using cross-cultural psychology to design afterschool educational activities in different cultural settings. In Wolfgang Friedlmeier, Pradeep Chakkarth, and Beate Schwarz (Eds.), *Culture and human development: The importance of cross-cultural research for the social sciences* (pp. 53–71). New York: Psychology Press.

Coleman-Jensen, Alisha, Nord, Mark, & Singh, Anita. (2013). *Household food insecurity in the United States in 2012.* Economic Research Report No. (ERR. 155). Retrieved from http://www.ers.usda.gov/media/1183208/err-155.pdf

Collins, Gail. (2009). *When everything changed: The amazing journey of American women from 1960 to the present.* New York: Little, Brown & Co.

Coloroso, Barbara. (2011). Bully, bullied, bystander . . . and beyond. *Teaching Tolerance, 39,* 50–53.

Cook, Jiyon. (2012). Why do Korean listeners have difficulty recovering the meaning of casual speech in English? A study in pragmatics. *Asian Social Science, 8*(6), 40–51.

Corbett, Christianne, Hill, Catherine, & St. Rose, Andresse. (2008). *Where the girls are: The facts about gender equity in education.* Washington, DC: American Association of University Women.

Cornelius, Carol. (1999.) *Iroquois corn: In a culture-based curriculum.* Albany, NY: SUNY Press.

Corntassel, Jeff J. (2003). Who is indigenous? "Peoplehood" and ethnonationalist approaches to rearticulating indigenous identity. *Nationalism and Ethnic Politics, 9*(1), 75–100.

Council of the Haida Nation. (2013). *Raven creation story.* Retrieved from http://www.haidanation.ca/Pages/language/haida_legends/media/read/IllRaven.html

Courey, Susan Joan, Tappe, Phyllis, Siker, Jody, & LePage, Pam. (2012). Improved lesson planning with universal design for learning (UDL). *Teacher Education and Special Education, 36*(1), 7–27.

Crandall, Joann. (1994, January). Content-centered language learning. *Eric Digest,* pp. 1–5.

Crawford, James, & Krashen, Stephen. (2015). *English learners in American classrooms: 101 Questions, 101 Answers.* Portland, OR: DiversityLearningK12.

Crocco, Margaret Smith. (2007). Speaking truth to power: Women's rights as human rights. *The Social Studies, 98*(6), 257–269.

Cross, Jr., William E. (1991). *Shades of Black: Diversity in African American identity.* Philadelphia, PA: Temple University Press.

Cummings, Joe. (2008). Franciso "Pancho" Villa. *History of Mexico* Retrieved from http://www.mexconnect.com/articles/130-francisco-pancho-villa

Cummins, Jim. (1996). *Negotiating identities: Education for empowerment in a diverse society.* Sacramento, CA: California Association for Bilingual Education.

Cummins, Jim. (2000). *Language, power, and pedagogy: Bilingual children in the crossfire.* Bristol, UK: Multilingual Matters Ltd.

Cummins, Jim. (2011). Literacy engagement: Fueling academic growth for English learners. *The Reading Teacher, 65*(2), 142–146.

Cushner, Kenneth, McClelland, Averil, & Safford, Philip. (2012). *Human diversity in education: An intercultural approach.* New York: McGraw-Hill.

Danforth, Scot. (2008a). John Dewey's contributions to an educational philosophy of intellectual disability. *Educational Theory,* 58(1), 45–62.

Danforth, Scot. (2008b). Using metaphors to research the cultural and ideological construction of disability. In Susan Gabel and Scot Danforth (Eds.), *Disability & the politics of education: An international reader* (pp. 385–400). New York: Peter Lang.

Danforth, Scot. (2014). *Becoming a great inclusive educator.* New York: Peter Lang.

Danforth, Scot. (2015a). Private interview. May 30, 2013. San Diego, CA.

Danforth, Scot. (2015b). Social justice and technocracy: Tracing the narratives of inclusive education in the USA. *Discourse: Studies in the Cultural Politics of Education.* Retrieved from http://dx.doi.org/10.1080/01596306.2015.1073022

Daniels, Roger, & Kitano, Harry. (1970). *American racism: Exploration of the nature of prejudice.* Englewood Cliffs, NJ: Prentice Hall, Inc.

Danns, Dionne. (2002). Black student empowerment and Chicago: School reform efforts in 1968. *Urban Review,* 37, 631–655.

Dar-Nimrod, Ilan, & Heine, Steve J. (2011). Genetic essentialism: On the deceptive determinism of DNA. *Psychological Bulletin,* 137(5), 800–818.

Darder, Antonia. (1991). *Culture and power in the classroom: A critical foundation for bicultural education.* Westport, CT: Greenwood Press.

Delpit, Lisa. (1995). *Other people's children: Cultural conflict in the classroom.* New York: The New Press.

Delpit, Lisa. (2002). Language diversity and learning. In Enid Lee, Deborah Menkart, and Margo Okazawa-Rey (Eds.), *Beyond Heroes and holidays: A practical guide to K-12 anti-racist, multicultural education and staff development* (pp. 154–165). Washington, DC: Teaching for Change.

Delpit, Lisa. (2006). *Other people's children: Cultural conflict in the classroom.* New York: New Press.

Derman-Sparks, Louise, & Edwards, Julie Olsen. (2012). *Anti-bias education for young children and ourselves.* Washington, DC: National Association for the Education of Young Children.

Derman-Sparks, L., Higa, C., & Sparks, B. (1980). Children, race, and racism: How race awareness develops. *Interracial Bulletin for Children,* 11(3 and 4), 3–9.

DeSilver, Drew. (2014). 5 facts about Indian Americans. Pew Research Center. Retrieved from http://www.pewresearch.org/fact-tank/2014/09/30/5-facts-about-indian-americans/

Dessel, Adrienne. (2010). Prejudice in schools: Promotion of an inclusive culture and climate. *Education and Urban Society,* 42(4), 407–429.

Dewey, John. (1916). *Democracy and education.* New York: Macmillan.

Diaz-Rico, Lynne T., & Weed, Kathryn Z. (2010). *The crosscultural, language, and academic development handbook* (4th ed.). Boston, MA: Allyn and Bacon.

Dolores Huerta Foundation (n.d.). Dolores Huerta. Retrieved from doloreshuerta.org

Douglass, Frederick. (2003). *Narrative of the life of Frederick Douglass, An American Slave.* New York: Barnes and Noble.

Downs, Alan. (2012). *The velvet rage: Overcoming the pain of growing up gay in a straight man's world* (2nd ed.). Boston, MA: Da Capo Press.

Duberman, Martin. (2011). *A saving remnant: The radical lives of Barbara Deming and David Mcreynolds.* New York: The New Press.

Duckworth, Angela Lee, Kirby, Terri A., Tsukayama, Eli, & Ericsson, K. Anders. (2011). Deliberate practice spells success: Why grittier competitors triumph at national science bee. *Social Psychological and Personality Science,* 2(2), 174–181.

Durey, Emily. (2013). Muslim fraternity confronts negative stereotypes. ABCNews.com. Retrieved from http://abcnews.go.com/ABC_Univision/News/muslim-fraternity-confronts-negative-stereotypes/story?id=18906879#.UYbl67WR98E

Dusenbery, Maya, & Lee, Jaeah. (2012, June 22). Charts: The state of women's athletics, 40 years after Title IX. *Mother Jones.* Retrieved from http://www.motherjones.com/politics/2012/06/charts-womens-athletics-title-nine-ncaa

Eakin, Marshall C. (2007). *The history of Latin America: Collision of cultures.* New York: Palgrave.

Education Week. (2011, July 11). Achievement gap. *Education Week.* Retrieved from http://www.edweek.org/ew/issues/achievementgap/

Egan, Susan K., & Perry, David G. (2001). Gender identity: A multidimensional analysis with implications of psychosocial adjustment. *Developmental Psychology,* 37(4), 451–463.

Ehrenreich, Barbara. (2001). *Nickel and dimed: On (not) getting by in America.* New York: Metropolitan Books/Henry Holt.

Ehrenreich, Barabara. (2014, January 13). It is expensive to be poor. *The Atlantic.* Retrieved from http://www.theatlantic.com/business/archive/2014/01/it-is-expensive-to-be-poor/282979/2/

Ehrensaft, Diane. (2011). *Gender born, gender made.* New York: The Experiment LLC.

Eliason, Michelle J., & Schope, Robert. (2007). Shifting sands or solid foundation? Lesbian, gay, bisexual, and transgender identify formation. In Llan Meyers and Mary Northridge (Eds.), *The Health of Sexual Minorities* (pp. 3–26). New York: Springer.

Engle, Shirley, & Ochoa, Anna. (1988). *Education for democratic citizenship: Decision making in the social studies.* New York: Teachers College Press.

Erevelles, Nirmala, & Minear, Andrea. (2010). Unspeakable offenses: Untangling race and disability in discourses of intersectionality. *Journal of Literary & Cultural Disability Studies,* 4(2), 127–145.

Erickson, Frederickson. (2012). Culture in society and educational practices. In James A. Banks and Cherry A. Banks (Eds.), *Multicultural education: Issues and perspectives* (7th ed., pp. 33–57). Hoboken, NJ: Wiley.

Erickson, Frederickson. (2015). Culture in society and educational practices. In James A. Banks and Cherry A. Banks (Eds.), *Multicultural education: Issues and perspectives* (9th ed., pp. 33–57). Hoboken, NJ: Wiley.

Espinosa, Paul. (1986). *The Lemon Grove incident* [Film]. San Diego, CA: Espinosa Productions.

Fagan, Kate, & Cyphers, Luke. (2012). Five myths about Title IX. *The ESPN Magazine.* Retrieved from http://www.espn.com/espnw/title-ix/article/7729603/five-myths-title-ix

Fallace, Thomas D. (2011). Tracing John Dewey's influence on progressive education, 1903–1951: Towards a received Dewey. *Teachers College Record, 113*(3), 463–492.

Farrell, Noreen, & Scott, Tuti. (2016). For the girls who dream big, the 2016 Olympics delivered. *New York Times.* Retrieved from http://nytlive.nytimes.com/womenintheworld/2016/08/21/for-all-the-girls-who-dream-big-the-2016-olympics-delivered/

Fausto-Sterling, Anne. (2000). *Sexing the body: Gender politics and the construction of sexuality.* New York: Basic Books.

Ferguson, Ronald F. (1991). Paying for public education: New evidence on how and why money matters. *Harvard Journal on Legislation, 28*(2), 465–498.

Field, Douglas. (2004). Looking for Jimmy Bladwin: Sex, privacy, and Black nationalist fervor. *Callaloo, 27*(2), 457–480.

Fillmore, Lilly Wong, & Snow, Catherine. (2000). *What teachers need to know about language.* U.S. Department of Education: Office of Educational Research and Improvement. ED –99-CO-0008, http://www.cal.org/ericcll/teachers/teachers.pdf

Foner, Eric. (2010). *The fiery trial: Abraham Lincoln and American slavery.* New York: W.W. Norton & Company.

Frankenberg, E., & Orfield, G. (2012). *Resegregation of suburban schools: A hidden crisis in American Education.* Cambridge, MA: Harvard Educational Press.

Frankl, Viktor E. (2006). *Man's search for meaning.* Boston, MA: Beacon Press.

Franklin, John Hope. (1974). *From slavery to freedom: A history of Negro Americans* (4th ed.). New York: Alfred A. Knopf.

Freeman, Jo. (1988). Social revolution and the Equal Rights Amendment. *Sociological Forum, 3*(1), 145–152.

Freire, Paulo. (1970). *Pedagogy of the oppressed.* New York: Continuum Press.

Frey, R., & Kochhar, R. (2014). America's gap between middle-income and upper-income families is widest on record. Pew Research Center. Retrieved from http://www.pewresearch.org/fact-tank/2014/12/17/wealth-gap-upper-middle-income/

Fulghum, Robert. (1988). *All I really need to know I learned in kindergarten.* New York: Ivy Books, p. 6.

Fung, Grace. (1998). Meeting the instructional needs of Chinese American and Asian English language development and at-risk students. In Valerie Ooka Pang and Li-rong Lilly Cheng (Eds.), *Struggling to be heard: The unmet needs of Asian Pacific American children* (pp. 197–219). Albany. NY: SUNY Press.

Gainor, Kathy A. (2000). Including transgender issues in lesbian, gay, and bisexual psychology: Implications for clinical practice and training. In B. Greene and C.L. Croom (Eds.), *Education, research, and practice in lesbian, gay, bisexual, and transgendered psychology: A resource manual* (pp. 131–160). Thousand Oaks, CA: Sage.

Galchinsky, Michael. (1994). Glimpsing golus in the golden land: Jews and multiculturalism in America. *Judaism, 43*(4), 360–369.

Gándara, Patricia. (1994). Choosing higher education: Educational ambitious Chicanos and the path to social mobility. *Education Policy Analysis 8.* Retrieved from http://epaa.asu.edu/epaa/v2n8.html

Garbacik, Jimee. (2013). *Gender & sexuality for beginners.* Danbury, CT: For Beginners LLC.

Garcia, Eugene. (2002). *Student cultural diversity: Understanding and meeting the challenge* (3rd ed.). Boston, MA: Houghton Mifflin Company.

Garcia, Gilbert N. (2000). Lessons from research: What is the length of time it takes limited English proficient students to acquire English and succeed in an all-English classroom? *Issues and brief: National Clearinghouse for Bilingual Education, 5,* 1–15.

Garcia, Ofelia. (2009). *Bilingual education in the 21st century: A global perspective.* United Kingdom: Wiley-Blackwell.

Gay, Geneva. (1994). *A synthesis of scholarship in multicultural education.* Oak Brook, IL: North Central Regional Laboratory.

Gay, Geneva. (2010). *Culturally responsive teaching: Theory, research, and practice.* New York: Teachers College Press.

Gay, Geneva. (2013). Teaching to and through cultural diversity, curriculum, and inquiry. *Curriculum Inquiry, 43*(1), 48–70.

Gee, James. (1996). *Social linguistics and literacies.* Bristol, PA: Taylor and Francis.

Ghassemzadeh, Habibollah. (2005). Vygotsky's mediational psychology: A new concept of culture, signification and metaphor. *Language Sciences, 27,* 281–300.

Gilligan, Carol. (1998). *In a different voice: Psychological theory and women's development.* Cambridge, MA: Harvard University Press.

GLAAD. (n.d.). *GLAAD Reference media guide: Transgender issues.* Retrieved from https://www.glaad.org/reference/transgender

GLSEN. (2013). *Safe space kit.* New York: Gay, Lesbian and Straight Education Network.

GLSEN. (n.d.). GLSEN ally week. Retrieved from http://www.glsen.org/allyweek/organize

Goldstein, Lisa S. (1999). The relational zone: The role of caring relationships in the co-construction of mind. *American Educational Research Journal, 36*(3), 647–673.

Goldstein, Richard. (2012). Gordon Hirabayashi, World War II internment opponent dies at 93. *New York Times.* Retrieved from http://www.nytimes.com/2012/01/04/us/gordon-hirabayashi-wwii-internment-opponent-dies-at-93.html?_r=0

Good, Thomas L., & Nichols, Sharon L. (2001). Expectancy effects in the classroom: A special focus on improving reading performance of minority students in first-grade classrooms. *Educational Psychologist, 36*(2), 113–126.

Goodenough, Ward H. (1976). Multiculturalism as the normal human experience. *Council on Anthropology and Education Quarterly, 7*(4), 4–7.

Goodheart, Adam. (2011). *1861: The civil war awakening.* New York: Vintage Books.

Goodlad, John. I. (1979). *What schools are for.* Bloomington, Indiana: Phi Delta Kappa. Signature edition 2006.

Goodman, Mary Ellen. (1964). *Race awareness in young children.* New York: Collier Books.

Goodman, Yetta M., & Kenneth S. Goodman. (1990). Vygotsky in a whole language perspective. In Luis C. Moll (Ed.), *Vygotsky and education: Instructional implications and applications of sociohistorical psychology* (pp. 223–250). New York: Cambridge University Press.

Gonzalez, Gilbert. (2016). *Guest workers or colonized labor? Mexican labor migration to the United States* (2nd ed.). New York: Routledge.

Gonzalez, Norma. (1995). The funds of knowledge for teaching project. *Practicing Anthropology, 17*(3), 3–6.

Gordon, Milton M. (1964). *Assimilation in American life: The role of race, religion and national origins.* New York: Oxford University Press.

Gould, Stephen Jay. (1996). *The mismeasure of man.* New York: W.W. Norton & Company.

Gould, Stephen Jay. (2002). *I have landed: The end of a beginning in natural history.* New York: Harmony Books.

Gould, Stephen Jay. (2008). *The mismeasure of man.* New York: W.W. Norton.

Graham, David. (2015, June 15). Violence has forced 60 million people from their homes. *The Atlantic.* Retrieved from http://www.theatlantic.com/international/archive/2015/06/refugees-global-peace-index/396122/

Grambs, Jean Dresden. (1968). *Intergroup education: Methods and materials.* Englewood Cliffs, NJ: Prentice-Hall.

Grameen Bank. (2016). *Grameen Bank.* Retrieved from http://www.grameen.com/index.php?option=com_content&task=view&id=16

Grant, Carl A., & Sleeter, Christine. (1998). *Turning on learning.* Hoboken, NJ: Wiley.

Grassl, Gary. (1998). Joachim Gans of Prague: The first Jew in America. *American Jewish History, 86*(2), 195–217.

Gutiérrez, Rochelle. (2002). Beyond essentialism: The complexity of language in teaching mathematics to Latina/o students. *American Educational Research Journal, 39,* 1047–1088.

Gutstein, Eric, Lipman, Pauline, Hernandez, Patricia, & de los Reyes, Rebecca. (1997). Culturally relevant mathematics teaching in a Mexican American context. *Journal for Research in Mathematics Education, 38*(6), 709–737.

Hafiz, Dilara, Hafiz, Yasmine, & Hafix, Imran. (2009). *The American Muslim teenager's handbook: For Muslims and non-Muslims alike.* New York: Ginee Seo Books.

Hakim, Danny, & Dalby, Douglas. (2015, May 23). Ireland votes to approve gay marriage, putting country in vangard. *New York Times.* Retrieved from http://www.nytimes.com/2015/05/24/world/europe/ireland-gay-marriage-referendum.html?_r=0

Hale-Benson, Janice E. (1982). *Black children their roots, culture, and learning styles.* Baltimore, MD: Johns Hopkins University Press.

Hall, Stuart, Held, David, Hubert, Don, & Thompson, Kenneth. (Eds), (1996). *Modernity: An introduction to modern societies.* Hoboken, NJ: Blackwell Publishers.

Halpin, Sean A., & Allen, Michael W. (2004). Changes in psychosocial well-being during stages of gay identity development. *Journal of Homosexuality, 47*(2), 109–126.

Hardman, Michael L., Drew, Clifford, J., & Egan, M. Winston. (2011). *Human exceptionality: School, community, and family* (10th ed.). Belmont, CA: Wadsworth.

Harlem Children's Zone. (2014). Harlem Children's Zone fact sheet. Retrieved from http://hcz.org/wp-content/uploads/2014/04/FY-2013-FactSheet.pdf

Haynes, Charles. (2008). *A teacher's guide to religion in the public schools.* Nashville, TN: First Amendment Center.

Heath, Shirley Brice. (1983). *Ways with words: Language, life, and work in communities and classrooms.* New York: Cambridge University Press.

Helms, Janet. (Ed.). (1990). *Black and White racial identity: Theory, research and practice.* Westport, Conn.: Greenwood Press.

Henry, Annette. (2015). Race and gender in classrooms: Implications for teachers. In James A. Banks and Cherry A. Banks (Eds.), *Multicultural education: Issues and perspectives* (pp. 183–207). Hoboken, NJ: John Wiley & Sons.

Hiebert, D. (2009). Ethnicity. In *The dictionary of human geography.* Oxford, UK: Blackwell Publishers. Retrieved from http://libproxy.sdsu.edu/login?url=http://search.credoreference.com.libproxy.sdsu.edu/content/entry/bkhumgeo/ethnicity/0

Hoerig, Karl. (2002). Remembering our Indian school days: The boarding school experience. *American Anthropologist, 104*(2), 642–646.

Holloman, Hall, & Yates, Peggy. (2012). Cloudy with a chance of sarcasm or sunny with high expectations: Using best practice language to strengthen positive behavior intervention and support efforts. *Journal of Positive Behavior Interventions, 15*(2), 124–127.

hooks, bell. (2000). How do we build a community of love? *Shambhala Sun 8*(3), 32–40.

Hoover, Mary Rhodes. (1998). A recommended reading list for teachers of students who speak Ebonics. *The Journal of Negro Education, 67*(1), 43–47.

Hotz, Robert Lee. (2002, August 30). Baby's "goo-goo" a building block of human speech. *Los Angeles Times,* A16. Retrieved from http://articles.latimes.com/2002/aug/30/science/sci-babytalk30

Hughes, Langston. 1987. *Selected poems of Langston Hughes.* New York: Vintage Press.

Hursh, David, & Martina, Camille Anne. (2016). The end of public schools? Or a new beginning? *Educational Forum, 80,* 189–207.

Ianni, F. (1996). The caring community as a context for joining youth needs and program services. *Journal of Negro Education 65*(1), 71–91.

Irvine, Jacqueline Jordan. (1990). *Black students and school failure.* New York: Greenwood Press.

Irvine, Jacqueline Jordan. (2002). *In search of wholeness: African American teachers and their culturally specific classroom practices.* New York: Palgrave.

Jablonski, Nina G., & George Chaplin. (2002). Skin deep. *Scientific American, 287*(4), 74–81.

Jackson, Liz. (2010). Images of Islam in US media and their educational implications. *Educational Studies: A Journal of the American Educational Studies Association, 46*(1), 3–24.

James, Frank B. (1970). *The suppressed speech of Frank B. James Wampanoag.* Retrieved from http://www.uaine.org/wmsuta.htm

Japanese American Citizens League. (2011). *The Japanese American experience: Curriculum and resource guide* (5th ed.). San Francisco, CA: JACL.

John-Steiner, Vera, & Mahn, Holbrook. (1996). Sociocultural approaches to learning and development: A Vygotskian framework. *Educational Psychologist, 37*(3/4), 191–206.

Johnson, Lauri. (2002). "Making democracy real": Teacher union and community activism to promote diversity in New York public schools, 1935–1950. *Urban Education, 37*(5), 566–587.

Johnson, Lauri. (2002). "My eyes have been opened" White teachers and racial awareness. *Journal of Teacher Education, 53*(2), 153–167.

Jover, Juan Ahonen. (2014). *The gay agenda 2014: Don't stop.* Seattle, WA: Createspace.

Kallen, Horace. (1998). *Culture and democracy in the United States.* New Brunswick and London: Transaction Publishers (with new introduction by Stephen J. Whitfield).

King, Joyce E. (1991). Dyconscious racism: Ideology, identity, and the mis-education of teachers. *Journal of Negro Education, 60*(2), 133–146.

King, Joyce E. (1994). The purpose of schooling for African American children; Including cultural knowledge. In Etta R. Collins (Ed.), *Teaching diverse populations: Formulating a knowledge base.* Albany, NY: SUNY Press.

King, Joyce E. (2001). Facing the new millennium: A transformative research and action agenda in Black education. Report of the AERA Commission on Research in Black Education. Paper presented at the annual meeting of the American Educational Research Association, New Orleans, LA.

King, Joyce E. (2011). Who dat say (we) "Too depraved to be saved"?: Remembering Katrina/Haiti (and beyond): Critical studyin' for human freedom. *Harvard Educational Review, 81*(2), 343–370.

King, Mary-Claire, & Motulsky, Arno G. (2002). Human genetics: Mapping human history. *Science, 298*(5602), 2342–2343.

Kirby, Darrell, & Julian, Nancy B. (1981). Treatment of women in high school U.S. history textbooks. *The Social Studies, 72*(5), 203–207.

Kirby, Michael. (2007). Sexuality and global forces: Dr. Alfred Kinsey and the Supreme Court of the United States. *Indiana Journal of Global Legal Studies, 14*(2), 485–508.

Koch, Janice. (2014). *Teach* (2nd ed.). Belmont, CA: Wadsworth.

Kochhar, Rakesh. (2006). Foreign-born workforce and employment of native born. Washington, DC: Pew Hispanic Center. Retrieved from http://pewhispanic.org/reports/report.php?ReportID=69

Korematsu Institute for Civil Rights and Education. (2015). Fred Korematsu bio. Retrieved from http://korematsuinstitute.org/institute/aboutfred/

Kosciw, J. G., Greytak, E. A., Palmer, N.A., Boesen, M. J. (2014). *The 2013 National School Climate Survey: The experiences of lesbian, gay, bisexual, and transgender youth in our nation's schools.* New York: GLSEN.

Kozol, Jonathan. (1991). *Savage inequalities: Children in America's schools.* New York: Crown Publishers.

Kozol, Jonathan. (2005). *The shame of the nation: The restoration of apartheid schooling in America.* New York: Crown Publishers.

Kozol, Jonathan. (2010). No half steps, no equivocation. *Educational Leadership, 68* (3), 28–29.

Krashen, Stephen. (1981). *Second language acquisition and second language learning.* Oxford: Pergamon.

Krashen, Stephen. (1982). *Principles and practice in second language acquisition.* Oxford: Pergamon.

Krashen, Stephen. (1993, February 23). Second language education: The monitor model. Speech at the Multicultural Education Infusion Center, San Diego.

Krashen, Stephen. (1996). *Under attack: The case against bilingual education.* Culver City, CA: Language Education Associates.

Krashen, Stephen. (2011). *Free voluntary reading.* Santa Barbara, CA: Libraries Unlimited.

Krashen, Stephen, & Terrell, Tracy. (1983). *The natural approach: Language acquisition in the classroom.* London: Prentice Hall Europe.

Krogstad, Jens Manuel. (2014). Census Bureau explores new Middle East/North Africa ethnic category. Pew Research Center fact tank news in the numbers. Retrieved from http://www.pewresearch.org/fact-tank/2014/03/24/census-bureau-explores-new-middle-eastnorth-africa-ethnic-category/

Krull, Edgar. (2003). Hilda Taba (1802–1967). *Prospects: UNESCO, International Bureau of Education, 33*(4), 481–491. Retrieved from http://www.ibe.unesco.org/publications/ThinkersPdf/tabae.pdf

Kuykendall, Crystal. (2012). *From rage to hope: Strategies for reclaiming Black and Hispanic students* (2nd ed). Bloomington, IN: Solution Tree Press.

Ladson-Billings, Gloria. (1995). Toward a theory of culturally relevant pedagogy. *American Educational Research Journal, 32*(3), 465–491.

Lake, Robert. (2012). *Vygotsky on education.* New York: Peter Lang.

Lakhani, Nina. (2015, December 6). Carlos Slim: Biography of Mexico's richest man penetrates the "cloak of silence." *The Guardian.* Retrieved from http://www.theguardian.com/business/2015/dec/06/carlos-slim-biography-diego-enrique-osorno-interviews

Lareau, Annette. (2011). *Unequal childhoods: Class, race, and family life* (2nd ed.). Berkeley, CA: University of California Press.

Larke, Patricia, & Larke, Alvin. (2009). Teaching diversity/multicultural classes in the academy. *Research in Higher Education Journal, 3,* 1–8.

Lee, Carol D. (1995). A culturally based cognitive apprenticeship: Teaching African American high school students skills in literary interpretation. *Reading Research Quarterly 30*(4), 608–630.

Lee, Carol D. (2000). Signifying in the zone of proximal development. In Carol D. Lee and Peter Smagorinsky (Eds.), *Vygotskian perspectives on literacy research: Constructing meaning through collaborative inquiry* (pp. 191–225). Cambridge, UK: Cambridge University Press.

Lee, Carol D. (2008). The centrality of culture to the scientific study of learning and development: How an ecological framework in education research facilitates civic responsibility. *Educational Researcher, 37*(5), 267–279.

Leonardo, Zeus. (2013). *Race frameworks: A multidimensional theory of racism and education.* New York: Teachers College Press.

Leong, F., & Okazaki, S. (2009). History of Asian American psychology. *Cultural Diversity and Ethnic Minority Psychology, 15*(4), 352–363.

Lewis, Michael. (2010). *The big short: Inside the doomsday machine.* New York: W.W. Norton & Company.

Lipman, P. (1998). *Race, class, and power in school restructuring.* Albany, NY: SUNY Press.

Lipska, Jerry. (1996). Toward a culturally based pedagogy: A case study of one Yup'ik Eskimo teacher. In Etta Hollins (Ed.), *Transforming curriculum for culturally diverse society* (pp. 205–226). Mahwah, NJ: Lawrence Erlbaum Association Inc.

Liptak, Adam. (2015). Supreme Court ruling makes same-sex marriage a right nationwide. *New York Times.* Retrieved from http://www.nytimes.com/2015/06/27/us/supreme-court-same-sex-marriage.html

Litsky, Frank. (2003, July 12). Bush administration says Title ix should stay as it is. *New York Times.* Retrieved from www.nytimes.com/2003/07/12/sports/12TITL.html?th=&pagewanted=print&position=

Litton, Edmundo F. (1999). Learning in America: The Filipino-American sociocultural perspective. In Clara Park and Marilyn Mei-Ying Chi (Eds.), *Asian-American education: Prospects and challenges* (pp. 131–153). Westport, CT: Bergin and Garvey.

Loewen, James. (2007). *Lies my teacher told me: Everything your American history textbook got wrong* (2nd ed.). New York: The New Press.

Lomawaima, Tsianina, & McCarty, Teresa. (2002). When tribal sovereignty challenges democracy: American Indian education and the democratic idea. *American Educational Research Journal*, 39(2), 279–305.

Lyall, Sarah, & Bernstein, Jacob. (2015, February 6). The transition of Bruce Jenner: A shock to some: Visible to all. *New York Times*. Retrieved from http://www.nytimes.com/2015/02/07/sports/olympics/the-transition-of-bruce-jenner-a-shock-to-some-visible-to-all.html

Lyon, Cherstin. (2012). *Japanese American wartime citizenship, civil disobedience, and historical memory*. Philadelphia, PA: Temple University Press.

Macgillivray, Ian K., & Jennings, Todd. (2008). A content analysis exploring lesbian, gay, bisexual, and transgender topics in foundations of education textbooks. *Journal of Teacher Education*, 59(2), 170–188.

Machamer, Ann Marie, & Gruber, Enid. (1998). Secondary school, family, and educational risk: Comparing American Indian adolescents and their peers. *The Journal of Educational Research*, 91, 357-69.

Manglitz, Elaine. (2003). Challenging White privilege in adult education: A critical review of the literature. *Adult Education Quarterly*, 53(2), 119–134.

Mann, Charles C. (2011). *1491: New revelations of the Americas before Columbus* (2nd ed.). New York: Vintage.

Marshall, Hermine H. (1996). Implications of differentiating and understanding constructivist approaches. *Educational Psychologist*, 31(3/4), 235–340.

Maslow, A. (1999). *Toward a psychology of being* (3rd ed.). New York: John Wiley & Sons.

Masse, Don. (2015). Not just the dead guys: Focusing on 21st-century arts in the art room. *Arts Activities*, 158(2), 24–25, 32.

Matriano, Estela. (2000). The impact of global changes on teacher education: Challenges, opportunities and a vision for a culture of people. *International Journal of Curriculum and Instruction*, 2(1), 85–91.

McCarty, Teresa L. (2002). *A place to be Navajo: Rough Rock and the struggle for self-determination in Indigenous schooling*. Mahwah, NJ: Lawrence Erlbaum Associates.

McClung, Merle. (2013). Repurposing education. *The Phi Delta Kappan*, 94(3), 37–39.

McGarry, Robert. (2013). Build a curriculum that includes everyone. *The Phi Delta Kappan*, 94(5), 27–31.

McIntosh, Peggy. (1992, January/February). Unpacking the invisible knapsack: White privilege. *Creation Spirituality*, 33–35.

McKinley, Jesse. (2015, November 10). Cuomo to raise minimum wage to $15 for all New York state employees. *New York Times*. Retrieved from http://www.nytimes.com/2015/11/11/nyregion/andrew-cuomo-and-15-minimum-wage-new-york-state-workrs.html?_r=0

McLaren, Peter. (1997). Decentering Whiteness: In search of a revolutionary multiculturalism. *Multicultural Education*, 5(1), 4–11.

Meier, Matt S., & Ribera, Feliciano. (1993). *Mexican American/American Mexicans: From conquistadors to Chicanos*. New York: Hill and Wang.

Meier, Terry. (1998). Kitchen poets and classroom books: Literature from children's roots. In Theresa Perry and Lisa Delpit (Eds.), *The real Ebonics debate: Power, language, and the education of African-American children* (pp. 94–104). Boston, MA: Beacon Press.

Mejia, Brenda X., & Gordon, Edmund W. (2006). Human learning and cognitive development: conceptual foundations of multicultural education. In Valerie Ooka Pang (Ed.), *Race and ethnicity in education: Principles and practices of multicultural education*, (Volume 1, pp. 45–64). New York: Praeger Publications.

Melendez, Joe. (2015). Oral history: The Arawaks and Puerto Rico. Private interview, September 16, 2015.

Menesini, Ersilia, Palladino, Bernedetta Emanuela, & Nocentini, Annalaura. (2015). Emotions of moral disengagement, class norms, and bullying in adolescence. *Merrill-Palmer Quarterly*, 65(1), 124–143.

Merryfield, Merry. (2001). Moving the center of global education: From imperial world views that divide the world to double consciousness, contrapuntal pedagogy, hybridity, and cross-cultural competence. In William B. Stanley (Ed.), *Critical issues in social studies research for the 21st century* (pp. 179–207). Greenwich, Conn.: Information Age Publishing.

Migration Policy Institute. (2015). Top languages spoken by English language learners nationally and by state. *ELL Information Center Fact Sheet Series*, 4, 1–6.

Milk Foundation. (2015). The official Harvey Milk biography. The Milk Foundation. Retrieved from http://milkfoundation.org/about/harvey-milk-biography/

Miller, James. (2008). What does it mean to be an American? The dialectics of self-discovery in Baldwin's "Paris Essays" (1950–1961). *Journal of American Studies*, 42(1), 51–66.

Mio, Jeffery Scott, Barker, Lori A., & Rodriguez, Melanie M. Domenech. (2016). *Multicultural psychology: Understanding our diverse communities*. New York: Oxford University Press.

Moll, Luis. (1990). *Vygotsky and education: Instructional implications and applications of sociohistorical psychology*. New York: Cambridge University Press.

Moll, Luis. (2000). Inspired by Vygotsky: Ethnographic experiments in education. In Carol D. Lee and Peter Smagorinsky (Eds.), *Vygotskian perspectives on literacy research* (pp. 256–268). Cambridge, UK: Cambridge University Press.

Moll, Luis, Amanti, Cathy, Neff, Deborah, & Gonzalez, Norma. (1992). Funds of knowledge: Using a qualitative approach to connect homes and classrooms. *Theory into Practice, 31*(2), 132–141.

Moll, Luis, & Greenberg, James. (1990). Creating zones of possibilities: Combining social contexts for instruction. In Luis Moll (Ed.), *Vygotsky and education* (pp. 319–348). New York: Cambridge University Press.

Moll, Luis, Vélez-Ibáñez, C., & Greenberg, James. (1988). *Project implementation plan. Community knowledge and classroom practice: Combining resources for literacy instruction*. Tucson, AZ: College of Education and Bureau of Applied Research in Anthropology.

Monaghan, Peter. (2015, January 19). The Kinsey Institute moves beyond the study of sex: Now it's love. *The Chronicle of Higher*

Education. Retrieved from http://search.proquest.com.libproxy .sdsu.edu/pqrl/docview/1648349129/6218793D837B476CPQ /1?accountid=13758

Moore, James R. (2009). Why religious education matters: The role of Islam in multicultural education. *Multicultural Perspectives, 11*(3), 139–145.

Morris, S. L., Foster, C. J., Parsons, R., Falkner, M., Flakner, T., & Rosalie, S. L. (2015). Differences in the use of vision and proprioception for postural control in autism spectrum disorder. *Neuroscience, 307*(29), 273–280.

Moses, Robert P., & Cobb, Charles E. (2002). *Radical equations: Civil rights from Mississippi to the Algebra Project.* Boston, MA: Beacon Press.

Moses, Robert P., Kamii, M., Swap, S. M., & Howard, J. (1989). The algebra project: Organizing in the spirit of Ella. *Harvard Educational Review, 59*(4), 423–443.

Muller-Wille, Staffan. (2014). Race and history: Comments from an epistemolgical point of view. *Science, Technology, and Human Values, 39*(4), 597–606.

Mundy, Peter, Sigman, Marian, Ungerer, Judy, & Sherman, Tracy. (1986). Defining the social deficits of autism: The contribution of nonverbal communication measures. *Journal of Child Psychology and Psychiatry, 27*(5), 657–669.

Munson, Barbara. (1999). Not for sport. *Teaching Tolerance, 15.* Retrieved from http://www.tolerance.org/magazine/number-15 -spring-1999/not-sport

Murphy, Kim (2012, May 20). Oregon forbids Native American mascots. *Los Angeles Times,* A16.

Myers, Walter Dean. (1994). *Malcolm X: By any means necessary.* New York: Scholastic.

NAACP. (2016). NAACP History: Lift Ev'ry Voice and Sing. Retrieved from http://www.naacp.org/pages/naacp-history-lift -evry-voice-and-sing

Nakano, Mei. (1990). *Japanese American women: Three generations 1890–1990.* Berkeley, CA: Min Press Publishing and the National Japanese American Historical Society.

Naranjo, Melissa, Pang, Valerie Ooka, & Alvarado, Jose Luis. (December 2015/January 2016). Summer melts immigrant students' college plans. *The Phi Delta Kappan, 97*(4), 38–41.

Nasir, Na'ilah Suad, Cabana, Carlos, Shreve, Barbara, Woodbury, Estelle, & Louie, Nicole. (2014). *Mathematics for equity: A framework for successful practice.* NY: Teachers College Press.

Natanovich, Gloria, & Eden, Dov. (2008). Pygmalion effects among outreach supervisors and tutors: Extending sex generalizability. *Journal of Applied Psychology, 98,* 1382–1389.

National Center for Education Statistics. (2013). *NAEP 2012 Trends in Academic Progress Reading 1971–2012 Mathematics 1973–2012.*

National Congress of American Indians. (2003). An introduction to Indian Nations in the United States. Retrieved from http://www .ncai.org/about-tribes/indians_101.pdf

National Congress of American Indians. (2013). Ending the era of harmful "Indian" mascots. Retrieved from http://www.ncai.org /proudtobe

National Council of Women's Organizations. (2013). *The Equal Rights Amendment.* Washington, DC: National Council of Women's Organizations. Retrieved from http://www.equalrightsamendment .org/misc/ERA_overview.pdf

National Governors Association Center for Best Practices, Council of Chief State School Officers. (2010). *Common Core State Standards.* Washington, DC: National Governors Association Center for Best Practices, Council of Chief State School Officers.

National Museum of the American Indian. (2007). *Do all Indians live in tipis?* Washington, DC: Smithsonian.

National Park Service. (2015). Quaker influence. National Park Service, U.S. Department of Interior. Retrieved from http://www .nps.gov/wori/learn/historyculture/quaker-influence.htm

National Portrait Gallery. (2015). Seneca falls convention July 19–20, 1848. Washington, DC: National Portrait Gallery, Smithsonian Institution. Retrieved from http://www.npg.si.edu/col/seneca /senfalls1.htm

National Women's Law Center. (2012). *Title IX 40 years and counting.* Retrieved from http://www.nwlc.org/sites/default/files /pdfs/nwlcathletics_titleixfactsheet.pdf

Nelson, Jack L., & Pang, Valerie Ooka. (2013). Prejudice, racism, and the social studies curriculum. In E. Wayne Ross (Ed.), *The Social Studies Curriculum* (4th ed., pp. 203–226). Albany, NY: State University of New York Press.

Nembhard, Jessica Gordon. (2014). *Collective courage: A history of African American cooperative economic thought and practice.* University Park, PA: The Pennsylvania State University Press.

Ng, Wendy. (2002). *Japanese American internment during World War II: A history and reference guide.* Westport, CT: Greenwood Press.

Nieto, Sonia. (2004). *Affirming diversity: The sociopolitical context of education* (4th ed.). Boston, MA: Allyn and Bacon.

Nisbett, R. (2003). *The geography of thought: How Asians and Americans think differently and why.* New York: The Free Press.

Nisbett, Richard E., Pen, Kaiping, Choi, Incheol, & Norenzayan, Ara. (2001). Culture and systems of thought: Holistic versus analytic cognition. *Psychological Review, 108*(2), 291–310.

Noblit, G., Rogers, Dwight, & McCadden B. (1995). In the meantime. The possibilities of caring. *Phi Delta Kappan 76*(9), 680–85.

Noddings, Nel. (1984). *Caring: A feminine approach to ethics and moral development.* Berkeley, CA: University of California Press.

Noddings, Nel. (1992). *The challenge to care in schools: An alternative approach to education.* New York: Teachers College Press.

Noddings, Nel. (2002). *Starting at home: Caring and social policy.* Berkeley, CA: University of California Press.

Noddings, Nel. (2013). Caring: A relational approach to ethics and moral education. Berkeley, CA: University of California Press.

Nothdurft, William E. (1989). *Schoolworks: Reinventing public schools to create the workforce of the future.* Washington, DC: The Brookings Institution.

Nussbaum, Martha C. (1997). *Cultivating humanity: A classical defense of reform in liberal education.* Cambridge, MA: Harvard University Press.

Oakes, Jeannie. (1992). Can tracking research inform practice? Technical, normative and political considerations. *Educational Researcher, 21*(4), 12–21.

Oakes, Jeannie. (2005). *Keeping track: How schools structure inequality* (2nd ed.). New Haven, CT: Yale University Press.

Ohlheiser, Abby. (2015, May 13). Harriet Tubman is your potential replacement for Jackson on the $20 bill. *The Washington Post.*

Retrieved from http://www.washingtonpost.com/blogs/the-fix /wp/2015/05/12/your-potential-replacement-for-andrew-jackson -on-the-20-bill-harriet-tubman/

Olson, Carol Booth, & Land, Robert. (2007). A cognitive strategies approach to reading and writing instruction for English language learners in secondary schools. *Research in the Teaching of English, 41*(3), 260–303.

Olson, Steve. (2002). *Mapping human history: Genes, race, and our common origins.* Boston, MA: Houghton Mifflin.

Orellana, Marjorie Faulstich. (2001). The work kids do: Mexican and Central American immigrants. *Harvard Educational Review, 7,* 366–390.

Ormrod, Jeanne Ellis. (2006). *Educational psychology: Developing learners.* Upper Saddle River, NJ: Pearson.

Ormrod, Jeanne Ellis. (2013). *Educational psychology: Developing learners* (8th ed.). Upper Saddle River, NJ: Pearson.

Oser, Rick. (2008). *Keeping it real.* Lemon Grove, CA: Golden Avenue Elementary.

Oser, Rick, Beck, Ellen, Alvarado, Jose Luis, & Pang, Valerie Ooka. (2014). School and community wellness: Transforming achievement using a holistic approach to learning. *Multicultural Perspectives, 16*(1), 26–34.

Oyserman, Daphna, Sorenson, Nicholas, Reber, Rolf, & Xiaohua Chen, Sylvia. (2009). Connecting and separating mind-sets: Culture as situated cognition. *Journal of Personality and Social Psychology, 97*(2), 217–235.

Özlem, Sensoy, & Marshall, Elizabeth. (2009–2010). Save the Muslim girl! *Rethinking Schools, 2*(2), 14–19. Retrieved from http://www .rethinkingschools.org/archive/24_02/24_02_muslim.shtml

Pak, Yoon K. (2004). Teaching for intercultural understanding: A teacher's perspective in the 1940s. In Joseph Watras, Margaret Smith Crocco, and Christine Woyshner (Eds.), *Social education in the twentieth century: Curriculum and context for citizenship* (pp. 57–75). New York: Peter Lang Publishing, Inc.

Pak, Yoon. (2006). Multiculturalism matters: Learning from our past. In Valerie Ooka Pang (Ed.), *Principles and practices of multicultural education* (pp. 3–22). Westport, CT: Praeger.

Pak, Yoon, & Johnson, Lauri. (forthcoming). *The history of intercultural education in the public schools, 1930's–1050's.*

Palmer, Parker. (2007). *The courage to teach for reflection and renewal, tenth anniversary edition.* San Francisco, CA: Jossey-Bass.

Pang, Valerie Ooka. (1994). Why do we need this class?: Multicultural education for teachers. *The Phi Delta Kappan, 76*(4), 89–92.

Pang, Valerie Ooka. (2005). *Multicultural education: A caring-centered, reflective approach* (2nd ed.). Boston, MA: McGraw Hill.

Pang, Valerie Ooka. (2006). Fighting the marginalization of Asian American students with caring schools: Focusing on curricular change. *Race, Ethnicity & Education, 9*(1), 67–83.

Pang, Valerie Ooka. (2010). *Multicultural education: A caring-centered, reflective approach.* San Diego, CA: Montezuma Publishing.

Pang, Valerie Ooka, & Cheng, Li-rong Lilly. (1998). *Struggling to be heard: The unmet needs of Asian Pacific American children.* Albany, NY: SUNY Press.

Pang, Valerie Ooka, Gay, Geneva, & Stanley, William B. (1995). Expanding concepts of community and civic competence for a multicultural society. *Theory and Research in Social Studies Education, 23*(4), 302–331.

Pang, Valerie Ooka, Han, Peggy P., & Pang, Jennifer. (2011). Asian American and Pacific Islander students: Equity and the achievement gap. *Educational Researcher, 40*(7), 378–389.

Pang, Valerie Ooka, & Jones, Evangelina Bustamante. (2004). Caring-centered multicultural education: Addressing the academic and writing needs of English learners. In Kathleen Kesson and E. Wayne Ross (Eds.), *Defending Public Schools: Teaching for a democratic society* (Volume 2, pp. 137–147, 204–206). Westport, CT: Praeger Publishers.

Pang, Valerie Ooka, Lafferty, Karen E., Pang, Jennifer M., Griswold, Joan, & Oser, Rick. (2014). Culture matters in science: Culturally relevant teaching. *Science and Children, 51,* 44–49.

Pang, Valerie Ooka, & Park, Cynthia D. (2003). Examination of the Self-regulation mechanism: Prejudice reduction in pre-service teachers. *Action In Teacher Education, 25*(3), 1–12.

Pang, Valerie Ooka, & Rámon, Valle. (2004). A change in paradigm: Applying contributions of genetic research to teaching about race and racism in social studies education. *Theory and Research in Social Education, 32*(4), 503–522.

Pang, Valerie Ooka, Rivera, Juan John, & Mora, Jill K. (1999). The ethic of caring: Clarifying the foundation of multicultural education. *Educational Forum, 64*(1), 25–33.

Pang, Valerie Ooka, & Sablan, Velma. (1998). Teacher efficacy: How do teachers feel about their abilities to teach African American students? In Mary E. Dilworth (Ed.), *Being responsive to cultural differences: How teachers learn* (pp. 39–58). Washington, DC: American Association of Colleges for Teacher Education.

Pang, Valerie Ooka, Stein, Rachel, Gomez, Mariana, Matas, Amanda, & Shimogori, Yuji. (2011). Cultural competencies: Essential elements of caring-centered multicultural education. *Action in Teacher Education, 33*(5–6), 560–574.

Pang, Valerie Ooka, Stratton, Tamiko, Park, Cynthia D., Madueño, Marcelina, Atlas, Miram, Page, Cynthia, & Oliger, Jennifer. (2010). The American DREAM and immigrant students. *Race, Gender, and Class, 17*(1–2), 180–193.

Park, Caryn C. (2010). Young children making sense of racial and ethnic differences: A sociocultural approach. *American Educational Research Journal, 48*(2), 387–420.

Park, Clara. (1997). Learning style preferences of Asian American (Chinese, Filipino, Korean and Vietnamese) students in secondary schools. *Equity and Excellence in Education 30*(2), 68–77.

Park, Cynthia D. (1998). Private communications.

Park, Youngmee K., Sempos, Christopher T., Barton, Curtis N., Vanderveen, John E., & Yetley, Elizabeth A. (2000). Effectiveness of food fortification in the United States: The case of pellagra. *American Journal of Public Health, 90*(5), 727–738.

Parkins, Irina Sumaji, Fishbein, Harold D., & Ritchey, P. Neal. (2006). The influence of personality on workplace bullying and discrimination. *Journal of Applied Social Psychology, 36*(10), 2554–2577.

Perry, Theresa. (1996). *Teaching Malcolm X.* New York: Routledge.

Perry, Theresa, & Delpit, Lisa. (1998). *The real Ebonics debate.* Boston, MA: Beacon Press.

Pew Research Center. (2011). *Muslim Americans: No signs of growth of alienation or support for extremism.* Retrieved from http://www

.people-press.org/files/legacy-pdf/Muslim%20American% 20Report%2010-02-12%20fix.pdf

Pew Research Center. (2015). *America's changing religious landscape; Christians decline sharply as share of population; Unaffiliated and other faiths continue to grow.* Washington, DC: Pew Research Center. Retrieved from http://www.pewforum.org/files/2015/05 /RLS-08-26-full-report.pdf

Pewewardy, Cornel. (n.d.). Why educators can't ignore Indian mascots. Retrieved from http://www.aics.org/mascot/cornel .html

Philips, Susan Urmston. (1993). *The invisible culture: Communication in classroom and community on the Warm Springs Indian Reservation* (reissued). Prospect Heights, IL: Waveland Press.

Pomerantz, Shauna, Raby, Rebecca, & Stefanik, Andrea. (2013). Girls run the world? Caught between feminism and postfeminism in the school. *Gender & Society, 27,* 185–207.

Postman, Neil. (2013). Whatever I call it, it is. *ETC: A Review of General Semantics, 70,* 310–317. First appeared March 1974, *ETC, 31*(3), 37–44.

Poteat, V. Paul, & Russell, Stephen T. (2013). Understanding homophobic behavior and its implications for policy and practice. *Theory Into Practice, 52,* 264–271.

Price, Michael. (2008). Case closed: Famous royals suffered from hemophilia. *Science.* Retrieved from http://news.sciencemag.org /sciencenow/2009/10/08-02.html

Proctor, Sherrie L., Graves, Scott L., & Esch, Rachel C. (2012). Assessing African American students for specific learning disabilities: The promises and perils of response to intervention. *Journal of Negro Education, 81*(3), 268–282.

Pryun, Marc. (2013). Critical social studies: Towards education for critical citizenship and thick democracy. *The Social Educator, 31*(1), 4–21.

Puentes, Jennifer, & Gougherty, Matthew. (2011) Intersections of gender, race, and class in introductory textbooks. *Teaching Sociology, 41*(2), 159–171.

Quinn, Daniel. (1995). *Ishmael.* New York: Bantam Books.

Ragosta, Michael. (2013). *Religious freedom: Jefferson's legacy, American creed.* Charlottesville, VA: University of Virginia Press.

Raise the Minimum Wage. (2015). *What's the minimum wage in your state?* Retrieved from http://www.raisetheminimumwage.com /pages/minimum-wage-state

Ramirez, Pablo A. (2010). Towards a borderlands ethics: The undocumented migrant and haunted communities in contemporary Chicana/o fiction. *Aztlan: A Journal of Chicano Studies, 35*(1), 49–67.

Rank, Mark Robert. (2005). *One nation, underprivileged: Why American poverty affects us all.* New York: Oxford University Press.

Rauf, Feisal Abdul. (2011, April 1). Five myths about Muslims in America. *Washington Post.* Retrieved from https://www .washingtonpost.com/opinions/five-myths-about-muslims-in -america/2011/03/30/AFePWOIC_story.html

Rea Salisbury, Vista. (1980). Columbus's Arawaks. *Sea Frontier, 26,* 279–286.

Rebora, Anthony. (2011, October 12). Keeping special ed in proportion. *Education Week.* Retrieved from http://www.edweek.org/tsb /articles/2011/10/13/01disproportion.h05.html

Reilly, Ryan J., & Siddiqui, Sabrina. (2013, June 26). Supreme Court DOMA rules federal same-sex marriage ban unconstitutional. *Huffington Post.* Retrieved from http://www.huffingtonpost .com/2013/06/26/supreme-court-doma-decision_n_3454811 .html

Renn, Kristen A. (2010). LGBT and queer research in higher education: The state and status of the field. *Educational Researcher, 39*(2), 132–141.

Reynolds, Daniel. (2014, June 26). Survey: Same-sex couples spend less, innovate more in weddings. *The Advocate.* Retrieved from http://www.advocate.com/politics/marriage-equality/2014/06/26 /survey-same-sex-couples-spend-less-innovate-more-weddings

Rickford, John. (1998). Holding on to a language of our own: An interview with linguist John Rickford. In Theresa Perry and Lisa Delpit (Eds.), *The real Ebonics debate: Power, language, and the education of African-American children* (pp. 59–70). Boston, MA: Beacon Press.

Riley, Richard and Cantú, Norma. (1997). Title IX: 25 years of progress. U.S. Department of Education and Office for Civil Rights. Retrieved from http://www2.ed.gov/pubs/TitleIX/title.html

Rivera, John, & Poplin, Mary. (1995). Multicultural, critical, feminine and constructive pedagogies seen through the eyes of youth: A call for the revisioning and beyond: Toward a pedagogy for the next century. In Christine Sleeter and Peter McLaren (Eds.), *Multicultural education, critical pedagogy and the politics of difference* (pp. 221–247). Albany, NY: SUNY Press.

Robinson, Carole A., York, Kaley, Rothenberg, Alexandra, & Bissell, Laura J. L. (2015). Parenting a child with Asperger's syndrome: A balancing act. *Journal of Child Family Studies, 24,* 2310–2321.

Rogers, Carl R., & Freiberg, H. Jerome. (1994). *Freedom to learn for the 80's* (3rd ed.). New York: Merrill.

Rogoff, Barbara. (1984). Introduction. In Barbara Rogoff and Jean Lave (Eds.), *Everyday cognition: Its development in social context.* Cambridge, MA: Harvard University Press.

Ronfeldt, Matthew, Loeb, Susanna, & Wyckoff, James. (2013). How teacher turnover harms student achievement. *American Educational Research Journal, 50*(1), 4–36.

Rosenwald, Michael. (2015). How Jim Obergefell became the face of the Supreme Court gay marriage case. *The Washington Post.* Retrieved from https://www.washingtonpost.com/local/how-jim -obergefell-became-the-face-of-the-supreme-court-gay-marriage -case/2015/04/06/3740433c-d958-11e4-b3f2-607bd612aeac _story.html

Ross, E. Wayne. (2014). *Social studies curriculum: Purposes, problems, and possibilities.* Albany, NY: State University of New York Press.

Ryan, William. (1976). *Blaming the victim.* New York: Vintage Books.

Sack, Kevin & Thee-Benan, Megan. (2015, July 23). Poll finds most in U.S. hold dim view of race relations. Retrieved from http:// www.nytimes.com/2015/07/24/us/poll-shows-most-americans -think-race-relations-are-bad.html

Sadker, Myra P., & Sadker, David. (2000). *Teachers, schools, and society.* Boston, MA: McGraw-Hill.

Sadowski, Michael. (2010). Beyond gay-straight alliances. *The Education Digest, 76,* 12–16.

Salamone, Frank. (Ed.). (2013). *The Native American identity in sports: Creating and preserving a culture.* Lanham, UK: Scarecrow Press.

Salmivalli, Christina. (2015). Bullying and the peer group: A review. *Aggression and Violent Behavior, 15*, 112–120.

San Miguel, Guadalupe. (2001). *Brown not White: School integration and the Chicano movement in Houston.* College Station, TX: Texas A&M Press.

Sandberg, Sheryl. (2013). *Lean in: Women, work and the will to lead.* New York: Random House.

Sanelli, Maria, & Perreault, George. (2001). "I could be anybody": Gay, lesbian and bisexual students in U.S. schools. *NASSP Bulletin, 85*(622), 69–78.

Saxe, Geoffery B. (1988a). Candy selling and math learning. *Educational Researcher, 17*(6), 14–21.

Saxe, Geoffery B. (1988b). The mathematics of street vendors. *Child Development 59*, 1415–1425.

Saxe, Geoffrey B. (1994). Studying cognitive development in sociocultural context: The development of a practice-based approach. *Mind, Culture, and Activity, 1*(3), 135–157.

Scarcella, Robin. (1999). *Academic English: A conceptual framework.* Santa Barbara, CA: University of California Language Minority Institute.

Scarcella, Robin. (2000). *Effective writing instruction for English learners.* Conference on English Learners, Sacramento, CA.

Scarcella, Robin. (2011). Good instruction: The key to ELLs' success. Retrieved from http://www.colorincolorado.org/article/good-instruction-key-ells-success

Scarcella, Robin. (2013). Language objectives and math. La Jolla, CA: University of California Professional Development Institute Training Video. Retrieved from http://www.colorincolorado.org/webcast/academic-language-and-english-language-learners

Scheurich, James Joseph. (2002). *Anti-racist scholarship: An advocacy.* Albany, NY: SUNY Press.

Schniedwind, Nancy, & Davidson, Ellen. (1998). *Open minds to equality.* Boston, MA: Allyn and Bacon.

Schocker, Jessica B., & Woyshner, Christine. (2013). Representing African American women in U.S. history textbooks. *The Social Studies, 104*(1), 23–31.

Schuman, Howard, Schwartz, Barry, & D'Arcy, Hannah. (2005). Elite revisions and popular beliefs: Christopher Columbus, hero or villain? *Public Opinion Quarterly, 69*(1), 2–29.

Scribner, Sylvia. (1984). Studying working intelligence. In Barbara Rogoff and Jean Lave (Eds.), *Everyday cognition: Its development in social context.* Cambridge, MA: Harvard University Press.

Scribner, Sylvia, & Cole, Michael. (1981). *The psychology of literacy.* Cambridge, MA: Harvard University Press.

Secret, Carrie. (1998). Embracing Ebonics and teaching Standard English: An interview with Oakland teacher Carrie Secret. In Theresa Perry and Lisa Delpit (Eds.), *The real Ebonics debate: Power, language, and the education of African-American children* (pp. 79–88). Boston, MA: Beacon Press.

Selwyn, Ben. (2012). Beyond firm-centrism: Reintergrating labour and capitalism into global commodity chain analysis. *Journal of Economic Geography, 12*, 205–206.

Sewall, Gilbert. (2008). *Islam in the classroom: What the textbook tells us.* New York: American Textbook Council.

Shannon, Janet Harrison. (1998). Family and community secrets: Secrecy in the works of James Baldwin. *Western Journal of Black Studies, 22*(3), 174–181.

Sheets, Rosa Hernández, & Fong, Adrienne. (2003). Linking teacher behaviors to cultural knowledge. *The Educational Forum 67*, 372–379.

Shelton, Jim. (2015, September 30). We already know how to close the achievement gap. *Education Week.* Retrieved from http://www.edweek.org/ew/articles/2015/09/30/we-already-know-how-to-close-the.html

Shriver, Maria. (2014). *The Shriver report: A women's nation pushes back from the brink.* New York: St. Martin's Press.

Siebers, Tobin. (2008). *Disability theory.* Ann Arbor, MI: University of Michigan Press.

Siek, Stephanie. (2012, May 4). New prosthetic limbs "celebrate" bodies, personalities instead of hiding lost limbs. Retrieved from http://inamerica.blogs.cnn.com/2012/05/04/new-prosthetic-limbs-celebrate-bodies-personalities-instead-of-hiding-lost-limbs/

Silver, Edward A. (1997). "Algebra for All": A real-world problem for the mathematics education community to solve. *NCTM Xchange, 1*(2), 1–4.

Singer, Alan. (2014). *Social studies for secondary schools: Teaching to learn, learning to teach* (4th ed.). New York: Routledge.

Sleeter, Christine. (1994). White racism. *Multicultural Education, 1*(4:5–8), 39.

Sleeter, Christine, & Grant, Carl A. (1987). An analysis of multicultural education in the United States. *Harvard Educational Review, 57*, 421–444.

Smith, Frank. (2005). *Reading without nonsense.* New York: Teachers College Press.

Smith, James F. (1999, August 4). The lowly tortilla gets a boost. *Los Angeles Times*, A1, A6.

Snowman, Jack, & McCown, Rick. (2013). *Ed psych.* Belmont, CA: Wadsworth Cengage Learning.

Somaiya, Ravi. (2015, June 1). Caitlyn Jenner, formerly Bruce, introduces herself in Vanity Fair. *New York Times.* Retrieved from http://www.nytimes.com/2015/06/02/business/media/jenner-reveals-new-name-in-vanity-fair-article.html?_r=0

Somashekhar, Sandhya. (2014, July 15). Health survey give the government its first large-scale data on gay, bisexual population. *The Washington Post.* Retrieved from http://www.washingtonpost.com/national/health-science/health-survey-gives-government-its-first-large-scale-data-on-gay-bisexual-population/2014/07/14/2db9f4b0-092f-11e4-bbf1-cc51275e7f8f_story.html

Southern Poverty Law Center. (2007). *Close to slavery: Guest worker programs in the United States.* Montgomery, Alabama: Southern Poverty Law Center.

Southern Poverty Law Center. (2016). *Latino civil rights timeline, 1903 to 2006.* Teaching Tolerance. Retrieved from http://www.tolerance.org/latino-civil-rights-timeline

Souto-Manning, Mariana. (2008). Teacher inquiries into gay and lesbian families in early childhood classrooms. *Journal of Early Childhood Research, 6*(3), 263–280.

Souto-Manning, Mariana. (2013). *Multicultural teaching in the early childhood classroom.* New York: Teachers College Press.

Stack, Liam. (2016). Light sentence for Brock Turner in Stanford rape case draws outrage. *New York Times.* Retrieved from http://www.nytimes.com/2016/06/07/us/outrage-in-stanford-rape-case-over-dueling-statements-of-victim-and-attackers-father.html?_r=0

Stanford, John, & Simons, Robin. (1999). *Victory in our schools.* New York: Bantam Books.

Steele, Claude M. (1997). A threat in the air: How stereotypes shape intellectual identity and performance. *American Psychologist, 52,* 613–629.

Steele, Claude M., & Aronson, Joshua. (1995). Stereotype threat and the intellectual test performance of African Americans. *Journal of Personality and Social Psychology, 69,* 797–811.

Stephan, Walter. (1999). *Reducing prejudice and stereotyping in schools.* New York: Teachers College Press.

Stratton, T., Pang, V. O., Madueño, M., Park, C. D., Atlas, M., Page, C., & Oliger, J. (2009, November). Immigrant students and the obstacles to achievement. *Phi Delta Kappan, 91*(3), 44–47.

Subedi, Binaya. (2006). Preservice teachers' beliefs and practices: Religion and religious diversity. *Equity and Excellence, 39*(3), 227–238.

Swim, Janet, Aiken, Kathryn, Hall, Wayne, & Hunter, Barbara. (1995). Sexism and racism: Old-fashioned and modern prejudices. *Journal of Personality and Social Psychology, 68,* 199–214.

Swim, Janet, Mallett, Robyn, & Stangor, Charles. (2004). Understanding subtle sexism: Detection and the use of sexist language. *Sex Roles, 51,* 117–128.

Swisher, Karen, & Deyhle, Donna. (1992). Adapting instruction to culture. In Jon Reyhner (Ed.), *Teaching American Indian students* (pp. 81–95). Norman, OK: University of Oklahoma Press.

Sykes, Bryan. (2001). *The seven daughters of eve: The science that reveals our genetic ancestry.* New York: W. W. Norton & Company.

Szasz, Margaret Connell. (1977). *Education and the American Indian: The road to self-determination since 1928* (2nd ed.). Albuquerque, NM: University of New Mexico Press.

Taba, Hilda. (1953). Research oriented programs in intergroup education in schools and colleges. *Review of Educational Research, 23*(4), 362–371.

Takaki, Ronald. (1993). *A different mirror: A history of multicultural America.* Boston, MA: Little, Brown, and Company.

Takaki, Ron. (1998). *Strangers from a distant shore: A history of Asian Americans.* New York: Little Brown.

Tatum, Beverly Daniel. (1992a). Talking about race, learning about racism: The application of racial identity development theory. *Harvard Educational Review, 62*(1), 1–24.

Tatum, Beverly Daniel. (1992b). African-American identity, academic achievement, and missing history. *Social Education, 56*(6), 331–334.

Tatum, Beverly Daniel. (2003). *Why are all the black kids sitting together in the cafeteria?* (Revised). New York: Basic Books.

Tatum, Beverly Daniel. (2010). Insist on excellence for all. *Educational Leadership, 68*(3), 29–30.

Teaching Tolerance. (1999). *Starting small: Teaching tolerance in preschool and the early grades.* Montgomery, AL: Southern Poverty Law Center.

Teaching Tolerance. (n.d.). Bullying basics. Southern Poverty Law Center. Retrieved from http://www.tolerance.org/bullying-basics

Teaching Tolerance. (n.d.). School climate questionnaire. Southern Poverty Law Center. Retrieved from http://www.tolerance.org/sites/default/files/files/general/School%20Climate%20Questionnaire.pdf

Temple, Tobias, & Neumann, Roland. (2014). Stereotype threat, test anxiety, and mathematics performance. *Social Psychology of Education, 17,* 491–501.

Tharp, Roland, & Gallimore, Ronald. (1988). *Raising minds to life: Teaching, learning, and schooling in social context.* New York: Cambridge University Press.

Thomas, Walter, & Collier, Virginia. (1997). School effectiveness for language minority students. *NCBE Resource Collection Series,* Number 9. Washington, DC: National Clearinghouse for Bilingual Education.

Thompson, Audrey. (1998). Not the color purple: Black feminist lessons for educational caring. *Harvard Educational Review, 68*(4), 522–554.

Thornberg, Robert. (2015). School bullying as collective action: Stigma processes and identity struggling. *Children & Society, 29,* 310–320.

Thousand, Jacqueline A., Villa, Richard A., & Nevin, Ann I. (2015). *Differentiating instruction: Planning for universal design and teaching for college and career readiness.* Thousand Oaks, CA: Corwin.

Tomasetto, Carlo, & Appoloni, Sara. (2013). A lesson not to be learned? Understanding stereotype threat does not protect women from stereotype threat. *Social Psychology of Education, 16,* 199–213.

Tough, Paul. (2012). *How children succeed: Grit, curiosity, and the hidden power of character.* New York: Mariner Books.

Tran, MyLuong. (1998). Behind the smiles: The true heart of Southeast Asian American Children. In Valerie Ooka Pang and Li-rong Lilly Cheng (Eds.), *Struggling to be heard: The unmet needs of Asian Pacific American children* (pp. 45–57). New York: SUNY Press.

Transgender Legal Defense and Education Fund. (2013, February 26). TLDEF files complaint to protect transgender child from school discrimination. Retrieved from http://transgenderlegal.org/headline_show.php?id=395

Tuckman, Bruce W., & Monetti, David. M. (2013). *Educational psychology.* Belmont, CA: Wadsworth Cengage Learning.

Tyack, David, & Hansot, Elizabeth. (1990). *Learning Together: A history of coeducation in American public schools.* New Haven, CT: Yale University Press with Russell Sage.

United Nations. (1949). *United Nations declaration of human rights.* United Nations.

United Nations. (2013). *United Nations statistical yearbook: Displacement levels and trends.* New York: United Nations. Retrieved from http://www.unhcr.org/54cf99b69.html

U.S. Census Bureau. (2011). Facts for features: Asian/Pacific American Heritage Month May 2011. Retrieved from http://www.census.gov/newsroom/releases/pdf/cb11ff-06_asian.pdf

U.S. Census Bureau. (2014, December 29). Census Bureau projects U.S., world populations on New Year's Day. Retrieved from http://www.census.gov/newsroom/press-releases/2014/cb14-tps90.html

U.S. Department of Commerce, Census Bureau, American Community Survey (ACS). (2009 and 2014). *Digest of education statistics 2015,* Table 102.60.

U.S. Department of Health and Human Services. (2014). Federal laws. Washington, DC: U.S. Department of Health and Human Services. Retrieved from http://www.stopbullying.gov/laws/federal/

U.S. Department of Health and Human Services. (n.d.). What is cyberbullying? Washington, DC: U.S. Department of Health and Human Services. Retrieved from http://www.stopbullying.gov/cyberbullying/what-is-it/index.html

U.S. House of Representatives. (n.d.). Legislative interests and achievements. Retrieved from http://history.house.gov/Exhibitions-and-Publications/WIC/Historical-Essays/No-Lady/Legislative-Interests/

U.S. House of Representatives. (n.d.). The women's rights movement, 1848–1920. Retrieved from http://history.house.gov/Exhibitions-and-Publications/WIC/Historical-Essays/No-Lady/Womens-Rights/

Valle, Ramón. (1997). *Ethnic diversity and multiculturalism: Crisis or challenge.* New York: American Heritage Custom Publishing.

Van Til, William A. (1959). Instructional methods in intercultural and intergroup education. *Review of Educational Research, 29*(4), 367–377.

Voicu, Cristina-Georgiana. (2013). Cultural identity and disaspora. *Philobiblon, 18*(1), 161–174.

Vygotsky, Lev. (1997). *The collected works of Lev Vygotsky.* New York: Plenum Press.

Walker, D. J. R. (1992). *Columbus and the golden world of island Arawaks.* Jamaica: Ian Randle Publishers.

Walker, Nefertiti, & Melton, E. Nicole. (2015). Creating opportunities for social change in women's sports through academic and industry collaboration: An interview with Kate Fagan. *Journal of Intercollegiate Sport, 8,* 82–95.

Weatherford, Jack. (1988). *Indian givers: How the Indians of the Americas transformed the world.* New York: Fawcett Columbine.

Weatherford, Jack McIver. (2010). *Indian givers: How Native Americans transformed the world.* New York: Three Rivers Press.

Weisberg, Deena Skolnick, Zosh, Jennfer M., Hirsh-Pasek, Kathy, & Golinkoff, Roberta Michnick. (2013). Talking it up: Play, language development, and the role of adult support. *American Journal of Play, 6*(1), 39–54).

Westbrook, Robert B. (1991). *John Dewey and American democracy.* Ithaca, NY: Cornell University Press.

Wilson, William Julius. (2010). Why social structure and culture matter in a holistic analysis of inner-city poverty. *The Annals of American Academy of Political and Social Science, 629,* 200–219.

Wineburg, Sam. (2001). *Historical thinking and other unnatural acts: Charting the future of teaching the past.* Philadelphia, PA: Temple University Press.

Wink, Joan, & Putney, LeAnn G. (2002). *A vision of Vygotsky.* Boston, MA: Allyn and Bacon.

Winkler, Karen. (2003). Kinsey, sex research, and the body of knowledge: Let's talk about sex. *Women's Studies Quarterly, 33*(3.4), 285–313.

Yunus, Muhammed. (2003). *Banker to the poor.* New York: PublicAffairs.

Yunus, Muhammed. (2006, December 10). *Nobel lecture given by Nobel Peace Prize Laureate, 2006, Muhammed Yunus.* Oslo, Sweden. Retrieved from http://nobelpeaceprize.org/eng_lect_2006b.html

Yunus, Muhammed. (2007a). *Grameen Bank at a glance.* Retrieved from http://www.grameen-info.org/bank/GBGlance.htm

Yunus, Muhammed. (2007b, October 21). *Social enterprise: Doing well by doing good.* Presentation at the University of California.

Zhang, Sarah. (2015, September 2). The FDA may add a life-saving vitamin to tortillas. *Wired.* Retrieved from http://www.wired.com/2015/09/fda-may-add-life-saving-vitamin-tortillas/

Ziegler, Mark. (2003, January 30). Title IX panel to air dissent. *San Diego Union-Tribune,* D1, D3.

Index